FRANCE IN MODERN TIMES

FRANCE
IN
MODERN
TIMES

1760 to the present

⋙·⋘

By Gordon Wright

⋙·⋙·⋘·⋙·⋘·⋘

Rand McNally & Company : Chicago
John Murray : London

RAND McNALLY HISTORY SERIES

Rand McNally

FRED HARVEY HARRINGTON, *Consulting Editor*

GATZKE, *The Present in Perspective*

JONES, *Ancient Civilization*

MOSSE, CAMERON, HILL, PETROVICH
Europe in Review

PALMER, *Atlas of World History*

STARR, NOWELL, LYON, STEARNS, HAMEROW
A History of the World (2 vols.)

TREADGOLD, *Twentieth Century Russia*

WILLIAMS, *The Shaping of American Diplomacy*

WRIGHT, *France in Modern Times*

Preface

"On all great subjects, much remains to be said." Macaulay's dictum is comforting to one who seeks to survey the life of a great nation — and particularly that of France, on which so much has already been said so well. Because the writing of history is a matter of selection and interpretation, no book on a broad topic is ever likely to substitute for those that have gone before; it can only aim to supplement its predecessors. It can present the author's own views and judgments, which to him, at least, seem to have validity and value. And it can try to fuse into manageable form the changing and contradictory interpretations that hundreds of historians past and present have offered us. This volume is designed to be that kind of interpretive synthesis. Its stress is on what Fritz Stern has called "the varieties of history"; it seeks to draw into the story the great mass of monographic and interpretive writing on modern France that has appeared during the past generation.

No historian of our day likes to be accused of methodological naiveté. I ought to say at the outset, therefore, that at least some of the unorthodoxy of this book is quite conscious. If the canons of the profession are to be violated, it is probably safer to do so knowingly and even brazenly, with the warning *caveat lector*. I have indulged rather often in what Franklin Roosevelt might have called "iffy" history, despite Benedetto Croce's warning that "there is no room in history for the merely possible or the merely probable." I myself think that there

v

is room for it at times, and that reflection on what might have happened as well as on what did happen can be fruitful for an understanding of a nation's evolution. I have also injected some historical controversies into the body of the narrative itself, and have chosen to build parts of the story around conflicting points of view. Such a practice, though not usually considered good form among historians, seems to me far more enlightening than the custom of predigesting many contradictory interpretations into a single mishmash and relegating the real content of history — the rival interpretations themselves — to premature burial in the footnotes. Finally, I have chosen to write about a restricted segment of the life of a single nation, even though in our day it is no longer intellectually respectable to write national history. I am quite ready to admit that France is part of something much broader called Western culture or Western society, and that to focus on a single national group may have narrowing and distorting results. I am not ready to admit that it is useless, or that national differences would be insignificant if the historian would remove his blinders. Besides, even Arnold Toynbee admits, at the outset of his massive *Study of History*, that "France perhaps approaches nearer than any other national state to being co-central and co-extensive with the whole of our Western Society"; and the Frenchman Jacques Fauvet asserts proudly (though perhaps a little chauvinistically) that "France, like a microcosm, reproduces the problems of all humanity."

This book is not designed to be a portable encyclopedia. Indeed, if the question of including or omitting a given detail arose in my mind, my customary reflex has been to omit it. One besetting sin of synthesizing books in our time is, in my opinion, that they tend increasingly to become reference works or compendia of names, dates, and facts. I have tried to provide the essential framework of events, but I have chosen to concentrate on main strands and trends and on the differing viewpoints of historians and of political groups toward events.

The date 1760 has no mystical significance as a point of departure. Any date between 1750 and 1770 would have been just as satisfactory. But the mid-eighteenth century does have real significance, I think, when one is seeking to examine the character and evolution of modern France. For that nation in recent times, like so much of Western society, is in very great part the product of the Enlightenment, of its view of human society and of man. Of course, the older heritage has its importance as well; indeed, one of France's modern problems is the weight of its long history. But for the most part, the France of our era springs from the eighteenth century's synthesis of Renaissance and early modern attitudes.

The perceptive but caustic French journalist Raoul de Roussy de Sales once noted in his diary that ". . . there is not a single book written by an American on France which is worth reading. . . ." From the Frenchman's point of view, he may be right. Americans are likely, nevertheless, to go on writing about France, if only for American readers. They may even console themselves with the hope that some day, some Frenchman may have reason to take a more charitable view.

❧◦❧◦❧ ❧◦❧

Professor Joel Colton of Duke University, who read the manuscript for the publisher, made a number of valuable suggestions for which I am grateful. I am indebted also to Professors David Landes of the University of California and Val Lorwin of the University of Oregon for permission to quote from unpublished manuscripts; to Abbé F. Boulard and the Éditions du Cerf for authorization to reproduce the religious map of France; to M. Georges Dupeux and the Librairie Armand Colin for the maps of the 1849 and 1936 elections; and to the Institut national de la statistique et des études économiques for the economic map of France. The quotations introducing Chapters Two, Six, Fourteen, and Thirty-Four are reprinted from the following books by permission of their publishers: A. Mathiez, *The French Revolution* (New York: Knopf, 1928); A. Cobban, *History of Modern France* (London: Penguin, 1957); E. M. Earle, *Modern France* (Princeton: Princeton Univ. Press, 1951).

Table of Contents

I

ENLIGHTENMENT AND REVOLUTIONARY FRANCE
1760 – 1814

I. *The Nation's Heritage*
page 3

II. *Society and Economy: Structure and Trends, 1760–1789*
page 16

III. *Temper of the Age, 1760–1789*
page 28

IV. *The Decadent Monarchy, 1760–1789*
page 40

V. *Upheaval, 1789–1792*
page 51

VI. *Climax and Relapse, 1792–1799*
page 66

VII. *Dictatorship, 1799–1814*
page 86

TABLE OF CONTENTS

VIII.   *The Varieties of History, 1760–1814*
page 107

II

FRANCE IN SEARCH OF A NEW EQUILIBRIUM
1814 – 1870

IX.   *The Bourbon Experiment, 1814–1830*
page 121

X.   *The Orleanist Experiment, 1830–1848*
page 144

XI.   *The Republican Experiment, 1848–1852*
page 167

XII.   *The Imperial Experiment, 1852–1870*
page 184

XIII.   *Economy: Structure and Trends, 1814–1870*
page 196

XIV.   *Society: Structure and Trends, 1814–1870*
page 210

XV.   *Intellectual and Cultural Currents, 1814–1870*
page 227

XVI.   *France, Europe, and the World, 1814–1870*
page 241

TABLE OF CONTENTS

XVII.   *The Varieties of History, 1814–1870*
page 259

III

THE ROOTING OF THE REPUBLICAN SYSTEM
1870 – 1919

XVIII.   *The Monarchist Republic, 1870–1879*
page 271

XIX.   *The Opportunist Republic, 1879–1899*
page 296

XX.   *The Radical Republic, 1899–1914*
page 325

XXI.   *Economy: Structure and Trends, 1870–1914*
page 343

XXII.   *Society: Structure and Trends, 1870–1914*
page 354

XXIII.   *The French Mind and Spirit, 1870–1914*
page 366

XXIV.   *France, Europe, and the World, 1871–1914*
page 377

XXV.   *"The Grandeur and Misery of Victory," 1914–1919*
page 393

TABLE OF CONTENTS

XXVI. *The Varieties of History, 1870–1919*
page 409

IV

CONTEMPORARY FRANCE: AN ERA OF CRISIS
1919–1960

XXVII. *The Quest for Normalcy, 1919–1931*
page 423

XXVIII. *The Era of French Hegemony, 1919–1933*
page 437

XXIX. *Economy and Society in the Postwar Decade, 1919–1931*
page 453

XXX. *Depression Politics, 1931–1936*
page 464

XXXI. *Crisis and Collapse, 1936–1940*
page 483

XXXII. *Bifurcated France, 1940–1944*
page 510

XXXIII. *The Life and Death of the Fourth Republic, 1944–1958*
page 527

XXXIV. *Silent Revolution or Quiet Stagnation?*
Social and Economic Trends, 1945–1960
page 548

xii

XXXV. *Trends in French Thought and Expression, 1919–1960*
page 568

XXXVI. *The Fifth Republic, 1958–1960*
page 578

XXXVII. *The Varieties of History, 1919–1960*
page 588

List of Maps

1. *The French Colonial Empire in 1914*
pages 448–49

2. *The Left in 1849*
page 478

3. *The Left in 1936*
page 479

4. *Dynamic vs. Static France*
page 553

5. *The Dechristianization of Rural France*
page 557

I
ENLIGHTENMENT AND REVOLUTIONARY FRANCE 1760–1814

It is commonly said that in this fertile country, on this territory so well marked out by nature, the emergence of a great people was to be expected. Such a statement confuses result and cause. . . . France is the work of man's intelligence and will.

JACQUES BAINVILLE

The Nation's Heritage

France in 1760 had almost attained its modern territorial limits. The duchy of Lorraine was still a border enclave, but its absorption was only a matter of time; it was quietly annexed six years later. The island of Corsica, under Genoese rule, was to be purchased in 1768; while along the Alpine frontier, the province of Savoy and the city of Nice were not to come under the French flag for another century. If France had a territorial destiny, it was largely fulfilled two hundred years ago, much in advance of most European nations.

The phrase "territorial destiny" might have meant little to Frenchmen of 1760, but "natural limits" would have had a more familiar ring. It harmonized with the more general concept of natural law, so basic to Enlightenment thought. That each state had its natural limits was taken as an axiom by Montesquieu, Turgot, Rousseau. Though none of these *philosophes* chose to define just where France's proper frontiers ran, the politicians of the revolutionary era promptly leaped to an obvious conclusion. "The boundaries of France," cried Danton in 1793, "are marked out by nature. We shall reach them at their four points, the Ocean, the Rhine, the Alps, the Pyrenees." The legend was to be a powerful and enduring one. Frenchmen of the nineteenth century applauded Michelet's lyrical phrase that asserted France to be "not the work of men, but of Providence" and Albert Sorel's dictum that French foreign policy through the centuries had been "dictated by geography." Even as late as the Paris peace conference in 1919, the concept was far from dead.

The curious thing is that the natural frontiers doctrine gained currency and significance only after French territorial unity had been largely achieved. The kings and statesmen who had pushed French sovereignty out from the Île de France toward Rhine, Alps, and Pyrenees had done so as empirical rather than as doctrinaire expansionists; even Richelieu acted thus, despite the legend that he originated the natural frontiers concept. It is just as well that the territorial builders of modern France did not rely on so dubious a theory, for the case against France's alleged natural limits is overwhelming. It may have become a convenient fiction to justify expansionism in the modern era, it may have seemed consistent with common sense, but, in fact, it rested on no valid base in geography or economics.

Frenchmen could easily reach another conclusion as well: that nature had dictated the formation of a single state rather than several states in the area bounded by Rhine, Alps, and Pyrenees. Undoubtedly, geography had contributed something to French unity; but the natural forces for unity had been fairly well balanced by opposite forces working for division and diversity. The great river basins of the Seine, Loire, and Rhone were semidetached regions, neither isolated nor fused by nature. That Burgundy became attached to France rather than to the Low Countries or to no neighbor at all was certainly not the work of geography. Despite Michelet, French unity was the work of men, not of natural forces; and it was a heterogeneous rather than a homogeneous unity, within which regional diversities stubbornly survived.

One other geopolitical theory may have more merit. Some scholars have found in topography, location, and climate a set of factors that has contributed to shaping a nation's social and political structure, its attitudes, its "national character." This kind of geographical determin-

4

ism has more often been applied to Germany or Russia than to France; yet a plausible case can be made for the effect of location on the structure of France and the behavior of Frenchmen. No other major state opens out in three directions: on the Mediterranean world, on north central Europe, and on the Atlantic. It is at least a reasonable hypothesis that the impact of varied ideas and cultures over the centuries produced a uniquely cosmopolitan and diversified culture in France, and that French governments were faced with a variety of alternative national policies as well as with a wide choice of friends and enemies. The critical significance of geography for France may lie in the very fact that too many choices were open — that no clear path was dictated by nature. The new nation-state of France might have become a land power, with a strong army and a continental destiny; or it might have become a maritime power, with a powerful navy and merchant marine and a world destiny. The two alternatives implied quite different social structures, political systems, and even psychological frameworks. During the formative centuries, it was France's fate to hesitate or straddle rather than to be drawn ineluctably into a consistent course of development. Indeed, down to our own day there remains a certain ambiguity about France's proper nature — an ambiguity that conflicts with the passion of Frenchmen for coherence, clarity, and logic.

※○⊂※·※○⊂※·※○⊂※

Some Frenchmen in 1760, and in the two succeeding centuries as well, found the factor of "race" to be more important than geography in the shaping of the nation. The eighteenth-century aristocracy took for granted that its members were set off from the masses by a difference in blood; that they were descended from the conquering Franks who had overrun the indigenous Gauls twelve centuries earlier. Some commoners accepted this thesis, too, and viewed the great revolution as a kind of massive, if delayed, revenge of the Gauls at the expense of the "Goths." As late as 1871, so notable a scholar as Ernest Renan

5

was to find in race an explanation for France's defeat at the hands of Bismarckian Germany: the warlike and courageous Frankish strain, wrote Renan, had been too much diluted by Celtic blood, with its hereditary taint of effervescence and weakness.

Racial theories, however, have not had much political or psychological significance in France's modern history. Frenchmen of our era have readily admitted that they are hybrids in origin, as mixed as almost any people in Europe. From prehistoric times until the end of the first Christian millennium, invasion brought a series of injections of "new blood." Over the next eight or nine centuries, a rather complete blending process occurred; then, from the later nineteenth century onward, France was again to become the melting pot of Europe. Most of the components of the mixture are known; only the proportions, and the real significance of these proportions, remain unclear. Even "our ancestors the Gauls" (the stock phrase that used to introduce French grade-school textbooks in history) were not indigenous, but constituted a fusion of Neolithic stock with early Celtic invaders. Then were added, in turn, Roman immigrants, Franks, Burgundians, and Normans. On the northern plains, each wave of invasion rolled over the previous one and merged with it. In remote regions like the Auvergne highlands and the Basque country, a more nearly pure variety of the Neolithic or Neolithic-Celtic stock survived.

Modern Frenchmen have made a virtue of their mixed origin. "We are a race of half-breeds," wrote the republican historian Charles Seignobos, "but mongrels are often more intelligent than pure-breds." "France," declared the monarchist Jacques Bainville, "is better than a race; it is a nation." And André Siegfried only a decade ago summed up the case in this fashion: "To the Latins the French owe their gift for expression and their intellectual lucidity; to the Celts their artistic nature as well as their individual anarchism; to the Germans what they possess of seriousness and constructive capabilities."[1] There is a curious

[1] In E. M. Earle (ed.), *Modern France* (Princeton: Princeton Univ. Press, 1951), pp. 4–5.

flavor here of racism in reverse — a variety of racism, it ought to be added, that is far less dangerous than the usual sort.

In one fashion, however, France's heterogeneous origins may have made a genuine contribution to France's present. Whatever the significance (or lack of it) of the ethnic factor, no one can doubt the importance of a nation's cultural heritage; and it is clear that each wave of invaders in the early centuries brought its peculiar institutions and folkways. The components of the resultant blend have produced violent (and perhaps useless) controversy. The most violent dispute of all, the echoes of which persist to this day, was the product of the nineteenth-century Celtic revival. Until a century ago, the traditional view of Frenchmen had been that the Gauls were benighted barbarians who needed the civilizing influence of Roman rule in order to permit the building of a strong state and a brilliant culture in Gaul. A new school of historians passionately challenged this tradition; it argued that the Roman conquest had been one of the worst crimes and tragedies in all French history, involving the destruction of a culture even more advanced than Rome's and the systematic creation of a false legend by the official propagandists of the Roman state. Vercingetorix, leader of the Gallic resistance movement, became the tragic hero of this pro-Celtic school, the victim of " . . . the baldheaded Caesar, the wan proconsul . . . [who] rejoiced in the . . . morbid pleasure of blasting and trampling under foot human destinies . . . ."[2] Whatever the validity of the case, it is hard to deny the profound effects of the Romans' language, law, religion, and architecture on the subsequent development of France.

A controversy of somewhat less intensity surrounds the Frankish conquest. To what degree were Germanic institutions and folkways blended with, or superimposed on, the Gallo-Roman culture found by Clovis and his successors? Modern scholars have, in the main, rejected the older thesis of predominant Frankish influence and have concluded that the Gallo-Roman fusion survived under a Germanic veneer. Some Frankish law was introduced, but it was grafted onto a Roman root. In

[2] F. Funck-Brentano, *The Earliest Times* (New York: Putnam, 1928), p. 106.

religion, the Roman influence prevailed completely. In the same fashion, the ethnic contribution of the Franks seems to have been rather slight. But in the gradual process of fusion of Frankish and Gallo-Roman institutions and "blood," the already existing differences between northern and southern Gaul were increased. More Franks intermarried with the Gallo-Romans north of the Loire; the Frankish accent gradually converted the northern vernacular into the ancestor of modern French, while a purer southern vernacular developed into the quite distinct language of Provençal or *Langue d'Oc*.

By the year 1000 the phase of racial and cultural mingling through violent irruptions of invaders from east or south was over. The last such group, the Normans, added little or nothing to the cultural amalgam, though blond Nordic types still appear today in the valleys of northern France. For several centuries the process of cultural fusion went on, never in complete isolation from neighboring cultures, but never again through sudden submersion. In the course of events there emerged quite early both a French state and a consciousness of French nationality, primitive in nature yet none the less real.

The French state, according to the classic formula of Jacques Bainville, was the work of its forty kings. One need not be a monarchist like Bainville to admire their work, even though it might be argued that Frenchmen were no better off within a powerful unitary state than they would have been within a decentralized structure like that of the Germanies or the Low Countries. At any rate, a single dynasty ruled France, in either the direct or the indirect line, from 987 to 1789; and while there was the normal quota of weak or contemptible kings, the dynasty was fortunate in producing a great man or a clever man at most of the right times. The early Capetians were thoughtful enough to provide, without exception, a male heir; and they were shrewd enough not to waste their substance, as certain German princes did, in chasing phantoms like the crown of the Holy Roman Empire. They concentrated, rather, on building up the family's personal domain from its tiny original nucleus around Paris, until their holdings exceeded those of any other French feudal prince, and they could overawe all potential rivals.

According to an old and romantic theory, the kings were aided in the process of building national unity by an obscure but deep longing of the masses for strength, authority, and an embodiment of their instinct toward nationhood. Such a theory may have satisfied Michelet, but it no longer finds many defenders. If anyone helped the kings break down feudal weakness and build royal authority, it was not the mass of Frenchmen but rather the rising bourgeoisie and the Catholic clergy. From the thirteenth through the seventeenth century, French holdings were gradually pushed out in all directions, and royal agents were invested with a growing share of power. There is both paradox and truth in the remark that absolutism was the product of the crown's weakness rather than of its power; that ". . . absolute monarchy was . . . no more than a gigantic system of bribery of those whom the crown found it worth while to bribe."[3] But if the methods used by French kings were not always glamorous ones, they were none the less effective. By the seventeenth century, the way was open for Cardinal Richelieu to consolidate the work of his forerunners and to hand on to Louis XIV a functioning royal absolutism.

Although the record of the French kings was an admirable one in certain ways, it had its seamy side as well. The trend toward centralization and absolutism was not accompanied by either steady or adequate progress toward the creation of an efficient and enlightened despotism. Royal institutions grew up gradually, haphazardly, with a barnacle-like encrustation of overlapping functions and useless sinecures. Never — not even under Richelieu — was there a thorough house cleaning. By 1760 the administrative structure resembled a palace that had been built piecemeal by adding rooms and wings without any renovation of the

[3] M. Prestwich, in J. M. Wallace-Hadrill and J. McManners (eds.), *France: Government and Society* (London: Methuen, 1957), p. 121.

original structure or any attempt to harmonize the whole. One source of the trouble had been the state's constant need of money and its inability to establish an effective mechanism for getting what it needed. In the later Middle Ages the monarchy had hit on the easy device of selling government offices; and as time went by, the temptation was great to expand the bureaucracy in order to increase the royal income. There was another reason, too, for this bureaucratic inflation. From time to time, when a set of officials had become so solidly entrenched as to bridle at royal authority, the monarchy had brusquely superimposed a new set and had transferred to the latter the functions (but not the perquisites) of the first group. This old Capetian device had proved useful at times, but it was hardly a way to build an efficient bureaucratic system. Worse still, certain office-holders eventually demanded (and got, in 1604) a hereditary vested interest in the posts they held; such posts could be willed to an heir, sold outright, or used as security for loans. The monarchy, deprived of the right to resell offices to each new generation, was driven to subdivide functions and create sinecures in order to replenish the treasury.

The absolute monarchy failed also to carry centralization to its logical conclusion. Richelieu took the longest step in that direction when he appointed intendants to enforce the royal will in the various provinces; but these officials, despite their extensive powers, could not challenge many traditional practices and institutions. A tangled undergrowth of local rules, trade restrictions, and special law codes seriously hampered domestic commerce and made travel a test of patience. Even the scale of weights and measures varied in different parts of the country. A few provinces had retained a special kind of local autonomy in the form of provincial "estates," which were deliberative bodies representing the privileged orders. Deeper still, provincial loyalties and folkways stubbornly survived, along with some linguistic variations. If France in 1760 was a centralized despotism with a conscious sense of nationhood, there was a curious patchwork quality about both state and society.

Undoubtedly, the regime's greatest weakness was in the sphere of public finance. The old feudal dues of medieval times were never replaced by a modern tax system; both kings and ministers were reluctant to face the problem of reform head on, usually preferring to find new income through some devious trick. More than any other single factor, it was the failure to build an adequate structure of public finance that eventually destroyed the monarchy.

Furthermore, while the Bourbons and their ministers gradually tamed the old aristocracy and stripped it of any real share of power, they allowed two other groups to achieve a kind of special power role; and both groups used their advantage to challenge royal attempts at reform. The first of these obstacles was the Catholic hierarchy; the second was the *parlement* of Paris, buttressed by the lesser provincial *parlements*. Both agencies appeared to be major pillars of the system; both, in the end, contributed to its destruction.

In appearance, the king had brought the church to heel in 1516, for the concordat of that year was a compromise worked out by king and Pope at the expense of the high French clergy. The concordat ensured to the king the right to select bishops and archbishops and to dominate church affairs, while it ensured to the Pope a steady income from the French faithful. The concordat was Gallican in spirit, for it placed control of the French church in Paris rather than in Rome; but this was not the kind of Gallicanism that French churchmen had so long wanted. They had hoped to free the French church of papal control in order to place it under the authority of a church council, not of the king. The hierarchy was never fully reconciled to the new system, and in consequence, its loyalty was always rather grudging. Yet no king dared challenge the clergy too directly, for the church's annual "free gift" was essential state revenue, and the clergy's corporative spirit and spiritual influence made it a dangerous opponent.

The twelve *parlements*, headed by that of Paris, were semijudicial agencies that had gradually dug themselves into a position of almost unrivalled authority in the bureaucratic monarchy. The *parlement* of Paris not only handled legal cases, but it also had the function of registering royal edicts. It thus possessed a kind of suspensive veto over royal legislation, if it could show that the new edict violated long-established customs and privileges. The king could always enforce his will, however, by holding a royal session of the *parlement* (called *lit de justice*) and ordering that the edict be registered. Originally the officials of the *parlements* had been commoners who had bought office and, with it, noble status. They constituted the highest echelon of that newer branch of the aristocracy called the *noblesse de robe*. For several centuries they had been docile servants and effective agents in establishing royal power at the expense of the older feudal elements in society. But by the eighteenth century they had developed a sense of independence that made them increasingly bold and obstreperous as critics of royal actions. They posed as defenders of justice and constitutionalism; in fact, their caste spirit and their growing sense of solidarity with the old aristocracy turned them against the bureaucratic monarchy and its plans for governmental and fiscal reform.

France in 1760 was at war. To Frenchmen, that was not much of a novelty; since 1667, when Louis XIV embarked on his lifelong campaign to dominate Europe, France had been engaged in a series of seven major wars, broken only by armistices improperly described as peace settlements. True, there had been one long interlude of almost uninterrupted peace from 1713 to 1740, during which time the king's chief minister, Cardinal Fleury, had managed to repress the war hawks of the day. Then the almost irrepressible conflict had resumed once more and had filled most of the last two decades before 1760.

England was the principal enemy, allied for the moment with Prussia on the Continent; and the crux of the Anglo-French conflict was the contest for overseas empire. France probably could not have avoided the colonial aspect of the war, except by abandoning its holdings in America and Asia. The European phase of the conflict had a far less valid base in French national or dynastic interests. Intriguing courtiers at Versailles, tempted by the prospect of glory and influence held out by Austrian diplomats, had managed to pull the French government into an unaccustomed alliance with France's traditional rival Austria. The French stood to gain little and to lose much; by 1760 they were well on the way to a major defeat. The year 1759 had been the most disastrous of the century, with nothing but bad news coming in from all fronts.

Louis XV, now fifty years of age and in the forty-fifth year of his reign, had been vainly trying to serve as his own chief minister since the death of Fleury in 1743. The vanity of the effort sprang partly from the size of the task he faced and partly from his own limitations. Louis had inherited a realm as rich and populous as any in Europe, but one with an empty public treasury and a ramshackle administrative system. At court and within the bureaucracy, political factionalism exceeded that of twentieth-century France at its worst. A domineering ruler like Louis XIV had been able to overawe the factions; a shrewd manipulator like Fleury could somehow manage to keep them balanced. For a well-intentioned but weak man like Louis XV, the problem was insoluble.

The Louis of popular tradition was pure cynic and profligate, indifferent to the imminent disaster so long as it did not interfere with the chase after game and women. As a matter of fact, if Louis really said anything like "After us, the deluge" (and he probably did not), it would have been in a spirit of gloomy resignation rather than cynicism. There is an opposite legend — of more recent origin, in this case — that has sought to rehabilitate Louis and to make him an able king overwhelmed by the force of circumstance. But the evidence offered in support of this thesis does more to prove Louis's good intentions than his capacity for crisis leadership. It is true that when he chose to rule directly after 1743, he was guided by higher motives than a thirst for personal power. But he lacked the strength of will, the intelligence, and the character to shape a wise policy and to risk his crown in an effort to push it to completion. By 1760 he was discouraged and disillusioned, and he no longer seemed capable of offering much resistance to the factional pressures that surrounded him.

The strongest pressures were quite naturally exerted by those who were personally closest to the king: the queen's faction on the one hand, that of the official mistress Madame de Pompadour on the other. Pompadour had long since become a platonic mistress only, but until her death in 1764, she and her favorites were to exert direct though sporadic influence on public policy. In certain respects that influence was relatively enlightened: Pompadour's common birth and her fancy for being considered an intellectual made her susceptible to the reform ideas of Enlightenment thinkers. But she was also a charming and emotional woman who impulsively played favorites and thought of policy in terms of personality; her recommendations to the king were sometimes disastrous. Through the queen, on the other hand, was channelled the influence of the church hierarchy and the aristocracy — especially the more selfish, narrow-minded, and bigoted elements of the old elites.

Also impinging upon the king were pressures from within the administration. The chief career bureaucrats were eager to keep aristocratic factions and court favorites out of positions of power and to run the government themselves as direct agents of a royal despot. Some of them were sincerely moved by a concern for efficiency and continuity of policy, while others were merely ambitious self-seekers; but among them a statesmanlike king might have found the kind of agents who could have helped him shore up and reform the decadent regime.

The most influential pressure group within the bureaucracy — the two thousand officials of the *parlements* — constituted, however, a serious barrier to constructive reform. They had been cowed by Louis XIV but had regained their self-confidence and expanded their influence since 1715. A decade before 1760 the long-suffering Louis XV had at last sought to challenge the privileged interests for which the *parlements* spoke. In 1749 his controller-general Machault, a career bureaucrat, made the first serious effort at fiscal reform in almost a century. A royal decree instituted a new five per cent income tax, called the *vingtième*, and imposed it on all Frenchmen, even including the largely tax-exempt social elites. Unlike earlier tax proposals, this one was designed to be a permanent reform rather than a temporary wartime expedient. Three years of violent controversy ensued, with the *parlements*, the nobility, and the clergy challenging the measure as an infringement of vested rights. In this instance the church hierarchy leaped forward with such energy to lead the fight that the *parlements* could remain in the background and confine themselves to moral support. In 1751 the enemies of reform prevailed, thanks to the help of the queen's faction at court. Machault's decree was suspended, and the government once more fell back on a variety of fiscal expedients, barely adequate in time of peace and hopelessly inadequate in time of war.

Monarchist historians of France have commonly dwelt on those bits of evidence that show the later Bourbons' awareness of the need for sweeping change. Their suggested conclusion is that the kings, despite their deplorable lack of backbone, were more to be pitied than censured. The real troublemakers, according to this version of history, were the selfish bureaucrats of the *parlements*, whose narrow recalcitrance under-mined the monarchy while it opened the way to abstract theorists and political fanatics. This much can be said for the monarchist viewpoint: it serves to offset the legendary thesis of a simple two-way struggle in the eighteenth century, with king and nobility on one side and the rest of the nation on the other. The power struggle of the time was, rather, a three-cornered one, and the protagonists were the vested interests, the rising new classes of society, and the crown. By 1760 the tensions among them were severe, yet they did not make a violent revolution "inevitable." True, the crown and the rising classes failed to join forces to avert revolution, and it would not have been a simple matter for them to do so. Still, the possibility of doing so did exist, and a different kind of king — or a king surrounded by different pressures — could have seized the opportunity. The English monarchy reconciled itself with changing times and opened the way to a long era of peaceful evolution. The eighteenth-century kings of France, whatever may be said in their defense, failed to do what needed to be done.

TWO

> . . . The Revolution was not to break out in an exhausted
> country but, on the contrary, in a flourishing land on a rising
> tide of progress. Poverty may sometimes lead to riots, but it
> cannot bring about great social upheavals. These always arise
> from a disturbance of the balance between social classes.
>
> ALBERT MATHIEZ

Society and Economy:
Structure and Trends, 1760–1789

France in 1760 was the most populous of European states. Louis XV's
subjects totalled approximately twenty-two million, which meant that one
of every six Europeans west of the Russian frontier was a Frenchman.
Ever since the Middle Ages, Frenchmen had outnumbered Englishmen,
Germans, Spaniards, Italians, even Russians; and only the tsar's vast
realms seemed capable in 1760 of catching and surpassing France.

For several centuries the French population, like that of Europe
generally, had not grown very much; a harsh nature had provided its own
correctives for the high birth rate. No Frenchmen in 1760 could know
that the nation stood at a major demographic turning point and that the
century from 1760 to 1860 would bring an unprecedented population explosion. By 1789 the total had already reached twenty-six million; by 1860
it would approach thirty-six million. Even in retrospect, the reasons
for so dramatic a change are not entirely clear, though improved sani-
tation and medical science, a more varied diet, and a general rise in
living standards certainly had something to do with it. The single fact
that infant mortality in 1760 was 250 per 1000 births and that it had

16

fallen to 160 a century later suggests one explanation. Paradoxically, this century of France's most rapid population growth was to bring the first serious challenges to the nation's numerical predominance in Europe and the first signs of impending decline.

Of Louis's subjects, barely one in twenty belonged to the socially and legally privileged elite. The First Estate, which included members of the monastic orders as well as priests and hierarchy, numbered about 130,000; the Second Estate, the hereditary nobility, totalled 400,000. All the rest were commoners: either members of that ill-defined category called the bourgeoisie, or ordinary peasants, artisans, workers — *le menu peuple*, as they were usually called. Nine out of ten lived by agriculture, either on isolated farms or in small village clusters. Few of them ever saw a city; at most, they might look forward to a rare visit to the nearest *bourg*, a commercial town of five or ten thousand people. Paris, with a population of a half-million, was the only metropolis; no other city except Lyon exceeded a hundred thousand.

In the hierarchical society of the eighteenth century, the court aristocracy stood at the apex of the pyramid, just below the royal family itself. Since the unsuccessful revolt of the great lords against royal absolutism in 1648–53—the so-called Fronde rebellion—the nobility had been forced to acquiesce in a position of prestige without power. Generous royal pensions lessened the sting, and so did the pleasures of life at Versailles, where the court nobles filled their time with the pursuit of pleasure or with intrigue. The support of this leisure class put a considerable burden on the public treasury, though compared to other items of expenditure (such as interest on the public debt) it was a minor item. A more serious consequence was the atmosphere of factionalism that hung like a fetid miasma about the court, choking and stifling those who sought to give France a vigorous and efficient administration. Only the notables of the aristocracy lived at court; the vastly greater number of lesser nobles remained on their provincial estates, isolated from the course of events and from the main stream of ideas. Some of them enjoyed the comfortable life of the country gentleman in a society that retained much of its feudal tone; others barely managed to maintain themselves in a style not much above that of a prosperous peasant or bourgeois.

The nobility in 1760 was not a closed caste, though it seemed on the way to becoming one. Over the centuries, there had been a slow but steady upward flow into its ranks, through royal action or through the purchase of government offices that carried noble status. For a long time the newcomers who bought such offices (the *noblesse de robe*) had been treated disdainfully by the old aristocracy. By 1760, however, they had gained acceptance if not full equality with the oldest families. Some of them could now boast of several generations of aristocratic status; they no longer smelled of the counting house. Besides, the new nobility had promptly repudiated its bourgeois origins and had assimilated itself to the mores and standards of the old aristocracy. More important still, it was the *noblesse de robe* that furnished the ablest spokesmen for aristocratic privilege. In preparing a coherent argument and presenting it effectively, legal training or judicial experience was better preparation than court intrigue or the life of a gentleman farmer.

It may seem strange that the aristocratic elite in a semifeudal society felt any need for spokesmen or defenders. In part, that was because the aristocracy wanted to protect the *status quo*, some aspects of which (its tax exemption, notably) were under sporadic attack. But it was also because the eighteenth-century nobility was increasingly inclined to attack and destroy the *status quo*. The revolutionary goal of the discontented nobles was a return to a semimythical medieval system, to an unwritten constitution that had allegedly been torn up by the absolutist kings and their bourgeois ministers. The aristocrats talked of decentralization, of the restoration of provincial rights, of an end to royal and bureaucratic despotism, of a "return to legality." Under the same banner they began to resuscitate old feudal dues that had long since lapsed, and they set out to regain a monopoly of appointments to high posts in government, church, and army. The members of the *noblesse de robe* joined wholeheartedly in this campaign. Overlooking the recency of their own bourgeois origins, they were quite ready to pull up the ladder by which they had risen into the privileged caste and to shut the trap door against further ascension. The aristocrats' motives combined class snobbery with economic pressure; in an era of rising prices and competitive extravagance, every possible source of income had to be tapped if they were to "live nobly," as tradition required them to do. The effect was to nurture the resentment of those commoners who suffered the consequences: the peasant who was suddenly confronted with forgotten feudal dues, the aspiring bourgeois whose hope of social advancement was threatened.

Alongside the aristocracy as a privileged order stood the clergy, whose label "First Estate" seemed to suggest even greater pre-eminence. Although there was a clear line distinguishing the clergy from the other estates, its members by no means constituted a class, in any sense of the word, or even a homogeneous stratum of society. It was, rather, a professional category enjoying certain social privileges; its upper ranks came almost entirely from the nobility, its middle and lower ranks from the bourgeoisie and the peasantry. Although a strong corporative spirit — and in some cases a common intensity of faith — held these diverse elements together, the gulf between hierarchy and parish priests was growing steadily wider and more obvious during the eighteenth century. Many village curés resented the contrast in income between the upper and lower ranks — a contrast roughly of 140 to 1. The village priests were, however, better off than the average peasant or wage earner, and they enjoyed greater social prestige. Dissatisfaction was sharper in the middle ranks of the church hierarchy — the cathedral chapters, for example, and the seminary teachers. Many of these posts were held by bookish young men of bourgeois origin, who chose the clerical career for reasons similar to those that inspire their modern successors to become university teachers. There had been a time when the able and ambitious ones might hope to rise to so distinguished a post as a bishopric; but the increasing difficulties of advancement in the eighteenth century were producing a sense of exasperated frustration among them.

High standards of morality and fervency could hardly be expected of a hierarchy that had come to be (in Alfred Cobban's phrase) a system of unemployment relief for sons of the aristocracy. It is easy to cite such cases as that of Talleyrand, who lived at court and visited his bishopric only once — his sole purpose then being to gain election to the Estates-General; or the Cardinal de Rohan, key figure in the squalid Diamond Necklace scandal; or the Prince of Bourbon-Condé, abbot of four monasteries, whose nearest approach to a spiritual act was the construction of a marble tomb for his pet monkey McCarthy. The surprising thing is that the clergy contained so many pious and sincere men and so many who managed to combine faith with enlightened tolerance. A century later, Alexis de Tocqueville went so far as to write: "I am not sure whether, in spite of the crying faults of some of its members, there was ever a more remarkable clergy than that of France in 1789." Even the members of the Jesuit order, singled out by Voltaire for his bitterest sarcasm and invective, sometimes displayed a breadth of interest and an open-mindedness that contrasted sharply with Voltaire's inverted bigotry. To regard the clergy as a solid reactionary bloc fanatically committed to the defense of dogma and special privilege would be vastly unfair. If the Great Revolution ultimately united the bulk of the First Estate under the standard of reaction, the fault was at least partly that of the church's critics.

Below the line that separated privilege from non-privilege lived the great bulk of Frenchmen who made up the Third Estate. Most of its members were peasants, and most of those peasants were free men who had long since shaken off all but the annoying remnants of feudal servitude. It is not easy to reconstruct the rural life of the eighteenth century; travellers' accounts are sketchy and full of contradictions, and statistics are remarkably inadequate. Some of the evidence suggests an almost incredible degree of degradation and misery: mud-floored huts, ragged clothing, undernourishment, frequent famine. Other testimony supports the view that, however primitive the existence of the French peasantry, conditions had improved over the previous century and were probably better than in any other continental country.

Most peasants were tenants, crop-sharers, or day laborers on estates owned by the privileged orders or the bourgeoisie; but a great many— perhaps half of all the peasants—had achieved virtual ownership of at least a bit of land. A few of these, the so-called *laboureurs,* were on the way to becoming a kind of rural middle class; they were expanding their holdings, acquiring herds of stock, even hiring laborers and lending money. The great mass of *manouvriers,* on the other hand, lived at a precarious subsistence level, supplementing their meager crops by working part-time on the large estates or taking employment in the rural textile industry, which allowed them to spin or weave at home. Their eagerness to acquire land amounted to a passion; but they were even more dedicated to preserving such remainders of the medieval rural structure as the right to graze animals and collect firewood on the common land of the village. The bulk of the peasantry thus remained precapitalist and intensely traditionalist in outlook.

It was in the cities and towns, not in the countryside, that the ferment of social change was most active. The bourgeoisie, an amorphous and varied category that included industrial and commercial enterprisers, financiers, professional men, bureaucrats, shopkeepers, and some independent artisans, had been making steady economic gains during the eighteenth century. Some of this new wealth was plowed back into business expansion, but most of it was used to purchase town houses, country estates, government bonds, government or church offices, or army commissions. It is tempting to suppose that this self-conscious and aggressive bourgeoisie, eager for recognition, power, and greater economic elbowroom, quite naturally turned against the old order and began to agitate for social equality, constitutional government, and economic laissez faire. In the end it did so; but, on the whole, the members of the bourgeoisie seem to have been reluctant revolutionaries at best. Far from being eager to crusade for a new social and political order, many of them clung to the old class structure that separated the privileged from the unprivileged. What they wanted was not to destroy privileges but to share them. All they asked was the right to become aristocrats themselves, if they were wealthy or clever enough to achieve that goal.

Why the French bourgeoisie developed this curious set of mores is not an easy question to answer. In part, it probably derived from the fact that this was a white-collar rather than a business bourgeoisie; that most

21

of its members were professional men, bureaucrats, or small shopkeepers rather than industrial or commercial enterprisers. But to state that fact is only to push the problem farther back and to raise the question why the vigorous entrepreneurial class was so small in eighteenth-century France. The restrictive character of Colbert's mercantilist system certainly hampered business growth, but so did more amorphous factors in the French psychological and social heritage.

If France had possessed a rigid and impermeable caste system, no such idea as sharing aristocratic privilege would ever have occurred to the bourgeoisie. But over the centuries there had been opportunities to rise: difficult and devious perhaps, but always available to the opportunist. Some bought office that carried noble status; some married their daughters to an impecunious aristocrat (who might speak contemptuously of the need to "manure his land," but who nevertheless gave noble status to his half-bourgeois sons); some were content to move a few steps up the ladder by the purchase of a minor army commission or a middle-rank church post. Enough opportunities had been available in the past to keep the bourgeoisie satisfied with the system and to make them want to share its advantages. In the mid-eighteenth century, however, these upward channels of mobility were gradually and almost completely blocked. The aristocratic campaign to regain a monopoly of all high offices got results. By the 1780's only a single high bureaucrat (Necker) was of common birth; even the intendants, once solidly bourgeois, were all noble. There had been twenty non-noble bishops in 1740; the last one disappeared in 1783. The aristocrats' final victory was achieved in 1781 when a royal decree reserved all army commissions to men of noble birth. Slowly and reluctantly, the bourgeoisie was driven to abandon its aristocratic aspirations. By 1760 some of its members had already begun to accept equalitarian doctrines, either in a mood of bitter frustration or in the hope that the threat might make the aristocracy retreat. By the 1780's equalitarian phrases were in general circulation in bourgeois salons and publications. Like Molière's doctor, the French bourgeois was becoming a revolutionist in spite of himself.

At the very bottom of the social pyramid, marked off from the petty bourgeoisie by no clear line of division, was the small but growing category of urban wage earners. Only Paris and Lyon contained sizable groups of this sort. Most of them were skilled artisans or handicraftsmen who worked in small shops, in intimate association with a bourgeois employer. Frequently they crossed the line that separated them from bourgeois status simply by setting up shop as independent enterprisers, with one or two assistants. Below them, ranging down into a kind of urban underworld that lived by its wits, was an almost submerged category of unskilled laborers who worked irregularly at menial or rough tasks. Many of them could not have survived without regular recourse to charity; in periods of economic stress, half of them—indeed, half of the skilled workers as well—might be unemployed. Early in 1790, according to official records, one Parisian in five was on some kind of relief roll, public or private. Even in prosperous times, the line between human and subhuman conditions in the urban slums would have been hard to draw.

∞⊂⊃∞⊂⊃∞⊂⊃∞

France's favorite historian, Jules Michelet, believed (as did most of his contemporaries a century ago) that the Great Revolution was at bottom the product of generalized misery — of conditions that had grown steadily worse throughout the eighteenth century until they finally reached the limit of tolerance. Many historians since Michelet's time have rejected his thesis and have argued that the mass of Frenchmen were not only better off than the subjects of any other continental monarch, but were also making some significant gains as the century moved on. They have found it easy to prove that the bourgeoisie, spearhead of the revolution, was a long way from being miserable in the generation before 1789; and they have contended that the peasant masses as well enjoyed greater prosperity and freedom than any other peasantry in Europe. Indeed, Alexis de Tocqueville could write in 1856 that the revolution was the outgrowth not of increasing misery but of the very opposite condition — the steady improvement in living condi-

23

tions and the growth of France's national wealth during the eighteenth century.

The story of the prerevolutionary era, as recent economic historians have been reconstructing it, is too complex to coincide with either the Michelet or the Tocqueville position. Paradoxically, these recent researches suggest that both versions have some validity and that the revolutionary situation came at a moment when hope and despair were strangely compounded. Most of the long-term statistical trends support the Tocqueville thesis; they show that the half-century before 1789 was an era of prosperity and economic growth. Price studies indicate a long upward price swing from 1733 to 1817. From the second to the fourth quarter of the century, French industrial production doubled in value and French foreign trade tripled. Furthermore, this was not a case of artificial economic growth produced by fiduciary inflation. The French monetary unit, stabilized in value in 1726 after the disastrous experiment of John Law, was to remain steady from that date until 1914 (save for a brief interlude during the revolutionary era). France's business expansion of the eighteenth century was a healthy one, based on such solid factors as a rapid increase in the supply of precious metals and in population.

In an era of long-term price rise and business boom, profits tended to increase and new opportunities opened out before those who knew how to take advantage of them. The chief gains went, quite naturally, to that enterprising minority of the bourgeoisie engaged in industry, commerce, or finance. Business expansion would have been even more rapid if so much capital had not been siphoned off into government bonds, elegant town houses, and rural estates. Large-scale factories remained exceptional though not unknown in the years before the revolution.

Rising prices and a growing population did not, however, work to the benefit of all Frenchmen. While the bourgeoisie gained, the wage earners of the cities clearly lost ground, for prices far outstripped money wages and buying power dropped markedly. That the eighteenth century brought increasing misery to this submerged segment of the nation seems undeniable. A plausible conclusion might be that this misery constituted one of the principal driving forces of the revolution, and that it stimulated the emergence of an embryonic proletarian class-consciousness directed against the bourgeoisie. If the shock troops of the revolution after 1789 had been composed primarily of these depressed wage earners, the hypothesis would be hard to refute. But the evidence strongly controverts it: the revolutionary crowds were made up, rather, of the next higher social category — the skilled artisans, the shopkeepers, the petty bourgeoisie of Paris. To the extent that the wage earners joined the action, they were inclined to follow the lead of bourgeois agitators and to direct their joint hostility against the "aristos" who were believed to be responsible for food shortages and high prices. There is little evidence of emerging class tension between wage earners and bourgeoisie, either before or during the revolution.

Rising prices and a growing population meant a gradual increase of fifty to sixty per cent in the price of foodstuffs — an increase from which the landowners were likely to benefit. Who owned the land in prerevolutionary France? No sure answer can be given, though widely varying estimates have been made. If one ignores local variations, the rough average may have been something like this: the nobility a quarter of the total area, the bourgeoisie a quarter, the church ten or twenty per cent, the peasants thirty to forty per cent. The most obvious gainers from rising food prices were the nobility, the bourgeoisie, and the clergy, for much of their crop went onto the market. Not only did they receive more for what they sold, but the cost of production tended to drop as the rapid growth in rural population made more and cheaper labor available. The nobles and the bourgeoisie profited also by the rising pressure of the population on the land, as a result of which land rentals roughly doubled in value during the eighteenth century. The clergy shared the foregoing advantages with respect to church-owned land and enjoyed a special advantage of its own: rising food prices gave it a steadily larger income from the tithe *(dîme)* on non-church lands, amounting to about one-thirteenth of the gross harvest.

The peasants, although they owned more of the soil than any other social group and rented or sharecropped much of the remainder, rarely benefited from the economic expansion of the prerevolutionary era. On the contrary, most of them probably lost ground. Only a few had anything left to sell after making provision for family consumption, the next year's seed, church and feudal dues, and taxes. In difficult years, a great many had to buy some food to get through the winter, so that even rural villages were the scene of frequent food riots. The pressure of population growth made matters even worse, for neither the amount of land in cultivation nor productivity per acre increased very much. A tiny minority of the peasantry managed to pull itself up by its bootstraps and to prosper in the era of rising prices; but the economic trends of the century worked against most of the peasants, whether they were small-owners, tenants, or crop-sharers.

The over-all impact of a half-century of economic growth, then, was to bring about a gradual but significant redistribution of wealth. The rich on the whole grew richer and the poor poorer, while in the middle ranges there was continuous opportunity for a vigorous and imaginative minority of peasants, artisans, and bourgeoisie to rise in the economic scale. The general effects of this evolutionary process were mixed; but on balance, dissatisfaction and despair almost certainly outweighed confidence and hope. Within the Third Estate, a majority became increasingly hostile toward the semifeudal social order and the ineffective bureaucratic monarchy that perpetuated such a system.

Any analysis confined to long-term economic trends is certain to be unrealistic unless it also considers the short-term fluctuations in the general curve. Concealed beneath the long-range rise in prices and in national wealth after 1730 was a zigzag pattern of boom and slump. About every ten years, on the average, came a cyclical crisis, originating almost always from a poor harvest and spreading rapidly to all parts of the economy. The first stage was normally a food shortage that drove grain prices up, severely affecting the mass of urban and rural consumers; then the domestic market for such items as textiles dried up temporarily, leading many manufacturers to curtail or suspend production and to throw their workers out of jobs. Food riots followed in many cities and villages, with popular passions directed against grain speculators, the aristocrats, or the government. A rash of bankruptcies increased the uneasiness of the bourgeoisie.

The last of these cyclical crises in the old regime began in 1787 and was inaugurated, as usual, by a bad harvest. What made this crisis worse than most was the fact that it struck an economy already weakened and undermined by a decade of recession or stagnation. A whole series of difficulties had converged to produce this recession; some of them were accidental, like the interruption of cotton imports during the American Revolution. Since about 1778 French economic life had been suffering from this "persistent languor." The poor harvests of 1787 and 1788 therefore produced effects even more rapid and severe than was normally the case. Grain prices doubled in a year; textile production was reduced by half; a wave of bankruptcies occurred; unemployment among the wage earners in the major cities probably reached a figure of fifty per cent. Few Frenchmen understood the nature of the crisis, but this did not restrain their bitterness. They found it easy to load the blame on the government, which, in 1786, had lowered protective tariffs against British goods in the so-called Eden Treaty and had removed restrictions on the export of grain from France. Their complaints had at least some validity; French manufacturers did face increased English competition under the Eden Treaty, and grain exports did rise fourfold in 1787, sixfold in 1788. The government's decision to turn toward freer trade was undoubtedly a farsighted one for France's long-run prosperity and strength, but it came at an unfortunate moment when readjustments in the economy were especially painful. There can be little doubt that the economic stress of the 1780's contributed to the outbreak of the Great Revolution. But to describe it as the major contribution would be risky and probably inaccurate. Without the pervasive influence of new ideas since mid-century, without the political crisis that culminated in 1788, the downward business cycle of 1787 might have passed like its predecessors, leaving behind it the usual jumble of economic wreckage and the usual memory of temporarily intensified misery.

THREE

> Between the social or economic fact and the historic
> event it is necessary for the mind of man to intervene
> if the first is to lead to the second.
>
> GEORGES LEFEBVRE

Temper of the Age,
1760–1789

Social change, most historians agree, is the product of multiple causes. But when scholars begin to assign relative weights to these multiple factors, controversy begins. Historians with left-wing tendencies have usually been inclined to stress the role of conditions as fundamental; historians with right-wing leanings, the role of ideas and of individual men. The contrast is sharpest when the origins of a great political-social revolution are being sought. To an especially rigid variety of Marxist, the dominant ideas of eighteenth-century France were little more than an intellectual secretion of the bourgeoisie, a by-product of the rise of that class to power and self-consciousness. To a conservative like Hippolyte Taine, those ideas were ". . . the central motor of events; the morbid germ which, introduced into the blood of a . . . profoundly sick society, produces the resultant fever, delirium, and revolutionary convulsions."[1] Rightists from Edmund Burke to Pierre Gaxotte have held that the doctrines of the Enlightenment gradually

---

[1] A. Aulard, *Taine, historien de la révolution française* (Paris: Plon, 1907), p. 57.

28

corroded the old order by breaking down respect for authority and for established institutions and by proposing as a substitute a "natural" order based on reason. Some of them have even found in Freemasonry a subversive underground network that served to spread and popularize the new ideas.

It is clear enough that the eighteenth century brought a basic change of outlook among educated Frenchmen and that one product of this mental transformation was the "alienation of the intellectuals." The role of an intellectual elite in the maintenance of social stability or the furtherance of social change has often been underestimated or even ridiculed, yet there seems to be a remarkable correlation between the alienation of such a group and the outbreak of revolution. Perhaps the most important development of the period 1760–89 was the progressive transformation of France's educated elite from loyal supporters to hostile critics of the old regime. Chateaubriand was to remark in retrospect that "the revolution had been accomplished before it occurred." He meant, of course, that many men's minds had been conditioned in advance for the upheaval that began in 1789.

If it was the generation of 1760–89 that turned potentially subversive, that generation took over most of its ideas from its predecessors, and added only a few new ones of its own. The bulk of Voltaire's writings and all of Montesquieu's had been published before 1760. Quesnay's treatise on physiocratic doctrine had appeared in 1758; Rousseau's three major theoretical works *(The New Heloise, Emile,* and *The Social Contract)* were to come in a rush from 1760 to 1762. Diderot's great *Encyclopedia,* the most notable compendium of Enlightenment thought, was well along toward completion; the last volume was to come off the press in 1765. The next quarter-century brought few new works of basic importance. That was the period when the Enlightenment spirit gradually spread outward and seeped downward: outward into certain segments of the privileged orders, downward through the various levels of the bourgeoisie. That was also the period that brought the progressive disillusionment of those intellectuals who had been the earliest converts to the Enlightenment view of man and society, and who had

29

devoted a generation to propagandizing that view. In 1760 they had assumed that an enlightened political leadership, once it understood the new doctrines, would willingly make the necessary alterations in society and politics. By 1789 they were determined to see the changes accomplished in spite of the existing political elite, if there should be no other way.

Enlightenment doctrines had their roots in the seventeenth century, perhaps even in the Renaissance. By 1700 the works of John Locke had crossed the Channel and were offering Frenchmen a startling new concept of the nature of man — as a creature not of immutable inborn traits but of vast, almost unlimited potentialities. The writings of Pierre Bayle, exiled along with his fellow Huguenots to the Netherlands, arrived in France soon after the turn of the century and produced an even greater impact. In the personal libraries of educated Frenchmen of the eighteenth century, Bayle's *Historical and Critical Dictionary* appeared more frequently than any other book; it became a kind of arsenal of ideas for the *philosophes* and buttressed their growing skepticism of authority. Voltaire's and Montesquieu's first political writings were published soon after 1720, and by mid-century the trickle had grown into a torrent. The themes of the *philosophes* in the generation before 1760 clustered about the somewhat ambiguous concept of humanism. Man — individual man — became the central figure in the universe. He was viewed as basically (though not purely) rational in nature; he was essentially good and almost infinitely perfectible, if provided with the proper education and institutions; he had the right to expect freedom from arbitrary rules and restrictions and to develop his capacities to their ultimate limit.

Such a set of beliefs was not subversive in the sense that it dictated the overthrow of the monarchy, the repudiation of the church, or the destruction of the social order. A society without a king, a god, or an elite of birth was almost inconceivable to most intellectuals before 1760. Mably and Morelly might question the validity of private property, or even preach a kind of utopian communism; Holbach might denounce all religion as mere superstition; an anonymous agitator might look forward to the day when "the last king would be strangled with the entrails of the last priest"; but these were exceptions, men of the lunatic fringe. The Enlightenment temper as a whole retained its loyalty to the dynasty, its deep-rooted faith in God (if not always the God of the Catholic church, or even the Christian deity), and its conviction that social distinctions were natural and necessary things. Yet in a deeper sense, Enlightenment concepts were far more subversive than its proponents knew; they could scarcely be reconciled with the dominant ideas on which the old regime rested. The institutions of eighteenth-century France were still based on authority and tradition, not on any rational or utilitarian test; the old ideal of an organic society could not be harmonized with the new concept of an atomistic one made up of autonomous individuals. The post-1760 generation of intellectuals became increasingly aware of the irreconcilable differences between the Enlightenment temper and the basic assumptions of the old regime.

Although the new generation for the most part popularized the ideas it inherited and added few new ones, a certain change in spirit did set in after mid-century. The relative simplicity and consistency of the new humanism began to be corrupted by still newer and more contradictory doctrines impinging upon it. Rousseau was primarily responsible for these accretions, some of which could not be easily reconciled with the more coherent set of beliefs of the early Enlightenment thinkers. One such novelty was the idea of equality — the most ambiguous and potentially the most explosive concept produced in the eighteenth century. The meaning of equality in practice, the possible contradictions between equality and individual liberty — these were problems that did not begin to emerge clearly until after 1789, and they were to weigh heavily upon the subsequent course of French history. A second accretion was Rousseau's emphasis on emotion and sensibility rather than on reason, suggesting a fundamentally different psychological base for the new order. Still a third novelty was Rousseau's concern for community as well as for the individual — a concern that would eventually force French intellectuals to consider the unavoidable but insoluble problem of reconciling the rights of the group with those

31

of the citizen in the new free society. Many of Rousseau's ideas had little resonance in the prerevolutionary years, but after 1789 they were to gain general currency. No other Enlightenment thinker had so many dedicated disciples during the Great Revolution.

The precise impact of ideas on men's minds is difficult to measure even in the most favorable conditions. For eighteenth-century France, which had not yet come to know the blessings of public opinion polls, the task becomes almost impossible. Illiteracy (measured by a man's ability to sign his own name) ranged from twenty to ninety-five per cent of male Frenchmen in various parts of the country, and it is a safe guess that some of those who could read did not very often do so. Yet there is enough scattered evidence to suggest that most thoughtful Frenchmen of the pre-1789 generation, whether literate or not, had been exposed to the new doctrines, and that a great many of them had absorbed some of the effects of those doctrines almost as unconsciously as modern man absorbs radioactive fallout. In the age of Voltaire and Rousseau, as in the later ages of Darwin and Freud, it was not always necessary to read the masters in order to pick up the catchwords, slogans, and simple ideas that were explicit or implicit in their systems. Gradually, indirectly, those ideas permeated the mood or temper of the era.

The peasants were undoubtedly least affected, for there still existed no channel for the diffusion of ideas outside the cities and *bourgs*. The impact on the aristocracy, on the other hand, was direct and widely felt, though variable in its effects. Some nobles, like the young Marquis de Lafayette, were promptly subverted by the new doctrines. Others reacted strongly against them and found an antidote in religious faith or in the idea of a return to the old feudal monarchy. For most of the court nobles, however, Enlightenment ideas seem to have been picked up as amusing topics for modish conversation in the salons. Montesquieu's writings were taken more seriously, for they could easily be adapted to support the aristocratic campaign against bureaucratic despotism. There is no way to be sure whether the aristocracy's flirtation with the new ideas of the age seriously affected its capacity to resist revolutionary change. What is much more certain is that few nobles were very deeply infected. The revolutionary crisis was to peel off the Enlightenment veneer, revealing in most of the aristocracy a deep commitment to the defense of an old order that its errors had done so much to undermine.

The most dedicated adherents to the Enlightenment temper were undoubtedly drawn from the educated bourgeoisie and the middle ranks of the church hierarchy. The Abbé Sieyès, whose career after 1789 was to make him the most prominent of these frustrated church intellectuals, was by no means an isolated case. Even that eminent revolutionary terrorist, policeman, and cynic, Joseph Fouché, had begun his career as a teacher in a church school. As for the bourgeoisie proper, its more vigorous, ambitious, and thoughtful members were quite naturally attracted to the new currents of ideas that had been sweeping into western Europe during the past century. Men who were making their way upward through individual enterprise were likely to find the doctrines of liberty and tolerance appealing. Yet many members of the French bourgeoisie were late and somewhat reluctant converts to the Enlightenment temper. Only when their ambition to rise in the old order was frustrated did they begin to adopt the slogans of the *philosophes*. Even as late as 1789, many of them probably would have preferred a system based on privilege to a plunge into real social equalitarianism.

One important agency in the diffusion of Enlightenment ideas was Freemasonry, which came to France from England in 1725. By 1789 there were about six hundred lodges in France; scattered through their predominantly bourgeois membership were a number of aristocrats and even some churchmen. The rituals of Freemasonry were permeated with the humanist doctrines of the Enlightenment. But to call Free-masonry an organized international conspiracy working for revolution is a grotesque distortion. The members were loyal monarchists and had with the humanist doctrines of the Enlightenment. But to call Free-masonry's violent republican and anticlerical tinge was to be acquired much later, in the mid-nineteenth century. Indeed, when the whirl-wind of revolution struck after 1789, the lodges assumed no role of leadership. On the contrary, they were quickly swept out of existence and disappeared for a generation or more.

⁂

Modern France and the modern Western world as a whole are in large measure products of the Enlightenment temper. Yet that temper has never won universal acceptance in a pluralistic and fragmented nation like France. From the very outset, a hard core of conservative critics rejected most of its premises and found in this set of ideas the source of France's gravest problems. The twentieth century has brought new recruits to this little anti-Enlightenment army and has added new variations to the attack. Alongside the traditional conservative position, with its emphasis on society's organic nature, on man's inherently evil tendencies, and on rationalism's evasion of reality, there has emerged a series of hostile views sprung in part from the Enlightenment tradition itself.

One such view, Marxian in inspiration, characterizes Enlightenment ideas as the reflection of bourgeois class interest. The ideas themselves are seen as natural products of changes in Europe's economic structure; the *philosophes* are viewed as class-bound propagandists. That the bourgeoisie seized upon the new outlook and used it, consciously or unconsciously, for its own ends, is taken to be the normal and inevitable behavior of a rising class. Exponents of this thesis single out as partial exceptions Rousseau, the theorist of egalitarianism, and a few lesser *philosophes* who were materialists and atheists. Their argument combines some validity and much plausibility — enough to permit its widespread acceptance, usually in a more muted form, by non-Marxians. But this premise that ideas must always be rigidly class-bound, that the Enlightenment temper was bound up with bourgeois interests alone, has too often been accepted without careful examination. The Enlightenment temper was produced by other factors besides the rise of capitalism; it was shared by other groups besides the bourgeoisie; and it was

34

broad and rich enough to fertilize much of European political and social thought for the next two centuries.

A second line of attack on the men of the Enlightenment has charged them with naive credibility, with the unconscious substitution of a new set of superstitions for the old discarded ones. The *philosophes,* according to this thesis, prided themselves on putting enlightened reason in the place of blind faith, but in actuality they only built themselves a new heavenly city based on little more than the will to believe. Their new faith rested on the untested premise that men would make rational choices if given free access to the truth; that man was basically good and was rendered evil only by bad institutions; that progress was a kind of law of human development, an inevitable process if the artificial roadblocks could be cleared away. The *philosophes* scoffed at people who believed in miracles, yet they built their whole system on faith in the miracle of human perfectibility.

Closely related to the foregoing criticism is the charge that the *philosophes* preached tolerance but neglected to practice it. Voltaire is the most vulnerable target of this school of critics, who insist that his scurrilous vilification of his opponents (especially the Jesuits) made the replies of the latter seem eminently fair-minded by contrast. Voltaire and other leading *philosophes* engaged in a concerted attack on one Catholic journalist that wrecked his reputation and his career; at one point these defenders of free speech called on the governmental censors to suppress his newspaper. On controversial issues of the time, the *Encyclopedia* was often more bigoted than the leading Jesuit journal.

There is a good deal of validity in this case against the intellectual leaders of the Enlightenment. Like crusading reformers of other eras, they often displayed a curious kind of inverse fanaticism, distorted the motives of their opponents, and showed signs of persecution mania. As a matter of fact, Enlightenment thinkers and publicists were rarely molested for their ideas after mid-century; and if the official censorship continued to operate right down to the revolution, it functioned sporadically and ineffectively. Frenchmen of the generation after 1760 were surprisingly free in both thought and action; it was the annoying

35

remnants of regimentation that lent color to the continuing fears and accusations of the Enlightenment intellectuals.

Whether this reform generation really substituted a new blind faith and dogma for the old is a more questionable charge. Few of its thinkers really believed in the unmixed rationality or the unlimited perfectibility of men; they were aware that irrational motives were intertwined with rational ones in human beings. Nor is it certain that they were mere ideologists, abstract system-builders, drafters of rationalistic blueprints largely unrelated to the facts of life. Defenders of the *philosophes* make a strong case for the empirical, utilitarian spirit of these thinkers and contend that most of them were, in fact, breaking the chains of abstract rationalism.

One other variety of modern anti-Enlightenment thought has directed its criticism at individual theorists of the eighteenth century. The two most common targets have been Montesquieu on the one hand and Rousseau on the other.

Montesquieu's critics have portrayed him as a kind of wolf in sheep's clothing — a concealed enemy of Enlightenment principles masquerading as a spokesmen for these principles. Montesquieu belonged to that judicial aristocracy whose interests were being fused with those of the old nobility; his real purpose, so the argument goes, was to substitute an aristocratic for a bureaucratic monarchy. His masterpiece *The Spirit of the Laws* is supposed to have been designed as a kind of handbook for those who would restore France to the pre-Richelieu system; his praise of English government is alleged to have sprung not from its liberal character but from the aristocracy's continuing power role across the Channel.

This much can be said in support of Montesquieu's critics: he did adopt some of the feudal arguments against despotism, the aristocracy did rely heavily on his book, and many *philosophes* of the next generation did find his ideas uncongenial. But the assumption that Montesquieu's motives were hypocritical is purely conjectural. It is just as plausible to regard him as a man of moderate, pluralist temper who sensed the danger of concentrating power in any one man or group of men, and who aimed to lessen this risk by a check-and-balance system of distributing power. No other thinker of the Enlightenment so completely eschewed pure reason in favor of the empirical spirit; his system was built not on logic but on the study of real examples chosen from history. If it is true that the aristocracy seized upon Montesquieu's arguments, so did other more forward-looking reformers. His ideas, more than those of any other Enlightenment thinker, seem to have inspired France's new political elite during the most constructive phase of the Great Revolution — the moderate phase from 1789–92.

No other figure of the Enlightenment has drawn such frequent and such vindictive attacks as Rousseau. One school of critics has denounced him for exalting the non-rational impulses of man and for allegedly preaching a kind of flamboyant self-indulgence; they find in him ". . . clashing phantasms in the guise of reason and a deadly virus oozing from a sick soul in lieu of moral principle."[2] A more recent manifestation of anti-Rousseau thought is that which condemns him as an ancestor of modern totalitarianism.

Rousseau not only shifted his emphasis from reason to sensibility and emotion, but he also added the doctrine of equality to the liberty and tolerance preached by his predecessors. When he chose to become the protagonist for equality and democracy, Rousseau went out looking for trouble, for these were concepts that were inherently ambiguous. According to his critics, Rousseau worsened that natural ambiguity by introducing the concept of the general will, one of the most easily corrupted phrases ever coined by a political thinker. If Rousseau never adequately defined the general will, he did specify that it was not synonymous with the will of all or with the will of a majority. He seems to have conceived it in a moralist's sense, as the spirit that would inspire all men if they were rightly and fully informed, and if no distorting factors existed to mislead them.

Some of Rousseau's disciples could conclude, therefore, that pending the arrival of those utopian conditions, the general will might be em-

---

[2] E. H. Wright, *The Meaning of Rousseau* (London: Oxford Univ. Press, 1929), p. 3.

bodied temporarily in a minority of men — even a small handful of them. That minority alone would know what all men would desire if they were not misled by evil institutions and by the psychological distortions produced by those institutions. The duty of such a vanguard would be to seize and hold power, if necessary in spite of the majority; to make men happy and virtuous by setting up new institutions and carrying out a thorough process of re-education; to "force men to be free," in Rousseau's own phrase. Rousseau's modern critics find in the climactic phase of the Great Revolution the earliest examples of this fanatical, crusading application of Rousseauan doctrine: first with Robespierre and his faction, then with the futile scheming of Babeuf. They find, too, a continuing current of Rousseauan influence in a series of exalted thinkers and activists of the nineteenth century, and a modern embodiment of the theory in Lenin's and Stalin's Russia.

Rousseau's defenders are appalled at this version of Rousseauan thought and brand it as sheer distortion. They insist that Rousseau's writings show a hatred of despotism of all kinds and an unwillingness to sanction the use of brutality to drive men even toward a desirable goal. By his phrase, "force men to be free," he meant only to create the kind of social environment in which no one would be tyrannized and in which man's native goodness would blossom naturally. These defenders see the general will as a kind of moralist's ideal, a symbol of the goal to be attained; they insist that for Rousseau a regime founded on tyranny and corruption could never, even in transitory fashion, embody the general will. Some of these Rousseauans prefer to regard the general will as no more than a bit of jargon to represent the generous social tendencies within each man, as opposed to his selfish tendencies.

The defenders of Rousseau probably have the stronger case. But they are not always ready to admit that Rousseau's ambiguity did leave his ideas open to distorted interpretations. His disciples and readers, left to wrestle with the meaning of the general will as well as with the more basic ambiguities of equality and democracy, almost inevitably divided into two factions and ended as polar opposites: on the one hand, as liberal, empirical democrats like Gambetta, Jaurès, Léon Blum; on the other, as totalitarian democrats such as Robespierre, Blanqui, and Maurice Thorez. Both of these streams might have risen out of Enlightenment thought and eighteenth-century conditions had no Rousseau ever lived. The fact is that he did live and write and shape men's thinking, that he did provide an intellectual pedigree for divergent democratic dogmas throughout the course of modern French (and Western) history. Certainly Rousseau was one of the most effective pamphleteers of all time; and "unfortunately," as one of his critics has ironically remarked, "he had a first-class mind."

From Edmund Burke's time to our own day, men have debated the validity of Enlightenment thought and the practical impact of those concepts on French society and politics. Recent criticism of the eighteenth-century temper has sometimes tended to obscure its admirable side. Perhaps the *philosophes* and their disciples were sometimes simple and naive; perhaps they put too much trust in man's natural goodness and rationality; perhaps they indulged in some self-deception and unwittingly furnished a theoretical foundation for a worse kind of tyranny than the sort they were trying to destroy. Yet the Enlightenment spirit also helped to break men free from arbitrary controls, gave them a chance at fuller self-development, and encouraged the introduction of humanitarian reforms. If the Enlightenment image of man's true nature was too simple to fit the reality, the older image against which it was set was surely even less adequate. If totalitarian democracy sprang from Enlightenment thought, it was neither the inevitable product nor the only product of that thought. Alongside it emerged the enduring stream of liberal, empirical democracy as well: the kind of undoctrinaire doctrine that inspires men to work in skeptical and cautious fashion, via trial and frequent error, toward a more humane society; the kind that doubts the imminence of any utopia, yet never abandons utopia as a theoretical long-term goal. For good or ill, the next two centuries of French history were to be pervaded by the ideas of Enlightenment.

FOUR

> . . . Experience teaches us that, generally speaking,
> the most perilous moment for a bad government is
> when it seeks to mend its ways.
>
> ALEXIS DE TOCQUEVILLE

The Decadent Monarchy, 1760–1789

In the late spring of 1774 a disgraceful scene occurred in the streets of Paris. As the funeral procession of Louis XV passed on its way to the royal tomb in Saint-Denis, the route was lined not with weeping mourners but with tipsy celebrants shouting such inappropriate comments as "Tally-ho!" Fifty years earlier, when the boy-king had begun his reign, he had been Louis the Well-Beloved. He had long since used up his credit and his popularity, though the fault was not entirely his own. Louis's mistakes and his character flaws had contributed much to the disintegration of his prestige; but he was burdened from the outset with almost insoluble problems inherited from his brilliant predecessor, and he faced growing and convergent pressures during his reign — pressures that even a greater man might have found overwhelming.

Part of the king's unpopularity at his death stemmed, ironically enough, from the wisest and most courageous act of his reign. In 1771 he had finally lost patience with the obstructionist *parlements* and had moved to break their power once and for all. His principal adviser at the moment was a minister named Maupeou, a career bureaucrat dedi-

40

cated to the ideal of an efficient bureaucratic monarchy and known to be capable of ruthless action. Maupeou purposely goaded the *parlement* of Paris into resisting a decree that reduced its powers. When the *parlement* struck back by refusing to transact business, Maupeou exiled the magistrates to the provinces, stripped them of their powers, and transferred some of those powers to new courts with more restricted authority. Then he plunged without delay into the pressing task of fiscal reform. The long struggle, it appeared, was over, and the worst obstacle to efficient government was cleared away.

Maupeou's action (which had the king's firm support) was not a popular one, however urgent it may appear in retrospect. A few prominent intellectuals like Voltaire and Turgot approved it, but the great bulk of opinion was outraged at what seemed to be a case of despotic repression. The *parlements* profited by the shrewd public relations campaign that they had conducted during the eighteenth century, which had enabled them to win the sympathy of both the exponents of aristocratic reaction and the advocates of enlightened reform. Which of these two contradictory programs they really represented was not yet clear in 1771; the *parlements*, by using ambiguous and emotion-loaded phrases, somehow managed to combine the opposites as they talked of constitutional rights and essential liberties. The king's initial decision, therefore, was much to his credit, and so was his stubbornness in supporting Maupeou after 1771 against the latter's almost hysterical critics.

French monarchist historians believe that the death of Louis XV at this critical juncture was the old regime's greatest disaster; that "only then did the Revolution become inevitable."[1] Their case rests on the assumption that the old king, had he lived another decade, would have pushed ahead with further reforms and would have managed to win the country's support for his program. They insist that the monarchy was still sound in 1774; that the discontent revealed at Louis's funeral was superficial and narrowly restricted, and that it indicated no real revolutionary spirit. Their thesis is plausible even if unprovable.

[1] J. Bainville, *Histoire de France* (Paris: Fayard, 1924), p. 291.

Ten years of firmness might have given the new institutions time to take root; Frenchmen might have tired of the *parlements'* outcries, especially if the king had countered with his own public relations campaign. Whether Louis possessed the requisite vigor and imagination is, of course, a purely speculative matter. His prior record as king hardly suggests it, and the monarchy had never shown much talent for explaining its program to the people. True, the popular welcome given to his successor, Louis XVI, in 1774, supports the view that the monarchial institution was still solidly rooted in the public affection. At least part of that enthusiasm, however, may have stemmed from a hope or belief that the new king would reverse rather than continue the policy of his grandfather and would resuscitate the suppressed *parlements*.

— That, in any case, is what Louis XVI promptly did. His good intentions were epitomized in the remark he is supposed to have made on his accession: "What I should like most is to be loved." Some of his initial actions were remarkably enlightened: he reduced royal expenditures, talked of the need to bring bread prices down, and made some of the best ministerial appointments in many years. But his most popular decision was undoubtedly the dismissal of Maupeou and the reversal of the great minister's work. The *parlements* were restored to their old status, much to their own satisfaction and that of the public; someone enthusiastically chalked on the statue of Henry IV, most popular of all French kings, the Latin phrase "He is resurrected."

Two years sufficed to prove the lack of wisdom of Louis's act. The king's most significant new appointment had been that of Turgot as controller-general. Turgot was both an eminent economic theorist (the most notable spokesman of the physiocratic school) and a career civil servant with a reputation as a practical reformer. During his term as royal intendant at Limoges, he had made notable progress in cleaning up abuses and invigorating the economy of a backward province. His nomination caused a sensation, and Turgot lost no time in embarking on an equally sensational new deal. His goal was to strengthen royal absolutism by making it efficient and enlightened. In the process, it was necessary for him to restore public credit and to clear away a thicket of outmoded economic restrictions. His program, if accomplished, would undoubtedly have revolutionized the old regime; for it involved abolition of tax exemption for the privileged classes, abolition of the restrictive guild system, drastic cuts in sinecures and pensions, and the creation of a national elective body empowered to deliberate on taxes (though not to legislate).

Turgot's failure has usually been attributed to his rashness, his lack of tact, his eagerness to get things done in a hurry. Such a view has at least some validity, for, as Turgot remarked, "in my family we die of the gout at fifty." But gradualism and tact might have been no more effective in furthering a program that directly challenged almost every powerful vested interest in France. Turgot's only chance of success lay in the unlimited and undeviating support of the king, buttressed perhaps by a direct appeal to the bourgeoisie and the peasants for mass support. Turgot doubted the feasibility of a massive public relations campaign; he believed that time was of the essence, and that it would take a generation or two of enlightenment to bring the masses around. He relied, unfortunately, on the king alone. For two years Louis held up remarkably well against the powerful convergent pressures that bore down upon him from the vested interests, from the circle around Queen Marie Antoinette, even from certain reform ministers who were offended by Turgot's tactlessness and his domination of policy. In the end Louis succumbed, with the disillusioned remark that "only Turgot and I love the people." The new deal was swept away in 1776, leaving scarcely a trace of effect.

Turgot's successor in the controller-general's office was a man of quite a different type. Jacques Necker, a Swiss Protestant banker who had settled in Paris and had made a fortune in speculation, was generally believed to be a financial wizard. Besides, he had friends among the *philosophes* and the physiocrats and was reputed to share some of their ideas of enlightened reform. Historians have not been kind to Necker, and probably with good reason. Though he was incorruptible and a man of moral courage, his self-image was a highly inaccurate one. He thought of himself as France's greatest statesman since Colbert, and unfortunately, many Frenchmen came to share his view. In fact, he possessed neither a long-range policy nor a clear understanding of what the nation needed and how it might be accomplished. For several years this millionaire with the soul of a bank manager managed to please everyone by talking reform but refraining from any real challenge to the antireform interests. While his popularity reached incredible heights, he continued to "live on borrowed time and capital."

A policy of expediency has its limits. By 1781 the enthusiasm for Necker was being offset by rising dissatisfaction. One principal source of trouble was the financial drain resulting from France's participation in the war of the American colonies against England. Foreign Minister Vergennes, with Necker's support, plunged into the war in 1778, primarily in the hope of getting revenge against England and recovering the colonial possessions lost in 1763. As a foreign policy gamble the venture proved reasonably successful, but the impact on the French treasury was disastrous. By 1781 Necker felt it necessary to take drastic action at last. The financial statement that he proceeded to publish was both unprecedented and shocking. For the first time, Frenchmen were given a glimpse into the mysteries of public finance; they could get a rough idea of how much tax money was being wasted in futile expenditures. Any good that might have been accomplished by this act was undone, however, by Necker himself; he juggled the figures to show an excess of income over expenditure and thus concealed the desperate need for tax reform. Necker's dramatic action brought his prompt downfall; there was an outcry from all the vested interests, and the king shortly found an occasion to ask for Necker's resignation. Necker left office a public hero, in the opinion of "enlightened" Frenchmen. His reinflated reputation was to have unfortunate results several years later when crisis leadership was required; for Necker was mistakenly assumed to have the necessary qualities.

After a brief interlude of drift, Louis found an able successor for Necker in the career bureaucrat Charles Calonne. The new controller-general was more intelligent than Necker and more diplomatic than Turgot; what he lacked was a stiff backbone. As a former intendant

in the provinces, Calonne understood as well as Turgot what was wrong
with the royal finances. Past extravagances had saddled the treasury
with such a heavy public debt that the interest on it consumed half of
the government's total revenue. There were only two ways out of the
impasse: the first, a repudiation of the public debt, openly or through
the concealed method of inflation; the second, a broadening of the tax
base to include the privileged classes. For several years Calonne avoided
either solution. Instead, he set out to restore public confidence by borrowing heavily and by embarking on a major public works program.
His methods produced a brilliant surface prosperity but did nothing
to correct past evils. By 1786 Calonne had come to the end of his rope;
he was forced to approach the king with a proposal to broaden the tax
base and a scheme by which the privileged classes might be persuaded
to accept it. Instead of the usual futile attempt to bully the *parlement,*
Calonne suggested that Louis convoke an Assembly of Notables, a hand-
picked body of aristocrats, churchmen, and bureaucrats, summoned to
hear their sovereign's needs and to grant him financial aid.

Louis accepted the idea with enthusiasm, thanks to Calonne's confident assurance that the privileged classes would welcome the plan and
would hail the king as a public savior. When the Assembly met in
February, 1787, Calonne appeared before it with an intelligent (though
not entirely frank) exposé of the government's financial situation and
with a well-conceived program of reform. But for once his remarkable
powers of persuasion failed. The Notables stubbornly refused to vote
any funds to the king unless the latter would first agree to revolutionize
the governmental system. They wanted the conversion of bureaucratic
despotism into aristocratic monarchy, with both central and local decision-making controlled by a national assembly and a series of provincial assemblies drawn from the privileged classes. Calonne, with the
king's support, stood surprisingly firm against these demands; but pressure from the queen and her advisers (who belonged to the most bigoted
element of the privileged caste) finally led Louis to repudiate and dismiss Calonne. The Notables adjourned shortly with nothing accomplished, except that the session had stimulated widespread discussion of

the fiscal abuses that had brought France to the verge of crisis. A flood of pamphlets inundated the country, many of them only distantly related to the issues discussed by the Notables, but all of them revealing a deep undercurrent of dissatisfaction.

Calonne's successor, Archbishop Loménie de Brienne, owed his appointment to the faction around the queen. Whether the archbishop believed in God was a matter of interested discussion among his contemporaries. Whether he was competent in financial matters could arouse no debate at all. His talents were those of the consummate courtier; his standing as a financial technician was strictly amateur. Even an amateur, however, could not evade the fact that every easy solution had been used and that only drastic and painful ones remained. The baffled minister promptly adopted the central idea in Calonne's program — a new land tax, to be levied against all classes without exception. But he decided to resort to the old-fashioned method of putting it into effect: an edict by the king, followed by due registration of the edict by the *parlement* of Paris. Now, at last, Louis was to suffer the consequences of his earlier error, the re-establishment of the *parlements*. Not only did the *parlement* of Paris refuse to register the edict, but it continued to balk even when the king appeared before it in formal *lit de justice* session. For a year the deadlock went on, the *parlement* clothing its motives in the usual disguise of righteous phrase. New taxes, it declared, could not be levied without the consent of the nation through its duly chosen representatives; only the Estates-General, an institution dead since 1614, could give validity to the king's decree.

In calling for an Estates-General, the *parlement* was merely repeating a suggestion made by the Assembly of Notables when it adjourned in 1787. In retrospect, it is easy to see that this proposal opened the door to revolution in France, and that it was the French aristocracy, not the unprivileged Third Estate, that took the fatal initiative. The aristocrats assumed that they could control the Estates-General and use it as a device to transform the monarchy, after which they would vote the king enough money to save the government from bankruptcy. Their long campaign for a revolution in reverse, for a return to the

46

quasi-feudal monarchy of pre-Richelieu days, seemed to be reaching its point of culmination.

The king, however, had one other alternative. It was still in his power to return to the Maupeou policy of 1771–74 and sweep the *parlements* out of existence. In 1788 he chose that course, though only in limited form. Instead of abolishing the *parlements*, he stripped them of much of their power, including their right to register royal edicts. The popular outcry that followed was spontaneous and overwhelming; it far exceeded the protest caused in 1771 by Maupeou's more drastic measures. The contrast indicated the change of mood in France in only seventeen years, though it may also have reflected the economic stress of the late 1780's. The public clamor confronted Louis with a risky decision: he must either carry his policy to its logical conclusion by dissolving the *parlements*, or else he must capitulate to the opposition. The tougher course he dared not try; the *parlements* had succeeded in making themselves too widely popular. Besides, he had no able and forceful adviser to bolster his determination; at court he was surrounded by critics of his new policy, and the queen's faction kept up a constant drumfire of misguided counsel. Reluctantly, Louis capitulated in July, 1788; he issued an edict convoking the Estates-General for the following spring, restored the rights of the *parlements*, and recalled Necker in a desperate attempt to stave off bankruptcy through the winter.

This time the edict was registered promptly and enthusiastically by the *parlement* of Paris. But the magistrates added a kind of postscript of their own: they shortly ruled that the Estates-General must be organized in the same manner as its predecessor of 1614. By that act, the magistrates cast off their disguise as defenders of Enlightenment doctrines. The 1614 assembly had been dominated by the privileged classes; the representatives of the three estates had sat as separate houses, and any action had required the approval of all three branches. The *parlement's* ruling outraged those bourgeois intellectuals who, since an Estates-General was first mentioned, had been urging and expecting that the new model would sit as a single house, in which the unprivi-

47

leged Third Estate would possess the dominant influence. Overnight the *parlements* lost most of their popular following; it became clear that they were really spokesmen for the aristocratic cause. Bourgeois reformers, who had assumed till now that the magistrates would lead their fight, began to seek out their own spokesmen to challenge inefficiency and privilege.

The winter of 1788–89 brought the first signs of active political organization by the men of the Enlightenment. The story remains obscure, but a mysterious Committee of Thirty seems to have assumed a directing role in the election campaign. It sent agents to the provinces, circulated pamphlets (like the Abbé Sieyès' *What is the Third Estate?*) as guides to the voters, and furnished interested groups with model grievance petitions *(cahiers de doléances)*. The most notable members of the Committee were not drawn from the bourgeoisie but were maverick aristocrats like Lafayette and Condorcet, or unorthodox churchmen like Talleyrand and Sieyès. Whether it received subsidies from the Duc d'Orléans, the ambitious and scheming cousin of the king, remains uncertain; but Orleans undoubtedly was involved in the election campaign through his own separate network of agents.

It was still not too late for the king to regain the initiative. If his chief adviser at this juncture had been a Turgot rather than a Necker, he might have won the enthusiastic support of the reformers by issuing his own reform program and embarking on a personal electoral campaign to get a majority committed to that program. Such a strategy would have required a kind of alliance between king and Third Estate, buttressed by the proreform minority within the privileged classes; it would have required the king to accept the Third Estate's demand for a one-house Estates-General in which the commoners would have as many seats as aristocracy and clergy combined. Not very much reform would have been needed to win the support of the educated elite; no more, certainly, than the restored Bourbons were to have to accept in 1814. Unfortunately, neither Necker nor the king perceived the possibilities of such a plan. Instead, Necker wasted those critical weeks in elaborate, too-clever schemes designed to get a tax reform through the Estates-

General while leaving all other issues in the king's control. Eventually the king and Necker did authorize double representation for the Third Estate, but they evaded any clear decision on the vexing problem of one versus three houses, and they neither announced nor prepared a program of reforms. Opportunity knocked at the door of Versailles palace; it produced little more than empty, reverberating echoes within.

Early in 1789, after much delving into ancient documents to discover proper election procedures, the voters met in the chief town of each district to choose their representatives. Both the First and Second Estates used a system of direct election, with an equality of suffrage that enabled parish priests and lesser nobles to outvote their hierarchical and caste superiors. Two-thirds of the clergy's elected representatives were parish priests of common social origin; only a handful were bishops, among them being Talleyrand. Most of the Second Estate's representatives were drawn from the country nobility or the *noblesse de robe* rather than from the great court aristocrats; a handful of liberal nobles like Lafayette also managed to win election. The Third Estate, though granted almost universal suffrage for male citizens aged twenty-five or over, chose its delegates by an indirect process involving two, three, or even four stages. Partly because of this screening process, the Third Estate's representatives were drawn from its educated elite rather than from the mass of commoners. Most of the delegates came from the middle or upper bourgeoisie; the bulk of them were lawyers or career bureaucrats. There were almost no peasants, and no wage earners at all. The Third Estate was also represented by a few renegade priests like Sieyès and a few renegade nobles like the Comte de Mirabeau (neither of whom could hope for election by his own privileged order). If the resulting body of delegates necessarily lacked experience for its imminent task, it certainly did not lack talent. Some historians believe that the level of ability in the Estates-General exceeded that of any elected body in French history.

Each group of electors, after choosing its representatives, performed a second traditional task: it drafted a *cahier* or grievance petition designed to call to the king's attention the abuses that needed correction.

None of the *cahiers* of 1789 challenged such basic institutions as the monarchy, the church, or private property. Those of the Third Estate were, however, filled with phrases from the *philosophes* about natural rights and social equality. All three estates agreed in condemning such obvious abuses as the *lettre de cachet*, which permitted indefinite imprisonment without formal charge; and they spoke often of such practical reforms as the unification of weights and measures and the abolition of internal tariffs. They called, too, for more local autonomy and for some kind of constitution that would limit royal power and ensure to the nation a voice in taxation. On these latter issues, however, the privileged and unprivileged classes used similar words but meant quite different things. The aristocratic idea of a constitution and of increased local autonomy implied a transfer of power from king and bureaucrats to privileged classes, not to the nation. Nor was there the least sign that the nobility was prepared to grant the commoners' demands for social equality.

Perhaps the most remarkable aspect of the *cahiers* was their moderate tone. The winter preceding the election had been a terrible one: food had been scarce, prices high, and the weather unseasonably severe. Unemployment in the major cities probably reached a figure of fifty per cent, and the meager charitable facilities of the time were overtaxed. Yet little of this misery was reflected in either the *cahiers* or in the choice of representatives. The dominant mood was not one that presaged revolution; it was rather a mood of buoyant enthusiasm, of confidence that at last something was about to be done and that a new and better future was in prospect for France.

FIVE

> Whoever wishes to avert a revolution must desire
> it enough to carry it out himself.
>
> RIVAROL

Upheaval,
1789–1792

Someone has observed that in the greatest of American university libraries, there are as many books on the French Revolution as on all the rest of French history combined. As tourists flock to Niagara rather than to Mud Creek Falls, so historians and readers of history have naturally been attracted to an episode that contains in concentrated form the action, the passion, the glamor that can be found in man's past. But glamor alone does not explain the appeal of this monumental upheaval. As one of the few great political-social revolutions in modern history, it constitutes a rare laboratory for analysis and comparison. And by its very scope and depth, its impact was to shape the course of French development from that day to this.

Yet it may be pertinent to remark, at the very outset, that both the uniqueness and the enduring effects of the Great Revolution can be — and have often been — exaggerated. The episode of 1789–1814 was, in a sense, only the cuminating phase in several interlocking revolutions that had been changing the character of France and Europe for a century or more. Some of these revolutions were social, economic, or intel-

lectual rather than political; but all of them interacted, and none of
them can be dismissed as of minor importance. Nor was the revolution
of the late eighteenth century a uniquely French experience. The upheaval in France was only one phase of a broader movement which some
recent scholars have labelled "the world revolution of the west" or "the
Atlantic revolution," and which dominated the period from about 1760
to 1815.

Most common of all the exaggerations or distortions is the one that
finds in the Great Revolution a simple key to all French history since
that time. It is tempting, but misleading, to accept the dictum of the
historian who declared that "as a consequence of the Great Divide
created by the French Revolution, a chasm yawned between the two
Frances, so deep and so wide that all attempts to bridge it failed. . . ."
It is easy to believe that France's modern problems stem from an almost
congenital conflict between defenders and enemies of the revolutionary
heritage. There is this much truth in the thesis: France's Great Revolution, unlike those of England and the United States, did produce a
permanent heritage of division rather than a powerfully-unifying national myth. But that this particular division has been the only one,
or even the most essential one, from 1789 until our day is a doubtful
proposition. Possibly it *was* the basic issue dividing Frenchmen for a
generation or two after 1814 — until the mid-nineteenth century, perhaps even until 1875. But in more recent times the defenders of the
revolutionary tradition have far outnumbered its enemies, and other
divisive issues of far greater importance have been superimposed upon
the original one or have cut diagonally across it. France during the past
century has become much too complex to fit into the easy set of categories provided by the doctrine of the "two Frances."

And yet, one can still find in the revolutionary experience an important key for understanding the evolution of modern France. The real
source of instability and division stemming from the Great Revolution
has not been the conflict between its enemies (a shrinking faction) and
its defenders (a vast majority) but rather the conflict within the revolutionary tradition itself. Georges Clemenceau might contend a century

later that "the Revolution is *un bloc*," to be accepted or rejected as a whole; the fact is that it was never a monolithic and homogeneous unity, and no objective viewer could ever see it as such. Clemenceau failed (or refused) to see that the revolutionary myth might have different meanings to different Frenchmen. Some of them looked back to the revolution of Mirabeau — to a constitutional monarchy rooted in the older tradition. Some were inspired by Danton's revolution — moderate, bourgeois, empirical. Others meant by the revolution the Robespierrist system and spirit — egalitarian, uncompromising, filled with crusading zeal. Still others found their model in Napoleon's revolution — in an efficient "authoritarian democracy," with the end justifying the means. To some extent, these different branches within the revolutionary tradition were to remain in agreement on ideology or values; they simply differed concerning techniques, on how best to achieve a commonly held goal. But there was a deeper division as well — one that concerned the goal itself, the nature of the future good society. The conflict might be summed up as one that brought into sharp contrast the libertarian and the egalitarian ideals: the one giving free play to individual talents, with little restriction by government or society; the other ensuring the rights of the weak as against the strong, through the agency of powerful, positive government action. Both attitudes could quite convincingly claim to find their origin in the revolutionary tradition, but they could not easily be reconciled in a nation whose intellectual formation did not incline its members to empirical compromise.

Temperamental differences were to reinforce, and at the same time complicate, this ideological division within the revolutionary heritage. The libertarians often (though not always) were men of the type that Lenin once labelled "softs": men of moderate, empirical, tolerant temper, inclined to favor gradualist methods and to doubt the imminence of the millennium, content to grope by trial and error toward a utopia without ever believing that it could be wholly achieved. The egalitarians often (though again not always) were the kind of men Lenin called "rockhards": rabidly fanatical, convinced of the oneness of truth, dedicated to the achievement of a perfect society without compromise or delay, willing to sacrifice the happiness of one or more generations for the sake of all those to come.

This complex set of inner contradictions involving techniques, ideologies, and temperaments suggests why there was never to be a single, unified revolutionary heritage in France during the nineteenth and twentieth centuries. All of them stemmed in one way or another from the experience of the Great Revolution, and, somewhat less distinctly, from the Enlightenment doctrines that preceded it. In that sense, the significance of the revolution as an enduring divisive force is real enough. But the study of the revolutionary episode becomes a far more complex task than if one could cling to the stubborn legend that classifies all Frenchmen as for or against the revolution *en bloc*.

Early in May, 1789, the delegates to the Estates-General straggled into Versailles for the opening session. The atmosphere was cordial and full of hope. The American ambassador, who heard the king's welcoming address, found himself choking with emotion at the warm applause and cheers that repeatedly interrupted Louis's remarks. The king spoke well, but, unfortunately, he said nothing; once again he had missed his historical cue. What he provided was a vacuum, and the more vigorous and imaginative representatives of the Third Estate promptly rushed in to fill it. Their strategy was remarkably shrewd; instead of turning to violent demagoguery or noisy complaints, they quietly announced their determination to do nothing at all until the king would agree to fuse the three estates into a unicameral assembly. They knew that unless they could win that initial victory, the privileged orders would block any reform program except that of the aristocratic faction.

The war of nerves lasted for six weeks. The delegates of the Third Estate met daily but refused to elect officers or conduct formal business. Their strategy began to show results in June when a few parish priests deserted the meeting hall of the First Estate and joined the Third. To hasten the process, the Third Estate on June 17 voted to call itself the

National Assembly and urged the privileged orders to join it. The king meanwhile had been subjected to intense pressure from aristocratic leaders and from the queen's faction, who wanted him to break the general strike. At last Louis gave in to their demands and scheduled a new joint session of the three orders for June 23.[1] This time, in the course of a long-winded speech, he went so far as to express his support of a whole series of reforms; but in the end he asserted that the vested rights of the privileged orders must remain intact and that the three estates must meet as separate houses. When the king had retired and the First and Second Estates had gone off to their meeting halls, the delegates of the Third Estate refused to budge. This was the occasion that won for Mirabeau his first fame as the revolution's spokesman; he rose and thundered at a royal official in his stentorian voice: "We will not leave except by force of the bayonet!" The stalemate lasted for four more days; then it was the king, not the Third Estate or the aristocracy, that gave in. On June 27 Louis reluctantly ordered the three estates to meet as one house; and the privileged orders even more reluctantly obeyed. No adequate explanation of Louis's capitulation has ever come to light. The most plausible explanation is that the motive was fear: rumors had reached the court that a Parisian mob was being organized to march on Versailles, with a view to forcing action. Whatever the reason, popular enthusiasm was mingled with relief. The English traveller Arthur Young, who had been waiting about the Paris region in anticipation of trouble, went off to the provinces, noting in his diary: "The whole business is now over, and the revolution complete."

The new unicameral body at Versailles could now properly call itself the National Assembly, and it set out at once to provide the monarchy

---

[1] In order to prepare the hall for the royal session, the king's officials on June 20 locked out the delegates of the Third Estate who had been meeting there. The angry delegates, suspecting that the Estates-General was about to be dissolved and sent home, met in a nearby covered tennis court and swore a solemn oath to remain in session — against the king's will, if necessary — until they had given France a constitution. The episode had little effect on the course of events, but it caught the public imagination and became an important part of the revolutionary myth.

with a constitutional base. The road seemed clear at last; but the next four months were to bring a whole series of unexpected obstacles. Most of them were put there by the privileged classes, who had awakened at last to the fact that their harassment of the king and their demands for an Estates-General had opened the way to a quite unexpected kind of revolution. Indeed, the aristocracy's shortsightedness during the preceding generation was to be matched only by its glaring lack of leadership in the tumult. Its spokesmen now urged the king to stop what they themselves had started: they wanted the National Assembly broken up, by force or threats, and sent home without delay. Whether they won Louis over to their plan is not quite certain; at any rate, he behaved in such a way as to make him appear a convert. Fresh mercenary troops began to arrive in Versailles early in July, and when the Assembly protested, only lame excuses were offered by the court. Then on July 11 Necker, still a theoretical symbol of reform within the government, was brusquely dismissed and replaced by a reactionary.

Nothing else in Necker's career produced such consequences as his dismissal. It crystallized the suspicion and resentment of the Assembly's leaders and brought the active elements of the Third Estate in Paris into action for the first time. The origins of the disorders that promptly developed, and that led to the mob attack on the Bastille on July 14, are still obscure. Whether there were paid agitators at work behind its apparent spontaneity, it is impossible to say; but there is at least some reason to suspect that the Duc d'Orléans was involved, and possibly a group of financiers who feared that the king might be preparing to repudiate the public debt. The crowd — made up primarily of artisans and shopkeepers rather than wage earners and unemployed — initially went into the streets in search of arms to defend Paris against the rumored plots of the "aristos." This was its motive when it converged on the Bastille on July 14; the attack on the fortress was accidental rather than premeditated.

The fall of this symbol of tyranny (which had long since been virtually abandoned as a place to incarcerate political prisoners) had repercussions far out of proportion to the incident itself. Its long-term

56

effect was to produce a revolutionary myth of spontaneous popular action against despotism and injustice — a myth so appealing that the French republic a century later made July 14 its national holiday. Its short-term effect was to unnerve the king and cause him to reverse his policy. Louis's reactionary advisers tried to persuade him to strike hard against the rioters of Paris; they proposed that he leave for the provinces to rally loyal citizens and the army, and that he then lead a march on the capital to dispense awful justice. After some hesitation, the king decided on appeasement rather than force. He restored Necker to office, made a personal visit to Paris to show that he held no grudges, and assured the National Assembly that there was no truth in the rumors of an impending royal coup d'état. "From this moment," wrote the British ambassador, "we may consider France a free country, the King as a very limited monarch." Many of the leading court aristocrats, led by the king's younger brother the Comte d'Artois, packed up and left the country in disgust to wait until this foolishness should blow over. Unfortunately, the queen and some members of her faction did not join this first phase of the emigration. Had she, too, departed, there might still have been a faint chance for a workable alliance between king and National Assembly.

Louis's capitulation enabled the National Assembly to settle down to its long task of converting France into a constitutional monarchy. But the next three months were to be marked by a sporadic continuation of the violence that had erupted on July 14. The first and gravest problem was posed by the disintegration of public order in many rural districts — a disintegration that reached the point of near-anarchy by August, 1789. Rural riots had begun to occur several weeks before the Bastille affair; a kind of mass hysteria brought them to a climax in the latter part of July. Confused rumors circulated that the "aristos" were planning some kind of reactionary coup or were hiring bands of unemployed vagrants to roam the countryside, raid granaries, and disrupt the public peace. The aroused peasants, assembled by tocsin to deal with the mythical invaders, found release for their fury by attacking local chateaux and burning records of feudal obligations.

The National Assembly, disturbed at this spontaneous insurrection, talked of appealing to the peasants for patience until their demands could be taken up in due form. Some members realized, however, that further delay might bring general chaos and decided on immediate action to calm the countryside. The upshot was the dramatic night session of August 4, when the Assembly voted by acclamation to sweep away the remnants of feudalism. Most of the aristocratic members went along with the decision in the hope of saving something from the wreckage; the next day the Assembly voted that the feudal dues should be commuted by a cash payment. In reality, the peasants paid no such indemnity; the progress of the revolution was too rapid. But the reform of August 4 proved to be one of the most durable of all the revolutionary changes. The wave of rural anarchy subsided, never to recur on such a scale during the next decade. The peasantry was converted from a potentially revolutionary into a conservative force. A year or so later, many peasants were to gain further satisfaction when church lands and some noble estates were made available for purchase. The poorer peasants were pacified, meanwhile, by being assured continued use of their traditional rights in the common land of each village — the right to graze animals, gather firewood, and so on.

No sooner had the countryside been quieted than the Paris crowd went on the move again. By the end of summer, economic stress in the cities was severe: bread was scarce, prices high, and unemployment general. Besides, Paris now had a new set of tabloid newspapers and a collection of popular agitators whose warnings of dastardly plots at court kept suspicions aroused. Such men as Camille Desmoulins and Jean-Paul Marat were gaining notoriety as self-appointed guardians of the public welfare. Early in October rumors again spread that the court was plotting a coup against the National Assembly. The evidence to support the accusation was much less convincing this time than it had been just prior to Bastille Day; but the Paris crowd no longer needed much evidence.

The great riot of October 5, like its predecessor in July, seems to have been produced by a mixture of spontaneity and *sub rosa* planning, in undetermined proportions. A mob of women demonstrating for cheaper bread was somehow diverted into marching on Versailles and was accompanied by a mixed group of agitators and curiosity-seekers. The unruly crowd spent the night in the palace courtyard and was in so ugly a mood by morning that the king capitulated to its demand. Court, government, and National Assembly, he announced, would all be transferred at once to Paris, presumably to remove them from the dangerous influences at work in Versailles. The Tuileries palace in Paris was hastily cleared of its occupants to make room for the royal family, and the Assembly shortly took up quarters across the street. Some members of the Assembly, angry or fearful at these events, re-signed their seats and returned home. Perhaps they foresaw that the atmosphere surrounding the government would be quite different in Paris, where public opinion could no longer be ignored, and where the possibility of direct mob pressure would be a constant threat.

Paradoxically, however, this October riot was to mark the end of violence for the next two years and the beginning of the longest period of quiet in the whole revolutionary decade. By 1790 a gradual im-provement in economic conditions had relieved the worst stress among the masses. The most determined enemies of reform had emigrated or had gone back to the provinces. The formation of rival political fac-tions in Paris, though it had begun, had still not reached the point where factional leaders could call out their followers to threaten or to attack their opponents. The Assembly was able to proceed in leisurely fashion with its task of drafting a constitution and with the even more pressing task of clearing up the financial mess which it had inherited. The king, though he had sacrificed some of his independence by moving to Paris, remained popular and respected. The time had passed when he might hope to reverse the revolution, but he was still in a position to guide its course through intelligent action.

This first phase of the revolution was to be its most constructive period, in the sense that many of its reforms were to endure.[2] The

[2] It is true that many of these reforms were interrupted during the years 1792–1814, but they reappeared thereafter in somewhat modified form.

principal change was the creation of a political system that may or may not have been inspired by Montesquieu, but that certainly reflected some of his ideas. It was a system replete with checks and balances, based on the concept that power ought to be distributed in order to avert its abuse. The constitution (of 1791) provided for a balance between king and legislature and between central and local authority. Attached to it as a preamble was a declaration of rights — not of the rights of French citizens, but of "man." It was a classic statement of the Enlightenment's natural-rights ideal, and it was permeated by the libertarian spirit. Historians have often been cynical about the allegedly class-bound bourgeois spirit that produced this declaration and made the possession of property one of the sacred rights of man. But if the tone of the document seems today to place excessive stress on liberty, on rugged individualism, that' was probably natural enough at a time when men were reacting against an arbitrary, caste-bound system that still contained many outmoded restraints. If equality received less attention than liberty in this first declaration of rights, it was not ignored; social equality, the end of legal privilege, was asserted without equivocation.

The most controversial action of the National Assembly was the series of decisions respecting the church — decisions that stripped away its special privileges, confiscated its landed wealth, and converted the priesthood into a kind of branch of the governmental bureaucracy. The law establishing the new church organization was labelled the Civil Constitution of the Clergy. It provided that men of the cloth, bishops as well as priests, were henceforth to be paid like postmen by the state, according to a fixed salary scale. More startling still, all church officials were to be chosen by popular election in the parish or diocese. A subsidiary change was the Assembly's decision to sell church lands to private buyers. The gradual disposal of these lands, most of which went to well-to-do peasants or bourgeois speculators, speeded the expansion of the small-owning peasantry and committed it strongly to revolutionary principles.

The church settlement was closely interlinked with the Assembly's attempt to solve the problem of public finance. As the presumed value of church lands approximately equalled the public debt, the Assembly issued certificates (called *assignats*) based on the church lands as security. The *assignats* would presumably be retired as fast as the lands were sold. Instead, they promptly began to circulate as paper currency; and the Assembly (along with subsequent legislative bodies) could not resist the temptation to issue more and still more of them. They were eventually to lose more than ninety-nine per cent of their value; succeeding governments sank deeper into the financial swamp, until Napoleon at last dictated a solution. The inflation of the 1790's had one hidden virtue, however. It wiped out much of the public debt inherited from the old regime, for the government could repay its creditors with ever cheaper money.

Among the National Assembly's reforms, some were so ill-conceived as to be totally unworkable. The church settlement was undoubtedly the worst example; it brought down the Pope's anathema upon the revolutionary leaders and turned most of the clergy into stubborn opponents of the new system. After only a few years the arrangement had to be abandoned in favor of complete separation (1795) of church and state. Still, one can understand the Assembly's mistakes even if one does not condone them. The traditional role of the church in France was such that no conceivable reform could have worked smoothly; the Assembly's plan was merely the worst of several bad alternatives. As for the financial problem, it had become too grave for any government except a ruthlessly authoritarian one. A decade or two of peace and prosperity might conceivably have allowed a solution less drastic than Napoleon's; it was not the National Assembly's fault that France plunged into a generation of war instead.

❧❧❧

On the whole, the reforms worked out during this initial phase of the revolution fitted together to form a coherent pattern, a system that ought to have functioned successfully. Why, then, did the new constitutional monarchy break down almost at once? Inaugurated in 1791, it was in ruins only a year later. Its collapse seems all the more regrettable when one considers that the next seven years, from 1792 to 1799, were to contribute little in the way of permanent reforms (though much in the way of revolutionary mythology). Most of the durable changes of the revolutionary generation were the work of the National Assembly (1789–91) or of Napoleon's early years in power (1799–1804). If the situation could somehow have been stabilized in 1791, Frenchmen might have been spared twenty years of domestic strife and foreign war.

The problem thus posed is one that arises in the study of almost any great social upheaval. It can be argued that the failure of the moderates results from a kind of law of revolution, from a dynamic process which, once begun, develops its own irresistible momentum and runs its natural course from moderation to radicalism to extremism to reaction. The theory is bolstered by the fact that moderates are not always good crisis leaders, since they lack the fanatical determination that would enable them to override opponents and doubters. Once in power, they are subject to the onslaught of the reactionaries, on the one hand, and of the "rock-hard" extremists, on the other. Caught in this fashion between ruthless elements on both right and left, moderate leaders may be doomed by their own moderation.

A less deterministic theory would trace the failure of the moderates in all great modern revolutions to individual human shortcomings—to a lack of adequate leadership at the critical moment or to an unlucky turn of chance that prevented the emergence of the right man at the right time. It has been argued, for example, that the fatal factor in the French Revolution was the death of Mirabeau in 1791, at the early age of forty-two. He has been described as the only moderate possessing the requisite ability and charisma to make the new system succeed and to mediate between king and popular assembly. So great was his prestige that the National Assembly entombed his body in the Pantheon; he was the first Frenchman to achieve that honor. The case for Mirabeau is seriously weakened, however, by the fact that the king refused to trust him as a potential chief minister, and by the further fact that

Mirabeau's real ambition was to serve an autocratic rather than a constitutional king. Toward the end, Mirabeau privately urged Louis to repudiate the almost-completed constitution and to leave for the provinces to rally loyal support there.

There is an easier and more convincing explanation for the failure of the constitutional monarchy: it puts the blame primarily on the king himself. Although Louis was well-meaning and showed occasional flashes of insight, his narrow mind had a stubborn and devious quality about it, too. The king did little to consolidate the new system, even though it left him a role of real importance. His most flagrant attempt at open sabotage was his attempted flight with the royal family in June, 1791. His purpose was to rally loyal supporters near or beyond the frontier and to march on Paris at their head. Such a scheme had been urged by the queen's faction as early as July, 1789; it was much less likely to succeed by 1791. Apprehended and brought back under guard before he could reach the border, Louis was nevertheless forgiven for his escapade and was shortly installed as constitutional monarch. But the king's indiscretions were not to stop there. During the subsequent months he used his legal power to veto far too often and much too unwisely; and he topped it off by repeated secret appeals to his fellow monarchs to intervene in his behalf.

This was curious behavior for a king who before 1789 had shown an inclination to challenge the vested interests and to carry out essential reforms. The explanation may lie in the constant pressure of the queen and her advisers, which weakened Louis's resolution and changed his flabby mind. Or it may be that this pious king had serious pangs of conscience at some of the reforms built into the new system — notably the reforms affecting the church. Or again, perhaps the course of events brought out his own true character as an irritable, small-minded, stubborn man who built up a neurotic resentment at his loss of initiative after 1789. It is true that even if Louis XVI had been ideally suited to his new role, the system might have broken down nevertheless. The reformers of 1789–91, immersed in the general theories of the Enlightenment, had groped in rather empirical fashion for ways to convert those theories into a precise and workable mechanism of government. Differences of opinion over both ends and means had begun to emerge early; the National Assembly had begun to divide into factions, each of them linked with one or more of the emerging political clubs in Paris. Still, these differences were not yet overwhelming, and the unavoidable clashes between factions might still have been kept within the bounds of peaceful discussion if the king had made a sincere effort to play his assigned role.

The crisis that wrecked the system was brought on by the outbreak of war against Austria and Prussia in April, 1792. Tensions had been building up for several months, partly through the machinations of French émigrés in the German states. No issue was involved that was serious enough to require war to resolve it; but both Louis and the dominant faction in the new French legislative body (now called the Legislative Assembly) wanted war, though for different reasons. The king favored war because he expected it to bring disaster; he believed that the French army, deprived of its aristocratic officers, would collapse before the invader and that the French people would call on Louis to save the country. The controlling faction in the legislature, the so-called Girondins or Brissotins, wanted war because its leaders expected victory. An aroused sense of patriotism, they believed, would solidify the nation behind the government. Besides, they had begun to suspect the king of treasonable foreign contacts, and they hoped that war might smoke him out. There was also an ideological side to this warmongering attitude. Some French politicians thought that the rest of Europe would eagerly welcome a libertarian crusade by French troops, who would serve as midwives in the birth of constitutional systems everywhere. This illusion contained just enough truth to make it attractive; it was fostered by political refugees (like the eccentric Dutchman Anacharsis Cloots), who flocked to Paris and assured Frenchmen that the Continent was panting for freedom. Only a few skeptics spoke out in opposition as the Assembly enthusiastically adopted its declaration of war. Not even those skeptics had any idea that the war would drag on for a quarter-century; but they did believe that it might play into the king's hands and destroy the constitutional experiment.

In this latter expectation, they were quite right. The French armies near the frontier disintegrated on the approach of the invaders. Ministers, generals, and king bickered angrily over responsibility for the disaster. In the end the king dismissed the leading ministers (who represented the dominant Brissotin faction) and substituted pliable nonentities. This rash act produced a series of disorders in Paris that culminated in what has been called "the second French revolution." On August 10, 1792, a mob led by some of the new radical politicians and club orators of Paris moved against the royal palace and took it by storm, after a bloody fight with the Swiss guards assigned to protect it. The royal family had escaped just before the crowd arrived and had sought the temporary security of the Legislative Assembly's meeting hall across the street. The Assembly, unwilling to resist this mob action, voted the deposition of the king and the immediate convocation of a National Convention to decide France's future. The royal family was placed in custody pending a later decision about its fate; the Assembly handed over interim authority to a small executive committee drawn from its own membership and from the Parisian radicals. On this note of violence and improvisation, with foreign armies on French soil and with all the gains of the revolution gravely threatened, the experiment came to a jarring end.

SIX

> The tragedy of the French Revolution lay not in the reaping of a crop of dragon's teeth, but in the frustration of so many noble and apparently practicable aspirations. It was, in the words of Albert Schweitzer, a fall of snow on blossoming trees.
>
> ALFRED COBBAN

Climax and Relapse,
1792–1799

No phase of the revolutionary epoch was so complex or so controversial as the climactic period between the fall of Louis XVI (1792) and the fall of Robespierre (1794). For almost the first time in European history, a major nation tried the experiment of government without either a monarch or a hereditary governing class. That nation quickly became involved in war against most of Europe and, at the same time, in civil war. Class tensions and ideological conflict rapidly grew more severe. They were embodied in the emergence or the consolidation of a whole series of factions and organized political groups. Of these organizations, the most remarkable was the network of Jacobin clubs — some two thousand of them, linked together under a tight central leadership, and anticipating in many ways the totalitarian parties of the twentieth century. Under Jacobin leadership, France was to try a series of economic and social experiments almost unprecedented in Europe and was to resort to outright terror and the purge as instruments of government. Throughout these two climactic years, a constant factor in the background or the forefront of affairs was the Parisian crowd, acting either spontaneously or through manipulation to shape the course of events. So tumultuous a period is bound to produce a wide variety of sharply contradictory historical interpretations. Not only the significance of the events, but some of the events themselves have been the subjects of bitter controversy.

Within a month after the suspension of the king, the citizens of France were once again summoned to the polls, this time to elect a National Convention whose sole purpose was to frame a new governmental system for France. The Convention gathered in September, but so pressing were the issues facing France that constitution-making was postponed for a time. Even when a new constitution was hastily adopted in 1793, the Convention voted to put it on ice until the end of the national emergency. For three years the Convention governed the country on an *ad hoc* basis, unhampered by constitutional limitations of any kind; it simply made its own rules as it went along. Absolute power rested in its hands; there was no check or balance in this system of government by assembly.

The Convention, elected by universal and direct manhood suffrage (though nine out of ten voters had not taken the trouble to go to the polls), was a more radical body than either of its predecessors. It no longer contained any professed monarchists but only different varieties of republicans. The two most important organized factions were the moderate Brissotins and the radical "Mountain" (so called because its members sat in the upper tier of seats in the Convention). The bulk of the Convention's membership fluctuated between these two poles. The Brissotins, who had dominated politics during the brief constitutional period, were coming to be known by the newer label of "Girondins," from the fact that several of their leaders came from the Gironde region near Bordeaux. Whether the Girondins really existed as a coherent organization is open to some question; the men so labelled varied rather widely in their views, and some of them (including their original leader Brissot) actually belonged to the Jacobin club. Still, they thought and acted in common enough of the time to be regarded by contemporaries as a loosely articulated group or party. "The

Mountain" was coming to be known as the Jacobin party, even though its membership did not coincide exactly with that of the Jacobin club of Paris. Its most notable leaders were, however, prominent members of the latter organization. The Jacobin club had first been formed in 1789 by certain representatives in the National Assembly as a forum for political discussion. Over the years its structure had become more rigid and its ideology more coherent. In addition, local branches had sprung up in hundreds of provincial cities and towns. Speaking broadly, the Girondin outlook was strongly libertarian, and its leadership was drawn from the prosperous middle bourgeoisie; the Jacobin worldview contained a stronger dash of egalitarianism, and its leaders came from a slightly lower stratum of the bourgeoisie. The difference between Girondin and Jacobin was more often one of temperament than one of class or doctrine.

The Convention lost no time in involving itself in an all-out war against most of Europe. The French armies had already checked the invading Prussian forces at Valmy, on the very day in September when the Convention had first met. By the end of the year French forces had pushed across the frontier into Savoy, the Rhineland, and the Austrian Netherlands; and the Convention enthusiastically announced that it would go on crusading for freedom so long as there were peoples in Europe who thirsted for liberation. To make sure that the already conquered territories would remain free, the Convention decreed their annexation to France. These measures alone would have been enough to arouse Europe; but the Convention promptly added another — the execution of Louis XVI. The margin in favor of the death penalty was narrow; most of the Girondins would have preferred to banish the exking to the United States.

These defiant acts ensured a foreign war; they also ensured the outbreak of civil war at home. Those friends of the martyred king who had not emigrated rose up now to defy the regicides and to resist government agents sent to draft their sons and to tax their purses for the conduct of the war. The Convention's new foreign policy, active and ideological in spirit, required a large army; its decision to conscript

300,000 men aroused far more hostility than did the execution of the king. Much of western France was soon aflame with revolt; it was natural for fervent patriots of Jacobin temper to see royalist agents everywhere.

A crisis so serious quite naturally played into the hands of the more fanatical element in the Convention and in the reorganized Paris municipality (now called the Commune). The Mountain, aided by pressure from the Paris crowd, hounded the Girondin leaders out of office in June, 1793; the mob besieged the Convention for three days running and refused to leave until the Girondins were arrested or agreed to resign. A few were imprisoned; the rest went off to their provincial homes and in some cases joined the spreading rebellion against the Convention's rule. By midsummer half of France was affected by insurrection. Meanwhile, the foreign war took a serious turn for the worse; the French armies were driven out of the Low Countries and their commanding general, Dumouriez, deserted to the enemy.

The threat of disaster abroad and at home opened the way to un-restricted authoritarian rule. The Convention had already established two potentially powerful executive organs: the Committee of General Security, to deal with police matters; and the Committee of Public Safety, to shape general policy. Although the committee members were elected for terms of only a month, the Convention gradually abdicated power into their hands, and re-election became an empty formality. The twelve-man Committee of Public Safety quickly became the effective governing authority; it was composed of ". . . perhaps the ablest and most determined men who have ever held power in France."[1] Within it, Maximilien Robespierre and his henchmen emerged as the dominant faction. Robespierre, a young and impecunious lawyer from northern France, had been an obscure member of the National Assembly from 1789 to 1791 and an active figure in the Jacobin club from the outset. He had made his way upward not by charm or brilliance or oratorical power, but by sheer persistence, dogged consistency, fanatical convic-

---

[1] A. Cobban, *A History of Modern France* (London: Penguin, 1957), I, 213.

tion in the rightness of his own ideas. A man of little warmth, lightness, or humor, "priggish on a heroic scale," he nonetheless managed to win the admiration and respect of his fellow Jacobins and of the lower middle-class elements of the Parisian population. To these disciples, he was the Incorruptible, the voice and conscience of the revolution, the spokesman for the egalitarian spirit of Rousseau. Backed by his handsome, brilliant, and absolutely ruthless young lieutenant Saint-Just, Robespierre embarked on a policy of repression and regimentation that dimly foreshadowed those of twentieth-century totalitarian regimes. The new ruling clique mobilized the nation's manpower and resources for war; it imposed strict economic controls, including price ceilings; it sent special agents to the provinces to enforce its will; it developed large-scale purge machinery to deal with "bad patriots." The provincial rebellion was ruthlessly repressed, though not extinguished; the tide of foreign war began to turn again in favor of the French. By the spring of 1794 the most critical moment had passed.

But Jacobin unity could not long stand so severe a test. Signs of dissension began to appear within the Jacobin leadership; one faction, headed by Georges-Jacques Danton, hinted that it was time to soften the regime and slow the machinery of terror. Conflict developed, too, between the Committee of Public Safety and the Committee of General Security over rival claims to police power. At the same time new threats were emerging to the left of the Jacobins. Various factions of extremists, notably the followers of a Parisian demagogue named Hébert, demanded an intensification of the terror, more rigid economic controls, an all-out attack on religion, and a transfer of real power to the activist citizens of Paris, organized in the forty-eight wards called *sections*.

Robespierre struck back ruthlessly against his critics. In March the Committee arrested and guillotined the Hébertist leaders; in April it was the turn of the Dantonists to be "shaved by the national razor." It seemed that the Robespierrists had cleared the path of all possible rivals and that no one could now stand in the way of their determination to establish utopia on earth, to create the Republic of Virtue. At that triumphal point, the Robespierre faction itself began to show signs of internal dissension. Simultaneously, many Convention members who had hitherto supported the Robespierrists developed an acute attack of nerves; there were rumors that sweeping new purge lists would include even those suspected of tepidity and doubt. A Robespierrist decision in June to step up the terror machinery by adding more courts and by stripping accused citizens of even the forms of judicial protection seemed to confirm the fears of those who were not intimate members of the power group. The outcome was a plot within the Convention itself, with the ex-terrorist Joseph Fouché as its key figure. Late in July, 1794, the plotters challenged the man whom they now secretly called "the dictator." They howled him down on the floor of the Convention and voted the arrest of the whole Robespierrist group. In the midst of a night of confusion, during which the Robespierrists vainly tried to mobilize the Paris crowd to save them, the leaders were captured; and at dawn they were carted off to the guillotine.

The victims of Thermidor were Jacobins; but so were most of the victors. The purpose of these victors was not to slow the course of the revolution, nor to stop the Reign of Terror that had already sent almost twenty thousand citizens to the guillotine, nor to return to a system of moderation and compromise. Yet their action produced all of these results. Thermidor marked the climax of the terror and the beginning of a gradual relaxation. Most Frenchmen were tired of the tension and violence that had gripped the country for a year; they began to realize, too, that the threat of foreign invasion and of internal upheaval was no longer great enough to justify emergency measures. The Committee of Public Safety was hobbled, the purge machinery and the economic controls gradually dismantled, and a new constitution drafted. The rump Convention adjourned at last in 1795, making way for the Directory — a structure of government that strongly resembled the one built in 1789–91, save for the fact that it provided for no king,[2] and that the

---

[2] Some Thermidoreans hoped to restore the monarchy in 1795, with the ten-year-old son of Louis XVI as king. They presumed that a regency council of good revolutionaries could raise the child as a constitutional monarch. The boy's death in prison in June, 1795, wrecked the scheme.

church was cut adrift from the state to enjoy the uncertain blessings of freedom.

The surviving members of the Robespierrist faction made one last attempt in 1795 to block this return to moderate government. The removal of price ceilings by the Thermidorians had brought a sharp jump in food prices and severe distress among the underprivileged urban groups. The resultant discontent was crystallized by one of the Convention's last acts — a decree requiring that two-thirds of the members of the next legislature be chosen from among the membership of the Convention. This convenient scheme for staying in office (or for keeping experienced men in office, if one prefers to be charitable) played into the hands of Parisian agitators. Once again they aroused the crowd and led it in a march on the Convention. But, for the first time since 1789, the mob failed to get its way. The Convention called on the regular army to break up the threat to peace and order; a young unemployed general named Bonaparte received the assignment and scattered the attackers with a whiff of grapeshot. The incident gave clear proof that the pendulum was no longer moving jerkily toward the left but had begun to swing back to the right. And more ominous still, it presaged the emergence of a new force in French political life: the army, and its new crop of revolutionary generals.

✥◦✥ ✥◦✥ ✥◦✥

Historians by the dozen have analyzed and narrated the French Revolution's climactic years; but somehow the story emerges in a wide variety of quite different forms. Here, as always, the facts do not speak for themselves; or at least they fail to speak with the same voice to all men. Although the various interpretations shade into one another, most of them can be fitted into four major categories: conservative or monarchist, liberal, radical, Marxian.

To conservative and monarchist historians, it was logical and almost inevitable that the revolution reached a climax in dictatorship and terror. If fanatical extremists achieved power and bathed the country in blood, it was because the so-called sensible moderates had opened the way to them, and because the *philosophes* had even earlier subverted the legal order. Enlightenment thinkers, ignoring the facts of history in favor of the attractions of pure reason, corrupted the nation's intelligentsia and undermined a legitimate system that was capable of being reformed. Edmund Burke had warned as early as 1790 that to uproot a social and political system and to seek to create a brand-new substitute was certain to bring disaster. Once the first steps had been taken in 1789, only one uncertainty remained: how much bloodshed and anarchy would be needed to produce a healthy revulsion among decent people? At what point would the nation call on a strong man to step in and clear up the wreckage?

In the conservative view, Robespierre was the disciple of Rousseau, the first in a long line of demagogues capable of translating Rousseau's ideas into action. The motive of this fanatic was not so much thirst for blood or power as for perfection; this zealot was prepared, for the good of mankind, to destroy wrong-headed people and to force men to be free. He found (or thought he found) in Rousseau the lesson that in times of crisis the general will may be embodied in a small minority, a vanguard, whose members can and must make decisions for a whole people. To attain his end, Robespierre built his vanguard into a disciplined organization, a kind of totalitarian party. He gradually converted the Jacobin clubs from free debating societies into a regimented clique of rigidly orthodox believers, imbued with a sense of duty to make men virtuous and free.

The conservative analysis of the revolution rarely pays much attention to class tensions or to economic and social forces. The decisive factors shaping the course of events are seen as psychological, temperamental, ideological; the explanation of terror is found in the distorted mind of the neurotic or the psychotic leader. When the revolution attained its paroxysm under "the sea-green Robespierre" and that "icy monster" Saint-Just, it had come to depend on outcasts ". . . recruited from that human trash which infests capital cities, from the epileptic and scrofulous rabble which . . . imports into civilization the degener-

73

acies, the imbecility, the defects of . . . its retrogressive instincts and its ill-formed heads."[3]

The liberal view of the revolution begins with a quite different set of preconceptions. It sees the old regime as hopelessly outmoded, far too weak and too rotten to reform itself. The revolution, therefore, was necessary, and most of its early leaders were admirable and high-minded men. Some liberal historians have singled out the Girondins for special praise and have described them as the cream of France's educated elite, honestly seeking a middle way. More commonly in recent years, the liberal interpretation admits that the Girondins were not much good at anything but making speeches and getting elected; it finds the real hero of the epoch in Danton, spokesman for the more moderate wing of the Jacobins. Here was a man who could act as well as talk; here was a charismatic figure, a crisis leader, and above all a master of the political art of compromise. Danton more than any other revolutionary politician was equipped to unify all French patriots and to find a true middle way.

If this estimate is sound, then why did Danton fail to hold power for more than a few months? The liberal answer is likely to be that Danton was destroyed by the villainous, scheming Robespierre, "the most hateful character in the forefront of history since Machiavelli . . . ."[4] Danton's defenders see Robespierre as a small-minded, jealous man who thirsted for power but possessed no talent for managing men, and who could not even comprehend Danton's statesmanlike policy of conciliating rival groups. The selfish plot of the Robespierrists disrupted revolutionary unity at the worst moment of national crisis and made that crisis far more serious than it needed to be. If it is true that Danton flaunted his weaknesses of character — his lack of integrity in financial matters, his lax personal habits — these were minor sins, the personal idiosyncrasies of a great man. In Victor Hugo's phrase,

[3] H. Taine, *Les origines de la France contemporaine: la révolution* (Paris: Hachette, 1890), II, 471.
[4] Lord Acton, *Lectures on the French Revolution* (London: Macmillan, 1910), p. 300.

"Danton [was] venal but incorruptible. He took bribes but didn't deliver the goods."

The liberal interpretation of the revolution, like the conservative, subordinates or oversimplifies the economic aspect and the issue of class conflict. The whole revolutionary era is seen as a two-way struggle between the privileged caste and the Third Estate; by implication at least, it seems that all commoners, from millionaire to beggar, joined forces to build and defend a new system. There is not much sign of a clash of interest between bourgeoisie and masses or of any conscious attempt by one social group to use another as a tool for achieving its aims.

When one moves from the liberal to the radical or "common man" view of the revolution, one crosses a kind of historiographical divide. Beyond that barrier, the emphasis shifts to the theme of class conflict. Individuals and ideas take on significance only as they reflect class interests; such factors as psychology and temperament are relegated to a secondary position. To the radical historian, it was the upper bourgeoisie that inaugurated and carried forward the revolution. Its aim was to take over the place of the aristocracy as the privileged class in the state and to combine with privilege a share of political power even greater than the nobility had possessed. Bourgeois leaders used the common man, consciously and even cynically, as the cannon fodder of the revolution; the *sansculotte* crowd was persuaded to do the fighting and dying that was needed to attain bourgeois ends. The conversion of the bourgeoisie to republicanism was a piece of sheer opportunism, when bourgeois leaders found that the king would not accept their domination.

But in the process of winning its fight (so runs the radical thesis), the bourgeoisie found itself threatened by two new dangers. The common man grew vaguely dissatisfied at being exploited and developed a tinge of antibourgeois class consciousness. On top of that, fissions began to occur within the bourgeoisie itself; some bourgeois leaders developed a sympathy for the condition of the underprivileged and became committed to a kind of primitive concept of social justice. The most

75

notable examples of this conversion were Robespierre and Saint-Just, the real heroes of the revolution. Their aims were high-minded and pure, their methods were dictated by the seriousness of the crisis. The Reign of Terror was essential to break the selfish resistance of re-actionaries and profiteers and to save the nation from its foreign enemies; the economic measures of the Robespierre era were not mere wartime expedients, but part of a conscious plan to build a welfare state. If Robespierre purged such social reformers as the Hébertists, that was because their dangerous demagoguery was frightening the bourgeoisie, arousing the animal instincts of the still unenlightened dregs of society, and endangering the great experiment of the Robes-pierre faction. But the liquidation of the Hébertists did not suffice to allay the fears of the bourgeoisie, whose selfish interests were threatened by the Incorruptible's plans for a welfare state. At Thermidor the class that had launched the revolution regained the initiative once more.

The Marxian view of the revolution, at one time almost undistin-guishable from the radical view, has more recently diverged somewhat from it. Orthodox Marxists find the origins of the revolution not in the aristocrats' misguided activities nor in the decreased social mobility of the eighteenth century, but in the increasing tension between dynamic forces and static forms. The forces were those of capitalism; the forms (of both state and society) those of feudalism. Part of the upper bourgeoisie had been absorbed into the feudal system, but those who had not been bought off in this fashion were driven by class interest to challenge all feudal limitations on emergent capitalist production. One after another, the various strata of the bourgeoisie assumed leadership in the revolution, always directing their efforts toward the same general end.

Until 1791 the upper bourgeoisie clung to power and to the futile hope that the feudal aristocracy might agree to a compromise. From 1791 to 1793 a slightly lower stratum of lawyers and commercial capitalists (the Girondins) took over; but they were doomed by a spirit of "class egoism" that made them incapable of appealing for popular support in the antiaristocratic struggle. Power therefore passed in 1793 to the Jacobins or *"moyenne classe"* — an ambiguous and not entirely homogeneous group, yet one that was bound together by class ties rather than by temperament or ideology. Jacobin aims seemed sufficiently like those of the *sansculotte* masses to make them natural collaborators. The *sansculottes* as a group were even more ambiguous than the Jacobins; they were not an embryonic proletariat, or even a coherent social class at all, but rather a kind of popular-front coalition drawn from the petty bourgeoisie, artisans, and wage earners. Together, Jacobins and *sansculottes* became the "essential motor" of the revolution. But there could be no real mutual comprehension or compromise between them once the aristocratic threat was destroyed. For their class aims were completely contradictory: the Jacobin bourgeoisie wanted to break all chains on capitalist enterprise, while the *sansculottes* wanted to set up a network of new controls guaranteeing the survival of the small independent operator, relic of the precapitalist era. Although the *sansculottes* were admirable men with progressive political ideas, their economic doctrines were retrograde, and they had inevitably to be pushed aside by the triumphant bourgeoisie.[5] Robespierre himself shared responsibility for destroying the momentum and the cohesion of the *sansculottes,* by paralyzing their chief agency of political action (the *sections* or wards of Paris) and by putting a ceiling on wages. He could not do otherwise, given his lack of real contact with the masses, his ignorance of economic and social issues, and his position as spokesman for a bourgeois-dominated government. That the masses lost confidence in him and failed to save him at Thermidor is, therefore, hardly surprising. Yet in spite of his natural defects, he remains the hero of

[5] According to the Marxians and near-Marxians, a similar conflict had been developing in rural France, but it had a somewhat different outcome. The rural parallel to the urban bourgeoisie was the emergent group of prosperous small-owners called *laboureurs;* they, too, wanted to break all traditional shackles on individual enterprise. The rural equivalent of the *sansculottes* was the mass of poorer peasants, who clung to all the ancient regulations (such as the right to use the village common land) that would protect the marginal family farm. The poor peasants, unlike the *sansculottes,* got at least part of what they wanted and managed to preserve some aspects of the precapitalist rural structure for another century.

the period, "incorruptible animator of the revolutionary government ..., artisan of national independence."[6]

The radical interpretation of the revolution and some aspects of the Marxian interpretation have won widespread acceptance in recent decades. Both views are plausible ones, and their special value is that they have given greater depth to the study of the crisis by their concern for social forces and relationships. The older liberal view of the Third Estate as a solid bloc, almost undifferentiated within by social or economic variations, is no longer tenable. On the other hand, the Marxian view forces the facts into a much too rigidly deterministic framework of theory and reads far too much into the minds of bourgeois leaders. The very concept of "class" itself remains too indistinct, and the boundaries between classes in that epoch too ambiguous, to serve as an adequate model for a thorough understanding of the revolution. The liberal thesis may be outmoded, yet, in fact, the various segments of the Third Estate had a great deal in common throughout the revolutionary

[6] A. Soboul, "Maximilien Robespierre (1758-1794)," *Cahiers du communisme,* XXXIV (1958), 820. In 1958 (the bicentenary of Robespierre's birth), the Communists in parliament proposed that the state erect a monument to Robespierre in Paris. The bill failed to reach the floor for discussion. Robespierre remains, therefore, one of the few first-rank figures in modern French history who has neither a statue in Paris nor an important street bearing his name. He also remains the only revolutionary leader about whom Frenchmen are still deeply divided. According to a recent opinion poll, Robespierre-admirers and Robespierre-haters are almost evenly balanced in France.

There is a second Marxian version of the revolution — Trotskyite in spirit — that views the *sansculottes* as an embryonic but genuine proletariat, whose incipient class-consciousness was, by 1794, beginning to be directed against the bourgeoisie. According to this version, the real heroes of the epoch were such left-wing extremists as Jacques Roux, spokesman for a faction called the *Enragés* or Wild Men. Robespierre, on the other hand, is regarded as nothing more than a hypocritical demagogue engaged in a contest for personal power against other bourgeois politicians. After he had tricked and betrayed the *sansculottes,* Robespierre was in turn mercilessly betrayed by powerful bourgeois interests that no longer needed him, and that resented his refusal to pursue an expansionist foreign policy designed to conquer new seaports and markets for the business class. When the bourgeoisie a few years later again needed protection against the resurgent masses, they turned to a military dictator rather than a politician.

upheaval. All commoners had much to gain by preserving the major achievements of 1789. No doubt the bourgeoisie profited most by the revolution, both at the time and over the succeeding century. Yet in the even longer run, it is hard to believe that the common man did not gain just as much as the bourgeoisie from the Great Revolution, or that these gains for the common man were not implicit in the Enlightenment doctrines accepted by the bourgeoisie.

❧◦❦◦ ❧◦❦◦ ❧◦❦◦

With the establishment of the Directory in 1795, France embarked for the second time on an experiment in balanced constitutional government. This time it was to last for four full years — an endurance record in that revolutionary decade. Yet in the end it, too, failed; and that failure raises once again the question of responsibility. Was the breakdown of the Directory traceable to a bad constitution, to ineffective leadership, to moral corruption, to class conflict, or to sheer bad luck? Was the regime wrecked not by its own shortcomings but by an overwhelming set of convergent problems, combined with the fateful appearance of a power-hungry genius?

Napoleon himself, like most of his admirers since, always insisted that his coup d'état of 1799 really destroyed nothing except a rotten facade; that his seizure of power merely averted other dangerous alternatives — the rise of a new Robespierre, or rapid disintegration into anarchy, or the resurrection of the old monarchy. Perhaps one ought to be skeptical of such a justification, since it resembles the excuses commonly offered by men who destroy constitutional systems. Yet many of Napoleon's enemies and critics, men of republican and liberal temper, have agreed that the Directory was a futile and contemptible regime. They have described it as rotten and impotent; as a system shot through with graft and controlled by a licentious ruling group whose appropriate symbol was the Director Barras, an unparalleled cynic "surrounded by crooked men and fallen women." These critics have called the regime a failure in economic policy, since the govern-

79

ment constantly skated on the thin ice of bankruptcy; a failure in foreign policy, since it could neither win the war against Europe nor get out of that war by negotiation; a failure in domestic politics, where its leaders zigzagged between enemies of left and right and repeatedly saved themselves by openly violating the constitution and by gradually abdicating into the hands of the military.

Few kind words have been said by historians about the Directory. Yet perhaps there is a case to be made for it, as for some other weak and short-lived regimes in modern history — Weimar Germany, for instance, or the Second and Fourth French republics. Such a case would not rest on a denial of the regime's shortcomings but rather on an affirmation of the difficulties inherent in representative government in times of stress and crisis, when a nation is deeply divided over both aims and methods. In circumstances of that sort, a middle-of-the-road group possessed of a bare majority and belabored by extremists of right and left is not likely to be effective, or even to survive, unless it is fortunate enough to turn up remarkably statesmanlike leaders and to profit by an upward economic trend. Perhaps flabby moderate republics like the Directory fall not because of their own internal weaknesses, but because they have the bad luck to be challenged by a strong, ambitious, unscrupulous critic — by a man who can make the system appear worse than it is, who can persuade the citizens to overlook its virtues and to concentrate on its faults, who can convince them that authority and efficiency are more to be desired than liberty combined with weakness.

If this hypothesis has any validity at all, it would follow that without a Napoleon Bonaparte the Directory might have survived for years or decades; or, more probably, that it might have given way to a modified monarchy something like that of 1791, with a king committed this time to accept his role as constitutional monarch. France was eventually to arrive at that kind of solution in 1814, but only after experiencing the fifteen years of glory and tragedy that were Napoleon's gift to Frenchmen.

The constitution of 1795, like that of 1791, put the government into the hands of an educated and well-to-do minority. More than a million Frenchmen were deprived of the right to vote, though they kept the juridical equality won in 1789. A five-man board of Directors elected by the bicameral legislature took the place of the king. In an effort to ensure stability, both executive and legislative terms were staggered; one Director and one-third of the members of the legislative councils were to go out of office each year.

The group in power — men of Thermidor, for the most part — was faced from the outset with constant sniping by the revived Jacobins and with backstage intrigues conducted by the royalists (who enjoyed British subsidies). Hardly a year passed from 1796 to 1799 when the Directors were not confronted by a serious threat from one side or the other. Sometimes the threat took the form of a conspiracy, as in the case of Babeuf's egalitarian plot in 1796 and General Pichegru's royalist intrigue in 1797. Such a danger could be handled rather easily as long as the political police remained alert. The threat was more serious when it took the form of an electoral victory by the left or right opposition, which could then disrupt or hamstring the government. "Third force" governments in such circumstances have few real alternatives. They can try for a coalition with one extremist faction, in the hope of absorbing its dynamism. Or they can cling to power without a clear majority, in the hope that the two extremes will balance each other. The Directors usually chose to follow neither course. Instead, they resorted to flagrant violations of the constitution in order to retain a majority; they invalidated the election of opposition legislators and suppressed their newspapers. Such tactics are risky ones, even when based on a sincere conviction that the opposition's purpose is to use its constitutional foothold for anticonstitutional purposes. They are doubly risky when the government must depend on army support to accomplish its ends, for at some point decisive power passes from the civilian to the military authorities. By the later 1790's the revolutionary army of volunteers, conscripts, and old-line officers had shaken down into a career force whose members remained in uniform because they chose to do so. Most of these troops had been continuously on

81

campaign for several years, and much of that time had been spent
outside France. The soldiers lost touch with events at home; they
grew increasingly dependent on and loyal to their commanding officers.
Among these officers there were some who were developing a sense of
intrigue and a taste for politics — partly, it must be said, because
certain Paris politicians tempted them to indulge that taste. In the end,
Bonaparte himself was to strike for power not on his own initiative,
but at the invitation of a political faction in Paris.

The Directors' increasing dependence on the military proved fatal
in the end. Yet even in retrospect it is not easy to suggest alternatives
that might have ensured the survival of the regime. A really first-rate
set of leaders would have been needed to find and follow such an alternative; and the Directory turned up no statesmen of that caliber.
A vigorous, coherent attack on the worst problems of the time —
notably on the problem of inflation, inherited rather than created by the
Directory — was essential. By 1795, a flood of *assignats* was in circulation, so many that they had become almost valueless. The Directory was
no more capable than the old monarchy of setting up and enforcing a
rigorous system of tax collection. Nor could it find new revenue
through borrowing from its own citizens; bond issues found few takers.
The Directors' only feasible solution was a kind of concealed declaration of national bankruptcy. The *assignats* were repudiated in piecemeal fashion, slowly enough to give clever speculators a chance to buy
up much property with the nearly worthless currency. By the end of
1797 they were out of circulation, and the Directors could proceed to
a masked repudiation of about two-thirds of the state's internal debt.
These measures, though unavoidable, were painful to many Frenchmen
and added to the unpopularity of the regime. Besides, there was no
guarantee that the bankruptcy procedure would not be followed by a
new inflationary spiral, for the government was still spending more
than it took in.

The chief reason for the continuously unbalanced budget was
France's persistent war. Like the inflation, it was not the Directors'
war; they had inherited it from previous regimes. But they failed to

understand that domestic problems were simply insoluble so long as the war dragged on. Their most disastrous mistake, therefore, would seem to have been in the sphere of foreign policy, where for reasons of obtuseness or weakness they did not face facts.

The Convention's armies had managed to conquer virtually all the territory up to the Rhine, thus rounding out the so-called natural frontiers. Several smaller states had withdrawn from the war, leaving only Austria, England, and Russia in the coalition. Might the Directors have negotiated peace at that point, retaining the revolutionary acquisitions? The issue has been bitterly debated by historians. Some of them argue that the English would never have agreed to let France keep conquered Belgium with its excellent seaports. They contend that since no patriotic Frenchman could think of giving up the natural frontiers once they had been attained, the Directory had no choice but to carry on the war. Other historians insist that both the English and the Austrians were war-weary and financially hard pressed and that both governments might have been persuaded to accept a *status quo* peace. They point out that in 1797 Pitt's government actually put out feelers indicating that it might be willing to see a trustworthy French government keep the Rhine frontier. What the English meant by "trustworthy" was not defined, but it probably implied a restored monarchy.

Pitt's suggestion came at an opportune time. The royalists in France had just made important gains in the legislative elections of 1797; it seemed possible that the Directors might join forces with the royalist faction, re-establish the constitutional monarchy, and get out of the war. They seriously considered the prospect but ended by deciding to challenge the royalists and continue the war. Most of the new royalist legislators were excluded from parliament; Pitt's agents went home empty-handed. It was not mere chance that one of the generals who urged and actively supported this course was Napoleon Bonaparte.

Here, it would seem, was a crucial example of bad judgment and weakness on the part of the Directors. Their critics believe that they misunderstood British war aims and exaggerated British weakness.

They assumed that the English business class, aroused at the loss of profits caused by wartime trade disruption, would soon force Pitt out of office and would allow the French to dictate terms. In defense of the Directors, it has been argued that they had no way of penetrating the real mood and motives of the English and that they simply took the wrong calculated risk. Their task was complicated, too, by the behavior of General Bonaparte, who exceeded his orders in Italy and set up satellite states there well beyond the natural frontiers. Finally, as the Directors weighed the prospect of a peaceful return to constitutional monarchy, they received little help from the exiled Bourbons. On the contrary, the pretender had recently issued an untimely manifesto announcing his determination to restore the old regime intact. Nothing could have been better calculated to wreck the hope of stabilizing France and Europe through compromise.

By 1799 the English, aided by the Directory's unwise and unpopular policy of plunder in the new satellite states (Holland, Switzerland, and northern Italy), had managed to organize a new anti-French coalition and to invade the French sphere of influence. Meanwhile the ex-Jacobins won enough legislative seats in 1798 and 1799 to challenge the faction that had controlled the government since 1795. Pressure and intrigue enabled the new majority to replace four of the five Directors. The Jacobin club was once again legalized, and it embarked on a noisy propaganda campaign in favor of a return to the Robespierrist system. At the other extreme, royalist intrigues reached a new pitch of intensity. At the very heart of the government, a third variety of intrigue developed around the ex-Abbé Sieyès, who had become a Director in June, 1799. Sieyès' aim was a bloodless coup d'état that would permit him to head off both right- and left-wing threats; he proposed to draft a new constitution that would give the republic a strong executive. All he needed for this end was an excuse to act and a general to serve as a sword. The excuse was easily trumped up; an alleged Jacobin plot would serve the purpose. The general was less easily found; it was only after a few false starts that Sieyès hit on Bonaparte as the right man and got his consent to participate.

The coup of the 18th Brumaire (November 9, 1799) came near misfiring. Some suspicious legislators saw through the plotters' flimsy scheme and were on the verge of ordering the arrest of Bonaparte and his fellow conspirators. Quick action by the general's younger brother Lucien, president of the lower house of the legislature, saved the day. Bonaparte's soldiers cleared the hall of all but a dependable rump faction, which promptly voted the desired full powers to the intriguers. The constitutional system was once again swept away — this time in favor of a barely-concealed military dictatorship.

The coup of 1799 was bloodless and was met by general indifference, even on the part of those segments of society upon which it had been based. The evidence is unmistakable that the Directory, whatever its modest virtues, had failed to win the affections of any important group of Frenchmen. Yet it was not this lack of public support that doomed the Directory. It is unlikely that Bonaparte could have succeeded if the system's own leaders had not opened the way to him. The political elite of the time had, for the most part, lost confidence in the system and had abandoned its attempt to make it work. Such is often the fate of weak compromise regimes — not only in the eighteenth century and not only in France.

SEVEN

> There will always be Frenchmen who subordinate
> social and spiritual needs to power and glory, to
> authority and order.
>
> PIETER GEYL

Dictatorship,
1799–1814

In all the history of modern France — indeed, of modern Europe — few
men have aroused more controversy than Napoleon Bonaparte. Passions
in the debate run strong even after a century and a half. To his
bitterest critics, he was a grasping, cynical, power-hungry despot, a
distorted genius whose taste for brutality and tyranny grew more intense with the years. These critics see him as essentially a counter-
revolutionary who diverted France from its proper course of absorbing
and consolidating the revolution's gains; as a ruler who chose to govern
through the twin devices of propaganda and terror, and who crushed
out liberty as thoroughly as any of history's dictators. To his admirers,
he was the national hero who preserved the essential achievements of
the revolution, who brought their blessings to the rest of Europe, and
who came nearer than any other political leader of modern times to
solving the problem of government in France. "He was not [wrote one
admirer] . . . for the Revolution of Marat and Saint-Just, for the
Revolution of assassination and plunder. With all his earnest fiery
heart he was for the Revolution of liberty and justice, for the Revolu-

tion of national honor. . . . But when the Revolution became a sewer of anarchy, a dung-hill of ferocious demagoguery . . . , he reared against it, brushed it aside with the flat of his sword, bent over a France that lay prostrate in the gutter, lifted her to her feet and held her there with arms that had suddenly grown strong enough and proud enough to support his country."[1]

To summarize even the high points in Napoleon's career as it impinged on the history of France is a formidable task. Born in Corsica just thirty years before his seizure of power, he became a Frenchman and a career soldier largely by accident. Corsica had become a French territory only a year before his birth; and the royal decree that enabled young Bonaparte to obtain a scholarship at a French military school was issued in the 1770's, just in time to make him eligible. In 1789 he was an obscure lieutenant in the royal army, with slight prospect of advancement but with a restless urge to action. The revolutionary era suddenly opened new vistas. For a time Bonaparte seemed inclined to plunge into the maelstrom of Corsican politics, but the broader opportunities in France brought him back to the mainland. His Jacobin friendships and his talents as artillery commander brought him rapid distinction during the Robespierre era, and near-disaster after Thermidor. Imprisoned briefly, dropped from the active army, he spent an obscure year or two in Paris remaking his fortune. His acquaintance with Barras opened the way to a command in the armies of the Directory; in 1796 he took over the army of northern Italy, one of three French contingents assigned to converge on Vienna. His brilliant campaign of 1796–97 enabled him to dictate peace to the Austrians and to convert part of northern Italy into satellite republics.

The Directors, unnerved yet impressed at Bonaparte's talents, next assigned him to lead an invasion of England. Bonaparte persuaded them to let him sail instead to Egypt, whence he might cut English trade routes, threaten England's control of India, and begin the construction of a new French empire in the Middle East. Cut off in Egypt when

---

[1] O. Aubry, *Napoleon, Soldier and Emperor* (Philadelphia: Lippincott, 1938), p. 17.

Admiral Nelson destroyed the French fleet that had landed his troops, Bonaparte spent almost a year in futile and costly desert expeditions, awaiting his chance to return to the European scene. Bad news from Paris strengthened his conviction that his star would soon lead him out of the Egyptian trap that threatened to wreck his career. A new European coalition had been formed, and its armies were not only overrunning the French satellite states but seemed to be threatening France itself. Seizing upon this excuse, Bonaparte secretly embarked for France in August, 1799, leaving his Egyptian army to its inevitable tragic fate.

The French public, unaware that the Egyptian adventure had turned into a disaster, welcomed Bonaparte as a national hero and as a potential savior from the menace of invasion. Many Frenchmen did not know that they had already been saved; that French armies in Holland and Switzerland had won notable victories, and that in Italy the coalition members had begun to quarrel over the spoils. What the nation wanted was security and peace; and it was beginning to think that only a general could achieve them. Against this background, Bonaparte received and accepted Sieyès' proposal to sweep away the flabby Directory and to replace it with a firm authoritarian republic. Though Bonaparte almost bungled the job on the crucial day, he made no false moves once power had fallen into the hands of the conspirators. Sieyès' new constitution provided for a powerful executive board of three consuls. Bonaparte, by a few deft suggestions, persuaded the other plotters to alter the draft in such a way as to vest virtually unlimited powers in the hands of the First Consul — Bonaparte himself. The other two consuls, Sieyès and Ducos, promptly faded into obscurity. So great was the enthusiasm for Bonaparte's leadership that a national plebiscite produced a majority of 99.999 per cent in favor of the new system. "What's in the new constitution?" one citizen is supposed to have asked another. "Bonaparte," came the simple and accurate answer.

For several years the nation's confidence seemed to be well justified. By luck and shrewdness, Bonaparte managed to get the Russians to withdraw from the war; by a victorious though costly new campaign into northern Italy, he restored the French satellite states there and forced the Austrians to surrender. Once again, England alone remained as an active enemy; and this time the English were ready to negotiate. By the Treaty of Amiens in 1802, France attained peace for the first time in a decade. True, the treaty left many critical points unsettled; but France retained control of the Rhine frontier as well as of northern Italy. So great was popular enthusiasm that Bonaparte's puppet senate proposed to lengthen his ten-year term as consul to twenty years. The First Consul modestly suggested that he would prefer to be consul for life; and almost without dissent the nation again approved his action by referendum.

Peace gave Bonaparte an opportunity to channel his overflowing energies into domestic reform. He had already moved, in 1801, to restore the tie between church and state; he persuaded the Pope to accept a concordat recognizing Catholicism as the religion of the majority of Frenchmen, placing priests once again on the state payroll, and providing for state nomination of bishops. The Vatican formally abandoned any claim to church property lost during the revolution. By this shrewd device, Bonaparte cut the ground from under clerical opposition to his regime. It was, as a royalist bitterly remarked, "a business arrangement between Christians and philosophers, made in the name of a government that was neither philosophic nor Christian."[2] A second set of reforms tightened and further centralized the governmental bureaucracy. A network of prefects, subprefects, and centrally-appointed mayors wiped out the last remnants of real federalism introduced by the revolution and carried the decisions of Paris into every hamlet. In the capital itself, a series of refurbished agencies like the Council of State and the Inspectorate of Finances provided vigorous, efficient bureaucratic leadership.

Authoritarian rule at last made possible a rigorous program of financial reform. Bonaparte found the treasury virtually empty and the government desperately dependent on loans from private bankers. He

[2] J. M. Thompson, *Napoleon Bonaparte: His Rise and Fall* (Oxford: Blackwell, 1952), p. 172.

encouraged his experts to revamp the system of direct taxation, and, through his new nation-wide bureaucracy, he succeeded in enforcing collection. To stabilize the currency and to ease the problem of government borrowing, he established the Bank of France and gave it control over the nation's credit system. The bank was owned and controlled by the leading financiers of France, who had a vested interest in checking inflation and restricting the issue of paper money; for the next century the franc was to become one of the most stable monetary units in Europe.

The law code that bears Napoleon's name also emerged during the era of the Consulate. Although the task of legal codification (like a number of other reforms attributed to Napoleon) had been begun by the Convention, it had dragged on until the First Consul inspired its rapid completion. Written into the code were some of the fundamental achievements of the Great Revolution — notably the principle of equality before the law. Another durable creation of this period was the Legion of Honor, designed to recognize achievement in every sphere and to harness the loyalty of an elite of talent. Education also drew Bonaparte's attention, though not so much because of his love of learning as because of his belief that educational discipline would produce good subjects and well-trained officers. He aimed to create a teaching hierarchy as rigid and obedient as the cadres of his army and a curriculum marked by absolute uniformity. A powerful board of education in Paris controlled the system, and Napoleon might have boasted (as did a later minister of education) that in every *lycée* in France every student at a given hour would be poring over precisely the same passage in the same book. The budget provided almost no funds for primary education (which was left to the local communes) or for girls' schools; Bonaparte was concerned with training a leadership elite, not with bringing literacy to the masses or diverting females from their proper functions. "What we ask of education," he wrote, "is not that girls should think, but that they should believe."

Bonaparte's only serious failure during the early years was the frustration of his colonial plans. His ambitions ranged to every conti-

90

nent, but only in America did he embark on a practical program. His attempt to reconquer the rich sugar island of Haiti ended in disaster; guerrilla warfare and fever decimated his troops. The renewal of war with England made communications impossible; Bonaparte withdrew the remnants of his expeditionary force and cut his losses by selling Louisiana territory (destined to be the granary for his West Indian sugar islands) to the United States.

The fragile peace between France and England broke down in 1803, after little more than a year. Superficially, the fault was England's for refusing to evacuate Malta in accordance with the peace terms. England's stubbornness, however, was inspired by the obvious fact that Bonaparte was not ready to rest content with the share of Europe he already controlled. During the year of peace he annexed Piedmont outright, tightened his domination of satellite Switzerland, embarked on a series of intrigues in the German states, and sent an agent to the Near East to explore possibilities for extending French influence there. It was not the kind of behavior to persuade the British that France was ready for peaceful coexistence.

With the renewal of war, Bonaparte threw himself into plans for a cross-Channel invasion. The British retaliated by occupying France's remaining colonial outposts and by smuggling agents into France to create a monarchist fifth column. The plot was detected just in time, and its leaders executed; but Bonaparte seized the excuse to convert the Consulate into an Empire. By founding a dynasty, he could assure France of long-range stability; even if an assassin were to destroy the emperor, a successor would be assured and the regime would survive. A plebiscite produced the usual massive majority, though there were graver reasons this time to doubt the integrity of the proclaimed results. On December 2, 1804, the coronation occurred in the cathedral of Notre Dame. The Pope, who had come all the way from Rome for the ceremony, was not even permitted to set the crown on the new emperor's head; it was Napoleon himself who did the crowning.

Through the early months of 1805 Napoleon waited anxiously for news that his Mediterranean fleet had sailed into the Atlantic, where it was supposed to decoy the English fleet into leaving the Channel unprotected for a few days. The cautious French admiral preferred to duck into a Spanish port and ignored the emperor's furious orders to come out at once. By summer the moment for a Channel crossing had passed, for England had managed to organize a new coalition against France. Napoleon, unable to risk an attack on England when Austria and Russia were again in the war, switched his plans with lightning speed and set off on the most brilliant of his campaigns. After his victory at Ulm in southern Germany, Vienna was taken without a fight, but the Austro-Russian forces fell back toward the east. The emperor caught them near the village of Austerlitz where, on December 2, 1805, he won his most famous single victory. The disaster left the Austrians no choice but to beg for peace. For the third time Napoleon dictated terms, this time much more severe than had been the case in 1797 or 1800. His foreign minister Talleyrand strongly urged a policy of generosity in order to win and keep Austrian friendship and to convert the Hapsburg empire into a bulwark against Russian encroachment into Europe. Napoleon unwisely ignored Talleyrand's counsel; he preferred to teach the annoying Austrians a lesson and to return home a triumphant conqueror.

England and Russia remained in the war, but the Russian forces had been so badly decimated that they withdrew from central Europe. As for England, Napoleon tried once more for peace based on the *status quo;* but the emperor's tightening grip on Europe made the *status quo* steadily more unacceptable to London. Late in 1806 the English persuaded Prussia, for the first time in a decade, to join the anti-French coalition. Once again Napoleon's armies went on the move; at the double battle of Jena and Auerstaedt, Prussian resistance was shattered and the road was opened to Berlin. Only a small fraction of the Prussian forces escaped to the east, along with the Prussian court.

By this time Russian armies were again in the field, thanks in part to English subsidies; and Napoleon's troops had to continue eastward despite the approach of winter. A bloody, icy, and inconclusive campaign ended at last in the summer of 1807, when the French managed to win the battle of Friedland. An even greater victory promptly followed: Russia was transformed by personal diplomacy from enemy into partner. At a meeting between Napoleon and Tsar Alexander on a raft moored in the middle of the River Niemen, the two sovereigns were reconciled and agreed to divide most of Europe (as well as parts of the Near East) between them.

By one of the clauses of the Treaty of Tilsit, the Russians agreed to close their ports against English goods. Napoleon thus plugged the largest single gap in his so-called continental system, his scheme for the economic strangulation of England. The system had been in effect since 1806, though certain earlier measures had anticipated it. Napoleon believed that by closing the Continent to British goods, the nation of shopkeepers would be driven to sue for peace. His commercial blockade lasted for eight years and severely damaged the British economy, but it failed to achieve its ultimate purpose. To some extent, leaks in the blockade were responsible; much contraband trade with England continued, and Napoleon himself eventually gave a quasi-legal base to this trade by granting licenses for the smuggling of certain British products. Far more important, however, was England's success in finding new markets (mainly in the New World) to compensate for its European losses. England's total exports therefore remained fairly stable throughout the period. But moral as well as economic factors wrecked Napoleon's scheme; the English will to resist at heavy cost was something that he had not anticipated and could never quite understand.

One fatal by-product of the continental system was a French expedition to Portugal in 1807 to force Portuguese participation in the trade blockade. Napoleon's armies got permission to cross Spain for this purpose, but some of them settled down on Spanish soil and refused Spanish requests to withdraw. Napoleon's intentions were obviously not honorable; he intended to convert Spain into a new satellite. By intrigue and threats, the weak Bourbon king was forced to abdicate and was replaced by a French puppet, Napoleon's brother Joseph. A spontaneous uprising of the Spaniards followed, with young army officers and the church hierarchy as the backbone of the rebellion. More and more French troops were poured into Spain in a vain attempt to repress the insurgent nation. Meanwhile the Spaniards received help from England; an army under Wellington landed in Portugal and crossed the frontier.

Napoleon's difficulties in Spain inspired a generalized unrest in Europe. The Austrians restlessly sought an occasion to get revenge; the Pope, increasingly discontented with the way Napoleon had interpreted the Concordat, was becoming obstreperous. Even in Paris itself, shrewd politicians like Talleyrand were engaged in devious intrigues aiming at a possible palace revolution. Reports of these intrigues brought Napoleon rushing home from Spain. In a whirlwind of furious action, he dismissed Talleyrand as foreign minister and ordered the annexation of the Papal States to France. The Pope himself was virtually abducted and was held a kind of prisoner near Paris. When the Austrians suddenly declared war in 1809, Napoleon eagerly marched off to the slaughter. For the fourth time the Austrian armies were crushed (this time at Wagram), and large chunks of Austrian soil were carved off for the benefit of neighboring states allied with France.

In 1810, at the end of his first decade in power, Napoleon's fortunes had reached their zenith. His domination of Europe was almost complete, and his position at home seemed unassailable. Annexations had carried the frontiers of France well beyond the Rhine and the Alps, all the way to Hamburg in the north and to Rome in the south. A series of satellite states, several of them ruled by Napoleon's brothers or brothers-in-law, adjoined all of France's land frontiers; there were outposts of this satellite empire as far distant as Poland and southern Italy. Most of the German states were fused into the so-called Confederation of the Rhine and subjected to the domination of Paris. Prussia was a mere shadow of its old self, Austria a landlocked empire shorn of much territory and prestige, Russia an ally. Only the stubborn resistance of England and the irritating guerrilla war in Spain remained to plague the emperor. It is not surprising that he foresaw the early capitulation of the British, whose morale was threatened by the long strain of war.

At home, the system seemed to have attained stability at last, after the constant upheaval of the revolutionary decade. The last of the royalist plots had been crushed in 1804, and so had a renewed peasant outbreak in the west in support of the royalist cause. Gradually, many of the émigrés had drifted back to France, to be given positions of prestige at court or, in some cases, ministerial posts of real responsibility. A new Napoleonic nobility was gradually created, and it mingled awkwardly with the old: most of the emperor's marshals became dukes or princes, and so did such ex-revolutionaries as Talleyrand and Fouché. Only the question of the imperial succession remained unresolved. In 1809 the emperor, eager for an heir, divorced his childless wife and persuaded the Austrian court to furnish him with a Hapsburg child-bride. In due course Marie Louise presented him with a son, thus apparently ensuring the perpetuation of the dynasty in a direct line.

Nothing, it seemed, was lacking; the regime had given France stability, efficiency, prosperity, glory. A vast building program in Paris stimulated business and added to the beauty of Europe's most beautiful capital. Government encouragement to industry through cheaper credit, better technical education, and productivity propaganda fostered the growth of factories; the blockade cut off English competition, and the needs of Napoleon's armies provided a huge market. For a decade business had been good (except in the hard-hit seaport cities); industrialists and bankers were content, and so were the workers, who had steady work at rising wage levels. The streamlined administrative system was operated by the most efficient bureaucracy France had ever known. Bonaparte had come to power without an organized faction of supporters; in filling key posts he had sought talent and energy alone and had ostentatiously ignored the political backgrounds of those who served him. It had been a shrewd gamble; the bureaucracy served him faithfully and well. Napoleon himself set the example for his officials by his almost inhuman capacity for sustained work. "Come, come, gentlemen, let's wake up!" he told his ministers at a night session, "It's only two o'clock; we've got to earn the salaries the French people pay us." The price of all these achievements — increasing regimentation and unceasing war — seemed to many Frenchmen well worth paying. If equality

95

of status and the fraternal unity of all Frenchmen survived from the revolutionary triad, liberty disappeared in all but name. The number of political journals in Paris was reduced from seventy-three in 1800 to four in 1811, and the content of those four was rigorously censored. A network of police agents under Fouché's orders unearthed subversives before they had gotten much beyond thinking dangerous thoughts. Napoleon's increasingly autocratic temper gradually turned his ministers into little more than errand boys; his unwillingness to share military glory led him to omit from the list of victories on the Arc de Triomphe the battle of Auerstaedt, where Davout had saved the day for his hard-pressed sovereign.

If Napoleon's power reached its peak about 1810, one can see in retrospect that the forces of disintegration were already at work. His continental system had not only failed to wreck Britain's economy, but it had also aroused European resentment toward France. Napoleon eventually had to depose his brother Louis as king of Holland because Louis could not and would not check the Dutch smuggling trade with England. There were other reasons, too, for the growth of dissatisfaction in the satellite states. Napoleon imposed heavy exactions in men and money for the conduct of his wars. When his brother-in-law Eugène Beauharnais wrote from Italy to protest this rapacious policy, the emperor replied brutally: "My principle is *France first*." By 1812 non-French conscripts made up almost half of Napoleon's forces. The flickering guerrilla war in Spain helped to keep discontent aglow everywhere and encouraged the hope of eventual resistance to the iron rule of the French. There were some faint signs of an emergent sense of nationalism in the Italian states, the Germanies, and the Austrian realm, though it probably affected only a rather small educated elite. Not even France itself was immune from the growth of discontent. A severe business recession that set in during 1810–11 cooled the enthusiasm of the bourgeoisie, which had been a solid pillar of the regime.

The signal for the revolt of Europe was given by Tsar Alexander. Whether he had really fallen under Napoleon's personal spell at Tilsit is an insoluble question; at any rate, by 1810 the friendship was fading fast. Napoleon made an effort to patch things up at a summit meeting at Erfurt in 1808, but the fundamental conflict was only deferred. Late in 1810 the tsar withdrew from the continental system and opened his ports to neutral ships carrying the goods of England or any other nation. Napoleon at once began to move men and supplies eastward to the Russian frontier. By early summer of 1812 he had collected the largest force ever to serve under his command, and the fateful invasion of Russia was launched. The retreating Russian forces evaded a pitched battle and scorched the earth as they withdrew, forcing the invaders to depend entirely on their own elaborate but inadequate supply system. Smolensk fell after two months, but Napoleon decided against going into winter quarters there and gambled on a lightning march toward Moscow. Early in September the Russians made their stand at Borodino and were beaten after a bloody all-day conflict. A week later the emperor rode into Moscow to dictate peace terms. But he found no one to hear his terms; tsar and court had withdrawn behind Moscow with the remaining Russian forces. Within twenty-four hours Napoleon, too, had left the city; fires, set intentionally or accidentally by the Russians, were whipped into fury by a high wind, and before rain fell to check the holocaust three-quarters of the city was destroyed. Deprived thus of winter quarters and supplies, unable to make contact with a Russian government that refused to ask for terms, Napoleon set out in October on the retreat to Smolensk. But by the time that city was reached, discipline had begun to disintegrate. The supply system, already overtaxed, broke down completely; soldiers roamed through the city looting or fighting over food and vodka. The weary forces headed westward again in mid-November, dragging their cannon and their booty, harassed by Cossack raiders, pierced by the incredibly severe cold. On December 14 Marshal Ney and three hundred and fifty half-frozen, half-starved men marched in good order across the border into Poland — the remnants of the Grand Army that had contained, only six months earlier, about a half-million men.

Napoleon had already abandoned his men in his haste to get back to Paris. Optimistic and cheerful in spite of the disaster, his central idea was to raise and train a new force for a second Russian invasion in 1813. This time, however, the task was to be far more difficult. There was open dissension in France and dangerous restlessness in Europe. For the moment, however, only the Prussians dared risk an open challenge to Napoleon by joining Russia and England in the war. By the late spring of 1813 Napoleon had recruited and trained a fresh army numbering a quarter of a million men, most of them French this time; and he set out once more toward the east "with his young guard and his long boots." He met the enemy in central Germany but was no longer strong enough to follow up his two inconclusive victories. From Vienna came disturbing indications that even his father-in-law, the Hapsburg emperor, might join the coalition against him. He spent a month in a desperate attempt to keep Austria neutral, but it was already too late. Secretly, Metternich had committed Hapsburg power to the enemy coalition and was only awaiting a safe moment to intervene. In August the Austrians cast off the cloak of neutrality; for the first time since his earliest campaigns, Napoleon faced a coalition whose armies outnumbered his own. His victims had learned at last, after far too much delay, that cooperation was the only way to defeat their oppressor. In October, at the Battle of the Nations near Leipzig, the French army was decimated, and its remnants forced to retreat. Word of disaster came from Spain as well; the last French forces were driven across the Pyrenees into France, and Wellington's army followed close behind. The Confederation of the Rhine collapsed, and its members joined the coalition; the Dutch called back the House of Orange; even King Joachim of Naples — Napoleon's brother-in-law — went over to the enemy.

Back in Paris, Napoleon could no longer ignore the threatening wave of discontent and weariness. He proceeded nevertheless to comb the country once more for troops. This time he could turn up nothing better than a meager force of teen-agers, untrained and appallingly outnumbered. Nevertheless, the armies of the coalition waited prudently along the Rhine in the hope that a full-scale campaign in France might be avoided. In November, 1813, the allied governments offered peace if

Napoleon would agree to stay within France's natural frontiers. Napoleon was both too proud and too suspicious of allied sincerity to accept this proposal; he turned instead to a vigorous diplomatic campaign designed to split the shaky coalition, and when that failed, to defensive war on the soil of France itself. His brilliant campaign of 1814 was, however, a hopeless one; the coalition armies crunched straight on toward Paris while the small French army buzzed angrily about them like a hornet before a tank. The city capitulated on the last day of March; on April 4 most of Napoleon's marshals abandoned his cause as futile and informed the emperor that they intended to surrender. The disillusioned ruler promptly abdicated in favor of his son, but the victors demanded (and got) an unconditional abdication instead. As a bitter joke they named him Emperor of Elba, a barren island of eighty-six square miles off the Italian coast. Two weeks later he left Paris for his new realm. On the way southward through France he was met with apathy, taunts, or threats from his former subjects. In the whole country, no voice was raised in his behalf except in the army, where most of the noncommissioned officers stubbornly asserted their loyalty to the commander they had served so long.

The fate of France lay in the hands of the coalition. A Bourbon restoration had not been one of the allies' war aims; the victors were not at all sure that such a solution would ensure a stable and peaceful France. The tsar had been inclined to favor promoting the Swedish crown prince, former Marshal Bernadotte of France, to the French throne. The Austrians had been tempted by the prospect of perpetuating the Empire, with Napoleon's little son on the throne and the Austrian-born empress, Marie Louise, acting as regent. The English had leaned toward the Bourbons, but they doubted the country's enthusiasm for a restoration. They were right in being skeptical; Frenchmen had lost their enthusiasm for anything except peace. The resultant vacuum provided a tiny organized faction of royalists with its opportunity. In an empty room small voices reverberate loudly; so it was with the Chevaliers de la Foi, a *sub rosa* organization of Bourbon supporters founded in 1810 to work toward an eventual restoration. As the in-

vasion proceeded, the Chevaliers had managed to stir up royalist demonstrations that impressed the allied statesmen. Just after Paris fell they
won an important new recruit — Talleyrand, still one of the highest
dignitaries of the Empire. Talleyrand's effective lobbying converted
the tsar and then the dominant faction in the imperial senate, which
voted on April 6 to call the Bourbon pretender to the throne of France.
Without much enthusiasm, the allied rulers concurred in the only course
that now seemed open. If any one man can be called the author of the
restoration, that man was Napoleon. By his stubborn determination to
fight to the bitter end, he had ruled out the only workable alternative —
a perpetuation of the Empire, with his child-son on the throne.

Across the Channel in exile, an aide burst in upon the pretender
with the joyous news: "Sire! You are king of France!" Coldly the new
sovereign replied, "And when have I been anything else?"[3]

❧◦❧◦❧◦❧◦❧◦❧

"What a romance my life has been!" These were Napoleon's words
as he reflected at St. Helena on his own career. Historians from his day
to ours have looked back on that career and have found no aspect of
it upon which they could all agree. "History," remarks Pieter Geyl,
"can reach no unchallengeable conclusions on so many-sided a character, on a life so dominated, so profoundly agitated, by the circumstances
of the time."[4]

Napoleon's right to be called a military genius probably draws the
greatest degree of consensus. Even if it is true that he was the last of
the eighteenth-century commanders rather than the first of the moderns,
he was, after all, still fighting an eighteenth-century war. Results
count in war; and Napoleon was rarely beaten. Few commanders in
history can point to so perfect a masterpiece of strategy and tactics as

[3] G. de Bertier de Sauvigny, *La restauration* (Paris: Flammarion, 1955), p. 72.
[4] P. Geyl, *Napoleon: For and Against* (New Haven: Yale Univ. Press, 1949), p. 15.

the battle of Austerlitz — second only, perhaps, to Cannae in the whole history of warfare.

Yet even in this sphere the critics have been severe. They have pointed out that Napoleon faced few opponents of first-rate ability; that the coalitions opposing him put as much energy into jealous squabbling as into the common effort; that his forces in the field usually outnumbered those of the enemy. They have observed that he made no original contribution to the art of war but was content to use a set of principles worked out by eighteenth-century strategists and taught to him at school; that his talent for handling armies grew less as his armies grew larger; that he was guilty of serious carelessness in his later years. They have charged that he sometimes made grievous mistakes and had to be saved by the heroism of a subordinate; that he would rarely share credit for any victory, unless one of his generals had been killed in action and was thus removed as a rival; that he consciously built up a false legend of his concern for the common soldier and his intimate knowledge of the men who fought for him; that, in fact, he had no more interest in his soldiers than a good workman has in his tools.

To Napoleon's admirers, his greatest and most durable achievement was in the sphere of domestic reform. The list of major reforms dating from the Consulate cannot be matched in any other brief period in French history; the administrative structure and the legal system have survived to this day. Napoleon's defenders insist that his actions preserved rather than destroyed the revolutionary achievements — notably civil and social equality and the revolutionary land settlement. They contend that a resurrection of the monarchy in 1799 or soon after would have meant a brusque return to the old regime; that by postponing the Bourbon restoration for another fifteen years, Napoleon provided time for the essential changes to take firm root. Some admirers even believe that by 1810 the emperor had virtually completed the difficult but all-important task of fusing the two traditions of old regime and revolution into a workable middle way.

An effective case can be made for this view. Napoleon was, in many respects, a son of the revolution; the great upheaval made his success possible, and he did preserve some of the revolutionary gains. More uncertain is the thesis that those gains would have been lost without him, and that a restored monarchy in 1800 or soon after would have been capable of resurrecting the old regime intact. The Bourbons undoubtedly nursed such illusions at the time; but they might have been forced to compromise once they tried to put their program into effect. It is true, too, that most of Napoleon's reforms had been instituted by the Convention or the Directory, and that his most striking personal contribution — the Concordat with the Vatican — was not an unmixed blessing for France. The Concordat replaced the Directory's experiment in the separation of church and state which, given time, might have won general acceptance in France. Eventually the French were to return to such a system; but only after a century of bitter conflict over the clerical issue, much of which might conceivably have been avoided had Napoleon not restored the tie between church and state. Perhaps, however, it was too early for separation to succeed in a country with France's Catholic heritage and in an era when the phrase "a free church in a free state" still had little meaning.

No aspect of Napoleon's career is more controversial than his foreign policy. To one school of historians, he was an aggressive expansionist incapable of being satisfied with what he had conquered; a man whose belief in his star meant that there could be no limits to his ambition and who therefore doomed Europe to a generation of war. To another school, he was no more than a patriotic Frenchman concerned with achieving national security and France's natural frontiers; this worthy goal was frustrated by self-seeking rival nations, notably England. Most of Napoleon's admirers insist that, if he pushed his territorial conquests beyond the natural frontiers and established there a cordon of satellite states, the purpose was purely defensive; he sought nothing more than buffers against enemies who would never be content to let France border on the Rhine and the Alps. Some of them add that the buffer-state policy was not Napoleon's creation but was inherited by him from the Directory. General Bonaparte, they say, merely helped to set up these satellites on orders from Paris, and once having taken power, could not abandon what the previous regime had passed on to him. Thus the whole epic of the Empire may be summed up as a defensive struggle to keep the conquests of the revolution — conquests that the kings of France had sought for centuries to achieve and that represented the fulfillment of France's historic destiny.

Napoleon's critics contend, on the contrary, that it was he who initially dragged the Directory into the buffer-state policy. They offer impressive evidence that the Directors intended to keep no territory beyond the Rhine and the Alps and that, if they ordered the conquest of northern Italy, it was only in order to trade that region for Austria's acceptance of the Rhine frontier. Napoleon, they insist, willfully ignored his instructions and conquered additional Italian territory. So glamorous were his victories, and so profitable the booty that the general sent home, that the Directors dared neither to challenge Bonaparte nor to abandon what he had taken. They were therefore trapped into a policy of conquest that ensured the hostility of the rest of Europe.

Many of Napoleon's critics further challenge the thesis that there were limits to his expansionism. It is true that until about 1805 he gave no clear indication of wanting to move beyond a buffer strip in Europe. After that date, however, he cast off any limitations. Much of the buffer area he annexed outright or handed over to some member of the Bonaparte clan. The rest of the Continent west of Russia gradually came into his grip in one fashion or another. Napoleon's critics conclude that this had always been his purpose, and that he had concealed his aims until his strength was great enough to let him move eastward. France, ringed about by a security cordon of buffer states, was simply too small for his vaulting ambition and vanity. His real dream was the domination of all of Europe — the construction of a new-model Roman empire ensuring peace, prosperity, and stability, with himself as heir of the Caesars.

There are a few admirers of Napoleon who accept this latter thesis, and who contend that the conquest of Europe was a high-minded and defensible program. France, they argue, was so far ahead of the rest of Europe that it was the duty of Frenchmen to speed the Continent's evolution by their benevolent rule. Both France and Europe, they suggest, would have had a happier and healthier future if Napoleon had managed to keep his conquests consolidated for at least a generation or two. The result in France would have been to ensure a permanent fusion of the revolutionary gains with a tradition of strong and efficient government. The result in the rest of Europe would have been to lay the foundations for a more nearly unified Continent. The next half-century was to be an era of critical importance, when the middle class everywhere was rising to power and liberal and national ideas were taking root. If these developments had occurred within a Napoleonic Europe rather than within separate and widely divergent political and social systems, the new governing class would have been more European than national. Its members would have found themselves constantly working on common problems, getting used to European-wide collaboration, and receiving their training in the most efficient of governmental bureaucracies. The hypothesis is an intriguing one; but it leaves open the question of Napoleon's willingness (or that of his successors) to relax his authoritarian grip as the new liberal and national forces gained strength.

Most of Napoleon's admirers have been somewhat more restrained than this. They have defended his purposes and actions prior to the fatal date of 1805, at which time they believe he made a disastrous error by pushing beyond the buffer region essential to France's security. The mistake, as they see it, was comprehensible; Napoleon can hardly be blamed for wanting to teach the Austrians a lesson after the latter had twice broken earlier treaty agreements with France. Besides, Corsican clan loyalty was deeply ingrained in Napoleon, and he was urged on to further conquests by his grasping brothers and sisters. But even though his motives were understandable, the conquest of Europe was pragmatically impossible to achieve.

These defenders-turned-critics point out that Napoleon's foreign minister Talleyrand warned him and sought to restrain him, arguing for a generous peace in 1805 that would have converted Austria into a grateful friend and an anti-Russian buffer. This policy, in turn, would have diverted Russia's attention eastward toward Asia, where a clash between Russia and England might have followed. In Talleyrand's mind was a complex balance-of-power arrangement that might have ensured to France the dominant role for decades to come. Perhaps it was sheer bad judgment that led the emperor to reject Talleyrand's advice; or perhaps it was Napoleon's excessive ambition and self-esteem. No man who believed so intensely in his star was likely to think that his star would lead him no farther than the Rhine. If Napoleon had some of the sense of balance and moderation so typical of the classical age, he also possessed the instincts of a gambler, an opportunist, a fatalist, unwilling to let himself be bound by a blueprint of long-range goals.

If Napoleon had really wanted peaceful coexistence within a balance-of-power system, he might have achieved it on two other occasions as well. The first was in 1802, after the English had agreed to peace. The English archives offer considerable evidence that both public and government were ready to try "appeasement," to let France keep the so-called natural frontiers, if Napoleon, in turn, would offer some guarantees of good behavior. Instead, the First Consul blandly proceeded to intrigue in the affairs of the rest of Europe and to disclose his further ambitions. A second possible opportunity came toward the end of 1813 when the allied sovereigns offered to let France keep the natural frontiers in return for appropriate commitments. Pride and suspicion combined to make Napoleon reject the offer. In this case, perhaps he was right to be suspicious; and probably it was as well for France and Europe that the drama was played out to the end.

One of the dogmas of Napoleon's admirers is that the emperor fell victim at last to the "awakening of Europe"—to the masses and nations of the Continent that rose against foreign rule, moved by a spirit of nationalism that they owed in large part to the French example. Napoleon was successful (the legend goes) so long as he fought against kings; he was beaten only when he had to fight against peoples—the peoples whom he had helped to free from their feudal chains. Napoleon himself contributed to this romantic legend after his downfall. It suited his ego to argue that no sovereign or combination of rulers could ever

105

match him; that he could be overwhelmed only by the great elemental force of the masses in motion. Napoleon's critics have offered persuasive evidence that the alleged awakening of Europe in the years before 1814 had scarcely begun. In the long run, French conquests doubtless inspired some growth in national sentiment everywhere; but there was little sign of it by 1814. The soldiers who destroyed Napoleon's system were almost all drill-hardened conscripts rather than volunteers. The crucial factor in Napoleon's defeat was the decision of Europe's monarchs to join forces, to suspend their jealous rivalries and cooperate for the duration of the war. Napoleon himself, by his ruthless and self-centered policies, had forged the iron ring of sovereigns that eventually choked and crushed his ambitions.

To judge the greatness of any eminent man of the past is a hazardous venture. If success and accomplishment are the tests of greatness, it must be admitted that Napoleon put his mark on French and European history to a degree seldom equalled by others and that he left behind a durable myth which, like so many myths, has had powerful effects. No one can question his charismatic qualities, his quick and keen intelligence, his capacity for sustained effort. Yet the flaws in his character were almost startling by contrast, for they were often so petty in nature. Napoleon was convinced that, as a man of destiny, he stood above any law; that he was not bound by ordinary moral standards in either his political or his personal life. His career was marked by a cynical realism, by a conviction that the end justifies the means. Was the end the greatness of France, the good of Europe, or the personal glory of Napoleon? Selfish and high-minded motives can rarely be disentangled in any man. One may best conclude with the perceptive phrase of an eminent historian: Napoleon Bonaparte was as great as a man can be without virtue.

EIGHT

The Varieties of History, 1760–1814

In one of Agatha Christie's whodunits, a disillusioned young lady fresh from her first year in college sagely remarks: "Such a lot of things seem to me such rot. History, for instance. Why, it's quite different out of different books." Her comment represents a long step toward historical understanding. If history is viewed not as a cut-and-dried series of indisputable "facts" but rather as a highly controversial set of judgments about past events, then its varied character can be taken as a matter of course. The purpose of this chapter, and of similar chapters terminating each part of this book, is to provide some guideposts through the historiographical maze by suggesting where controversial interpretations and supplementary information may be found. An exhaustive bibliography of primary sources and of books and articles about modern French history might be useful here, but it would consume far too much space. Besides, such bibliographies are available elsewhere — notably in the *Clio* series published by the Presses Universitaires de France: E. Préclin and V. Tapié, *Le XVIIIᵉ siècle* (Paris, 1952); Louis Villat, *La Révolution et l'empire* (Paris, 1936); Jacques Droz *et al.*, *L'Epoque contemporaine: restaurations et révolutions (1815–1871)* (Paris, 1953); Pierre Renouvin *et al.*, *L'Epoque contemporaine: la paix armée et la grande guerre* (2d ed.; Paris, 1960).

The Great Revolution, more than any other phase of French history, has been subjected to many and varied analyses. Paul Farmer, in his essay *France Reviews its Revolutionary Origins* (New York: Columbia University Press, 1944), summarizes these changing historiographical fashions, especially during the Third Republic. As early as the 1820's young historians like Mignet and Thiers were beginning to portray the revolution as a constructive experience; in the 1840's Louis Blanc, Lamartine, and Michelet were extolling its spokesmen and activists as heroes and martyrs rather than fanatics and cutthroats. Conservatives of that era preferred to read Thomas Carlyle's or Hippolyte Taine's version. Carlyle's *French Revolution* (London: Fraser, 1837) implanted for generations the legend of the revolution degenerating into a blood-thirsty orgy, one long reign of terror. Taine, in his *Origines de la France contemporaine: la révolution* (Paris: Hachette, 1878–84) took a similar view; he once described the upheaval as "the insurrection of donkeys and horses against men, under the leadership of monkeys with parrots' tongues." The more judicious liberal-conservative Alexis de Tocqueville took a middle position; he found that the revolution merely completed the monarchy's work of building centralized power in France. His *L'Ancien régime et la révolution* (Paris, 1856) remains a classic example of historical analysis.

By the end of the nineteenth century the revolution's defenders were firmly established in power and were shaping a quasi-official republican view of the great upheaval. That view was embodied in the *Histoire politique de la révolution française* (Paris: Colin, 1901) of Alphonse Aulard, first holder of the chair of history of the revolution at the Sorbonne. Aulard's work reflected the values of the dominant parties of his time, the Opportunists and the Radicals. His version was less impassioned and rhetorical than Michelet's (on whose works the republicans of 1850–90 had been weaned); he provided a soberer, more solidly documented analysis that glorified the moderate republicans of the pre-Robespierre years and that elevated Danton to the role of hero.

Soon after 1900 Aulard's ablest disciple, Albert Mathiez, broke with his mentor on the ground that Aulard's interpretation was too bourgeois and too narrowly political. Over the next quarter-century Mathiez developed what I have earlier (Chapter Six) labelled the radical or common-man interpretation of the revolution. Mathiez shifted his emphasis toward class conflict, attacked Danton as a corrupt bourgeois opportunist, and substituted Robespierre as hero. His culminating work was his three-volume *La Révolution française* (Paris: Colin, 1922–27). Many eminent historians since Mathiez's day have followed in his tradition, though they have added a greater depth and sophistication. The most notable figure is Georges Lefebvre, whose *La Révolution française* (Paris: Presses Univ., 1951, 1957) and *The Coming of the French Revolution, 1789* (Princeton: Princeton Univ. Press, 1947) are already classics. A somewhat similar approach marks the work of the Oxford historian J. M. Thompson: *The French Revolution* (New York: Oxford Univ. Press, 1945) and *Robespierre* (New York: Appleton, 1936). The more moderate Aulard tradition reappears in refined and enriched form in Crane Brinton's sparkling *Decade of Revolution, 1789–1799* (New York: Harper, 1934) — though perhaps De Tocqueville rather than Aulard is Brinton's spiritual ancestor.

Mathiez and his school were eventually outflanked on the left by Marxian scholars, who arrived late on the scene, and who have not yet produced many impressive works on the revolution. Marx himself intended to tackle the subject but failed to get round to it. The classic eight-volume *Histoire socialiste de la révolution française* (1901–6) of Jean Jaurès (ed. Mathiez; Paris: L'Humanité, 1922–24), though it stresses the class struggle, is obviously pre-Leninist in spirit. Albert Soboul has provided a brief and sketchy manual for the party faithful *(La Révolution française, 1789–1799* [Paris: Ed. Sociales, 1948]) and has recently added an exhaustive monograph on class relationships in Paris at the height of the revolution: *Les Sans-culottes parisiens en l'an II* (Paris: Clavreuil, 1958). A deviant Marxian version, Trotskyite in temper, may be found in Daniel Guérin's *La Lutte des classes sous la première république* (Paris: Gallimard, 1946). Guérin denounces Robespierre as the demagogic tool of the bourgeoisie and exalts Parisian extremists like Jacques Roux; he finds in the *sansculottes* an emergent class-conscious proletariat. Both Soboul and Lefebvre, on the contrary, defend Robespierre (with some reservations) and describe the *sansculottes* as a mélange of classes, a kind of popular front.

Recent decades have brought a renewal of the antirevolutionary interpretation, notably in the works of Jacques Bainville *(Histoire de France* [Paris: Fayard, 1924]) and Pierre Gaxotte *(La Révolution française* [Paris: Fayard, 1928]). Both authors were associated with the neoroyalist Action Française movement; both won election to the French Academy by their literary talents. Their versions are, however, sharply slanted interpretive accounts based on no fresh research; for the revolution itself, they merely bring Taine up to date.

A recent essay by the British historian Alfred Cobban reasserts a kind of Toquevillean position by contending that the revolution really made few basic changes in French society that would not have come through evolutionary processes *(The Myth of the French Revolution* [London: Lewis, 1955]). Cobban has also argued that the use of the term "Girondins" has long distorted our understanding of the revolution, since no such party or faction existed in organized form. Both of these themes recur in more muted form in Cobban's *History of Modern France: Old Regime and Revolution, 1715–1799* (London: Penguin, 1957), which presents the revolution as the culminating phase in a great age of social transformation rather than the introductory phase in an age of change. Cobban's remarkably concise synthesis combines great erudition with an elegant style and penetrating judgments.

⋙∘⋘ ⋙∘⋘ ⋙∘⋘

Interpretations of the prerevolutionary era (1760–89) are inextricably intertwined with those of the revolution itself. Conservatives and monarchists from Taine to Gaxotte, confronted by the question, "Was this revolution really necessary?" have usually answered with a vigorous negative and have been inclined to stress the role of subversive ideas in undermining a social and political order that needed to be re-

110

formed rather than destroyed. Taine's violent philippic *L'Ancien régime* (Paris: Hachette, 1875) contains the classic statement of this view; although he doubted the capacity of the old elite to reform the state, he considered the revolutionary doctrinaires far more incompetent and dangerous. Neomonarchists like Bainville and Gaxotte admit that the eighteenth-century monarchy had some shortcomings, but insist that it could have reformed itself had it not become infected with "political Fénélonism" (i.e., the limited-monarchy ideas of the old aristocracy). They seek to rehabilitate Louis XV as an intelligent, farsighted states- man who was hamstrung by vested interests, misunderstood by doc- trinaires, and weakened by his own self-doubts. Gaxotte's *Le Siècle de Louis XV* (Paris: Fayard, 1933, 1958) contains the most detailed ex- pression of this thesis.

Republican historians, on the other hand, have usually emphasized conditions rather than ideas as the principal causes of the revolution, and they have pictured the old regime as a decrepit and venal system headed by cynical or incompetent despots. They have rejected the mon- archists' conspiracy theory and have defended the *philosophes* against the charge of naive dogmatism. In recent years, however, they have come to accept the view that the eighteenth-century monarchy did make sporadic attempts at reform, and that these efforts were blocked not only by the aristocratic resurgence but also by judicial sabotage. The judges of the *parlements,* long regarded as spokesmen for enlightened reform, have thus been transmuted into self-seeking proponents of aristocratic reaction, in the benefits of which they hoped to share. Franklin Ford's *Robe and Sword: The Regrouping of the French Aristocracy* (Cam- bridge, Mass.: Harvard Univ. Press, 1953) shows how the barrier be- tween old aristocracy and newly ennobled bureaucrats was eroded away after Louis XIV's time and how the judges emerged as the most effective spokesmen for feudal interests. Elinor Barber's *The Bourgeoisie in Eighteenth-Century France* (Princeton: Princeton Univ. Press, 1955) draws on some sociological concepts to show how most of the bourgeoisie were content with a system of inequality so long as the "upward channels of social mobility" continued to permit some of them to rise into the

111

privileged caste. Only when these channels were blocked did the middle class turn reluctantly to egalitarian doctrines. Georges Lefebvre's *Coming of the French Revolution* demonstrates how the bourgeois revolution was triggered by the "aristocratic revolution" of 1787–89. A detailed study of this latter development is being made by Jean Egret; parts of his work have been published in French scholarly reviews.

The nature and the appeal of Enlightenment doctrines continues to be a subject of lively debate. Alongside the older right-wing criticism of the *philosophes* as impractical doctrinaires, two newer lines of attack have been opened in recent years. From one direction, Marxians or economic determinists (e.g., Harold Laski, in his *The Rise of Liberalism: the Philosophy of a Business Civilization* [New York: Harper, 1936]) have denigrated Enlightenment ideas as narrowly class-bound. From another direction, some disillusioned antirationalists of our age of anxiety accuse the men of the Enlightenment of ignoring man's non-rational side; or they hold that the *philosophes* were blind to their own myth-building proclivities. Carl Becker's *Heavenly City of the Eighteenth-Century Philosophers* (New Haven: Yale Univ. Press, 1932), though not the work of an antirationalist, lends effective support to these critics, for Becker argues that the *philosophes* were in fact "true believers" rather than coolly objective men of reason. R. R. Palmer's *Catholics and Unbelievers in Eighteenth Century France* (Princeton: Princeton Univ. Press, 1939) might be taken to support the same conclusion; it shows, at least, that the *philosophes* were sometimes more bigoted and fanatical than many of their Catholic targets. The case for the Enlightenment has been restated (though with some reservations) by Kingsley Martin in his *French Liberal Thought in the Eighteenth Century* (London: Turnstile, 1954) and (with fewer reservations) by George R. Havens in his *The Age of Ideas* (New York: Holt, 1955).

Controversy about the Enlightenment has also focussed on individual thinkers, and especially on Rousseau. The traditional criticisms of Rousseau by both conservatives and rationalists are well summarized in E. H. Wright's *The Meaning of Rousseau* (London: Oxford Univ. Press, 1929). The most recent denunciation, by J. L. Talmon in his *Origins of Totali-*

tarian Democracy (London: Secker and Warburg, 1952), portrays him as the fountainhead of left-wing totalitarian doctrines, the inspirer of Robespierre, Babeuf, Lenin, and Stalin. J. W. Chapman has come to Rousseau's defense in his *Rousseau: Totalitarian or Liberal?* (New York: Columbia Univ. Press, 1956). The traditional view of Montesquieu as a dedicated pluralist and libertarian has given way to a new orthodoxy that makes him a neofeudal reactionary, seeking to defend his own privileged caste: e.g., in Louis Althusser's *Montesquieu: la politique et l'histoire* (Paris: Presses Univ., 1959). The case for Montesquieu is reasserted in Havens' *Age of Ideas*. Voltaire, who has been frequently "exposed" as bigot, cynic, bootlicker of despots, or playboy-poet masquerading as serious political thinker, has been just as vigorously defended by his partisans —most recently by Peter Gay in his thoughtful study *Voltaire's Politics* (Princeton: Princeton Univ. Press, 1959). Gay asserts Voltaire's right to be considered a practical and effective proponent of "constitutional absolutism" and a sincere defender of free expression.

Still another disputed aspect of the prerevolutionary era has to do with economic conditions. Were Frenchmen prosperous or miserable; was their lot improving or growing worse? Michelet's is the classic statement of the thesis of increasing mass misery as a cause of the revolution; De Tocqueville first stated the contrary thesis that France's prosperity, rather, contributed to the great upheaval. The most influential recent contribution to the debate is that of C. E. Labrousse, in *La Crise de l'économie française à la fin de l'ancien régime* (Paris: Presses Univ., 1944). Labrousse's study of price trends in the eighteenth century shows a significant long-term rise, reflecting real economic growth. But it also reveals a cyclical pattern of boom and slump, with bad harvests setting off periodic depressions; and it shows that the 1780's was one of these periods of slump. The Labrousse thesis, which has gradually been absorbed into textbooks and lectures as the new orthodoxy, has been subjected to methodological criticism by David S. Landes in his "The Statistical Study of French Crises," *Journal of Economic History*, X (1950), 195–211; Landes objects to what he calls "the dangers of simplistic explanations of complex historical phenomena."

One of the most important recent reinterpretations of the revolutionary epoch as a whole is R. R. Palmer's *Age of the Democratic Revolution, 1760–1800* (Princeton: Princeton Univ. Press, 1959). Palmer demonstrates that the French upheaval must be viewed as part of a much broader ideological and social movement—that this was a revolution of the Western world and not simply a French affair. Jacques Godechot, in his exhaustive study *La Grande nation: l'expansion révolutionnaire de la France dans le monde, 1789–1799* (Paris: Aubier, 1956), likewise argues that if French influence quickly spread through much of neighboring Europe, it was because those areas were ready to receive the revolutionary ideology and not because French military power forced alien concepts on unwilling populations.

❧◦❧◦❧◦❧

Few men in history have been so much written about as Napoleon; few have drawn such bitter denunciation or such uncritical praise. The voluminous literature on the subject has been surveyed by Pieter Geyl in his *Napoleon: For and Against* (New Haven: Yale Univ. Press, 1949). The differences in viewpoint range over almost every aspect of Napoleon's career: his stature as a military commander, his role as domestic reformer, his claim to be "the creator of French industry," his hold on public emotions, and so on. But the most important foci of dispute are two: Was Napoleon the consolidator of the revolution or its destroyer? Were his expansionist ambitions responsible for the long war that eventually wrecked his Empire, or was he merely attempting to hold the legitimate gains won by his predecessors?

The debate over the first issue is probably a futile one, since it revolves in part around semantic difficulties. His detractors cannot deny that Napoleon carried to completion many of the administrative and legal reforms begun by the Convention; his admirers cannot deny that civil liberties were drastically curtailed in this authoritarian police state. The ambiguity lived on in the Bonapartist tradition of the nineteenth century; Bonapartism sometimes seemed to belong on the left, sometimes on the right, and usually it managed to draw support from both extremes.

On the foreign policy issue, the classic defense of Napoleon is that of Albert Sorel in his eight-volume *L'Europe et la révolution française* (Paris: Plon, 1885–1904). Sorel contended that Bonaparte inherited his policy from the old monarchy, the Convention, and the Directory; that, like any patriotic Frenchman, he considered it his mission to attain and preserve France's "natural frontiers"; and that those frontiers could be protected against English greed and incomprehension only by setting up a chain of buffer states beyond the Rhine and the Alps. Critics like Raymond Guyot, on the other hand, charge him with wilfully ignoring the Directory's orders to take no territory beyond the natural frontiers except for bargaining purposes; they hold that he dragged the country at once into a campaign of unlimited conquest *(Le Directoire et la paix de l'Europe* [Paris: Alcan, 1911]). A middle category of historians like Adolphe Thiers *(Histoire du consulat et de l'empire* [Paris: Paulin, 1845–75]) contends that Napoleon's aims were honest and defensible until 1805, at which time he made a crucial error by rejecting Talleyrand's policy of restraint and conciliation with Austria.

Among recent attempts to reassess the Napoleonic period, F. Markham's *Napoleon and the Awakening of Europe* (New York: Macmillan, 1954) is perhaps the most useful brief account. Markham describes the emperor as the last of the enlightened despots rather than the first of the modern dictators and discredits the legend that he was finally destroyed by the aroused nationalism of the European masses. He also makes the suggestion (heretical for an Englishman) that it might have been better for both France and Europe if Napoleon had been able to perpetuate his control of the Continent for a generation or two. Such a view seemed less startling when it appeared in the work of a French patriot like Edouard Driault *(Napoleon et l'Europe* [Paris: Alcan, 1910–27]). J. M. Thompson's *Napoleon Bonaparte, His Rise and Fall* (Oxford: Blackwell, 1952) is constructed primarily from the emperor's voluminous published correspondence. Félix Ponteil's *Napoléon Ier et l'organisation autoritaire de la France* (Paris: Colin, 1956) takes the view that Napoleon destroyed more than he preserved of the revolution's institutions and principles.

❖❦◦❦❖ ❖❦◦❦❖ ❖❦◦❦❖

Whole libraries could be filled with specialized monographs and works of synthesis on the period 1760–1814. One finds in the book stalls along the Seine erudite volumes on even such narrowly restricted topics as "Pregnant Women Before the Revolutionary Tribunal." To single out a few of them for listing here is doubtless unjust to those omitted; but to mention none at all might be even more unfair.

On the prerevolutionary generation: Leo Gershoy, *From Despotism to Revolution* (New York: Harper, 1944); R. Mousnier and E. Labrousse, *Le XVIIIe siècle* (Paris: Presses Univ., 1953); Daniel Mornet, *Les Origines intellectuelles de la révolution française* (Paris: Colin, 1933); Paul Hazard, *La Pensée européenne au XVIIIe siècle* (Paris: Bovin, 1946); Burdette Poland, *French Protestantism and the French Revolution* (Princeton: Princeton Univ. Press, 1957); H. Fréville, *L'Intendance de Bretagne (1689–1790)* (Rennes: Plihon, 1953).

On the revolutionary decade: A. Goodwin, *The French Revolution* (London: Hutchinson, 1953); Jacques Godechot, *Les Institutions de la France sous la révolution et l'empire* (Paris: Presses Univ., 1951); R. R. Palmer, *Twelve Who Ruled* (Princeton: Princeton Univ. Press, 1941, 1959); Marcel Reinhard, *Le Grand Carnot* (Paris: Hachette, 1950–52); Crane Brinton, *The Jacobins* (New York: Macmillan, 1930); George Rudé, *The Crowd in the French Revolution* (Oxford: Clarendon, 1959); André Latreille, *L'Eglise catholique et la révolution française* (Paris: Hachette, 1946–50); Paul Beik, *The French Revolution Seen from the Right* (Philadelphia: Am. Phil. Soc., 1956); André Fugier, *La Révolution et l'empire napoléonien* (Paris: Hachette, 1954).

Special mention should be made of Georges Lefebvre's influential monograph *Les Paysans du nord et la révolution française* (Lille: Marquant, 1924), which propounds the thesis that peasant solidarity in 1789 made the revolution possible, but that this solidarity was broken by the events of the revolution. The urban bourgeoisie, Lefebvre contends, shared its gains with the upper strata of the peasantry, while the lower strata gained little. This new urban-rural bourgeois alliance, according to Lefebvre, is what gave the revolution an essentially conservative character and produced conservative results. For an excellent summary of Lefebvre's work, see R. R. Palmer, "Georges Lefebvre: The Peasants and the French Revolution," *Journal of Modern History*, XXXI (1959), 329–42. Communist historians hold that the urban and rural bourgeoisie were forced to compromise with the poor peasants in order to keep the latter's support against the stubborn resistance of the landed aristocracy: A. Soboul, "La Communauté rurale française (XVIIIᵉ–XIXᵉ siècles)," *La Pensée*, LXXIII (1957), 65–81.

On the Napoleonic period: Geoffrey Bruun, *Europe and the French Imperium* (New York: Harper, 1938); Georges Lefebvre, *Napoléon* (Paris: Presses Univ., 1936, 1947); Odette Viennet, *Napoléon et l'industrie française* (Paris: Plon, 1947); François Crouzet, *L'Économie britannique et le blocus continental (1806–1813)* (Paris: Presses Univ., 1959).

8

II

FRANCE IN SEARCH OF
A NEW EQUILIBRIUM
1814–1870

NINE

> Louis XVIII has not been restored to the throne
> of his ancestors: he has simply ascended the
> throne of Bonaparte.
>
> JOSEPH DE MAISTRE

The Bourbon Experiment, 1814–1830

Restoration periods often strike posterity as tame and colorless. They usually follow upon an era of profound revolution or of prolonged war, and they naturally suffer by contrast. Efforts to return to normalcy, to recover a lost stability and to assure order, are not likely to be glamorous. Yet if they are less spectacular than times of upheaval, they are sometimes equally significant in the development of a nation.

French history from 1814 to 1848 is a case in point. Preceded and followed by major revolutions and by dramatic experiments in one-man leadership, that generation seems a dull and prosaic one. Yet specialists in the era are agreed that few periods have been of greater formative influence in the shaping of modern France; some of them even consider that influence more profound than the impact of the revolutionary epoch itself. This was a time of ferment—of intense intellectual and literary activity, of unprecedented richness in social theorizing, of fundamental economic change. It was a time of experimentation, too; France in these years tried out a kind of proto-parliamentary system of government and grew so accustomed to it that the parliamentary principle was rarely abandoned thereafter. It was an era marked by the attempt to find a stable compromise combining the principles of the old bureaucratic monarchy, the surviving feudal-aristocratic tradition, and the ideals of the revolution. The historian's problem is to judge how nearly the compromisers approached success, and why in the end they failed to create a durable constitutional monarchy.

When the Bourbons returned from almost a quarter-century of exile, they found a France that had been profoundly altered. A new social structure had replaced the old semifeudal system; equality of status had established itself in French law and mores. Juridically at least, special privilege survived only for the male sex, as the Napoleonic code enshrined "the rights of man and the wrongs of woman." True, Napoleon had begun to infringe the new equality by creating his own aristocracy, which clung to its titles after 1814. But these new nobles, like the old, possessed no special juridical status; before the law, all men were equal citizens.

The revolution had brought, too, a considerable redistribution of wealth through the sale of much large landed property. But legend has greatly exaggerated the extent of the social revolution involved. Land transfers did not change France overnight from a nation of large estates to one of small-owners. That process had been proceeding gradually for centuries; the revolution speeded it up, but left it still unfinished. Many small-owners after 1789 got clearer title to the land they already possessed and added more as well. But the great bulk of poorer peasants had no capital with which to make even a down payment on "aristo" land and, in any case, could not hope to bid on land that was not within walking distance of their cottages. Most of the transferred land went to the already well-to-do peasant minority or to the bourgeoisie, who became absentee owners in most cases, and who arranged to have the land worked by small-renters or crop-sharers. Furthermore, a considerable number of large estates survived the revolutionary epoch pretty much intact. Many nobles kept their land by refusing to emigrate; some émigrés found devious means to retain their property or got it back by serving Napoleon; some of the church lands were sold in large undivided tracts. The shift toward rural democracy was therefore relative; the French agricultural

122

structure remained exceptionally varied through the nineteenth century.

A more fundamental change was the highly centralized and relatively efficient administrative structure with which Napoleon had endowed the country. There was some irony in the fact that the revolution had accomplished in this sphere what the kings of France had been groping to achieve for centuries. Even more ironic was the fact that the revolutionists had done it rather in spite of themselves, for their initial program had aimed at decentralized local democracy. The Jacobin leaders had felt it necessary to create a rigid structure of centralized control, and this, in turn, had been consolidated by Napoleon. New or remodelled administrative agencies in Paris—the Council of State and the Inspectorate of Finance, for example—also proved to be both effective and durable.

France possessed, too, a new and sounder structure of public finance. Napoleon handed on to the Bourbons the privately owned and operated Bank of France, with control over the nation's credit system. With the bankers rather than the bureaucrats or the politicians in control, a debased or inflated currency was a much less likely prospect. A more curious heritage was the nation's financial soundness despite the drain of a twenty year's war. Much of the old public debt incurred by the monarchy had been liquidated by the inflation of the 1790's, and Napoleon managed to fight his wars without doing very much borrowing. Although the British finally triumphed, they emerged from the war with a per capita public debt twenty times as heavy as that of defeated France.

Still another change for the returning Bourbons was the new relationship between church and state. The clergy had been transmuted from a privileged corporation into a special branch of the bureaucracy, with its salaries paid by the state; and Catholicism now enjoyed a somewhat reduced status as the religion of a majority of Frenchmen, not of all loyal subjects. Church domination of education had also been reduced, though by no means broken. Napoleon's network of *lycées* provided for only a small proportion of young Frenchmen; primary education remained largely in the hands of the church. Finally, the revolutionary era had implanted a tradition now fairly well rooted in the public consciousness— that some sort of elected assembly was a normal and necessary part of the governmental machinery. Although Napoleon had stripped his legislature of most of its power, he had retained the principle of a representative body within his authoritarian system.

If Louis XVIII had felt completely free to follow his basic impulses, perhaps he would have begun his reign by wiping out all of these changes produced by the revolutionary whirlwind. Historians have disagreed sharply about the real character and motives of this complex monarch. For some of them, he was the personification of moderation and statesmanship, the prince who had absorbed the spirit of English institutions during his long exile, and who now set out to reconcile all Frenchmen. For others, he was a narrow and bigoted old man who chose the path of compromise only when he was pushed onto it by necessity. His ministers, according to this theory, made the key decisions of the reign, and Louis in the end got the credit for their wisdom. It is probably true that Louis had developed no real taste for English constitutional monarchy; but at least he was shrewd enough to recognize that, in the current state of France and Europe, an attempt to restore the old order might mean trouble. Whether he was really wiser and more flexible than his late brother Louis XVI is difficult to say; perhaps he was merely older and more cynical. When he failed to get his way, he found it easy to divert himself through other pastimes: gourmandizing, for example, and the platonic company of royal favorites.

Not all of the resurgent royalists were so reconciled to compromise. A faction of extremists, whom their critics called "ultra-royalists," was determined to root out the reforms of the revolutionary epoch and to purge the administration of those who had served the Corsican. Some of the ultra leaders were returned émigrés; but the faction was made up in large part of the lesser backwoods aristocracy, most of whom had stayed in France throughout the revolutionary epoch. Among them were the organizers of the Chevaliers de la Foi, who had done so much to bring about the restoration. These rural nobles were militant and uncompromising men, tinged by a strain of real fanaticism; they held that any compromise with evil (i.e., the revolution) would be a betrayal of principles. Their symbol and hope was the king's younger brother, the Comte d'Artois.

In prerevolutionary days Artois had been a court playboy of scandalous reputation; in his new incarnation he was a fervent and almost blue-nosed religious fanatic. Artois's conversion was not unique, for exile had brought many émigrés back to the church. The eighteenth-century court had been touched by skepticism, even cynicism; the nineteenth century was to bring a new interpenetration of royalism and Catholicism. If there was any Bourbon who resisted the trend and clung to the skeptical eighteenth-century tradition, it was Louis XVIII himself.

Although Louis owed his restoration in part to ultra propaganda activities, he owed it also to the allied powers and to that large group of Napoleonic peers and bureaucrats that had rallied to the Bourbon cause as the Empire collapsed. His initial policies were designed to satisfy all three groups but to let none of them get dominant influence. Instead of embarking on a major purge of Napoleonic officials, he maintained most of them in their posts. "Union and forgetfulness" was his motto. On the other hand, he brusquely rejected a constitution hastily drafted in April, 1814, by Napoleon's Senate and Corps Législatif; for that constitution was a bald attempt to tie his hands and to perpetuate the Napoleonic legislators in office. He promulgated instead a kind of pseudo-constitution called the Charter, which restored the principle of divine right but absorbed many of the revolutionary changes. His new bicameral legislature was granted more power than the Napoleonic legislative bodies had possessed; and its upper house, the Chamber of Peers, was packed not with loyal ultras but with Napoleonic officials who had climbed aboard the Bourbon band wagon. It is not surprising that a man of ultra spirit like De Maistre should remark acidly that Louis had not restored the Bourbon throne but had merely taken over that of Bonaparte.

But if some of the new king's actions infuriated the ultras, other decisions alienated the rest of the country. Thousands of army officers were brusquely retired on half-pay, and the crack regiments of the imperial guard were scattered among isolated provincial garrisons. Meanwhile, many émigrés demanded and got their old officers' commissions with appropriate promotions for seniority; almost four hundred new generals were created within a year. A series of public ceremonies in memory of victims of the revolution gave Paris a kind of permanent funereal air. There were indications that the king intended to restore the church to its old privileged role. Most disastrous of all, taxes were increased until they exceeded the exactions of Napoleon.

Before the Bourbons had been back in office for a year, unrest was so general that rumors of it began to reach the exiled emperor on his bucolic Mediterranean island. Bad British puns about Napoleon's lack of Elba-room had some basis in fact. The emperor found it hard to curb his energies; and he was disturbed also at reports that he might be banished to a still more distant island as a security measure. This combination of circumstances suggested to him that his star was rising once more and that destiny called on him to follow it in one last adventure. With a handful of followers, he evaded British surveillance and landed on the southern coast of France in March, 1815. Within three weeks he was in Paris, acclaimed by a hysterical crowd; all along the route northward, cities had opened their gates to him, troops sent to block his progress had fallen to their knees before him. Not a drop of blood had been shed in defense of the Bourbons — not even by Louis himself, despite his brave assertion that he would die if need be on the steps of the throne. Instead, the court had hastily departed to a new place of exile across the border in Ghent.

The failure of the nation to defend the dynasty, and of the dynasty to defend itself, reflected badly on Bourbon rule. On the other hand, the nation's hysterical welcome of Napoleon overlay a generalized mood of antagonism and suspicion. Napoleon sought to appease his opponents by announcing a program of liberal reform that contrasted sharply with his whole authoritarian record. He knew, however, that his only chance of regaining the country's affections would be a quick and cheap military victory. Such a prospect, in the face of an aroused and united Europe, would have seemed dim indeed to anyone without Napoleon's self-confidence; and Waterloo promptly shattered his chimeric dream.

Again he was forced to abdicate, and, after a hesitant attempt to escape to America, he threw himself on the mercies of his British captors.

❧⋄❧⋄❧⋄

Napoleon's mad gamble left the nation worse divided than before and gravely threatened the Bourbons' chances. For a time, the irritated victors of Waterloo hesitated to permit the dynasty to return; when they finally did so (for lack of a better alternative), Louis XVIII seemed to be the creature of the allied powers rather than the choice of the French nation. Furthermore, the second restoration, unlike the first, was followed by a wave of angry reprisals against those who had served Napoleon. Many high officials had compromised themselves during the Hundred Days and could not be forgiven a second time. Alongside the governmental purge, a more spontaneous "White Terror" occurred in certain monarchist regions; vigilante justice was freely dispensed. Above all, the episode played into the hands of the ultras, for it seemed to confirm their warnings that a policy of moderation would bring disaster. In the legislative elections that followed shortly, a large majority of ultras was swept into the Chamber of Deputies.

At first the king was pleased at this result, for he had feared that the elections might reveal the monarchy's unpopularity. In an unfortunate phrase, he referred to the new assembly as the Incomparable Chamber. On second thought, his pleasure was reduced by his concern at the possible effects of the ultra program; he chose as ministers, therefore, moderate royalists like the Duc de Richelieu and Élie Decazes. There followed a year of severe tension between king and ministers on the one hand and the ultra-dominated Chamber on the other. The ultras embarked on a drastic purge of regicides, Jacobins, and collaborators of Napoleon.[1] They agitated for the return of all property to the

---

[1] The dominant figure in a parliamentary committee set up to try suspects was a returned émigré named Count Robert Joseph MacCarthy, who attained quick but fleeting notoriety as a rabid hunter of subversives.

"rightful" owners, and abolition of Napoleon's administrative bureaucracy, and the return of education to church control. The long-range goal of the ultras, however, was not merely the repeal of the past twenty-five years of French history, but the repeal of the past two centuries. They still clung to the nostalgic program of the eighteenth-century aristocracy — the destruction of the centralized bureaucratic monarchy in favor of a quasi-feudal system. If there was anyone who had learned nothing and forgotten nothing since 1789, it was not the Bourbons but their dedicated ultra supporters.

The most curious aspect of the contest between ultras and moderates was the ultras' unprincipled espousal of certain liberal and even democratic ideas. They argued not only for the adoption of the parliamentary principle of legislative control over the ministry but for universal manhood suffrage as well. Since the ultras controlled the Chamber of Deputies but not the ministry, their advocacy of the parliamentary principle was at least understandable, if not very sincere. Their desire to give the vote to the common man may seem more surprising. It rested on the conviction that the "popular classes" were mostly loyal to their betters and to tradition, while the prosperous bourgeoisie had been tainted by un-French ideas. The moderate royalists preferred a rigorously limited suffrage, confined to men of high birth or great wealth; and in the end they got their way. By the system adopted in 1817, the vote was granted to only about ninety thousand Frenchmen. Some royalist historians contend that the ultras were right on this point; that universal suffrage would have rooted the monarchy firmly in the nation. If so, the fatal error of the Bourbons after 1814 (and of the Orleanist dynasty after 1830) was their fearful rejection of votes for the masses. But the hypothesis is not a very convincing one. Although some regions in southern and western France were still intensely royalist in the traditionalist sense, the ultras probably exaggerated the depth and extent of this mass sentiment. Wishful thinking made it easier for them to ignore the changes that had occurred in the outlook of many ordinary Frenchmen since 1789.

Perhaps it was the king's native good sense that led him to resist the ultras; or perhaps it was the rising pressure of the allied powers, whose nervousness increased as the ultras' demands grew louder. Wellington hinted that France might have to be saved from its own folly a third time. The tsar warned bluntly: "Either send your deputies home, or we'll keep all our troops in France." At last, late in 1816 Louis dissolved the Chamber and lent support to his moderate ministers as they manipulated the new elections. This time the moderates swept the major cities and most of northern and eastern France; ultra domination of the Chamber was broken. A few ultra hotheads talked angrily of a palace revolution against "King Voltaire"; but most of them preferred a policy of embittered sniping at Louis and his moderate advisers and warned gloomily that the Jacobins would soon be riding again.

In spite of ultra obstructionism and predictions of disaster, the Bourbon compromise functioned reasonably well from 1816 to 1820. Richelieu and Decazes, the two strong men of the ministry, steered successfully between reactionaries and reviving radicals; if their rule was not glamorous, it was, on the whole, effective. By 1818, thanks to large loans secured from English and Dutch bankers, France's war indemnity was paid and the allied occupation ended. Domestically, there were glimmerings of a true parliamentary system; ministries tended to become more homogeneous and *de facto* Chamber control over the ministry more real. The title *président du conseil des ministres* (or prime minister) came into common use, although Louis disliked it and sought to avoid it. The king had by now fallen almost completely under the influence of his current favorite, Élie Decazes, a shrewd and ambitious politician of bourgeois origin. Louis doted on his "darling Élie" in almost maudlin fashion; when a crisis eventually forced Louis to dismiss Decazes from the ministry, the king not only gave him a dukedom but took down the portrait of Francis I in the royal chambers to make way for that of Decazes. Whether Decazes was merely a scheming opportunist or one of the ablest middle-way politicians of the nineteenth century remains a subject of lively controversy.

The partial revival of representative government after 1814 led to the emergence of loosely organized yet on the whole durable factions or parties for the first time in a generation: ultras on the right, moderates in the center, and liberals on the left. None of these factions was rigid or homogeneous; none could face the test of power without being promptly riven by personal and doctrinal conflict. Such was the fate of the moderates after 1816, and of the ultras during the 1820's; such was eventually to be the destiny of the liberals as well, in 1848.

The ultras, doctrinally speaking, came closest to being homogeneous. Their tendency to divide into two wings derived from differences over means rather than ends; the extremists, the "ultra-ultras," were true fanatics in spirit, while a more restrained element preferred to regain and to hold power by political maneuvering. The ultras' principal theorist was the Vicomte de Bonald; their chief political leader, the Comte de Villèle; their symbol and voice, the eminent poet and essayist Chateaubriand.

The moderate royalists, like most middle groups, were less sharply defined in composition and doctrine. Such theory as they had was worked out by a small group of intellectuals who chose to call themselves the "doctrinaires": the philosopher Royer-Collard and the historian Guizot stood out among them. Royer-Collard as chief doctrinaire spokesman contended that the Charter of 1814 amounted to an ideal compromise, resting as it did on a strong king, a hereditary nobility, and an influential bourgeoisie whose wealthiest leaders were represented in parliament. The whole course of French history, pontificated this Sorbonne professor, had led up to this present pinnacle of perfection. Practical politicians like Decazes paid little attention to the doctrinaires; political realists, they accepted the existing system and adapted themselves to it.

The self-styled "liberal party" on the left was a complex mosaic of elements joined together by little more than common hostility to the Bourbons. Of their three most noted leaders, Lafayette was a republican, Jacques Manuel a Bonapartist, and Benjamin Constant a constitutional monarchist. None of the three possessed the qualities of effective political leadership. The republican element within the liberal faction was small. The very word republican suggested violence and anarchy to most Frenchmen; the republic implied Jacobinism, and "Jacobin" had a flavor like that of "Bolshevik" in our times. The liberal party's ablest spokesmen in this era were the constitutional monarchists, who stood for a parliamentary system like that of Britain, with individual rights protected by the state and suffrage limited to men of property alone. The most curious adherents to the liberal coalition were the Bonapartists. Their presence might seem to suggest a mere marriage of convenience, a hypocritical alliance of authoritarians and libertarians bound together by nothing more than their common desire to destroy the Bourbon compromise. In fact, both Bonapartists and liberals felt a strong common bond when the fundamental achievements of the revolution were thought to be in danger. Not even the harsh experience of the years 1789–1814 had yet fully clarified the fact that within the revolutionary tradition there were potential conflicts as deep as those separating the revolution from its enemies.

Four years sufficed to destroy the Bourbon experiment in moderate autocracy. The moderate politicians faced the same alternatives that normally confront any centrist group possessing no comfortable majority of parliamentary or public support. One possibility was to convert enough adherents of the right and left to give the center a solid majority; a second was to negotiate a firm alliance with either the right or the left. The moderate leaders of 1816–20 achieved neither goal. On the contrary, moderate support in the Chamber of Deputies shrank steadily after 1816; and neither right nor left showed any interest in a compromise alliance with the center.

Some historians have denounced the liberal left as principally responsible for the failure of the moderate experiment. A left-center alliance, they argue, might have opened the way to a gradual reform of the whole system and the emergence in France of a constitutional monarchy as durable as that of Britain. Other critics contend that it was the ultra right, rather, that committed the fatal error. They suggest that a right-center coalition might have developed into a genuine conservative party, the kind of political force that modern France has always lacked, the kind that could have ensured political stability. It would be hard to choose between the two extreme wings for factiousness and bigotry. This was not to be France's last experience with the distortion of a parliamentary or proto-parliamentary system through the obstructive tactics of large extremist minorities on right and left. A governing center, caught between groups that reject the rules of the system and the possibility of gradualist reform within the system, finds itself driven to abandon rational discussion of political issues and falls back into a position of sheer self-defense. At best, it seeks to defend the system; at worst, it defends nothing more than its personal position. Its shortcomings of leadership are therefore made to appear even worse than they are.

The political trend after 1816 was steadily leftward; at every partial renewal of the Chamber, more liberals gained election. By 1819 it was even possible for a regicide of 1793 to win a seat. The ultras hysterically predicted that a "revolutionary torrent" was about to engulf France; Decazes calmly ignored them and clung to his middle-of-the-road line in the belief that he could gradually convert the milder liberals to his cause. The effort may have been a futile one; perhaps it was the moderates who were on the way to being swallowed up by the left. At any rate, the experiment was wrecked by the assassination, in 1820, of the king's nephew the Duc de Berry. The assassin, a fanatical Bonapartist who had followed his hero to Elba and then to Waterloo, had hoped to wipe out the royal line by killing the last Bourbon still young enough to produce a male heir. He struck too late; eight months later the Duchesse de Berry gave birth to a son, "child of the miracle." What the assassin destroyed instead was the moderate regime. The ultras set out in full cry after Decazes, whose criminal laxness, they alleged, had encouraged the assassin. The king was reluctantly driven to part with Decazes; the electoral law was altered to weaken the chances of the left; and in the emotional wave that followed the assassination, the ultras swept back into control of the Chamber. They were to govern France, with only a brief interlude, for the entire decade.

132

The Bourbon Experiment, 1814-1830

One immediate result of the ultras' triumph was a turn to outright subversion on the part of the left. A series of underground plots culminated in the formation of a secret society called the Carbonari, whose name and ritual were borrowed from Italy. But the Carbonari lacked both skilled leadership and mass support. Its members were mostly intellectuals and army noncommissioned officers; it put down almost no roots among the city workers or the common soldiers. A successful uprising might have brought workers and soldiers to the banner of revolution; but the attempts of the Carbonari were ill-planned and futile affairs that gave rise to little more than durable legend. The effect, in fact, was negative; for subversion gave the government an added excuse for repression. The press was subjected to more severe controls and censorship; a dozen Sorbonne professors were dismissed, and a priest was installed as rector of the university. At the same time a stronger foreign-policy line was adopted, partly as a device to weaken the left by competing with the tradition of Napoleonic glory. The device succeeded; a French military expedition into Spain in 1823 culminated in glorious success rather than the disaster that had been predicted by the liberals. The army, mollified by the prestige and promotions that came out of the Spanish affair, became reconciled to ultra rule. For the rest of the decade the liberals had to abandon their plots in favor of a renewed effort at peaceful opposition.

To cap their Spanish success, the ultras in 1824 achieved their greatest electoral victory since 1816; the liberal opposition was reduced from one hundred and ten seats to twenty. A few months later the last feeble barrier to their complete triumph was cleared away when Louis XVIII at last expired. The aged king had confined himself to a largely inactive role since 1820, seeking diversion in the company of the new royal favorite, Madame du Cayla, an amateur agent of the ultras. He had made no serious attempt to hamper the ultra leaders; but the latter were sure to feel themselves on more solid ground once the Comte d'Artois was elevated to the throne as Charles X. Yet within six years

133

both the ultras and the dynasty itself were to find themselves dislodged from power — and largely through their own mistakes.

❧◦❧◦❧◦❧

Charles X has been roughly handled by historians for more than a century, and he has gone down in legend as a kind of paragon of bigoted ineptitude. In fact, he possessed almost all of the qualities of kingship except good judgment. There was much to be said for his character and his general comportment; certainly he looked and acted like a king, far more so than his obese and almost immobile predecessor. Nor did he dictate a sharp and sudden shift in policy, or even in the tone of politics, as soon as he took the throne. Yet several incidents early in the new reign seemed to imply a sharp thrust toward reaction and sufficed to arouse the mixed fears and hopes of the left.

One such incident, unimportant except for its symbolic character, was the new king's coronation at Reims. This five-hour ceremony of medieval splendor, climaxed by the anointment of the new sovereign with holy oil miraculously preserved from the revolutionary despoilers, seemed to suggest a will to return to the old regime in both form and spirit. More serious was a series of laws adopted by the Chamber in 1824–25 — laws that could easily be viewed by suspicious Frenchmen as inspired by a mood of black reaction. The most notorious of these was a measure to indemnify the émigrés for the loss of their property during the revolution. To finance the scheme, Finance Minister Villèle worked out a conversion of five per cent government bonds to a lower rate of interest and used the savings to issue new bonds which were handed over to the émigrés in question. The measure produced a bitterly partisan debate in parliament and in the press. The opposition charged that honest bourgeois bondholders were to be victimized for the benefit of a class that had deserted the country in time of crisis; the ultras replied that the émigrés' sole crime had been to run away from the guillotine. Only in later retrospect was it possible to see that the law labelled "the émigrés' billion" (the figure was a considerable exaggeration) was in fact a sensible compromise of a nagging issue. After 1825 there was no more talk of restoring the lost property itself; its new owners at last possessed safe title. The law thus consolidated, at rather low cost, one more important aspect of the revolutionary reforms.

There were other parts of the ultra program that were far less defensible. Such, for example, was a law to punish sacrilegious acts in churches by long imprisonment or even death — a law that Bonald defended with the curious argument that the death penalty was eminently fair because it would send accused persons before the natural judge of sacrilegious acts. The law produced bitter resentment, yet it was never enforced; its only victim, remarks one historian, was the regime. Equally unwise was a severe press law that virtually hamstrung the publishers of newspapers, pamphlets, and circulars — a bill that one minister described, with monumental ineptitude, as "a law of justice and love." Finally, there was a bill to restore (in aristocratic families only) the prerevolutionary rule of primogeniture in the inheritance of landed property. In fact, the measure's effects would have been slight even if it had not been rejected by the Chamber of Peers. But susceptible Frenchmen feared that it implied a continuing effort to restore the old regime by destroying the revolutionary principle of legal equality.

Not all of the ultras' program after 1824 was so bigoted and dangerous as the left asserted it to be. Neither did the program represent a brusque shift toward reaction, inspired by the accession of the new king. Several of the measures in question (notably the "émigrés' billion") were being drafted before the death of Louis XVIII. The fault of Charles X was a failure to sense the mood of the country and to take seriously enough the growing evidence of discontent. Several times, during or after vindictive debates in the Chamber, Charles made state visits to the provinces and received such a warm welcome that he returned with all his doubts relieved. Convinced that the country stood solidly behind him, Charles in turn stood solidly behind his chief minister Villèle. Unfortunately for the dynasty, Villèle's genuine abilities were balanced by equal shortcomings. His real talent lay in the sphere of public finance; he took a passionate interest in revising the government's accounting procedures and did it so scientifically that those procedures have been used in France ever since. Furthermore, he was more politician than fanatic; unlike some of his fellow ultras, he had at least a marginal propensity to compromise. What Villèle lacked was imagination, glamor, the indefinable qualities of real statesmanship; he had an accountant's soul. Honest and efficient, but petty and inclined to devious scheming, Villèle and the king together gradually frittered away the almost impregnable political power they possessed at the peak of ultra strength in 1824.

One might assume that the ultras' decline was the product of their own extremism, of a policy line that drove center and left to cooperate and that brought a revival of the left. To a much greater degree, however, that decline was the product of fissures within the ultra bloc itself. Men of extreme views and of fanatical temperament often find it easier to cooperate when out of power than when faced with the task of governing. Such, at any rate, was the case after 1824.

One source of conflict was Villèle's growing inclination to compromise. The necessities of governing softened his rigid views at least to a degree; he was willing to maneuver within fairly narrow limits. But to his fanatical supporters, the "ultra-ultras," any compromise at all was anathema; and there shortly emerged once again a right-wing opposition group that harassed the ministry and sometimes even collaborated with the left to stir up trouble.

A second divisive factor was a personal feud that developed between Villèle and Chateaubriand. The two men had worked in close harmony during the early restoration years; but once in power, neither of these ambitious egoists was willing to relinquish the spotlight to the other. Chateaubriand had always affected an artist's disdain for politics and had preferred to pose as an observer watching the game in tolerant amusement. In fact, his passionate interest and his personal ambition were too obvious to conceal. In 1822 Chateaubriand achieved the post of foreign minister, where he upset Villèle's cautious foreign policy and overshadowed Villèle by his flamboyant showmanship. His natural conceit was redoubled by his successes; he became an impossible subordinate. In 1824 he managed, by devious means, to defeat one of Villèle's finance bills. Perhaps he was scheming to upset the president of the council and take his place; Villèle, in any case, thought so and persuaded the king to dismiss him abruptly. Thereafter it was unlimited war between the two men. Chateaubriand embarked on a vindictive antigovernmental campaign in his newspaper, the effect of which was increased by his literary prestige and his ultra connections. No other man contributed so much to the downfall of the ultra government in 1828 and, eventually, to the fall of the dynasty itself. Too late, Chateaubriand was to realize what he had done. After 1830, as a point of honor, he refused to serve the new dynasty. "I'm still following that carrion [Charles X]," he would explain to questioning friends.

A third source of trouble within ultra ranks was the religious question, which produced a limited revival of the old Gallican spirit of hostility toward Rome. The Gallican mood had seemed well on the way to dying out by 1815. Both king and clergy continued to be Gallican by instinct, but the progressive weakening of the papacy had lessened the old fear that Rome might dominate the French church and France itself. Perhaps Gallicanism might have disappeared imperceptibly had it not been for the religious revival of the restoration period. That revival reflected the ultras' sentiment that France had sinned and must repent; that the nation must be brought back from its Voltairean skepticism to the true faith.

Certainly the church needed some kind of revival if it was not to wither away. The clergy was seriously reduced in numbers; recruiting had become extremely difficult after 1789. Most of the bourgeoisie had been weaned away from the faith, and Enlightenment skepticism was beginning to spread downward. An English traveller in 1818 found that "though the churches are still open, the congregations are gone"; and he concluded that French Catholicism was a mere vestige of the past.[2] Only in the aristocracy had the trend away from religion begun to be reversed.

[2] F. Hall, *Travels in France in 1818* (London, 1819), p. 364.

The first step in the effort to renew the faith was the organization of a kind of domestic missionary order in 1814. The Missions de France sent teams of evangelists into the countryside to hold open-air revivals. Some of them resorted to demagogic devices in an effort to stir up mass emotions; crosses were erected, books burned, sermons delivered at night in church cemeteries with weird lighting and sound effects. The campaign converted few apostates; but it did stir up both religious and antireligious fanaticism. A more important development was the rapid growth of extra-legal church schools. The church was permitted to establish a *"petit séminaire"* in each department for the preparatory training of priests; but the seminaries promptly turned into clandestine secondary schools, and by 1830 they were enrolling one-third of all the secondary students in the country. Fantastic rumors spread that the returning Jesuits were infiltrating everywhere, and that these agents of papal domination were on the way to taking over the country. Even the king was alleged to have become a secret Jesuit, committed to turning France over to "the men in black." There were, in fact, fewer than four hundred Jesuits in France, but the order always made an attractive target for anticlerical suspicions.

Still another legend of the 1820's concerned the Congrégation, which was alleged to be a kind of Catholic freemasonry controlled by the Pope, with secret agents strategically placed throughout the government and the administration making all decisions and destroying any official who defied its will. Most of the ultras ridiculed the charges as pure left-wing propaganda; the Congrégation, they said, was no secret society but an inoffensive organization of Catholic laymen dedicated to good works. But even some ultras grew disturbed and began to suspect their colleagues of responding to secret instructions originating in Rome.

These converging internal dissensions gradually broke up ultra solidarity and, at the same time, stimulated a revival of the center and left. When Villèle gambled on elections late in 1827, the venture brought political disaster. The liberal left and the moderate royalists (by now called the "right-center") together won as many seats as did Villèle's supporters, while Villèle's bitter enemies on the extreme right, the so-called ultra-ultras, held the balance of power. Reluctantly, King Charles had to part with Villèle in order to appease the moderate element.

The new ministry, a mélange of moderate royalists and Villèle supporters, was headed by a relative unknown named Martignac. The king made it clear that he regarded this government as a mere stopgap; he even refused to let Martignac use the title "president of the council." This lack of royal confidence, plus the ministry's own heterogeneity, made its task almost hopeless. Martignac's best chance for survival seemed to be to win the support of the liberal left; he sought to appease them by such measures as relaxation of the press law and reinforcement of controls over church schools. But the liberals refused to meet him halfway; they accepted his concessions, yet they systematically opposed him on every issue that arose. This persistent hostility of both the left and the extreme right finally gave the king the excuse he wanted to unload Martignac. In 1829 the ministry was dismissed, and Charles restored the ultras to power.

In itself, this decision was not necessarily fatal to the dynasty. The right kind of ultra might still have saved the system: a Villèle perhaps (despite his unpopularity), or, better still, a Chateaubriand. Whatever his failings, the aging poet did possess immense prestige. Instead Charles chose for key ministerial posts "the three most unpopular men in France": Polignac, the king's personal favorite; Bourmont, who had deserted to the enemy on the eve of Waterloo; and La Bourdonnaye, the most bigoted ultra-ultra in political life. The character of the new ministry transformed the temper of the opposition, turning it aggressive to the point of outright disloyalty. It brought, too, the emergence of younger, more vigorous spokesmen on the left. Early in 1830 a new liberal daily called *Le National* was founded, inspired by Talleyrand, backed by the liberal financier Laffitte ("the king of bankers and the banker of kings"), and run by a youthful team whose most remarkable member was Adolphe Thiers. This brilliant southerner, of common birth but uncommon ambition, had risen rapidly in Parisian society through sheer ability and energy. For a time he had grown discouraged at the prospect of political advancement and had talked of leaving France. The creation of the Polignac ministry gave him new hope; he and his friends plunged into a press campaign designed to bring about not a change of ministry but a change of dynasty and of constitution. "We must either cross the Channel or cross the Atlantic," Thiers asserted. It was clear that he preferred the shorter crossing, and that his group at *Le National* was committed to the king's cousin the Duc d'Orléans as candidate for the throne.

The best ally of the opposition was the Polignac ministry itself, which managed to commit virtually every possible mistake during its year in office. Some of the ministers had urged a royal coup d'état at the very outset. Perhaps decisive action in 1829, followed by rigorous repression of the left, might have succeeded in shoring up the monarchy for a time. But Polignac came round to such a policy only slowly and reluctantly; and when he finally did adopt it, the opposition was well organized and dug in. Through the winter of 1829–30, the ministry debated and marked time, giving no clear indication of a positive policy or of effective leadership. Polignac toyed with some fantastic schemes in the field of foreign policy, apparently in the hope that a great diplomatic victory might arouse the nation's enthusiasm.

When the Chamber met early in 1830, its majority was spoiling for a fight; it promptly voted an address to the throne denouncing the new ministry. Charles dissolved the Chamber without delay and ordered new elections in July. The outcome was ominous: 274 seats for the various opposition groups, 143 for the ministry. That Polignac was doomed was quite clear. That the Bourbon dynasty was doomed was much less clear, though its survival now probably would have required Charles to accept the role of constitutional monarch. Some of his advisers urged another alternative: why not buy off enough members of the opposition to get a majority in the Chamber? "We know the price of consciences — it's not too high," remarked one minister. But the king, as honest as he was bigoted, would hear of neither bargaining nor retreat. He chose instead a head-on challenge to the left: a royal coup d'état that would alter the Charter beyond recognition.

Ministry and king carefully and secretly prepared a set of decrees (the July Ordinances) that dissolved the new Chamber even before its convocation, altered the electoral system, deprived the wealthy bourgeoisie of the right to vote, and stripped the press of any semblance of liberty. In order to ensure surprise, no troops were moved to Paris to reinforce the small garrison there. King and ministry acted with incredible naiveté in assuming that no disorders would follow; the prefect of police proved his total incapacity by guaranteeing that there would be no trouble. The government was comforted, too, by good news that arrived opportunely from Algiers. A French expeditionary corps sent to punish the Dey had landed and swept to a conquest of the capital in only twenty days. This news was expected to smother discontent in a wave of patriotic fervor. Even so, Charles wavered at the very end and signed the July Ordinances only after some hesitation. Once the decision had been made, he abandoned all doubts and went off to the country to hunt.

During the "three glorious days" that followed, Charles lost his capital and his throne. The insurrection developed gradually: a few small demonstrations on the twenty-sixth, barricades in the working-class sections on the twenty-seventh, retreat of the royal garrison in the face of rebel attacks on the twenty-eighth and twenty-ninth. The whole operation was largely spontaneous and lacked organized leadership. A group of liberal politicians met sporadically from the outset of the crisis but took no real action until the twenty-ninth, when the city had been virtually cleared of royal troops. Faced by the prospect that the republicans might move into the vacuum, the liberal leaders hastily named a governing committee for Paris and transformed it the next day into a provisional government. Its members were constitutional monarchists; its aim was to substitute a new dynasty for the old. On the morning of July 30 the walls of Paris were adorned with posters (the works of Thiers and his friends) calling for the transfer of the crown to the Duc d'Orléans.

The duke, however, showed some reluctance in mounting the throne, which had not yet been formally vacated by his royal cousin. Orléans had prudently left Paris for the suburbs when the disorders began, and it took a series of urgent missions by liberal leaders to persuade him to return to the capital. A confusing set of contradictory negotiations ensued; but the outcome, on the morning of July 31, was an agreement that the duke would become "lieutenant-general" of the kingdom. That afternoon the duke ventured to the Hôtel de Ville through glowering street crowds of Parisian workers, students, and shopkeepers — the revolutionaries who could see that their revolution was being confiscated. Their hero, Lafayette, had already privately refused a proposal that he become president of a republic; now he publicly reaffirmed that decision by appearing on the balcony with the Duc d'Orléans and by uttering his classic phrase: "Here is the best of republics!" On August 2 Charles abdicated in favor of his grandson and called on the new "lieutenant-general" to make way for the legitimate king. The duke professed lack of authority to decide the country's fate; but the next day, when the two chambers of parliament met, the duke baldly announced to them that Charles had abdicated without condition. The ex-king, after some thought of further resistance, ended by accepting his fate and departed for a second exile in England.

Though the Bourbon experiment ended in failure, there is no reason to suppose that it had to end thus. Frenchmen were, on the whole, well governed, prosperous, contented during this fifteen-year period; one historian even describes the restoration era as "one of the happiest periods in [France's] history."[3] It was not an easy task to blend two traditions as incompatible as those inherited from the revolution and the old regime; yet blending them ought not to have been beyond human capacity. Some of the responsibility for the failure of the experiment certainly belonged to the extremists of both right and left — to those elements that had no sympathy for gradualism or compromise. The greater fault, however, must be laid at the door of the king and his advisers — better men, but not wiser men, than they have customarily been described. It has sometimes been argued that the failure of the

[3] Bertier de Sauvigny, *La restauration*, p. 628.

Bourbon experiment was one of modern France's major disasters; that this failure ruled out the development of a durable constitutional monarchy, one that might have given France the kind of stability based on legitimacy that has distinguished modern England. Perhaps so; but if it is true, the dynasty itself must bear most of the blame. Besides, a second experiment in compromise, less legitimate yet possibly better adapted to changing times, still remained to be made — the Orleanist system.

TEN

Stagnation is perhaps the only practical way of remaining faithful to one's principles.

R. DE JOUVENEL

The Orleanist Experiment, 1830–1848

Some months after the revolution of 1830 a deputy arose in the Chamber to complain that not very much had changed in France. The Charter of 1814 still existed, slightly revised; the suffrage had been broadened only from 90,000 to 170,000 voters; ministers were still not responsible to the Chamber; nothing had even been done to punish that evil man Polignac. Casimir Périer, president of the council, answered bluntly: "The trouble with this country is that there are too many people like you who imagine that there has been a revolution in France."

To men like Périer, there had, in fact, been no revolution but only a change of dynasty, a return to the balanced compromise that had operated in the years 1816–20. They saw no real flaw in the Charter of 1814; all it needed to function successfully was the right sort of king.

Not all of the Orleanist politicians shared this view. It was easier to put Louis Philippe on the throne than to agree on his proper function once he was there. Two principal factions emerged almost from the outset and came to be known by the ambiguous labels right-center and left-center. The former group, represented by such men as Casimir Périer and the former doctrinaire François Guizot, saw 1830 as a culmination, not as a beginning. The regime, they believed, should be based on the upper bourgeoisie alone; and the king, as an active executive, should govern as well as reign. The left-center, with Adolphe Thiers and Alexis de Tocqueville as representative spokesmen, saw 1830 as the beginning of an evolutionary process. They aimed to broaden the base of the regime to include the middle and lower ranks of the bourgeoisie; and they held the king's role to be (in Thiers's classic phrase) to reign but not to govern.

It was the right-center that dominated the ministry through most of the Orleanist period, partly because the king so largely shared its views of the meaning of 1830. Louis Philippe, who had played so hesitant a role during the revolution, proved to be a much more complex and positive person than appearances might have indicated. He was the son of that Duc d'Orléans who had flirted with revolution after 1789 but had ended on the scaffold. He himself had passed through a youthful republican phase: at eighteen he had fought in the republican army at Valmy, and he had even joined the Jacobin club for a time. The Terror had driven him into exile, but he had carefully remained aloof from the émigré group. Even during the Hundred Days he had chosen to seek his own place of refuge in England rather than to follow the court to Ghent. After Waterloo the British had seriously considered setting him on the French throne in place of Louis. During the Bourbon era his house in Paris had been a gathering place for liberals — but he had played the liberal role with restraint, in moderation. It seemed safer to aspire than to conspire; and so he struck a democratic pose, kept a wide circle of varied acquaintances, and avoided committing himself to any cause.

Transmuted suddenly into king of the French, Louis Philippe continued to look and act like a typical Parisian bourgeois. He rose early, shaved himself, and put in a long day at the office; he broke royal precedent by sending his sons to one of the public *lycées* founded by Napoleon; he invited business men and their wives to palace functions;

he showed a strong instinct for thrift and prudently invested part of his income in British bonds. A certain lack of aristocratic dignity made it easy to scoff at him as "the shopkeepers' king" and to caricature him as the Crowned Pear. Even Thiers remarked acidly that the king's morning prayer began with the phrase: "Oh Lord, give us this day our daily platitude." His coronation was in startling contrast to that of Charles X: instead of the glamorous ceremony at Reims, there was a simple formality in the chambers of parliament, with the emphasis on the contract between king and people rather than between king and God.

But beneath this unimpressive exterior, Louis Philippe concealed a stubborn determination to be a king rather than a figurehead. He showed no sympathy for the idea of broadening the suffrage, or for making the ministry responsible to the Chamber, or for permitting the president of the ministerial council to be the real executive. Instead, he assumed an active role in the governing process; he tried when possible to choose ministers who would take orders, and there is even some evidence that he liked to provoke quarrels among his ministers so that he might step in with a dictated solution. Despite appearances, Louis Philippe had no sympathy with the view of many Orleanist politicians that the institution of monarchy had outgrown its mystical significance and now possessed only a purely utilitarian value. Perhaps it is true that the king suffered from a deep "illegitimacy complex"; that he was determined to establish his right to rule by heredity, as head of the younger branch of the Bourbon family, and not merely by the choice of parliament. In short, the king was not willing to regard 1830 as a French 1688. In some ways, Louis Philippe was a remarkable astute monarch; but he was not the kind of king who was likely to make a system of constitutional monarchy function smoothly, or who would be inclined to adapt it to the changing needs of society. From the outset the throne rested squarely on a double ambiguity — the source of the king's authority and the extent of that authority.

The Orleanist period has commonly been described as a completely class-bound era: as "the bourgeois monarchy," run by and for the plutocrats. The description is not entirely false. The mass of the population — peasants, urban workers, lesser bourgeoisie — still had no voice in politics, while the bulk of the old aristocracy withdrew disdainfully to its provincial chateaux or to its Parisian town houses in the Faubourg Saint-Germain. It was a kind of second emigration, psychological this time rather than physical. Even the new Orleanist aristocracy created by Louis Philippe was drawn almost entirely from the upper bourgeoisie.

But it would be wrong to conclude that Orleanism was completely identified with the well-to-do business class. Some members of the older aristocracy who possessed liberal leanings — the Duc de Broglie, for example — rallied to the new monarchy; and some able young men of common birth, like Thiers, were able to rise into the governing group. One historian has characterized the system as not so much a government of a single class as a "government of elites" — of all the elites, whether of birth, money, or intelligence.[1] Rarely before or since has there been so intimate a tie between the government and the universities. Many high posts went to Sorbonne professors; Guizot was simply the best-known political figure among them, while the philosopher Victor Cousin became a kind of quasi-official theorist of the regime. The French Academy, that group of forty immortals, became so thoroughly Orleanist that "for half a century it remained an Orleanist salon." Thus the regime possessed an intellectual tone (or perhaps it was only a veneer) that dignified its more crassly materialistic base.

If the Orleanist system had an ideology, a distinctive spirit or outlook, it was best summed up in the phrase *"juste milieu,"* or golden mean. A regime marked by such a mood is an easy target for ridicule; the middle-of-the-road virtues are rarely glamorous, and the ideal itself suggests a fuzzy ambiguity, a tendency toward flabby compromise. "Any regime," it has been said, "faces the threat of degenerating into a parody of its intentions; a middle-of-the-road regime faces it more

[1] R. Rémond, *La droite en France de 1815 à nos jours* (Paris: Aubier, 1954), pp. 80–81.

than most."[2] The Orleanist system has received its full share of such criticism, both from its contemporaries and from posterity. Some of the charges were undoubtedly well founded; but some of them have just as certainly distracted attention from the virtues of the regime. Peace abroad, stability at home, prosperity and at the same time an active intellectual life — these things France enjoyed during the Orleanist era, whether or not it was the Orleanist system that produced them.

⊷⊷⊷⊷⊷⊷

The political history of the July Monarchy falls naturally into two contrasting periods: the decade of instability (1830–40), when ministries averaged less than a year in duration; and the era of rigidity (1840–48), when the regime's governing personnel and policies became almost petrified.

The ministerial instability of the first decade strikes one as incongruous at a time when the extremes of left and right had little influence in politics, and when the dominant center groups prided themselves on their attachment to the spirit of the golden mean. On the right, the old ultras had withdrawn from political life, and no extreme left was likely to emerge in parliament as long as the suffrage was so narrow. The Chamber of Deputies was filled with men of middle-class virtues, men of education and of oratorical talent, men inclined to judicious moderation rather than to demagoguery and political bulldozing. Yet by the end of the decade the Chamber was sometimes torn by tumult as great as in the cruder era of universal suffrage; the deputies bombarded ministerial orators with interruptions and insults, and one speaker who complained of fatigue was even greeted by the unmannerly cry "Drop dead, dog!"

This anomalous condition was the product of the chronic conflict between right-center and left-center, a conflict intensified by the

[2] R. Rémond, *La droite . . .* , p. 73.

emergence of sharp personal rivalries and ambitions and by the king's habit of interfering in periods of crisis. Because the Chamber contained no well-defined parties but only amorphous factions, clear majorities were rare and homogeneous ministries exceptional. Right-center domination was broken by occasional interludes of left-center control, but such interruptions were brief. Adolphe Thiers, whose brilliance was exceeded only by his ambition and his conceit, twice managed to attain the post of president of the council, but he failed to hold power for more than a few months. Louis Philippe was not the kind of king to let himself be overshadowed by a politician, even one as clever as Thiers. The right-center, though it controlled the ministry most of the time, produced no really outstanding leader except the banker Casimir Périer, a domineering figure who could overawe both Chamber and king; but Périer fell victim to the 1831 cholera epidemic, much to Louis Philippe's secret satisfaction.

That first decade brought instability not only within the parliamentary arena but outside it as well. Only a few months after the 1830 revolution some of the ultras (who now began to call themselves Legitimists) attempted to oust the "usurper" from his throne. The Duchesse de Berry, mother of the "miracle child," landed in southern France in 1832, expecting to be welcomed by a general insurrection in favor of the Bourbons; but division among the Legitimists, coupled with amateurish planning, turned the affair from drama into farce. The duchess escaped to the Vendée in peasant disguise and again called vainly for a rising, then eluded the Orleanist police for several months before an informer revealed her hiding place. The Legitimist cause, bolstered somewhat by the duchess' daring, was severely shaken a few months later when the duchess (still in custody) was found to be pregnant. Not even the evidence of her secret marriage to an Italian count sufficed to restore her tarnished reputation; the Bourbon cause languished during the rest of the reign.

Meanwhile, republican agitation was raising an even more serious threat. Though the republicans were probably less numerous than the Legitimists, they were more concentrated and, for a time, more united.

A whole series of *sub rosa* organizations began to spring up in Paris, with branches in other major cities. New leadership was emerging, too: a younger generation of bourgeois intellectuals and artisans, idealistic and romantic in temper, filled with the doctrine of the common man. Out of this inchoate movement came a series of large-scale riots and insurrections in the years 1831–34. They were usually touched off by labor discontent and took on political overtones as they developed. In the most serious of these affairs, the Lyon insurrection of 1831, at least fifteen thousand workers engaged in a pitched battle with the National Guard; the casualty figure exceeded six hundred. The fact that the National Guard (a kind of bourgeois honor society) was called out to help repress the disorders gave a strong color of class conflict to these episodes.

The effect of all this unrest was to weaken the republican movement through the arrest of its leading figures and to drive it underground through the adoption of more severe laws on press and associations. Only scattered and small-scale disorders occurred thereafter, as in 1839 when that dedicated conspirator Auguste Blanqui tried one of his many abortive coups in Paris. But the gradual decline of violence on the left did not mean that the republican element was becoming reconciled to the regime and had decided to work within it. Rather, republican leaders were now aware that the time had not come when violence would be effective; and they turned by necessity to a sustained propaganda campaign instead. But as they did so, they began to lose some of their troops. The urban workers showed signs of swinging away from the bourgeois republican leaders in favor of newer crusaders for sweeping social reform. This cleavage between bourgeois and proletarian republicans was not clearly recognized at the time, but 1848 was to make it dramatically evident.

Alongside the Legitimist and the republican threats to the regime there developed still a third active challenge to the reigning dynasty, in the form of a Bonapartist campaign. By 1830 the Napoleonic legend was taking the form of a vague but widely generalized sentiment. To many Frenchmen, Napoleon was no longer the ruthless dictator who

150

had sacrificed an entire generation of young Frenchmen, but the "Little Corporal" who had made his own way up the steps of the throne and had finally died a martyr to British francophobia and greed. The legend made him always the defender of the common man — the commander who knew each of his soldiers by name, the ruler who gave every citizen a voice at the polls. But while the legend had gained in strength, Bonapartism as an organized political movement had been steadily disintegrating. The leading figures of the Empire were disappearing one by one; the imperial heir presumptive, Napoleon's only legitimate son, died, too, in 1832. It seemed that Bonapartism was on the way to becoming nothing more than a special variety of republicanism; Bonapartists began to resemble the partisans of other defunct dynasties, clinging more stubbornly to their lost cause as its futility became more obvious.

The new pretender, Louis Napoleon Bonaparte, seemed an unlikely prospect to crystallize this amorphous sentiment. He was alleged to be the son of Napoleon's brother Louis, although doubts about his paternity made it uncertain that he was a Bonaparte at all. Even more doubtful were his qualities of leadership and his potential appeal to the French nation. Louis Napoleon had grown up in exile; even the French language was to him a foreign tongue that he never learned to speak without a German accent. In his youth he had fought briefly for Italian freedom as a Carbonaro; and in 1831, shortly after his arrival in Paris, he was expelled from France for associating with republican subversives. Frenchmen knew little more than this about the young man until his farcical attempt in 1836 to invade France with a handful of partisans. He appeared dramatically at a barracks in Strasbourg and persuaded its commander (who had served under his uncle) to follow him with troops and band into the heart of the city. There he was promptly arrested, given a trial that made his cause seem ridiculous, and shipped off to exile in the United States. Undismayed, Louis Napoleon got himself back to England and tried again in 1840. This time he crossed the Channel in a chartered launch with some fifty loyal supporters and a tame eagle. His hope that the army commander at Lille might rally to his cause was disappointed; again he was ignominiously arrested, tried, and this time sentenced to life imprisonment in the fortress of Ham. It was clear now to everyone, even to Louis Napoleon, that the Napoleonic legend alone was not enough to produce a successful revolution. That legend had somehow to be embodied in a person — in a man distinguished by qualities of leadership and possessed of a program as well as a name. Louis Napoleon was to use his six years in prison (which he called ironically "the University of Ham") to develop such a program and to publicize it in a series of pamphlets.

None of the abortive insurrections and coups of the 1830's seriously shook Louis Philippe's regime. More dangerous, in fact, were the attempts at assassination of the king that marked the unstable decade. Ten near misses within that short period constituted a kind of record and led Louis Philippe to remark philosophically that "there seems to be a closed season on all kinds of game except me." Luck or fate saw him through, and, though some of his escapes were so close as to seem almost miraculous, he survived without a scratch.

By 1840 the regime was settling at last into a kind of torpid stability. The country was prosperous and at peace; if the ruling elite was rigid and narrow, it was not fickle or tyrannical. Under the leadership of François Guizot, France was about to enter upon one of the longest periods of stable government in its modern history. The Orleanist monarch, it seemed, had found the key to success that had eluded the Bourbon dynasty.

Guizot, a talented historian turned politician, has always been a subject of controversy among his fellow historians. Some of them have called him the greatest statesman of the nineteenth century; others contemptuously rate him as "an outstanding mediocrity," or "remarkably second-rate." More than any other Frenchman of his time, he symbolized both the policy of the golden mean and the idea of government by all the elites. Guizot sincerely believed in the principle of equal opportunity; and he believed that the principle was fully operative in France. Every man, he held, was free to get rich; those who failed to seize the opportunity could no longer blame an unjust society but must face the fact of their own limitations. Although Guizot was a Protestant (and one of the first of his creed to rise high in government), he reflected the spirit and ideals of the Catholic bourgeoisie as well — especially that segment of the provincial bourgeosie that had never turned Voltairean. There was a strong tinge of Jansenism in the outlook of this group — a kind of quasi-Calvinistic view that the upper classes had a moral duty to govern and to protect the lower orders. Jansenism had long since disappeared as an organized sect, yet remnants of it survived as a set of moral and intellectual standards that colored French life for generations, and that pervaded the thinking of much of the provincial bourgeoisie throughout the nineteenth century.

Few nineteenth-century politicians were so unpopular as Guizot or so blandly indifferent to popularity. There was an irritating holier-than-thou quality about this cold and self-righteous man. To his critics in parliament he once remarked, "As for your insults, your calumnies, your venomous attacks, you may multiply them, pile them up as high as you like, yet they will never reach the level of my contempt." If he managed to retain power from 1840 to 1848, that was because the king lent him steady support and because Guizot was a clever practitioner of corridor politics. Louis Philippe's support was natural enough, for Guizot perfectly embodied the king's doctrine that the ministry should regard itself as the emanation of the monarch and not of the Chamber. Guizot's talent as a political operator may seem more surprising, for he was personally incorruptible as well as cold. There was something of the Robert Walpole about him; Guizot knew English history well and apparently took Walpole as a kind of model. His most effective device was to win the support of wavering or hostile deputies (who drew no salaries) by offering them salaried government posts on the side. At times, as many as one-third of the deputies were on the state payroll in this fashion. Recent scholarship suggests that the legend of Guizot's corrupt tactics has been much exaggerated; yet it is doubtful that he could have held office for eight years if the opposition had managed to push through a bill denying bureaucrats the right to sit as deputies. Eighteen times such a bill was introduced in the Chamber; eighteen times it was defeated.

Guizot's energies during his years in power were devoted mainly to encouraging business expansion (primarily through a hands-off policy, but in some cases through direct governmental aid) and to conducting foreign policy. Only one great legislative act remains associated with his name — and that one dated from an early period, when he was merely minister of public instruction. Guizot's educational reform of 1833 was a landmark in the field; it has been properly called the charter of French primary (i.e., elementary) education. Of the thirty-eight thousand communes in France, fifteen thousand had no school of any kind. Guizot's law obligated every commune to establish a public primary school and provided for expanded teacher-training facilities. The law did not yet guarantee free or compulsory education, nor did it eliminate church influence in the primary schools (though local school boards were to have a majority of laymen). Furthermore, the law was not implemented everywhere — notably in regions where the church had already set up its own primary schools. It was, nevertheless, an important step in the direction of mass education and in the direction of giving the teaching profession more status and better working conditions. By 1848 the number of teacher-training schools had risen from forty-seven to seventy-six, and enrollment in public primary schools had almost doubled.

Guizot's chief rival and most acerbic critic was Thiers, who likewise combined the roles of historian and politician. As one of the principal kingmakers of 1830, Thiers had expected far more than he got in the way of political power under Louis Philippe; and his wounded vanity drove him almost to the point of opposition to the Orleanist regime. Disappointed in his political hopes, Thiers devoted part of his enormous energy to journalism and to writing a massive history of the Napoleonic era. He had been prudent enough to marry money, which gave him independence and an entree into the best Orleanist society. The salon provided a forum for his sparkling monologues on every subject from

Japanese porcelain to differential calculus. But social and scholarly success left him unsatisfied; his ambition was not to write history but to make it. "Just think," he told a friend disconsolately, "how much a man must do to get half a line in a book on world history!" Thiers' neurotic self-esteem may have reflected his small stature (he barely topped five feet in height), or it may have derived from his irregular and humble birth. Whatever its origin, this egotism left little room for generous or humane inclinations. It is hard to avoid the conclusion that he was essentially an *arriviste* concerned with carving out his own career, indifferent to the welfare of any other human being or even of the nation. He lacked both understanding of and interest in social problems and social forces. His phrase for the masses was "the vile multitude"; to him, universal education would be "like building a fire under a great pot that is empty." His world was circumscribed by the halls of parliament and the salons, where his skills at repartee and debate were unsurpassed. No other French statesman of the nineteenth century was to have so long and distinguished a career, or would be remembered with greater admiration. Yet the essential flaw in his character offset his talents and kept him from attaining the highest level of statesmanship. Although he remained an Orleanist until 1872, his harassing tactics during the 1840's contributed much to the downfall of the regime that he had done so much to create.

⋖◦⋗ ⋖◦⋗ ⋖◦⋗

Religious issues, which had done so much to complicate the French political problem during the revolutionary and restoration epochs, seemed to be losing their intensity in the Orleanist era. It was not that French Catholicism was losing its hold on the nation; on the contrary, one might almost call this an era of Catholic renaissance. Two incidents that occurred in Paris in 1831 and 1848 provided a suggestive contrast. Early in 1831 some ultras arranged to celebrate a Mass in memory of the Duc de Berry. A mob of hostile Parisians broke into the church and dispersed the worshippers, then moved on to the archepiscopal palace, sacked the place, and threw the archbishop's library into the Seine. The Orleanist police made no serious effort to stop the riot; neither did Thiers, who was an interested eyewitness. But at the height of the revolution of 1848, when a mob broke into the royal chapel of the Tuileries palace, its behavior was quite different. Instead of desecrating the place, the crowd reverently carried the crucifix to the nearest church. The old cry *"A bas la calotte!"* ("Down with the priests") was no longer heard; onlookers in 1848 reported cries of *"Vive la religion!"* instead, or even, *"Vive Jésus Christ!"*

A remarkable change had occurred within two decades, and no simple explanation of it will suffice. One contributing factor was the church's loss of special privilege after 1830. In previous years its close tie with the ultras, its commitment to Bourbon reaction, its rapid gains in power and wealth, had made it an object of suspicion and hostility in many quarters. The Orleanists broke the alliance between throne and altar; the new regime took on a mildly anticlerical cast. Louis Philippe himself was a Voltairean who privately scoffed at religion but attended Mass as a social duty. Thiers was openly contemptuous of religious belief, except for the vile multitude. Victor Cousin held that the clergy would still be useful as "moral policemen and funeral directors," but assumed that the skepticism of the urban bourgeoisie would gradually spread downward as education did its work. Guizot, though a believer, was not a Catholic. At the very outset the regime pruned the state budget for religious activities and expelled some religious orders. In the end, this mild and rather painless persecution benefited the church. Perhaps the Vatican recognized this fact; at any rate, the Pope repeatedly advised the clergy to remain loyal to the Voltairean king.

More significant still was the gradual process of change that had set in within the church. New currents of thought were developing there, currents that seemed destined to rejuvenate Catholicism and that foreshadowed a reconciliation with the modern world. In a word, the church (or an important segment of it) was at last getting round to accepting the revolution of 1789. It may be true (as one impatient French Catholic has put it) that "the church in France is always one

156

revolution behind." At any rate, the Orleanist period did bring the beginnings of what has sometimes been called "neo-Catholicism."

In the church, as outside it, the older generation of leaders was rapidly disappearing; the unreconstructed ultras were being replaced — at least in part — by vigorous young priests and laymen attuned to their times. Some of them, like Frédéric Ozanam, were principally concerned with social problems and the alleviation of misery. Ozanam, while still a university student, brought together six friends to form the new Society of St. Vincent de Paul, an organization that rapidly expanded until it became nation-wide and then world-wide in scope. Ozanam was the fountainhead of the durable current called "social Catholicism" in nineteenth-century France. Although conservative in spirit, it refused to be satisfied with the mere practice of charity but insisted on seeking the reasons for poverty and on working toward greater social justice. Ozanam's was only the best known of a whole series of Catholic social-action groups, which blossomed in unprecedented fashion in this era.

Other Catholics were moving meanwhile toward a new and still hardier doctrine: one that would reconcile the church with political liberalism or even with democracy. In 1830 a little group of priests headed by Félicité de Lamennais founded the first Catholic daily newspaper in Europe, *L'Avenir,* and set out to preach political democracy mixed with some incipient social reform. Modern Catholicism has produced few figures so striking as Lamennais. A crusader whose enterprises always withered, a fanatically fervent believer who eventually left the church, he has been described as "a modern Savonarola," and as the only genius produced by nineteenth-century French Catholicism. Of Breton birth, Lamennais was a kind of "caricature of the Celt": a romantic, mystical, brooding, and undisciplined youth. In the Bourbon era he had been, like his fellow Breton Chateaubriand, an ultra-ultra royalist; but even more intense had been his ultramontane convictions, his hostility toward the Gallican tradition. Gallican kings and bishops, he argued, had long used the church as a tool of national policy; instead, they ought to serve the Pope, who alone could accomplish the regeneration of human society.

By 1830 Lamennais had become totally disillusioned with the Bourbons; he shifted brusquely from his program of "Pope and King" to a new program of "Pope and People." In *L'Avenir* he proposed to regenerate mankind by starting at the bottom, with individual and ordinary men. His fervent crusade, though it made him the idol of many young priests, promptly aroused the hostility of the hierarchy; and Lamennais went off to Rome to appeal his case to the Pope. His hopes were no more than illusions; he should have known that the Vatican could not adopt his cause when almost the entire French hierarchy opposed it, and that the Pope could not commit the church to the ideal of political democracy. Instead, he was instructed to recant and to suspend his newspaper. Lamennais submitted, but he stormed and brooded over the outcome; he soon broke with the Vatican as he had broken with the Bourbons. Thereafter he became increasingly isolated; as he moved farther left, he began to anticipate the Christian socialist position of the twentieth century. The revolution of 1848 brought him a brief period of glory — he was elected a deputy in Paris — but he soon slipped back into obscurity once more, to die a lonely old man almost without followers.

There is a dramatic contrast between Lamennais's career of repetitious failure and the long-range success of most of the ideas for which he fought. His ultramontane doctrine gradually gained strength until, by the end of the century, it had virtually wiped out all remnants of the Gallican tradition. His attempt to reconcile the church with political democracy was to be reflected in one of the most important political movements of twentieth-century France and Europe. His Christian socialism anticipated papal doctrine as expressed in the encyclical *Rerum Novarum* (1931), but it was to have an even more direct heritage in the emergence of labor-oriented Catholic movements with a strongly leftist slant. Lamennais and Karl Marx, someone has remarked, were the two greatest visionaries of nineteenth-century Europe.

The failure of Lamennais's campaign in the 1830's did not mean the immediate relapse of French Catholicism into a mood of reaction. Although such disciples as the young priests Lacordaire and Montalembert left him, they remained representative of what might be called a moderately liberal Catholic current, seeking to adapt the church to the new society that had emerged from the Great Revolution. Lacordaire's impact was exerted through his powerful sermons at Notre Dame, sermons that attracted thousands of hearers, including many young intellectuals and bourgeois Parisians whose parents were thorough Voltaireans. Montalembert meanwhile turned to politics as the most effective sphere of action. He set out in the 1840's to fuse all Catholics into a single political bloc, dedicated not to an attempt to restore the old regime but to effective political action within the existing regime. The practical issue on which he chose to fight was the school question. Montalembert demanded the right to establish Catholic secondary schools competitive with those of the state and to operate them without state interference. The church already had its network of primary schools and its seminaries for training priests; what it wanted now was legal authority to train the sons of the bourgeoisie, the nation's future governing elite.

Montalembert was shrewd enough to build his campaign around the attractive slogan "liberty of education" and to aim his arguments quite frankly at the literate public rather than at the politicians alone. The emotional impact was great: here at last was the church committed to the principle of liberty, to the principle of equal and fair treatment, rather than to the idea of monopoly or special privilege. Montalembert's campaign was not to succeed until 1850, but it probably contributed to the revived popularity of the church in the later Orleanist period. On the other hand, a tinge of demagoguery crept into the bitter debate between Montalembert's forces and the defenders of state schools; so vindictive were the charges and counter-charges that they intensified the hostility between Catholics and dedicated anticlericals. This was to be the first passage of arms in a century-long conflict over the school question — a conflict whose divisive effects have sometimes verged on the tragic.

If the Orleanist epoch brought fresh currents into French Catholicism, it also brought evidence that the old currents kept much of their force. Indeed, division within the church seemed to be attaining a new pitch of intensity. In 1842 a strange young man named Louis Veuillot took over the editorship of the Paris daily *L'Univers* and established himself over the next forty years as one of the most powerful figures in modern French religious history. Of common birth and Voltairean upbringing, his sudden conversion as a young man had turned him into a superheated fanatic. He was the bitterest enemy of the liberals and the compromisers. Intolerant of error, a master at the art of whipping up emotions, he set out (as Ozanam put it) "not to win back unbelievers, but to arouse the passions of believers." Veuillot possessed remarkable journalistic talent and a flair for speaking the language of the people; he has been called one of the most influential journalists of all time. His tireless activity gave promise that not all French Catholics would slip docilely into the liberal current. And the Vatican, for a generation at least, was to favor the Veuillot position against that of the liberal Catholics.

Statistically speaking, the number of churchgoers in France may not have increased very much during the Orleanist era. There is clear evidence that difficulties in recruiting new priests were increasing. Yet perhaps the turning point in the church's fortunes had already arrived by 1848, in the sense that a segment of the bourgeoisie was beginning to swing back from Voltaireanism to the Christian faith. It has often been alleged that the bourgeois outlook changed only after the traumatic shock of civil war in 1848; that fear of social revolution led the freethinking property-owners to reconstruct Catholicism as a bulwark of the social order. Some Frenchmen undoubtedly did react this way after the June Days. But there is good reason to believe that the Catholic revival was fed by other emotions than fear, and that its roots went deeper than 1848. The first signs of the bourgeois return to the

160

faith can be found in the Orleanist era; and that return was inspired or hastened by the forces of rejuvenation within the church.

❧❧❧

The revolution that destroyed the regime of Louis Philippe has often been called a result without a cause. A more appropriate phrase would describe it as a result far out of proportion to the cause. Frenchmen were not being oppressed or tyrannized; the government was not confronted by bankruptcy or undermined by a powerful subversive movement plotting its overthrow. Indeed, one of the two leading republican newspapers in Paris had so small a circulation that it was forced to suspend publication a few weeks before the upheaval. Until the very last moment most of the opposition leaders aimed not at revolution but merely at abdication. Some of them were even less ambitious; they meant only to give the king a scare.

But if a revolutionary temper was lacking, there was widespread irritation and discontent; so much of it that even court circles were nervous. The king's sons frankly expressed their concern; his widowed daughter-in-law, mother of the heir apparent, was reputed to believe that Louis Philippe's stubbornness was endangering her son's chances for the succession. The king was subjected to rising court pressure to sacrifice Guizot, chief symbol of the regime's unpopularity. Alexis de Tocqueville, in a prophetic speech delivered in the Chamber in January, 1848, warned that if trouble should occur, it was likely to have repercussions much more profound than a mere change of ministry.

Louis Philippe complacently ignored the prophets of doom. He sent his critical sons off to Algeria or to service with the navy; he let it be known that he considered his daughter-in-law dangerously disloyal. He refused even to consider parting with Guizot, whose presence he thought essential for the perpetuation of the system to which he had grown so much attached. A less dependable and pliable chief minister might embark on some risky foreign crusade or demand a beginning of political reform.

If there had been little talk of revolution or republicanism in the years before 1848, there had been much talk of reform. Throughout the decade opposition deputies had been introducing bills designed to broaden the suffrage or to deny deputies the right to hold salaried posts in the bureaucracy. This frustrated desire for reform had gradually corroded the middle and lower ranks of the bourgeoisie and had even found expression in that pillar of the regime, the National Guard. A second source of discontent, more imprecise but even more widely shared, was the regime's lack of glamor. "France is bored," remarked the poet-deputy Lamartine as early as 1839; by 1847 he was bold enough to predict a "revolution of contempt." Even the virtues of the regime were thus turned to its discredit; peace and stability seemed to suggest cowardice and stagnation. Still a third factor endangering public morale was the apparent evidence of dry rot within the ruling elite. A financial scandal in 1847 implicated two ex-ministers, who were charged with accepting bribes and playing favorites in the grant of government concessions. A prominent Orleanist peer, involved in a marital triangle, murdered his wife and then committed suicide. Cases of this sort gave some bourgeois supporters of the regime a bad conscience; they wondered whether the very base of the system was rotting away, and their will to defend it was undermined.

All these sources of irritation affected the bourgeoisie but left the masses largely indifferent. The discontent of the urban workers sprang from other sources: in part from the cumulative impact of socialist propaganda, but in the main from long-endured misery, compounded by the depression that began in 1846–47. This was the gravest economic crisis of Louis Philippe's reign. The same wave of bad weather that produced the great Irish famine brought a series of crop failures in France as well. Food became scarce and expensive; the price of wheat rose 250 per cent, and the government was driven to import foodstuffs. The agrarian crisis rapidly affected the whole economy; many mines and factories shut down, some of the new railway companies went bankrupt, unemployment spiralled upward.

The 1840's brought, too, a dangerous alienation of the intellectuals.

Novelists like Victor Hugo, George Sand, and Eugène Sue were developing a kind of mythology of the common man and were playing with
doctrines of democracy or socialism. The biting caricatures of Honoré
Daumier stripped the governing elite of its veneer of dignity and
respectability and suggested that men in authority ranged from petty
frauds to human vultures. Three notable historians — Michelet, Lamartine, Louis Blanc — produced in 1847 three striking new interpretations
of the Great Revolution, all of them glorifying some aspect of that
dramatic upheaval. Lamartine's heroes were the Girondins; Blanc
praised Robespierre; Michelet exalted the people, the revolutionary
crowd. "It is said everywhere," wrote Lamartine proudly, "that my
book fans the hard fires of revolution, and that it will inspire the
people for revolutions to come. May God so will it!"

Dissatisfaction took organized form in the summer of 1847.
Opposition leaders, denied the right to hold public political meetings,
evaded the law by scheduling a series of banquets in the major cities
and indulging in political oratory between courses. The novelist Gustave
Flaubert attended one in Rouen that lasted nine hours, and that
destroyed his enthusiasm for politics: "What abominable taste! [he
wrote to a friend] what wines! and what speeches! . . . I was nau-
seated." But Flaubert was the exception; most of Guizot's critics
wallowed enthusiastically in their opportunity to denounce the government and to drink toasts to reform. A huge banquet scheduled to be
held in Paris on February 22, 1848, with a hundred opposition deputies
on the invited list, finally broke the government's patience; orders
were issued to cancel the affair. Although most of its sponsors were
willing to give in, a few hotheads insisted on action and announced
that they would appear at the assigned place in spite of the government.

Their stubbornness sparked the crisis that followed. On the twenty-
second, students and workers congregated in the streets and began to
clash with the police. Louis Philippe showed a serene confidence in his
ability to handle the riots, which he thought would be minor in any
case. His army garrison in Paris was three time as large as that of
the Bourbons in 1830; it was well equipped, possessed carefully laid

plans to meet an insurrection, and could depend on the support of the bourgeois National Guard. Indeed, the king's confidence was well founded; and the regime almost certainly would have beaten back the uprising save for three crucial sources of weakness. One was the virtual desertion of the National Guard, whose loyalty was corroded by the growing desire of the lesser bourgeoisie for a share of political power. The second was the character of the army command in Paris; at its head were fourth-rate generals elevated to their posts for reasons of influence rather than of competence. The third was the king's own reluctance to be responsible for a blood bath — a reluctance that led him to suspend the army's prearranged plan at a critical moment, when the rebels seemed to be on the run and appeared ready to give in without further fighting.

Toward the end of the second day of rioting, the king reluctantly decided to sacrifice Guizot. Perhaps that decision might have saved the regime, had not an accidental clash occurred a few hours later between troops and rioters outside Guizot's office. Or perhaps that bloody incident only gave the more dedicated revolutionaries a better excuse for continuing the fight; for by now, the working-class quarters were speckled with street barricades. In any event, the situation had become critical; and at midnight on the twenty-third, Louis Philippe turned grudgingly to Thiers as a possible savior. Again, the possible effect of this gesture was nullified when the king at the same time named General Bugeaud to be army commander in Paris, for Bugeaud was probably the most hated general in the service. By morning the revolutionary tide was flooding toward the royal palace. Thiers, who fancied himself a new Napoleon in the sphere of military strategy, urged the king to leave Paris, organize an army of sixty thousand men, and besiege the city until it could be taken by storm. Louis Philippe refused to consider such a solution; after a futile attempt to rally the remnants of the National Guard in defense of the palace, he wrote out his abdication in favor of his grandson and departed by cab for the suburbs, whence he eventually made his way to English exile. The king's daughter-in-law remained behind with the ten-year-old heir apparent. While the mob ransacked the Tuileries and tested the contents of the royal cellar, the duchess and her children went to the Chamber of Deputies, hoping that the child would be accepted as king by acclamation. Many of the deputies were willing, but the Chamber was gradually inundated by waves of rioters who disrupted the proceedings. When Lamartine finally got the floor, his flamboyant oratory destroyed the dynasty's last faint hope; only that morning he had tentatively committed himself to the republic as the sole solution. As the disillusioned duchess and her brood departed in their turn for exile, the crowd and the deputies surged off across Paris to the Hôtel de Ville, the traditional seat of newly-founded republics.

Thus for the second time in a generation, and for the third time since 1792, constitutional monarchy had failed in France. Was this proof that such a system, in essence a pragmatic and somewhat incoherent compromise between rival doctrines, was unworkable for Frenchmen, with their passion for coherence and logic? Or was it simply the product of ill fortune, of the country's failure to turn up the kind of monarchs and politicians capable of making such a system function? Or, rather, was the heritage of conflict produced by the Great Revolution so intense as to make any kind of stable government impossible until time allowed passions to die down? A case can doubtless be made for an affirmative answer to each of these questions. Yet once again, as in 1792 and as in 1830, shortcomings of statesmanship seem to have been the crucial factor; and the thesis that any of these three experiments in constitutional monarchy was bound to fail in France is hard to defend. To ask whether the Orleanist experiment was better fitted to survive than its Bourbon predecessor (assuming in both cases a somewhat higher caliber of leadership) would probably be no more than an exercise in futility. The Orleanists lacked the Bourbons' aura of legitimacy and some of the glamor of ancient tradition. They possessed, on the other hand, a somewhat greater comprehension of the emerging nineteenth-century world; and, potentially at least, they should have been better able to base their rule on all segments of that broad amorphous category called the bourgeoisie.

It is tempting to conclude that no other regime in modern French history missed so good an opportunity to perpetuate itself as a durable political system. A little flexibility, a little imagination, a little capacity for self-criticism — only this, and France might have remained Orleanist for another century.

"Any immobile institution is vicious because it ends as privilege and contradicts the real state of the society it serves." The author of this perceptive comment was, strange to say, François Guizot.

ELEVEN

> Each revolution undertaken by the French people
> must establish a new philosophical truth in the
> world.
>
> *From the preamble to a*
> *governmental decree of 1848*

The Republican Experiment, 1848–1852

Karl Marx's first important venture into the writing of contemporary history was his account of the 1848 revolution and the Second French Republic. Although his two brief books on the subject fused propaganda with history, they contained such a remarkable combination of shrewd insight and plausibility that his analysis continues to be widely accepted in our day. In muted form, it reappears in many non-Marxian works.

The February revolution, according to Marx and his latter-day disciples, amounted to little more than the overthrow of the older financial bourgeoisie by the newer industrial bourgeoisie. That hard fact was concealed at the time by a brief interlude of confused class relationships, when the essential conflicts within society were temporarily clouded by a romantic haze of universal brotherhood. The bourgeois provisional government showed its good will by granting the vote to all men and by adding a workingman (Albert) and a prominent socialist (Louis Blanc) to the governing body of the new republic. The old feud over the church's proper role seemed to be ended; republicans and Catholics worked together more intimately than they had ever done before, or were to do again until the founding years of the Fourth Republic a century later. Parisian workers paraded to the Hôtel de Ville to offer the new republic a free gift of a day's wages each; during the first two months such voluntary contributions from the workers brought the government more income than it could raise through its first bond issue. The novelist Flaubert, in retrospect, sardonically summed up the spirit of '48 as an incoherent blend of religious fervor, romantic ardor, and thirst for progress. His fictional artist of 1848 dashed off a portrait intended to symbolize the new age; it portrayed Christ at the throttle of a locomotive, racing full speed through a virgin forest.

Then, according to the Marxian version, came a gradual clearing of the air, the emergence of suspicion and hostility, the recognition of true class relationships. The proletariat, aware that it had been duped, began to organize clubs on the Jacobin model, to march in street demonstrations, to threaten the government, to demand that the principle of "the right to work" be written into law. Its spokesmen urged that elections be postponed for a year or more, in order to permit the "education" of the benighted peasant masses; they called for an active ideological foreign policy to aid peoples' governments in Europe; they demanded immediate social as well as political reforms. Meanwhile, the increasingly nervous bourgeoisie was seeking ways to protect its special privilege. The poet Lamartine served for a time as a kind of oratorical lightning rod, diverting mass discontent by his florid and evasive speeches. A few meager bones were even thrown to the workers in an effort to keep them appeased. But gradually, as the Marxians see it, the bourgeois leaders recovered their self-confidence and abandoned sham. They resented the concessions that has been forced on them, and the continuing demands of the proletariat; they were upset at the business crisis produced in part by the uncertainty born of upheaval; they were angry when some republicans proposed to nationalize public utilities like the railways and the insurance companies; they were frightened at the success of a few producers' cooperatives that the skilled workers had managed to establish. By a series of hypocritical intrigues, the bourgeois politicians consciously provoked a workers' revolt in June, 1848, in order to provide an excuse for drowning the "reds" in their own blood.

The Marxist and neo-Marxist thesis suggests that the bourgeois leaders were not merely narrow-minded and selfish, but wicked as well; that most of their actions were inspired by greed and marked by low cunning. A typical act was the creation of the so-called National Workshops a few days after the revolution, under pressure from the workers' representatives in the government. The experiment, the Marxians contend, was purposely sabotaged from the outset by placing the Workshops under the control of a minister who was violently anti-socialist. That minister consciously set out to discredit social reform by making the Workshops a ridiculous caricature of the "social workshop" idea popularized in the 1840's by Louis Blanc. An even more discreditable trick, in the Marxian view, was the recruiting of a special armed police called the "mobile national guard," made up of the toughest young unemployed workers and hoodlums in Paris and dedicated to breaking up street demonstrations by the honest proletariat. The same low motives were supposed to have inspired the government's decision to hold elections without delay, so that the partisans of social reform might be inundated by a damp wave of peasant votes. Similar hypocrisy allegedly lay back of the republic's foreign policy of talk without action — a spate of fine words on behalf of revolutionary movements in Europe, cancelled out by a refusal to lift a finger in support of those revolutionary governments. In the end, the fearful bourgeoisie is charged with opening the way to a political adventurer named Louis Napoleon Bonaparte, whose system of authoritarian order it preferred to the risks of free government.

The Marxist version — especially in its slightly modernized neo-Marxist form — is an attractive one, for it ties the period into a neat bundle with no loose ends. Some aspects of it, moreover, are undoubtedly sound. Many members of the bourgeoisie were openly or hypocritically bigoted and subject to panic; too often the leading politicians were shortsighted or confused. Yet as a total explanation the thesis is more plausible than convincing. It is far too simple and systematized to fit a highly complex episode; many of its assertions are both unproved and unprovable. Its deepest flaw, however, is that it assumes far too much in the way of understanding bourgeois motivations. As a British historian has remarked, "Nobody claims to see further into the minds of people they dislike than these socialist historians."[1] A few hair-raising quotations from particularly bigoted politicians will not suffice in 1848 or in any other period to support a set of generalizations on the outlook of the political class. No one can sensibly deny that the story of the Second Republic was in part a story of emergent class conflict; but it was in some ways less than that, and in some ways more.

❧◦❧◦❧◦❧

The provisional government that was patched together in February, 1848, contained some estimable men, but there was no single figure who combined executive ability with charismatic appeal. Only Lamartine seemed to possess a touch of charisma, and he therefore emerged as symbol and spokesman for the government; but Lamartine clearly lacked the qualities of real crisis leadership. Perhaps no man could have managed so heterogeneous a group of ministers; or perhaps the issues of the time were too complex for settlement. Yet if the new republic had turned up an energetic, shrewd, and high-minded group of leaders at the very outset, it is at least possible that the whole history of the period might have been altered.

Except for the workingman Albert, the membership of the provisional government was solidly bourgeois. The bourgeoisie, however, was far from solid in outlook. Within the government two major factions promptly emerged: a moderate wing, dedicated to political reform, and a radical wing, committed to social experiments as well. Both elements did agree on one basic principle — that of universal

[1] J. Plamenatz, *The Revolutionary Movement in France* (London: Longmans, 1952), p. 77.

manhood suffrage, even though such an experiment was almost unprecedented in Europe, and even though more than a third of the prospective voters were still illiterate. Perhaps the government's action was naive; perhaps its decision to rush the elections was ill-advised. But there is not the slightest evidence that either decision was dishonest or inspired by shrewd class calculation.

Even on the issue of social reform, the basic division within the government did not show up very clearly at first. Both elements agreed to set up a large study commission directed by Louis Blanc to examine and recommend useful social experiments; both elements agreed to establish the agency misnamed the National Workshops. Neither of these decisions represented a clear governmental commitment to sweeping social reform; but neither one seems to have been designed as a hypocritical scheme for discrediting or sidetracking the social issue. It is true that Louis Blanc's Luxembourg Commission did end in total futility and that the National Workshops resembled an emergency relief agency of the leaf-raking variety rather than a revolutionary system of producers' cooperatives, as advocated by Louis Blanc. But there is only meager and shaky evidence for the view that the bourgeois ministers were inspired by ulterior motives. The provisional government was faced on its accession by a severe economic crisis that had gripped the country since 1846, and the upheaval of 1848 quickly made the situation even worse. As unemployment grew and as thousands of jobless workers flocked to Paris from the provinces, some kind of emergency measures had to be taken for both humanitarian and practical reasons. The Workshops provided such relief, however meager and badly administered it may have been. Alongside them, there did develop a few real producers' cooperatives of the Blanc variety — notably in the shoemaking and clothing trades.

The government's foreign policy, shaped mainly by Lamartine as foreign minister, was the source of sharper dispute between moderate and radical elements as the months went by. The radicals called for a crusade in support of revolutionary governments in central and eastern Europe. Lamartine gave the idea lip service but no material aid. Not even a huge street demonstration organized by the radicals in support of aid to the Poles succeeded in forcing Lamartine's hand. Perhaps this failure to act was really "the first step on the road to Munich";[2] perhaps, in retrospect, it would have been better if Frenchmen had died carrying liberty throughout Europe rather than fighting each other on the barricades in June. Yet the problem is too complicated for such an easy formula; and doubt must greet the charge that Lamartine's foreign policy was motivated by nothing more than a bourgeois fear of spreading social upheaval. It may be that Lamartine, instead of being wicked, was simply wrong; indeed, it is even possible that he was partly right. He believed that an ideological crusade might be disastrous, since it might drive the European powers into a new anti-French coalition like that of Napoleon's day. He probably suspected also that the crusading spirit of the noisy radical minority was not shared by Frenchmen in general. Lamartine was evidently misled into believing (as German liberals also believed) that the king of Prussia had rallied to the liberal cause and would be a dependable ally for the French republic. Together, these liberal states of western Europe could then free the Continent from the chief threat to liberalism — armed intervention by reactionary Russia. If Lamartine was wrong in this analysis, his motives would seem to have been above reproach, and his reasoning comprehensible at least.

On Easter Sunday (April 23) Frenchmen went to the polls to shape the destiny of the republic. There had been little time for nation-wide campaigning or for "educating" the rural voters. Most of the peasants and villagers, at a loss to make choices among candidates, ended by voting for lists of local notables — landlords, doctors, notaries — whose names were familiar but whose political affiliations were kept ambiguous. Frenchmen turned out on election day in surprising numbers: 84 per cent of the eligible voters cast ballots, a figure never again to be reached in any French election. The outcome confirmed the fears of the radicals: the rural vote went to moderate or conservative candi-

---

[2] A. J. P. Taylor, in F. Fejtö (ed.), *The Opening of an Era: 1848* (London: Wingate, n.d.), p. xxvi.

dates in all but a few regions. Of nine hundred seats in the new Constituent Assembly, fewer than one hundred were won by the radical republicans or socialists. Even in Paris candidates of the extreme left ran well behind the moderate republicans: Lamartine's name led all the rest, while the radical Ledru-Rollin ranked only twenty-fourth, Louis Blanc twenty-seventh, and Lamennais thirty-fourth. Moderate republicans numbered about five hundred in the new Assembly, monarchists three hundred, and radicals only eighty.

The moderate politicians, bolstered by the verdict of the country, unfortunately failed to show much wisdom in the way they used their new authority. When the Assembly met in May, its majority was determined to root the radicals out of the five-man executive council that was destined to replace the provisional government. Lamartine, fresh from an unprecedented electoral triumph that had seen him poll a million and a half votes in ten districts, took it upon himself to resist that pressure; he refused to accept membership in the new executive council unless the Assembly would elect the radical spokesman Ledru-Rollin as well. It may be that Lamartine's motives were demagogic; his angry moderate colleagues thought so, and so have neo-Marxist historians. But perhaps his action stemmed rather from his deep conviction that an open breach between moderate and radical republicans might bring disaster to the republic itself and that his unparalleled influence must be used to preserve the broad coalition between rival ideologies and classes. The Assembly resentfully bowed to his pressure but showed its anger by barely electing Lamartine and Ledru-Rollin to the new executive council.

During the month that followed, Lamartine proved incapable of dominating the new moderate majority. He failed, most notably, in his effort to provide an acceptable substitute for the National Workshops, the cost of which was bitterly resented by most bourgeois and rural politicians and taxpayers. His plan was to convert the uncompleted railway system into a great public works project and to transfer the unemployed from the Workshops to this more constructive enterprise. The Assembly's rejection of this proposal buttresses the Marxian view of the bourgeoisie's class-bound outlook; but it is worth noting that the idea of public works and of nationalization of the railways was accepted by a number of bourgeois politicians.

The outright abolition of the Workshops followed logically and speedily; young men on the state payroll were offered enlistment in the army as an alternative, older ones were faced by the prospect of departing for the provinces to drain pestilential swamps. The almost immediate consequence was the three-day civil war in Paris known as the June Days — next to the Commune of 1871, the bloodiest episode in the history of modern France.

Two grave charges have been made against the men who abolished the Workshops: that they consciously aimed to provoke the Parisian proletarians to revolt, and that they gave the rebels two full days to assemble and build street barricades so that they might then wipe out the reds en masse. Neither charge can be convincingly defended. Beyond doubt, there were a few rabid red-haters who thought in terms of provoking the radicals to a bloody showdown; but there is no proof that this sentiment was strong among the bourgeois politicians in general, or even that this sentiment existed at all among most of the deputies. The principal bourgeois motive, rather, seems to have been a shortsighted impulsion to cut taxes and to end the boondoggling that allegedly marked the operation of the National Workshops. As for the second charge, there is some reason to believe that prompt army action at the very outset of the June Days might have gotten the rebellion quickly in hand without much bloodshed. General Cavaignac, who was charged with the defense of Paris, refused to take such prompt action despite the urging of Lamartine. His motives remain unplumbed; but the most plausible explanation is that Cavaignac's rigid mind had been set by his experience in repressing Algerian disorders. His practice there had been to let the rebels commit themselves to strong positions and then to blast them out with artillery. Such tactics used in Paris had savage results: at least fifteen hundred rebels were killed on the barricades or in the settling of accounts that followed, and unofficial estimates put the figure at three thousand or more. Twelve thousand others were arrested, and many were subsequently transported to Algeria.

The effects of the June Days were calamitous. One immediate result was the replacement of the five-man civilian executive council by a temporary military dictatorship under Cavaignac. The general became the idol of the more bigoted element of the bourgeoisie, while Lamartine plummeted into political obscurity. The Parisian radical movement was decapitated by the death, imprisonment, or exile of most of its leading figures. Class hostility reached a new pitch of intensity. While bourgeoisie and aristocracy developed an unreasoning terror of the reds, the workers retreated into silent and embittered opposition to the regime. If the June Days did not doom the Second Republic to extinction, they undoubtedly lengthened the odds against the system's survival.

Comparative quiet descended on the country after the catastrophic June crisis. Gone was the constant effervescence of the republic's early months; gone also the euphoria, the enthusiasm, that had been the hallmark of '48. Cavaignac as temporary executive remade the ministry to suit more conservative tastes. Many of the reform decrees of February and March (e.g., the reduction of the working day in Paris factories to ten hours) were repealed. Louis Blanc's Luxembourg Commission had already been abolished in May. By the end of the year the sum total of surviving social reform — despite an unprecedented flowering of proposals — was virtually zero. The Assembly turned meanwhile to its allotted task of drafting a constitution. Six months of discussion produced the inevitable compromise document designed to satisfy a variety of rival factions and theories. In form at least, it was unambiguously democratic, for its unicameral legislature was to be chosen for a three-year term by universal male suffrage and its president for a four-year term by the same voters. For the first and last time a French republic chose to experiment with a presidential rather than a parliamentary system.

What the constitution of 1848 left unclear was the relationship between president and legislature, both of which were to be emanations of the popular will. One sanguine deputy offered this prediction: "The executive and legislative powers will clash and balance each other under the nightly and daily surveillance of the press. If they are jealous of each other, that's no matter; if they dispute,. so much the better. When you hear them squalling, you'll know they're not dead." A strong minority of the constitution-makers was much more skeptical about the benefits of squalling controversy. An obscure young deputy named Jules Grévy had even sought to abolish the office of president entirely and to provide no executive except a committee of the legislature. Grévy's fear of a strong executive, given consistency a few years later by Louis Napoleon's coup d'état, was to lend him an appearance of prescience that would eventually carry him to the presidency of the Third Republic in 1879.

Other nations have proved that a constitutional system like that of the Second Republic can be workable—in other nations, at any rate. Perhaps the system was doomed in France by the peculiar political heritage of the country. Or perhaps it might have been workable there except for the presence of a glamorous presidential aspirant with autocratic ambitions. The constitution-makers were not aware that such an aspirant was at hand (though some of them were suspicious of the aims of Cavaignac and Lamartine). Few of them would have thought of Louis Napoleon Bonaparte as a serious threat, for his beginnings in politics had resembled farce rather than high drama.

Louis Napoleon had returned from British exile[3] soon after the revolution, accompanied by a motley group of supporters and subsidized by his blonde English mistress, the actress Miss Howard. He had been elected to the Constituent Assembly in a by-election in June, but his first speech at the tribune had ended in grotesque failure. Some politicians were sensitive to the curious appeal of his name and got early seats on his band wagon; but few of them believed him capable of aggressive leadership. Indeed, that was precisely why some of them joined him. Thiers, for example, backed him for the presi-

[3] He had escaped from the fortress of Ham in 1846 after serving six years of his life term.

176

dency in the hope that a weak executive might open the way to the return of the Orleanist monarchy (and the return of Thiers to the ministry). Not even the shrewdest politician could have foreseen the extent of the Bonapartist landslide in the December presidential election: Louis Napoleon polled 5,500,000 votes compared to 1,500,000 for Cavaignac, 370,000 for Ledru-Rollin, 37,000 for the radical Raspail, and an almost insulting 17,000 for Lamartine. Five months later the election of the Legislative Assembly produced almost as great a shock. The moderate republicans who had shaped the new republic were almost wiped out. The radical left made impressive gains, winning almost two hundred seats; but it was the monarchist right that could claim the real triumph. With its four hundred seats it possessed a clear majority, though that majority was divided into Legitimist and Orleanist factions. A republic whose president was a Bonaparte and whose legislature was dominated by monarchists seemed predestined to disaster. Disaster was indeed to be its fate—and within three years.

❦❦❦

Any coherent account of the Second Republic's constitutional phase must depend on a prior judgment of Louis Napoleon's aims and character. Some historians have seen him as an unprincipled schemer interested in little except women, race horses, and power and determined from the outset to destroy the republic at the appropriate moment. Others take the view that he was a sincere idealist who sensed the trend of his age and who sought to give France the vigorous leadership it needed. Some of his defenders believe that if the president always meant to convert the republic into an empire, it was only for high-minded reasons. Others remain convinced that until late in 1851 he remained loyal to the republic and sought only to get the constitution amended so that he might run for additional terms. If Louis Napoleon has been something of an enigma to historians, perhaps that is because he was an enigma even to those who knew him best. His niece Princess Mathilde, one of the shrewdest of the Bonapartes, once remarked im-

177

patiently: "If I had married him, I think that I would have broken his head open to find out what's inside."

During the early phase of Louis Napoleon's presidency he seemed inclined to collaborate with the conservative majority in the Legislative Assembly. He catered to conservative views in his foreign policy — notably by sending aid to the beleaguered Pope, driven from Rome by republican revolutionaries — and by his acceptance of a Catholic-sponsored educational reform, the Falloux Law of 1850. He also signed into law bills that deprived one out of three Frenchmen of the right to vote and that restricted the press and the right of political assemblage.

Yet Louis Napoleon had long since indicated his sympathy for ideas that ran counter to the whole conservative doctrine. During his imprisonment at Ham in the 1840's he had published several pamphlets of vaguely Saint-Simonian flavor — notably a work entitled *The Extinction of Poverty*. Bonapartist candidates, when they ran for the Legislative Assembly in 1849, had usually chosen to stand on a platform of dynamic change rather than one of static defense. Monarchist candidates in 1849 had been inclined to talk of order, family, property, religion; their Bonapartist rivals preferred to urge the importance of rural roads, railways, canals.

Karl Marx contended (and neo-Marxist historians echo his view) that Louis Napoleon's leftist leanings were mere sham; that he resorted to pseudo-socialist phraseology as a demagogic device to frighten the bourgeoisie. His attempt to win the genuine affection of the propertied class had failed, according to Marx, and so Louis Napoleon shifted to a kind of blackmail by hinting that he might turn sharply left and use the *lumpenproletariat,* the scum of the cities, to establish a kind of socialist dictatorship. By this tactic, according to Marx, the bulk of the bourgeoisie was not so much won over as neutralized; and the country's fate was left in the hands of the "inert" classes — the most backward and superstitious elements of the peasantry and the petty bourgeoisie. Only after Louis Napoleon had repressed the proletariat and neutralized the bourgeoisie, argued Marx, did he consider it safe to challenge the conservative majority in the legislature. But the Marxist

thesis that Louis Napoleon looked to the ignorant, the inert, the "trog-
lodytes" of French society for his chief support can hardly be reconciled with what Louis Napoleon said throughout his life, or with what
he did as emperor, or with the kind of support he got from certain
dynamic elements in the population.

If President Bonaparte went along with the conservative majority
until 1851, he did so not by choice but by what seemed to be necessity.
He needed funds from the Assembly, and he needed also a constitutional reform that would enable him to run for a second term. He
signed the Assembly's bill restricting the suffrage, but with great reluctance; and he was not much more enthusiastic about the Falloux
Law in 1850. That law, a major event in the nineteenth-century religious, educational, and political history of France, marked the successful conclusion of a ten-year Catholic campaign to secure greater
influence in education. It gave the church the right to operate secondary schools (*collèges*) alongside those of the state, and it increased
church influence in the supervision of state primary schools. Similar
bills had been defeated four times during the 1840's by the skeptical
Orleanist politicians. In 1850 many of those same politicians (Thiers,
for example) swung over to join the conservatives in its support.

The motives that produced this change of mind were not all admirable ones. The hysterical red scare produced by the June Days led
Voltaireans like Thiers to acclaim the church as "the last bulwark of
the social order." "Every Voltairean in France with a few thousand
pounds of income," remarked Ozanam bitterly, "wants to send every-
body to Mass, provided that he himself doesn't have to go." Thiers
even talked of giving the church a total monopoly of primary education.
The mood of the moment benefited Catholic reactionaries like Veuillot
and led even a mildly liberal prelate like Montalembert to declare:
"There is only one recipe for making those who own nothing believe
in property-rights: that is to make them believe in God, who dictated
the Ten Commandments and who promises eternal punishment to those
who steal." The trend in France was furthered by a swing toward
reaction in the Vatican; Pius IX, after recovering his lost throne in

179

1849, abandoned his earlier liberal inclinations. It was clear by the end of 1848 that the Christian democratic current, so prominent in the early months of the revolution, had in fact touched only a small elite within the church. Not until the twentieth century was it to know a significant revival.

The Falloux Law has been described as the greatest clerical victory of the nineteenth century. Although the confirmed Voltaireans among the bourgeoisie remained skeptics, they nevertheless began to send their sons to Catholic *collèges;* within a generation, half of the secondary students in France were enrolled in Catholic schools. The return to the faith that had revealed itself within the aristocracy after 1814, and that had begun to affect the middle classes in the 1840's, now made rapid progress among the bourgeoisie. This process of rechristianization was to give Catholicism a solid bourgeois base in twentieth-century France. The church's problem henceforth would be to check the trend toward unbelief that had already set in strongly among the urban workers and that was to make serious inroads among the peasantry as well after the mid-nineteenth century.

If the Falloux Law was a victory for the clericals, it was in some ways a costly one. Its effect was to intensify the anticlerical spirit of the left and to infect the whole republican movement with an almost unreasoning suspicion of the church. It was no accident that the next generation brought the conversion of Freemasonry from its mildly deist and liberal outlook to a mood of violent republicanism and bigoted anticlericalism, or that an obscure politician in 1863 coined the durable battle cry, "Clericalism, there is the enemy!" Anticlericals became convinced that the church's purpose was to achieve a complete monopoly of education in order to tighten its grip on the state; they believed that church schools were "mental incubators" whose existence would divide French youth into two irreconcilable camps. The Falloux Law became a kind of symbol of the conflict, a bogey to frighten the left. Thus the Second Republic, which at the outset had brought republicans and Catholics together in a flush of fraternity and good will, ended by making the religious problem a major political issue destined to poison the atmosphere in France for generations. Objectively, the Falloux Law scarcely deserved such opprobrium, for it was a compromise that infuriated Catholic extremists like Veuillot as much as it aroused the anticlericals. The real tragedy for France was that this relatively moderate Catholic victory came at a moment when passions were building up on both sides. During the subsequent generation the loudest Catholic voices were to be those of the Veuillot faction, while the most vocal republicans would be turning to a dogmatic and materialistic doctrine called positivism. Neither faction was inclined toward peaceful coexistence or was ready to let the Falloux Law, in either its original form or a revised version, be given a fair trial.

By the summer of 1851 the relationship between Louis Napoleon and the Legislative Assembly had reached total stalemate. Despite the president's efforts to appease the conservative majority, it stubbornly refused to grant him the two things he most wanted: a constitutional revision to permit a second presidential term, and a vote of funds to enable him to pay his personal debts. At some undetermined point in 1851 Louis Napoleon evidently gave in to the pressure of his entourage and, with apparent reluctance, turned to planning a coup d'état.

In this scheming, the army was destined to play a key role. Since 1799 the officer corps had remained aloof from politics and had served each successive regime in docile fashion. Its morale and prestige had fallen sharply since the great days of the Napoleonic empire. If the military life and the ideal of patriotic glory still had defenders in France, they tended to cluster on the left, among Jacobin republicans and chauvinistic Bonapartists. Yet a segment of the officer corps showed signs of abandoning its neutrality after 1848 and ended by participating — for the first time in the nineteenth century — in the overthrow of a regime. Most of the officers, even though the bulk of them were commoners promoted from the ranks, disliked the republic as a regime of squabbling lawyers; they leaned toward a return to the monarchy, and some of them engaged in intrigues with the monarchist majority in the Assembly. A smaller group of officers — mostly below the top echelon — found themselves attracted to the prospect of a restored empire. Louis Napoleon quietly shifted these men into key posts and entrusted to one of them, General Saint-Arnaud, the task of ensuring the success of the coup d'état.

Early on the morning of December 2, 1851 (the anniversary of Austerlitz, and of the great Napoleon's coup in 1804), the leading legislators were routed out of bed and arrested, and a drastic revision of the 1848 constitution was announced by the president. It provided for a ten-year presidential term and a sharp cut in the legislature's powers. The nation was called upon to approve the new authoritarian order by plebiscite and proceeded to ratify the change by a massive majority of ninety-two per cent. Louis Napoleon's only disappointment came from the fact that his coup had not been unopposed and bloodless. Despite Saint-Arnaud's military precautions, barricades had gone up on December 3 in the working-class quarters of Paris, and rioting crowds had clashed with troops and police in a number of cities. Before quiet could be restored in the country, several hundred Frenchmen had been killed and twenty-six thousand arrested. Almost ten thousand were subsequently transported to Algeria, and three thousand were interned in France. Although workers and bourgeois republicans took a leading part in these hopeless attempts to preserve the republic, they were not alone in resisting the coup d'état. Some of the bitterest protest came from Orleanists, dedicated to the ideal of the *juste milieu,* and from Legitimists, who had been looking forward to an early restoration. There is at least some validity in Pierre Gaxotte's remark that Louis Napoleon strangled not a republic, but the foetus of a monarchy.

The authoritarian republic was obviously nothing more than a stopgap arrangement. On December 2, 1852, Louis Napoleon took note of what he called the nation's desires and converted himself from president into emperor. This time there was no trace of open protest; the decisive step had been taken in 1851. The docile voters once again approved by plebiscite, this time by an increased margin of ninety-seven per cent.

The brief episode of 1848–52, shortest of France's four completed republics, cannot be explained without an analysis of class antagonisms; nor can the social stresses of the next half-century be fully understood without an analysis of the events of 1848, which intensified those stresses. Class conflict alone, however, furnishes only a restricted explanation of this or any complex upheaval. Individuals act for other reasons than class interest; nations are something more than congeries of classes. Perhaps, as the historian Ernest Labrousse suggests, the tragedy of 1848 was that a set of twentieth-century problems suddenly faced a society with an eighteenth-century structure, and that the leaders of the time had no real understanding of the emergent industrial age.

TWELVE

> The empress is legitimist, my cousin is republican,
> Morny is Orleanist, I am a socialist; the only Bona-
> partist is Persigny, and he's crazy.
>
> *Attributed to* NAPOLEON III

The Imperial Experiment,
1852–1870

Only twice in the century and a half since 1815 has parliamentary or quasi-parliamentary government in France been interrupted by frankly authoritarian systems. These two exceptions, the Second Empire and the Vichy regime, both appear to be aberrations from the country's norm, and both were generally denounced as such after their overthrow. In the case of the Second Empire, however, the passage of time eventually brought a revisionist current and suggested to many Frenchmen that there had been unsuspected virtues in Napoleon III's system. Some biographers converted the emperor from an unscrupulous tyrant into an almost visionary reformer and patron of progress. Many economists pointed out that the period of the Second Empire brought the most rapid economic and social change in French history, and that it strikes the retrospective observer as a kind of watershed between the France of the old regime and the France of the twentieth century. Some historians even suggested that Napoleon's system came nearer than any other to reconciling the diverse traditions — libertarian, equalitarian, authoritarian — left to posterity by the Great Revolution. The new legend has doubtless been exaggerated in some respects, but it does permit a more balanced view than was possible in the years after Napoleon's fall.

Built into the empire were a number of inconsistencies that have always made it difficult to analyze. The regime's emphasis on glory stood in at least potential contrast to Napoleon's enduring interest in the right of nationalities to self-determination. Its stress on the defense of order and stability seemed incompatible with Napoleon's encouragement of dynamic change. Its authoritarian beginnings are hard to reconcile with its gradual liberalization, a process that eventually turned it into a quasi-parliamentary system resembling that of 1814–48. Perhaps these inconsistencies prove that the imperial regime was nothing more than a haphazard jumble, reflecting the confused welter of ideas within the opportunistic emperor's mind, and prevented by its very nature from arriving at any sort of harmonious fusion. But an even more persuasive hypothesis is that Napoleon, a man of complex and imaginative temperament, sensed some of the trends of his times and sought, in quite un-Cartesian fashion, to adapt an old and complex nation to those trends. If his course was sometimes illogical and his system hybrid, it can only be said that perfect symmetry and logic have not always been the hallmarks of durable systems.

The Second Empire divides itself into two major periods: the authoritarian phase to 1859, the liberal phase thereafter. The transition from one to the other was closely linked with a change in foreign policy that sharply affected Napoleon's relations with the church, and a change in tariff policy that affected his relations with the business group. The new foreign policy grew out of the emperor's decision to help Cavour drive the Austrians out of northern Italy in 1859. The fillip thus given to Italian nationalism endangered the Pope's temporal control of Rome and alienated French clericals who had hitherto supported Napoleon. The new economic policy was embodied in Napoleon's surprise negotiation of a low-tariff treaty with England in 1860. It aroused widespread concern among French manufacturers, who had hitherto applauded the empire's economic policies and had profited greatly from the remarkable boom of the 1850's.

Napoleon's turn toward domestic liberalization that began late in 1859 and continued jerkily throughout the next decade may have been merely an attempt to find a new base of support in place of that lost through his foreign and economic policies. Perhaps the emperor and his advisers slipped into this dangerous current under pressure of circumstances, through mere opportunism or sheer weakness, somewhat against their own preferences and without any clear idea of where the current might carry them. But it is equally possible that the evolution of the 1860's was both planned and desired; that it had been, from the very outset of the empire, the more or less conscious intention of Napoleon and of certain advisers like Morny; that it was the product of an ambition to reconcile the conflicting political traditions inherited from France's past. A choice between these interpretations depends on an estimate of motives and therefore permits no sure or easy answer. But a second problem is equally crucial. Whatever the motivation of Napoleon and his entourage may have been, was their new course after 1859 a sensible and realistic one? Was it, by 1870, on the way to producing a viable compromise system of government, or was it dragging the regime into a morass of hopeless contradictions? Was this kind of authoritarian system capable of mellowing without destroying itself? Here again, no easy or certain answer is possible; yet some answer must be attempted if the record of the empire is to be judged as well as narrated.

❖➣◦⟶❖ ❖➣◦⟶❖ ❖➣◦⟶❖

The political system of the authoritarian phase requires only brief analysis. Its institutions were frankly borrowed from those of the First Empire: the façade of legislative organs without much prestige or power, the ministry responsible to the emperor alone, the plebiscite as an occasional device to give the illusion of popular control. Napoleon justified this attempt to resurrect the past by remarking that for fifty

186

years France had retained the administrative, judicial, religious, and financial structure established by Napoleon I, so that a return to his political institutions was only logical and consistent. In a relatively mild sense, the new empire was a police state. Opposition to the regime was possible, but it was narrowly restricted by controls on the press and on the right to hold public meetings. The modern concentration camp did not yet exist, but there was its primitive equivalent in the penal colonies of Guiana and Algeria. Most of the regime's outspoken critics had chosen exile in preference to prison or deportation: among them were such notables as Thiers, Victor Hugo, and Louis Blanc. Silent but bitter antagonism persisted among diehard republicans, Legitimist aristocrats, and most Orleanist politicians, though some Orleanists were converted by Napoleon's policy of aid to enterprising business men.

Support for the regime during its authoritarian decade came not only from the business class but also from the church hierarchy, from the bulk of the peasantry, and from a considerable minority of the urban workers. Churchmen knew that Napoleon was a freethinker, but they applauded his support of the Pope's temporal power and his defense of social order; some bishops heaped on their adulation with a trowel, publicly comparing the emperor to Constantine and Saint Louis. Napoleon's proletarian support came from those workers who were embittered and disillusioned with the republicans after 1848. Bonapartist candidates who promised vigorous measures of economic expansion caught the fancy of at least some working-class elements, and the boom of the 1850's kept them relatively content. The peasants, save for those few who voted red or the larger number who remained subservient to local aristocrats, contributed the regime's mass base. Many of them were moved by considerations of glamor and glory, many by a conviction that Napoleon would repress radicals and *partageux*. But there were some who clearly betrayed quite opposite motives — who voted for Bonapartist candidates as a kind of declaration of independence from the local notables who had dominated them for so long. At least the beginnings of peasant education in the use of the ballot can

187

be traced to the era of the Second Republic and the Second Empire; as early as 1849 peasant voters in certain regions had shaken off the docility that marked their voting behavior in April, 1848, and had turned to republican or Bonapartist candidates. This rebellious sense of independence benefited Bonapartism in the early years, but in the long run it was to undermine the regime's support in the countryside. Once a stiff-necked peasant had learned that he could safely ignore the admonitions of the local aristocrat, priest, or notary, he was likely to rebel against the pressures of Napoleon's prefects as well.

The authoritarian empire left only a restricted sphere for active political life. Sessions of the Corps Législatif (the new lower house of parliament) were closed to the public, and only a brief summary of its proceedings was made available in the press. Although the Corps was elected by universal manhood suffrage, Napoleon was careful to space the elections at intervals of six years. "I am prepared to be baptized with the water of universal suffrage," he is supposed to have said, "but I don't intend to live with my feet in a puddle." The plebiscite, a device theoretically designed to indicate the responsibility of the emperor to the people, was actually used only three times: in 1851, 1852, and 1870.

Yet it would be unjust to conclude that the authoritarian empire anticipated the totalitarian system of Hitler, or that the empire was run by a hand-picked collection of Bonapartist fanatics and puppets. In creating the new political class whose function it was to shore up and administer the empire, Napoleon and his advisers did not confine themselves to "pure" Bonapartists, nor did they seek to sweep away the old elites in favor of a new privileged caste. Instead, they drew heavily on the existing elites, in an effort to combine aristocracy with democracy. "Official candidates" for the Corps Législatif — i.e., those who were actively patronized by the government — were not hand-picked in Paris but were often selected by the imperial prefects from among the local notables whose influence might get them elected and whose support (if it could be won) would be valuable to the regime. Although many of the notables resisted the government's blandishments and remained loyal to a previous regime, a fair number of ex-Legitimists and ex-Orleanists gradually let themselves be converted. The effect was to shunt aside many of the early Bonapartists of more modest social origins who had rallied to Louis Napoleon's cause in 1848 and had begun to build local party machinery. The Second Empire thus came to be a curious alliance of old and new forces, and it represented neither a total break with France's political past nor a revolutionary change in the locus of power within French society. The lower middle class, so heavily represented in the political elite of twentieth-century fascist states, got little satisfaction out of Napoleon III's revolution. Not until the middle years of the Third Republic did this segment of society work its way up into the controlling circles of the state.

Napoleon's ministers and high administrative officials also represented a mixture of old and new. Some, like Persigny, were personal henchmen whose loyalty had been tested in the early days of adversity. Some, like the Duc de Morny and Comte Walewski, were kinsmen of the emperor — illegitimate ones, it is true, but kinsmen nevertheless. Some, like Achille Fould, came from powerful banking families. Some, like Eugène Rouher, Jules Baroche, and Michel Chevalier, were ex-Orleanist lawyers, politicians, or intellectuals. Some, like the prefect Haussmann who rebuilt Paris in its modern form, were career bureaucrats who had served both the monarchy and the republic. Critics of the regime alleged that it was run by a band of shady and unscrupulous adventurers whose qualities reflected the shoddy artificiality of the system. There were men around Napoleon who did fit that description; but the empire had a broader and more reputable base than its enemies' charges would suggest. If the regime was not served by all the elites, that was not because the emperor preferred adventurers to solid citizens, but rather because so many prominent Frenchmen remained irreconcilable after 1851.

❦━━❦━━❦

Napoleon's first steps toward softening the authoritarian system in 1859 were relatively hesitant ones. Political exiles were amnestied and allowed to return; the Corps Législatif was given the right to present an annual "address" or set of formal resolutions to the emperor, and its sessions were opened to the public. More important, however, was the fact that additional reforms followed at irregular intervals throughout the decade. In 1867 Napoleon restored freedom of the press and of political assemblage and granted parliament the right to interpellate the ministers. Meanwhile he had given the workers the right to form trade unions and to strike and had approved a significant program of broadening public education, drafted by his aggressive minister of education, Victor Duruy. The whole process reached a startling culmination on New Year's Day in 1870, when Napoleon decreed the establishment of a quasi-parliamentary system. The cabinet was henceforth to be a homogeneous body, responsible to the Corps Législatif and subject to overthrow by it. To indicate his sincerity, the emperor chose as prime minister Émile Ollivier, a moderate republican who had been a leading figure in opposition circles for a decade. Ollivier was permitted to staff his cabinet with ex-republicans and ex-Orleanists, most of whom had long been exponents of parliamentary government. True, the revised sytem contained a serious ambiguity: it provided no solution in case there should be a deadlock between emperor and parliament. But a similar ambiguity had existed from 1814 to 1848 and had not prevented a gradual evolution toward something very much like a parliamentary monarchy.

This jerky progress howard "liberalized authoritarianism" during the 1860's cost Napoleon much of his conservative support, yet failed to win him enough new friends on the left to counter-balance the loss. Instead, the opposition steadily gained strength at each legislative election. In 1857 opposition candidates had polled only three-quarters of a million votes; in 1863 they got two million, and in 1869 three and a half million, or almost 45 per cent of the total vote cast. On the face of things, it would seem that the emperor's liberal gamble had failed, and that he might have been wiser to revert to a purer form of authoritarianism, buttressed by the support of the church and the business group. Some of his advisers (Persigny, for example) had so argued all along, and they fought a steady rear-guard action to check the liberal trend before it was too late.

But though the empire's downfall seems to justify Persigny's warnings, it would be risky to conclude that Napoleon destroyed himself by attempting to graft liberalism onto an authoritarian root. Those critics who prophesied disaster offered no real alternative except stand-pattism — a policy that has rarely succeeded for very long in any modern and dynamic nation. Successful regimes have ordinarily been the ones with enough flexibility to adapt themselves to changing economic, social, and psychological conditions. It may be that Napoleon's reforms were not intelligently conceived, or that he lacked a sense of timing and a knack for public relations and thus lost the benefit that should have accrued from his concessions. At any rate, it does seem certain that after 1859 Napoleon was moving in the right direction so far as the bulk of French opinion was concerned. There can be little doubt that by the end of the decade most Frenchmen favored the establishment of some kind of parliamentary system, whether labelled monarchy, republic, or empire.

There is an apparent contradiction here. If Napoleon was moving in the right direction to satisfy Frenchmen, why did the opposition grow steadily larger and more obstreperous? Partly, no doubt, because greater freedom made it safer to indulge in the pleasures of vocal opposition, so long denied to an assertive people. Still more, perhaps, because many Frenchmen were not satisfied with piecemeal reforms and felt that only a powerful opposition movement could push the emperor all the way to a full-scale parliamentary system. The purpose of much of the opposition in the later 1860's was not to overthrow the dynasty but rather to speed the process of liberalizing the empire; many monarchists, many republicans were prepared to leave Napoleon III in office if he would only accept the principle of responsible government.

The most effective support for this interpretation is offered by the outcome of Napoleon's plebiscite of May, 1870. The emperor had just taken, on New Year's Day, his longest step toward a full-fledged parliamentary regime; and he called on the voters to approve or repudiate that reform. The opposition vote, which had climbed to three and a half million in 1869, plummeted to one and a half million; the progovernment vote rose from four and a half to seven and a half million. No greater victory had been won by the regime since the days of the authoritarian empire. Even though the persistent hard core of opposition was still disturbingly large, it seemed clear that Napoleon had at last found a formula satisfactory to the bulk of the nation. Seven Frenchmen out of nine were ready to support the quasi-parliamentary experiment of 1870, combining an autocratic monarch with a responsible cabinet. The record of the liberal decade thus suggests that Napoleon III did grope his way toward a workable governmental system: a system lacking in inner logic, yet potentially capable of reconciling and balancing the nation's most important conflicts.

One crucial question remains, however: Was Napoleon III capable of heading that kind of regime? A compromise system that lacks inner logic, that combines Caesarism and responsible government, calls for exceptionally shrewd, adaptable, pragmatic leadership. The flaws in Napoleon's character make it doubtful that he could have furnished that kind of adept yet vigorous statesmanship. His intimates knew that he had an indolent streak, that he was inclined to vacillate, that he indulged at times in wishful thinking in preference to facing hard facts. "Napoleon the Well-Meaning," someone sarcastically called him. If there had been time to try the new experiment in quasi-parliamentary government, Napoleon might have been confronted quite soon with a major challenge to his personal authority; for many of his new supporters were determined to complete the process of liberalization by converting the emperor into a British-type monarch, subordinate to parliament's wishes. No one can be sure that Napoleon would have been flexible enough to take that final logical step in a process that he himself had voluntarily begun. Indeed, his next step might possibly have been in quite the opposite direction — a brusque repudiation of the trend of the 1860's, a virtual coup d'état against the liberal empire.

Events were not to permit the testing of the new hybrid regime; only five months after the triumphant plebiscite, it had collapsed, and the emperor was on his way to exile in England. What doomed the empire was not its internal evolution but rather the cumulative results of a series of errors in foreign policy. By 1870 France found itself isolated and confronted by a powerful new rival across the Rhine. Napoleon had failed to intervene in central Europe in 1866 when it might have been easy to check the growth of Prussian power. He had failed in his subsequent efforts to secure face-saving compensations in the form of territorial gains along the Rhine. He had failed once more when he sought to bolster French military power by introducing a new army bill into parliament in 1867. His proposal, which would have brought a larger annual contingent of draftees into the army and would have increased the cost of preparedness, aroused a political storm; in the end the bill had to be so watered down that it became innocuous. Meanwhile the failure of Napoleon's "great idea" — the building of a Catholic empire in Mexico allied with France — had divided the nation and provided his critics with effective ammunition. Efforts after 1866 to negotiate alliances with Italy and Austria-Hungary produced no result except to arouse false hopes in Paris.

War with Prussia was not the only possible outcome of the crisis that erupted suddenly in July, 1870. Either Bismarck or Napoleon III could have averted a test of arms. Bismarck had no desire to avert it; Napoleon lacked the foresight to do so. Chronic illness during the last years of his reign probably lessened his capacity to devote sustained attention to the developing crisis or to make difficult decisions; he was unwise enough to let authority slip into the hands of his second-rate foreign minister, Gramont. The French government, aroused at the news that Spain had secretly arranged to place a Hohenzollern prince on the Spanish throne, put such heavy pressure on the king of Prussia that the latter persuaded the Hohenzollern nominee to withdraw his candidacy. Gramont had thus won a notable diplomatic victory, but he was not intelligent enough to be satisfied with it. Instead, he demanded still further Prussian assurances for the future, and thus gave Bismarck an opportunity to play the picador to "the Gallic bull." On July 19 the French government, angered at Prussia's apparent flouting of French demands, slipped into war — unnecessarily, unwisely, and with inadequate preparation for so severe a test.

Few Frenchmen except Adolphe Thiers (who had been issuing gloomy warnings ever since 1866) fully understood the threat that France faced. Prime Minister Ollivier encouraged the nation's illusions by announcing that he accepted war "with a light heart," and his war minister even more recklessly assured parliament that the army was ready "to the last gaiter button." What the army lacked in 1870 was not gaiter buttons but something far more serious: efficient, vigorous, and imaginative leadership. The officer corps, though honorable and loyal, had slipped into a rut of routine-mindedness and smug complacency that contrasted sharply with the tough and keen mentality of the Prussian staff. France's clumsy and antiquated process of mobilization had not even been completed when the first German troops crossed the frontier. Within a month the great border fortress of Metz was cut off by the invaders, and the army of Marshal Bazaine besieged therein. Napoleon, who had gone to the front to share the perils of war with his soldiers, refused to adopt the one strategic plan that might still have averted defeat — a slow retreat to Paris and a stand outside the walls of the capital. Fearing the political repercussions of such a strategic withdrawal, he accompanied his remaining army under MacMahon in an attempt to relieve Metz. The Prussians cornered MacMahon's force at Sedan on August 31 and broke its resistance in a brief battle fought the next day. Napoleon, aware that the fight was hopeless, sought a hero's death in the front lines, on the theory that his martyrdom might save the throne for his adolescent son. Even that consolation was denied him; and he fell ignominiously into the hands of the Prussians.

The emperor, but not the empire, survived the carnage of Sedan. When the news reached Paris on September 3, the regime's political leaders tried desperately to prop up the imperial system by arranging an interim government under a military leader. Even the republican politicians were willing; most of them were not eager to take power at so gloomy a moment. But it was far too late to save the empire; its prestige and glamor had vanished in defeat. On September 4 demonstrating crowds converged on the Corps Législatif and demanded the proclamation of a republic. Napoleon's system disintegrated without bloodshed, and almost without regret.

The Second Empire outlasted any other governmental experiment that had been tried in France since 1814. Whether it achieved more than its predecessors and whether it came nearer to producing a durable compromise are controversial issues. For two generations after its fall the empire was bitterly vilified by all good republicans. Yet by the middle 1870's Bonapartism had revived sufficiently to become an important political force in France; in 1877 there were 104 Bonapartists in the Chamber of Deputies. So quick a recovery (even though it proved fleeting) may suggest that many Frenchmen remembered the days of Napoleon III with nostalgia. Some twentieth-century critics of the parliamentary republic were to find a retrospective utopia in the Second Empire: a middle way, they said, between the divisive weakness of multiparty democracy and the oppressive tyranny of modern totalitarianism. Yet it is quite possible that the consequences of the empire were more destructive than constructive; that this interruption in the nineteenth-century trend toward responsible government created as many problems as it tried to solve, and that some of France's contemporary ailments are at least partly traceable to it. Certainly it deepened the neurotic fear of the strong man among French republicans and liberals and reinforced the sentiment that authority must be both suspected and resisted. After 1870 the new republic was shaped, its institutions were built in an atmosphere of violent revulsion against the Second Empire — even against those aspects of it that might have helped France adapt its political, social, and economic structure to the needs of modern times.

THIRTEEN

... Despite a contrary view that has been too long
accepted, economic life is in large measure what
governments make it.

J.-M. JEANNENEY

Economy: Structure and Trends, 1814–1870

The changes wrought in France's economic system by the upheaval of
the Great Revolution were probably less sweeping than those effected
in the political, the social, or even the psychological spheres. True, the
revolution bulldozed away many of the tangled restrictions on domestic
trade that had grown up in the old regime and destroyed the remnants
of the corporative system that had still hampered production. It thus
cleared the way for a fundamental change in economic structure and
for the arrival of the industrial age. But no more than the faint
beginnings of anything like an industrial revolution had occurred in
France by 1814, and another full generation was to pass before French
enterprisers were to take much advantage of their new freedom.

Napoleon, to be sure, claimed credit for great advances and boasted,
"It is I who created French industry." His regime did in fact stimulate
some progress toward mechanization, and, by providing a huge protected continental market, it offered French business men an unprecedented opportunity for expansion. Some of them took advantage of it;
a good many fortunes were founded in the Napoleonic era. Yet the

196

emperor's industrial policy was so narrowly military in purpose that what he achieved was rarely durable; and the business crisis that set in after 1811 undid much of what had been done. Furthermore, finance rather than industry attracted the ablest enterprisers during the Napoleonic era. Except in banking, the over-all effect of the revolutionary era may even have been negative rather than positive; some historians have argued that the experience actually impeded the nation's economic growth.

The restored Bourbons after 1814 might have chosen any of three possible economic patterns. One of these would have involved a return to the rigid and hierarchical structure of the old regime, based on gilds or corporations. A second would have been the adoption of economic liberalism, the doctrine that had seemed to represent the wave of the future in the later eighteenth century. The old monarchy had established some precedent for such a policy when it negotiated the Eden Treaty of 1786, and after 1789 the revolutionary leaders had at first seemed inclined to perpetuate it; but liberalism had soon been submerged in a generation of war. The third possible alternative was to continue the system that had developed under the stress of protracted war, and that had been consolidated by Napoleon: a system of "national economics," whose regulations and controls were designed to make France as nearly self-sufficient as possible.

The idea of a return to the old corporative system found few defenders in Bourbon France, even among the ultras. A brusque turn toward laissez faire was not much more popular, even among the bourgeoisie. Louis XVIII and his advisers, urged on by the British, made a timid initial effort to edge in that direction by reducing trade barriers somewhat; but an influx of British goods followed and quickly forced the government back to the wartime policy of controls on trade. Pressure in the direction of tariffs was exerted by the two most powerful interest groups in France: the larger landowners and the business class. Their vigorous lobbying ensured steadily rising tariff rates after 1816, to the point of total exclusion of some items. The duty on iron goods, for example, eventually reached 120 per cent.

The defensive attitude of French producers of basic items like textiles and iron goods was understandable. British industry, already advancing rapidly before war broke out, had spurted so far ahead under wartime conditions that it had left its French competitors out of the running. More surprising was the fact that French agrarians joined in the demand for high tariffs. France in the past had never needed barriers against incoming farm products; the only restrictions, indeed, had been against the *export* of grain. France, as a great agricultural nation, seemed to possess the same kind of competitive advantage that the British now enjoyed in industry. The new defensive stance was the outgrowth of a dual change. First, wartime shortages had driven grain prices up, and agrarian interests believed that protection might keep them there. Second, France faced for the first time the threat of quantity imports from the steppes of Russia. As British landlords got their corn law in 1815, so French landowners won the same kind of victory in 1819; and protection for other farm products followed in series. Even the winegrowers climbed aboard the tariff band wagon, though they faced no direct foreign competition. Their aim was a high duty on tea, to avert what they described as a threat to French morals as well as French prosperity. "Tea," declaimed one agrarian deputy, "breaks down our national character by turning those who use it often into cold and stuffy Nordic types, while wine arouses in the soul that gentle gaiety . . . which gives Frenchmen their amiable and witty national character."

Few voices were raised in opposition to the steady spiral of tariff increases, even to suggest that other nations might retaliate and thus injure French exports. Any possible concern on this point was quieted by the customs officials, who annually presented figures that showed a steady growth in both exports and imports, with the balance always "favorable." Recent studies suggest that these figures were systematically falsified for political reasons, and that more dependable statistics indicate a growing stagnation in trade and a disturbing decline in exports. For the protective system not only kept French domestic prices high and slowed up modernization; it also brought reprisals abroad.

By the end of the Bourbon era some Frenchmen were becoming aware of this fact. An economic crisis that set in from 1826 to 1829 caused enough stress to arouse serious questioning of the system, especially on the part of the winegrowers, shipping interests, and other seaport groups. Nothing in the way of change was accomplished under the Bourbons; vested interests were too numerous and too strong. Besides, a governmental study commission rejected the idea of a turn toward lower tariffs on the ground that it would work an injustice to men who had, in good faith, gone into business with the expectation of continuing tariff protection. Here was a classic example of special privilege crystallizing promptly into vested interest. The doctrines of economic liberalism nevertheless began to make serious progress for the first time during the late 1820s. Professor J.-B. Say, the French popularizer of Adam Smith, began to get a hearing at last, even in parliament. The discontent produced by the recession of 1826–29 undermined the nation's previous solidarity on economic policy and doubtless contributed to the unrest that produced the revolution of 1830.

France's economic structure changed remarkably little during the Bourbon restoration. The government's attitude toward business was epitomized in the accountant's outlook of Villèle: his goal was a balanced budget with the lowest possible expenditure. Government aid to industry or agriculture or commerce, except through tariff protection, was almost nil. No French regime has ever offered so perfect an antithesis to the twentieth-century Keynesian ideal. While industrial production and commercial enterprise made slow progress, French bankers consolidated their position as the real business elite of the era; as in Napoleon's day, finance continued to attract the nation's most vigorous enterprisers. Perhaps it was in part their discontent with the regime's narrow lack of imagination that drove a number of wealthy bankers — Jacques Laffitte and Casimir Périer, for example — into the liberal opposition and led some Frenchmen to call the 1830 upheaval "the bankers' revolution."

Something resembling an industrial revolution began at last during the reign of Louis Philippe, though it did not reach its apogee until the Second Empire. It was natural enough that a bourgeois monarchy should favor the interests of the business class (or what the business group thought to be its interests). That favoritism was reflected in a continuance of high tariffs, almost without change; in a low level of taxation; in a policy of governmental noninterference in business operations; and in generous government aid to private enterprise through grants of concessions and financial guarantees. The Orleanist monarchy also spent more freely than its Bourbon predecessor. Public expenditures were doubled: larger sums were allotted to the army, to agricultural development, to the building of schools, but above all to public works — canals, roads, railways. The public debt increased, since taxes remained almost stationary; but public credit remained sound.

The result of the government's policies was a steady but not spectacular growth in production and trade, particularly in the 1840's. The increase in national income during Louis Philippe's reign probably averaged two or three per cent yearly. Coal production tripled, but continued to lag behind that of Belgium and far behind that of England (the ratio in 1846 was one to ten). Pig-iron output doubled, but still amounted to only a quarter of England's output. Imports doubled, though exports rose only about half as much. Railway building was begun at last, but even now it proceeded less rapidly than was the case in several rival nations, including the German states. Some of the first rails had to be imported from England despite the heavy tariff, for most French iron was still being smelted on small charcoal furnaces, inadequate for the purpose. Large industrial plants continued to be rare in 1848, and even where mechanization had been introduced, the machines remained small. The Alsatian textile industry was the most notable exception: the Protestant entrepreneurs of Mulhouse led the way in modernization. Some Catholic textile families of the Roubaix area in northern France, and a few ironmasters like Schneider and Wendel, were not far behind.

Despite these signs of progress, France in the era of Louis Philippe still showed a resistance to change, a relative lack of dynamism, that was to continue persistently throughout most of the modern era. This state of affairs has led to a lively controversy among economic historians. Through the centuries preceding the industrial revolution French artisans and handicrafters had outproduced any other European nation; and France entered the industrial era prepared, it would seem, to meet the challenge of any competitor. Instead, the nineteenth century was to see France gradually outstripped by a whole series of rivals, and the twentieth was to complete the process of turning France into a second-rank (though still important) industrial nation.

In the opinion of one school of historians, France's handicaps in the new era were primarily technical and structural ones: expensive fuel, cheap labor, and inadequate risk capital. Because labor was plentiful and cheap (France then being a crowded country), the introduction of machine methods was no pressing necessity. Because some of France's coal deposits were still undiscovered, part of the nation's fuel had to be imported at high cost. Because commercial capitalism had developed more slowly in France than in England, the impetus to produce in quantity for large overseas markets was less intense, and the amount of liquid capital accumulated by the trading class was more limited. Because French banking developed late, the capital that did exist in France was not properly mobilized for investment purposes until the last half of the nineteenth century.

There is a second school that sees France's relative lack of dynamism as the product of psychological and sociological handicaps rather than technical and structural ones. Its exponents grant that Frenchmen faced some technical difficulties (as in lack of coal and inadequate mobilization of capital), but they contend that the principal missing factor in the new age was a lack of vigor, of the spirit of risk, of entrepreneurial drive on the part of French business men, combined with a social atmosphere that was uncongenial to business enterprise. The business tradition in France, according to this thesis, was one of conservatism and caution. The goal was security rather than expansion; the ideal was one of preserving rather than creating wealth; the ethical code favored coexistence rather than competition. The customary business structure was the "family firm," small enough to be operated without any sort of outside interference. Expansion beyond a certain point, or even investment by outsiders, was to be avoided because it would undermine the family's independent control. Furthermore, the idea of seeking to destroy weaker competitors or to monopolize the market would have outraged most French business men even if it had occurred to them. During a tariff inquiry in 1832 the large and prosperous Anzin firm of ironmakers actually opposed a reduction in duties on iron on the ground that it would wipe out some of Anzin's weaker competitors.

A contributing factor in this lack of aggressive entrepreneurial drive, according to this school of historians, was the social ethos inherited from the old regime. The business man had traditionally ranked low in prestige; the way to gain status in prerevolutionary France had not been to succeed in business but to get out of business somehow, or to get one's sons out. "In the bourgeoisie," ran the eighteenth-century maxim, "only the fool remains a bourgeois." Balzac's novels reflect (though in rather distorted form) the persistence of an anticapitalistic atmosphere even in the nineteenth-century era of bourgeois rule. Dislike and contempt for the vigorous enterpriser marked the outlook not only of the old aristocracy but also of the governmental bureaucracy. If an exceptional young man did turn up, full of imagination and aggressive ambition, he was likely to face the massed hostility of the entire business group and to find sources of risk capital (which were meager enough, at best) closed against him. As a result, most business expansion of the era was the work not of new men but of old families gradually expanding their plants through reinvestment of profits (as the De Wendels) or moving out from banking into industry (as the Périers). Successful new operators like the Schneider brothers at Le Creusot, whose ironworks was founded in 1836, were rare exceptions to the rule.

Some light may be shed on the debate by a brief reference to railway development, the most important new field of enterprise in the era of Louis Philippe. In 1842 the government laid out a plan for a national network and assigned the task of construction to private firms through a system of concessions. Large-scale government aid was provided; the state first took on more than half the construction cost by providing the land, the roadbed, and the bridges, and later shifted to a kind of cost-plus arrangement by which it guaranteed to the private firms a fixed return on their investment. But the decision in favor of private rather than state construction and operation of the railways was not reached automatically, despite the predominant influence of the business group in this era. The ministry leaned at first toward a governmental monopoly of the railroads, and a vocal minority in parliament (headed by Lamartine) fought for that solution on the ground that private control would lead to profiteering and the emergence of a new class of "feudal" tycoons. Such an antibusiness attitude suggests that even some members of the political elite in the bourgeois monarchy reflected the traditional ethos of hostility toward the entrepreneur.

On the other hand, French business men lost no time in taking advantage of the opportunities offered by railroad building; there was sharp competition among financial houses for the concessions that seemed most likely to be profitable. In the end the concessions were shared out among the principal financial groups by pragmatic arrangements among the business men themselves. No powerful new category of rail tycoons of the Jim Hill type emerged during the railway-building era in France; the old guard of banking divided the spoils.

But the railway age, and the beginnings of industrial expansion, quickly revealed a serious weakness in France's banking structure. The existing banking firms like Rothschild and Hottinguer constituted what the French still call *la haute banque*. These institutions were, in David Landes' phrase, "small, exclusive credit clubs"; they were owned by a family or a small well-knit group of financiers, who contributed all the funds and doled them out to only the safest borrowers. Business men without access to the "club" had no recourse except to turn to a usurer at excessive interest rates. The old banks had no machinery by which to mobilize risk capital for the kind of large-scale investment that began to demand huge funds in the 1840's. Besides, most of them preferred smaller and safer operations and concentrated their efforts on buying government bonds. Rothschild, for example, got a near-monopoly of government loans during the Orleanist epoch. Some members of the *haute banque* clique nevertheless wanted to engage in railway and industrial financing, and they sought to set up new credit institutions of the joint-stock variety in an effort to mobilize idle capital. They got little encouragement from the state, and the old banking structure remained largely intact under Louis Philippe. Of the billion francs invested in French railways before 1848, only four hundred million was contributed by Frenchmen; most of the remainder came from England. Yet even that contribution strained the existing credit resources of the old banks; the growing distortion between an outmoded credit system and an expanding economy contributed to the business crisis of 1846–51 and, indirectly, to the revolution of 1848. Not until the Second Empire was a solution to be found.

Until 1846 the Orleanist monarchy enjoyed economic stability and rather steady growth. The end of the reign, however, brought the most severe depression in a generation. Bad weather was partly responsible; there was a series of crop failures throughout western Europe in 1845–47. The agrarian crisis and the rapid rise in food prices that resulted produced a creeping paralysis of business that sharply reduced production in the nation's factories and mines, that bankrupted several of the new railway companies as well as many small local banks, and that led to widespread unemployment. The revolution of 1848, far from solving the problem, only compounded it; the political upheaval added to business uncertainty and intensified the depression. The Second Republic, after an initial series of expedients to alleviate the crisis, returned to the well-rooted tradition of domestic laissez faire — combined, of course, with a continuing high level of tariffs. The depression dragged on nevertheless, shrouding the whole history of the Second Republic in its gloom. Sizable numbers of Frenchmen turned to overseas emigration as a solution, for almost the only time in the modern history of France; a quarter of a million left between 1846 and 1851.

Although the effects of the mid-century crisis appeared to be most intense in the industrial cities, they were in fact much deeper and more enduring in certain densely populated rural areas where the domestic system of handicraft production had been combined with part-time farming. For more than a century this combination of activities had supported (at a marginal standard) a rural population far larger than primitive agriculture alone would have allowed. The depression of 1846–51 hastened the ruin of rural handicrafts, already threatened by the rise of the factory system; and it gave a great impetus to the flow of population out of the depressed rural areas. The crisis thus brought to an end a whole economic era, an era whose structure had been carried over from the eighteenth century.

⋙○⋘ ⋙○⋘ ⋙○⋘

It was Louis Napoleon's good fortune that the business slump was coming to an end at the moment when he seized power in 1851, and that the first decade of his rule coincided with the most remarkable period of economic growth and change in modern French history. Although the boom was to be checked somewhat in the 1860's, the Second Empire stands out in the nineteenth century as a time of exceptional economic vigor. Statistics, though dull, are revealing. Industrial production doubled between 1852 and 1870; foreign trade tripled, outstripping the growth of any other European nation; the use of steam power rose fivefold; railway mileage was increased sixfold. The intriguing question here is this: To what degree were imperial policies responsible for this growth and for the sudden emergence of a remarkable group of entrepreneurs? Did the empire merely ride the crest of a world-wide boom in the 1850's? Was the appearance of vigorous entrepreneurs nothing more than a fluke, a kind of un-French deviation from a basic norm?

Undoubtedly the European climate was favorable to economic growth in the 1850's. Prosperity was general throughout the world, stimulated in part by a rapid rise in the available gold supply from

Californian and Australian mines. New technical methods made their appearance in industry; new kinds of business organizations were emerging, based on the principle of limited liability and favoring the growth of large-scale enterprise. But it is clear that Napoleon would not have been content to relax and enjoy the fruits of general prosperity. He intended to stimulate economic growth; he believed (in his own classic mixed metaphor) that it was the function of government to be "not a necessary ulcer, but rather the beneficent motor of any social organism."

This repudiation of the laissez faire ideal might seem to suggest a kind of state-socialist philosophy. In fact, what the imperial government did was not so much to engage in public spending (though both budgetary expenditures and the public debt did rise) as to encourage private speculation and investment. For example, the regime guaranteed a minimum interest rate on railway securities; it sponsored the merger of many small and shaky railway companies into six large ones; it authorized the creation of the first investment banks (notably the Crédit Mobilier); it stimulated the building trades by a vast state-financed plan to reconstruct Paris, along with lesser plans in most major cities. For the most part, the state avoided direct economic activity, preferring to create a favorable climate for private enterprise.

More significant than the new government's tendency to favor business was the fact that so many Frenchmen took advantage of the opportunities offered. Perhaps this meant that the French as a whole were not so deeply rooted in an older tradition after all and were not so ill-adapted to the demands of entrepreneurship; or perhaps this particular crop of Frenchmen happened to be unique. At any rate, they proceeded to establish not only investment banks but also most of the great deposit banks (like the Crédit Lyonnais) that have endured to this day; they created the first department stores (notably the Bon Marché) and the first chain groceries, selling their own packaged products (Félix Potin); they modernized the bulk of the iron and textile industries; they completed the network of major railways and telegraph lines; they expanded the stock exchange in such fashion as to mobilize the savings of small investors; and they started France on its long career of foreign investment.

It is true that some of the older business families disliked and resisted the new men and the new methods. It is true also that much small old-style enterprise survived alongside the new firms and found ways to protect itself until the mid-twentieth century. It is true, finally, that many of the new entrepreneurs of the empire were of Protestant or Jewish background, and they may have been naturally inclined to repudiate the standard French cultural heritage and the antibusiness social ethos. But the struggle between old and new was not simply a contest between a dominant national culture and a frustrated, resentful subculture. Among the older business and banking leaders, committed to the traditions of family enterprise and cautious conservatism, there were many of Jewish or Protestant origin; among the modernizers there were at least some members of old Catholic families. Furthermore, the struggle of old against new was less clear-cut than it has often seemed to economic historians. According to the standard legend, for example, the old families of the *haute banque* bitterly opposed the new joint-stock investment banks that mobilized vast sums of idle French capital and poured them into industrial development; and in the end (still according to the legend) they managed to destroy the Crédit Mobilier, bellwether of the new banking system. As a matter of fact, many representatives of the *haute banque* had been experimenting for years with primitive forms of the new investment bank, and after 1852 most of the old firms bought into the new banks as devices to achieve what the old banks could not do. By 1870 France's credit system had been almost completely renovated; a real financial revolution opened the way for the nation to play a major role in industrial expansion both abroad and at home.

Of all the actions of Napoleon III in the economic sphere, the most hotly disputed was his turn toward lower tariffs in 1860. There are Frenchmen still who regard that date as the critical turning point in French economic progress, as the "black day" of the century — just as there are others who see 1892 (the decisive return to high tariffs) as the real disaster. The so-called Chevalier-Cobden Treaty with England, followed by similar pacts with other nations, introduced the only period of relatively free trade in modern French history.

The origins of this sudden shift are somewhat controversial. The new policy was certainly urged on the emperor by Saint-Simonian advisers like the economist Michel Chevalier. Enemies of the treaty charged at the time that Napoleon's purpose was far less idealistic; they held that his aim was to buy back England's cooling friendship through economic appeasement. The emperor's long-standing Saint-Simonian leanings make the former theory more plausible. At any rate, the new policy either caused or coincided with a slackening in France's prosperity and economic growth; a severe slump occurred in 1862, and full recovery was never achieved in Napoleon's time.

Economic liberals could and did argue that the slump was due at least in part to the interruption of American cotton shipments during the Civil War, and to a general world-wide slackening after the boom of the 1850's. Still, they could not deny the fact that the Chevalier Treaty did severely affect enterprises like iron and textiles that had to face stiff British competition; and a fair number of marginal firms were forced out of business. The government had foreseen the need for readjustment and had set up a special loan fund to aid the industries affected; but the sum provided was too small to shield all those in trouble. In justification of the turn toward freer trade, it may be said that the policy forced many French business men to consolidate, enlarge, or modernize their plants, so that these firms emerged healthier than before. Thus some segments of business were helped, others hurt, by the new liberalism of 1860. There is no easy criterion for judging the over-all results for the nation. If the long-run gains outweighed the immediate pains and stresses of readjustment, it is nevertheless likely that the imperial regime was, on balance, the loser; for much of its backing in business circles was alienated by the brusque turn to freer trade.

The years from 1814 to 1870, taken as a unit, constituted a time of reasonably successful adaptation to changing times. France had been the world's wealthiest nation in 1814; it was still a close second to England in 1870. No nation except Great Britain enjoyed greater economic growth in those years; the average increase in national income since 1814 has been estimated at between two and three per cent per annum. An effective new banking structure had been built, and basic transportation facilities had been completed. About mid-century the value of industrial production had at last caught up with and surpassed the value of agricultural production. Textile production was still far and away ahead of any other sector of industry, but the foundations had been laid in metallurgical enterprise as well. In 1870 there seemed to be no reason to suppose that France during the century to follow would slip from its traditional status as one of the world's great economic powers.

FOURTEEN

> The paradox of French history is that a revolution-
> ary settlement was to provide the basis for a pro-
> foundly conservative pattern of society.
>
> ALFRED COBBAN

Society: Structure and Trends, 1814–1870

"The social history of nineteenth century France," remarks an eminent French historian, "is still 'terra incognita'."[1] If this is so, one reason for it may be the lack of consensus as to the boundaries and content of that amorphous but important subject called social history. As some-times practiced, it can degenerate into a conglomerate mass of hetero-geneous details about bathtubs and gas lights, fused together by nothing more than the pious hope that the whole kaleidoscope will somehow show "how ordinary people lived." On the other extreme, it can become so systematized and abstract, so concerned with artificial constructs like classes, strata, and elites, that individuals and events disappear into vapor.

An effort to reconstruct in systematic fashion the habits, customs, and mores of a past era is undeniably a valid enterprise, for a nation's history is rooted in such aspects of its collective life. Even more useful, potentially at least, is the effort to examine group relationships and to

---

[1] Bertier de Sauvigny, *La restauration*, p. 319.

analyze "power structures," provided that the tentative and hypothetical nature of such analyses is recognized. Karl Marx was one of the first to make this latter attempt and to provide what modern scholars call a "model" for the investigation of nineteenth-century French society. But the oversimplified character of his model makes it more misleading than enlightening when one seeks to take a cross-cut slice through any modern society at a given point in time. Indeed, any model complex enough to fit French society in the early nineteenth century would, in turn, be too complex to be very useful. It may be better, therefore, to avoid formal model-building in favor of a more loose-jointed and descriptive survey of social groupings and of the relationships between them.

Juridically speaking, France emerged from the revolutionary era a society of atomized equals, with no intermediate groups intervening between the whole society and its individual citizens. In reality, it remained a complex tapestry of classes, groups, and professions, the outlines of which are difficult to distinguish clearly. Many of France's prerevolutionary social distinctions survived in custom if not in law; and superimposed upon them were new distinctions of more strictly economic character. The diversity thus produced was still further increased by persistent regional differences in speech, culture, and outlook. Although the revolution had swept away many artificial barriers to national unity and had intensified the sentiment of nationalism, several generations would still be needed to erode away deeply etched provincial traits. Indeed, that process of erosion has never been completed to this day.

Restored to the top of the social pyramid in 1814 was the old aristocratic caste, undiminished in its pride of birth though no longer privileged in a legal sense. The prerevolutionary gap between the court nobility of Versailles and the lesser provincial aristocracy of the backwoods had been narrowed considerably by the revolutionary experience. The playboys and skeptics of Versailles had been converted into solid pillars of morality and religion; the country nobility had never ceased to be such pillars. Political leadership during the restoration era was shared by both groups: alongside great émigré nobles like the Duc de Richelieu sat obscure country gentlemen like the Comte de Villèle. The old court aristocracy did face serious problems of readjustment, notably of an economic nature. Most of them had lost their prewar estates and — more serious still — the royal subsidies that had once supported them in frivolous leisure at Versailles. They looked to the public treasury for help; what they sought was either compensation for lost properties or some kind of salaried government post, even if it might involve menial duties. In the 1820's many aristocrats moved into such bureaucratic positions as justices of the peace, tax collectors, even postmasters. The fact that they often served honorably and efficiently did not reconcile the sons of the bourgeoisie, many of whom emerged from university or law school to find no official posts left open to them. The resentment of this latter group contributed to bourgeois antagonism toward the Bourbon dynasty.

From the outset the old aristocratic families were forced to share the top rung of society with those members of Napoleon's peerage that had rallied to the Bourbon cause in 1814. As one historian succinctly puts it, "Napoleon I was overthrown but his followers were not. They arranged the Bourbon restoration and were absorbed into the new system."[2] Contempt for these upstarts was general among the "real" aristocrats, who nevertheless had to confine themselves to grumbling about it. Their bitterness was to be even greater toward the new peers named by "the usurper" Louis Philippe after 1830. Relations between the two branches of the nobility were frigid; the old families ignored these social climbers (most of whom had been promoted from the upper bourgeoisie) and isolated themselves in their Legitimist salons in the Faubourg Saint-Germain. The Orleanist peers therefore had Louis Philippe's court to themselves, and they developed their own salons across the Seine in the commercial quarter of Paris. Louis Philippe's peerage was not intended to be hereditary. It became so, by a curious irony, through the fall of the dynasty that had created it;

[2] T. Zeldin, *The Political System of Napoleon III* (London: Macmillan, 1958), p. 4.

there was no sovereign after 1848 who could deny to an Orleanist peer the right to hand on his title to his son. Although such titles lacked any juridical base, custom made them as permanent as the titles of the oldest families. After 1852 Napoleon III once again inflated the nobility by elevating his favorites to the peerage. The nineteenth century thus produced a far more complex aristocracy than that of the old regime — one that by 1870 was divided into categories almost as distinct as geological strata.

Until 1830 the aristocracy both dominated politics and set the tone of society. After 1830, save perhaps for a brief interlude in the 1870's, it was never again to play either role. Henceforth it was the bourgeoisie that set the tone, no longer in brazen imitation of the nobility but in conformity to its own developing set of semiaristocratic, semibourgeois standards and ideals. Henceforth it was the bourgeoisie that provided France's political as well as economic elite.

Few terms are more ambiguous or amorphous than the word "bourgeoisie." The range of variation from the millionaire banker or industrialist of Paris or Lyon to the village grocer or postal clerk of Clochemerle renders almost meaningless any label that seeks to classify them in a common category. Nineteenth-century custom tended increasingly to distinguish various subdivisions — usually an upper, a middle, and a petty bourgeoisie; but the three groups shaded imperceptibly into each other, just as the petty bourgeoisie merged into the category of workers just below it. To speak of the nineteenth century in Europe as "the bourgeois century," or of Louis Philippe's regime as "the bourgeois monarchy," therefore begs the essential question: Which stratum of the bourgeoisie dominated, and how did it assert its power? Or, to put it another way, from which stratum was the political elite drawn, and which strata were capable of influencing the decisions of that elite?

One fact is clear: the upper bourgeoisie shared power in varying but unbroken fashion from 1814 to 1870. Its role was secondary to that of the aristocracy so long as the Bourbons reigned; but the wealthy business class did have the right to vote and to sit in parliament, and its spokesmen made up the liberal opposition there. Its members clearly dominated the political scene from 1830 to 1848 and, somewhat less obviously, from 1849 to 1870; for a brief interlude in 1848 they shared control with representatives of the middle bourgeoisie. Direct and sustained access to political power for the middle bourgeoisie was not to come until the Third Republic, and for the petty bourgeoisie, until the end of the century.

Both the Bourbon and the Orleanist regimes drew a quite arbitrary line between those privileged to share political power and those denied it, and that line was based frankly on birth and wealth. Louis Philippe reduced the entrance fee slightly in 1830; the number of eligible voters at the outset of his regime was increased to 168,813. As thus revised, the line may serve as a kind of pragmatic dividing point between upper and middle bourgeoisie. The former included both old and new banking families like the Rothschilds and the Périers, together with industrialists like the Schneider brothers and De Wendel, and professional men like Thiers and Guizot. For the most part, their rise to wealth and status was recent. "It is scarcely an exaggeration to say that the French *grand bourgeois* . . . seemed new-rich alongside the English *grand bourgeois* whose fortune had been made over a period of a hundred fifty years. The roots of the new society developed in the hothouse of imperial protectionism [i.e., of Napoleon I]."[3]

The middle bourgeoisie, insofar as it can be distinguished from the upper bourgeoisie, was a larger and more varied category. Included in it were the middle-rank industrialists and traders, most members of the liberal professions, and the upper levels of the governmental bureaucracy. No barrier prevented their rise into the upper bourgeoisie; it was primarily to this group that Guizot addressed his famous admonition, "Get rich!" Many of them profited by the opportunities that came their way with the business expansion of the 1840's and after; a steady though slow process of upward mobility marked the whole nineteenth century.

The petty bourgeoisie was more heterogeneous still. It included

---

[3] C. Morazé, *Les bourgeois conquérants* (Paris: Colin, 1957), pp. 151–52.

the mass of little independents of city, town, and village — small enter-prisers, shopkeepers, artisans, clerks, schoolmasters, petty employees of the state. Some of them inherited an old family tradition of shopkeep-ing or craftsmanship; their fathers or grandfathers had been the *sansculottes* of the Great Revolution, the partisans of Danton, Robes-pierre, Marat. A far greater number had recently made the transition from what the eighteenth century had called *le menu peuple* or the "popular classes." Those who came of peasant origin usually took two or three generations to penetrate the lower levels of the bourgeoisie; the process of direct promotion from peasant to bourgeois was to remain uncommon until the later nineteenth century, when access to the bourgeoisie became a matter of educational level and achievement. The more common upward route before 1870 was from skilled workman to petty entrepreneur, or from shopkeeper's son to the liberal professions or the state bureaucracy. "The nineteenth century," says Charles Morazé, "is filled with striking examples of shopkeepers' sons arriving at the very highest honors via science or industry."[4] The process was usually a great deal slower, however; and the petty bourgeoisie as a whole could not yet foresee the time when it might dominate political life or even share political power.

One source of pride the petty bourgeoisie did possess: namely, membership in the National Guard, whose origin dated from the Great Revolution. No institution, perhaps, was more representative of the era 1814–48. All citizens who paid a direct tax were automatically enrolled in the Guard and were required to furnish their own uniforms and weapons. Here was the clerk's or the shopkeeper's most glamorous mark of distinction, setting him off from the common people and establishing him as a defender of the social order. The fact that some contemporaries scoffed at these "greengrocer janissaries" detracted nothing from their pride. Charles X infuriated its members in 1827 when he brusquely dissolved the Guard for its lack of discipline and its "subversive" attitude during a review. Louis Philippe was shrewd

4 C. Morazé, *Les bourgeois conquérants*, p. 415.

215

enough to reconstitute it in 1831 and to appear on frequent occasions in National Guard uniform. But by 1848 indiscipline and political discontent had again weakened the Guard as an effective defender of the monarchy. It was the Guard's impending defection just outside the Tuileries that led the king, in February, 1848, to abandon his last hope of repressing the revolution. Thereafter it was never again to play a significant role. The regular army and the new uniformed police took over the function of preserving public order.

Whether France possessed a true proletarian class during the early nineteenth century is largely a matter of definition. If one essential aspect of proletarian status is psychological, involving the development of a clear sense of class-consciousness, then one can find little sign of a real proletariat in France before 1848 and virtually no sign at all before 1830. The suggestion has even been made that 1880 would be the most accurate date for the appearance of a proletariat. If, on the other hand, the test is merely one of economic function — if men who have nothing to sell but their labor are *ipso facto* proletarians — then an embryonic proletariat had existed in the larger French cities for centuries and in rural districts ever since the end of serfdom. Probably the most accurate conclusion would be that the period 1814–70 gradually converted the urban workers into class-conscious proletarians but left the process incomplete.

Labor's heritage from the revolution was a mixed one, combining as it did the liberalism of the men of 1789 with the regimentation of Napoleon. The Le Chapelier law of 1791 had outlawed labor organizations and strikes in the name of liberty; Napoleon in 1803 had reimposed on every worker the obligation of carrying a workbook, a kind of labor passport, in which each change of domicile or of job had to be recorded by employers. A few anemic mutual-aid societies survived the revolutionary period and were tolerated extra-legally after 1814; so did those curious medieval remnants called the *compagnonnages,* which

216

were fraternal societies of skilled artisans. Exclusive in spirit, open only to bachelors, each one had its elaborate rituals, its ancient traditions, its bloody feuds with rival trades. New members normally spent several years in a tour of France, working for a time in each major city. Although these vestiges of a past era were decaying rapidly by 1850, some remnants of them were to endure even into the twentieth century and were to complicate the task of forming modern trade unions.

The artisans of the *compagnonnages* were the aristocrats of labor. In contrast, the domestic handicrafters (who were usually part-time peasants) and the new stratum of factory workers faced an existence that was often subhuman. If Karl Marx had written his *Kapital* in the Bibliothèque Nationale rather than in the British Museum, he might have buttressed his argument with French examples just as appalling as those which he drew from official British surveys. In those cities where the factory system was emerging, a working day of fifteen hours or even more was normal during the Bourbon and Orleanist epochs. Wages rarely sufficed to keep a family alive, even if both parents and children worked; a supplement from private charity was common. In the Lille area in 1828 two-thirds of the workers were carried on some kind of relief roll. Only a minority of workers could expect to eat meat more than once or twice a year. From 30 to 50 per cent of a working family's budget went for the purchase of bread; it was quite literally the staff of life. Contemporary descriptions of housing conditions in the slums of Lille or Nantes are almost beyond belief. At Mulhouse about 1830 the average life expectancy for children of the bourgeoisie was thirty-one years; for children of weavers, less than four years. In Louis Philippe's reign nine-tenths of the army draftees from industrial areas had to be rejected for physical deficiencies. Alcoholism and promiscuity were common; in one representative year, one-third of all births in Paris were illegitimate. Illiteracy among the workers was almost universal. Price and wage studies for the period 1814–48 are undependable, but real wages almost certainly fell during the Bourbon era and barely held their own under Louis Philippe. Until the 1840's at least, population growth far outstripped economic growth, and the workers of both city and countryside suffered the consequences.

In face of such conditions, the workers behaved with surprising docility. The Bourbon period produced few serious labor disorders, and there were only 382 strikes (most of them minor) during the whole reign of Louis Philippe. The only major outbreaks were those of the Lyon silk weavers in 1831 and 1834; they produced severe repression and an enduring legend, but nothing in the way of improved conditions. Some historians have seen the Lyon insurrections as nothing more than spontaneous hunger riots; others contend that they embodied a burgeoning class-consciousness and a bitter resentment at the unfair practices of the industrial employers or middlemen. It may be pure legend that the 1831 rioters carried a black flag bearing the phrase "Live working or die fighting"; whether true or not, it eventually became part of labor's myth. The 1834 outbreak had repercussions in Paris as well; there, too, labor protest was repressed in bloody fashion, and the episode was immortalized by Daumier in his powerful caricature entitled "The Massacre of the Rue Transnonain."

Premier Casimir Périer told parliament in 1831, just after the first Lyon insurrection had been put down, "The workers have got to get one thing through their heads: their only remedies are patience and resignation." His statement epitomized the outlook of most political leaders and most industrialists of the time. There were exceptions, however. Some sensitive Catholics, like the Vicomte de Villeneuve-Bargemont, prefect at Lille during the late 1820's, exposed the miserable conditions of life among the workers and asked (as did the archbishop of Cambrai in 1845): "Is it necessary that the worker perish, body and soul, so that the master may climb faster to the summit of opulence . . . ?"[5] Not even a regime committed to laissez faire could ignore forever such evils as slum conditions, absenteeism, and the high rate of draft rejections. In 1837 and 1840 the government conducted investigations of child-labor conditions, and in 1841 it pushed through

[5] In V. Lorwin, "Labor and Economic Development in France" (unpublished manuscript).

parliament the only labor reform of the period. This measure outlawed the employment of children below the age of eight and shortened hours for those below sixteen. The bill aroused bitter opposition in parliament, not only from factory owners but also from such notables as the philosopher Victor Cousin and the scientist Gay-Lussac; they declared that it violated the sacred principles of liberty and justice. The opposition managed to attach an amendment that pulled the teeth in the bill; it provided that factory inspectors must be unpaid volunteers, chosen from among retired manufacturers. In consequence, the law had little practical effect. By 1848 France had fallen far behind England in the sphere of social legislation.

The 1848 upheaval seemed destined for a time to reverse the order of precedence and to make France the world's model for social advance. The working day in Parisian factories was reduced to ten hours; several large producers' cooperatives were organized with state aid; a government commission to study labor problems was set up, with two hundred employers and two hundred workers as members. There was much talk of guaranteeing the right to work and of adding a minister of labor to the cabinet. But by the end of the year the proposals had been abandoned and the reforms repealed. The vanished mirage of a new utopian era left the workers more bitter and frustrated than ever.

In this state of disillusionment, a great many workers could easily be attracted to Napoleon III, who was supposed to be an advocate of Saint-Simonian policies and a friend of the common man. During his first decade in power, however, Napoleon was too dependent on the support of the business class to embark on any startling social reforms. Labor profited indirectly from the remarkable economic expansion of the 1850's, though probably not in proportion to the gains of the business group. After 1860 Napoleon turned to more direct measures of social reform. In 1862 he provided a subsidy for a workers' delegation to attend the London Exposition and to observe English labor conditions; in 1863 he set up a credit agency to finance cooperatives; and in 1864 he granted labor the right to strike. The last years of the empire brought a rash of strikes, far more extensive than France had ever known. They brought, too, the first important steps toward the organization of labor. A delegation of French workers helped establish Marx's First International in 1864, and by 1870 the French branch of the International was larger than that of any other nation. More important still, Napoleon let it be known in 1868 that he would permit (but would not legally authorize) the formation of unions, and workers from the skilled trades promptly took advantage of the opportunity. It was only "a blinking and uncertain tolerance," however, that labor got from the Second Empire. French leaders of the International, for example, were repeatedly prosecuted for their activities. This curious mixture of liberty and repression probably had the effect of driving the most active elements of French labor toward more radical doctrines and aided the Marxians in their contest with the milder Proudhonians.

One imperial reform that did produce lasting effects on class relationships was Haussmann's rebuilding of Paris. The effect was to produce, for the first time, a kind of generalized social segregation in the capital. Hitherto, in most parts of Paris, workers and bourgeoisie of all levels had resided in the same buildings, with social status in inverse proportion to the floor occupied. Prior to the social revolution introduced by the elevator, the wealthy lived on the lower floors, families of moderate income on the middle floors, and the poor in the garret. Haussmann's face-lifting of the city destroyed large areas of mixed housing and replaced them with new apartment houses far too expensive for the workers. A general exodus toward the suburbs followed: the heart of Paris, largely bourgeois henceforth, was to be surrounded by a largely proletarian red belt. The long-range effects of this segregation on class relationships are difficult to measure, but they may have gone deep.

In some parts of France, on the other hand, the generation after 1850 brought scattered efforts at paternalistic social reform by certain employers. The Protestant textile magnates of Mulhouse led the way in the 1850's by providing model housing and by pioneering in efforts to prevent work accidents. Some employers, whether through humanity or self-interest, began to establish a variety of social-welfare services. By 1875 a parliamentary committee inquiring into labor conditions could report proudly that France had outstripped all other countries in such employer-sponsored welfare schemes. Yet many employers clung to the idea that short hours and higher wages would only debauch the inherently inferior working man, whose fate it was ". . . to support with resignation the privations and sufferings which our social conditions are powerless to spare him."[6] Paternalistic reforms, in such an atmosphere, could scarcely suffice to satisfy labor.

There can be little doubt that the position of French workers began to change markedly during the Second Empire, and that by 1870 a considerable nucleus of the labor movement had become self-consciously proletarian. Outward appearances seemed to suggest that the workers were also better off: that their living standards had risen since 1848, for the first time in the nineteenth century. Whether there was really any net gain is a highly controversial point; some scholars contend that price increases wiped out money-wage increases. What is certain is that the urban working class had grown in size, had begun to organize, and was becoming class-conscious by 1870. Unfortunately, its class feeling was "deeper in resentments than in solidarity, better defined in its alienation from other classes than in its own organization."[7] This was a condition that was destined to persist for decades, with serious effects on both social relationships and political stability in France.

❦◦❧◦❦◦❧◦❦◦❧

Nineteenth-century France was still a peasant nation, so far as its mass base was concerned. In 1814 three out of four Frenchmen lived by farming; by 1870 the proportion had dropped, but only to 52 per cent.

Surprisingly little is known about rural life in that epoch. History,

[6] In V. Lorwin, "Labor and Economic Development in France."
[7] V. Lorwin, "Labor and Economic Development in France."

it seems, was made in the cities and bypassed the countryside. There is even a lack of adequate statistics, for agricultural surveys before 1870 were rare and incomplete. No accurate estimate can be made, for example, of the number of landless peasants who became small-owners as a result of the Great Revolution. What does seem certain is that the peasantry changed less than any other segment of society in the years 1814–70, and that rural life remained pretty much as it had been in the eighteenth century, save for the legal abolition of feudal relationships.

If the period was marked by any constant trend, it was the steadily increasing subdivision of the soil, produced in part by the new law codes that required equal shares to all heirs, but produced primarily by the growing pressure of population on the land. France's rural population reached an all-time peak in the late 1840's, and even the drift to the cities that set in thereafter did not suffice to reduce the pressure very much by 1870. The total number of farms operated in France kept growing throughout the period and was to continue to increase until about 1890. Some new land was brought into cultivation, but not enough to prevent a shrinkage in the average size of farms. The bulk of the peasantry remained, therefore, on a marginal standard that permitted little improvement in either living conditions or in agricultural techniques. Millet's famous painting of "The Man with the Hoe" probably represents no grotesque caricature of rural life but a faithful reproduction of an "average" peasant of the time (1862). That "average" peasant was only a little better off than he had been a century earlier. At best, he had raised himself one notch economically — from the level of misery to that of poverty.[8]

In part, the peasants were responsible for their own backwardness. There seems to have been widespread resistance to the idea of change in either techniques or mores. Furthermore, most peasants suffered from what has been called "the proprietary illusion" — the desperate desire to own a piece of land or to add to that already owned. Instead

[8] M. Augé-Laribé, La révolution agricole (Paris: Michel, 1955), p. 181.

of devoting their meager savings to better housing or improved techniques, they were inclined to scrape and borrow in order to invest in a piece of the soil. Nothing was left for raising living standards or experimenting with new methods; and besides, a burden of indebtedness was built up over the years — a load made heavier by the lack of adequate sources of farm credit. Not until Napoleon III's time was an institution set up to rescue peasant borrowers from the usurer, and even then it failed to provide much help. Nothing like adequate farm credit was to become available until the burgeoning of mutual credit associations in the 1890's. Most peasants suffered also from the complex pattern of land division that forced them to farm tiny scattered parcels of land and to spend as much time travelling from one to another as in fruitful labor.

The fault was not entirely theirs, however. Large landowners in France offered much less vigorous leadership toward a modernization of techniques than was the case in England; and successive governments offered scarcely any leadership at all. Until 1848 at least, the politicians appeared to believe that high tariffs on foodstuffs gave the peasants all the help they needed. The Second Republic established at last a chain of schools for specialized agricultural training, but the Second Empire undermined this promising new effort when it reduced the budget for agricultural education by half. The peasantry got little from the state except the ballot plus slowly improving facilities for basic education. By 1870 the number of children in primary schools had more than doubled since 1830, though 30 per cent of French army conscripts were still illiterate, and most of those were peasants' sons.

Generalizations about the peasantry are, however, likely to be misleading; for the farm population in the nineteenth century certainly did not constitute a single homogeneous class or stratum. Large landowning continued to coexist with small farming; sizable groups of tenants and crop-sharers survived alongside the independent owners; and there was an important population of landless farm laborers. Significant regional variations continued to mark the countryside. Even before 1789 the intensity of religious belief had varied markedly,

223

and the areas that had been least fervent then were the first to show signs of abandoning the faith entirely in the mid-nineteenth century. Likewise, there were old variations in educational level, mores, and habitat. After 1814 a new source of regional differentiation began to emerge. Certain areas in the north and east — notably the region adjoining the Belgian frontier — began to move steadily ahead of the rest of France in the adoption of new techniques. The resulting contrast between dynamic and stagnant sectors was to become a permanent feature of France's agrarian structure and was to be intensified rather than softened during the century after 1870. It was only partially offset by the introduction, after 1850, of the practice of liming the soil in certain infertile regions of the center and west. That practice reclaimed for the plow vast areas of "acid" soil, notably in Brittany, that had never before been cultivated.

Even though no sweeping agricultural revolution had occurred in France by 1870, and even though rural life remained primitive and isolated, events were conspiring to prepare a fundamental change. For one thing, the use of the ballot and the gradual spread of literacy were providing the peasants with a slow course in political education — one that would eventually give them, after 1870, a powerful hold on the machinery of the state. Meanwhile, the penetration of many parts of the countryside by the new railway network was opening the way to a real social revolution. Most villages until now had been almost hermetically sealed off against the world and had lived largely untouched by outside currents of ideas. Some peasants and village artisans had travelled during the slack season in search of work, but these adventurers were exceptions to the rule. Nine out of ten Frenchmen in the census of 1861 were living in the department where they had been born; it seems a safe guess that seven or eight out of ten had never even journeyed outside their natal region. By 1870, however, the major rail lines were complete, and in the 1880's additional secondary lines were to reach all but the most remote sectors. Men, ideas, products, could at last flow both into and out of the village. Rural

France was about to become, not overnight but over a half-century, an active and organic part of the nation.

≈⊃◦⊂≈ ≈⊃◦⊂≈ ≈⊃◦⊂≈

France's population in 1814 — twenty-nine million — exceeded that of any other European nation save Russia. The figure had increased almost 30 per cent since 1760; it was destined to grow another 30 per cent by 1870. In retrospect, the century from 1760 to 1870 stands out as unique in French demographic history; it was the only long period that produced a sustained and sizable population increase. Until about 1850 the effects were felt primarily in the country districts, where population density reached a peak about mid-century. A serious threat of overpopulation was checked by the exodus toward the cities that began with the depression of 1846–51, and that was to continue sporadically thereafter. The process of urbanization, exceptionally slow until this time, got under way at last during the Second Empire.

France's remarkable population growth in the early nineteenth century concealed from contemporaries the first signs of an opposite trend, whose full impact was not to be felt until after 1900. The decade of the 1820's was the last one to show a large excess of births over deaths; thereafter, the birth rate declined more sharply than the death rate. The severe depression of 1846–51, complicated by a cholera epidemic in 1849, produced a kind of demographic disaster. Annual population growth fell during those years to 2.2 per thousand, the lowest figure since the French had begun to keep statistics; in a number of regions, population actually declined. The Second Empire brought some recovery; but explosive growth was never again to recur until the years after the Second World War. In retrospect, the crisis of 1846–51 can be seen as marking the end of one demographic era and the beginning of another. Before 1846 the nation's reproduction rate had rarely fallen below 1.00 (the level theoretically required

225

for a population to replace itself without decline). After 1846 the rate tended increasingly to fall below that figure.[9] In 1814 one of every seven Europeans west of Russia had been French; in 1914 the proportion was to be only one in ten. At midcentury, however, the trend was not yet clear. No Frenchman in 1870 foresaw that the demographic problem would strike his grandchildren as one of the most severe threats to the nation's vigor and greatness.

[9] The annual net reproduction rate, which fell below 1.00 during most of the period 1846–59, rose again during the generation 1860–89. But in 1890 it dropped below 1.00, and stayed there almost constantly until 1946.

FIFTEEN

> The more I study . . . , the more I become convinced
> that everything in politics is only consequence and
> symptom, that it is the ideas and sentiments which per-
> vade a people that are the true cause of everything else.
>
> ALEXIS DE TOCQUEVILLE

Intellectual and Cultural Currents, 1814–1870

The years of the revolution and the empire had diverted most French-men's minds from intellectual and cultural pursuits. But it was not mere contrast with that relatively barren era that made the postwar decades seem a time of such intense productivity, of such "prodigious intellectual ferment." No French generation since that of 1660, says Pierre Gaxotte, had been so creative, so rich in artistic and literary genius. "With tame rabbits in the seats of the mighty [remarks Albert Guérard] the age was, intellectually, a glorious jungle."[1] Just as striking was the rapidity of change in mood and taste, in intellectual climate. Rationalism in thought and classicism in the arts still seemed almost unchallenged at the end of the Napoleonic era; but by 1830 the romantics had clearly won the battle for predominance. The elec-tion of the young romantic poet Lamartine to the French Academy in 1830 symbolized the victory. From the 1820's until about 1850

[1] A. Guérard, *France, A Modern History* (Ann Arbor: Univ. of Michigan Press, 1959), p. 290.

romanticism was to pervade the modes of thinking and feeling of most sensitive Frenchmen.

This is not to suggest that romanticism was a peculiarly French product. Indeed, it came to France years later than to either England or Germany, and it was regarded by some old-guard Frenchmen as a degenerate foreign import. Such a view was clearly improper, not only because romanticism had its own French pedigree in the works of Rousseau and others, but still more because it would doubtless have dominated the age even if France had been sealed off tightly from foreign ideas. This was so not because of any "natural swing of the pendulum" away from arid rationalism and classical regularities, but rather because a generation of tension and upheaval had undermined the solid base of certainty and security upon which the age of reason had rested. Doubt and pessimism displaced hope and optimism; men felt a deepened concern for the metaphysical problems of existence, death, and eternity. The twentieth-century age of anxiety offers some insight into the *mal du siècle* of early nineteenth-century Europe.

The term romanticism has been loosely used to describe a wide variety of things. That could hardly fail to be the case, for its essential spirit was one of revolt against an established order — against rigid rules, laws, dogmas, formulas. It is not easy to define a mood or movement whose central characteristic is revolt, and whose stress is on self-expression and individual uniqueness. For the most part, romantics held that man is and ought to be guided by warm emotions rather than by cold reason, by the heart more than by the head. Their preferred image of the world was not a static and mechanical thing, a Newtonian machine, but an organism in process of uninterrupted change, growth, evolution. In their search for beauty, action, glamor, romantics often felt the need to escape from the ugly reality of the present into some distant time or place: the exotic East or Africa, the mountain wilderness, the Middle Ages, a future utopia. Yet they were not, with rare exceptions, mere escapists; they wanted to be, and were, an organic part of the life of their times. For a decade or so, romanticism was rather incongruously linked with political reaction in Bourbon France. Ultra political theorists like Bonald, ultra literary figures like Chateaubriand, could view the restored dynasty as the spearhead of their rebellion against the established order of rationalism and classicism — against an intellectual tyranny that had gripped educated Frenchmen for a century, and that had led (they believed) to illusion and disaster. The early romantics found their utopia in France's distant past; they put their faith in such age-old institutions as monarchy and church, whose glamorous appeal was emotional more than rational. "I wept, and I believed" — so Chateaubriand described his reconversion to Christianity. Nations are organisms rather than machines, argued Bonald; therefore ". . . to ask an assembly to write a constitution is like a patient asking his doctor to make a temperament for him."

For a decade or more the defenders of rationalism and classicism fought back successfully against the new mood. Rationalism found its chief support on the liberal left, among the adherents of the revolutionary tradition. To the liberals, the romantics were permitting themselves to wallow in sentimentality and to indulge in an emotional orgy: "Romanticism is not merely ridiculous," they declared, "it is a disease, like sleepwalking or epilepsy." They tried to sabotage Victor Hugo's play *Hernani* on its opening night; they accused Delacroix of painting with a broom while drunk; they derided the unconventional bohemianism of the young rebels, their morbid self-pity, their cadaverous heroes and fragile, swooning heroines. The passion of controversy led them to exceed the bounds of reason and to equate all romantic works with modern soap operas.

It is really not very surprising that men of rationalist outlook were unfair toward the romantics. Rationalists were temperamentally unfitted to appreciate the passionate force of a Delacroix canvas; or the lines of a Gothic cathedral restored by Viollet-le-Duc; or the mood of the composer Berlioz, who boasted of loosing "floods of sinister vibrations" in the concert halls of Paris, and who verged on passionate frenzy as he listened to the premiere performance of one of his own works ("It's superb! It's sublime! How monstrous, colossal, horrible!").[2] What the rationalists failed to perceive was the "constructive destruction" of the romantic spirit, its clearing away of rules and restrictions that had hampered the free expression of men's imagination and sensibility. With all its excesses and excrescences, romanticism was to have a liberating impact almost unparalleled in modern cultural history.

There was another aspect of romanticism, too, that the liberals overlooked at first. They failed to realize that the central characteristic of the new spirit — its intense individualism and its mood of revolt — might soon lead to a natural alliance between the romantics and the political opposition. Even before 1830 that alliance had begun to develop; a decade had been enough to destroy most of the romantics' illusions about the Bourbon dynasty. Not even Charles's fantastic coronation ceremony in 1825 could do more than create a shoddy façade of ersatz medievalism, behind which could be detected a most unglamorous reality. Chateaubriand, the living embodiment of romanticism, was already deep in intrigue with the liberal opposition; Victor Hugo in 1829 executed a complete about-face with his new manifesto that "romanticism is, at bottom, nothing more than liberalism in literature." For the utopia of the past, the romantics began to substitute one in the future — an era of harmony, brotherhood, and universal peace. By the time this literary generation came to an end, some of its leading figures had moved all the way to the extreme left, where they combined republicanism with a variety of socialist doctrines. George Sand, professional novelist and amateur feminist, was the most prominent of these intellectual socialists; but there were many others by the 1840's who were in full rebellion against the bourgeois era. Victor Hugo, though a peer of the realm, preached the brotherhood of nations and the instinctive goodness and justice of the common man; Lamartine implied a belief in the cleansing virtues of violence; the historian Michelet found the Great Revolution to be a magnificent epic, with its hero "the people"; the best-selling

[2] Bertier de Sauvigny, *La restauration*, p. 492.

novelist Eugène Sue, who kept Paris on tenterhooks for the next chapter in his serialized romances, crusaded for the regeneration of society through Fourier's brand of utopian socialism. A few romantics resisted the leftward trend and clung to reactionary views or withdrew (like Alfred de Vigny and Théophile Gautier) into an ivory tower of devotion to pure art. But on the whole, romanticism by 1848 was as closely intertwined with democratic and socialist doctrines as the earlier romanticism had been committed to reaction.

Even at the height of the romantic age, the rationalist mood of the Enlightenment continued to dominate some French minds. There was an old-fashioned variety of liberal, deeply rooted in the classical and rationalist heritage, who found the romantic temper fundamentally alien whether linked with right-wing reaction or with left-wing radicalism. The liberal outlook, as it evolved into its early nineteenth-century form, still displayed some tendency toward ideological narrowness and rigidity; but just as deep or even deeper was its spirit of moderation and balance. Many nineteenth-century liberals in France as well as in England were suspicious of impassioned crusading for causes and of immoderate appeals to the heart in defiance of the head. George Sand appalled them as much as Bonald had done. Perhaps this liberalism made its greatest appeal to the bourgeoisie, but it was far more than merely a congealed class dogma. What separated liberal rationalists from romantic democrats throughout the century seems to have been not class interest so much as temperament. In much the same fashion, temperament was to be the decisive factor in the choice of twentieth-century French leftists as they faced the alternatives of socialism and communism.

French liberals of the early nineteenth century did not form a solid bloc. One variety early became reconciled with the monarchical compromise of 1814–48 and sought to provide a doctrine for this fusion of revolution and old regime. The mark of any such doctrine was inevitably a kind of eclecticism, pragmatic rather than rigorously logical in nature. During the Bourbon period it was the so-called doctrinaires who represented this right wing of liberal thought: men like the philosopher Royer-Collard and the historian Guizot. Under Louis Philippe, Guizot continued the tradition, but it was the Sorbonne philosopher Victor Cousin, semiofficial theorist of the regime, who provided the most elaborate statement of what he called "enlightened eclecticism." Cousin produced an attractively blended cocktail of ideas borrowed from every kind of philosophical and religious system. "The Good, the True, and the Beautiful" — these were to be the eternal axioms on which the social order should rest.

Alongside the eclectic right wing, a somewhat more rigorously consistent left-wing current of liberal thought persisted throughout the period. Its partisans were less easily satisfied by the monarchical compromise and more inclined to cling to the heritage of the Enlightenment. Cousin's ideological cocktail they found completely unpalatable; but they showed little creative talent in presenting a substitute. Their most notable thinkers were Benjamin Constant and J.-B. Say during the Bourbon era; Adolphe Thiers, Charles de Rémusat, and Frédéric Bastiat in the Orleanist period; Lucien Prévost-Paradol under the Second Empire. Their total intellectual contribution to the development of liberal theory was remarkably meager — especially when contrasted with the richness of French liberal thought in the age of reason and with the vigor and variety of the English contribution in the era of Bentham, Mill, and Ricardo. French liberalism in the nineteenth century could do little more than produce pale imitators or dilettantes. Somehow it seemed that the liberal ideology had gone to seed in France, after its unprecedented flowering before the Great Revolution.

Yet there was one figure of remarkable stature whose contribution seems to contradict these generalizations about the barrenness of French liberal thought. Whether Alexis de Tocqueville truly embodied the liberal temper has been much debated; the twentieth-century neoconservatives have made a concerted effort to claim him as their

232

ancestor. But if Tocqueville, like the conservatives, was deeply concerned at the potential dangers built into democratic thought — the threat of mediocrity, of mass tyranny, of a kind of totalitarian distortion of the democratic ideal — his solution was not to build a barrier against the natural growth of democracy or to return to some kind of organic and hierarchical society. It was, rather, to ensure the survival of liberal values and minority rights in an age predestined to become democratic. Tocqueville claimed to possess no foolproof solution but proposed instead a set of psychological and structural safeguards. He advocated a kind of pluralism — a scattering of authority both within the governmental structure and between the state and private associations. And he warned his contemporaries, in effect, that vigilance is the price of freedom. Few other liberals of his century saw so far into the future or sought so intelligently to ensure the long-range protection of constitutional government and individual rights.

❖⊃◦⊂❖ ❖⊃◦⊂❖ ❖⊃◦⊂❖

No current of thought in early nineteenth-century France ran so strongly or so deep as the current of social theory. From 1814 to 1870 an unbroken series of French thinkers ". . . carried on a continuous debate on the basic premises of social organization that was unequaled for the range of views expressed and the sharpness of analysis, and this debate laid bare most of the issues that have concerned the Western world ever since."[3] This burgeoning of social theory was the more remarkable in the light of France's relatively late and slow conversion to industrialism. If it is rapid social change that produces new currents in social thought, England rather than France ought to have led the way.

The two great precursors, the Comte de Saint-Simon and Charles Fourier, reacted to the impending industrial era in quite opposite ways. Saint-Simon's was a creed of progress, through the application of

---

[3] P. Farmer, in H. S. Hughes (ed.), *Teachers of History* (Ithaca: Cornell Univ. Press, 1954), p. 59.

science and technology to social problems. He combined his gospel of productivity with that of brotherhood; in his hierarchical society of unequals, guided by an elite of engineers and entrepreneurs, classes would collaborate for the common welfare. He foreshadowed, even though in impractical and romantic fashion, such modern concepts as technocracy, the managerial revolution, and "enlightened capitalism." Saint-Simon died in 1825 obscure and almost unknown, and some of his disciples came near wrecking the tiny movement that survived him. Their effort to win over the workers by persuasion (mainly through courses of lectures) failed dismally; and their attempt to organize a kind of semireligious communal sect only made them seem ridiculous. Saint-Simonianism as an organized movement lacked impact; but its ideas, propagated by individual converts, infiltrated the thinking of a great many Frenchmen over the next generation. Indeed, the ferment produced by the doctrine was almost unique in its effect, for it influenced a wide variety of reformers who rejected or moved on from the Saint-Simonian faith. A number of vigorous entrepreneurs as well as intellectuals were attracted by the gospel of productivity and welfare, and so were a few politicians — notably Louis Napoleon. Its appeal to the workers, however, was meager. It offered them neither liberty nor equality, but only what struck them as the dubious privilege of being led by a priesthood of dedicated capitalists and technicians.

Fourier's creed was harmony rather than productivity; he combined a reluctant acceptance of the industrial age with a desire to get back to a simpler life. Like Saint-Simon, he stressed the idea of class collaboration, but without a managerial elite to guide the new society. Fourier's idea, rather, was free and voluntary association of capital, labor, and talent. He proposed to check the oppressive growth of large cities and of mass-production methods by scattering industry in small communities where modern techniques might be combined with country life. Fourier's ideal community or "phalanx" was designed to contain 1620 people, or a complete assortment of the 810 different species of male and female temperament that he believed to exist in humankind. Life in these utopias would be so pleasant that the residents would rise at three in the morning and would rush to work with passionate enthusiasm. Labor would no longer be onerous, for there would be a variety of work assignments, and ingenuity would make even the unpleasant jobs seem fascinating. Garbage collection, for example, would be entrusted to hordes of small boys mounted on Shetland ponies and dressed in colorful costumes, with full freedom to indulge their natural propensity to dirt.

Some modern scholars have found in Fourier a precursor of contemporary industrial decentralization, of suburban garden cities, and even of Freudian themes of individual neurosis as the product of frustration. His doctrines, like those of Saint-Simon, produced no organized movement and won him no labor support. All of the experimental communities set up in France and elsewhere promptly failed. Yet the Fourierist doctrine survived and spread, especially among intellectuals and petty bourgeois converts. Fourier's principal disciple, Victor Considérant, who tried to bring his ideas down to earth by linking them with political action, was popular enough to be elected a deputy in both 1848 and 1849.

Of all the utopians, it was Étienne Cabet who came nearest to arousing mass enthusiasm. Some estimates (probably exaggerated) have given him as many as two hundred thousand disciples during the 1840's; one historian attributes to Cabet's influence the fact that there was no violent clash between workers and bourgeoisie in Paris in February, 1848. Cabet was a gentle and harmless socialist of the seraphic school; he preached the ideal of a classless society and complete communal ownership, to be achieved by persuasion and example. His doctrines were in fact neither very consistent nor very original; he had absorbed many of them from the Owenites, while in exile in England. The 1848 episode burst Cabet's bubble; by April he was not even able to win election to the Assembly. Disheartened, he departed with his disciples to establish an unsuccessful utopia across the Atlantic.

Even before 1848 a new mood was beginning to make itself felt within utopian socialism: a mood that was more intransigent and less idealistic. The evils of the early industrial age could not be entirely

ignored; the fact of class conflict was growing obvious; the attractions
of state action, or even of violence, were becoming more tempting. One
representative of this new outlook was Louis Blanc. At the base of
Blanc's doctrine was the producers' cooperative — an idea already advanced by such predecessors as Philippe Buchez, a onetime Saint-
Simonian turned Catholic. Blanc gave the idea more systematic treatment and suggested a practical mechanism through which the workers
might take over ownership of a factory. His device was to be state aid:
the government would lend capital to the workers, who would gradually
repay it from the profits of the enterprise. His "social workshops"
vaguely foreshadowed the later syndicalist ideal. Although no organized
movement was created by Blanc, he had won wide support among the
workers by 1848. His phrase "the organization of labor" was one of
the most popular slogans of the revolutionary year.

Other thinkers who reflected the new and tougher outlook were
Constantin Pecqueur, Auguste Blanqui, and Pierre-Joseph Proudhon.
Pecqueur, a "socialists' socialist" whose influence was felt by other
thinkers rather than by the mass of workers, began as a Saint-Simonian
but ended with a doctrine somewhere between Marxism and modern
Christian socialism. He advocated a kind of Christian collectivism,
with the state owning the means of production and operating them in a
democratic and humanitarian spirit. His system contained tinges of the
corporative ideal, but it was also marked by the idea of class conflict
and by an economic interpretation of history. Auguste Blanqui was the
principal heir to the Babeuf tradition of direct revolutionary action, as
carried down into the nineteenth century by that first of professional
revolutionaries, Filippo Buonarroti. Blanqui refused to waste time
blueprinting the new utopia: it would be enough, he argued, to seize
control of the state and then to sweep away all barriers to reason,
education, true enlightenment. Blanqui's repeated attempts at a coup
d'état against monarchy, empire, and republic failed for lack of adequate planning and support; forty of his seventy-nine years were to be
spent in the prisons of Louis Philippe, Napoleon III, and the Second
and Third republics.

Of all these mid-century theorists, Proudhon was clearly the most paradoxical. He called himself an anarchist; Marx labeled him a petty bourgeois utopian; some modern scholars have described him as a proto-fascist, others as a rugged individualist opposed to all tyrannies. Proudhon brought on most of the confusion by his refusal to knit his ideas together into a system and by his volcanic tendency to toss off striking epigrams. He created no organized movement, and his only attempt at practical reform — a free-credit system in 1848 — failed completely. Yet his long-range impact was to exceed that of almost any other contemporary French social theorist; it can be argued that the French labor movement through most of its history has drawn as much of its inspiration from Proudhon as from Marx. Proudhon stated his anarchist position as a purely theoretical ideal, not as a practical possibility; he saw it as preferable to its theoretical opposite, an arbitrary and all-powerful state. The heart of his doctrine lay in its syndicalist and its pluralist aspects. As a forerunner of syndicalism, Proudhon rejected Marx's idea of a political revolution led by professional agitators; he held that the workers must depend on themselves and must resort to economic rather than political methods. As a pluralist, Proudhon rejected the idea that power in the hands of a new class or elite would be any less dangerous than power in the hands of the old vested interests. At the heart of his thinking was the conviction that all men are complex animals, capable not only of goodness and justice but also of evil and injustice; like Lord Acton a good many years later, he believed that power must always tend to corrupt its holders, no matter what their origin. His solution was "federalism," a scattering of power and property in such fashion that no power group could dominate all the others. Whether or not Proudhon's doctrine deserves the label "petty bourgeois socialism," it did prove attractive to the kind of workers who organized and led the French trade-union movement in the Third Republic.

Not all of the social-reform ideas in nineteenth-century France came from the left. Just as in England during the same era, there was a current of conservative social thought, inspired in part by Christian principles and in part by a sense of outrage at the abuses produced by laissez faire. Left-wing Catholics like Lamennais and Buchez did not belong in this current; they were, rather, isolated ancestors of modern Christian socialism. The true conservative reformers were essentially paternalists, moved by a sense of moral obligation or by a conviction that the principles of 1789 had atomized and destroyed society.

Frédéric Ozanam and his followers in the 1840's represented the moral impulse in pure form; they preferred to put their energies into social action rather than into theorizing. The shaping of a doctrine of conservative social reform was left to Frédéric Le Play during the Second Empire. Like so many other men of his time, Le Play's interest in social issues had been aroused by his youthful contact with the Saint-Simonians. During his lifetime of extensive travel as an engineer, Le Play developed the thesis that the family rather than the individual must be the ultimate unit in a healthy society. He pioneered the technique of sociological case studies of families and built upon his findings both a theory and an organized movement to propagate it. His goal was to substitute for the "unstable" family of the modern era a somewhat broadened and more tightly-knit family unit, dedicated to the common good and capable therefore of achieving happiness. His ideal of virtual self-sufficiency for such family groups could not, however, be adapted to the conditions of wage earners, whose fate inevitably depended on the employer group. Le Play's only remedy for the ills of the proletariat was a paternalistic one; he preached the obligation of employers to ensure their workers steady jobs and decent wages and to set them an example of hard work and probity. Le Play was a major contributor to the late nineteenth-century conservative school of social Catholicism in France.

✥◦❧ ✥◦❧ ✥◦❧

The transition from romantic utopianism to a tougher-minded mood was not confined to the social theorists of the 1840's. A similar transition was also in progress in the main current of French thought and

238

culture and was preparing the way for the new mid-century *Zeitgeist* of materialism and realism.

A few forerunners of the new mood had appeared at the very height of the romantic era. Stendhal, whose masterpieces anticipated the psychological novels of the late nineteenth century, observed severely in 1821 that "imagination must learn to respect the iron laws of reality," and he described his own work as "a mirror rambling along a highway." Honoré de Balzac, that gigantic figure who sought to portray in his hundred-volume *Human Comedy* every aspect of the society of his time, combined the romantic and the realistic moods much as Dickens was doing across the Channel. Friedrich Engels was to remark that he had ". . . learned more from Balzac than from all the works of the historians, economists, and professional statisticians of the period taken together."

But the real turning point in French thought and taste came in 1848. If the revolutionary upheaval was in part the product of romanticism, it was also the culmination of that movement; the tone and temper of literature, the arts, philosophy, changed drastically in the 1850's. Gustave Flaubert best reflected the new mood in literature; resisting a deep inner compulsion toward romantic self-expression, he drove himself to dissect in almost clinical fashion the characters and the society that he portrayed in objective if somewhat sordid detail. In painting, Gustave Courbet led the revolt against the dominant school of Delacroix and sought to reproduce real scenes and people with photographic accuracy. It was Courbet who first proudly adopted the label "realist" flung contemptuously at him by his rivals. In social theory, the positivist doctrines of Auguste Comte began to win wide acceptance in the decades after his death (1855). Michelet might still be the great national historian, but alongside his impassioned rhetoric a more rigorously scientific kind of history was winning readers. Renan's *Life of Jesus,* the sensation of the 1860's, represented this changing mood. In architecture, Napoleon III's builders chose an eclectic style in place of the pseudo-Gothic that remained so popular across the Channel and the Atlantic. Only in music did the romantic temper remain almost unchallenged right down through the nineteenth century. Offenbach and Meyerbeer, purveyors of the light romantic operetta, seemed even more representative of the rather gaudy and superficial gaiety of the Second Empire than did the native-born romantics Gounod and Bizet.

Frenchmen had not awaited the era of positivistic scientism to turn their talents to science and pure scholarship. As early as 1817 at least one American visitor found Paris to be not the literary and artistic but the scientific capital of Europe. For training in pure science and mathematics, few institutions anywhere could rival the École Polytechnique. Nor could many nations boast so remarkable a collection of creative thinkers and scholars as Ampère, Fresnel, Gay-Lussac, Laplace, Lamarck, Cuvier, Berthelot, Bernard, Pasteur, Champollion, Guizot, Michelet.

Taken as a whole, the half-century from 1814 to 1870 had been a brilliant one in the intellectual and cultural realms. If the achievements of Frenchmen did not lead the world in every field — the fine arts, literature, music, science, philosophy, political and social theory — it would be hard to name a rival nation whose citizens had done so much in so many activities of the mind and the spirit. If Frenchmen were guilty of a certain complacency, of a kind of cultural chauvinism, it was not entirely without justification. Even in retrospect, it is difficult to accept the caustic verdict of an English historian, to whom the brilliance of the era was merely "the iridescence of decay."[4]

[4] A. F. Thompson, in J. M. Wallace-Hadrill and J. McManners (eds.), *France: Government and Society*, p. 224.

SIXTEEN

> For a nation that has known greatness and glory,
> there is no middle ground between the maintenance
> of its old prestige and complete impotence.
>
> LUCIEN PRÉVOST-PARADOL *(1868)*

France, Europe, and the World, 1814–1870

France, in the eyes of most Europeans during the first half of the nineteenth century, was the potential troublemaker of the Continent. It could hardly be otherwise, after a generation of French crusading for liberty or for conquest. Although defeated and chastened, the French were suspected of subversive inclinations that might lead them to aid liberal and national movements elsewhere; and they were suspected, too, of an ambition to recover the Rhine frontier. These apprehensions were kept alive by the fact that some Frenchmen over the years did keep urging an ideological or an expansionist foreign policy, and by the vocal resentment of French patriots toward the "humiliating" treaty settlement of 1815. The fears of the Europeans contributed eventually to their willingness to let Bismarck shift the balance of power against France by creating a powerful state in the heart of the Continent.

The curious thing was that French governments, from 1814 to 1852 at least, rarely behaved according to the European stereotype. They were inclined to walk softly and to carry a small stick. Caution,

241

restraint, an avoidance of crusades of all kinds — these were the hall-marks of French policy until the accession of Napoleon III, and even Napoleon indulged in no rash attempt to restore French grandeur at any cost. Perhaps the French governments of the era were merely timid, unimaginative, even pusillanimous; perhaps, on the other hand, they contributed to the stability of Europe in its most peaceful century of modern times.

Throughout the Bourbon period the monarchy faced a double pressure for a more active policy; from the ultras on the one hand, from the liberals on the other. The ultras felt the need for a strong and glamorous foreign policy to overcome the sentiment that the regime had been imported in the saddlebags of the conquering allies and dared not stand up for French interests. The ultras wanted a firm commit-ment to the Metternichean principle of antirevolution, with France lead-ing the way as defender of continental stability. The liberals likewise urged an active foreign policy, but of quite the opposite sort: they wanted France to serve as symbol and sponsor of liberal movements everywhere. Ultras and liberals agreed on one point only: that French self-respect required a revision of the 1815 treaty settlement. A chau-vinistic tinge was given to this campaign (and a word added to the language) by the agitation of such Napoleonic veterans as Nicholas Chauvin.

Both of the Bourbon kings and most of their ministers avoided either the ultra or the liberal line, preferring a cautious, noncommittal neutralism. For several years any other policy might have brought new foreign intervention; indeed, both the British and the Russians in 1816 privately exerted pressure to get the ultras out of office in favor of more moderate and restrained leadership. The return of the ultras in 1820 brought no real change, mainly because Villèle, strong man of the new government, was stubbornly opposed to adventures of any kind. Adven-tures might upset his program of financial stabilization and might bring trouble with England; Villèle's foreign policy was therefore limited to a single principle — to stay out of trouble.

The only important deviation from this line was France's expedition into Spain in 1823. Villèle had tried to evade ultra demands that France, on behalf of the Concert of Europe, go to the aid of the Spanish king against his liberal ministers. In an effort to frustrate the war hawks in his cabinet, he named Chateaubriand foreign minister; but Chateaubriand promptly switched sides and announced that a French army of a hundred thousand men would be sent into Spain. The venture seemed a foolhardy one, not only because the English were hostile to it, but also because no Frenchman could forget the reception that Napoleon's invading army had received in Spain. If France's greatest military genius had been unable to break Spanish resistance, how could a Bourbon-led army do so? The French liberals hopefully predicted disaster, and Villèle half believed them. Instead, the expedition developed into a triumphal military parade; Madrid fell within a month, with only a handful of French casualties. Bourbon prestige was reinforced, and so was the French army's loyalty to the regime; the soldiers revelled in the glamor born of victory and in the promotions and decorations that followed it.

It was Chateaubriand, however, who deserved much of the credit for the triumph, and who claimed all of it. "My Spanish war, the great political event of my life" (he wrote in his memoirs) had done more to stabilize the regime than all the other politicians of France had managed to do in eight years. "The youth of France had come in a body to my side, and never afterward left me. . . . I could not step into the street without attracting a crowd."[1] The victory encouraged Chateaubriand to push ahead toward a new kind of French foreign policy, adventurous rather than cautious in spirit. The Spanish expedition he conceived as only the first step toward freeing France for action; his next move would be to secure an alliance with Russia, which would enable him to tear up the treaties of 1815 and to recover the Rhine frontier. But Villèle proved to be a shrewder political infighter than Chateaubriand. The rivalry between the two men pro-

[1] R. de Chateaubriand, *Mémoires d'outre-tombe* (Paris: Garnier, n.d.), IV, 284-85, 313.

duced a crisis in 1824, and Villèle got the furious foreign minister dismissed from office.

Not until Polignac's accession in 1829 was the policy of caution infringed again.[2] As an ultra-ultra, Polignac hoped for a great diplomatic victory that would restore the popularity of the regime. His aim was to sweep away the treaties of 1815 and to recover the Rhine frontier; and he could manage this only by getting Russian support. The scheme which he concocted was certainly one of the most remarkable in French diplomatic records. The partition of moribund Turkey was to furnish the occasion for a Franco-Russian agreement and for a complex series of territorial exchanges through which every nation would be bought off. Russia and Austria would receive sizable chunks of Turkish territory; Prussia would annex the Dutch Netherlands and Saxony; England would get the Dutch colonies; France would receive the Dutch-ruled provinces of Belgium. The expropriated Saxon king would be transferred to a new state carved out of the Prussian Rhineland, while the Dutch monarch would rule a new Byzantine-Greek empire at Constantinople. Polignac tried out this fantastic scheme on the Russians, but it got a cold reception. As a substitute, he hit on the idea of an expedition against the Moslem ruler of Algiers. A long-standing economic and diplomatic controversy furnished an excuse for action, but British opposition to any European intervention had led Polignac's predecessors to confine themselves to angry words. The expedition of 1830, which at the outset seemed as risky as the Spanish venture of 1823, proved to be an equally striking success. Algiers fell only three weeks after the French force landed, and news of the triumph encouraged Charles X to proceed with the domestic coup d'état of July that led to his overthrow. Polignac's active foreign policy thus contributed to the fall of the Bourbons, and at the same time gave France an unintended dividend — the opportunity to acquire a new colonial empire in North Africa. For the Orleanist monarchy, after

[2] France's involvement in the naval battle of Navarino (1827) was not a very important exception, since the battle developed accidentally out of a Franco-British naval demonstration against the Egyptian fleet.

much backing and filling, chose to stay in Algiers and to conquer the vast hinterland as well.

⋙◦⋘ ⋙◦⋘ ⋙◦⋘

The wave of emotion that produced the revolution of 1830 was accompanied by an upsurge of nationalism and a demand for a more aggressive foreign policy. The moment seemed ripe for a change, for revolution spread through much of Europe in a kind of chain reaction, and the foundations of the 1815 settlement appeared to be seriously undermined. The revolt of the Belgians against Dutch rule encouraged those Frenchmen who wanted to recover the Rhine frontier, while Polish and Italian outbreaks against their Russian and Austrian masters offered tempting opportunities for crusades of liberation. Not only the republican left, but some of Louis Philippe's supporters as well, urged action.

The new king faced a difficult choice. The powers were tense and hostile to the revolutionary usurper; a false move might bring disaster both to France and to his new dynasty, which had been received coolly by the other monarchs. Yet he dared not grovel too obviously because of the surge of patriotism among his own partisans at home. Discreetly, he announced a policy of nonintervention in the Belgian crisis, and he resurrected Talleyrand as a special emissary to London, with instructions to work out a face-saving solution of the Belgian problem. Talleyrand's aim was an agreement dividing Belgium among all its neighbors; in the end, he had to settle for an independent Belgium, committed to choose its monarch from one of the minor royal families of Europe. The compromise disappointed the chauvinist element in France; and what followed infuriated them even more. The Belgians, ignoring instructions from the powers, invited one of Louis Philippe's sons to become their king; Louis Philippe, after some hesitation, sidestepped the opportunity as too risky. Meanwhile, the French government was evading domestic pressure for an expedition to help the Poles; several months of temporizing gave the Russians time to crush the insurrection.

245

"Order reigns in Warsaw," announced the French foreign minister. Advocates of a strong policy on both left and right were beside themselves. "Philippe is a police officer," wrote Chateaubriand, "Europe can spit in his face; he wipes himself, offers his thanks, and displays his royal certificate." The king's critics believed, both then and later, that an unparalleled opportunity had been missed in 1830. A vigorous French government, wrote Louis Blanc a decade later, could have made over the whole Continent on liberal lines and could have raised France once again to the position of leader of Europe. The Belgians, he insisted, had been eager for annexation; in Italy, Poland, Spain, the liberals had needed only a French gesture to ensure victory; the Turks were looking for a patron and protector. France would have faced no serious opposition, according to Blanc, for the great powers were too preoccupied, or too hesitant, to interfere.

There is good reason to think that Blanc was much too sanguine both about the probable reaction of the powers and about the prospects of the central European liberals. Indeed, Louis Philippe's "weak" foreign policy probably saved the dynasty from disaster, and it produced some constructive results in the process. If France failed to recover the Rhine frontier, it got the next-best thing: an independent and friendly Belgian state, whose new king shortly married a French princess. The establishment of Belgium also meant that France might hope for a gradual, peaceful revision of the 1815 treaties, which were thus infringed for the first time. And France secured, finally, a chance to try the experiment of an entente with England.

This Franco-British alignment was the most important aspect of Orleanist foreign policy, but it proved to be much less durable and useful than Louis Philippe had hoped. Although it survived sporadically from 1830 to 1846, it lacked much substance after the first few years. No formal alliance was ever signed, despite a French effort in 1833 to negotiate a defensive pact. Some scholars believe that economic rivalries were responsible for its breakdown; that only a sharp reduction in French tariffs could have overcome British reluctance and could have given the diplomatic entente an essential base in economic collaboration. Others hold that trade rivalries and tariff conflict were merely contributing factors in the cooling of the new friendship. Much more basic, they argue, were such things as Palmerston's personal hostility toward Louis Philippe and a series of Anglo-French controversies involving prestige rather than commerce, in areas ranging from Spain to the Pacific Ocean.

The Near East had been a potential source of tension from the outset. Turkey's defeat at the hands of Russia in 1829 suggested that the Ottoman empire might be on the verge of collapse. But Russian policy over the next generation was designed to bolster Turkey in order to make it a satellite state, while the British aimed to bolster Turkey for just the opposite reason — to make it an anti-Russian bulwark. Only the French showed an active interest in at least a partial dismemberment of Turkey. They were engaged in carving off Algeria (still theoretically subject to Turkish control); and they had built up special influence in the Egyptian province ruled by Pasha Mehemet Ali, who was challenging the sultan's suzerainty. The French sent officers to train Mehemet's army, granted him loans, and supported him when the sultan set out in 1839 to chastise him.

Unfortunately for France, British and Russian interests converged on one vital point: namely, their antagonism toward Mehemet Ali's pretensions to independence and conquest. Louis Philippe might have been inclined to abandon Egypt had it not been for the pressure of public and parliamentary opinion in Paris, which drove him for a brief period to try a tough policy. Early in 1840 he appointed Adolphe Thiers head of the ministry. Thiers combined the qualities of a bantam rooster with a passionate interest in military strategy; he took an intransigent stand in support of the Egyptians. Once again, the French faced a general European coalition headed by England. Thiers rashly pushed ahead with a policy of bluff, apparently on the assumption that the powers would not really face war; but neither French opinion nor the French king was willing to run so great a risk. Thiers was dismissed late in 1840, and the way was opened for a revival of the English entente. The prospect of such a revival seemed especially good since Guizot, the new strong man of the ministry, wanted England's friendship and opposed foreign adventures.

But a whole series of plaguing issues kept the waters roiled during the 1840's. A conflict between British Protestant and French Catholic missionaries in Tahiti (the so-called Pritchard Affair) led to years of bickering, and resentment persisted even after a compromise settlement was arranged. The British blocked a French plan to intervene in Morocco and warned Paris against a projected Franco-Belgian customs union. But the incident that finally swept away the remnants of the entente occurred in Spain. Both the French and the British had been jockeying for position at the Spanish court, each one with a view to diplomatic and commercial advantage. Their rivalry came to focus upon the young queen, who was eventually to achieve well-earned notoriety as Isabella the Amorous. The French were eager to provide her with one of Louis Philippe's sons as a husband; the British candidate was a German prince, a relative of Victoria's consort. After a long deadlock the French proposed a compromise: a Spanish duke would marry the queen, while Louis Philippe's son would marry Isabella's younger sister. The British angrily denounced the plan as a clever French trick; they charged that the French had carefully handpicked an impotent husband for Isabella. Guizot pushed ahead with the scheme nevertheless and brought on the inevitable disruption of the entente. It was a sad commentary on Guizot's statesmanship that he considered the Spanish marriage plan his diplomatic masterpiece; even worse was the fact that French opinion also received it with enthusiasm. Perhaps Guizot had in mind the creation of a new alliance system linking France, Spain, the kingdom of Naples, and even Austria. Or perhaps his sole purpose was to win French applause for a successful finesse against England. Neither purpose would justify the price Guizot had to pay — the bitter hostility of the British.

The Orleanist era illustrates the difficulties involved in conducting a pacific, prudent foreign policy marked by the spirit of the *juste milieu* and of compromise. It gave France a generation of peace, with some territorial gains and no territorial losses. Yet the policy contributed to the downfall of the regime, for it lacked glamor and offered the opposition a handy stick with which to beat the government. Meanwhile, it won the monarchy no real friends abroad; by 1848 France was almost totally isolated. Critics of the regime both then and later argued that an ideological foreign policy would have been both more admirable and more profitable for France. The first and best chance was missed, according to them, in 1830; a second opportunity was developing after 1845, as serious unrest began to grow in Italy, Switzerland, and Poland. But the king and Guizot, instead of encouraging this liberal unrest, chose to collaborate with Metternich in a policy of repression. The door was left open for Palmerston to emerge as champion of liberal movements and to win for England the moral and diplomatic leadership that rightly belonged to France. At the very least, argue these critics, Paris ought to have expressed its sympathy with the liberals of the 1840's. Instead, Guizot concentrated his energies on the Spanish marriages and on controlling unrest in Europe. The Orleanist record in foreign affairs has sometimes been used as evidence that any foreign policy marked by caution and restraint, by a spirit of *juste milieu,* is bound to be flabby and futile. A fairer conclusion might be that such a policy requires extraordinarily shrewd and flexible leadership if it is not to end in general disillusionment.

⋘∘⋙⋘∘⋙⋘∘⋙

The 1848 revolution, even more than that of 1830, brought a wave of crusading fervor in France. Central Europe's insurrections were far more fundamental ones this time, and the prospect of renovating the whole Continent seemed far brighter. It is not surprising that the republican left wing put heavy pressure on the new provisional government to send armies of liberation marching across France's frontiers. Was this the great lost opportunity of the modern era? That question was later to obsess such eminent French Socialists as Jean Jaurès and Léon Blum. It has obsessed French historians as well. One of them asserts flatly that if Frenchmen had seized their chance in 1848 to

249

wipe out feudalism in central Europe, they would have been spared the disasters of 1870, 1914, and 1940; and a British historian adds that the decision not to act marked the abdication of France as a great power.

The thesis is tempting, but its validity is open to at least some doubt. The provisional government of 1848 could not be sure that Frenchmen in general shared the activists' eagerness for a crusade on behalf of freedom. It knew that the interventionist current was offset by a strongly pacifist or isolationist stream, not only among the peasant masses but even among the Paris republicans. Perhaps the crusaders themselves would have been less enthusiastic if they had faced up to the possible consequences of their policy — the re-creation of the anti-French coalition of 1815 and a general war against the monarchs of Europe. It is true enough that the policy of inaction had unhappy results; the new regimes in central Europe were destroyed, and so was the French republic itself. It may be argued that a crusade could hardly have produced worse results. But it is unfair to ignore (as some historians have done) the hazards of a strong foreign policy in 1848, or to suggest that the provisional government's cautious line was nothing more than the product of blindness and class bigotry.

With Napoleon III came the first fundamental change since 1814 in the temper and conduct of French foreign policy. Although Napoleon announced just before the coup d'état of 1851 that "the Empire means peace," no ruler bearing his name was likely to rank peace higher than glory. Nor could any Napoleon fail to regard the treaties of 1815 as a humiliating *Diktat* that must be revised for the sake of national and dynastic prestige. One might think that the task of characterizing the Second Empire's foreign policy would be an easy one; yet quite the contrary is true. Napoleon's conduct of affairs aroused more controversy among contemporaries, and has been more diversely judged by historians, than any other phase in the foreign policy of nineteenth-century France.

To some historians, the emperor was a dreamer hypnotized by the principle of the rights of nationalities; a man whose idealism was not adequately balanced by a sense of realism, and who failed to understand how his dreams might impinge upon the interests of his country. To others, he was a calculating schemer concerned above all with prestige, aiming to dazzle the French people by his exploits, utilizing the nationality principle as a mere pretext to justify his meddling tactics. To still others, he was an admirably farsighted and intelligent statesman who foreshadowed the modern ideals of self-determination and European federation, who wanted France to lead Europe toward that brighter destiny. Finally, there are those who conclude that he had no clear aim at all; they see him as buffeted about by conflicting currents within France and concerned primarily to keep himself in power through shrewd manipulation.

Not only Napoleon's motives, but his alleged errors of judgment as well, have been subjects of continuing controversy. Some critics have charged him with focussing too narrowly on Italian questions, perhaps because his early experiences as a Carbonaro there left a kind of emotional residue. German scholars have accused him, rather, of a persistent determination to recover the Rhine frontier at almost any cost and to keep Germany weak enough to be subservient. Other historians allege that he failed to raise his eyes from the European scene and see that a vast colonial empire could be had for the taking. Still others believe that the emperor's central purpose was to build a great alliance system led by France, and that he bungled the task through his inability to choose among potential allies.

The controversy doubtless stems from Napoleon's complex and contradictory nature and from his habit of secretive, tight-lipped diplomacy. Probably the emperor was neither a rigid doctrinaire, nor an idealistic dreamer, nor an unprincipled opportunist. His interest in the rights of nationalities seems to have been genuine; but almost certainly it was not the core of his policy, the central aim for which he would sacrifice all else. He made no effort, for example, to push that principle in the Balkan region, where it would have interfered with his ambition to arrange an Austrian alliance. A reasonable conclusion might be that his central aim was a very broad and general one: to restore French prestige in Europe and to give his dynasty a solid base. Napoleon's revisionist attitude toward the treaties of 1815 was almost as fundamental as that of the Germans toward Versailles many decades later. Apparently the emperor had shaped no rigid program but intended to feel his way in pragmatic fashion toward a restoration of national prestige. His primary goal was neither territorial expansion nor European federation, but a balance-of-power system under France's diplomatic leadership.

During his first decade in power Napoleon sought to achieve this end through close collaboration with Britain. To win London to such a policy was probably his principal motive in entering the Crimean War of 1854–56; certainly French interests in the Near East offered no adequate justification for war with Russia. A warm relationship did develop for a time; the period brought the first use of the phrase "entente cordiale."[3] But the entente gradually cooled after 1860 as the result of a series of minor squabbles, in spite of the closer trade relationships made possible by the Chevalier-Cobden Treaty.

As a kind of substitute for the Anglo-French alignment, Napoleon turned to a device that had long attracted him: a revival of the European congress system of the Castlereagh era. The emperor's interest in diplomacy by conference (a practice for which there was little precedent in periods of peace) lends some plausibility to the thesis that he was a kind of European federalist. He conceived of the congress system, however, much as Castlereagh had done — as a mechanism for operating a balance-of-power system. His scheme got little support from the other powers, who usually evaded his invitations to settle problems around a table. Simultaneously during these middle years of the empire, Napoleon was embarking on a whole series of enterprises that

[3] Napoleon tried to avoid conflicts with the British, even to the point of what might be called appeasement. For example, he gave little support to Ferdinand de Lesseps' company organized to build the Suez Canal, since he knew that the British opposed the project. If the canal was finally constructed the credit must go to De Lesseps rather than to Napoleon. P. Renouvin, *Histoire des relations internationales, le XIXe siècle* (Paris: Hachette, 1954), I, 331–35.

aroused the suspicions of the rest of Europe and that produced division at home: aid to Piedmont in creating a north Italian federation, intervention in Mexico to carve out a sphere of influence there, an expedition to Syria (1860) with the declared purpose of protecting Christians against Moslem persecution, penetration of Indo-China as a base from which to tap the Chinese market.

From 1866 onward the empire entered a third phase, during which Napoleon was increasingly preoccupied with the German problem. This was not to be the most brilliant phase of Napoleonic diplomacy; indeed, the disaster of 1870 was prepared in considerable part by the mistakes of the prewar years. The emperor seriously underestimated both Prussia's potential power and Bismarck's skill and ruthlessness. He even helped the Prussians get a treaty with Italy in 1866 — a treaty that was essential to Bismarck's plans for an armed showdown with Austria. It is quite clear that he expected a standoff fight between Prussia and Austria, with France stepping in at the proper moment to mediate and to dictate terms. A few Frenchmen perceived the danger more clearly: Thiers, for example, who publicly warned the government on May 3, 1866. Napoleon ignored the warning; but even when the battle of Sadowa proved Thiers right, he failed to intervene while there was still time. After some hesitation, he gave up the idea of concentrating an army on the Rhine — probably because most French opinion was so vigorously and vocally hostile to the idea.

The fatal error of inaction in 1866 was compounded during the years that followed. Napoleon's clumsy efforts to get territorial compensation along the Rhine only played into Bismarck's hands. His attempts to negotiate alliances with Italy and Austria dragged on to an empty conclusion; and his desperate attempt to build up France's military power was defeated by an irritated public opinion at home. By the time of the decisive crisis in July, 1870, Napoleon seems to have let the power of decision slip almost entirely out of his hands — the result, at least in part, of chronic illness. It may be that the emperor saw more clearly than either his advisers or his subjects during the last years before his downfall. But even if that was the case, he no longer showed the leadership and the determination required to conduct an unpopular but hardheaded policy. Napoleon's inadequacy as a crisis leader left the nation, at the end of his eighteen-year reign, reduced in prestige, isolated in Europe, and threatened with demotion to the status of a second-rate power. Perhaps that decline was not entirely chargeable to him; perhaps the facts of geography, resources, and population were beginning to catch up with the French. But it would be futile to deny that Napoleon deserved an important share of the blame. Confronted by a rival as able and unscrupulous as Bismarck, the emperor's shortcomings as a shaper of foreign policy could no longer be concealed.

❧꧁◦❧꧁◦❧꧁◦

European interest in empire-building reached its lowest point in the first half of the nineteenth century. France, like the other powers, showed only sporadic flashes of interest in colonial expansion during the years 1814–70. Yet the imperial impulse never died out entirely; on the contrary, a beginning was made toward creating a new overseas empire in place of that lost to the English in the eighteenth century.

The treaty of 1814 restored to France the scattered remnants of the old empire, consisting of little more than a few tropical sugar islands plus some trading stations on the west coast of Africa. The Bourbons were content with what they had; their one overseas expedition (to Algiers in 1830) was not intended as a colonial venture. Louis Philippe absorbed the rest of Algeria, rather in spite of himself, and also added Tahiti and the Comoro Islands, off Madagascar. Napoleon III contributed Cochin-China, a protectorate over Cambodia, and control of the west African hinterland of Senegal. This scattered and incoherent list suggests that chance rather than any conscious goal governed these acquisitions. Only in the Second Empire were the first anticipatory signs of the new imperial age to be seen: national prestige, humanitarian drives, and economic motives seem to have been interwoven in Napoleon's mind.

254

If most Frenchmen had no clear idea of why (or whether) they wanted colonies, they were scarcely clearer on how to run an empire once they had gotten it. Until 1848 they fell back rather automatically into the mercantilist tradition of the old regime, according to which the colonies were mere appendages of the mother country, destined to contribute to France's well-being. The revolution of 1848 brought a brief experiment in humanitarianism a century ahead of its time. Napoleon III restored authoritarian control from Paris, but combined it with an unprecedented liberalism in the economic sphere, and capped all this with some rather ambiguous talk about building an Arab kingdom in Algeria.

The old colonies (like Martinique and Guadeloupe) continued to be run after 1814 by a planter class, set atop a population of slaves. Their trade, as mercantilist doctrine required, was completely monopolized by France. This system was already beginning to decay well before 1848 destroyed it. Colonial cane sugar was running into new competition from French beet sugar, developed on a large scale during the Napoleonic wars; the importation of slaves had been outlawed in 1815, and the institution of slavery itself was under rising attack. A far-sighted policy in Paris would have broken the grip of mercantilism at the earliest possible date, in order to permit a gradual shift in the colonies from sugar plantations to new products adapted to the French or the world market. But the planters and, even more, powerful shipping interests in Bordeaux managed to block any change.

The acquisition of Algeria burdened the French with a brand-new problem, for which the old colonial system was in no way adapted. Here for the first time was a large indigenous population to be ruled; here, too, was potential space for French colonization on a large scale, at a time when France was threatened by overpopulation; here, finally, was an area whose agrarian products would compete with rather than supplement those of the mother country. France's conquest of Algeria was largely accidental. The Bourbons had no intention of empire-building in 1830; Charles X had apparently planned that a congress of European powers would decide the country's fate. Louis Philippe kept troops there primarily because the British were so eager to get them out; he had knuckled under to England on the Belgian issue, and he had to resist British pressure somewhere to placate opinion at home. Then, having decided to retain a strip along the coast, the French were gradually sucked into a conquest of the hinterland as well in order to stop constant harassment by Algerian tribesmen. The cost of the conquest brought repeated complaints in the French parliament; it is likely that the critics would have had their way except for the prestige factor. By 1848 the conquest was complete except for the rugged Kabylia region; another generation of *razzias* (lightning raids, complete with burning and looting) was required before the Berbers there could be subdued. The process of colonization had already begun in the 1840's; by 1848 about a hundred thousand Europeans (only half of them French) had settled in Algeria. There was still no clearly conceived plan of development to govern such matters as the size of holdings or relationships between European and Algerian farmers.

The revolution of 1848 brought the most drastic change in the history of French colonialism. The republicans of that era, though not much interested in colonies, did have a clear-cut policy toward them. That policy was one of assimilation: it rested on the assumption that all men are free and equal, and that the overseas possessions ought to be integral, self-governing parts of France. One of the very first steps was to free the slaves, with a small indemnity to the owners. The ex-slaves were converted into citizens at once; and several of the old colonies were given the right to elect deputies to the Paris parliament. Northern Algeria was assimilated even more completely (in formal structure, at least); it was converted into three French departments complete with prefects and many of the formal appurtenances of departments in continental France. Most of the reforms of 1848 were to prove permanent, save for a partial interruption during the Second Empire. Economically, the reforms had a severe impact on the sugar islands, where the planters were already in difficulties. Production dropped sharply and did not regain the 1848 level for a generation. Gradually, however, the islands managed to convert to a new and healthier economic base. One further consequence of the 1848 upheaval was a new spurt of emigration to Algeria. After the National Work-shops were closed, about twenty thousand settlers moved down with government aid; and the coup d'état of 1851 produced another im-portant wave of emigrants. By 1860 the European population in Algeria had risen to two hundred thousand, and by 1870 to three hundred thousand.

Napoleon III's colonial policy, like almost every aspect of his reign, defies any simple description. In some ways, it foreshadowed the great age of European imperialism in the late nineteenth century; in other respects, it seemed tinged with the humanitarian outlook of the twentieth. The idea of assimilation was promptly abandoned, and the colonies were restored to the status of political appendages governed from Paris. On the other hand, the colonies gained a new freedom of trade when the emperor turned toward economic liberalism in 1860. Important new acquisitions were added to the empire in Indo-China and west Africa; but often they were not so much the product of conscious policy in Paris as of independent action by French army and navy officers on the spot. This was notably the case in Senegal, where French control of the hinterland was won by that remarkable soldier and empire-builder, General Faidherbe. It was less true in Indo-China, where the decision to intervene was made in Paris. A small force landed at Saigon in 1859 to protect Catholic missionaries and began a piecemeal conquest of Cochin-China. The real purpose was to get a naval base and to gain access, via the Indo-Chinese river valleys, to the supposedly fabulous Chinese market. At one point Napoleon was on the verge of withdrawing this expeditionary force, for there were rising protests in Paris about the cost involved, and his more important Mexican venture was running into difficulties. Pressure exerted by the clergy, by Bordeaux shipping interests, and by spokesmen for the French navy averted the withdrawal and committed France to a century of imperial activity in southeast Asia. Here was an early example of the complex blend of humanitarianism, prestige-seeking, and special interest that was to become so common in the new imperialistic age.

Napoleon's most curious overseas ventures were his Mexican expedition and his scheme to convert Algeria into an Arab kingdom under French protection. The excuse for intervention in Mexico (which began in 1861) was to force the Mexican revolutionary republic to honor certain debts owed to Europeans. The real reason appears to have been Napoleon's belief that Mexico might be turned into a kind of satellite state or sphere of influence of great economic value to France. Perhaps he hoped also to appease the French clergy by breaking the power of the Mexican anticlericals and to please French patriots by a display of French energy. The venture proved to be, instead, an unmitigated disaster; Mexican resistance, United States warnings after the end of the Civil War, and the new Prussian threat across the Rhine forced a humiliating evacuation of Mexico in 1867.

Napoleon's Arab-kingdom plan bore at least a superficial resemblance to the projects of those twentieth-century French progressives who defend the Algerians' right to autonomy and who hope to see Arabs and European settlers living harmoniously side by side. The emperor twice visited Algeria to study its problems on the spot and came away fascinated by the Arab people and Arab ways. For a time he stopped the flow of colonists into Algeria and talked of preserving the indigenous society with its feudal structure and leadership. The Algerian dream, like that of Mexico, ended in total frustration and was promptly abandoned by the Third Republic. Like so many other enterprises of the Second Empire, it can be used to buttress either of two theses about the emperor: Napoleon the humanitarian idealist, or Napoleon the well-meaning chaser of chimeras.

SEVENTEEN

The Varieties of History,
1814–1870

Historical controversy is a natural by-product of upheaval; agitated periods like the Great Revolution lend themselves to sweeping and doctrinaire interpretations. Controversy is less often associated with periods of relative quiet, when fundamental changes occur in gradual and undramatic fashion. There are clear-cut schools of thought about the 1789 crisis; there are only overlapping differences of opinion about the dominant trends of the nineteenth century. Indeed, few historians have even tried to examine the years 1814–70 as a coherent period with its own distinguishing traits. More often they have been diverted into piecemeal study of shorter segments of time, perhaps because the political chronology of early nineteenth-century France lends itself so well to such subdivision. It is as though Frenchmen had thoughtfully sawed up their history like cordwood into lengths of fifteen to twenty years, in order to make them more easily manageable to the historian. What is lost in the process is continuity, an overview of the significance of the times.

Divergent viewpoints emerge, nevertheless, as one reads the relevant chapters in general histories of France, or the relevant volumes in collaborative multivolume works. Monarchists like Bainville, Gaxotte (*Histoire des français* [Paris: Flammarion, 1951]), and Lucien Romier (*History of France* [New York: St. Martins, 1953]) offer a rather grudging defense of a restored monarchy that made the fatal error (if

259

we are to believe Gaxotte) of refusing to trust the masses with the ballot. Albert Bayet's *Histoire de France* (Paris: Sagittaire, 1938) provides a rigorously leftist and anticlerical view; Jacques Madaule's *Histoire de France* (Paris: Gallimard, 1943) offers the judgments of a Christian democrat. Volumes IV through VII in Ernest Lavisse (ed.), *Histoire de la France contemporaine* (Paris: Hachette, 1920–22), express the outlook typical of firm republicans writing in an era when scientific objectivity was still the historian's supreme but elusive goal. Somewhere in the middle, politically and philosophically speaking, fall the works of André Maurois (*Histoire de la France* [Paris: Wapler, 1947]), Albert Guérard (*France: A Modern History* [Ann Arbor: Univ. of Michigan Press, 1959]), and D. W. Brogan (*The French Nation, 1814–1940* [New York: Harper, 1957]). All three are remarkably literate and well informed but somewhat idiosyncratic accounts. There is no Communist survey of nineteenth-century France, though Communist scholars have worked on specific periods and topics (notably the 1848 revolution). Marxian and quasi-Marxian interpretations are cogently criticized in John Plamenatz's *Revolutionary Movement in France, 1815–1871* (London: Longmans, 1952). J. P. T. Bury's *France, 1814–1940* (London: Methuen, 1956) is an accurate and dispassionate survey that eschews interpretation.

Some of the most thoughtful and provocative of recent books about nineteenth-century France are those that trace a single thread of development from 1815 to the present; they manage thus to reveal the continuity that is concealed beneath changes of regime. One of the best is René Rémond's *La Droite en France de 1815 à nos jours* (Paris: Aubier, 1954), which examines the evolution of right-wing groups and doctrines. Rémond detects three principal strands within the right-wing tradition: traditionalist, conservative-liberal, and nationalist. Varying in strength, changing in character, they persist and recur throughout the modern era. Adrien Dansette studies the relationship between church and state in his lively *Histoire religieuse de la France contemporaine* (Paris: Flammarion, 1948–51). For so explosive a subject, the tone is quite dispassionate; the casual reader might find it hard to detect that

Dansette is a Catholic. Raoul Girardet traces the fluctuating social and political role of the army in his *La Société militaire dans la France contemporaine* (Paris: Plon, 1953); by implication, the contrast with the more influential and active role of the German army is striking.

Charles Morazé's highly original essay *La France bourgeoise (XVIIIᵉ–XXᵉ siècles)* (Paris: Colin, 1946) contains some stimulating ideas on social and economic structure and demographic trends, but it provides no real synthesis of the role and development of the French middle classes. His more recent *Les Bourgeois conquérants: XIXᵉ siècle* (Paris: Colin, 1957) is equally original in treatment, but it subordinates the socio-economic development of France to that of the Western world as a whole. Labor history is surveyed from a moderately leftist viewpoint in Edouard Dolléans's *Histoire du mouvement ouvrier* (Paris: Colin, 1948–54) and in Georges Lefranc's more all-inclusive *Histoire du travail et des travailleurs* (Paris: Flammarion, 1957). Val Lorwin's unpublished manuscript "Labor and Economic Development in France" is replete with fresh information and provocative ideas. Emmanuel Beau de Loménie's curious and doctrinaire three-volume work *Les Responsabilités des dynasties bourgeoises* (Paris: Denoel, 1943–54) endeavors to prove that a close-knit caste of business and banking families managed to entrench itself during the Great Revolution and has dominated the nation ever since through its shrewd manipulation of politics. The author (whose pedigree is Orleanist) contends that the narrow egotism and hypocritical careerism of the "bourgeois dynasties" have been responsible for most of France's modern ills, for they allegedly implanted a tradition of cynical opportunism instead of attachment to firm principles. Although his conclusions far outrun his evidence, Beau de Loménie's book has had a surprisingly wide impact both on writers who have absorbed and reproduced his thesis and on those who have felt impelled to weigh and refute it.

The thread of economic development, with special stress on governmental policies and their effect, has been traced by Shepard B. Clough in his *France: A History of National Economics* (New York:

Scribner, 1939). The relatively slow rate of growth of the French economy during the nineteenth and twentieth centuries has produced a lively controversy in recent years. J. H. Clapham's classic *Economic Development of France and Germany, 1815–1914* (Cambridge, Eng.: Cambridge Univ. Press, 1936) attributes France's relative retardation to an inadequate supply of critical raw materials and an excessive supply of labor. David S. Landes has been the most vigorous exponent of the newer Schumpeterian view that psychological and sociological factors were more important: "French Entrepreneurship and Industrial Growth in the Nineteenth Century," *Journal of Economic History*, IX (1949), 45–61, and "Business and the Business Man: A Social and Cultural Analysis," in E. M. Earle (ed.), *Modern France* (Princeton: Princeton Univ. Press, 1951). A forthcoming book by Rondo Cameron, foreshadowed by a series of articles in specialized periodicals, takes a position somewhat akin to Clapham's, but it adds much new information about France's nineteenth-century leadership in the economic development of central Europe (through providing capital and technicians).

Political structures and doctrines are traced through the nineteenth century by J.-J. Chevallier in his *Histoire des institutions politiques de la France de 1789 à nos jours* (Paris: Dalloz, 1952). A lucid and balanced synthesis of modern scholarship on French foreign policy may be found in Volume V of Pierre Renouvin's *Histoire des relations internationales: Le XIX*ᵉ *siècle, de 1815 à 1871* (Paris: Hachette, 1954).

Demographic trends and their significance have been examined by C.-H. Pouthas in his *La Population française pendant la première moitié du XIX*ᵉ *siècle* (Paris: Presses Univ., 1956). His statistics emphasize some rather neglected contours of the history of the period: notably the importance of the economic-demographic crisis of 1846–51 as a kind of watershed between the old France and the new. An even more unorthodox work is that of the demographer-historian Louis Chevalier: *Classes laborieuses et classes dangereuses* (Paris: Plon, 1958). By investigating what he calls the biological foundations of social history, Chevalier gives a new dimension to the period 1815–48. The prevalence of crime in Paris (the Chicago of that era) he traces to a pathological state induced by demographic changes — notably by the rapid influx of population and the resulting lack of social integration. So bitter were class antagonisms that it was almost as though two hostile civilizations were confronting each other in Paris. Another kind of sociological history, bearing on the evolution of religious attitudes, has been pioneered by Gabriel Le Bras in his *Introduction à l'histoire de la pratique religieuse en France* (Paris: Presses Univ., 1942–45).

◈⋙◦⋘◈ ◈⋙◦⋘◈ ◈⋙◦⋘◈

Most historians who deal with the nineteenth century have been content to examine a single political regime — though it has been fairly common to combine the Bourbon and Orleanist periods for joint analysis. Félix Ponteil's *La Monarchie parlementaire, 1815–1848* (Paris: Colin, 1949) views the epoch as one of almost unprecedented intellectual ferment and of significant institutional development. This was the time, says Ponteil, when parliamentary government became permanently rooted in France. Paul Bastid, in his *Institutions politiques de la monarchie parlementaire française, 1814–1848* (Paris: Sirey, 1954), likewise stresses the flexibility of institutions that permitted the gradual emergence of cabinet homogeneity and responsibility.

On the Bourbon monarchy, G. de Bertier de Sauvigny's broad synthesis *La Restauration* (Paris: Flammarion, 1955) is a remarkably good introduction. His account, though balanced in tone, is a kind of restrained rehabilitation of the Bourbon regime. Its shortcomings, he argues, were by no means fatal ones; indeed, its overthrow inflicted an "irreparable wound" on the nation, for it destroyed the last chance of blending monarchical tradition with emergent democracy in British fashion. F. B. Artz's *France Under the Bourbon Restoration* (Cambridge, Mass.: Harvard Univ. Press, 1931) is the most detailed general account in English. The ablest defense of Louis XVIII as a statesman-

like moderate is Pierre de la Gorce's *La Restauration: Louis XVIII*
(Paris: Plon, 1926); a hostile view is presented by C.-H. Pouthas in his
Sorbonne lectures, *Histoire politique de la restauration* (Paris: C.D.U.,
1938). The nearest approach to an effective defense of Charles X is
Bertier de Sauvigny's account, cited above.

On the Orleanist period, there is no detailed and up-to-date synthesis like that of Bertier de Sauvigny. Biographical studies do something to fill the gap: Pierre de la Gorce, *Louis-Philippe* (Paris: Plon,
1931); J. Lucas-Dubreton, *Monsieur Thiers* (Paris: Fayard, 1948) and
Lamartine (Paris: Flammarion, 1951); Henri Malo, *Thiers* (Paris:
Payot, 1932).

Interpretations of the 1848 revolution and the Second Republic
have gone through a complete cycle during the last century, beginning
with Karl Marx's *The Class Struggle in France, 1848 to 1850* (first
published 1850; Moscow: For. Lang. Pub. House, 1948) and ending
with a return to the Marxian viewpoint in many of the books written
for the centennial celebration in 1948. During the middle phases of this
cycle, monarchist and republican historians competed in denouncing or
defending the men of 1848. The most important monarchist work was
Pierre de la Gorce's *Histoire de la seconde république française* (Paris:
Plon, 1887), which portrayed a stable and successful constitutional
monarchy destroyed by impractical doctrinaires who could only prepare the way for a dictator. Republican historians (like those who
wrote the collaborative Lavisse series) justified the overthrow of the
July Monarchy, but they lacked much enthusiasm for the leaders and
achievements of the Second Republic. They were inclined to belittle
those leaders as the last of the romantics — as well-meaning men
whose naive errors permitted clerical reactionaries like Falloux and
ambitious schemers like Louis Napoleon to destroy the republic.

Most books written to celebrate the centennial turn their attention
to social and economic factors and make class relationships the key to
the course of events. Communist historians have taken special interest
in this episode; the best of the party-line studies is Jean Dautry's
1848 et la IIe république (Paris: Éditions Sociales, 1948, 1957). Other

leftist viewpoints, less doctrinaire than that of the Leninists, may be found in Georges Bourgin's chapters in F. Fejtö (ed.), *The Opening of an Era, 1848* (London: Wingate, n. d.) and in Georges Duveau's contribution to Charles Moulin (ed.), *1848: le livre du centenaire* (Paris: Atlas, 1948). There are a number of lively accounts by such Anglo-Saxon scholars as Arnold Whitridge (*Men in Crisis* [New York: Scribner, 1949]) and Priscilla Robertson (*Revolutions of 1848: A Social History* [Princeton: Princeton Univ. Press, 1952]). A vigorous but belligerently one-sided account of the decline and overthrow of the Second Republic is Henri Guillemin's *Le Coup d'état du 2 décembre* (Paris: Gallimard, 1951). The author, a maverick left-wing Catholic, has collected every scrap of available evidence to support the thesis that the panic-stricken bourgeois notables of the time threw themselves into the arms of Louis Napoleon in order to preserve their privileges. Napoleon in turn is portrayed as an unprincipled schemer surrounded by a "band of racketeers."

Guillemin's denunciation of Napoleon III represents a kind of throwback to the classic caricatures of the emperor contained in two contemporaneous pamphlets: Victor Hugo's *Napoleon the Little* and Karl Marx's *The Eighteenth Brumaire of Louis Bonaparte*. Republican historians for a generation or two after 1870 were not much more flattering. On the other hand, most twentieth-century biographers have been strongly revisionist, and some of them have presented Napoleon as one of France's most admirable and farsighted statesmen. The most effective of these rehabilitations are Albert Guérard's *Napoleon III* (Cambridge, Mass.: Harvard Univ. Press, 1943) and Paul Guériot's *Napoléon III* (Paris: Payot, 1933). A more critical view of Napoleon as a modern Hamlet appears in J. M. Thompson's *Louis Napoleon and the Second Empire* (Oxford: Blackwell, 1954), while a younger British historian returns to the tradition of Hugo and calls Napoleon "a tawdry, pitiable derivative": "A late Romantic who must have made Stendhal turn in his grave, he was the truly weak man, sustained by a legend stemming from true greatness and vitality. . . . Drifting from failure to failure, feebly compromising and conciliating, this Chekhovian dictator ruled virtually without opposition. . . ." (A. F. Thompson in *Manchester Guardian Weekly*, LXXI [Dec. 30, 1954]).

The "standard work" on the empire is the seven-volume account of Pierre de la Gorce: *Histoire du second empire* (Paris: Plon, 1899–1905; the work of a monarchist critic). The best up-to-date synthesis of modern scholarship is Marcel Blanchard's *Le Second empire* (Paris: Colin, 1950). Louis Chevalier's unpublished Sorbonne thesis entitled "Les Fondements économiques et sociaux de l'histoire politique de la région parisienne, 1848–1851" offers impressive evidence to show that Bonapartism directed its appeal not to the most conservative and the most ignorant elements (as Marx held), but rather to those interested in dynamic economic growth and social flux and to small farmers in revolt against the local oligarchies of notables. On the other hand, Theodore Zeldin's *Political System of Napoleon III* (London: Macmillan, 1958) contends that after 1852 the emperor sought to win converts from the established social and political elite rather than to base his rule on the new men from the lower middle class that had begun to build the Bonapartist political machine in 1848–51.

On Napoleon III's foreign policy, there is an excellent summary of various conflicting interpretations in the *Clio* volume by J. Droz *et al.*, *L'Epoque contemporaine: restaurations et révolutions*. Lynn M. Case's *French Opinion on War and Diplomacy during the Second Empire* (Philadelphia: Pennsylvania Univ. Press, 1954) provides a link between foreign policy and public attitudes.

❧◆❧◆❧◆

The following list offers a representative sampling of recent monographs. On labor conditions: Jean Bruhat's *Histoire du mouvement ouvrier français* (Paris: Éditions Sociales, 1952) provides the official Communist viewpoint. Labor unrest has been studied in detail by J.-P. Aguet (*Les Grèves sous la monarchie de juillet* [Geneva: Droz, 1954]) and by F. L'Huillier (*La Lutte ouvrière à la fin du second empire* [Paris: Colin, 1957]). Georges Duveau's *La Vie ouvrière en France sous le second empire* (Paris: Gallimard, 1946) contains a wealth of detail on the workingman's condition at mid-century and argues that the boom of the 1850's brought no real gain in wages.

On social theory and radical thinkers in this era of unexampled richness: C.-E. Labrousse, *Le Mouvement ouvrier et les théories sociales en France de 1815 à 1848* (Paris: C.D.U., 1954); Maxine Leroy, *Histoire des idées sociales en France* (Paris: Gallimard, 1947–54); Frank E. Manuel, *The New World of Henri Saint-Simon* (Cambridge, Mass.: Harvard Univ. Press, 1956); Alan B. Spitzer, *The Revolutionary Theories of Louis Auguste Blanqui* (New York: Columbia Univ. Press, 1957); Elizabeth Eisenstein, *The First Professional Revolutionary: Filippo Michele Buonarroti* (Cambridge, Mass.: Harvard Univ. Press, 1959).

On economic development: A. L. Dunham, *The Industrial Revolution in France, 1815–1848* (New York: Exposition, 1955); Bertrand Gille, *Recherches sur la formation de la grande entreprise capitaliste (1815–1848)* (Paris: SEVPEN, 1959) and *Banque et crédit sous la monarchie censitaire* (Paris: Presses Univ., 1959); Louis Girard, *La Politique des travaux publics sous le second empire* (Paris: Colin, 1951); Claude Fohlen, *L'Industrie textile au temps du second empire* (Paris: Plon, 1956); David Pinkney, *Napoleon III and the Rebuilding of Paris* (Princeton: Princeton Univ. Press, 1958).

For the life of the times (social history in its more popular sense) there are two entertaining volumes by Robert Burnand (*La Vie quotidienne en France en 1830* [Paris: Hachette, 1943]) and Maurice Allem (*La Vie quotidienne sous le second empire* [Paris: Hachette, 1948]).

On religious issues and leaders: J.-B. Duroselle, *Les Débuts du catholicisme social en France* (Paris: Presses Univ., 1951); F. Veuillot, *Louis Veuillot: sa vie, son âme, son oeuvre* (Paris: Alsatia, 1937); Philip Spencer, *The Politics of Belief in Nineteenth Century France* (London: Faber, 1954).

On intellectual trends: Stanley Mellon, *The Political Uses of History: A Study of Historians in the French Restoration* (Stanford:

Stanford Univ. Press, 1958); D. O. Evans, *Social Romanticism in France, 1830–1848* (New York: Oxford Univ. Press, 1952); D. G. Charlton, *Positivist Thought in France during the Second Empire* (Oxford: Clarendon, 1959).

On politicians and political issues: Irene Collins, *The Government and the Newspaper Press in France, 1814–1881* (London: Oxford Univ. Press, 1959); Jean Fourcassié, *Villèle* (Paris: Fayard, 1954); Roger Langeron, *Royer-Collard* (Paris: Hachette, 1956); Emmanuel Beau de Loménie, *La Carrière politique de Chateaubriand* (Paris: Plon, 1929); J. M. Chapman and Brian Chapman, *The Life and Times of Baron Haussmann* (New York: Macmillan, 1958); Pierre Guiral, *Prévost-Paradol* (Paris: Presses Univ., 1955).

III

THE ROOTING OF
THE REPUBLICAN SYSTEM
1870–1919

EIGHTEEN

> If the Republic isn't the right system for France,
> the surest way to get rid of it is to establish it.
>
> HENRI WALLON *(1875)*

The Monarchist Republic,
1870–1879

The dramatic phases in a nation's history are not always the ones that do most to shape that nation's destiny. There was not much drama in the decade of the 1870's in France; it suffers by contrast with the somewhat meretricious glitter of the empire just before it and with the generation of political turmoil, crisis, and scandal that immediately followed. Yet it constitutes a vital and formative period in the political development of modern France. It saw the establishment of the governmental framework that has served the nation, with minor changes and brief interruptions, ever since. It produced the beginnings of the modern party system and of the basic political divisions that were to harden and endure for decades. More fundamentally still, it brought the conversion of a majority of Frenchmen to the republican ideal. Republicanism, ever since the Great Revolution, had been a minority current in the country, though its size and strength could not be precisely measured. In February, 1871, not more than a third of the nation's votes were cast for declared republican candidates. But by the middle of the decade, and certainly by the end of it, that minority had become a permanent majority.

Such a transition to republicanism may seem quite normal to one who lives in the twentieth century. In the mid-nineteenth it was exceptional. No other major nation in Europe became republicanized so early as the French; the only existing republics on the Continent were Switzerland, Andorra, and San Marino. The reasons, therefore, deserve examination.

One shaping factor was negative in character: the monarchist majority that existed in 1870 helped to cancel itself out by its own internal rivalries. The three competing dynasties never quite managed to reconcile their differences; and obviously, as Thiers indelicately put it, there was not room on the throne for three backsides. But there was a positive factor at work, too; French republicanism in that decade seemed to be taking on a new look. From the outset in 1871 it was the moderate, libertarian wing that got control of the republican movement. In the past, whenever the French republicans had achieved power, this moderate element had been promptly challenged by a smaller, but noisier and more aggressive, egalitarian or Jacobin wing; and the challenge had usually produced a bloody clash between the two factions. So it had been in 1792–94, and so again in 1848. Any prospect that the radicals might get control would have terrified France's socially conservative elements, notably the peasants and the middle classes. They were reassured to find the republicans headed by a set of solid, stable, even stuffy men, who at the very outset met and mastered the left-wing activists. In that era at least, Thiers was surely right in his dictum that "the republic will be conservative or it won't be at all."

In the consolidation of the moderate republic, many men had a hand; but two of them played indispensable roles. One of these — Adolphe Thiers — was a late convert from the monarchist right; the other — Léon Gambetta — came over from the radical left. Rarely has France produced a pair of leaders so remarkable, and rarely have two men offered so striking a contrast. They shared a southern temperament and common birth. In almost every other respect, they were at opposite poles. Thiers was a patriarch of seventy-three, a veteran of four full decades of political life; Gambetta at thirty-two was a mere beginner who had barely had time to make his maiden speech in parliament when the empire fell. Neither man was made to understand the other; Thiers was to refer to his junior colleague as a "raging madman," while Gambetta labelled Thiers "that sinister antique." Yet the two careers converged in the 1870's to consolidate the new republic.

Thiers's role was to furnish leadership and stability at a critical moment, just after the disaster of 1870. His prestige in the country had reached its peak; and that prestige this lifelong monarchist put at the service of the provisional republic. The moderate republicans had other leaders as safe and sound as Thiers; but none had his glamor, his faint touch of charisma. Gambetta's role was to rally a sizable segment of the Jacobin left wing to the moderate, libertarian program, and thus to avert a potentially disastrous faction-fight among republicans over the nature of the republic. The irrepressible firebrand, the demagogic orator and patriot became the conciliator, the "opportunist," the practitioner of politics as the art of the possible.

❧◦❧◦❧◦❧◦❧◦❧

When the Paris crowd burst into the hall of the Corps Législatif on September 4, 1870, it was to Léon Gambetta that the rioters looked for leadership. He it was who led the revolutionists' march across town to the Hôtel de Ville, where, by long-established ritual, it was customary to proclaim republics. He it was who promptly became the spark plug of the new provisional government, composed for the most part of deputies from Paris constituencies. In this Government of National Defense, Gambetta chose the key post of minister of interior. Because that ministry controlled the administrative bureaucracy and the police, Gambetta believed that he could use it to consolidate the republican victory. He promptly installed a new set of fervently republican prefects throughout the provinces and argued for postponing the election of an assembly until these new officials might have time to "prepare" the voters.

The immediate problem, however, was to expel the invader from the sacred soil of France. Some members of the new government hoped at first that Bismarck might offer soft peace terms to the new republic or that a European league of neutral states might put pressure on the Prussians to retire. These vain hopes quickly evaporated. By September 23 Paris was surrounded and besieged by the Prussian forces. If France was to continue resistance, at least part of the government had to be transferred to the provinces. Gambetta volunteered; he took over the ministry of war in addition to his previous post, and on October 7 he and a friend dramatically escaped from beleaguered Paris via balloon. After a hazardous trip that saw the adventurers blown in the wrong direction almost to the Belgian frontier, Gambetta managed to make his way to southwestern France to organize some kind of armed force.

Over the next four months all his unbounded energy and powers of persuasion were thrown into the task of national salvation. His mind was suffused with the myth of Valmy, with the passionate conviction that an aroused nation in arms could throw back any invader. All Frenchmen, he proclaimed, must shelve political issues until the war was won. These were noble sentiments — a bit too noble, indeed, for Gambetta himself to accept without mental reservations. Military victory meant to him not only saving France from the Prussians but also rooting the republic in French affections. To evoke the myth of Valmy was one thing; to repeat the "miracle" of 1792 was another. Gambetta might measure up to Danton, but Danton had not been faced by a Moltke and a Bismarck. Within a few weeks Gambetta managed to patch together several makeshift armies. All were inadequately trained, equipped and led; yet they put up a surprisingly good fight in several skirmishes with the Prussians. But the futility of the enterprise grew increasingly clear to all but Gambetta and his loyal disciples. Europe would offer no aid; France's last trained army was lost when Marshal Bazaine, besieged in Metz, capitulated without a fight late in October;

in Paris the threat of starvation and epidemic grew ominous. The provisional government's will to resist rapidly withered away. Besides, some members of the government had been growing suspicious of Gambetta's flamboyant activities in the provinces. Jealous of his glamor and his popularity, they could easily persuade themselves that his goal was a kind of Robespierrist dictatorship. Late in January, over Gambetta's furious objections, Minister of Foreign Affairs Jules Favre approached Bismarck to seek an end to hostilities; and on the twenty-eighth, a three-weeks' armistice was signed. Some of Gambetta's entourage urged him to proclaim a dictatorship; he refused, but he angrily resigned his post in this government of capitulation.

The central purpose of the armistice, as both the French government and Bismarck saw it, was to allow time for a kind of plebiscite on the issue of war or peace. Orders went out at once to convoke the voters on February 8 for the election of a National Assembly, empowered to make peace in the name of the French people. The election proved to be the most curious one modern France has known. The campaign lasted only a week. Half the country was occupied by Prussian troops; public meetings were virtually impossible; mail service was in chaos; and any semblance of a nationally-organized campaign was out of the question. The electoral system of the Second Republic was resurrected for use; it provided for large multimember constituencies in which the voters would select a whole party list. Candidates had to be chosen hastily by impromptu local committees, often without informing the candidate that his name had been put up. The most eminent figures, or those best known locally, were usually chosen to head each ticket. One result was that Thiers was elected in twenty-six districts, Gambetta in ten.

More important still was the unique influence of local factors in the choice of candidates. That fact contributed to the election of a great many aristocrats; for in rural areas the *châtelain* was the man most generally known. But there was an added reason for this aristocratic resurgence: most of them ran on tickets ambiguously labelled "list of peace" or "peace and liberty," whereas their republican rivals were

275

viewed by the electors as war hawks. As a matter of fact, most moderate republican candidates were also eager to end the war; but the Gambettist agitation for a bitter-end fight clouded the issue and aided the antirepublicans. Although few of the latter openly campaigned as advocates of a restoration, their tactics turned the election into a sweeping monarchist triumph. When the new Assembly convened in Bordeaux a week later, it contained more than four hundred monarchists to only two hundred republicans and a handful of Bonapartists. Both Bismarck and the Government of National Defense had correctly judged the country's temper. Everywhere except in Paris and a few scattered provinces, the nation had voted for peace on any reasonable terms. Whether the nation had voted for a monarchical restoration was, however, much more ambiguous.

❧◦❧◦❧◦❧◦❧◦❧

The Assembly's first obligation (and its only clearly defined duty) was to make peace. It acted with dispatch; Adolphe Thiers was chosen as provisional executive and was sent at once to negotiate with Bismarck. The Prussian terms were severe; Thiers fought hard to get them softened, but with slight effect. His suggestion that Bismarck take part of Indo-China instead of Alsace was not even discussed. In the end Thiers had to accept a preliminary peace that required France to pay a war indemnity of five billion francs, that provided for the occupation of eastern France until payment was complete, and that transferred all of Alsace save Belfort, and one-third of Lorraine, to Germany. On March 1 the Assembly reluctantly approved this settlement, whereupon Gambetta and his followers, together with most of the deputies from Alsace and Lorraine, walked out of the hall and handed in their resignations. Gambetta, thoroughly disillusioned, went into voluntary exile in Spain, his career apparently finished. Six months later, however, he was to be back in politics, a successful candidate in a by-election. The most colorful phase of his career was over, but the more important part was still to come.

276

The Assembly's choice of Thiers as provisional executive had seemed to be dictated by the results of the elections. His prestige, however, only half-explained his success; he had also played his cards with remarkable skill. Although a lifelong Orleanist, he had carefully adopted a kind of neutralist position in politics after the fall of the empire, and he had cultivated friendships in all groups. When the Assembly convened, he seemed to stand above political divisions; and he encouraged this idea by urging the need for a political truce during the months of peacemaking and reconstruction. All groups therefore agreed unanimously to let him serve as a kind of combined president and premier. The monarchist majority reluctantly agreed to let the regime be called a provisional republic, partly because their plans for a restoration of the king were not yet quite mature, partly because they were relieved to let the republic be made responsible for signing a severe peace.

Early in March the Assembly voted to transfer the seat of government to Versailles. Before it could reconvene in the new temporary capital, it found its authority repudiated by Paris and several other major cities, and it was drawn into a large-scale civil war. The sixty-two-day episode of the Paris Commune in 1871, bloodier than any other civil clash in modern French history, was to leave a lasting imprint on the nation. On the hill of Montmartre the exotic Byzantine bulk of the Church of the Sacré Coeur rises today to commemorate the Commune's victims; it was built in the 1870's by French conservatives as a kind of atonement for the nation's sins. In the cemetery of Père Lachaise, the "wall of the federals" (i.e., Communards) serves as a shrine to the Commune's martyrs, who were executed there by government troops at the end of the revolt.

The bare facts of the affair are far simpler than the interpretations they have elicited. Paris since the armistice had been in a state of agitation that verged on collective neurosis. The excitement and tension of the siege culminated in an explosion of fury when the government suspended hostilities; and this sense of outrage was redoubled when the provinces voted massively for peace. Republican Paris also resented the monarchist character of the new Assembly, its decision to make Versailles the capital in place of Paris, and its prompt cancellation of such wartime emergency measures as moratoria on debts and rents and a daily dole to members of the National Guard. An explosion was almost inevitable; it came on March 18 when Thiers's government attempted to disarm the city by hauling away two hundred cannon that had been cast during the siege and had been paid for by public subscription. Angry mobs of Parisians dragged the cannon to the heights of Montmartre, drove off the Versailles troops, and lynched two generals unfortunate enough to be caught in the vicinity. Thiers refused either to strike back at once or to negotiate with the rebels; he withdrew all government officials and armed forces from the city, in preparation for a siege and an eventual full-scale showdown. This isolation of the rebellion threw control of it into the hands of the more extreme element, which proceeded to organize the city as a self-governing "Commune" and called for the conversion of all France into a decentralized federation of such free municipalities.

The second siege of Paris, this time by Frenchmen, lasted for nine weeks. By May 21 Thiers had collected enough troops to strike. Sympathizers inside the city let the attackers through the outer fortifications; the Communards dug in and fought back street by street. At the end of a week of bloody conflict, faced at last by imminent defeat, they set fire to most public buildings in the center of Paris: the Tuileries palace and the Hôtel de Ville were burned, the Louvre and Notre Dame barely saved. Little quarter was given on either side; the attackers summarily shot anyone caught with weapons, while the Communards executed a whole group of hostages headed by the archbishop of Paris. Twenty thousand died in the repression of the Commune — several times as many as in the June Days, more even than the number of Parisian victims in the Reign of Terror. Thousands of surviving Communards were deported to the penal islands, while others escaped into exile.

A whole tissue of legend has grown up about the Commune. Some years ago a Soviet journalist visiting Paris asked a small boy in a working-class quarter what he knew about the Commune. "Do you mean what they teach you in school," asked the child, "or what papa says?" "Papa" doubtless followed the line laid down by Karl Marx himself, according to which this was the first clear-cut case of the class struggle erupting into violence. This proletarian rising, the Communists argue, was doomed to failure because the proletariat still lacked maturity and adequate leadership; but it offered a foretaste of the future. They see the bourgeoisie, hysterical with fear and hate, indulging in shameless butchery; and they contend that the international bourgeoisie stood together in support of Thiers's effort to defend class privilege. Bismarck helped the government cause by releasing prisoners of war for Thiers's use; and Communist scholars have recently added the charge that the American minister in Paris hypocritically helped to undermine the Commune by posing as a mediator but acting secretly as a class enemy.

Non-Marxian historians, however, find little evidence for the view that this was a class-conscious proletarian rising, or that it was clearly socialist in inspiration. Its leadership included a few professed followers of Marx, but the impact of Proudhon's and Blanqui's ideas was far more direct. Its deeper spirit was egalitarian and anticlerical rather than socialist; its driving force was injured patriotism and anti-ruralism more than a desire for economic and social change. It is commonplace to point out that the Commune's most radical measure was to prohibit night work in bakeries, and that its leaders scrupulously respected the contents of the Bank of France. A victorious Commune would surely have gone much farther toward social change; even so, its prudence is suggestive of its spirit.

Non-Marxians would also challenge the Marxist interpretation of "bourgeois" motives in 1871. Probably Thiers was wrong in refusing to try for a negotiated settlement with the Commune's leaders, some of whom would have asked for nothing better. But if he was wrong, it does not follow that bourgeois hysteria and class hatred accounted for his error. One consideration that almost certainly motivated Thiers was his belief that negotiating with the rebels would be risky — that it might look like appeasement, might encourage the spread of rebellion to other cities, might bring on a nation-wide civil war. A probable second factor was more personal in nature. Thiers fancied himself something of a military genius, scarcely less brilliant than his hero Napoleon. His formula for mastering a rebellious Paris had long since been worked out; he had vainly proposed it to Louis Philippe in February, 1848, and again to Cavaignac in June of that year. His plan called for prompt evacuation of the city, a tight siege until rebel enthusiasm began to dim, and then a lightning stroke by the armies massed around the walls. The Commune finally offered this frustrated strategist a chance to try out his infallible recipe for victory. As for the severity of the repression that followed the victory, that, too, may represent something other than bourgeois blood lust. The Communards contributed something to this "hysteria" by their executions of hostages and their attempts to burn public monuments. Perhaps Thiers himself was too much affected by the news that the Communards, during the siege, had pulled down his house in Paris stone by stone.

No doubt a greater man than Thiers would have shown more mercy. After "bloody week" it is scarcely surprising that his name long remained anathema to Parisians; that he, almost alone among France's notable statesmen, never had a statue or monument raised to him in the city; that when the city council, after many decades, finally gave his name to a thoroughfare, it chose not a broad boulevard but a minor street one block long.

"The Commune," remarks one French historian, "is the key to our contemporary history." What he means, presumably, is that the episode left a kind of psychological scar; that it permanently divided republicans, embittered the workers, and intensified class conflict. There is much truth in this view; the long-range effects were deep and severe. There is a striking parallel between the Commune and the June Days of 1848, which also exacerbated social tensions and encouraged the radical workers to justify the use of violence as a political weapon. Yet there is also a curious contradiction between these two episodes. The June Days contributed to the early overthrow of the Second Republic by a strong man; the Commune, on the contrary, did not wreck the Third Republic, and it may even have helped it to survive for seventy years. To socially conservative Frenchmen, especially in the provinces, the government's victory suggested that the republic could be tough and effective and could handle serious threats to public order. Furthermore, republicanism was purged of its radical leaders by execution or exile and fell for a decade into the unchallenged grip of safe moderates like Favre, Simon, Grévy, and Ferry. The rooting of the republic in the countryside was certainly made easier and more rapid under such leadership. Perhaps the June Days might have had a similar effect if republican leadership after 1848 had been equal to that after 1871, and if there had been in 1848 no young and glamorous aspirant dictator on the scene, ready to take advantage of republican division and conservative fears. In 1871 Napoleon III was old and ill, his son young and untried; and luckily for the republic, no other substitute turned up.

∻⋙∘⋘∘∻⋙∘⋘∘∻⋙∘⋘∘

It may seem strange that an Assembly dominated by a large monarchist majority had not moved without delay to restore the king. The most plausible explanation is that the monarchists were divided into roughly equal and completely irreconcilable factions, the Legitimists and the Orleanists, each with its own rival pretender. Still, both dynasties had been so long out of power that all but a few diehards were ready to seek a compromise. Furthermore, a solution lay naturally at hand. The Bourbon pretender, the Comte de Chambord, was aging and childless; the Orleanist Comte de Paris was young and prolific. Nothing seemed simpler than to unite behind Chambord as king, with the Comte de Paris as heir apparent.

The latter was willing, but Chambord brutally scuttled the plan. In July, 1871, he returned to France for the first time since 1830, and he issued a manifesto calculated to upset all but the most hard-shelled Legitimists. He would accept the throne, he declared, only on his own terms; and those terms seemed to imply a return to the pre-1830

281

restoration era, if not to the old regime itself. His statement said nothing of a responsible ministry; it placed much stress on a kind of quasi-feudal decentralization; and it bluntly ruled out the tricolor flag in favor of the fleur-de-lis.

The issue of the flag, insignificant in itself, stood as a symbol of Chambord's whole outlook. He failed to realize that the tricolor had taken root in French affections and could not be so easily replaced. But more important still, Chambord's apparent intention to restore arbitrary, paternalistic rule outraged even the great bulk of the monarchists themselves. Indeed, one reason they had not moved more impulsively toward a restoration was that the monarchist politicians wanted the king to return on their terms, not on his. Most of them wanted a British-type monarch, symbol of order and stability but subject to parliament's domination. For the time being, therefore, they suspended their planning and contented themselves with Thiers's provisional rule.

Only a few days before Chambord's manifesto, another severe blow had been dealt the monarchists. More than a hundred vacancies existed in the Assembly, thanks to multiple elections of certain candidates in January and to resignations since then. All these by-elections were held simultaneously on July 2, with startling results. Ninety-nine seats were won by republican candidates, twelve by monarchists, and three by Bonapartists. A more complete reversal in six months' time would have been hard to imagine. In reality, however, the result did not imply a dramatic conversion of the nation from monarchism to republicanism. The most important factor was that since January the monarchists had lost their trump card: their demand for immediate peace. Indeed, the republicans managed to steal that card in July; they accused the monarchists of favoring an armed crusade to Italy to recover Rome for the Pope. The electoral outcome proved nevertheless that many Frenchmen were ready to accept a republic that existed and that was directed by a man like Thiers.

Thiers's position, meanwhile, had become almost unchallengeable. The period from 1871 to 1873 has sometimes been called "the reign of

Adolphe I." It was one of the rare interludes in modern French history when the republic has possessed a strong executive; Thiers combined in his person the functions of president and of premier, much as General de Gaulle was to do in the first biennium of the Fourth Republic. True, the Assembly had the right to replace Thiers at will, but in fact it dared not do so. His prestige in the country was too great, his skill as a parliamentary debater too awesome to encourage any critic to challenge him on the floor of the Assembly. Thiers was well aware of his strategic position and made the most of it. When the Assembly grew restive or balky, he talked of resignation and got his way. Thiers had spent a lifetime waiting to enjoy such untrammelled power; liberal in theory but authoritarian in temperament, he did not hesitate to use that power, and on the whole he used it well. He gave France almost two years of vigorous and effective leadership; if his "reign" redounded to his own glory, it also consolidated the emergent republic.

What Thiers managed to do was to restore some of the nation's shaken self-confidence and to convince Frenchmen that a republic could be safe and sane. He moved promptly to reorganize the army and to restore its morale. Within six months after utter defeat he was able to stage an impressive military parade through Paris; and within four years France's standing army was almost as large as that of Germany. He called on Frenchmen to restore the nation's credit by subscribing to two large bond issues; they responded by oversubscribing the first loan twofold, the second fourteenfold. By 1873 the indemnity was completely paid off, and French soil liberated eighteen months ahead of schedule. Much more questionable were his actions in the economic and social sphere, where he beat back proposals for an income tax and took the first steps away from Napoleon III's experiments in free trade. Both decisions reassured the propertied classes but had regrettable social effects and long-term political results.

Thiers's vigorous leadership and domineering manner won him support in the country but lost him friends in the Assembly. Many deputies muttered privately against "the dictator," and monarchist suspicions were aroused by indications that Thiers was flirting with the republicans. They accused him of conniving with the latter in by-elections and of undermining monarchist chances by refusing to install good monarchists as prefects. It was clear enough that Thiers was becoming reconciled to a Thierist republic. In 1872 he said so openly, thus repudiating his initial promise to remain politically neutral. But if the republicans continued to win in by-elections, it was not so much through Thiers's connivance as through their own shrewd electoral tactics. Sensing the temper of the country, they took care to choose moderate candidates; one of these even campaigned on the slogan, "I'm the biggest taxpayer in the district." They continued to accuse the monarchists of warmongering on behalf of the Pope and frightened voters by warning them of a subversive clerical conspiracy with its headquarters in the Vatican. So well organized was their whole campaign that it may suggest the existence of some kind of *sub rosa* republican central committee. If such a body existed, it is at least possible that Thiers was somehow in touch with it.

As the monarchist majority was steadily whittled away in by-elections, the angry and desperate monarchist faction decided that Thiers must be unseated and the king restored without further delay. Several months of planning and maneuvering went into the plot before they dared challenge the great man. Above all, they needed to have a substitute ready and willing to replace Thiers, and a candidate was not easy to find. They finally managed to persuade the commander of the army, Marshal MacMahon, to sacrifice himself for his country. In May, 1873, they manufactured an excuse to push Thiers out of the presidency and hastily substituted MacMahon before the latter could change his mind. One aspect of the change, scarcely noticed at the time, had long-range effects on the republic's political structure. Thiers had combined the functions of chief of state and prime minister; he had been a real presidential executive. MacMahon chose to confine himself to the role of chief of state and turned over the active task of forming and directing a cabinet to the ablest monarchist politician, the Duc de Broglie. This separation of formal from actual executive functions was to last as long as the Third Republic, and it was to reappear in the Fourth as well.

The monarchists' purpose, however, was not to perpetuate the republic, but to replace it without delay. This time they succeeded in arranging a meeting between the two pretenders and thought they had managed to work out a compromise on program and doctrine. So sanguine were they that they began to prepare the carriages in which King Henry V would enter Paris. Then, at the last minute, the Comte de Chambord again sabotaged the plan; once more he issued a kind of manifesto announcing that he would return only on his own terms, and under the fleur-de-lis flag. The monarchist leaders, convinced that the country would reject such a symbol, and committed themselves to the ideal of divine right of parliament rather than divine right of kings, abandoned their plans in disgust. The only hope, they decided, was to wait until death removed this stubborn Bourbon. To give themselves an adequate margin, they voted MacMahon a seven-year term as president. As if to spite them, Chambord lived on until 1883, long after the chance of a monarchist restoration was utterly dead.

Chambord managed to furnish one more evidence of his quixotic temper when, late in 1873, he sought to carry out the restoration in his own way. Secretly he re-entered France and went to Versailles, hoping that MacMahon might be persuaded to appear with him before the Assembly and to call on the latter body to acclaim Chambord as sovereign. The marshal, to Chambord's indignation, refused to go along on the ground that such an act would be illegal. Chambord waited vainly for several days, then slipped back into exile with the bitter remark: "I thought I would be dealing with a Constable of France; instead, I found a captain of gendarmes." Thiers remarked that Chambord ought to go down in history as the French George Washington, the real founder of the republic.

Chambord's stubborn blindness has inspired a number of fanciful theories about his motivation. The most plausible explanation roots it in the curiously isolated life he had led since childhood. For thirty years he had lived in an Austrian chateau, surrounded by loyal émigré aristocrats who were nourished on illusions rather than reality. These retainers had convinced themselves and Chambord that the French masses still yearned in almost mystical fashion for their true sovereign. Chambord himself was marked by a deeply pious and mystical strain, a conviction that God would eventually open the eyes of Frenchmen. That such a man should have chosen to call himself Henry V was truly ironical; no one could have been more different from the last Henry, that genius of flexible opportunism.

The problem of giving France some kind of permanent or quasi-permanent political structure could not be postponed much longer. In 1873 the Assembly set up a committee to prepare a constitutional draft. It began in leisurely fashion by collecting and analyzing all republican constitutions of both past and present, in an effort to find those principles that ensured durability. But speedier action became essential as the trend in by-elections continued to flow toward the republicans.

Finding a majority for any draft was, however, not so easy; for already the Assembly's simple monarchist-republican-Bonapartist division was evolving into a more complex pattern of factions that foreshadowed a party system. Among the monarchists, two principal groups could be distinguished: (1) an extreme right-wing faction called the *chevau-légers* or "light cavalry," rigid and stubborn supporters of the Comte de Chambord's ideals; (2) the Right-Center, larger, more flexible, and mainly Orleanist by tradition. On the republican side there were three subdivisions: (1) the Republican Union (popularly called "Radicals") on the extreme left, led by Gambetta and marked by a sectarian Jacobin and egalitarian spirit; (2) the Republican Left, containing the bulk of moderate bourgeois republicans like Grévy, Ferry, Simon; (3) the Left-Center, a smaller faction of ex-Orleanists like Thiers and Casimir Périer who had recently crossed the line from monarchism. There was still a handful of Bonapartist deputies, but the death of Napoleon

III in 1873 had cut them adrift from any firm policy or leadership. Thereafter they entered into an uneasy coalition with the monarchists.

The deepest line of cleavage no longer ran down the middle of the Assembly, separating monarchists from republicans. More significant were those that divided the diehard *chevau-légers* from the Right-Center, and (to a lesser degree) the diehard Radicals from the moderate republicans. In other words, there was emerging a strong tendency toward a coalition of the center groups — toward what the jargon of French politics was later to call a policy of *concentration*. From the 1870's onward this often-frustrated impulse toward *concentration* was to be one of the most marked and enduring aspects of French political life. Its first product was to be the constitution of 1875, a curious compromise document that was republican in name but monarchist in form. A patchwork affair, little more than a framework of basic law, it established a two-house legislature, a cabinet responsible to that legislature, and a presidency designed for easy conversion into constitutional kingship.

Some historians have argued that the compromise of 1875 was the product of conscious and selfish scheming on the part of France's most powerful social class — the well-to-do upper bourgeoisie that had risen to power and affluence during the Great Revolution and had dominated politics and society through the nineteenth century. These families, it is alleged, consciously or instinctively spotted some of their leading representatives in both the monarchist and the republican movements, so that the entrenched social elite could retain control no matter what the form of government. The most intriguing bit of circumstantial evidence was the link between monarchist Right-Center and republican Left-Center factions in the Assembly; the parliamentary leaders of those two factions had married sisters and lived in twin houses with adjoining gardens in Paris. The thesis is plausible, however, rather than provable. Right-Center and Left-Center were separated by a genuine difference in principle — the issue of monarchy versus republic. Yet in practice, their common outlook could transcend that basic difference. Both groups held firmly to the parliamentary system and to libertarian

287

ideals; no Machiavellian scheming was needed to show them that the kind of regime they desired could exist in either monarchical or republican form.

The chief problem was how to bring the moderate Republican Left faction into association with the two Centers; for without the moderates' votes, no constitution could be adopted. That problem was easily solved, however, for the moderates likewise wanted a parliamentary system operated in a libertarian spirit. The label "republic" attached to the constitution sufficed to win their adherence. More surprising and more important was the decision of Gambetta and most of his Radical supporters to rally to the constitution. Until 1875 the Radicals had steadily denied that this Assembly had any right to draft a constitution. Besides, they were vigorously opposed to the kind of constitution that the center groups would support. The Radicals' ideal was the constitution of 1793, concentrating all power in a one-house assembly rather than scattering authority through several balanced organs of government. Nevertheless, Gambetta refused in the end to embark on a course of intransigent (and probably sterile) opposition to the constitution of 1875. He persuaded most of the Radical group that the new system was the best they could get at the moment. At least it would continue to bear the republican label; and within it, the Radicals might continue to broaden their following until some day the system might be amended to fit the Radical ideal. Part of the Radical group resisted; led by Louis Blanc inside the Assembly and Georges Clemenceau outside it, this faction clung to its intransigence and denounced Gambetta as a turncoat. The Republican Union split permanently into factions labelled "Radical" and "Opportunist"; after some years the latter group gradually merged with the Republican Left of Grévy and Simon.

Gambetta's action astonished many Frenchmen who had thought of him as a noisy and dangerous demagogue, a kind of aspiring dictator. They had failed to realize that temperament often outweighs ideology. Gambetta, by origin and inclination, was a Jacobin and an egalitarian; but by temperament and instinct, he was a moderate and gradualist.

Beneath his flamboyant language, there were deeper traits of flexibility
or "realism." His enemies believed that his flexibility was mere hypocrisy, that he was a schemer ready to sell his principles in return for
power. In fact, he was a man who liked to remark that "politics is the
art of the possible," and who chose the label "Opportunist" to illustrate
his belief that each advance must await the opportune moment. Gambetta was convinced that the republic, if it was to endure, had first to
be formally established and must not be made the subject of argument
for a decade. He believed that it would have to be operated cautiously
until the mass of voters were reassured as to its stability and balance.
Only then could the ideal of equality be implemented, in gradual
fashion. If the republicans remained deeply divided, if the Radicals
boycotted the new system and sought to destroy it, he believed that the
outcome would be disastrous; another Bonaparte or some other authoritarian substitute would find the way paved for him. By his new Opportunist line, Gambetta contributed as much as Thiers to the doctrine that
the republic — at the outset, at least — must be conservative or must
perish. It can be argued, too, that he contributed as much as Thiers to
the consolidation of the Third Republic. A different policy might have
led the republicans, like the monarchists, to cancel themselves out by
internal division.

❧◦❧◦❧◦❧

Its work done at last, the National Assembly adjourned on the last
day of 1875 to make way for the new constitutional system. Its
members could look back on their five years of service with good consciences. Blind though they were to social and economic issues, they
had achieved much in the political realm. Many of the Assembly's
abler leaders were destined to play leading roles over the next two
decades.

Four years still had to elapse, however, before the republicans could
get control of the new republic. The presidency was safely monarchist
until 1880, when MacMahon's term was due to expire. The new Senate,

289

as expected, was dominated by monarchists as a result of the system of indirect election designed for just that purpose. In each constituency, senators were chosen by an electoral college made up primarily of delegates from the various local councils, (notably the municipal councils). Each municipality (or "commune") provided one delegate, no matter what its population; so Paris with two million inhabitants and St.-Jean-du-Doigt with a few hundred enjoyed a curious kind of equality. This system of weighting the vote in favor of small-town and village France ensured that the Senate would always be a rural body, inclined to check what rural France regarded as the dangerous passions and impulses of the cities. The system also seemed to ensure right-wing control of the Senate, since most rural towns and villages were traditionally administered by the local aristocrats or notables.

The republicans' best hope at the outset was to win control of the new lower house, elected by universal manhood suffrage. There had been no real nation-wide test of public sentiment since 1871; even the most sanguine republican could not be too confident. Gambetta, in an effort to maximize republican chances, proposed that all republicans pool their strength by agreeing on a single candidate in each district. His proposal failed, and for a quite simple reason: any attempt to unify the republicans implied a leader, and the obvious leader would be Gambetta himself. He stood midway between Moderates and Radicals; he almost alone possessed a touch of charisma, the traits of popular leadership. Too many republicans, however, disliked this rumpled bohemian, or were jealous and suspicious of his demagogic flair. Rather than accept his leadership, the republicans chose to go to battle in three separate phalanxes: Moderates, Opportunists, and Radicals.

Perhaps Gambetta might have achieved his goal of republican unity, in spite of jealousy and suspicion, if the National Assembly had endowed the Third Republic with a different electoral procedure. One of the Assembly's final acts had been to set up the system used in most elections from 1876 to 1936: it provided for small single-member constituencies, with a run-off ballot if no candidate received a clear majority on the first ballot. The monarchists chose this scheme as

290

likely to be profitable to them; it would give local notables a clear advantage. The republicans had tried unsuccessfully to perpetuate the system used in 1849 and 1871, with large multimember districts and no run-off ballot. The latter system, if preserved, might have prevented the fragmentation of the republicans into rival factions at the very start and might thus have given modern France a quite different party structure. It might also have elevated Gambetta into the dominant role in the years after 1876.

In spite of their division, the republicans won a decisive victory in 1876; the new Chamber of Deputies contained 340 republicans and only 155 monarchists or Bonpartists. No one, it seemed, could any longer doubt the nation's conversion to the republican ideal. Gambetta, who had dominated the electoral campaign, was the logical choice to form the new regime's first cabinet; but MacMahon refused even to call him in, choosing instead a colorless centrist named Dufaure. When Dufaure was overthrown a few months later, MacMahon continued to ignore Gambetta, this time in favor of the moderate Jules Simon. MacMahon's monarchist advisers acted thus with an ulterior motive: they hoped to anger Gambetta, split the republicans, and force Simon's moderate group to turn to the monarchists as partners in the new government. They underestimated their enemy. If Gambetta had been a small-minded man, moved by personal ambition and resentment, the scheme might have succeeded; but instead, he announced his loyal support of the Simon cabinet on major issues of policy, and he lived up to that promise.

The new premier's task was an almost hopeless one. Caught between a republican Chamber and a monarchist Senate, he could not avert serious friction on any important policy decision. Simon was well suited to the task; his flexibility approached the level of genius. For a few months he managed to straddle with great skill, but a whole series of pressing issues demanded action. The monarchists, for example, were urging a foreign policy of aid to the Vatican in its contest with the Italian state; and the republicans were agitating for legislation to unshackle the press. MacMahon's advisers began to urge him to find an excuse to unload Simon and to put a good monarchist in his place. A crisis was made more certain by the new constitution's ambiguities about the proper role of the president. MacMahon's conception of the presidential prerogatives was, on the whole, much like that of Charles de Gaulle eighty years later. The president, MacMahon believed, was intended to be the equal of parliament; he ought to be able to choose his ministers freely, without toadying to parliament's wishes; if a clash should occur, it would be his privilege to dissolve the Chamber and let the voters decide the issue. Only if the will of the people were made absolutely clear would the president be obligated to retreat. The republicans, on the other hand, held that the president was supposed to be a kind of formal figurehead; that he was obligated to appoint a ministry acceptable to the Chamber; that he had no right to set himself up as the rival and the equal of parliament. Both interpretations were plausible, since the constitution itself was so unclear; and there was no supreme court to decide the issue.

MacMahon grew increasingly irritated at Simon's straddling, and his monarchist cronies fanned that irritation. On May 16, 1877, he decided to act, as he believed he had a right to do: he sent Simon a sharply critical letter that virtually invited the premier's resignation. After a night's sleep MacMahon thought better of his impulse and sent a messenger to recover the letter before it reached the recipient. Unluckily, Simon had arrived at his office early that morning; he read the letter and immediately submitted his resignation.

The outcome was total deadlock between president and Chamber of Deputies. MacMahon nominated a monarchist as premier; the Chamber refused to approve him and announced that it would engage in a kind of sit-down strike until the president named an acceptable premier. MacMahon struck back by dissolving the Chamber (with the consent of the compliant Senate) and called on the voters to settle the dispute. But the president, prodded by his advisers, was not willing merely to state his case and let the voters have free choice. In the campaign that ensued, he used every kind of pressure to influence the outcome. He toured the country indefatigably as chief campaigner; his figure on horseback appeared on wall posters everywhere; he suspended or transferred seventy-seven of the eighty-seven prefects, substituting men of "correct" opinions; he accepted the active aid of priests and bishops who spoke from the pulpit in favor of monarchist candidates.

Whether MacMahon's activities helped or hurt his cause is hard to say. He was not an effective campaigner; indeed, his slow wit and bumbling comments made him an easy target for republican ridicule and quickly became part of France's political folklore. The church's unwise interference also boomeranged; republican orators frightened their hearers with predictions of a government run by the men in black. Furthermore, the campaign drove all republican groups together; for a few brief months France had its nearest approach to a two-party system. Gambetta stumped the country as chief spokesman; Thiers was put forward as the republicans' symbol and as MacMahon's putative successor. Thiers died midway through the campaign, but the republicans managed to use his prestige even in death; they staged a great public funeral for the grand old man, with the republican deputies, headed by Gambetta, walking bareheaded behind the coffin.

"We departed 363," Gambetta liked to declaim, "we will return 400." The republican victory proved to be less sweeping; indeed, their numbers fell from 363 to 320. But their margin in the Chamber and in the country was nevertheless clear-cut, and it had been won against the monarchists' best efforts. Some of MacMahon's cronies urged him to turn to force and to use the army to sweep away the republic; but his legal scruples were too great, and a number of monarchists shared those scruples. Gambetta summoned him to "give in or get out"; he gave in, accepted the republican interpretation of the president's proper role, and proceeded to name a premier acceptable to the Chamber. He was increasingly irritated, however, at his powerless role and at serving a regime that he detested. The final blow came in 1879, when partial elections to the Senate brought such sweeping republican victories that the latter achieved control of the upper house. This success was the most remarkable achievement of the decade, for it meant that the republicans had somehow infiltrated hundreds of small town and village councils and had taken control away from the older notables who had always run local affairs. Evidently some effective political action had been occurring at the grass-roots level through the 1870's; the result had been, in the words of one historian, "a quiet village revolution."

Within a month MacMahon found an excuse to resign; "I've had enough toads to swallow," he remarked to friends. The republicans promptly chose as his successor the moderate Jules Grévy, an able but colorless career politician. That choice was consciously symbolic; one of Grévy's chief claims to eminence was the fact that in 1848 he had sat in the Constituent Assembly and had proposed that the Second Republic get along with no president at all. Such a man was unlikely to emphasize the potential prerogatives of his office.

The so-called *seize mai* crisis of 1877 has been called the decisive incident that converted the mass of Frenchmen to republicanism. Until that time a vote for a republican candidate might not mean very much of a commitment. But in 1877 the issues were clear, the chips were down; every voter had to choose between one course or another. Perhaps it would be more accurate to say, however, that the *seize mai* did not convert Frenchmen but rather furnished proof that the conversion had already occurred.

The long-range effects of the 1877 crisis are clear and can be easily summarized. It ended for many decades the attempt to make the presidency a powerful office capable of balancing parliament's authority. It weakened the cabinet as well as the president, for it deprived the premier of the important right to request the dissolution of parliament. Dissolution remained theoretically possible, but in practice it was never again used in France until 1955; MacMahon had poisoned it by giving it an odor of antirepublicanism. The crisis tended to weaken the parties as well, by contributing to the development of flabby and undisciplined groups. Without the use of dissolution, deputies were safely ensconced in their seats for four years and could not be brought in line by party whips threatening them with electoral disaster. In addition, the crisis further embittered France's religious feud; there followed almost immediately a showdown fight over church influence

294

in education. A shorter-term effect of the *seize mai* affair was that it interrupted the parliamentary trend toward a *concentration des centres;* it drove a wedge between moderate monarchists and moderate republicans, who might otherwise have been inclined to collaborate in coalition governments. The old line of cleavage down the middle of the Chamber was deepened and broadened by the events of 1877; the effects were not to be fully overcome until the 1890's.

The year 1879 thus marked the end not only of a decade but also of an epoch in the Third Republic's history. In outward appearance and in social and economic structure, France had changed little in that decade. Yet a kind of divide had been crossed, irrevocably this time. The era of experiment and uncertainty was over; France was permanently a republic.

NINETEEN

How beautiful was the Republic under the Empire!
ALPHONSE AULARD *(1885)*

The Opportunist Republic, 1879–1899

The abdication of MacMahon in 1879 completed the process of putting the republicans in control of the republic. For the next two decades, almost without a break, political power remained in the hands of the moderate or libertarian wing of republicans — the element currently called Opportunists and composed of a fusion of the old Republican Left with the Gambettist ex-Radicals.

In retrospect, it is hard to resist the sentiment that the Opportunist era represents one of the great wasted opportunities of modern French history. The monarchists, except for brief periods, were no longer strong enough to threaten the regime; the Radicals on the other wing could not hope to dislodge the Opportunists but only to share power at best. Two things might have been accomplished by the Opportunist leaders, if they had been men of imagination and foresight. In the political sphere, they might have given the republic a backbone and sinews by developing a vigorous executive and a more stable party system; in the social-economic sphere, they might have taken at least some cautious steps toward social reform and economic modernization.

296

The Opportunists did neither, and France ever since has been paying the penalty for their shortsightedness. Instead, the Opportunists wasted most of their energies in what might be called France's last religious war. That feud between clericals and anticlericals poisoned the atmosphere for a generation and left a heritage of bitterness that has not been entirely dissipated to this day.

To some degree, the Opportunists' error was embedded in their view of man and the world, in their libertarian spirit and their somewhat arid rationalism. Their prejudices, their preconceptions, left little room for an understanding of the forces at work in France and Europe — forces that would require men to adapt their institutions to a more complex age. There were partial exceptions: Gambetta, for example, did recognize the need for an effective political system, with an executive that could act and with a majority that would support its action. His goal continued to be the fusion of all republicans into one large and coherent party that could defend the regime against its enemies; and he still thought that it could be achieved through the use of an electoral system based on multimember districts. But Gambetta also continued to be his own worst enemy; his political rivals were too jealous, or too suspicious of his aims, to adopt his electoral reform plan or to let him take power as premier. To some extent, it was a case of men without glamor fearing and resenting one who possessed it; mediocrity, someone has said, tends to seek its own level. To a colorless and routine-minded politician like President Grévy, Gambetta's free and easy ways and flamboyant personality were anathema. Grévy's values were reflected in his comment to the director of the annual art exhibition, who had told him: "No extraordinary paintings this year, but a good average." "A good average!" responded the president, "Just what a democracy ought to have." Although Grévy posed as a do-nothing president, he was an old hand at manipulating affairs behind the scenes; he managed to keep Gambetta out of the premiership for almost three years and helped to block Gambetta's political program.

The need for governmental action in the social and economic

spheres was even more alien to the Opportunist leaders. Gambetta himself asserted: "There is no social question — there are only social questions." The idea of state action to alleviate misery, to correct inequities, or to modify the structure of the nation's economy collided head-on with the Opportunists' libertarian principles. Such heresies they associated with the name of Napoleon III, or with the gradually reviving reds on the left. Gambetta and his wing of the Opportunists did continue to exalt the little man as symbol and spirit of democracy; Gambetta announced the emergence of what he called *les nouvelles couches* — new layers of society that deserved a share of power. But the little man to Gambetta was not the underprivileged and increasingly discontented proletarian but the small independent operator — peasant, artisan, shopkeeper. To this kind of Frenchman, the threat of oppression came not so much from big business as from the state or, perhaps, from foreign competitors. His ideal, therefore, was high protection and invertebrate government.

The Opportunists were not alone in reflecting the prejudices of the little Frenchman; their Radical rivals were not much more sincerely committed to a program of social and economic action. The Radicals did talk of a mild income tax and of laws to protect labor; but few of them showed any crusading zeal for reform. No republican group in that era had any real understanding of, or interest in, social or economic issues. Only the Catholic paternalists, the declining Bonapartists, and the emerging socialists took such problems seriously.

❧◦❦◦❧◦❦◦❧◦❦

These were the negative factors that explain why the Opportunists wasted their two decades in power. But there is another side to the problem. The political elite of the time underacted in the social and economic sphere; why did it overact in the religious sphere? What produced its excessive, almost neurotic stress on the clerical problem as the fundamental issue of the age?

In a sense, the religious conflict was an almost inevitable product of France's past. Any country with an old and deep Catholic heritage, and with a church that once possessed a unique power role, must face severe stresses in a secularizing age. Memories of the good old days were likely to attract some Catholics and to frighten most non-Catholics. But this factor alone does not suffice to explain the intensity of the conflict in the late nineteenth century. For a religious war there must be not one faith but two — faiths that are militant, hostile, and mutually exclusive. That kind of rivalry developed in France after the mid-nineteenth century; and each camp was dominated by a loud extremist minority too bigoted to think of compromise. Catholicism's rival in this era of conflict was the dogma that chose to label itself positivism.

Positivism's impact in France was first felt in the 1850's, but it arrived in full strength after 1870. The trend was not merely French; this was part of a general European movement toward materialism and scientism, one that spread as far eastward as Russia. But it took its most virulent form in France — perhaps because the founder of positivism was a Frenchman, perhaps as a reaction against the excesses of French romanticism, or perhaps because French republicans were most eagerly searching for a system, a doctrine, a faith. They found that system in Auguste Comte's teachings, with their vast panorama of human history moving upward through successive stages of superstition to a utopian future. Comte taught the inevitability of progress as men managed to strip away those remnants of superstition called theology and metaphysics, and as they turned instead to a positive approach through science. Man, said Comte, was like any other animal the product of physical, chemical, and biological factors; and the laws of his behavior and of social organization could be discovered through scientific method.

There was little in all this that was really new; in most ways, it amounted to a restatement and elaboration of eighteenth-century ideas, with a touch of evolutionism grafted on. Its impact resulted from the fact that it came at just the right time to find a ready-made clientele. What French republicans found here was a consistent and complete set of ideas, a philosophical substructure, for their materialist and agnostic leanings. It supported their optimistic hope that men, through science, could remake the world. Most republican leaders, whether Opportunists or Radicals, absorbed some of it even when they did not swallow it whole. Gambetta expressed a generalized view when he declared soon after 1870, "What we propose to do is to apply positivism to the political order."

Positivism thus developed into a militant faith in brutal opposition to Catholicism. And like the latter faith, it had its organized arm, its militant counter-church, in Freemasonry. Until the mid-nineteenth century French Masonry had been relatively mild and tolerant in outlook; its spirit was deistic, not agnostic. The positivist temper produced a basic change; Masonry was rapidly converted into a crusading order dedicated to rooting out clericalism. The organization was never very large; estimates range from 24,000 to 50,000 members at the end of the century. But its rolls included an important proportion of republican politicians; by 1900 almost every Radical deputy was a Freemason. More crucial still, most local republican party officials, whether Radical or Opportunist, were members of a lodge.

The most eager converts to the new faith and its new church came from the white-collar strata: there were doctors, pharmacists, notaries, village schoolmasters in profusion. The classic caricature of the type appeared in Flaubert's *Madame Bovary;* his pharmacist M. Homais was the narrowest of bigots, whose prejudices were covered by a thin veneer of learning. Georges Clemenceau's father, a country doctor, was a representative figure; he used to tell his son: "Remember, Georges, there is only one thing worse than a bad priest — and that's a good priest." A lunatic fringe of anticlericals found Masonry too mild and organized Freethinkers' associations with chapters in many villages. On "so-called Good Friday," they arranged banquets at which they "avenged themselves on clericalism by stuffing themselves with sausage."

Religious wars, as earlier observed, require two rival sets of fanatics. So it was in France: a segment of Catholics in this era played into the hands of their critics, and the Vatican contributed to the strife.

Pope Pius IX, after the revolutionary upheaval of 1848–49, was transmuted into the epitome of everything the positivist spirit execrated in the church; Vatican policy in his day took on a strongly intolerant and obstructionist cast. Meanwhile the Christian democratic current within the French church almost dried up after 1848; its importance had been temporarily exaggerated by the revolutionary crisis, and it returned to obscurity for several more decades. In place of these left-wing Catholics who had seemed to represent the new voice of the church in 1848, there emerged as a more influential spokesman one of the most fanatical and violent agitators French Catholicism has ever produced: the journalist Louis Veuillot.

Veuillot, a self-educated commoner, had been raised an unbeliever. Suddenly converted while still a young man, he became overnight a superheated zealot. In 1842 he became editor of the Paris newspaper *L'Univers,* and for the next forty years his voice thundered out from that lay pulpit. Veuillot was a rabid hater of the Christian democratic tendency in the church and of liberals and compromisers of all sorts. Absolutely intolerant of error, he "wielded the crucifix like a bludgeon, and mixed vitriol with his holy water." His only regret about the Reformation, someone remarked, was that John Huss had not been burned sooner, and Luther not at all. He crusaded vindictively against the republicans, all of whom he considered to be antisocial and fomenters of disorder. The idea of social reform was to him a dangerous delusion. "Some men," he wrote, "must work hard and live badly. Misery is a law of God to which they must submit. Society needs slaves." When the church won victories (as in the Falloux Law of 1850), Veuillot was rarely satisfied; what he wanted was not a partial but a complete success — in this case, complete and unrestricted control of education by the church.

Veuillot's campaigns served ideally to encourage the fears of the anticlericals, who suspected that whatever churchmen might say, their real aim was to get a stranglehold on both education and politics. And unfortunately for French civil peace, the Vatican for a generation threw its weight behind the Veuillot faction. Such behavior confounded those liberal Catholics and mild anticlericals who hoped for a compromise, who sought some middle way between the spread of complete materialism on the one hand and a revival of a kind of medieval theocracy on the other.

Veuillot's influence was strengthened in the 1870's by the remarkable rise of a new religious order, the Assumptionist Fathers. This order, though founded in 1845, had been little heard of until after 1870; then it suddenly rocketed into prominence and played a first-rank role until expelled from France in 1901. Unlike the older monastic orders, the Assumptionists had no glorious past and produced no great thinkers; yet they put a deep mark on French Catholicism for two generations. Their spirit was mystical, emotional, fanatical; their purpose was to appeal to the masses through the more primitive emotions. Their remarkable success is not easy to explain. In part it grew out of the shock of national disaster in 1871; the Assumptionists called on Frenchmen to recognize that defeat was a natural product of seventy-five years of error and sin. They took the lead in a national campaign to collect funds for the building of the Church of the Sacré Coeur, as a sign of the nation's penitence. They turned, too, to mass action through modern methods. The practice of pilgrimages to holy places, moribund since the end of the Middle Ages, was resuscitated by them in the 1870's. Aided by the railway system (which was persuaded to grant special low rates to pilgrims), they were able to rally mammoth crowds from all parts of France. They moved also into popular journalism: they founded a daily called *La Croix*, to be sold at low cost and to be read by the common man. Its growth was phenomenal; soon it had over a hundred provincial editions and claimed a circulation of more than a half-million. Its tone resembled that of Veuillot's *L'Univers*, but its audience was far wider. To most parish priests in rural areas, it was the sole source of contemporary truth, as implicitly accepted on matters of politics as was the Vatican on matters of faith and morals.

This Assumptionist-led agitation of the 1870's was something new in scope and spirit; France had known nothing like it for a half-century at least. It was enough to frighten many good republicans, who in turn could use it to terrify the peasantry with threats that feudal privileges were in danger of being restored. All this was made still worse by the *clerical extremists' efforts to influence French foreign policy. The republicans were convinced (or claimed to be convinced) that a powerful subversive group was seeking to get a stranglehold on the French state, with a view to using it in the service of a foreign potentate.

By no means all French Catholics or freethinkers were such bigoted obscurantists as Veuillot and Homais. Within the church both the tiny Christian democratic and the larger liberal Catholic current persisted, and both were appalled at the extremes of the new Assumptionist spirit. Thus the ablest monarchist politician, the Duc de Broglie, refused to read *La Croix* or to join in Assumptionist-sponsored pilgrimages; he held that religion's place was in the heart and home, not in public places. Among republican freethinkers, too, there was an important moderate current. Some anticlerical republicans found themselves dissatisfied with positivism and agnosticism and sought to fill their spiritual need by turning to Protestantism. A neo-Kantian revival led by the philosopher Renouvier asserted the idea that beneath the world of the senses there existed an ultimate reality, too deep to be comprehended by human reason and the scientific method. Still others, like Gambetta, remained freethinkers yet felt the need for some kind of reconciliation with Catholicism — a kind of peaceful coexistence, perhaps. They remained essentially anticlerical nevertheless, for they believed that the church should possess no special position in education or in the state.

But the extremists in both camps were louder and more aggressive; they looked on the moderates with suspicion as "soft," as fellow travellers of the enemy. Their mutual provocation was to dominate the political life of France from the 1870's to the end of the century, and to some degree even until the First World War. It is not surprising that the first years after the republicans' conquest of the republic were filled with a bitter squabble over church influence in education. Out of this controversy emerged a series of laws adopted piecemeal from 1879 to 1886, and usually called the Ferry Laws after their cabinet sponsor, Jules Ferry.

＊ᔐｏᗭ＊ ＊ᔐｏᗭ＊ ＊ᔐｏᗭ＊

France's educational system on the eve of the Ferry reforms consisted of two parallel sets of schools — Catholic and public — at every level from primary to university. In the Catholic system the primary schools were oldest and deepest-rooted; they had existed since prerevolutionary times. In many villages the Catholic primary school had no competitor. At the secondary level Catholic *collèges* (high schools) had spread rapidly since their legalization by the Falloux Law in 1850; they now attracted almost half the male secondary students in France, and they almost monopolized secondary education for girls. Catholic universities, on the other hand, were new and weak; they had been authorized only in 1875, by one of the last legislative acts of the rightist National Assembly.

The more rabid anticlericals aimed at nothing less than the suppression of all church-controlled schools and the establishment of a state monopoly of education. They were convinced that Catholic schools were "mental incubators" designed to breed antirepublican and antimodernist ideas; and they further alleged that educational standards there were deplorably low. Ferry and most of the Opportunist leaders were not ready to go so far, at least in the foreseeable future. Their goal was not to outlaw Catholic schools but rather to expand the rival public-school system. They were determined, too, to secularize or "laicize" the public schools by rooting out religious teaching and clerical influence therein.

That influence had been strong since 1850 (except in the universities, the chief strongholds of positivism). In all public primary and secondary schools religious education was required by the Falloux Law; and in addition, parish priests were ensured a kind of ex-officio membership on local public-school boards. Even more important, many public-school teachers were members of the Catholic teaching orders, for the state simply did not recruit or train enough secular teachers to do the job.

The impact of the Ferry Laws was slightest at the university level; Catholic institutions of higher learning were merely denied the right to call themselves universities and had to be satisfied with the label "Catholic Institute" instead. It was the primary and secondary schools that felt the full force of the Ferry reforms. The new legislation outlawed religious training in the public schools and substituted civic education. It denied to members of Catholic orders the right to teach in public schools after a five-year transitional period, which would presumably give the state time to train replacements. The Chamber provided funds to build many new public schools, especially for girls, and to create vastly expanded facilities for teacher training. A normal school to prepare primary teachers was to be established in every department; and two advanced normal schools were set up in the suburbs of Paris to train those who would teach the teachers.

The impact of this new public educational system on French attitudes and behavior is not easy to estimate, but there is good reason to believe that it was a major shaping force over the next half-century. The centralized, standardized nature of the system tended to make for uniformity rather than variety—uniformity not only in teaching methods but also in teachers' attitudes. Catholics were convinced from the outset that the public schools would be consciously converted into mental incubators breeding materialism and positivism. Whether or not this was the conscious purpose, it was, in many cases, the result of the Ferry Laws. Village teachers, already inclined toward the positivist outlook, frequently became the self-appointed challengers of the village priests. Someone has described them, ironically but not inaccurately, as a "positivist priesthood," or as "the black hussars of the republic." Another consequence of the highly centralized teacher-training system was that it tended to indoctrinate each generation of elementary teachers with a kind of standard outlook. That first generation of 1885–1914 was militantly patriotic and infected the children in its charge with the same enthusiasm. The dominant attitude of the next generation of teachers, between the wars, was to be quite the opposite — pacifist and internationalist, skeptical and even cynical. The *instituteurs* of France both reflected the temper of their times and reinforced that temper.

Although French Catholics feared that the Ferry Laws were only a first step toward complete suppression of church schools, no such action followed. Indeed, the state even failed to enforce all the provisions of the Ferry Laws. When the five-year transitional period ended, many Catholic brothers and nuns continued to teach in public schools; indeed, some were still there a half-century later. This lax enforcement may indicate a growing tolerance among republican leaders. But it also suggests that the republican politicians might have been wiser if they had drafted the laws in milder compromise form. The effect of the bitter debate over the Ferry Laws was to encourage the extremists on both sides, and thus to keep the religious war aflame.

Although the school laws dwarfed other political issues during the early 1880's, two other significant episodes also marked those years. One was Gambetta's brief fling at the premiership; the other was Ferry's sponsorship of colonial expansion.

The Gambetta cabinet, though a complete fiasco, was notable as the last serious attempt to check the trend toward a weak executive and a flabby party system. If successful, Gambetta might have converted the Third Republic into something more like the parliamentary system of Great Britain. The republic was still new, and political habits not yet so deeply rooted as to resist all change. Gambetta's enemies, notably President Grévy, had managed to keep the great tribune out of power for almost three years after the republican triumph of 1879; but the parliamentary elections of 1881 forced their hand. The Opportunists won their greatest victory ever; with some three hundred and fifty seats, they possessed a clear majority in the Chamber. Monarchist strength was reduced to fewer than a hundred seats, while the Radicals

on the left had almost the same number. Among the Opportunists there
could be no doubt that Gambetta stood out as the most forceful leader,
the only man of really national stature.

Gambetta's purpose, as he prepared to take power for the first time
since 1870–71, was not to avenge himself on his jealous rivals, but
rather to win them over to his cause. He proposed to include every
republican ex-premier, every important figure in political life, in his
cabinet. He himself proposed to assume a new kind of role, as prime
minister without portfolio; unlike his predecessors, he would not combine his post with the interior ministry or the foreign ministry but
would undertake to direct and coordinate all governmental activities.
In discussing his hopes with his friends, he revealed an even more
ambitious goal; he hoped not only to give the republican system vigor
and authority, but also to reconcile the deep divisions that marred
France's heritage. Somehow, he thought, Frenchmen could be bound
together into a real national unity: monarchists and republicans,
Catholics and anticlericals, bourgeoisie and working men might be reconciled in a harmonious society and an effective state. Perhaps it was pure
illusion to suppose that this could be done. Or perhaps it was a mark
of real statesmanship to set up such a long-term goal. At least Gambetta
had no illusions about the difficulties of his program; his plan, he said,
was to *"sérier les questions"* — to take up one issue at a time, in the
order of their urgency.

Gambetta's dream was clouded from the start. The various ex-pre-
miers refused to join his cabinet — possibly because Gambetta had
impulsively announced his plans to the press before explaining them to
the politicians concerned, or possibly for less admirable reasons. Gambetta was forced, therefore, to form a cabinet of his own youthful
disciples — many of them able men with brilliant futures in politics, but
little known at the time save for their reputations as Gambetta's
henchmen. The premier set out at once toward his goal of national
reconciliation by appointing men of all political backgrounds to high
posts in the administration, the army, and the diplomatic service. Such

broad-mindedness offended many loyal Opportunists and increased their suspicions of Gambetta's motives.

The premier, sensing that his rivals were closing in for an early kill, chose to move rapidly and dramatically: he proposed a constitutional amendment to strengthen the government's authority. His plan was to reduce the power of the Senate so as to deny it the right to block legislation adopted by the lower house, and to write into the constitution a new electoral system that would, he thought, encourage the growth of fewer and stronger parties. An angry outcry followed; Gambetta was denounced as an incipient Caesar. He struck back with a remarkably prophetic speech on the dangers of drift and the need for effective government in a republic. But his enemies were too strong; he was beaten and overthrown after three months in office. With him disappeared the last real chance for the Third Republic to alter its constitution without abandoning republican principles.

If Gambetta had lived another twenty years, perhaps he might have gotten a second chance. But only a few months later he was dead, at the age of forty-four. Though some mystery and a great deal of rumor surrounded his death, the truth was less dramatic: he suffered a ruptured appendix.[1] The tragedy shocked even the enemies of the great tribune. All the republicans went into mourning and voted him a state funeral. Into his grave they poured earth from Alsace, smuggled across the frontier at night. His body was buried at Nice, his heart extracted and placed in an urn in the Pantheon. The politicians were so shaken that as a kind of expiation they proceeded to adopt the electoral reform for which he had fought so vigorously. By a strange irony, it went into effect just in time to aid the enemies of the republic, resurgent in the elections of 1885.

Gambetta's death left Jules Ferry as the only first-rank moderate

[1] Most of the rumors stemmed from the fact that Gambetta had accidentally shot himself in the hand ten days earlier. Many Frenchmen believed that he had been shot by an agent of the Jesuits or the Germans; or by an abandoned mistress; or even by his mistress *en titre*, Léonie Léon. Madame Léon's influence over Gambetta during their twelve-year liaison may have contributed heavily to his increasingly moderate views on the church and other issues.

republican leader; and Ferry proceeded to give France three years of remarkable governmental stability. It began to seem that Gambetta's urgent call for constitutional reform had been premature, and that a stronger executive was emerging by natural processes. In fact, this period of stability was a kind of fluke: it was made possible by the Opportunists' clear majority in the Chamber, and by the fact that Ferry was both able enough and colorless enough to keep that majority intact. If Ferry succeeded so well, it was precisely because he lacked Gambetta's glamor; rival politicians felt neither fear nor jealousy. Unlike Gambetta, he had no interest in popularity; he preferred to ignore the voters and to work behind the scenes with other professional politicians. Gambetta had hoped to strengthen the executive branch by linking it to the mass of citizens; Ferry further rooted the tradition of an executive dependent on parliament.

In other respects, too, Ferry was Gambetta's perfect opposite. Ferry had a curious way of doing things piecemeal; his reputation as one of the half-dozen ablest statesmen of the whole Third Republic was largely *ex post facto*, for the importance and coherence of his achievements could be seen only in retrospect. It would never have occurred to him to follow Gambetta's example: to lay out a clearly defined program, to go directly to the nation in search of support ·for that program, to regard political leadership as a process of educating the whole electorate.

Ferry followed his piecemeal technique in getting the school laws adopted; he used it again in laying the foundations for a new colonial empire. Ferry's chief claim to greatness, in the eyes of modern Frenchmen, was that during his years in power France absorbed Tunisia, took over most of Indo-China, got a foothold in Madagascar, and moved out into the Sahara from bases along the coast. There is a powerful textbook legend that the whole enterprise was a kind of one-man operation conducted by Ferry; that he won an empire not only in spite of French public opinion, but behind France's back; that the bulk of Frenchmen were indifferent or hostile to colonies because their eyes were fixed on Alsace or on their own pocketbooks. Ferry was allegedly shrewd enough to recognize this fact and therefore cagily wheedled small sums from parliament by concealing his real aims. When the politicians and the country discovered what he had been doing, he was driven from office in disgrace.

Much of this standard account is certainly myth. Ferry was a late convert to colonialism; as an old republican of 1848 vintage, he was instinctively hostile to it. When the issue of sending a French force into Tunisia came up, he was one of the last members of the cabinet to agree to it. He initiated almost none of the colonial expeditions of the 1880's; most of them were the work of army officers or traders on the spot. If Ferry asked for small driblets of funds and never clearly laid out an imperial program, it was not so much because he feared parliamentary and popular opposition as because he habitually did things that way. If he was twice overthrown as premier on colonial issues, it was largely a matter of chance; in both cases his majority had been disintegrating, and he was due to fall on the first issue that might arise. When Ferry did fall, furthermore, his successors and critics continued what had been begun: there was no great revulsion in the Chamber or in the nation against colonial ventures.

Ferry has often been described as the conscious agent of powerful economic pressure groups whose imperialistic motive was sheer profit. Some colonialist pressure groups did exist, but it is difficult to gauge either their strength or the manner in which their influence was channelled into politics. The imperialistic drive in France seems to have been more often psychological and emotional than economic. The empire, someone has said, was built primarily by "bored army officers looking for excitement." Even Ferry himself appears to have been converted more for reasons of national prestige than in search of economic advantage.

✢◗◦◖✢◗◦◖✢◗◦◖✢

Jules Ferry's greatest shortcoming was his utter lack of popular appeal. The dull grayness of his leadership contributed at least something to that first great challenge to the new republican system, the semicomic-opera Boulanger affair. A general election occurred in 1885, shortly after the Ferry cabinet's fall, and that election produced one of the most startling reversals modern France has known. On the right, monarchists and Bonapartists more than doubled their strength and captured over two hundred seats; on the left, the Radicals made less spectacular gains but ended with more than a hundred seats. Opportunist strength fell to about two hundred seats; their formidable majority was wiped out. Few political experts had foreseen a shift so drastic. In retrospect, it seems to have been the product of a whole series of confluent factors, none of them very important if taken alone. One factor was the rising agitation of diehard patriots like Paul Déroulède — war hero, poet, professional chauvinist, exponent of *revanche*. Another was the rising dissatisfaction of the workers, who began to sense that they were the republic's forgotten men. The school squabble had deepened the hatred of monarchists and clericals for what they began to call *la gueuse* — that slut, the republic. And suffusing it all, there was the factor of sheer boredom with the regime's lack of color.

The Opportunists, incapable of forming a cabinet without either left or right support, turned by a kind of automatic reflex to their fellow republicans on the left; for the first time the Radicals entered a coalition government. They arrived in a chip-on-shoulder mood. Their gains had made them aggressive; they demanded, in return for their cooperation, two revolutionary changes — an income tax and a stiffer policy toward Germany. Few things could have frightened the Opportunists more than those twin scourges, war and the income tax. The Radical demand soon wrecked the coalition cabinet, and the Opportunists turned to a segment of the monarchist right as safer partners. This was not to be the last occasion when a center-left coalition, dictated by the outcome of an election, shortly gave way to a center-right coalition.

The new combination proved to be as shaky as its predecessor. Now it was the monarchists who expected to be paid for their support, and their price was a drastic revision of the Ferry school laws. Few good

Opportunists were willing to abandon what they had just won. The Opportunists, condemned thus to operate a weak and unstable government under fire from both left and right, suffered a further blow by the untimely occurrence of a minor scandal in high places. President Grévy's son-in-law, a politician named Daniel Wilson, was found to have set up shop in the presidential palace as an influence-peddler; he had been unwise enough to solicit business on the presidential letterhead. Efforts to hush up the affair failed; the Opportunists persuaded the reluctant Grévy to resign and put an inoffensive politician named Sadi Carnot in his place.

Enough discontent of various sorts existed in 1887 so that the right chemical agent could easily crystallize it. That agent turned up in General Georges Boulanger. A newcomer to politics, Boulanger had gotten his start through the aid of prominent Radicals like Georges Clemenceau, who regarded him as one of the few true republicans in the officer corps. When the center-left coalition was formed in 1885, the left had insisted that Boulanger be included as minister of war. He would protect the republic, they said; and he would stand up to Bismarck as well.

It is clear in retrospect that the Radicals did not really know their man. As war minister, he made himself a national hero almost overnight. He won the army's affection by instituting a whole series of reforms in barracks conditions, food, weapons; he won the general public by restoring the custom of military parades and by riding at the head of the troops on a handsome black horse; he won the business men by sending troops to control a strike; he won at least some workers by ordering the soldiers to share their rations with the strikers; he won all patriots by issuing a public challenge to Bismarck. An orgy of personal publicity accompanied all these acts; by 1886 Boulanger was the most popular figure in France.

Boulanger's tub-thumping behavior contributed to the breakdown of the center-left coalition; the Opportunists were not only nervous about his popularity but also frightened at his warmongering. When the cabinet fell, the new government reassigned him to an obscure provincial command. By this time many of his original Radical sponsors like Clemenceau had lost their illusions about the general. Other Radicals, however, were more enthusiastic than ever. Here, they thought, was the man who might rescue the republic from the impotent lawyers, who might give it vigor and color. They kept him informed of the rise of discontent in Paris and continually urged him to take up the crusade.

Boulanger reacted cautiously at first; but the Wilson scandal finally encouraged him to come out of the wilderness. Although he listened to his old Radical backers, he began listening also to new voices on the right. Some of the more rabid monarchists, and some Bonapartists as well, had decided that Boulanger might be their man and might pave the way to a restoration. Boulanger, in disguise, visited Switzerland and talked to both pretenders; he secretly accepted their money to conduct a political campaign. His new sponsors got him a campaign manager who had learned electoral tactics in the United States. Beginning in 1887 Boulanger's name began to be entered in a series of by-elections; and almost always he was triumphantly elected. The government sternly warned him that a soldier on active duty could not run for office; Boulanger blandly replied that his name had been put up without his permission and pointed out that after each election he had promptly resigned. It was clear, nevertheless, that a piecemeal plebiscite was under way.

The government was convinced that Boulanger was directly involved, but it was unable to uncover his tracks. In an effort at punishment, the cabinet put him on the retired list. Nothing could have been more unwise; for now he was free to campaign actively and openly. He issued a program marked by calculated vagueness: it called for a sweeping revision of the constitution, though without indicating the nature of the projected changes. He sought and got support from a mixture of left and right elements; in many cases Boulangism was strongest in the areas that had been strongly Bonapartist. But in one notable respect Boulanger differed from Napoleon III: his program included no social or economic reforms. He continued to run for the Chamber in a series of by-elections, but his real aim was to build up support for the general elections of 1889. His plan was to enter a list of candidates in every district, with his own name at the head of each list. He would then presumably take over as the beneficiary of a kind of national plebiscite. Some of his backers urged him to more rapid action — to a coup d'état without delay. Boulanger resisted their pressure and chose to try for power through the forms of legality.

The shaky center-right coalition meanwhile collapsed again, and the desperate Opportunists turned back to the anti-Boulangist Radicals for help in saving the republic. In January, 1889, a few months before the scheduled general elections, a by-election occurred in Paris; and government leaders challenged Boulanger to a contest there. They believed that a victory over the general in this oldest of republican strongholds would burst the Boulanger bubble. Boulanger accepted the challenge; he took on the strongest candidate the republicans could find and defeated him badly. The moment was ideal for a coup d'état; the regime would probably have collapsed almost without resistance. But Boulanger chose once more to stay within the forms of legality; in a few months, he believed, the voters would sweep him into power.

The government had been saved by Boulanger's inaction, but its chances of winning the coming general elections seemed slight. Some desperate republican politicians wanted to steal Boulanger's thunder by revising the constitution at once. Others, more cynical and certainly more realistic, argued that the best course would be to discredit the general personally. Somehow they had detected the real nature of the man and the real psychology of the movement. Minister of Interior Ernest Constans managed to trick Boulanger into believing that the government had evidence of his treason to the republic, and that he would shortly be put on trial before the Senate. The plan succeeded: Boulanger fled to Belgium and announced lamely that his political enemies had planned to railroad him into prison.

Few political bubbles have ever burst so completely or so quickly. In the elections only a few weeks later, a handful of declared Boulangists (notably the novelist Maurice Barrès) managed to win seats; but most of those who still used the label were badly beaten. The general's disgusted followers began to tell the inside story; soon his secret dealings with both monarchists and Bonapartists came into the open and the remnants of his prestige disintegrated. A year or two later he committed suicide at the grave of his mistress in Brussels.

The surprising fact, in view of the brevity of the episode and the mediocrity of its leader, is that Boulangism had deep and enduring consequences. The short-term effect was to give the beleaguered Oppor tunists a new lease on life; they were ensured another ten years in office, almost unchallenged. Their Radical rivals were divided and discredited; the monarchists and Bonapartists also lost prestige by having involved themselves in such an adventure. Some monarchists decided to make the best of a bad business and converted themselves into conservative republicans. These converts shortly got encouragement from the Vatican, when Pope Leo XIII through a spokesman recommended the policy called *ralliement,* or acceptance of the republic.

More striking still were the long-term results of the Boulanger affair. The most obvious of these was the deepened neurosis of republicans with respect to strong men in politics and to the reinforcement of the executive. The libertarian ideal of negative government henceforth had greater charm than before; even immobility seemed better than adventure. Less clear, but perhaps just as important, was the effect of the episode on the temper of the right wing in politics. For almost a generation the dominant current within the right wing had been moderate and parliamentarian in spirit, peaceable and compromising in foreign policy, mainly rural in its support. An English-type conservatism had seemed to be emerging in France in place of the older traditionalist right. But the Boulanger episode either produced or reflected the rise of a quite different kind of rightist group—more authoritarian, more violent, more demagogic and emotional in nature. Its militant spirit was accompanied by a new chauvinism; the right henceforth took over from the Jacobin left the tradition of superheated patriotism and blind confidence in the army. This new right also found its strongholds in the cities rather than the rural districts. Until Boulanger's victory in the Paris by-election of 1889, Paris had always been considered the

315

"reddest" city in France; henceforth it was to remain predominantly right-wing in politics. The existence of this new variety of rightist doctrine, a permanent current in twentieth-century France, was bound to have a significant impact on French political life. Perhaps it would have arrived without Boulangism as its midwife; perhaps such a movement is an unavoidable product of the mass age throughout the Western world. But that Boulangism speeded its emergence and helped to shape its character in France can hardly be denied.

The decade of the 1890's, seen in retrospect, stands out as an era of political transition, a time of general shifting of political forces. Party labels changed, and so did party attitudes. Gambetta's term "Opportunists" took on unpleasant connotations and gradually gave way to "Moderates" — a term that has endured ever since as a generic name for mildly conservative bourgeois republicans. More fundamental than the change in name was a kind of reversal in attitude: the Moderates showed a growing tendency to look toward the right rather than toward the left for their political allies. Heretofore, during the first republican generation, the standard slogan had been "no enemies to the left"; each crisis found all republicans joining in defense of the regime. By the end of the 1890's, however, the Moderates were more inclined to form coalitions with a segment of the ex-monarchist right. It was, according to one historian, ". . . the most significant political realignment that occurred between the 1870's and the First World War."

The Moderates' new outlook derived in part from changes on the right; a good many monarchists became ex-monarchists during the 1890's. It is tempting to assume that the Vatican's new line, the policy of *ralliement,* was responsible for the conversion of the right. Superficially at least, the facts do not support this theory; most monarchist politicians, most prominent Catholics in France, rejected the idea of *ralliement,* open criticized it in their press, and ignored the Vatican's suggestion that Catholic politicians seek a merger with the Moderates to form a large and solid conservative party. The only Catholic politician who tried to carry out the Pope's plan — Albert de Mun — failed dismally in the attempt. So bitterly did many rightists resent the Vatican's shift of policy that some of them swallowed rumors of an alleged kidnapping of the Pope by Freemasons. The plotters (so went the story) had imprisoned Leo XIII in the Vatican dungeons and had put up an impostor to issue false instructions to the faithful.

Beneath the surface, however, the *ralliement* was much more effective that it seemed to be. Catholic leaders might say "no" to the Vatican, but Catholic voters proceeded to say "yes." Through the 1890's Catholic electoral support steadily drained away from monarchist candidates to the advantage of Moderate republicans, who were regarded as a more effective barrier against the rise of the left. As the monarchist bloc in parliament declined, the Moderate republicans no longer saw it as a grave danger. Indeed, as Moderate deputies came to draw more and more of their support from these ex-monarchist voters, they naturally developed a greater sympathy with conservative and Catholic ideas. The *ralliement* may have failed as a formal policy, but it succeeded in a more important sense; it hastened the erosion of the old barrier between republican center and monarchist right. The trend of the 1890's foreshadowed the decline of the church question as a critical political issue; France's religious war might have lost much of its intensity had it not been revived in the late 1890's by the Dreyfus Affair.

The Radicals, it is true, refused to abandon their suspicions of clerical motives. They warned that the church, unable to win in an open fight, had returned to tactics of infiltration in an effort to recover its lost influence in politics and education. Clemenceau called the *ralliement* a Vatican trick, and warned his colleagues against trying to do business with Rome: "You say that the Catholics have held out a hand to you. Put your own in it; it will be so firmly held that you can never draw it back. . . . You will be the prisoner of the church."

Although the Radicals clung stubbornly to their anticlerical convictions, in other ways they, too, showed signs of a changing outlook in the 1890's. Many of them were watering down their egalitarian and Jacobin heritage; if they still gave lip service to the old Radical program of political and social reform, they no longer took it very seriously. More and more, they were becoming the heirs of the Gambetta tradition, with its opportunism and its commitment to defend the little Frenchman. A more intransigent wing, revolted at this softening of the doctrine, broke away and chose the label "Socialist Radicals"; its members still prided themselves on their Jacobin heritage and clung to the principle "no enemies to the left." Even after the two wings fused again into a single group (called henceforth the Radical and Socialist-Radical party), they continued to look in opposite directions for political allies. The party was able to bear these internal tensions only because its discipline was so lax; the Radicals had almost no central organization, and they remained "less a party than a state of mind."

The 1890's brought not only change in the old parties, but the emergence of a potentially powerful new force — socialism. Its rise was still another factor that turned the Moderates toward the right; they began to fear a new threat to the established order, a graver threat than that posed by declining monarchism.

Socialism's roots in France were old and deep, but as an organized political force it was relatively recent in origin. The repression of the Commune in 1871 had set back its growth for a decade; but the repression also had the curious effect of strengthening the Marxian variety of socialism at the expense of other, more moderate kinds. Most of the leaders killed or exiled in 1871 were non-Marxians: Proudhonians, Blanquists, and so on. With the ground pretty well cleared of these native socialist movements, Marx's disciples could step into the vacuum and seize the initiative in evangelizing the working class. When the first "socialist workers' congress" met in 1879, the fanatically Marxian convert Jules Guesde was able to take the leading role and shape the doctrine of the French Workers' party that emerged.

This is not to suggest that Guesde had a clear field. His party, like all socialist movements, soon ran onto the shoals of doctrinal con-troversy and shattered into several mutually antagonistic fragments. Some adherents found Guesde's party too rigid, others not rigid enough; some wanted to admit any sympathizer, others insisted on proletarian purity; some favored orthodox Marxism, others wanted to fuse it with the Blanquist tradition. Despite these conflicts, a few socialist candidates won seats in the Chamber in the 1880's; and in 1893 the number jumped suddenly to about forty. They represented, however, five different organized socialist parties as well as an unor-ganized collection of "independent socialists" like Jean Jaurès with vaguely egalitarian and humanitarian ideas. The principal goal of the next decade was to be the fusion of all these factions into one large unified party; it was eventually accomplished in 1905, thanks largely to the work of Jaurès.

❧◦❧◦❧◦❧

Both the rise of socialism and the general shifting of political forces in the 1890's were hastened by that fragrant episode known as the Panama Scandal. Ferdinand de Lesseps, the builder of the Suez Canal, had organized the Panama Company in 1880 to dig a canal through the isthmus. Frenchmen rushed to invest in a firm headed by one of France's national heroes; but mismanagement and poor planning soon got the company into hopeless difficulties. The promoters, in a desperate effort to mobilize new capital, sought the consent of the Chamber to issue a lottery loan. In 1888 agents of the firm bribed enough politicians to get the scheme approved and paid off enough journalists to get favorable press publicity. The loan nevertheless failed dismally, and the company collapsed.

Embittered shareholders set up a cry for an investigation. In 1892 a poison-pen journalist named Edouard Drumont took up their cause in an effort to prop up his sagging newspaper. Anti-Semitism was his stock in trade, and Drumont therefore concentrated his fire on two Jewish agents of the company who had allegedly bought off the poli-

ticians: Baron Reinach and Dr. Cornelius Herz. His two victims had a
falling-out, and each one privately began to feed information to Drumont in the hope of buying protection from the latter's attacks. At the
height of the agitation, Reinach committed suicide; and the scandal
reached such proportions that parliament had to set up an investigating
committee. Eventually the committee recommended that the directors
of the company, together with ten deputies who were seriously compromised, be tried for bilking the public and accepting bribes. The trial
ended in 1893 with an almost complete whitewash. A verdict of guilty
against the directors was promptly quashed on a technicality; and all
the accused deputies were acquitted save one who was imprudent
enough to confess.

Superficially, the political consequences of the affair seem to have
been slight. Most of the deputies tainted by the scandal were re-elected
in 1893; the one notable exception, Georges Clemenceau, was beaten
for other reasons. The Moderates who had dominated politics throughout the Panama period continued in power through the rest of the
decade. Some Anglo-Saxon purists have concluded that Frenchmen have
no ethical standards in politics and take graft to be a matter of course.
French monarchists offer a somewhat related thesis: the republic, they
assert, had corrupted the country's morals and had implanted the
doctrine that anything goes if one can get away with it.

The effects of the scandal in fact went much deeper than they
appeared to be on the surface. Most of the leading Moderate politicians,
though re-elected to parliament, prudently withdrew into the background to let the dust settle. In their places there emerged a new
generation of Moderates: young men, untouched by the scandal. This
renewal of personnel in turn strengthened the tendency of the Moderates to make political alliances on the right. Unlike their predecessors,
the new men were too young to remember the heroic struggles of the
1870's when all republicans had stood together to avert the monarchy.
The memory of the *seize mai* had been a powerful emotional cement,
binding together the center and the left; that memory meant little to
the new generation.

The scandal contributed also to the shift of rural France toward the left. It reinforced the old provincial suspicion that Paris was a sink of corruption, and that even the most honest provincial deputies could rarely resist that fetid atmosphere for very long. Common sense, therefore, seemed to call for a frequent change of deputy, and normally a change toward the left — since the chances of remaining pure were likely to be greater on the left margin of the political spectrum. Panama thus speeded a political trend that was already in progress in the Third Republic. That the republic survived the crisis without much trouble was in part a matter of luck; the enemies of the regime, still divided and staggering after the Boulanger episode, could not yet put together a serious threat to the system. A few years earlier or later, Panama might have had far more disastrous results.

The republic was not to enjoy a very long breathing spell. From 1896 until the end of the century France was sucked into the vortex of an almost unprecedented crisis — a crisis that deserves the name of a bloodless but no less intense civil war. This was the Dreyfus case; or, in French usage, simply *l'Affaire*.

Few fictional whodunits are more complex than this real-life case of alleged treason. Any attempt to summarize the story is therefore a kind of exercise in futility. Apparently, in 1894 a French staff officer and man-about-town, Major Esterhazy, began to sell information to the German military attaché in Paris. French counter-intelligence found in a German Embassy wastebasket an unsigned letter probably written by Esterhazy; but in searching for the culprit, they wrongly accused another staff officer, Captain Alfred Dreyfus. They failed, however, to find any evidence confirming Dreyfus' guilt, and they probably would have abandoned the accusation had not that professional anti-Semite, Edouard Drumont, gotten wind of the affair and raised a public outcry. Drumont, whose best-selling book *Jewish France* (1886) has been called "the first great explosion of modern anti-Semitism," charged that wealthy Jews were trying to buy the freedom of a traitor. Army authorities decided, therefore, to proceed with a court-martial, during which they accepted as evidence certain documents that were later proved to be forgeries. Dreyfus was sent to Devil's Island for life, while Frenchmen applauded the army's efficiency and toughness.

Military secrets nevertheless continued to flow to the German Embassy; and new evidence in 1896 at last cast suspicion on Esterhazy. The new chief of counter-intelligence, Colonel Picquart, re-examined the Dreyfus file and concluded to his dismay that Dreyfus had been innocent. Army authorities, convinced that he was mistaken, transferred Picquart to the Tunisian desert; but something of what he knew began to leak out to the press, and a few newspapers (notably Clemenceau's) launched a crusade for a new trial. Meanwhile another counter-intelligence officer, Major Henry, fed bits of anti-Dreyfus information to Drumont and others, so that the controversy became increasingly public and bitter. On the side, Henry took the precaution of forging some new documents to strengthen the case against Dreyfus, and he easily convinced his army superiors of their validity. The army therefore resisted all demands for a reopening of the case — the more so because it resented civilian interference in a matter of military justice.

By 1898 virtually the entire educated elite of France was committed to one side or the other. Families were split; there were frequent clashes in the streets, and duels were fought daily. Intellectuals led the fight for Dreyfus; but a smaller group of intellectuals joined monarchists and right-wing Catholics to resist revision. The Assumptionist organ *La Croix* leaped into the forefront and campaigned for stripping all Jews of citizenship. Most politicians still tried to quiet the storm and to stay aloof from any commitment; but there were notable exceptions like Clemenceau, Jaurès, and Scheurer-Kestner who held that party interests should give way to the overriding principle of justice for the individual citizen.

A major break in the case came suddenly late in 1898, when a new counter-intelligence officer accidentally detected Henry's forgeries in the Dreyfus file. Henry confessed and that night committed suicide. Esterhazy fled to England and gave out contradictory stories about his role in the case. Although the anti-Dreyfus faction still insisted that Dreyfus was the culprit, and that top-secret documents in the possession of counter-intelligence would prove it if they could only be released without causing war, they could no longer avert a new trial. Late in 1899 Dreyfus was again court-martialled, but again the military judges found him guilty (though with extenuating circumstances). He was promptly pardoned by the president of the republic and was vindicated by a civilian court several years later.

There are enough gaps and contradictions in the evidence to leave it still partially shrouded in uncertainty. A few Frenchmen still believe that Dreyfus was guilty and was saved by Jewish influence and money. Some think that there may have been two traitors — Esterhazy and a second officer who, to avoid discovery, continually fed in false leads to distract the pursuers. Still others suggest that there may have been no traitor at all. Their hypothesis is that Major Henry had a little evidence of military leaks and wrongly suspected Dreyfus; that he persuaded Esterhazy to write the original note of 1894 and "planted" it in the German Embassy as evidence to buttress his suspicions.

More important, however, was the impact of *l'Affaire* on French political life and the enduring myth that it left behind. Its immediate effect was to bring the Radicals into power and to keep them there for most of the time until the Great War. The Moderates were badly split over the Dreyfus issue and were mainly concerned to keep things quiet; the Radicals profited by the opportunity to come out on the right side when victory for the Dreyfusards was almost certain. They convinced themselves, and a great many voters, that they had saved the republic from a clerico-monarchist plot, and that they must be kept in office to protect the republic. The new Waldeck-Rousseau cabinet (1899–1902), though headed by a Moderate, was dominated by Radicals and supported by Socialists; it was a kind of popular front ahead of its time, comented by the presumed right-wing threat to the regime.

The Affair also sharpened the suspicions of French leftists toward both the army and the church. A new wave of antimilitarism and anti-clericalism followed; steps were taken to republicanize the army and to weaken church influence. Both the general staff and certain elements in the church had blundered badly in their handling of the Dreyfus controversy; their behavior had seemed to justify the republicans' suspicions. The effect was to deepen the existing division within France and to set back the growth of something like national consensus.

Like most great emotional upheavals, this one was significant mainly for the mythology it inspired. Most French republicans saw the Affair as a contest between the forces of righteousness and progress on the one hand and those of bigotry and obscurantism on the other. The Dreyfus camp clung to the principle of justice for every man, even though the coherence of society and the prestige of its institutions might be temporarily shaken. The anti-Dreyfusards stood for the principle of *raison d'état*, of the end that justifies the means; they rejected the idea that the individual citizen possessed any sacred rights superior to those of the state. To some degree, the controversy *was* rooted in this conflict between values, and the victory of the Dreyfusards did reinforce the libertarian ideal. But the case was also heavily encrusted with less admirable motives of political advantage and bigoted loyalty; and in large part the story was one of fallible human beings sucked into the maelstrom without quite knowing how they got there. One curious by-product was the strengthened self-image, and popular image, of intellectuals as incorruptible men of virtue, untouched by prejudice and able always to detect the right and just cause. Along with it went the legend of honesty and justice as characteristics of the left, and selfishness and bigotry as qualities of the right. Both illusions were of strictly limited validity and were to produce some unfortunate consequences in twentieth-century French politics. Thus the complexities of the case itself were hardly greater than the complexities of the heritage left by it. One might almost epitomize *l'Affaire* as "the shame and glory of modern France."

TWENTY

Radicalism: no term so necessary to comprehend if
one is to understand contemporary France; no term
whose comprehension is so difficult.

MAURICE SORRE

The Radical Republic,
1899–1914

When René Waldeck-Rousseau took office as premier in 1899, the Third
Republic reached a major political turning point. Waldeck himself was
a Moderate, of the same stripe as the men who had been governing
France for twenty years (though superior to most of them in ability).
A wealthy lawyer of austere temperament, who fixed on his colleagues
"the cold eye of a jellied fish," he was one of the few surviving representatives of the *haute bourgeoisie* in politics. What distinguished his
cabinet from its predecessors was that the key posts were held by
Radicals, and that it even contained one Socialist, Alexandre Millerand.
Henceforth the Radicals were to replace the Moderates as the fulcrum
of republican politics; from 1899 to 1940 they were rarely out of power
(usually in coalition with a segment of the Moderates), and for most
of that time they were the largest group in the Chamber. Their conquest
of the Senate followed more slowly, but no less surely; after the First
World War, the upper house was to become the Radicals' chief fortress.

The transition from Moderate to Radical rule, however, brought no
sharp change in the republic's structure or spirit. There had been a

time when the Radicals were ferociously Jacobin and egalitarian, but they had been gradually drifting away from that heritage. The source of Radical strength, which had once been urban, was coming to be mainly rural and small-town in character; the party had come to represent the interests of the little independent producer or trader, who might still be strongly egalitarian in theory but who was much more inclined to be libertarian in practice.

One development that helped to reshape the Radical outlook in the 1890's and after was the rise of socialism. As the Radicals found themselves outflanked on the left by a more dynamic and aggressive faction, they began to feel that segments of the Moderate group were more congenial neighbors. This turn toward the right was also strengthened by the Radicals' accession to power after 1899. The responsibilities of office had their customary effect; and in addition, success brought a new current of conservative converts into the party. Many aspiring young politicians who might have chosen to be Opportunists or Moderates a generation earlier now found the Radical label to be the best guarantee of electoral success. These "immigrants" had little in common with the generation of intransigent doctrinaires that had denounced Gambetta for his opportunism. Yet the Radical party — or a large segment of it, at any rate — never shook off a kind of nostalgic yearning after its lost virtue. The party still prided itself on its leftist character; many of its members were never quite reconciled to the idea of collaborating with the Moderates and almost instinctively hoped that somehow the old slogan "no enemies to the left" might be rejuvenated. Thus the party remained an ambiguous, loose-jointed organization, still deeply anticlerical, still theoretically egalitarian, yet no longer really committed to any social reform more drastic than the income tax — and, indeed, no longer sure that this ancient Radical panacea would be quite safe.

The Radical temper was both reflected in and reinforced by the writings of their favorite philosopher-journalist, the man who called himself Alain. His epigrams were widely quoted and savored. "Obey, but resist — there is the whole secret," wrote Alain. "Anything that destroys obedience is anarchy; anything that destroys resistance is tyranny." Basic in Alain was a fear and suspicion of leadership, a conviction that the good citizen is not the one who conforms and co-operates, but the one who resists authority. To him, the function of the deputy was "to represent the ordinary undistinguished citizen against the eternal conspiracy of the strong, the rich, the powerful" — those who have been corrupted by power and success.[1] The function of the minister, likewise, was not to govern but to keep a watchful eye on the bureaucrats. Alain's disciples gradually overran the teaching profession and taught the new generation to distrust all leaders, to regard patriotism as the last refuge of a scoundrel, to scoff at talk of sacrifice or discipline as sheer hypocrisy, to see as the highest symbol of civic virtue the gesture of thumb-to-nose. If ideas and attitudes shape human events, there is much to be said for the thesis that the doctrines of Alain had a grave demoralizing effect in twentieth-century France. His brand of libertarianism — negative, desiccated, small-minded — brought to a sad culmination that admirable current of ideas that had done so much to free men in an earlier age. That it was the natural, the inevitable culmination of liberal thought is, however, by no means self-evident.

⋘⋙ ⋘⋙ ⋘⋙

The left-wing coalition of Radicals, Socialists, and Waldeck Moderates welded together by the Dreyfus crisis gave the republic an almost unique experience in stability from 1899 to 1905. Five and a half years with only two cabinets (and those two almost identical) constituted an all-time record; some Frenchmen even began to believe that a cure had been found for the disease of governmental weakness. The new stability, however, proved to be no more than an interlude, and the system soon reverted to type. From time to time a strong premier backed by a fairly coherent majority could temporarily reinforce the

[1] P. Williams, in J. M. Wallace-Hadrill and J. McManners (eds.), *France: Government and Society*, p. 229.

executive branch, but the institutional framework went on unchanged, and the republic's political mores were not seriously altered. Indeed, the coalition of 1899–1905 lacked even the vigorous centralized authority essential to an effective functioning of the cabinet system; for behind the premier, and restricting all his acts, hovered a permanent steering committee called the *Délégation des gauches,* representing the various component parties in the coalition. Policies were made by this unofficial body operating behind the scenes and reaching decisions through a kind of diplomatic negotiation; premier and cabinet had only to execute policies handed down to them.

When the coalition took office France appeared to be on the verge of civil war. For several months the regime seemed constantly in danger; then, suddenly, with Dreyfus' pardon, the agitation faded away as though by magic. A few diehards on both sides continued to bicker, but they quickly found themselves isolated; *l'Affaire* disintegrated with astonishing speed. The explanation, François Goguel suggests, is that the agitation of 1898–1900 had not been based on a hard substratum of economic discontent. Once the fate of the man Dreyfus was decided, the one crystallizing factor in the conflict was gone.

Yet in a deeper sense the Dreyfus crisis faded out much less quickly; indirectly, it pervaded political life for most of the next decade. Such passions had been aroused that either side, if victorious, was likely to abuse its victory. The new governing coalition was determined to hobble and punish those groups that had threatened the republican regime and the ideals that it represented. The chief offenders, as the coalition saw it, had been the army and the church; the government was determined to republicanize the one and to hamstring and isolate the other.

The new minister of war, General André, set out to destroy the army's right to run its own affairs (and also, perhaps, hoped to avenge himself on those fellow officers who had long cold-shouldered him for his republican views). André reformed the system of promotion by taking it out of the hands of the officer corps and vesting it in the ministry of war. He set up a kind of private espionage system to keep track of officers' opinions and habits: Freemasons in many cases served as volunteer agents, sending their reports to the central Masonic headquarters in Paris, whence they went to the war ministry. A card file indicated the officers who attended Mass and who expressed their antirepublican views too freely. Eventually the details of this amateur spy system leaked out and produced such an uproar in parliament that André had to be dismissed. Although he had not completed his task of democratizing and republicanizing the general staff, enough was accomplished so that by 1914 the high command was no longer a solidly monarchist-clerical stronghold.

The Dreyfus upheaval and its aftermath contributed to reshaping the officer corps, but the cost was high. Army prestige and morale, which had reached their peak during the generation after 1871, fell to a new low after 1900. Applications for entrance into Saint-Cyr military academy fell by half; a great many officers resigned their commissions or retired. In part, the change in mood resulted from dissatisfaction at the army's long inactivity, at the low levels of pay, at the slowness of promotion. The challenge of constant tension, the hope of imminent revenge against Germany, had begun to disintegrate by 1890. The officer corps gradually slipped again into a rut of inertia and conformity. If this mood had lasted until 1914, the German onslaught might have brought a repetition of 1870. Luckily for the nation, however, the resurgence of national spirit that set in after 1910 was to be reflected in the army. A new vigor and toughness pervaded the officer corps just in time to prepare it for the great test; although unaccompanied by any increase in imagination or by fresh strategic thinking, the revival of morale enabled the army to survive the shock of the German attack.

The Waldeck government's second target was the church. Unfortunately, many priests and members of religious orders had plunged into the Dreyfus controversy, even though no basic issue of faith or morals had been involved. The left's bitterness was focussed on certain congregations like the Assumptionists, who had crusaded most violently against Dreyfus, and the Jesuits, who had always been fair game when the church came under fire. Dreyfusards were persuaded that a clerical-military plot lay behind the whole Dreyfus affair; they believed that most of the officer corps had been educated and consciously corrupted in Catholic schools. Waldeck-Rousseau himself favored rather mild measures of repression; he proposed to exile only those orders that had gone to fanatical extremes during the Affair. But the Chamber was far more intransigent; it amended Waldeck's bill to provide for the expulsion of all orders save those that might be granted special authorization by parliament. In practice, few authorizations were granted; thousands of monks and nuns set off into exile in Spain, the United States, and elsewhere.

The reprisals against the church were intensified after Waldeck voluntarily retired from the premiership in 1902 and suggested as his successor Senator Émile Combes. Waldeck evidently misjudged his man; Combes shared none of Waldeck's spirit of moderation but was a dedicated fanatic who saw clerical plots and intrigues everywhere. As a young man, Combes had almost completed his training for the priest-hood when he lost his faith and turned to medicine instead. This "heretic theologian" made the works of Voltaire his new Bible and embarked on a single-minded campaign against the church. As a one-time seminarist, he could claim a special insight into Catholic intentions. "Raised in the harem," he used to say, "I know its inner secrets."

Combes's total achievement in his two and a half years as premier (1902–5) was to continue and expand the anticlerical program begun by Waldeck. He evicted most of the remaining religious orders; he engaged the Vatican in a series of jurisdictional disputes over the appointment and disciplining of bishops. His purpose was to drive the Pope into denouncing the Concordat (which quickly became, as someone has put it, a Discordat). In the end it was his own patience that gave way first, and in 1905 he persuaded the French parliament to denounce the century-old agreement. By the separation laws that followed, all ties between church and state were severed. Priests and bishops were taken off the state payroll; title to all church property was transferred to the state; committees of Catholic laymen were to administer church affairs in each parish.

Most Catholics bitterly resented this treatment and feared its effects on the church in France. The unilateral denunciation of the Concordat struck them as a calculated insult to the Vatican. They were disturbed at the problem of finding private financial support for the church establishment; since clerical salaries were certain to drop, the recruitment of new priests might become almost impossible. Nevertheless, most bishops were convinced that they had no choice, and that they had better make the best of a bad business. A few liberal churchmen even found a silver lining in the cloud, foreseeing a new era of vigorous growth for a free church, untrammelled by official bonds. But the French hierarchy was promptly overruled by the Vatican. The Pope issued strict orders that Catholics should resist the new legislation and should refuse to participate in the new parish committees of laymen. At the same time he excommunicated every deputy who had voted for the separation laws.

For a year or two France again faced a threat of generalized violence. In the Chamber the more rabid anticlericals welcomed the Vatican's intransigence and wanted to seize the opportunity for a showdown fight with the church. If Catholics refused to set up laymen's committees, they argued, then Catholics had no legal right to function as an organized group or to use the churches for worship. They insisted that the government proceed at once to take inventory of its new properties, as provided by an apparently inoffensive clause in the new laws. But the civil servants sent to "count the chandeliers," as Clemenceau put it, met violent resistance from the embattled congregations. In some areas Catholics guarded their churches with shotguns; in remote hill regions they set wolf traps or even chained a wild bear at the church door. Several were injured, and at least one killed, in the scuffles that followed. Luckily, the Socialists withdrew from the coalition at this point, and Combes fell from power. His successor was less extreme; and Aristide Briand, the new minister of cults, relaxed the enforcement of the new church legislation. Ignoring anticlerical protests, he authorized extra-legal arrangements that permitted parish priests to lease church buildings and equipment from municipalities for a nominal sum. Gradually the new system rooted itself in French mores.

The impact of separation on the church was quite as severe as Catholics feared it might be. Heretofore, the average priest's income had made him slightly better off than most of his parishioners; now, except in a few rich parishes, he was near the very bottom of the scale in economic status. Recruiting became much more difficult; within a few years the number of young men entering the priesthood had dropped by half. Catholic schools were hard hit, too, for contributions now had to go to support the church itself, and often no money was left to operate a school. In a short time the number of children in Catholic primary schools fell by more than a third; in secondary schools, by a quarter. Separation also speeded up the process of dechristianization that was already well under way in the working-class suburbs and some rural areas. The impact was especially great on the peasants, in whose minds Catholic observances had often come to be matters of custom or habit rather than an expression of genuine faith. So long as the church was linked to the state, it retained a kind of official prestige; in 1905 that prestige was suddenly destroyed. An example of the effect may be found in the Limoges area, where the proportion of nonbaptized children rose from two to forty per cent between 1899 and 1914, and the number of civil marriages from fourteen to sixty per cent.

At the same time the church did gain something from the separation. A greater liberty of action was one such gain. The state could no longer intervene in church affairs; it could no longer cut off an offending priest's salary, or deny priests the right to exert active pressure in elections, or protect a bishop against the Vatican's disciplinary action. Separation thus wiped out the last feeble remnants of the Gallican tradition. A second long-range gain was in the character of the priesthood. After a decade of drastic decline recruiting gradually rose again to the previous level in quantity and attained a much higher level in quality. Young men who entered the church henceforward could no longer hope to find there a relatively soft berth carrying official status; if they entered now, it was by fervent conviction. Here was a case where pruning the tree had certainly rendered it healthier. Finally, separation opened the way to the possibility of harmonious coexistence of Catholics and freethinkers in France. The clerical threat gradually lost most of its potency after 1905, not only because some members of the new generation were beginning to drift away from positivism, but also because even positivists found it harder to believe that the men in black were about to take over the country. The old feud was slow in dying; indeed, remnants of it still survive to plague present-day politicians. Certainly, however, the separation of 1905 hastened its decline.

❧◦❧◦❧◦

Meanwhile, the long era of stable coalition government had broken down in 1905, when the Socialists withdrew their support. Many Socialists had been urging such a withdrawal ever since the end of the Dreyfus crisis. Once that battle was won, they argued, the Socialists had nothing to gain by giving their votes to a bourgeois cabinet — especially to one that had no interest in social reform. It had taken all the persuasive powers of Jean Jaurès, the party's ablest spokesman, to keep his group in line behind the Waldeck and Combes cabinets. Behind the scenes, in the *Délégation des gauches,* his influence over the government had exceeded that of any other man.

Republican France has produced few political leaders more remarkable or more appealing than Jean Jaurès. Almost every French town has a street or square named for him; every leftist party quotes him or claims him as an ancestor. Jaurès was a man of the south: a warm, expansive personality, a spellbinding orator. Some skeptics believed that he was inclined to inebriate himself with his own rhetoric and to dazzle his hearers more often than he enlightened them. He was nevertheless a man of brilliant mind, and the lucidity of that mind was further sharpened by exposure to the best training offered by the French educational system. In his class at the École Normale Supérieure — a kind of forcing-ground for the best intellects in France — his only serious rival had been the philosopher Henri Bergson. He taught philosophy briefly in the south; but the lure of politics had soon tempted him out of the classroom. In 1885, at the age of twenty-five, he became the youngest member of the Chamber of Deputies.

Jaurès entered politics as an Opportunist whose political heroes were Gambetta and Ferry. In a sense, that was what he always remained. He was at heart no doctrinaire but a humanitarian — a liberal idealist who believed in the essential goodness of man, and who was persuaded at first that a bourgeois elite could and should lead the way toward social justice. He suffered some disillusionment when his bourgeois backers, irritated by his passionate appeals for the alleviation of human misery, helped to defeat him in the 1889 elections. But a man so intensely optimistic by nature could never become really disillusioned. His rival, Clemenceau, a convinced cynic, once snorted: "Do you know how you can always recognize a speech by Jaurès? All the verbs are in the future tense."

In the nineties Jaurès began calling himself an Independent Socialist, and he returned to the Chamber in 1893 on the rising Socialist tide. Though he had been reading Marx and henceforth called himself a Marxist, he never really succumbed to the master's system or dogma; always he sought to reconcile it with his own liberal idealism. His socialism, such as it was, sprang from the heart rather than the head.

When Jaurès entered the Socialist movement, he found it split into six competing segments: five organized parties, plus a number of Independent Socialist deputies like himself. From the outset he was convinced that unity was essential if the proletariat were to use what he called "the revolutionary instrument of universal suffrage" to bring about the new era. In addition, he believed that socialism must set out to attract as many bourgeois sympathizers as possible. It took him more than a decade to accomplish Socialist unity, so deep were the schisms within the movement. Jaurès' chief rival was Jules Guesde, founder of the first Marxian party in France. The contrast between the two men could hardly have been more complete. They shared intelligence and sincerity; but Guesde was dogmatic and doctrinaire, intensely suspicious of the bourgeoisie (from which he himself had come), cold and austere in temperament. Jaurès was robust and earthy; generous, impulsive, naively optimistic; as careless in dress and personal habits as a four-year-old child. Guesde was "the ferocious sectarian, sharp-featured and bilious," whose piercing eye and long beard made him resemble (as a contemporary put it) "either Christ or Alphonse Daudet." In those early years of socialism in politics Jaurès and Guesde clashed on almost every major policy decision: on whether to commit the movement to the Dreyfusard cause, on whether to support Waldeck-Rousseau in 1899, on whether to let a Socialist enter that cabinet, on whether to abandon the apocalyptic vision of eventual class violence. Yet the two men did in the end reach an accommodation that permitted the creation of a united Socialist party. And there survived in both men a powerful residue of patriotism, despite the Marxist dogma that the worker has no country.

On the issue of supporting the Radical-dominated cabinets of 1899–1905, however, Guesde never became reconciled to Jaurès' views; indeed, his antagonism increased with the passage of time. Guesde insisted that the Socialists would get nothing in return for their support; that the Radical politicians were concerned only to harass the church and not to aid or protect the proletariat. He steadily argued for an ultimatum to the cabinet: either real social reforms or an end to the coalition. Jaurès could not deny the fact that the workers had gotten nothing from the Waldeck and Combes governments, but he continued to insist that his strategy would produce long-range results. He contended that once the Radicals had completed their anticlerical program thanks to Socialist support, they would be willing to turn to social reforms — both because they would have no program of their own left to accomplish, and because they would have learned to trust the Socialists through long experience in collaboration.

It would be pleasant to believe that Jaurès' program, if continued for a few more years, might have brought an enduring coalition or even a merger of Radicals and Socialists into a broadly-based leftist party like British Labour. But his strategy rested on some shaky assumptions. It took for granted that the Radicals, once their own program was accomplished, would naturally turn to the left for allies and a program. Jaurès failed to see that the Radicals were sliding toward the center and were coming to share much of the Moderate outlook. In any event, his tactics never reached the point of being tested, for in 1904 Guesde finally managed to force Jaurès to abandon the bourgeois coalition. Guesde won his victory by carrying his fight to a higher authority, the Socialist International, as its Amsterdam congress in 1904. There the two French spokesmen publicly argued the case: could a Socialist party cohabit with bourgeois politicians without losing its virtue? In the end, it was the powerful German delegation that decided the issue in favor of Guesde; for the German party was already committed to a Guesdist line at home. Jaurès almost carried the day by his eloquence, arguing that what was good for the German Socialists was not necessarily good for other national groups. In France the party could find some really dependable allies among the progressive bourgeoisie, and together they could get control of parliament and of the state itself. In Germany a different strategy was quite proper, since the Reichstag was so weak and the bourgeoisie so uncooperative that the prospect of attaining real power via elections was slight.

Jaurès took his defeat at Amsterdam in good spirit; he obediently put an end to Socialist support of the Combes cabinet. He was convinced that proletarian unity was all-important, and that it could at last be achieved in France if he would knuckle under. He was right: in 1905 the Guesdist and Jaurèsist factions were merged into the unified Socialist party, henceforth called the S.F.I.O. From 1905 to 1936 (save for an interruption during the Great War) the party clung doggedly to its policy of nonparticipation in "bourgeois" cabinets. In that sense, Guesde's influence dominated French socialism for a generation. But it was the spirit and outlook of Jaurès that steadily pervaded the party in the years after Jaurès' defeat at Amsterdam. On almost

every major party issue that arose down to 1914 the reformist, anti-
doctrinaire faction triumphed. French socialism developed into a constitutional party, the advance guard of the democratic groups, and not
into a dogmatic class-bound revolutionary movement. Its gains were
steady; its percentage of the popular vote rose in every prewar election,
until in May, 1914, it emerged as the second-largest single group in
parliament with one-sixth of the nation's votes and one-sixth of the
seats in the Chamber. One did not have to be a Jaurèsian optimist to
conclude that France's future lay in socialism.

The new Socialist line brought an end to the post-Dreyfus era of
cabinet stability. Henceforth the Radicals were driven to collaborate
with the Moderates, which most of them did without reluctance. For
the next generation, from 1905 to 1936, France was governed by a
kind of permanent though shifting coalition; sometimes the premier
was a Radical, sometimes a Moderate, sometimes a hybrid like Aristide
Briand, with friends in all camps.

Curiously, the two most notable Radical premiers in the prewar
decade — Georges Clemenceau (1906–9) and Joseph Caillaux (1911–
12) — could hardly have been more atypical of the Radical temper.
Indeed, only a loose-jointed and amorphous group like the Radical
party could have contained such a maverick as Clemenceau for so long.
In a sense, he was the last survivor of an earlier phase of radicalism,
when the leaders had been tough-minded, doctrinaire zealots, filled
with Jacobin patriotism and egalitarian convictions. The party's trend
toward libertarian views, toward flexibility and compromise in politics,
had left Clemenceau untouched. By temperament he had always been
harshly authoritarian, and this trait grew more marked with advancing
age. His specialty in political life had been the destruction of cabinets,
which gave him his sobriquet "the Tiger." No other politician possessed
a sharper tongue or sword; Clemenceau counted his duels by the dozen.

The aging Jacobin got his chance at last in 1906. The record of his premiership contained little that was consistent with Radical tradition. His initial program did call for several measures of social reform, but they remained stillborn. The period was marked, rather, by the most severe labor unrest France had ever known, culminating in an attempted general strike in 1909. Clemenceau, who insolently described himself as "France's number one cop," ruthlessly repressed the disorders by using troops. Such behavior cost him some of his support; but his caustic tongue irritated even more of his partisans. This abrasive quality finally brought him down in 1909, barely short of Waldeck-Rousseau's record of three years in office. Most Frenchmen concluded that Clemenceau's first chance at power would also be his last. One thing was certain: the Radicals would no longer mistake him for one of theirs.

Joseph Caillaux, premier in 1911–12, was even less representative of his party. Frustrated ambition had led him to defect from the Moderate camp, but he remained a Moderate in all but name. A financial expert of strictly orthodox economic views, his ties were mainly with influential banking circles. Only a few weeks after joining the Radicals he had become their party leader; a few more weeks and he was head of a Radical cabinet. Like Clemenceau, Caillaux was a man of authoritarian temper; but he outdid the Tiger in personal vanity, and he lacked any trace of Clemenceau's savagely Jacobin patriotism.

Caillaux's soft line toward Germany infuriated Clemenceau, but another trend of the epoch irritated the Tiger even more. This was the growth of antimilitarism and antipatriotism on the left. The spread of Marxism contributed to this trend, and so did the Dreyfus Affair. But the spearhead of the antimilitarist campaign was to be found in the labor movement, with its syndicalist tradition, its antipolitical outlook, and its stress on violence. Soon after the turn of the century a *lycée* professor named Gustave Hervé began a vindictive crusade in the trade-union press. Hervé denounced the officer corps and scoffed at the ideal of patriotism; he called on French soldiers to throw off their shackles, to rip the flag from the barracks and plant it on the nearest dunghill. Some segments of the Radical party were gradually pulled into this campaign, though in a milder way. Radical politicians soon learned that their peasant and small-town voters disliked military service and retained an old prejudice against the officer class. Since re-election often seemed to depend on catering to these views, most of the Radical deputies from rural districts began to denounce the army and to support a reduction in the term of military service.

The change in mood that set in about 1911 was primarily the product of European tensions, and it was stimulated by what most Frenchmen took to be the aggressive and unreasonable behavior of the German government. The nationalist revival of 1911–14 pervaded almost every segment of society — the political elite, the army, the bureaucracy, the urban bourgeoisie, even the labor movement. The Moderates, whose ancestors had been horrified at Boulanger's jingoism, shared the new temper as strongly as anyone; so did many Radical politicians, though the bulk of the Radicals lagged behind the trend simply because their home districts in rural France were less quickly affected. That rural lag was reflected in the last prewar elections (April-May, 1914), when the country chose a Chamber whose majority was committed to a reduction in military service and a pacific foreign policy. Meanwhile, however, the nationalist revival had swept Caillaux and the Radicals out of office in favor of a more intransigent Moderate government headed by the Lorraine patriot Raymond Poincaré; and a year later (1913) it had carried Poincaré to the presidency of the republic. It had also bolstered the sagging morale and prestige of the army and had given the officer corps a new sense of confidence and purpose at a moment when that was desperately needed.

❧❧❧

Two new political movements, small in numbers but in both cases durable and significant, were added to the existing parties during the

339

prewar decade in France.[2] One was the Action Française; the other, the Christian democratic Sillon.

 Charles Maurras, a young classical scholar brought out of his ivory tower by the Dreyfus Affair, founded the Action Française in 1898 as a weapon for fighting the Dreyfusards. The organization survived *l'Affaire*, and developed into an intensely nationalistic and authoritarian movement of the extreme right, dedicated to saving France from such un-French elements as the Protestants, the Freemasons, and the Jews. Maurras soon grafted both monarchism and Catholicism onto his movement, on the ground that both institutions were needed in order to restore national unity and to rebuild an organic society. Though membership remained small, the impact of the organization was far out of proportion to its size. It attracted an active and vocal group of intellectuals and young people: the historian Jacques Bainville, the journalist Léon Daudet, the novelist Paul Bourget were among them. Its newspaper was brilliantly written and scurrilously shocking; its young activists kept Paris in an uproar by battling Socialists in the streets and persecuting unpatriotic professors at the Sorbonne.

Though the movement in many ways foreshadowed later totalitarian groups, its doctrine as defined by Maurras contrasted with those of later irrationalist leaders. Maurras thought of himself as the purest of rationalists and positivists, as a defender of France's true Greco-Roman heritage against the corrupting influence of Teutonic mysticism. His goal was to restore traditional institutions and mores, those that France had known before the disaster of the Great Revolution; it was not to go forward by disintegrating the old society and establishing a new elite, in modern totalitarian fashion. Yet despite his purposes and the disclaimers of his later disciples, it is clear that the product of his

[2] The Dreyfus Affair crystallized a whole series of political parties and movements, some of which had existed as amorphous factions without much organizational structure. Thus in 1901 the Socialist-Radical party was given nationally organized form for the first time, and the Moderate faction gave birth in 1901–2 to two organized parties: the Democratic Alliance (which supported Waldeck's coalition with the left) and the Republican Federation (which opposed it).

agitation was a proto-fascist mood. Maurrassism reinforced the rabid right-wing temper that had emerged from Boulangist agitation, and ensured its persistence in France. While Alain was demoralizing a large segment of young Frenchmen on the left, Maurras was corrupting an important part of the right. In the wealthy, well-born, right-thinking classes that dominated industry, the upper bureaucracy, the army and navy, Maurras got a wide hearing. He indoctrinated them with a violent contempt for the masses as degenerate, for the republic's leadership as rotten; he persuaded this segment of the French elite that the nation faced catastrophe unless "the real country" could seize control from "the legal country." Thanks to Alain and Maurras, ". . . the masses distrusted those who might have led, and the classes hated and despised those who might have followed."[3]

Catholics in the old Veuillot and Assumptionist tradition welcomed the Maurrassian agitation. Another segment of Catholics found it nauseating. They found their apostle in young Marc Sangnier, a crusading idealist who in 1898 brought together a little group of fellow students eager to find a way to live as well as to practice their faith. From a discussion group the Sillon (Furrow) turned to social action; it attracted a small but devoted band of young laymen and parish priests. In 1907 Sangnier began to convert the Sillon into a political movement and to put up candidates for the Chamber. The organization was frankly committed to a reconciliation between church and republic; its leaders rejected control by the hierarchy and opened their ranks to all well-wishers, whether Catholic or not. In that era the enterprise was far too daring to achieve success. Both Catholics and freethinkers remained warily aloof; yet the Vatican (influenced, possibly, by Action Française advisers) viewed it as potentially dangerous. In 1910 Pope Pius issued a virtual death warrant, in which he described the Sillon as "that miserable tributary of the great stream of apostasy." Sangnier

---

[3] P. Williams, in J. M. Wallace-Hadrill and J. McManners (eds.), *France: Government and Society*, p. 242.

submitted and liquidated the organization. But its small elite continued to work through other less vulnerable agencies; many of them (including Sangnier) were to see their dream of a great Christian democratic movement become reality.

TWENTY-ONE

> A huge factory isn't my idea of the model for a
> perfect society.
>
> "ALAIN" *(1907)*

Economy: Structure and Trends, 1870–1914

Frenchmen of our time look back on the years before 1914 as *"la belle époque"* — roughly translatable as "the good old days." Any era tends to take on increased glamor and appeal in retrospect; as an ironic Frenchman once remarked, people are rarely able to conjugate the verb "to be happy" in the present tense. Yet the pre-1914 generation probably came closer to that fortunate state than has any other in modern French history.

During the half-century of peace that intervened between the Prussian war and the 1914 conflict, the nation enjoyed a remarkable combination of stability and expansion. The old France survived, yet alongside it a new France was obviously emerging. Industrial output tripled between 1870 and 1914; total national income probably doubled; French investments abroad increased sixfold. The process of urbanization continued steadily, though not so rapidly as to destroy the older rural society. In 1870, 52 per cent of the active population was engaged in agriculture; in 1914, the figure still exceeded 40 per cent. Living standards, though difficult to measure, were on the rise for the bulk of the population and put Frenchmen ahead of any other continental people.[1] Although mass housing conditions (both urban and rural) remained antiquated and uncomfortable, levels of consumption steadily rose, and real wage rates in industry increased by something like 50 per cent between 1870 and 1914. Most of the peasants, after surviving a period of serious difficulties in the seventies and eighties, were better off, too. Average crop yields improved a little, farm prices began to rise again in the mid-nineties, and a falling birth rate combined with a drift to the cities to cut the pressure of population on the land. The only statistics that were beginning to disturb Frenchmen were those in the demographic sphere. From 1871 to 1914 the total population rose only from thirty-six to thirty-nine million. Even before the carnage of the First World War, France as a nation was falling behind its more prolific neighbors, and the population pyramid was beginning to show the first signs of a middle-age bulge.

Any graph of French economic activity from 1870 to 1914 would be likely to show two major phases: an era of relative slackness from the Prussian war to the mid-nineties, followed by a period of impressive vigor and growth from 1895 until the First World War. The first phase did not bring either absolute decline or stagnation; rather, it was marked by a slowing of the remarkable expansionist trend of the Second Empire. The most notable phenomenon was a jerky decline in price levels, which fell about 40 per cent between 1876 and 1896. Industrial growth continued, but at a more gradual rate, while agriculture found itself in almost constant difficulties caused by the competition of overseas imports and by the disastrous impact of a disease called phylloxera that destroyed a third of the vineyards in France. Then, in the mid-nineties, the upturn came; prices rose again by 40 per cent from 1896 to 1914, output jumped dramatically, foreign trade increased by about 75 per cent, and the national income made its most phenomenal growth since the days of Napoleon III. Those were the

[1] Some authorities disagree and believe that by 1914 per capita income in France was lagging behind that of Germany, Switzerland, the Low Countries, and most of Scandinavia. The statistics are obviously inadequate and controversial.

years that brought to France its share of the second industrial
revolution.

The reasons for the shift from slackness to boom about 1895 are not
easily discoverable. To some degree, France merely reflected a European-wide trend: the seventies and eighties had been a time of slackness
and declining prices everywhere, and the upturn was general from the
mid-nineties. But some special factors seem to have been operative in
France to make the boom there even greater than it was across the
Channel in Britain. One such factor was the opening of the vast Briey
iron-ore fields in French Lorraine. The Germans had drawn the 1871
frontier between French and German Lorraine in such a way as to
annex most of the known iron deposits of the area, but what they had
gotten proved to be the outcroppings of a huge subterranean deposit,
the bulk of which lay on the French side of the frontier. The Lorraine
ore, though rich, contained impurities that made it almost unusable
until English experimenters developed a new smelting process in 1878.
French engineers began at once to drill in the area and shortly made
a rich strike in the Briey basin, only four miles from the German
frontier. Technical difficulties interfered for a time with the exploitation
of the new ore, but these were solved shortly before 1900, and the iron
and steel industry of the region expanded at a remarkable rate. By
1914 there were twenty iron and steel works in French Lorraine, producing more than two-thirds of France's total pig iron and steel. In
addition, large quantities of raw ore and pig iron were sold to Germany
and Belgium; France became the world's largest exporter of iron ore.

A second factor, much more controversial in its impact on economic
growth, was France's decision in 1892 to adopt a high-tariff policy on
both industrial and farm products. Napoleon III's turn toward freer
trade had never been widely popular with the French business class,
though it had forced much of French industry to modernize itself
during the sixties. The revulsion against the empire after 1870 provided an added reason for a return to higher tariffs, and so did the
general European trend toward protectionism beginning in the seventies. When Napoleon's low-tariff treaties expired, the Opportunist poli-

ticians re-established duties on many industrial products; but it was not until the so-called Méline Tariff of 1892 that all-out protectionism was adopted. The Méline rates were boosted again in 1910, making French tariff rates the fourth highest in the world.

Whether the Méline Tariff marked a return to good sense or the beginning of French decadence is an issue that has divided Frenchmen ever since. Its defenders assert a direct causal relationship between the tariff law and the boom that followed shortly after; they point out that protectionist France from 1900 to 1914 enjoyed a more rapid rate of growth in production and foreign trade than did free-trade Britain. They point also to the fact that the Méline Tariff, by setting up duties on imported foodstuffs, enabled France to preserve a healthy and balanced economic and social structure. French farmers, instead of being driven off the land as in Britain, managed to survive and, in some cases, to prosper. France was able to remain 90 per cent self-sufficient in foodstuffs and to keep third rank among the wheat-producing nations of the world. Furthermore, according to the defenders of the tariff, this large farm population constituted a steady home market for French industrial goods.

Critics of the Méline Tariff deny that it contributed very much to the subsequent boom, which, they say, was the product of European and world-wide economic trends. They admit that the tariff enabled many French producers to survive, but at a heavy cost to the economy and to society as a whole. France continued to raise much wheat, for example, but at a cost twice that of more efficient countries. The rate of economic growth after 1895, the critics insist, could and should have been much faster than it was; without tariffs, exports might have been expanded far more rapidly, and a bigger and healthier domestic market might have been developed. They believe that the effect of the tariff was to produce a stagnant rather than a vigorous economy. Inefficient plants and farms could survive without having to modernize; the cost of production remained high, consumption levels low, and France's competitive trade position bad.

This debate has hinged largely on the kind of society preferred by

the two camps. If the central goal is a system built around small independent producers and distributors — if the aim is a kind of Jeffer-
sonian social stability rather than a technocratic social fluidity — then
the Méline policy was wise and healthy. If the goal is a vigorously
competitive economy, capable of adapting and keeping up with other
nations in a fluid world, then the Méline Tariff certainly had long-
range results that have weighed on France ever since. It was not that
the Méline Tariff rendered impossible the modernization and expansion
of French plants and farms; some industrialists and farmers undertook
such modernization voluntarily. The trouble with the tariff was that it
encouraged the tendency of most business men, peasants, and politicians to avoid changes in the established routine and strengthened
their conviction that France had attained a kind of beatific state of
perfect harmony and balance. The effect of the republic's tariff policy
was to encourage the division of twentieth-century France into two
sectors: a dynamic, modern, efficient sector that increasingly dominated
the nation's production figures, and a static, backward, unadapted
sector that scarcely changed at all and that continued to dominate the
nation's political machinery.

The survival of this large static sector in France nevertheless raises
some important questions. Other nations also turned protectionist in
the late nineteenth century, yet they saw their static sectors rather
thoroughly squeezed out by dynamic competitors. Indeed, this latter
process was so rapid in the United States that antitrust laws were
finally adopted to check the trend toward monopoly. France needed no
such laws. Two factors there blocked what might seem to be a natural
trend: one of them was political, the other psychological.

Politically, most of the Third Republic's leaders consistently tended
to favor the little man — both by necessity and by choice. A successful
politician could hardly avoid such an attitude in a country with so
many voters who were little men. But it was a genuinely appealing
attitude as well, for it fitted the honest prejudices of most French
politicians, the bulk of whom were themselves of middle- or petty-
bourgeois origin. The Opportunists and Moderates, with their con-

servative social philosophy, saw the small producer and distributor as the source of social stability. The Radicals were even more deeply committed to defending the little man, by doctrine and interest as well as by family background.

But the survival of static France was ensured also by a psychological factor. Most of the efficient industrialists and farmers in France were not strongly impelled to expand production, to corner the market and to destroy their small competitors. Perhaps they restrained themselves because they thought it wise to preserve a large buffer element of small producers and distributors as a sort of "social umbrella" beneath which their own power and profits could be dissembled. Or perhaps they saw here a simple device for keeping their profit margin high. By permitting prices to stay at a level that would keep the small inefficient producer in business, the dynamic manufacturer or farmer could enjoy the pleasant condition of operating without much risk or effort, and he could count on a handsome income from a limited but stable market.

These factors kept the new dynamic sector of the economy from overrunning and crushing out the static sector. Yet they could not prevent a gradual erosion of static enterprise and a steady concentration of economic power, especially in the industrial sphere. By 1914 more than half of the total output of many items was being produced by four or five firms, and small marginal enterprises were steadily dropping in number. Still, small firms did survive in far larger proportion than in other western nations. In 1914 one-third of France's industrial workers were still employed in shops with no more than ten workers each, and more than half were still in plants with no more than a hundred employees. The survival of the static sector was even clearer in agriculture, where the excessively slow drift to the cities (amounting to about one per cent of the rural population per year) left far too many marginal farms operating, and where most peasants had no easy access to capital for improvements. French agriculture increasingly became a museum with exhibits ranging from the medieval to the ultra-modern.

In a sense, the most remarkable successes of French business men after 1870 were achieved outside the frontiers of France. French bankers and engineers played an active part in the industrial development of the rest of the European continent. Already, between 1850 and 1870, French investments abroad had risen from two billion to fifteen billion francs; by 1914 the total had reached forty-five billion francs, two-thirds of which had been placed in Europe or in the Mediterranean basin. The largest single recipient was Russia, with 25 per cent of the total; the French colonial empire, in contrast, attracted only 10 per cent. Almost one-third of France's available liquid capital had gone into foreign investment by 1914 — a proportion higher than that of England. Most of these funds were funnelled abroad through powerful new investment banks founded during the generation after 1870: the Banque de Paris et des Pays-Bas (1872) was the best known. Along with French cash, French technicians were also items of export. One historian has estimated that French capital and engineers built about 90 per cent of the trunk railway lines on the Continent (Germany and Scandinavia excepted).

Whether this foreign activity benefited or harmed the nation is a controversial issue, the answer to which depends partly on the perspective of the viewer. Frenchmen after 1914 would undoubtedly have been better off if most of this exported capital had been invested at home — especially since so much of it was lost through Russian default after 1917. On the other hand, Frenchmen before 1914 probably gained more than they lost by foreign investment, which brought them higher returns in interest than they could have gotten through domestic use of the funds. In the short run, the national income and standards of living were increased thereby.

In the years before 1914 few Frenchmen believed that the nation had taken the wrong economic path since 1870. They possessed stability, prosperity, a solid currency, and a balanced budget; what more could they want? If the per capita income of Frenchmen lagged behind that of Englishmen and was only half that of Americans, it still ranked among the highest on the Continent. They could smugly observe that the

German epigram to describe an idyllic existence ran thus: "to live like God in France." Yet even in that pre-1914 era a handful of French business men and economists were less sanguine and were beginning to voice fears of French decadence — fears inspired largely by the astonishing gains of Germany next door. There were some labor leaders, too, who complained of the sluggishness of the French economy and the lack of dynamism displayed by French entrepreneurs. American employers, they observed, were just as antilabor as French employers, but at least they were men of imagination and energy. If France only had an American-type business group, they argued, the aggressive attitude of these bosses might strengthen the feeble trade-union movement by shaking the French worker into a more active class-consciousness.

Another full generation was to elapse, however, before Frenchmen in large numbers would critically re-examine their nation's economic record in the pre-1914 era. When they did so, some of them concluded that the decline of French power in the twentieth century was not merely the product of two disastrous world wars but had deeper roots in *la belle époque* itself. France's rising production and trade figures between 1870 and 1914 had concealed from contemporaries a relative decline that was dramatic. In 1870 France was still the world's second industrial producer and trading nation; in 1914 it had fallen to a poor fourth in both respects. The French share of world industrial production dropped during those years from almost 10 per cent to 6 per cent.

That Frenchmen failed to compete successfully with the most dynamic industrial nations is clear; the reasons for that failure remain controversial. Some economic historians have taken the position that the French did about as well as they could with what they had; that the nation's structural and technical weaknesses were simply too great to permit effective competition with rival states better equipped by nature for the industrial age. The chronic shortage of coal — especially good coking coal — was one such handicap; another was the deep-rooted tradition of luxury manufacture that hampered rapid conversion to production-line methods. A second school of historians has argued that the principal factor hampering France's economic growth, after 1870 as well as before that time, was the continuing lack of a real entrepreneurial spirit. They observe that other nations managed to find ways to compensate for their lack of essential raw materials or succeeded in uprooting an older manufacturing or farming tradition in favor of a new. They point out that France no longer lacked liquid capital after mid-century, but that French investors preferred to invest it in underdeveloped countries rather than at home. They point to the persistence of the family firm in France — to the stubborn conviction of many business men that no outsider should even be permitted to invest in the enterprise, and that the owner's duty was to protect and hand on his patrimony rather than to risk losing it in an effort to double its size. They note the French inclination to take smallness as an ideal — an inclination deeply rooted in French mores, business or otherwise. "Mon verre est petit, mais je bois dans mon verre" ("My cup may be small, but I drink from my own"): few French maxims are more revealing of a generalized attitude toward life.

To a lesser degree, French entrepreneurship after 1870 continued to be hampered by the old heritage of social values — a heritage that had been generally uncongenial toward the ideas of business expansion and monetary success. There were still remnants of the traditional attitude that the way to attain status was to escape from business, not to succeed within it. The escape route, which had once led into the aristocracy, now led into politics or the professions. More common still was what one historian has called "a genteel pattern of entrepreneurship," whose ". . . ideal model is that of the businessman as a 'rounded,' civilized individual, not enslaved by his wealth, but master thereof to spend it in the fashioning of an elegant, cultivated existence."[2] Many of the values contained in this ideal of the good life were the values of a precapitalist age; and there is some evidence to support the view that this ethos gained new strength in the pre-1914 years. It provided a kind of self-justification for French business men as they saw them-

[2] David Landes, "Religion and Enterprise: The Case of the French Textile Industry" (unpublished essay).

selves being outstripped by crassly materialistic rivals in "less civilized" societies. On the other hand, the business man or banker in the Third Republic no longer needed to feel ashamed of his calling, provided he stayed within the bounds of propriety.

France's notable business expansion after 1895 might seem to suggest a fundamental change in the nation's attitudes and mores. Yet even in this highly favorable era, French business leaders failed to take full advantage of their opportunities. For example, instead of expanding the new Lorraine steel industry to its greatest potential capacity, the French preferred to export much of their raw ore and pig iron to German and Belgian manufacturers for processing and finishing. No doubt that decision was dictated in part by France's lack of coke, which had to be imported from the Ruhr at high cost; but it was also the product of the unwillingness of French enterprisers to gamble, of their lack of interest in expansion. Other opportunities, too, were missed. This was an era of transition to new products: new materials like rayon and aluminum, new finished goods like the automobile. In many of these fields the French got an initial advantage and then promptly lost it. Frenchmen in the nineties set up the first rayon mill, and in 1901 led the world in rayon production; by 1914 France had fallen to third rank. The same advantage was lost, or missed, in aluminum production, in automobile building, and in electrical products. The notable growth of French industry between 1895 and 1914 did not change the fundamental structure of the industrial system. Textiles — the chief product of early industrialism — continued to dominate French production right down to 1914; textile mills still employed the largest number of workers and furnished the largest item of export. Not until the impact of the First World War was France propelled into the second stage of industrialism, the metallurgical age.

If French business psychology was partly responsible for the retarded growth of industry, the politicians of the time also bore their share of the blame. The new republican political elite was largely untrained and uninterested in economic problems and adopted a kind of neutral attitude toward the business world. It has been said that no statesman of the Third Republic left his name attached to a significant piece of legislation in the economic sphere. There are two possible exceptions to this generalization — Méline and Freycinet — but whether the effects of their contributions were positive or negative is open to debate.[3] On the whole, the politicians of the era probably did more to retard than to promote economic growth. But if that was the case, they were surely not being unrepresentative of their electors. Like most successful politicians of all eras, they shared the mores of their time and place.

[3] Méline's achievement was the tariff of 1892; he is the patron saint of agrarian protectionists in France. The Freycinet Plan (1879) laid out an elaborate program of state-subsidized railway construction, confined to secondary lines in areas still remote from the completed trunk system. Although the plan still awaits its historian, it has often been criticized as a costly piece of pork-barrel legislation that endowed France with a largely useless network of uneconomic lines and that played into the hands of shady speculators.

Society: Structure and Trends, 1870–1914

The Third Republic, a lover of paradox might say, was created by the aristocracy, administered by the upper bourgeoisie, operated by the lower bourgeoisie, and dominated by the peasantry.

The interrelationships between social realities and political mechanisms or forces are never easy to untangle, save perhaps in the kind of system that the Germans call a *Staendesstaat*, where social categories are pretty much fixed and functions are rigidly defined. In a modern social system of relatively open and fluid character, however, even its component categories, strata, or "classes" defy clear definition. Throughout modern French history these categories merge and overlap, so that commonly used terms like "bourgeoisie" and "proletariat" may mislead more than they enlighten. Even more ambiguous is the relationship between rural and urban dwellers in a changing society. The practice of lumping together the whole rural population under the collective label "the peasantry" lacks validity; yet an attempt to assimilate farm laborers with urban factory workers, or proprietors of small farms with the urban middle classes, runs into important contra-

354

dictions. Perhaps these difficulties help to explain why so little significant work has been done in the social history of modern France.

Of all social categories in late nineteenth-century France, the aristocracy is most easily dealt with, for it was the smallest, the most clearly defined, and the least important group. The decade of the 1870's represented its last brief resurgence in politics. Since 1830 most of the old Legitimist families had been sulking in domestic exile; they had lived on their country estates or in the Saint-Germain quarter of Paris and had ostentatiously disdained official society and politics. The newer aristocracy created by Louis Philippe had been out of power only since 1848 and had been less inclined to turn its back on life. Many Orleanist notables had remained active in business during the Second Empire, and some had re-entered politics as well — usually as members of the liberal opposition. The fall of the empire brought both groups flooding back into dominant roles in national as well as local politics; but their triumph was short. By 1879 they had been dislodged from one position of strength after another, and their subsequent attempts to recover influence only reaffirmed their permanent eclipse as an important organized group. For a time the sons of aristocrats continued to enter the diplomatic service and the army in disproportionate numbers, but those services, too, had become rather thoroughly republicanized by 1914. In the church hierarchy, the aristocrats' grip had long since been broken; as early as 1889 eighty-six of the ninety bishops and archbishops were of humble origin. The voters of a few rural areas in western France stubbornly continued to send aristocrats to parliament throughout the period of the Third Republic, and even into the Fourth. On the whole, however, aristocratic titles in the twentieth century had taken on an archaic and anachronistic flavor.

※◦✍◦※◦✍◦※◦✍◦

In France, as in all the Western world, the nineteenth century was the era of the bourgeoisie; and the Third Republic represented its ultimate triumph. But its steady growth in size and power made both

355

the label and its content more and more amorphous and ambiguous. "Vast and multiform as the nation itself," the bourgeoisie ranged from a millionaire banker like Henri Germain to the village druggist or postal clerk of Claquebue. Such great variety permits no very useful common classification, though a good many efforts have been made to identify the bourgeois spirit. André Siegfried once sought to define the bourgeois as "a man who has something in reserve"; more recently, he has suggested that bourgeois status might better be considered a state of mind, a particular set of mores, a type of behavior. Siegfried and others have also proposed a subclassification of the bourgeoisie into four or possibly five categories: *grande, haute, moyenne, petite,* and possibly *très petite.* An increasing number of scholars has tried to evade the ambiguities by abandoning the term "bourgeoisie" entirely and substituting "middle classes," with the emphasis on the plural form of that term. In the confused state of the question, perhaps historians must be content with a loose-jointed analysis that uses the terms "middle classes" and "bourgeoisie" interchangeably.

In the early years of the Third Republic the political and economic elite of the regime was drawn for the most part from the upper middle classes: from Siegfried's *grande bourgeoisie* (old, wealthy families like the Rothschilds) and, even more commonly, from the *haute bourgeoisie* (men like Thiers, Casimir-Périer, Henri Germain). Most of them were Orleanist by tradition, though a few had rallied to Napoleon III. After 1870 they proved more flexible and adaptable than the aristocracy; most of them, like Thiers, were converted to republicanism during the first decade and retained important roles in economic and political life. Politically they straddled the center, from which strategic position they were able to help shape the constitution of the new republic. After 1880, however, few members of the *haute bourgeoisie* remained in parliament. Their political influence henceforth was exercised indirectly, through the action of pressure groups like the Comité des Forges (an iron and steel makers' trade association, set up in 1864) or through personal contacts with prominent politicians. Moderate premiers like Maurice Rouvier, Radical premiers like Joseph Caillaux, were

356

linked closely to Parisian bankers of the *grande* and *haute bourgeoisie*. Intermarriage was common within this social group, and the world of banking and business took on a kind of clannish character through the development of what one historian has called "bourgeois dynasties."

Although their ancestors had been Voltairean anticlericals in the eighteenth and early nineteenth centuries, most members of the upper bourgeoisie had by now reconciled themselves to the church as a respectable and necessary institution. If many of them were still religious skeptics, they were willing to see their wives go to Mass and their children to Catholic schools. A powerful minority of the upper bourgeoisie, however, was Protestant; and that group had always clung more fervently to its faith. The role of what the French called the "H. S. P." (*haute société protestante*) in industry, banking, politics, and journalism was far out of proportion to its size. For one brief period there was even a Protestant majority in the cabinet.

No sharp barrier marked off the upper from the middle bourgeoisie; the structure of society was fluid (if somewhat viscous), so that there was a constant though slow upward trickle into the *haute bourgeoisie*. The *moyenne bourgeoisie*, numbering perhaps two or three millions, was much more varied in character. Its members were not newcomers to economic affluence and social status. Most of them had become solidly established in business or in the professions during the early nineteenth century; they were well-to-do, well-educated, and respected citizens. Most of the republican leadership in 1848 had come from the middle bourgeoisie; many of its members had also done well in business and government under Napoleon III. But its apogee was still to come. Economically, it profited both by the era of falling prices from 1876 to 1894 and by the boom that followed. During the first phase its members piled up savings and got control of much of the nation's liquid wealth, while during the second phase they invested abroad or participated cautiously in business expansion.

Politically, the triumph of the middle bourgeoisie was even clearer. From about 1879 onward its representatives dominated parliament and cabinet, although after the turn of the century they began to be edged out of this dominant role by men of lower social origin. The middle bourgeoisie got an even firmer and more durable grip on the higher posts in the civil service; efficient and well-trained, these middle bourgeois officials went on quietly administering the republic long after political power proper had shifted downward in the social scale. From the middle bourgeoisie there also came an influential group of lobbyists or intermediaries between the worlds of business and politics: *politiciens d'affaires* they were called, in the curious French phrase. Their nebulous activities occasionally emerged out of the shadows into public view, as during the Panama Scandal, and clouded the reputation of the regime. The contrast between the pure, romantic, even naive spirit associated with the 1848 republic and the unscrupulous affairism that came to be much too common in the political life of its successor impressed and disturbed many Frenchmen.

If the era of the Third Republic brought any really fundamental social change in France, it was probably the active emergence into roles of political and social importance of the lesser bourgeoisie — *petite* and even *très petite*. These were the elements whose rise Gambetta had foreseen when he spoke of the *nouvelles couches* that would soon be demanding recognition. They were the "little Frenchmen" *par excellence:* the small shopkeepers, clerks, white-collar employees, schoolmasters, petty civil servants of city, town, and village. Already before 1870 they had begun their ascent into the middle classes; the first and essential step in this process of upward mobility had come when their peasant or artisan fathers had put aside enough money to give them a secondary education. No other social group had so many fervent disciples of the revolutionary tradition — and especially of its Jacobin, Robespierrist phase. Ferociously egalitarian, positivist, anticlerical, and patriotic, their theoretical utopia was a republic purged of "superstition" and dedicated to the protection of the little man. Although their rise into the middle class was recent and their personal ties with the peasant and artisan world remained close, few members of this petty bourgeoisie had much comprehension of social issues. They wanted equality of status and careers open to talent, not equality of condition or state action to protect the weak and "lazy." If they had a social program, it was summed up in a moderately progressive income tax and the expansion of mutual-aid societies.

It was the lesser bourgeoisie that flooded into both Opportunist and Radical ranks from the seventies onward, and that got an unshakable grip on the Radical movement by the end of the century. Its greatest strength was in local politics; its members, fervent and dedicated men, became the active militants of the Radical party and of Freemasonry — the ward heelers, town councillors, village mayors, and members of electoral committees that chose candidates for parliament. The ablest of them began to rise into national politics as well; by 1914 a large proportion of the Radical deputies came of petty bourgeois origin. These were the new notables of the regime, the men who dominated political life in the middle years of the Third Republic, and who continued to constitute the bulk of the political class down to the collapse of 1940. The eventual decline of the republic, as some scholars see it, was intimately associated with the fading influence of this petty bourgeois political class after 1918 — or perhaps with its stubborn and narrow-minded inability to adapt to changing times. If the Third Republic, then, may properly be called a bourgeois democracy, that phrase tends to hide a steady evolutionary process within the middle classes themselves: a gradual downward shift in the locus of political power, from *haute* to *moyenne* to *petite* bourgeoisie.

Aristocracy and bourgeoisie combined made up only a small fraction of the French population before 1914 — perhaps 15 or 20 per cent in all. Alongside them, or below them, was the great mass of workers and peasants, sometimes lumped together as *les classes populaires* — ill-defined, poorly organized, and only vaguely class-conscious. Between them and the bourgeoisie the line of separation was indistinct. It was not an economic boundary, for there were workers and peasants who were better off than some of the lesser bourgeoisie. Perhaps the clearest distinction by this time was educational: the "popular classes" had no more than an elementary education (if they received any at all), while the bourgeois was the product of a secondary school, either *lycée* or *collège*.

Within this mass the peasantry was in steady but slow decline, and the industrial workers in constant numerical progress. In 1870, 52 per cent of Frenchmen had made their living by agriculture, while only 23 per cent were industrial workers or artisans. By 1914 the farm population had dropped to 44 per cent, and the number of urban workers had risen to 39 per cent. Another 10 per cent in 1914 were commercial employees, and 6 per cent were civil servants. Thus the peasantry, by a narrowing margin, still formed the largest single element; and in addition, the unequal distribution of population gave the peasants an outright majority in more than half the departments of France. The potential political power of this rural mass is obvious; some scholars have concluded from it, with at least partial validity, that the Third Republic may have been operated by the bourgeoisie but was in fact dominated by the peasantry.

The truth is somewhat more complex, largely because the peasantry was too heterogeneous to constitute a solid bloc. For one thing, the number of independent farmers in 1870 was balanced by an almost equal number of farm laborers, whose outlook did not necessarily coincide with that of owners and operators. Furthermore, the independent farmers were subdivided into owners, tenants (*fermiers*), and crop-sharers (*métayers*), and their holdings ranged from several hundred acres to miniscule plots too small to support a family. Finally, in some parts of France the peasants lived clustered together in villages or even sizable towns, while in other sections they were isolated in separate farmhouses scattered through the countryside. Such diversity virtually ruled out any common outlook, except perhaps a set of negative attitudes — a deep-rooted suspicion of the city-dweller and a desire to be left alone by the tax collector and the army recruiter.

Although peasant diversity did not grow less between 1870 and 1914, the period did see the beginnings of gradual changes, some of which foreshadowed a kind of rural revolution in the twentieth century. Until about 1890 the dominant nineteenth-century trend continued; a steady subdivision of the land increased the number of farms until the figure reached an all-time peak of six million. This trend was the product of rural overpopulation; in many regions population growth was still not being offset by the drift to the cities. Land hunger remained intense; peasants scraped and saved to buy bits of large estates or to develop new marginal land. While the independent peasantry thus reached its maximum size about 1890, the cost of that process was heavy, for most of these six million farm operators were primitive in their methods and marginal in their standards. Their precarious state furnished a good argument to the proponents of the Méline Tariff in 1892 — although in fact most peasants sold little or nothing on the market and stood to lose more than they gained by high tariffs on farm products.

Sometime in the nineties came a reversal of the trend; the number of farms operated began to drop, and it has continued to decline almost without interruption ever since. From almost six million in 1890 it fell to five million in 1911, four million in 1929, and two and a half million in 1946. This trend may seem to reinforce the Marxian thesis that sooner or later big capitalist enterprise ruthlessly drives the little farmer off the soil. In certain limited areas of France (notably in the wheat and sugar-beet country that runs from the Paris basin to the Belgian border), there were real signs of such a tendency toward capitalist concentration both before 1914 and after the war. But for most of France, the post-1890 process was rather one of gradual consolidation of dwarf holdings into middle-sized family farms in the 25-to-100 acre class. The rural exodus at last offset rural population growth; many small-owners, or sons of small-owners, began to sell or rent their bits of soil to a neighbor or, in some cases, let it go back to nature. This process presaged the rise of a healthier and more prosperous peasantry, although there continued to survive a great many of the older marginal farms too small and too poorly equipped to furnish more than a meager subsistence.

A second healthy trend was the spread of education and an increase in rural permeability to outside contacts. In 1870 probably a third of the peasants were still illiterate; by 1914, thanks to the Ferry school laws, almost all could read and write. In 1870 the inhabitants of three out of four rural communes still lived in almost total isolation from the outside world; by 1914, thanks to improved rail and road communication and the growing use of the bicycle, most peasants had come to know something beyond their own villages. It was an era, too, of continuing political education in the countryside. In the elections of 1871 many peasants still were uncertain about the use of the ballot; they fell back on voting for, or accepting the guidance of, the local notables — the châtelain or the curé. That habit persisted in 1914 in a few areas like the Vendée; but in most of France the peasantry had long since gained at least a primitive degree of political sophistication. Republican prefects and subprefects had their share in this educational process; so did returning country boys who had gone to the cities to work or had served in the army; so did urban newspapers, as they began to penetrate the countryside. But most important of all was the action of republican militants — the village school teacher who challenged the local curé to doctrinal combat; the village politician, whether doctor or pharmacist or veterinarian or notary, who labored assiduously to indoctrinate the peasants and to line up the vote. Few French peasants by 1914 had learned much about economics, or agronomy, or the importance of organization; but they had learned to listen to the new notables in place of the old, and they had discovered that most politicians were dependent on peasant votes to stay in office.

⇒∘⇐∘⇒∘⇐∘⇒∘⇐

If France had a forgotten man in the pre-1914 era, it was surely the urban worker. The expansion of the working class since 1870 had brought rising unrest and violence but not very much in the way of social gains. In 1884 trade unions had finally been formally legalized; in 1900 women and children were restricted to a ten-hour day; in 1906

Sunday rest was made obligatory; in 1910 an optional social insurance plan was established. Almost no other industrial state in those years granted so little to its labor force.

Bourgeois and peasant shortsightedness was partly responsible for this lack of progress. Neither middle classes nor farmers had developed much of a social conscience; they clung to the doctrine of laissez faire and to the ideal of the lowest possible tax bill. Together, these two segments of society formed a solid phalanx in parliament against which labor demands could beat in vain. Almost the only signs of interest in social problems in the later nineteenth century turned up on the extreme right, among Catholics and Legitimists. Even the Comte de Chambord, for all his obtuseness in political matters, had some inkling of the need for social reform. The attitude of these rightists, however, was excessively and naively paternalistic. Efforts by such Catholic conservatives as Comte Albert de Mun to develop what they called "social Catholicism" ran up against the incomprehension of most French employers and the suspicious hostility of the working class.

But labor shared at least some responsibility for its failure to get more from the politicians. Much of its potential influence as a pressure group was wasted by the workers' reluctance to join trade unions, and by the antipolitical bias of the unions that did exist. The Confédération Générale du Travail (C.G.T.), although it was by far the largest union organization, had several rivals; and five million out of the six million industrial workers in 1914 still preferred no union at all. In part, labor's resistance to organization may have derived from the excessive individualism that is supposed to be typical of French workers (and of Frenchmen in general). More probably, it grew out of the character of French industry, so much of which remained small and semiartisanal in structure. In shops with only a dozen employees, *patron* and laborer remained both physically and temperamentally close; class-consciousness sprouted slowly there. Furthermore, even large enterprise had a special character in France; 40 per cent of French workers were still employed in the textile and clothing trades in 1914, and more than half of these worked at home rather than in

363

factories. Such a labor force was far more resistant to organization than a mass of production-line workers in vast impersonal plants.

Labor discontent was softened, too, by the slow but real upward trend in living standards. All statistics suggest that the second half of the nineteenth century was more favorable to the workers than the first half had been, and that the working man was better off in 1914 than ever before. True, after 1894 the rising price curve almost offset wage increases, so that real wages rose little in the two decades before 1914. This meant that the labor force was not sharing in the benefits of French economic growth during those boom years; the increase in the total national income (which has been estimated at 37 per cent for the decade 1902–12 alone) concealed from labor the fact that its share of that income was getting relatively smaller. No adequate statistics were available in those days to awaken them to such painful facts; indeed, even today statistics on the pre-1914 national income and its distribution are so uncertain as to make any conclusions hazardous. But even if it is true that labor was getting a steadily smaller slice of cake, the whole cake was quite obviously getting larger, so that the worker found himself gaining a little in absolute terms. No sense of desperate urgency drove him to join a union or to further the growth of socialism by any action more drastic than voting for Socialist candidates (most of whom were petty bourgeois in origin). Despite the fact that strikes were frequent during the prewar decade, there was actually less labor violence in France than in the United States during that period.

Paradoxically, the militant minority within French labor was one of the most violent in Europe — in doctrine, at any rate. From the time of its organization in 1895, the C.G.T. adopted an ideology of direct action through strikes, sabotage, and boycotts and an attitude of hostility toward participation in the political process. Its founders had been influenced by the ideas of Proudhon and the anarchists; long before Georges Sorel came along, they had developed the thesis of the general strike as the ultimate weapon. Political action, they held, would be futile and corrupting; "to send workers into parliament," asserted one C.G.T. leader, "is to act like a mother who would take her daughters into a house of prostitution."[1] The union resisted the Socialists' efforts to annex it as a kind of factory branch of the party; in its Amiens Charter of 1906 the C.G.T. asserted a rigidly apolitical position that it was to retain for forty years. Relations between the unions and the Socialist party were, in consequence, worse in France than anywhere else in Europe before 1914. The C.G.T.'s extremism probably helped to keep it small; its numerical weakness in turn almost certainly helped to keep it extreme. It was easy for labor leaders without many troops to seize upon the romantic thesis that a small but militant vanguard would one day lead the unorganized mass of workers in a spontaneous movement to achieve its proletarian destiny.

Although the doctrine of revolutionary syndicalism remained the C.G.T.'s official line until 1914, there were clear signs that the trend within labor was away from violence and toward reformism. The attractions of collective bargaining and of parliamentary labor legislation were undermining the apocalyptic dogma of the old-guard union leaders. On the eve of the war the C.G.T. seemed to be moving toward a working alliance with the Socialist party in an effort to achieve piece-meal reforms. The myth of the general strike was losing its appeal; the crusading antimilitarism of the C.G.T. was being challenged by a current of revived patriotism within the unions. Had it not been for the disruptive impact of the Great War, and the new set of myths that grew out of the Russian Revolution, perhaps French labor might have been drawn into the dominant Western tradition of reformist action within, rather than against, the existing state.

[1] In V. Lorwin, "Labor and Economic Development in France."

TWENTY-THREE

> We are viewing the prologue of an incredible
> drama, such as no one has seen for several
> centuries.
>
> LÉON BLOY *(1906)*

The French Mind and Spirit,
1870–1914

Frenchmen in the decade before 1870 had already entered upon a new phase in their intellectual evolution. The formidable figure of Victor Hugo still loomed up to overshadow all rivals as the symbol of French cultural achievement; but, although he lived on until 1885, he had become a kind of gigantic anachronism, an object of mixed admiration and tolerant cynicism. The time had passed when the romantic mood was congenial to men's spirits; this was a harder, less frankly emotional age, attuned to the rise of science and materialism. Science alone, wrote the chemist Marcellin Berthelot in the sixties, possesses ". . . a moral force powerful enough to bring about without delay the blessed era of equality and fraternity." "The trend of the times is toward science," added Émile Zola; "we are driven in spite of ourselves toward the exact study of facts and things." This change of mood that set in after mid-century was, of course, not uniquely or even especially French; it was shared with the rest of the Western world. Yet as always, when refracted through French minds and adapted to the French cultural heritage, it took on a special coloration.

366

Three men stand out as the high priests of that first republican generation from 1870 to 1890: Auguste Comte, Hippolyte Taine, and Ernest Renan. It would be hard to exaggerate the impact of Comte's ideas; rarely in history has a thinker of such indifferent talent managed to indoctrinate so thoroughly the whole political class of the next generation. This success was due not so much to Comte's originality as to his talent in systematizing and modernizing the doctrines that had sprung up during the Enlightenment era. These ideas he wove together into a consistent and all-embracing philosophy or world view; and he combined them with the faith in science and inevitable progress that was burgeoning throughout the West. This combination was produced at just the moment to catch on, for the anticlerical republicans of France were seeking a doctrine, a philosophy, upon which to build their new world. By 1870 Comte's positivism had become the quasi-official philosophic system of almost every republican, whether Opportunist or Radical; and many monarchists like Thiers were infected as well. Comte's dedicated disciple Émile Littré, (most celebrated as compiler of a dictionary) devoted a lifetime of pamphleteering to the task of indoctrinating the educated French elite.

Ernest Renan, though he refused to call himself a positivist and though he was only a late and reluctant republican, was another powerful inspirer of the new generation in France. Like the positivists, he preached and practiced the cult of reason and science. A devout Breton by birth, he had almost completed his training for the priesthood when he lost his faith and left the church. His *Life of Jesus*, published in 1863, brought him overnight fame (or infamy, depending on the point of view); it was a brilliant attempt to write the life of Christ as a human being, through the use of the most rigorous methods of scientific research. Renan spent a lifetime crusading for the introduction of German scientific methods into French education; he traced the disaster of 1870 in part to France's backwardness in this sphere, though he found it also in the excesses of universal suffrage and in racial degeneration. As late as 1889 he published a book called *The Future of*

Science (written forty years earlier) that was a hymn to reason and progress: "Science," he declared, "is my religion."

Renan represented a deep-rooted tradition in the French outlook: the spirit of skepticism. His contemporary, Hippolyte Taine, literary critic and historian, epitomized an equally ancient heritage: the rationalist or Cartesian cast of French thought, with its stress on order, clarity, and logic. In a book published in 1870, Taine denounced the futility of metaphysical speculation and proclaimed it man's duty to study facts alone. Alongside the natural sciences Taine set what he called the "moral sciences"; he advocated the use of similar methods to seek laws in history and in human behavior. The same attitude was reflected in his literary criticism: books were to him, like any other product of the human spirit, the outgrowth of race, milieu, and moment, and he added that "vice and virtue are products like vitriol and sugar." As a true Cartesian, Taine had a passion for formulas, for reducing ideas to their essentials; every man and every book, he remarked, could be summarized in three pages, and every three pages in three lines. A mathematical theorem seemed to him the ideal of perfect beauty. Like Renan, Taine after 1871 set out to analyze the reasons for the nation's disgraceful military failure; he found the origins of French decadence in the ideological abstractions and the revolutionary myth that had seduced the nation since 1789. There is some irony, therefore, in the fact that both Taine and Renan were so admired and lionized in the new republic, and that both men had so deep an impact on the mood of that republican generation.

The dominant mood of positivism and scientism in the 1870's and 1880's was reflected in literature and the arts almost as clearly as in philosophy and politics. In literature, two major currents stemmed from Renan and Taine, respectively, and ran parallel until the end of the century. Renan's skepticism pervaded the work of such novelists as Anatole France; Taine's Cartesian rationalism carried over into the naturalistic school headed by Émile Zola. Anatole France, perhaps the most widely-read literary man of the era, was a kind of mild successor to Voltaire — a master of wit and irony, "a humanitarian dilettante with a choice style and no very deep convictions." Perhaps his skepticism did go so deep that it seemed to leave him a total agnostic; yet underlying France's gentle mockery of human foibles there persisted a deep though vague attachment to the principles of 1789, to the ideals of liberty and justice. That attachment brought him eventually to a kind of humanitarian socialism, best reflected in his own ironic comments on bourgeois institutions. "I have pondered the philosophy of law," remarked his character Monsieur Bergeret, "and I recognized that all social justice rests on these two axioms: theft is reprehensible, the product of theft is sacred." Equally typical was France's comment that "the law in its majestic impartiality forbids the rich as well as the poor to sleep under bridges, to steal purses and to beg for bread."

Zola, the greatest and most representative figure of the naturalistic school, sought quite frankly to apply the scientific method to fiction. Like Taine, he saw men as products or playthings of powerful forces beyond their control; a pessimistic determinism pervaded his works. Zola believed that the novelist should attack his subject with the objectivity of a chemist in his laboratory. Massive research went into his books, for he believed that novels, like histories, should be written from documents. Almost annually, beginning in 1871, he produced a volume in his massive Rougon-Macquart series, examining in vast detail the development of a family in mid-nineteenth-century France. His concentration on the seamy side of human existence only added to the brutal power of his works. Many readers thought that they found here a kind of untouched photograph of life beneath the false surface of bourgeois society.

Even in poetry, the scientistic spirit of the age had its impact. The school of Parnassian poets that stemmed from Leconte de Lisle resurrected the classical tradition but thought of themselves as aloof observers of life, as representative voices of a scientific era. In painting likewise, the dominant school of impressionism sought to go beyond Courbet's realism to a more accurate approach to reality. Recent advances in optics furnished these artists with a better understanding of the nature of light, and they sought to apply this knowledge by the so-

369

called impressionistic technique. The leading impressionists, men like Manet, Monet, Degas, and Renoir, set up as their ideal the artist as a "disembodied eye," as aloof from his subject as any laboratory experimenter.

A scientific age ought properly to reveal itself not only through the impact of science on thought and the arts, but also through a heightened interest and more rapid advances in science itself. Such was the case in France in this era; in pure science, and even in many of its applied branches, Frenchmen competed successfully with almost every rival nation. Their achievements were the more striking in light of the inadequate resources available to them; university laboratories were meager and primitive, industrial research almost nonexistent. A catalogue of names would be of little use, save perhaps to indicate the variety of French interest in the sciences. Among the eminent figures of the age were Louis Pasteur in medicine; Marcellin Berthelot in chemistry; Pierre and Marie Curie and Henri Becquerel in physics; Jean Charcot, Freud's predecessor and teacher, in psychopathology; and Henri Poincaré in mathematics. Frenchmen began to pioneer also in the newer social sciences and to apply the spirit and even the methods of science to such humanistic disciplines as history and literary criticism.

⟡◦⟢ ⟡◦⟢ ⟡◦⟢

Yet even at the height of the scientistic-positivistic age contrary trends persisted from a past era, and premonitory signs of a new mood began to appear. If the year 1879 brought the first novel of Anatole France, it also brought the first work of Pierre Loti, whose lush and exotic romanticism clashed strangely with the temper of the times, but whose books found a wide public for several decades. The new republican class might find its inspiration in Comte's arid positivism, but it could never escape its youthful impregnation with Michelet's passionately romantic version of French history. Flaubert and Zola might pride themselves on confronting life with cold detachment, yet even

370

these giants of realism and naturalism could not successfully repress their own frustrated romanticism. Good republicans might reject the "superstitious obscurantism" of the church, yet some of them were repelled by total agnosticism and sought a compromise in conversion to Protestantism or a return to Kant as a substitute for Comte.

Alongside these surviving currents from the past, new ones of even greater import began to emerge in the 1880's and 1890's. In 1886, at the very height of the positivist age, the new school of symbolist poets got its name and began to attract a few avant-garde readers. In 1889 Paul Bourget, in his best-selling novel *Le Disciple*, challenged all the basic assumptions of the era and founded a traditionalist cult based upon authority, the family, and social order. In his didactic preface Bourget warned young Frenchmen of his generation against two temptations: "brutal positivism" and "disdainful sophism," and he bemoaned the corrupting influence of universal suffrage, "the most monstrous and iniquitous of tyrannies." Over the next two decades Bourget and Anatole France were to engage in an impassioned fictional debate involving every major political issue as well as the rival doctrines underlying those issues. It was in 1889, too, that the young philosopher Henri Bergson produced his first book, little noticed at the time but a harbinger of real intellectual revolution. There was a kind of symbolism in the fact that the two remaining high priests of the scientific age, Renan and Taine, disappeared from the scene in 1892 and 1893, respectively. New idols, new sources of inspiration took their place; from the mid-1890's onward Bergson and Maurice Barrès became the standard-bearers of the revolt against positivism and scientism.

Barrès, a brilliant young Lorrainer whose first novel appeared in 1888, spoke out passionately for a repudiation of the stultifying doctrines that had dominated republican thought. He called for a return to "the sources of national energy" and sought to found a cult of the self, of the soil, of *la patrie*. An "integral nationalist" (the phrase was coined by Barrès), a life-long republican who preached authoritarianism, a mystical unbeliever who deeply admired the church, a spokesman for the extreme right who advocated a kind of socialism, Barrès epitomized in his person many of the complexities and contradictions of the new era and of the new right wing in politics. A fervent supporter of General Boulanger, he was elected to parliament just as Boulangism disintegrated; and over the next two decades he remained an isolated but influential voice. That influence, however, defies precise analysis; it was never focussed, but always curiously diffused. Barrèsism did not become embodied in a formal, enduring organization; rather it infiltrated the ideas and emotions of a whole generation. Few men did so much to consolidate the new mood of chauvinistic authoritarianism on the extreme right; few men found such a devoted following among young intellectuals; few men have written novels that so successfully reflected a vital aspect of their times. "Without Barrès," a French scholar has recently remarked, "it is impossible to study France's domestic history from 1880 to 1914."

The influence of Bergson, though it developed more gradually, proved in the end to be both broader and deeper than that of Barrès. His ideas "powerfully shaped not only the thought but the sensibility of a whole generation of Frenchmen"; he has even been called the Descartes of the modern era. Bergson undermined the very foundations of positivist thought and offered a new set of doctrines to take its place. He attacked the determinism and the scientific dogmatism of the age; he shifted attention to man's nonrational drives, to intuition as the proper path to truth. In his phrase *élan vital* (vital urge), he characterized the creative force that, according to him, makes men and nations great. Our real selves, Bergson taught, are not represented in our clear ideas, the product of rational reflection; they lie buried in those subconscious tendencies that rarely emerge from the depths. Bergson's full impact came after the publication of his best-known work, *Creative Evolution*, in 1906; by 1910 Bergsonism had become a kind of new gospel. His lectures at the Collège de France were social events where serious students and the *beau monde* competed for classroom space; his ideas penetrated almost every intellectual discussion in prewar Paris. As Taine's ideas had led to Zola and Renan's to Anatole France, so Bergson's had their literary reflection in Marcel Proust. The first

372

volume of Proust's massive novel, however, went almost unnoticed in 1913; his appeal, like that of Bergsonism generally, was to reach its climax in interwar France.

The literary and artistic revolt that accompanied Barrèsism and Bergsonism had begun even before the impact of these men was felt. The symbolists — Verlaine, Rimbaud, Mallarmé — led the way in the mid-eighties; they rebelled against the dry rigidity of science, yet they had no desire to return to the turgid eloquence of Hugo's romanticism. Symbolist poets, as Rimbaud proudly asserted, sought "to regard as sacred the disorder of their minds." Their aim was not to express clear ideas, or even to evoke precise images, but merely to give verbal form to the confused sentiments arising from the subconscious. Symbolist influence was felt also in music with Claude Debussy and somewhat less strongly in prose and painting. Its day had passed by the turn of the century, but its powerful liberating and renovating effect continued to be felt for decades in French literature and the arts. Many of the ablest writers of the new generation, men like Paul Claudel and André Gide, got their literary baptism in the symbolist movement. The new schools of painting that proliferated in Paris from the 1890's onward—cubism, fauvism, and all the others that were often lumped together as "post-impressionist" — also reflected the general revolt against positivism and science. These painters scoffed at the impressionists' futile attempts to reproduce light and flesh in oil and pigment; they had no interest in becoming mere scientific observers of nature, mere "disembodied eyes," but wanted rather to express on canvas their own emotions and perceptions. Here again the irrational, the subconscious returned to the place of honor.

Even in political theory, the Bergsonian outlook had its impact in the work of that curious figure Georges Sorel. Sorel was a retired engineer and ex-Marxist who, partly under the influence of Bergson's teachings, turned violently against Marxism and sought a new path of salvation for the worker and for society. His creation, the doctrine of syndicalism, represented a partial return to nineteenth-century anarchist ideas, but re-established those ideas on a new irrationalist foundation.

373

Direct action alone, he argued, could save the proletariat; theoretical discussions, political activity, were mere diversions. No great movement, he asserted, had ever succeeded without its myth; and the myth that grips and inspires the working class should be the general strike, out of which may emerge the new society. Sorel attracted few proletarian readers; when the head of the C.G.T. was asked by a parliamentary investigating committee whether he had read Sorel, the witness answered wryly: "No, I read Alexandre Dumas." Indeed, French labor leaders had no need to borrow a doctrine from Sorel; in a sense, it was the C.G.T.'s existing doctrine that Sorel borrowed and systematized, after attaching some effective slogans or catch phrases. His readers, in the long run, turned out to be right-wing activists rather than workers. Nevertheless, his concept of the myth as a drive to action clearly reflected the turn to irrationalism that marked his age.

But if the dominant mood in thought, in literature, and in the arts showed a sharp change after 1890, the grip of positivism and scientism remained almost unshakable in the educational establishment, and probably in most of the literate population as well. The prewar years brought a widening gulf between an intellectual avant-garde on the one hand and the world of scholarship, business, and politics on the other. Not until after the Great War did the avant-garde revolt against rationalism and science spread out into other social and intellectual strata. To Frenchmen generally, the symbolists were "the decadent school," the cubists and fauvists unbalanced exhibitionists, the ideas of Barrès and Bergson curious excrescences of right-wing thought. Anatole France continued to be the literary idol of republicans; Comtean positivism persisted as the quasi-official doctrine. In the universities the great names were those of Émile Durkheim in sociology, Vidal de la Blache in human geography, Fustel de Coulanges and Ernest Lavisse in history — all of them men who sought to apply the most rigorous scientific method to the study of human affairs. The impact of Durkheim's thought was especially great, though indirect in nature: as a kind of official sociology, it reinvigorated and modernized Comtean positivism. Durkheim, like Comte, saw human history as a kind of slow, inevitable rise from primitive superstition to rational understanding of man and the universe. No place was left in his system for institutions or ideas based on mystery or emotion rather than reason; religion itself became merely a device for social control, a phenomenon to be examined and explained by scientific analysis alone. By 1914 Durkheimism dominated the universities and secondary schools, and after the Great War it also penetrated deeply into the normal schools that trained French primary teachers. Thus a whole generation of French school children between the wars was to get a watered-down dose of Durkheim's neopositivist and scientistic outlook.

Since the republican political class remained committed to positivism, one might presume that the post-1890 intellectual revolt should have found its special following among the antirepublican monarchists and Catholics of the right. On the whole, that was the case; yet some of the loudest exponents of the new irrationalism claimed to be republicans (Barrès and Sorel, notably), while some of the sharpest resistance to the irrationalist mood appeared within the extreme right and within the church. Charles Maurras, founder of the neoroyalist Action Française, professed the greatest contempt for the antirationalist outlook and claimed as his intellectual master none other than Auguste Comte. Maurras persuaded himself that his doctrine had been worked out in Comtean fashion, through a rigorously scientific study of the facts; his attempt to harness his new authoritarian nationalism to the monarchy and the church was not the product of emotional fervor but of hard-headed analysis, of "political science." Where Maurras went wrong was in assuming that his doctrines and his methods would appeal to other Frenchmen through their rational rather than their emotional force. In fact, Maurras encouraged the very mood he professed to abhor.

An even more serious kind of opposition to the new irrationalism was beginning to develop meanwhile within the church, in the form of neo-Thomism. Intellectually speaking, French Catholicism during most of the nineteenth century had been remarkably sterile; there had been some remarkable pioneer ventures into the sphere of social action but little in the realm of thought. Seminary education had grown narrow and routine in character; fresh ideas, if they appeared, were viewed with suspicion. Toward the end of the century this relative stagnancy began to be stirred by several new currents. One group of "modernists" sought to reconcile church doctrines with the positivists, rationalist outlook. Another group of "fideists" turned in the opposite direction, arguing that religion should be separated completely from science and should be quite frankly rooted in purely irrational faith. But far more influential (and more acceptable to the Vatican) was the return to the doctrines of St. Thomas Aquinas that centered in France from the 1880's onward. The Thomists, following Aquinas, refused to accept the view that faith and reason were irreconcilable; and they sought to buttress the validity of the Catholic position by appeals to Aristotelian metaphysics. In 1906 the conversion of a young freethinker named Jacques Maritain (partly through the preparatory influence of Bergson's teaching) brought to neo-Thomism its most lucid and prolific exponent. By 1914 this was to be the most vigorous intellectual current within the church, with an even more notable future before it.

The rich variety and individuality of French intellectual life still made it possible, too, for paradoxical figures like Charles Péguy to appear and to resist inclusion in any school or category. Poet, essayist, and editor, Péguy began as a Marxian Socialist and ended as the most fervent of Catholic converts. He denounced the republican politicians with the intensity of a Maurras, yet steadily defended democratic processes and the republican system. An intense nationalist and a sincere admirer of the army, he crusaded ardently against nationalists and army during the Dreyfus case and died as a volunteer soldier at the Marne. No Frenchman of his generation so thoroughly embodied the irrational spirit of the era; both his faith in God and his passionate patriotism were those of a mystic. He belongs, no doubt, in that long tradition that runs from Pascal to Emmanuel Mounier, and that makes of French intellectual history so complex a mosaic.

TWENTY-FOUR

> To forget is as impossible as to pursue revenge.
> D'ESTOURNELLES DE CONSTANT *(1913)*

France, Europe, and the World, 1871–1914

The inception of the Third Republic found French prestige in Europe and the world at its lowest point since 1815. On the Continent, France was without friends or allies; overseas, France possessed only scattered remnants of a once-great empire. The contrast in 1914 was striking. France had become the keystone of one of Europe's principal power blocs and had brought under the tricolor the world's second largest colonial empire. In the light of this record, the historian Maurice Reclus may be right when he remarks that if a king or an emperor had ruled France between 1870 and 1914, it would be considered one of the great reigns in the nation's history.

The era was obviously one of notable achievement in foreign and imperial affairs. There is special irony, therefore, in the fact that few Frenchmen had any real interest in either foreign policy or colonial expansion in those years. Neither topic was an important issue in electoral campaigns; parliament rarely debated problems of foreign policy or empire; between 1885 and 1912 no cabinet was overthrown on such an issue. Most politicians and most citizens had their minds

377

fixed on such domestic issues as the church-state conflict or the Dreyfus drama. This widespread indifference left a fairly free field of action to those few politicians and those specialized interest groups that looked beyond France's frontiers. The roles of such men as Ferry, Delcassé, Caillaux, and Poincaré therefore take on special significance.

French policy throughout the period 1871–1914 has often been described as dominated by a single passion: the thirst for revenge against Germany, the determination to recover Alsace-Lorraine. French diplomacy, according to this legendary view, was simply the story of a slow, steady, single-minded effort to break out of the isolation imposed by Bismarck and to encircle Germany for the final reckoning by force. Much has been made of the black crepe in which Parisians veiled their statues of Metz and Strasbourg after 1871, and of the pathetic appeal of Daudet's classic story "The Last Class," and of Gambetta's pungent phrase, "Never speak about it, always think about it." The *revanchard* thesis was perpetuated in many of the histories of diplomacy written after 1918; it was buttressed also by the tone of postwar French schoolbooks, which were inclined to see the Great War as the inevitable climax of a kind of Greek drama.

A variant form of this simple legend was the thesis advanced by the monarchist historian Jacques Bainville. To him, the Third Republic's political leaders were divided into heroes and villains: on the one hand, farsighted patriots; on the other, weak-kneed appeasers. The men in the former group — Delcassé, Clemenceau, Poincaré — courageously faced the fact that permanent coexistence with a dominant Germany was impossible, and that a new war must come eventually; they concentrated on building up French strength so that the disaster of 1871 would not be repeated. The second category of politicians, the appeasers, included most of the republic's prominent leaders: Thiers, Gambetta, Ferry, Hanotaux, Waldeck-Rousseau, Rouvier, Caillaux. These men, according to Bainville, lacked either courage or vision and were prepared to see France sink into the role of second-class state or even German satellite.

The story of French foreign policy was in fact more complex than either of these theories would suggest. France's feud with Germany over Alsace was not the only issue of importance, or even the central issue in that era; and French political leaders cannot be so easily separated into heroes and villains. A. J. P. Taylor has suggested that the whole record of European diplomacy in the prewar years resembles a quadrille more than a tug-of-war; and his metaphor is well adapted to the role of French diplomacy.

The legend nevertheless contains at least a kernel of truth. For one thing, Alsace-Lorraine was the only important issue that never disappeared from the minds of French policy-makers from 1871 to 1914. It persisted, however, as an irritant rather than as a poison; it affected policy, but it was not the key to an understanding of all French attitudes and actions. If most Frenchmen never really forgave the Germans after 1871, the idea of *revanche* had clearly lost most of its appeal by the nineties, and even prior to that time references to the lost provinces had taken on a character that was often more ritualistic than passionate. Black crepe on the statue of Metz, a special color for Alsace-Lorraine on maps — these manifestations were enough to soothe the injured pride of most Frenchmen. What persisted was a refusal to forget the two lost provinces, to accept their loss as final and unalterable. That refusal weighed on French policy-makers and narrowed the choices open to them. But it did not produce the kind of national psychosis that has sometimes been attributed to the French in those years.

There is a kernel of validity in the Bainville thesis too. If French political leaders cannot properly be divided into patriots and appeasers, they can be separated into exponents of two different methods in seeking some kind of coexistence with Germany. Alongside the Delcassés and the Poincarés, who doubted the Germans' willingness to tolerate a France of equal strength and prestige, there existed an almost unbroken series of politicians who hoped that a real reconciliation with Germany might be possible. A few of these men (although they dared not admit it publicly) were prepared to write off the lost provinces, provided that the Germans would grant the Alsatians real autonomy or would return a strip of Lorraine as a kind of gesture. Some of them advocated schemes of economic collaboration — notably the development of Franco-German banking consortiums to invest in Africa. Some of them — notably the rising Socialist leaders — were impressed by the size and apparent power of German socialism and foresaw as an imminent reality the friendly coexistence of several proletarian states in western Europe. If all of these hopes for reconciliation failed, that failure probably resulted from the erratic and shortsighted policies of the German government more than it did from the persistence of irreconcilable anti-German feeling in France. There is some reason to believe that a more receptive and imaginative attitude in Berlin might have pulled France into the German power bloc.

For the first twenty years after 1871 French diplomatic isolation remained complete, and no leader or group made any real effort to break out of that isolation. While both Thiers and Gambetta hoped for an eventual understanding with either Britain or Russia, no good opportunity for such a rapprochement occurred. The price of an entente with Russia would have been a French promise of support to the Russians in their conflicts with Britain in the Middle East and the Far East; the price of an entente with the British would have been similar support in reverse. In both cases the risks seemed out of proportion to possible French gains. Besides, neither Russia nor Britain appeared very receptive, and the French themselves were not agreed as to which of these two potential allies they preferred. For ideological reasons, part of the monarchist right was inclined toward Russia, and the constitutional monarchists plus most of the Radical left toward Britain.

A third possible alternative did exist even then, in the form of a reconciliation with Germany. The price in this case, however, was far too high; France would have been required to renounce Alsace-Lorraine and to accept the status of client or veiled satellite, after the fashion of Austria-Hungary. The surprising thing is that the principal Opportunist leaders of the period nevertheless did toy with the idea of

380

seeking some sort of understanding with the Germans. Gambetta, in spite of his intransigence in 1871 and his general reputation as a fire-eating patriot, went so far in 1878 as to consider a secret meeting with Bismarck, but he gave up the idea as premature. Ferry went even farther; he was prepared to accept occasional collaboration with Germany on precise and limited issues. Ferry, like every other French-man of his day, could not accept the loss of Alsace-Lorraine, but as a hard-headed realist he declared that it would be senseless for France to keep its whole attention fixed on "a wound that will never stop bleed-ing." He was ready to divert some French strength to overseas expan-sion — not because Bismarck urged such a diversion, but in spite of the fact that Bismarck urged it. When Bismarck in 1884 hinted that he might welcome a Franco-German alliance aimed against Britain, Ferry ignored the feeler, probably because he quite rightly distrusted Bis-marck's motives. Even if Bismarck had been sincere in wanting an alliance, it is unlikely that a formal reconciliation would have been possible so soon after 1871 unless the Germans had been remarkably generous. An active and vocal minority of Frenchmen remained in-transigent toward Germany; indeed, the *revanche* idea really emerged in organized form at just this time, with the formation of Paul Déroulède's League of Patriots in 1882. This upsurge of chauvinism contributed to Ferry's downfall and to the Boulanger craze that fol-lowed. But if Frenchmen — politicians as well as common citizens — were still unwilling to accept anything that looked like renunciation of the lost provinces, they were no more enthusiastic about an armed crusade to recover them; and so Boulanger promptly followed Ferry into political oblivion.

If a reconciliation with Germany was still beyond the reach of the Opportunists, an entente with Britain seemed to be a more attainable alternative. The idea of forming a bloc of liberal states had an ideolog-ical appeal to most Opportunists even though, like Frenchmen gen-erally, they were inclined to distrust the British. But any real hope of a Franco-British entente was destroyed for a generation by the emer-gence of an almost accidental conflict over Egypt. British forces landed there in 1882 to repress nationalist disorders and to protect British lives and property. Once there, they stayed, much to the irritation of the French political world. Frenchmen in general — both common citizens and business groups with interests in the eastern Mediterranean — seem to have been largely indifferent to the Egyptian imbroglio, but the Paris politicians somehow persuaded themselves that the nation had lost face. Over the next two decades French cabinets wasted much effort in a policy of pinpricks vainly intended to dislodge the British from Egypt. Repeated attempts to find a solution never quite succeeded; it was not until 1904 that this "absurd impasse" was resolved in the negotiations that led to the Entente Cordiale. The most ironic aspect of the whole affair was the fact that the British had landed in 1882 at the suggestion of French Premier Gambetta, and that Gambetta's purpose had been to use joint intervention as a first step toward creating an Anglo-French entente. After his fall from office the Chamber refused to vote funds for French participation in the landings, and somehow the device that was intended to produce an entente turned into a device that postponed one for a generation.

Meanwhile, the French had embarked on their new course of imperial expansion in Africa and Asia. Jules Ferry, who usually gets the credit or the blame, has often been described as the political spokesman for business groups that were beginning to see vast potential markets and investment possibilities in the underdeveloped areas. Some colonialist pressure groups did exist in that era, but it is difficult to gauge either their strength or the manner in which their influence was channelled into politics. For the most part, the new imperialism of the 1870's and 1880's seems to have reflected noneconomic motivations: the hope of Christianizing and "civilizing" backward peoples, the desire to rebuild French prestige by proving the nation vigorous and virile.

Ferry evidently came to share these psychological and emotional drives, and he used the economic argument mainly as an ex post facto justification. When he first took office as premier in 1881, he lacked interest in colonial expansion; and his decision to take over Tunisia in 1882 was reached rather reluctantly, under pressure from certain

382

foreign office and army officials who had been preparing the coup. Once converted, however, Ferry became a consistent and enthusiastic expansionist. During his second ministry (1883–85) he pushed a whole series of expeditions that had already been launched on a small scale by French traders, explorers, or army officers. Savorgnan de Brazza was sent into the Congo to carve out a vast equatorial colony; Djibouti on the Red Sea was annexed as a coaling station; expeditions were sponsored in Madagascar and Tonkin.

Ferry was probably ahead of both public and parliamentary opinion. Yet succeeding cabinets abandoned none of his acquisitions; and the process of absorbing bits and pieces of Africa and Asia continued, mainly through the autonomous action of traders and soldiers on the spot who pushed ahead without awaiting instructions from Paris. In the 1890's imperialism began to win broader popular support. Probably it was not mere chance that the same decade brought a rapid decline in the appeal of *revanche,* though which was cause and which effect is not clear. New and more vigorous pressure groups began to emerge: notably the Committee on French Africa in 1890 and the Colonial Union in 1895. These organizations were backed by textile exporters and investment banking groups as well as by the older colonialist elements in the church, the armed forces, and the patriotic societies. The economic factor thus assumed a steadily growing importance in French expansionism, even though it probably remained secondary throughout. General public interest, however, was still relatively slight and superficial when compared with British enthusiasm in the last years of the century. Jules Ferry, strolling past a lurid side show at the Paris Exposition of 1889, remarked bitterly: "There's all *they* know about the empire — the belly dance." Yet despite this indifference and the continued hostility of much of the left, the building of the empire was almost complete by the turn of the century.

The economic impact of empire on France was not very great in the pre-1914 era, for the French neither put much into their colonies nor got much out of them. Most of the colonial budget went for the salaries of administrators and for support of the army; public expenditure on public works, schools, and so on was meager. Private capital also shied away from the colonies; only 10 per cent of France's overseas investments went there, as compared to 25 per cent to Russia alone. Although the French reserved most of the imperial trade for themselves, the total remained small because most of the colonies were still so underdeveloped. The empire took only 13 per cent of France's exports, and it furnished little in return except foodstuffs. A few French companies and banks made handsome profits (notably in Indo-China); but for Frenchmen as a whole, the golden age of imperialism was largely gilt.

❧❦❧❦❧❦

In the midst of all this overseas activity, the French had achieved a major victory in Europe itself: a political accord signed with Russia in 1891 ended their long period of diplomatic isolation. The principal author of this pact, someone has said, was not a Frenchman at all, but the German foreign-office expert Baron von Holstein, on whose recommendation the Germans had abandoned their secret tie with Russia in 1890. But even before that date tensions between Germany and Russia had been growing, and French policy-makers had been moving to take advantage of this change. When Bismarck closed the German money market to the tsar's government in 1887. French lenders had stepped in as substitutes; and this flow of private funds, approved and encouraged by the French government, gradually thawed the tsar's frigid hostility toward the republic. More important still, the Russian government after 1890 began to fear that the Germans might decide to court France, and thus leave Russia in total isolation. In 1891 the tsar reluctantly approved a Franco-Russian agreement that was really nothing more than a friendly entente; the two nations agreed to consult together to maintain the peace of Europe and to take joint action if either party were attacked. French policy-makers set out at once to add a more precise military agreement, to which the tsar acceded only after long hesitation. A pact was drafted in 1892, but the tsar was so upset by reports of the Panama Scandal that he sought to restore the old tie with Germany instead. German obtuseness, however, drove the Russians back into French arms, and the military pact was signed in 1894. Although neither party used the word "alliance" for several years, an alliance in fact existed; and for the next decade it was to be the cornerstone of French foreign policy.

In France the Russian pact was welcomed enthusiastically by almost everyone except the left-wing Radicals and the Socialists. Over the next few years, however, some of its initial popularity ebbed away, for the Russian government showed little inclination to back French diplomatic action either on the Continent or in Africa. Some Frenchmen who wanted to take a stronger line in dealing with Germany felt that the Russian pact actually hampered them more than it helped them, for the Russians wanted no trouble with the Germans. The French, in turn, had no enthusiasm for supporting Russian ambitions in Turkey, where French investors held 60 per cent of the state debt, or in the Balkans, where the French had nothing to gain if their allies stirred up a crisis. Nevertheless, in 1899 Foreign Minister Delcassé decided to tighten France's rather lax ties with Russia. His motives have never been fully clarified; in any case, he went to St. Petersburg and negotiated an additional accord that committed the two parties to collaborate in maintaining not only peace but also the balance of power in Europe. The new terms implied that France would back Russia if the Balkans *status quo* were upset (presumably by Austria), and they also implied that Russia would help France recover Alsace-Lorraine if the Central Powers sought to upset the European balance. The pact also added a provision for joint action if either party were attacked by the British. Without this reinforcement of the Franco-Russian alliance in 1899, the pact might have disintegrated before 1914.

The weaknesses of the Franco-Russian alliance during the 1890's kept two alternative schemes alive in Paris — an entente with Britain, or a reconciliation with Germany. Each of these alternatives is supposed to have had its vigorous proponent in the French foreign ministry: Gabriel Hanotaux for the pro-German orientation, Théophile

Delcassé for the pro-British. Certainly both of these men had a remarkable opportunity to shape French policy; Hanotaux served as foreign minister from 1894 to 1898 with only one brief interruption, while Delcassé broke all durability records by holding the post from 1898 to 1905. They enjoyed other advantages too: the pattern of European power relationships was still somewhat fluid, and the French political world was so preoccupied with domestic problems that both men had a fairly free hand in foreign affairs.

Hanotaux, according to some of his admirers, came nearer than any other French statesman to settling the old quarrel with Germany. He supported a scheme to challenge British power in Egypt by dispatching a French expedition across Africa to the upper Nile, consciously ignoring British warnings that this would bring trouble. Meanwhile, he avoided clashes with the Germans and was even on the verge of accepting a German proposal to collaborate against British expansion in Africa when he fell from office in 1898. Some historians conclude that Hanotaux's fall was a disaster that led eventually to the 1914 war; for he was replaced, they say, by a vindictive faction of Germanophobes, headed by Delcassé, who spent the next few years preparing the encirclement of Germany.

This thesis, though simple and appealing, has never been supported with adequate proof. There is no evidence that Hanotaux was systematically pro-German; indeed, at least twice he ignored German feelers for active collaboration against the British in South Africa. As for the Marchand expedition to challenge Britain in the upper Nile, Hanotaux was not its only or even its principal sponsor. Although Hanotaux's real aims have never been fully clarified, it seems probable that his policy resembled that of Jules Ferry: he was willing to consider occasional collaboration with Germany on precise issues but not a general reconciliation on German terms. Perhaps what he wanted was just enough Franco-German cooperation to frighten the British into letting France expand in Africa and Asia.

The traditional view of Delcassé's role after 1898 is even more controversial. His critics see him as the warmonger who took office with a single-minded purpose — to build an alliance system that would isolate Germany and open the way to revenge. Some of his admirers accept the same view but justify it: "France's answer to Bismarck," one of them has called him. Indeed, some of Delcassé's closest collaborators later lent support to this thesis by drawing a direct line from his aims in 1898 to the victory of France in 1918. Yet it is by no means so clear that Delcassé was systematically anti-German from the start. He seems to have been as much anti-British as anti-German when he took office; and this hostility toward Britain was intensified when his first act as foreign minister was a humiliating retreat before British threats in the upper Nile. The Marchand expedition, which had arrived at the town of Fashoda on the Nile, was ordered home in order to avoid possible war with Britain. "Fashoda," wrote the German ambassador in Paris triumphantly, "has made Frenchmen forget Alsace-Lorraine." It is true that Delcassé is supposed to have said privately: "As long as the Germans remain at Strasbourg and Metz, France will have but one permanent enemy: Germany." Yet several of his actions between 1898 and 1901 suggest a continuing hostility toward the British and a willingness to collaborate with Germany in a kind of continental league against Britain. How far he would have been willing to go in this direction cannot be guessed, as the Germans failed to seize the opportunity. The only certainty is that by 1902 Delcassé had definitely decided to play the British rather than the German card and to prepare a Franco-British entente that finally materialized in 1904. German leadership, he had concluded, was so unstable that it would probably force France into a war sooner or later. This view of Delcassé would suggest that the British entente was not the central goal of his whole career, but simply one move in a complex chess game whose only goal was to further French national interests (as Delcassé saw them). Probably his tightening of the Russian alliance had the same motivation, and so did his successful attempts to detach Italy from full membership in the German alliance system.

Whatever the truth about Delcassé, he did rigidify France's rather amorphous foreign policy into a pattern that was to endure for the next decade. Delcassé himself lost control of that policy in 1905 when German pressure forced him out of office. His error had been to push France along too far and too fast toward a set of commitments that involved serious risks, without making sure that the nation was ready either morally or materially to assume such risks. When the threat of war came, and Delcassé insisted on facing it, France's unreadiness emerged with disastrous clarity. Even the cabinet to which he belonged voted unanimously against him.

How responsible Delcassé was for bringing on that 1905 crisis is again unclear and controversial. For several years the French had been preparing to absorb Morocco, the last rich territory still open to domination in north Africa. One great power after another was bought off or gave its consent; even the British finally approved in 1904, as part of the Entente Cordiale arrangements. When the French took steps to move in, however, the German government intervened by sending the kaiser on a state visit to Morocco. Delcassé's critics contend that he had consciously sought to insult Berlin by buying off every power except Germany. His defenders reply that he had sounded out the German ambassador in Paris as early as 1901 and had been assured of German indifference toward Morocco. They see him as puzzled and upset by the Germans' sudden interference but as willing to placate them by offering such assurances as the maintenance of the open door for German trade. When it became clear that they were not willing to be placated, but aimed to use the crisis as a lever to disrupt the new Franco-British entente, Delcassé grew angry and stubborn and insisted that France face Germany down.

Delcassé believed (or professed to believe) that the Germans were merely bluffing, and he insisted that the British had assured him orally that they would help France if it came to war. His cabinet colleagues were unwilling to take the risk, and in this they were probably right. War in 1905 would have been, as D. W. Brogan puts it, "deeply unpopular and certainly disastrous"; the nation was still seriously divided by the Dreyfus Affair and the church-state controversy, and army morale had reached its lowest point for decades. Ten years later a remarkable national and military revival had set in, and the chance of victory was much more real.

Most of Delcassé's work survived, despite his fall. Premier Maurice Rouvier, who took the lead in forcing him out of office, had not intended that the Delcassean system should continue. Rouvier not only feared that war would bring defeat, but he hoped that war might not be necessary at all; his ambition was to achieve a reconciliation with Germany through developing financial collaboration between French and German investment groups. An ex-banker himself, Rouvier remained in close touch with certain Paris banking circles that favored the creation of a Franco-German consortium to develop Africa and Asia. His hopes quickly evaporated, however; the German government proved much more difficult to deal with than he had expected. Berlin rejected his proposal of direct negotiations to liquidate the crisis and insisted on a full-scale international conference to exploit its diplomatic victory. Within six months Rouvier had concluded that France's security required the maintenance of Delcassé's alliance system. Neither he nor his immediate successors as premier made any attempt to carry out a diplomatic revolution. The most striking case was that of Clemenceau, premier from 1906 to 1909. The Tiger had been, ever since 1891, one of the bitterest critics of the Russian alliance. Once in power, though, he made no attempt to undermine the Russian pact, but rather he approved its expansion into the Triple Entente in 1907. He sought also to reinforce the Entente Cordiale by urging the British to build up an army to go with their fleet. He and other Frenchmen feared that an armyless Britain in case of war might sink the German navy and let the French fight the rest of the war alone. On the other hand, the Clemenceau cabinet refused to expand its support of Russia to the point of risking war on behalf of the Russians in the Bosnian crisis of 1908–9.

Although the Delcassé policy was maintained by a series of Radical-led cabinets, the idea of reconciliation with Germany never died out. Its appeal was strongest among the left-wing parties. The Socialists were dazzled by the strength of the German Socialists, by far the largest Marxian party in Europe; and they continued to despise Russia as the heart of reaction. One segment of the Radical party also clung to the idea of reconcilation, mainly through the device of Franco-German financial collaboration in underdeveloped areas. Just as Maurice Rouvier had been spokesman for this viewpoint in 1905, now Joseph Caillaux sought to move toward the same end. Caillaux, a former treasury official turned politician, had kept many close ties with Parisian banking circles. His purpose, when he became premier in January, 1911, was to reduce Franco-German tensions through business collaboration. Some British diplomats at the time suspected him (probably unjustly) of aiming at a real diplomatic revolution that would jettison the Entente Cordiale and substitute a similar pact with Germany.

If Caillaux really hoped to carry through a major change in foreign policy, his plan was disrupted at the very outset. On the day that he took office a new Franco-German crisis over Morocco began; the German gunboat *Panther* arrived at Agadir to protect the lives and interests of German nationals (none of whom, incidentally, lived anywhere near Agadir). This German action was in fact a clumsy protest against a French move (ordered by Caillaux's predecessor) to convert Morocco into a protectorate. Several months of tension followed; eventually Caillaux, behind the back of his own foreign minister, tried a kind of appeasement by ceding a large slice of the French Congo to Germany in return for a free hand in Morocco. Perhaps he hoped that this might be a first step toward a broader rapprochement with Berlin. Instead, it produced just the opposite result. The angry Chamber of Deputies ratified the cession of the Congo strip but then overthrew the cabinet. A wave of anti-German feeling swept across the country; and partly in response to it, the politicians replaced Caillaux with Raymond Poincaré. This rigid and rather narrow Lorrainer, widely respected for his personal integrity, was to be both symbol and spokesman for the nationalist revival of 1911–14.

Both the origins and the character of this nationalist revival have been disputed. Was it aggressive or defensive in spirit? Was it the product of German saber rattling or of some native-born chauvinistic hysteria? Recent studies of the phenomenon (by German and American as well as French scholars) strongly support the view that it was primarily defensive; that it was the patriotic reaction of politicians and citizens who were baffled, upset, and increasingly resentful at the behavior of Berlin. This was not merely a revival of the *revanchard* chauvinism of the previous generation, the mood of Déroulède, Barrès, and Boulanger. The importance of the new spirit was that it affected precisely those kinds of Frenchmen who a generation earlier had opposed the chauvinists and had hoped for some kind of peaceful coexistence with Germany. Poincaré was not the political heir of Déroulède but rather of the Ferrys and the Gambettas — of those middle-of-the-road republicans who had been hostile to Boulanger's tub-thumping. And while the nationalist revival impinged most strongly upon the Moderates, it also affected a considerable segment of the Radicals, and even a few maverick Socialists.

It would be easy to conclude that the leaders in France's nationalist revival, whatever their motivation, contributed directly to the outbreak of war in 1914 by their intransigence, their chip-on-shoulder attitude in every international crisis. Poincaré especially, in his post as premier in 1912–13 and then as president of the republic, has often been denounced as a warmonger, a practitioner of what a later generation of Americans came to call "brinkmanship." The full evidence suggests a much less damning conclusion. There is very little proof, indeed, that Poincaré and the men around him were eager for an armed showdown with Germany; but they believed that it was likely to come, and they were determined to build up France's material, moral, and diplomatic strength so that out of war might come victory. They strengthened the standing army in the only way still open to them — by keeping draftees under arms for three years rather than two. They sought to persuade the British to accept more precise commitments and managed to get at least a little satisfaction. They took steps to reinvigorate the sagging Russian alliance by promising to support Russian diplomatic action in the Balkans. This did not involve goading the Russians to adopt a positive Balkan policy; rather, it meant abandoning direct attempts to restrain Russia there. As the Poincaré group saw it, the greatest danger facing France was not that Russia might drag France into an unnecessary war, but that Russia might desert France and rejoin Germany. Such a diplomatic revolution, French leaders believed, would leave France no alternative but to accept the role of a dependent power, subject to the unreasonable whims and dictates of an almost incomprehensible German governing elite.

This Poincaré policy would be open to serious criticism if there had existed at the time a sound and workable alternative. Some Frenchmen of that era did believe that such an alternative existed, and many historians have sided with them in retrospect. It was Caillaux who continued to be the chief representative of a softer policy of reconciliation. Caillaux retained most of his influence in the left-wing parties and managed to regain a cabinet post late in 1913. After the victory of the Radicals and Socialists in the parliamentary elections of April-May, 1914, he ought to have been in line for a return to the premiership. His restoration to power would presumably have meant a reversal of the Poincaré policy of preparedness and tightened alliances, and a renewed effort at a Franco-German rapprochement. The experiment might have been forced on President Poincaré save for two assassinations: that of a Parisian editor by Madame Caillaux in March, that of the Archduke Franz Ferdinand at Sarajevo in June. Madame Caillaux's rash act temporarily clouded her husband's political chances; the archduke's death produced general war. Whether the Caillaux policy could have succeeded at that point in history is an unanswerable problem. One thing only is sure: that its success would have depended more on men and moods in Berlin than on choices and attitudes in Paris.

TWENTY-FIVE

> When a man dies, I suffer. When fifteen hundred
> thousand die, that's statistics.
>
> PHILIPPE BERTHELOT

"The Grandeur and Misery of Victory,"
1914–1919

No historian has yet managed to measure the effects of the First World War — "the great war," as Frenchmen still call it — on the French nation. It is easy to cite statistics of physical damage or loss of life or decline in industrial production; it is much harder to assess the moral and psychological impact of this vast calamity, its permanently debilitating results, its traumatic effect on large parts of the population. Nations, like the individual human beings that compose them, are remarkably resilient things; history furnishes many examples of their vigorous recovery from periods of disaster. Perhaps that very resilience tends to conceal some of the deeper effects that endure beneath the surface of the system and that surprise observers by their long-range consequences. Such lesions are more likely to be concealed when a nation seems to triumph over disaster — when the long strain of war ends in what men call victory. Nations that are beaten undergo long examination and self-examination; the effects of the war may even be exaggerated to the point of producing a kind of national neurosis. Nations that triumph are generally assumed to be, and assume them-

393

selves to be, healthy organisms that have somehow been spared by the plague.

The real significance of the Great War for the student of French history lies not so much in the dramatic details of the military effort or the tensions of wartime politics as in the total impact of the experience on the France of the next generation. That impact can hardly be overrated. More often, it has been underrated — especially during the interwar era, when it seemed that France had survived the crisis almost unchanged, had emerged even stronger than before, and had recovered its position as the dominant power of Europe. Some of the effects of this misconception will be examined in succeeding chapters.

The test of war presents any democratic system with difficult and paradoxical problems: problems that are intensified when no one has foreseen a long war and when the fighting occurs on the nation's own soil. That the French republic survived this kind of test is in some ways astonishing. The fact of victory in 1914–18, contrasted with disastrous defeat in 1870–71 and 1939–40, suggests some intriguing problems of comparison. One explanation would find the difference in the realm of national morale: in the fact that Frenchmen in 1914 were more united, more enthusiastic, more determined than in 1870 or 1939. This was probably the case at the outset, and it contributed much to France's success in checking the initial German drive; but as the Great War dragged on, disunity and defeatism did grow to serious proportions without producing military collapse. Another explanation might trace the difference to the realm of equipment and manpower: to the fact that in 1914 France was better prepared materially and was less heavily outnumbered than in the earlier and later wars. It is probably true that in relative numbers of men under arms the French were somewhat better off than they had been in 1870, in spite of the fact that population trends had favored the Germans. Universal military service and the three-year service law had partially redressed the balance. But the most notable advantage the French possessed in 1914 was that only in that war could they count on Russian manpower to divert much of Germany's striking force.

Still a third explanation would attribute France's success in the 1914 war to better military leadership, to the vigor and imagination of French generalship, which proved more than a match for that of the enemy. Such a thesis is both highly controversial and difficult to test. There had undoubtedly been a notable current of rejuvenation and of new energy in the French high command just before 1914, and this current surely contributed to the victory. But there is not much evidence of imaginative thinking or of strategic genius in the army's planning just prior to the war. Plan XVII, in effect when the war broke out, was no better adapted to the times than was the French war plan of 1940; it involved an immediate offensive into Alsace and Lorraine and left Paris exposed to a German drive through Belgium. French intelligence reports about German strength and plans seem to have been little better or worse than those of 1940 (though certainly better than those of 1870). The high command had shown little inclination in the prewar years to experiment with new kinds of weapons; advocates of more heavy artillery were brushed off by those who considered the smaller, more mobile 75mm. cannon adequate for all purposes — "the Father, Son, and Holy Ghost of warfare," as someone put it. To the extent that new ideas about strategy and tactics had affected the army, they tended to be the wrong ones for the kind of war that was impending. The most vocal and vigorous faction in the officer corps was preaching the virtues of all-out attack by masses of infantry unencumbered by any other equipment than a rifle and a mood of exaltation. The *furia francese*, these doctrinaires contended, would more than offset the enemy's superior numbers. A good many French soldiers were sacrificed to this religion of the offensive during the Great War; but luckily, the dominant faction in the high command viewed it with some skepticism and was flexible enough to adapt its strategy to the needs of a stalemated defensive war.

The army's commander-in-chief, General Joffre, belonged to that new group of republican (and perhaps Freemason) officers elevated to

395

top command posts after the Dreyfus Affair. The Radical cabinet of
1911 had chosen him in preference to such officers as Philippe Pétain,
a freethinker who was reputed to be a monarchist, and Ferdinand Foch,
a fervent Catholic with Jesuit training and a Jesuit brother. Joffre's
interest was the army, not politics; and if he lacked imagination and
flair, he had the kind of stolid, imperturbable temperament that adapted
him well to a dragging defensive war. Although his Plan XVII put the
French armies at an initial disadvantage, Joffre was far less deeply
committed than the Germans to a single recipe for victory. When the
German forces drove through Belgium into France, Joffre acted in time
to shift troops back to Paris, where they successfully checked the
German attack at the Marne River in September. Joffre and the French
high command undoubtedly deserved much of the credit for this
decisive success; but they were aided by the fact that the German
army's former commander General Schlieffen had endowed the attackers with an impossibly risky plan. If superior French generalship was
partly responsible for victory in the Great War, it was mainly because
German military leadership fell so far below the standards of 1870
and 1940.

At the outset of war both politicians and public in France had
temporarily abdicated into the hands of the high command; the country
was ruled for the first few months by a tacit military dictatorship. The
war of 1914 has been called the last popular war in history. Frenchmen,
like Germans and others, greeted its outbreak with enthusiasm — partly
because it came as a kind of emotional release after a long period of
pent-up tension, partly because none of them foresaw its scope and
duration. Even the antimilitarists, so vocal in past years, forgot their
suspicions of the army. The spirit of *union sacrée*, while it lasted, was
intense. On the floor of the Chamber of Deputies, Edouard Vaillant, a
Communard in 1871, and Albert de Mun, an officer in Thiers's army
that repressed the Commune, shook hands for the first time in their
political careers. The cabinet was broadened to include every group; it
ranged from the Socialist Jules Guesde to the conservative Denys
Cochin, "the first qualified representative of Catholic interests" to enter

a French cabinet since MacMahon's day. Prewar plans for the preventive arrest of a thousand trade union and extreme-leftist leaders were cancelled as unnecessary. The laws exiling the religious congregations were suspended, permitting many Jesuits and Assumptionists to return for army service.

Joffre's success at the Marne temporarily strengthened the high command's authority and enabled him to keep the post of commander-in-chief until 1916. As the months passed, however, the politicians gradually recovered their voices and began to chip away at the high command's power. Some of the friction that developed between Paris and Joffre's headquarters was political in character; it derived from a conflict between Joffre and his subordinate Albert Sarrail, "the Jacobin general," hero of the more doctrinaire Radicals and the Socialists for his vigorously leftist views. A personal conflict between the two men, caused by Sarrail's ambitious intrigues and Joffre's jealousy, led to Sarrail's demotion in 1915. The parliamentary left thought that it smelled a reactionary plot; the incident almost turned into a crisis and seriously shook the "sacred union" for the first time. Other complaints by the politicians were better founded: they were inspired by growing dissatisfaction with Joffre's conduct of the war. His "nibbling policy" of limited attacks on the German trenches bled the army without producing much in the way of results. Meanwhile his refusal to strengthen the defenses of the great fortress city of Verdun, based on his conviction that the Germans would not attack there, also brought rising criticism. When the Germans did strike early in 1916 and overran most of Verdun's outer defenses, Joffre proposed to abandon the city and retreat to a shorter defense line. The politicians openly rebelled against this scheme on the ground that it might lead to disintegration of the army's and the nation's morale. The formidable task of saving Verdun was turned over to the sector commander, General Pétain, who managed to blunt the German offensive in perhaps the most critical action of the whole war. It was clear that Pétain's victory owed little to Joffre. Late in 1916 the accumulated dissatisfaction in Paris led to

Joffre's transfer to a desk job in the war ministry and his replacement by a junior general named Nivelle.

Joffre's fall marked the end of the long struggle between military and civilian authorities that had gradually eroded the initial predominance of the high command. From late 1916 to late 1917 the politicians were in the saddle; the Chamber and Senate exercised direct and constant control over both headquarters and cabinet. Nivelle was parliament's man; his vigor and charm had impressed touring politicians at the front, and his plan for an all-out series of coordinated attacks to win the war at once appealed to men who were growing war-weary. Unfortunately, Nivelle overlooked one essential factor: to succeed, his plan needed large reserves of manpower, which in the spring of 1917 simply did not exist. The attack was a bloody fiasco and was followed by a near-collapse of morale in parts of the French army; whole companies "mutinied" in the sense that they refused orders to go over the top.

The disaster led to the substitution of Pétain for Nivelle. Pétain got the mutinies in hand by a policy of mixed repression and generosity. He immediately cancelled any further offensive actions and decided to mark time until large-scale American aid could arrive. "Squat, do little, and keep the losses small" — such was his doctrine. But if the French army had reached and survived its low point in the spring of 1917, behind the front the nadir was still to come. By the autumn of 1917 there was a serious current of defeatism in Paris and rising pressure for an immediate white peace. This sentiment was strongest among the Socialists and left-wing Radicals. The outbreak of the war had led the entire left to rally solidly to the nation's defense; the Socialist deputies had voted unanimously for war credits, and some of them had gone off to the front to die at the Marne. In 1915 came the first few defections, and from that time onward defeatism grew steadily. By 1916 the white-peace advocates within the Socialist party were almost strong enough to control the organization; only the influence of men like Guesde kept the Socialist delegation in parliament from going into open opposition. The events of 1917 — the Russian upheaval and gen-

398

eral war-weariness — played into the hands of the defeatists, but it was not until the party congress of July, 1918, that they got control of the Socialist party machinery and policy. By that time the moment had passed when they might have done serious damage to the French war effort.

The potential symbol and spokesman for the defeatists was not a Socialist, however, but the Radical Joseph Caillaux. The ex-premier was still convinced that the war might have been averted had he been in power in 1914. During several wartime trips abroad he allegedly made contact with German agents to discuss the possibility of a negotiated peace. Meanwhile, Caillaux's friend Jean-Louis Malvy, minister of interior, fed secret subsidies to defeatist newspapers in Paris. Even Aristide Briand, after his overthrow as premier early in 1917, apparently had "fugitive contacts" with German agents in Switzerland.

By the autumn of 1917 there was grave doubt of France's ability or willingness to fight on toward victory. Squabbling had become so bitter, suspicion so widespread, that President Poincaré faced a dramatic choice: either a Caillaux government that would presumably try for a white peace at once, or a Clemenceau cabinet that would stand for a fight to the finish. For three years Clemenceau in his newspaper had been denouncing with equal vehemence the defeatists and the leaders of France's war effort — including Poincaré himself; but Poincaré's resentment was outweighed by his revulsion against Caillaux's defeatism. When the shaky Painlevé cabinet was overthrown in November, 1917, the president promptly called Clemenceau to the premiership. Abruptly, the period of parliamentary domination ended; France entered upon a kind of civilian dictatorship, or the nearest thing to it that the republic had known since the days of Gambetta in 1870.

Clemenceau was the last survivor of the old Jacobin tradition that had once been the hallmark of the Radicals. He and his old political colleagues had long since parted company; his support in 1917 came almost solidly from the parties of center and right. Clemenceau angered the left by his prompt and brutal suppression of defeatists of all kinds;

he made no distinction between disreputable German hirelings like the journalist Almereyda and idealists or imprudent schemers like Caillaux and Malvy. The latter were both arrested, though they were eventually acquitted of the charge of illegal contacts with the enemy. Even Briand was threatened with prosecution unless he retired into the background. Many leftists never forgave Clemenceau; their chance for revenge was to come in 1920, when they helped to defeat the Tiger for the presidency.

Clemenceau's harsh obstinacy, much like that of Winston Churchill in a later war, injected a new spirit into the nation; morale stiffened just enough and just in time to allow France to survive the great German spring and summer offensives in 1918. Once again the enemy reached the Marne without being checked. At the critical moment Clemenceau managed to persuade his allies to accept the principle of a single command for all allied forces in the west; and it was largely his decision that gave this assignment to General Ferdinand Foch rather than to Pétain. The Tiger's feelings about Foch had always been mixed; he disliked the general's Jesuit connections, yet he was attracted by Foch's gamecock qualities and was put off by Pétain's defeatist tendencies. Within an hour after Foch had been named general-in-chief of the Allied armies in France, he and Clemenceau were engaged in a bitter controversy, and serious friction continued to mark their relationship throughout the last months of the war. Clemenceau repeatedly tried to give Foch suggestions or orders; Foch answered sharply or, worse still, ignored the premier entirely. The infuriated Clemenceau became persuaded that Foch and Poincaré had entered into a conspiracy against him. Yet to his credit, the Tiger let Foch have his way and backed him till the end. Undoubtedly, part of the explanation for France's victory in 1918 must be found in the kind of leadership France got at the critical moment. Probably a Clemenceau and a Foch would not have been enough to turn the tide either in 1870 or in 1940; but if there had been no Clemenceau and Foch in 1918, the outcome of the war might have been quite different.

Victory, like champagne, produces a certain temporary delirium in those who savor it. Not all Frenchmen resisted that delirium in 1918 and after; no people can easily endure such an ordeal, emerge victorious, and face the dismaying fact that they are worse off than before the war began. One effect of the conflict was to reassure Frenchmen about their governmental system. Before 1914 it had been widely criticized as ineffective and unstable; yet it had survived and beaten the great autocracies and had managed to turn up abler leadership than did the authoritarian regimes. The republic's greater flexibility quite rightly proved to be a virtue; the regime had managed to adapt itself to changing wartime circumstances. Unfortunately, it was easy to carry this reassurance too far and to conclude that critics of the system had no valid case whatsoever. The republic had admirably survived the terrible test of a long war, but it was destined to be less effective in facing the domestic problems of an industrial age.

Although many Frenchmen and foreigners assumed that France would now play the dominant role in Europe, taking the place of Bismarck's Germany, there were some who sensed that France could probably never again face another crisis like this one. No other warring nation had suffered such high proportionate manpower losses: of the eight million men mobilized, five million were killed or wounded. The dead alone amounted to 10 per cent of the active male population, and even more were partially or totally incapacitated. No nation could less afford such losses, especially when they were concentrated in the middle years of the male population. The demographic problem, already grave, threatened to become insoluble. Material losses were less critical, yet exceptionally severe; a large segment of France's best industrial and agricultural territory had been devastated. Industrial production, despite the building of new war plants, dropped to 60 per cent of the prewar figure; in later retrospect, it was estimated that French economic growth had been set back by almost a decade.

Still another war-born problem was that of public finance. From

401

one of the world's most solid currencies in 1914, the franc was suddenly transformed into one of the most unstable. So long as the war lasted, depreciation reached only 15 per cent, but within a year after victory it had passed 50 per cent. Wartime governments had preferred borrowing or inflation rather than a pay-as-you-fight policy; the tax yield during the war years scarcely exceeded the prewar level. True, parliament finally adopted an income-tax law in 1916, but the rates were too low to produce much revenue. In addition to the heavy load of domestic and foreign debt in 1918, France had lost much of its overseas investment, including the huge sums sunk in tsarist Russia. France's condition was by no means hopeless at the end of the war; the nation remained rich enough to recover financial stability if its leaders and citizens had seen the problem clearly and had acted with vigor and dispatch. But the financial impact of war plus postwar policy errors did turn the financial problem into a major source of French weakness during the interwar era.

In many ways the war did not so much alter basic trends in France as speed up trends already under way. Such was the case, for example, in the demographic sphere and in the nation's social and economic evolution. The wartime experience did profoundly transform France's industrial structure — more profoundly, indeed, than any other experience of war or depression in modern times. These changes derived not only from the army's need for war material, but also from an enforced shift in industrial location. Because the area that included most of French heavy industry was overrun and occupied, a new heavy industry had to be created in Paris and in central and southern France. For the first time Paris became a major center of large industry; until now it had been mainly small plants that had clustered around the capital. At the same time there occurred a rapid shift from textiles to metallurgy. In 1906 the balance had been three to one against metallurgy in percentages of industrial workers employed; by 1920 metallurgical workers outnumbered those in textiles. This change meant not merely new products, but a new kind of labor force — more concentrated, more unskilled, more inclined to radicalism. The war brought a million new members into the trade unions; most of them were fresh immigrants from rural districts, without the individualistic tradition of workers who came of artisanal backgrounds. The metallurgical workers became the most radical segment of labor, and the red belt of industrial suburbs around Paris became the chief Communist stronghold between the wars.

The effect of the war on the industrial ownership group is harder to assess. The army's insatiable need for munitions and supplies opened up easy avenues to men of enterprise; the number of millionaires sharply increased, for profit controls were inadequate to check the rise of great wealth. Yet there is not much evidence that the war stimulated the growth of a new kind of business elite. No significant group of self-made men rose to industrial prominence; rather, it was the established families of the upper bourgeoisie that profited by the opportunities offered. Perhaps that was because only the older families had ready access to credit for building new plants or converting to war production; perhaps it was because their political connections put them in touch with the government offices that controlled war contracts. At any rate, there was neither a notable broadening of the business elite nor a real change in the outlook of that elite. The cautious, conservative attitude typical of French business continued dominant into the postwar era.

The war's impact on the peasantry was clearer and more profound. No other segment of society was so hard hit by mobilization; few peasant boys were deferred, whereas a fair proportion of factory workers and miners had to be excused from duty at the front. It has been estimated that half of France's war casualties were peasants. Among those who survived, many had had a taste of city life and refused to go back to their isolated rural existence. On the other hand, peasants who stayed on the land during the war years attained a temporary prosperity such as they had never known. Many farmers paid off old mortgages and bought more land; many marginal farms were enabled to survive for an additional decade. Yet the long-range result of the war was to inject a new spirit of questioning and discontent — not only among those whom the army had uprooted, but also among those who stayed behind. The peasantry "went into the war docile and resigned; it came out resentful and ready to complain."

On the whole, then, the war's effect on France's social and economic structure was to shake it up without producing really revolutionary or fundamental changes. The country emerged still a curious blend of dynamic and static elements; the upheaval and its aftermath produced no large rootless element of *déclassés*, of "marginal men," as it did in Germany. The long-range effects seem to have been strangely mixed: on the one hand, an increased stability approaching the point of stagnation; on the other hand, a growth in stresses and tensions within this rigidified social and economic structure. Perhaps the upheaval was both too great and not great enough for a nation faced with the problem of converting itself to twentieth-century conditions.

France's role at the Paris peace conference forms a necessary addendum to any account of the war. At the time, and during the interwar years, the Anglo-Saxon world was inclined to view that role critically: France was seen as a kind of narrow-minded Shylock determined to get its pound of flesh and indifferent to the disastrous consequences of such an attitude. Hitler's aggressive career tended to reverse this view; during the Second World War the French began to seem the misunderstood heroes of the Paris conference, who alone had clearly perceived the German threat and had urged the creation of solid barriers on the Rhine and in eastern Europe. These fluctuating estimates tend to conceal the essential fact that the real errors of Western statesmen were committed not at the conference itself but during the two postwar decades, and that these mistakes did not grow inevitably out of the nature of the peace settlement. It can be argued, as a theoretical proposition, that if the French had been more generous and reasonable in 1919, a peaceful democratic Germany might have emerged and endured. It can be argued likewise that if the French had been allowed to write a really severe treaty, perhaps Hitler could have been stopped in time. Treaties, however, are less important for what they contain than for how they are applied; the effectiveness of either a soft or a severe treaty would have depended on the wisdom of interwar statesmanship. As it turned out, Western leaders were incapable of administering a compromise treaty like Versailles; there is no reason to suppose that they would have done much better with any other kind.

At the outset of the peace conference Clemenceau's program included the following essential points: the creation of one or several buffer states on the west bank of the Rhine, permanently occupied by French troops or linked with France; the establishment of strong new states on Germany's eastern border (notably a Poland *"forte, forte, et très forte,"* in Clemenceau's words); the payment of reparations by the Germans to cover the cost of restoring all war damage (the word "damage" being broadly interpreted). French negotiators were also determined to secure a share of the German and Turkish colonial empires, as provided by wartime secret treaties.

Not all Frenchmen were agreed on this program. Some of them (notably on the left) regarded it as too severe and likely to destroy the hope of building a new harmonious European order. Some of them thought it too soft: they favored the permanent dismemberment of Germany into several states and total disarmament of these states. As the conference proceeded, however, the bitterest criticism came not from those who had opposed the Clemenceau program but from those who had initially approved it, and who believed that the Tiger was sacrificing too much of it without a fight. These critics — men like Foch, Poincaré, Barrès — later argued that if Clemenceau had stood intransigently on his original demands, the British and Americans in the end would have accepted them, since both those nations had already achieved their war aims: control of the seas in the one case, national security in the other.

Clemenceau, however, at no time believed it possible for France to dictate the peace terms. He was aware that the French had not won the war alone; indeed, he was aware that France's victory had been in some ways a kind of lucky accident. Without British and American aid, the disaster of 1870 might have been repeated; and American aid had come not through clever French diplomacy, or even through French righteousness, but through German blundering. Neither did Clemenceau believe, deep down, that the permanent repression of Germany was possible. His anti-German epigrams have too often been taken as examples of a bigoted extremism: "There are twenty million Germans too many"; "The more Germany is split up, the better I'll like it." Less well known, but more revealing, were his remarks before the French Senate during the subsequent debate on treaty ratification: "Today, we are masters. Nevertheless, if we want conciliation in the interests of our children, we must use this superiority with moderation. . . . I do not want to run after their [the Germans'] good will — I don't have the proper feelings for that. Still, sixty million people in the center of Europe will take some room, especially when they are men of science, of method."

The division among Frenchmen over the peace settlement was most clearly revealed when the Versailles Treaty came before the Chamber of Deputies for ratification. The debate was no mere formality; it dragged on, interspersed with other business, for six full weeks between August and October, 1919. Criticisms were showered on Clemenceau from almost every side of the Chamber; from *Père la Victoire*, said the wits, he had been transmuted into *Perd la Victoire*. The Socialists took the line that the treaty was too harsh for the new democratic and peaceful Germany; French policy, they argued, ought to be based on collaboration with that Germany and on active participation in the League of Nations. But the center and right critics took exactly the opposite position and, by their skepticism toward both the new Germany and the League, revealed a deep strain of inferiority and defeatism. The treaty, they charged, contained no real guarantee against German recovery or rearmament and no assurance that the Germans would ever pay reparations. The American and British aid treaties were of doubtful value and would probably be repudiated by the Americans anyway. Only the annexation or indirect control of the Rhineland-Saar area would have provided security, they asserted. A few of these critics, more farsighted, complained also of the string of weak states set up in eastern Europe. "In reality," warned one of them, "you have Balkanized eastern Europe. If this continues, you may see them Bolshevized tomorrow."

Clemenceau himself sat grimly silent through most of the debate, while his younger lieutenants offered the government's rebuttal. The error of these spokesmen was that they went too far in defending the treaty as an almost foolproof instrument. They insisted that the critics' fears of German evasion or of future allied weaknesses were groundless; they argued that if the Americans should repudiate Wilson's military-aid treaty, France would be legally authorized to seize the Rhineland by force. What they failed to do was to face up realistically to any of the difficult problems, such as how Germany could pay large reparations without first getting a grip on much of world trade, and how France could checkmate German power if the wartime coalition disintegrated. The effect of their presentation was to mislead many Frenchmen both within and outside parliament about the impending problems of the postwar era.

Clemenceau alone sought to inject a more realistic note, when he rose to speak at the very end of the debate. "What you are about to vote on today," he told the Chamber, "is not even a beginning, but the beginning of a beginning." His critics were right, he asserted, when they found the treaty full of imperfections; but they had missed the real point. "M. Louis Marin [a right-wing deputy] went to the heart of the question when . . . he said with a touch of despair: 'Your treaty condemns France to eternal vigilance.'" That, said the Tiger bluntly, was exactly and unavoidably the case. "Peace is only war pursued by other means. . . . I see life as a perpetual conflict in war and in peace . . .; that conflict you cannot suppress." Like Winston Churchill a generation later, Clemenceau was offering his countrymen blood, toil, tears, and sweat, but in this case he was doing so just at the moment of triumph, when most Frenchmen desperately wanted to relax behind some puncture-proof barricade. If the Clemencist spirit, hardheaded yet not inflexible, had been widely shared by Frenchmen at the time and over the two decades to follow, the course of French and European history might have been quite different. But it would have required more than Clemenceau's valedictory speech to offset the illusions already implanted about the treaty and to alter the mood of the times. The interwar era was already committed to indulgence in wishful thinking and the propagation of myths. Perhaps, after such a war, nothing else could have been expected.[1]

[1] Three years later, a young admirer called on Clemenceau as the latter sat in embittered retirement. "Everything I have done has been wasted," growled the old Jacobin. "In twenty years, France will be dead."

TWENTY-SIX

The Varieties of History, 1870–1919

As perspective shortens, historians find it more difficult to characterize a past epoch, to see it in the round and to judge its significance within the total development of a society. Perhaps that is why a Frenchman has recently remarked that "no satisfactory over-all study of the Third Republic exists — or will exist for a long time to come" and why an American scholar has asserted that almost all of French history since 1870 ". . . has yet to be written, if only as a prelude to its being rewritten."

Yet if no "satisfactory over-all study" exists, certain segments and aspects of the Third Republic have been explored with considerable success. For political developments, D. W. Brogan's *France Under the Republic (1870–1939)* (New York: Harper, 1940) has already become a kind of classic. Packed with detail, illuminated by Brogan's wit, erudition, and insight, it suffers only from the unevenness produced by the author's inclination to write about what happens to interest him. It is Brogan commenting on French history, rather than French history by Brogan. The viewpoint is that of an urbane and cosmopolitan liberal, sympathetic toward the problems of the middle-of-the-road politicians. David Thomson's *Democracy in France* (London: Oxford Univ. Press, 1946, 1958) is a remarkably sophisticated analytical study of the political and social dynamics of the Third Republic. Thomson argues that the republic, by combining conservative institutions with

409

revolutionary ideas, was "the first successful attempt to reconcile the conservative and the revolutionary traditions in France," but he concludes that all of its assets turned into liabilities in the more complex twentieth century.

François Goguel's account is the best French study of the Third Republic's political history. His *La Politique des partis sous la IIIe république* (Paris: Seuil, 1946) is rather rigidly schematized; he finds the reality of French political life to lie in the conflict between two rival "political temperaments" — that of "Movement" and that of "Established Order." These categories he considers more fundamental than André Siegfried's classification of right-center-left, for he holds that on major issues the right and center always joined to defend the Established Order against the left. This schema, which is probably more provocative than really useful to the student of history, does not recur in Goguel's lectures at the Institut d'Études Politiques, which have been published as *Histoire des institutions politiques de la France de 1870 à 1940* (Paris: Cours de Droit, 1951–52). For a chronological analysis of the Third Republic's evolution, these lectures are unsurpassed.

The most ambitious narrative of the Third Republic is Jacques Chastenet's *Histoire de la troisième république* (Paris: Hachette, 1952–60), the first five volumes of which carry the story to 1931. A graceful and lucid account, it is primarily an interpretive synthesis that seeks to integrate all aspects of history. Its author, a representative right-of-center Moderate, has added his own insights to the work of the specialists on whom he draws. Maurice Reclus's *Grandeur de la troisième* (Paris: Hachette, 1948) is a spirited defense of the republic. He contends that it produced the ablest political personnel of the nineteenth century, and he suggests that if a king had ruled France from 1870 to 1918, royalists would exalt the period as a high point in France's past. Maurice Baumont's *Gloires et tragédies de la IIIe république* (Paris: Hachette, 1956) is sound but not very novel in treatment. Georges Duveau's *Histoire du peuple français de 1848 à nos jours* (Paris: N.L.F., 1953) is, on the contrary, an unorthodox and often provocative commentary by a maverick leftist. Paul Bouju and Henri Dubois's *La Troisième république* (Paris: Presses Univ., 1957) is a brief pamphlet bearing a weighty thesis: that the republic was dominated throughout by "the Interests" — a caste of scheming bankers, speculators, and monopolists who manipulated politics for their own ends. There is no general account of the period by a Communist historian. On the monarchist extreme, Jacques Bainville's *La Troisième république, 1870–1935* (Paris: Fayard, 1935) is a readable but slanted essay. How the defunct regime looked to at least some of its Vichyite successors may be seen in Léon Emery's *La Troisième république* (Paris: Inter-France, 1943), the work of a left-wing pacifist who chose to collaborate with the Germans.

⋘∘⋙ ⋘∘⋙ ⋘∘⋙

Many of the topical studies cited in Chapter Seventeen carry their particular threads through the Third Republic: Rémond on the right-wing groups; Girardet on the military; Dansette on church-state relations; Lorwin, Dolléans, and Lefranc on labor; Clapham and Clough on economic development; Morazé on the bourgeoisie; Beau de Loménie on the "bourgeois dynasties." The growth of Christian democracy is sympathetically traced in Maurice Vaussard's *Histoire de la démocratie chrétienne* (Paris: Seuil, 1956). On the church, Father Lecanuet presents a moderate Catholic viewpoint in *L'Église de France sous la IIIe république* (Paris: Alcan, 1930). Pierre Renouvin provides a skillful synthesis of modern scholarship on foreign policy in Volume VI of his *Histoire des relations internationales: le XIXe siècle, de 1871 à 1914* (Paris: Hachette, 1955). Richard D. Challener traces the evolution of French military doctrines in *The French Theory of the Nation in Arms, 1866–1939* (New York: Columbia Univ. Press, 1955) and suggests that the republic's preference for a noncareer army, composed mainly of civilian reservists, hampered military and foreign policy planning.

Most books on the Third Republic, however, confine themselves to a shorter time span or to a particular incident. The first few months of the republic have been examined by J. P. T. Bury in his *Gambetta and the National Defence* (London: Longmans, 1936; sympathetic to Gambetta) and by Henri Guillemin in his *Cette curieuse guerre de 70* (Paris: Gallimard, 1956). Guillemin seeks to prove the "collective treason" of the propertied classes, who allegedly capitulated to the Germans in order to be free to fight their real enemy, the people of Paris. On the Paris Commune of 1870, there have been sharp differences of view. Karl Marx's contemporaneous pamphlet *The Civil War in France* (Moscow: For. Lang. Pub. House, 1948) continues to inspire French Communist historians in our day; they find the incident a clearcut example of the class struggle erupting in violence. The recent Communist version, as expressed in frequent articles in the party's theoretical and intellectual organs *Cahiers du Communisme* and *La Pensée*, emphasizes the international solidarity of the bourgeoisie; it argues that both Bismarck and the American minister to France lent active assistance to Thiers, and that hysterical class hatred led to the butchery of thousands of Communards. Non-Communist historians take the position, rather, that the Communards were motivated by injured patriotism, antimonarchism, and antiruralism, and that the class-struggle aspect was a minor theme on both sides. Among the recent studies are E. S. Mason, *The Paris Commune* (New York: Macmillan, 1930); Frank Jellinek, *The Paris Commune of 1871* (London: Gollancz, 1937); Albert Ollivier, *La Commune (1871)* (Paris: Gallimard, 1939). Charles Rihs, in his *La Commune de Paris, sa structure et ses doctrines* (Geneva: Droz, 1955), emphasizes the doctrinal heterogeneity within the Commune's leadership and suggests that an internal crisis would have occurred if the Commune had survived much longer. Jean T. Joughin has traced some of the Commune's after effects in *The Paris Commune in French Politics, 1871–1880* (Baltimore: Johns Hopkins, 1955).

On the Republic's first decade, the liveliest accounts of political events are those of Daniel Halévy: *La Fin des notables* (Paris: Grasset, 1930) and *La République des ducs* (Paris: Grasset, 1937). Jacques Gouault has sought to explain *Comment la France est devenue républicaine* (Paris: Colin, 1954); he concludes that most Frenchmen were seeking a middle way between reaction and revolution, and that they found it in the petty-bourgeois republic. The conversion of the peasantry in 1871–75 was the fundamental change; it was not the product of republican propaganda but of a slowly acquired conviction that the old notables could never really defend the interests of the little man.

The issues and men of the Opportunist epoch (1879–99) have been studied in spottier fashion. The British historian A. F. Thompson severely castigates the ruling group for its "timid conservatism" and "drab complacency" (in J. M. Wallace-Hadrill and J. McManners (eds.), *France: Government and Society* [London: Methuen, 1957]). These "new Girondins," according to Thompson, were best personified by Jules Ferry, "the archetype of their evasive mediocrity." Antidotes for his caustic view may be found in Chastenet (*op. cit.*), to whom the Opportunist leaders were statesmen of stature, and in Maurice Reclus's *Jules Ferry* (Paris: Flammarion, 1947), which is almost adulatory in its praise. Ferry's role as the great builder of empire emerges somewhat shrunken from T. F. Power's *Jules Ferry and the Renaissance of French Imperialism* (New York: King's Crown, 1944) and C.-A. Julien's *Les Politiques d'expansion impérialiste* (Paris: Presses Univ., 1949). There are no adequate biographies of Gambetta or of most of the lesser Opportunist leaders.

The scandals and crises of the late nineteenth century have long fascinated historians as well as journalists. Adrien Dansette's *Le Boulangisme* (Paris: Perrin, 1938) is the liveliest account of that episode. Jacques Néré, in his unpublished Sorbonne thesis "La Crise économique et sociale de 1882 et le mouvement boulangiste" (1959), demonstrates how the economic stress of the decade contributed to Boulangism's success in Paris. Boulanger's vague slogans and his patriotic appeal pulled many working men away from radicalism; after the movement collapsed most of them turned to socialism. On the Dreyfus Affair, Joseph Reinach's seven-volume contemporaneous account (*Histoire de l'Affaire Dreyfus* [Paris: Fasquelle, 1901–8]) continues to be the basic work; it is strongly pro-Dreyfus. The best recent studies are Guy Chapman's *The Dreyfus Case* (London: Hart-Davis, 1955) and

413

Nicholas Halasz's *Captain Dreyfus: the Story of a Mass Hysteria* (New York; Grove, 1955). Halasz's account, though journalistic, rests on solid research. Chapman's much more painstaking study revises the old revisionists; it propounds the thesis that anti-Semitism played only a minor role in the Affair and that the legend of good, high-minded men struggling against evil bigots must give way to a more balanced and dispassionate estimate of both factions. Error, confusion, and prejudice, he contends, pervaded the atmosphere on both sides. On the other hand, Robert F. Byrnes, in his *Antisemitism in Modern France* (New Brunswick: Rutgers Univ. Press, 1950), reasserts the importance of anti-Semitic doctrines as background to the Affair, and analyzes their character and appeal in France. Pierre Miquel's *L'Affaire Dreyfus* (Paris: Presses Univ., 1959) is an excellent brief synthesis that stresses the role of the French press; while Maurice Baumont's *Aux sources de l'Affaire* (Paris: Ed. les Productions de Paris, 1960) clarifies the tangled diplomatic aspects of the crisis.

Politics and politicians in the Radical era (1899–1914) have received less attention. L. V. Méjan has painstakingly examined the resurgence of the church-state feud after the Dreyfus Affair, in her monograph *La Séparation des églises et de l'état* (Paris: Presses Univ., 1959). She contends that the separation issue aroused passions almost as intense as those surrounding the Dreyfus case, and that a major upheaval was averted only through the efforts of such compromisers as Briand and his advisers. There are few good biographies of statesmen of the period. The exceptions are J. H. Jackson's *Clemenceau and the Third French Republic* (New York: Macmillan, 1948); Geoffrey Bruun's *Clemenceau* (Cambridge, Mass.: Harvard Univ. Press, 1943); Jacques Chastenet's *Raymond Poincaré* (Paris: Julliard, 1948); J. H. Jackson's *Jean Jaurès, His Life and Work* (London: Allen and Unwin, 1943); and Marcelle Auclair's *La Vie de Jaurès ou la France d'avant 1914* (Paris: Seuil, 1954). All of the foregoing biographers are strongly sympathetic toward their subjects. The rise of socialism is examined by Aaron Noland in his *Founding of the French Socialist Party* (Cambridge, Mass.: Harvard Univ. Press, 1956) and by Marcel

Prélot in *L'Evolution politique du socialisme français* (Paris: Spès, 1939), while M. M. Drachkovitch severely castigates most of the Socialist leaders over the years in his *De Karl Marx à Léon Blum* (Geneva: Droz, 1955). Michael Curtis analyzes and compares the doctrines of three leading critics of the pre-1914 republic: *Three Against the Third Republic: Sorel, Barrès, and Maurras* (Princeton: Princeton Univ. Press, 1959). There are sympathetic accounts of Maurras's Action Française by Robert Havard de la Montagne (*Histoire de l'Action Française* [Paris: Amiot-Dumont, 1950]) and by Henri Massis (*Maurras et notre temps* [Paris: Palatine, 1951]).

On the First World War, Cyril Falls' *The Great War, 1914–1918* (New York: Putnam, 1959) synthesizes — from a British angle — the vast body of literature on the military campaigns. Henry Contamine's *La Revanche, 1871–1914* (Paris: Berger-Levrault, 1957) belies its title; it is a careful study, based on archival research, of French strategic concepts during the two generations before 1914. Contamine defends the French high command against the traditional charge of rigidity of mind and fanatical dedication to the doctrine of an all-out offensive; his account of the first six weeks of the war supports the view that French military leadership was more flexible and quick-witted than the German general staff. The crucial wartime relationship between government and high command in France has been lucidly portrayed by Jere C. King in his *Generals and Politicians* (Berkeley: Univ. of California Press, 1951). King has continued the story into the peace-making era in his *Foch versus Clemenceau* (Cambridge, Mass.: Harvard Univ. Press, 1960). There are some perceptive chapters on the conflict over French war aims in Arno Mayer's *Political Origins of the New Diplomacy* (New Haven: Yale Univ. Press, 1959).

On the Third Republic's foreign policy, there has been no general reassessment for many years. Pierre Renouvin's thoughtful synthesis (with an up-to-date bibliography) is the indispensable introduction. A. J. P. Taylor's *Struggle for Mastery in Europe, 1848–1918* (London: Oxford Univ. Press, 1954), though it focusses mainly on Berlin and London, contains some provocative judgments on France's role in

European affairs; its author is inclined to revise all "standard" interpretations, especially those that were labelled "revisionist" a generation
ago. Raoul Girardet is expected to publish shortly his study bearing on
the significance of Alsace-Lorraine in French opinion and policy-mak-
ing; his work may be expected to test, for the first time, the deep-
rooted legend that the urge for revenge dominated French minds from
1871 to 1914.

One of the most controversial issues in the foreign policy area con-
cerns the role of Delcassé as foreign minister. Both Delcassé's admirers
and his critics have long been inclined to describe him as a dedicated
Germanophobe who devoted himself to forging an iron ring about
Germany. More recently A. J. P. Taylor, J. D. Hargreaves, and others
have portrayed him as hesitating between an anti-British and an anti-
German position for several years; they conclude that only German
obtuseness drove him into an Anglo-French entente. In the realm of
curiosa, there is the line recently taken toward Delcassé by the ultra-
nationalist extreme right in France. On the fiftieth anniversary of the
Entente Cordiale (1954), the Parisian weekly *La France Réelle* described Delcassé as an inexperienced and obscure politician who was
hand-picked for the post of French foreign minister by the British
Foreign Office. The British, through their agents among the French
Freemasons, allegedly kept Delcassé in the cabinet for seven long
years — long enough to complete London's program of diplomatic revolution. Such legends require no historical evidence to support them;
they survive thanks to the sheer will to believe. For a more balanced
survey, C. W. Porter's *The Career of Théophile Delcassé* (Philadelphia:
Univ. of Pennsylvania Press, 1936) is still serviceable.

Eugen Weber's *Nationalist Revival in France, 1905–1914* (Berkeley: Univ. of California Press, 1959) provides a fresh insight into the
origins and character of the new intransigent mood that colored French
political life in the prewar decade. Weber shows that the new variety
of nationalism, unlike the earlier *revanchard* attitude of Barrès and
Boulanger, was the patriotic and defensive reaction of Frenchmen
aroused by what they considered to be the arrogant and incompre-

416

hensible behavior of the Germans. The politicians affected by it were the heirs of those who had opposed and restrained the chauvinism of the Boulangists a generation earlier. Gilbert Ziebura's monograph *Die Deutsche Frage in der Oeffentlichen Meinung Frankreichs von 1911– 1914* (Berlin: Colloquium, 1955), through a careful analysis of French publications of the time, reinforces Weber's conclusions about the nationalist revival.

On French colonial expansion there is an extensive monographic literature, but no really adequate synthesis. Stephen H. Roberts' *History of French Colonial Policy (1870–1925)* (London: King, 1929) is detailed but rather outdated. Shorter and more general accounts are Henry Blet's *Histoire de la colonisation française* (Paris: Arthaud, 1949–50) and Henri Brunschwig's *La Colonisation française du pacte colonial à l'Union Française* (Paris: Calmann-Lévy, 1949). Agnes Murphy has examined the doctrines behind the new imperialism in *The Ideology of French Imperialism, 1871–1881* (Washington, D. C.: Catholic Univ. Press, 1948).

There are few good monographs on the economic history of the Third Republic; as for the business history of the epoch, it is almost untouched. Michel Augé-Laribé has traced agricultural conditions and policies in his *La Politique agricole de la France de 1880 à 1940* (Paris: Presses Univ., 1950); Eugene Golob has studied *The Méline Tariff* (New York: Columbia Univ. Press, 1944). There are some interesting chapters on various aspects of business history in Jacques Boudet (ed.), *Le Monde des affaires en France de 1830 à nos jours* (Paris: S.E.D.E., 1952). Jean Bouvier's doctoral thesis, defended at the Sorbonne in 1959, examines the early growth of one of France's biggest deposit banks: "Le Crédit Lyonnais de 1863 à 1882."

On intellectual and cultural trends, Henri Peyre's *The Contemporary French Novel* (New York: Oxford Univ. Press, 1955) is a masterly analysis of main currents in prose fiction since 1890; an excellent supplement is Germaine Brée and Margaret Guiton's *An Age of Fiction: The Novel from Gide to Camus* (New Brunswick: Rutgers Univ. Press, 1957). Roger Shattuck's *The Banquet Years: The Arts in France,*

1885–1918 (New York: Harcourt, 1958), brilliantly written and filled with piquant anecdotes, examines the Bohemian world of writers and artists by focussing on the work of several avant-garde figures. There are some penetrating sections on such French thinkers as Sorel, Bergson, and Durkheim in H. Stuart Hughes's *Consciousness and Society* (New York: Knopf, 1959).

∞⤳✦∞⤳✦∞⤳

Although the study of history through fiction has its risks, there are times and places when the novel can illumine many obscure corners. Nowhere is this so true as in the history of France since the mid-nineteenth century (or even before, as the works of Stendhal and Balzac show). Perhaps the reason is that historians of modern France have left many glaring gaps which only the novelist has tried to fill; perhaps it is because French literary men have taken a lively interest in political and social issues; or perhaps (as Herbert Luethy puts it) "in France literature has taken the place of political economy, sociology, and statistics."[1]

For the general historian (as distinct from the student of literary history or belles-lettres), some of the works of Emile Zola, Maurice Barrès, Paul Bourget, Anatole France, and Roger Martin du Gard possess unique value. Zola's Rougon-Macquart series, though set in the time of Napoleon III, illumines the social history of the early Third Republic as well, and his *La Débâcle* is a remarkable commentary on the Franco-Prussian war. Barrès's trilogy *Le Roman de l'énergie nationale (Les Déracinés; L'Appel au soldat; Leurs figures)* focusses on intellectual and political life in the 1880's and 1890's. Bourget's *Le Disciple* (1889) was the manifesto of the resurgent conservatives

---

[1] H. Luethy, *France Against Herself* (New York: Praeger, 1955), p. 72. "Literature," adds Luethy, "is the only possible and adequate social science of a society organized in innumerable groups held together by personal ties, each small enough to be surveyable by all its members and private enough to be impenetrable by outsiders; while in the mass their infinite divisions and subdivisions make them totally unsurveyable and incalculable."

against the positivist mood of the republic; Anatole France's four-volume *Histoire contemporaine (L'Orme du mail; Le Mannequin d'osier; L'Anneau d'améthyste; Monsieur Bergeret à Paris)* was a kind of sustained rejoinder to Bourget, with the political events of the Dreyfus decade as its subject matter. Martin du Gard's *Jean Barois,* though an indifferent novel, portrays in remarkable fashion the conflict of ideas in France between 1890 and 1914.

Other useful novels are Paul Adam's *Le Mystère des foules* (on the Boulanger episode); Alphonse Daudet's *Numa Roumestan* (on politics in the 1870's); Georges Duhamel's *Chronique des Pasquier* (on the evolving fortunes of a bourgeois family); Romain Rolland's *Jean-Christophe* (on the pre-1914 generation); and Jules Romains's twenty-eight volume *Hommes de bonne volonté* (an attempt to do for the France of 1907–33 what Balzac had done for the age of Louis Philippe).

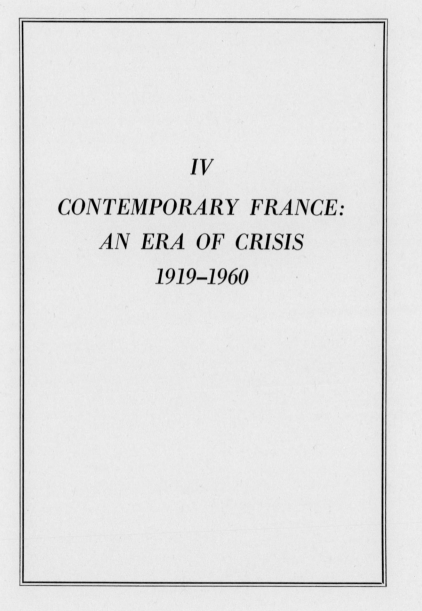

IV

CONTEMPORARY FRANCE:
AN ERA OF CRISIS
1919–1960

France contains two fundamental temperaments — that of the left and that of the right; three principal tendencies, if one adds the center; six spiritual families; ten parties, large or small, traversed by multiple currents; fourteen parliamentary groups without much discipline; and forty million opinions.

JACQUES FAUVET

The Quest for Normalcy, 1919–1931

The Third Republic, as seen in retrospect by observers of our day, seems to have passed through three distinct though interconnected phases: the heroic age from 1871 to about 1900, during which the republicans fought off all challenges and consolidated the regime; the stable era from 1900 to about 1930, when the system appeared to have won a degree of popular consensus unequalled by any of its predecessors; the period of disintegration that began about 1930 and ended in collapse a decade later.

If this broad pattern has any validity, it might seem logical to assume that something disastrous happened about 1930 to disrupt a popular and generally successful regime. That disaster, one might conclude, was the great economic crisis that not only created grave tensions within France but also opened the way for the rise of aggressive enemies across the Rhine and the Alps. Probably it is true that the Third Republic would have endured — by force of inertia, if nothing else — if spared the impact of depression and war. Yet the real test of any regime is how well it can face up to crisis. A nation that collapses

423

as quickly as France did in 1940, a nation where consensus disintegrates when confronted with the economic and social stresses of a depression decade, is clearly suffering from some deeper sources of weakness. Something was wrong well before the depression hit France — though just what was wrong is a complex and controversial question.

It has sometimes been argued that the source of the trouble can be traced to the Great War of 1914–18, with its terrible drain on French manpower, resources, and emotions. The remarkable economic recovery of the 1920's and the factitious hegemony of France in postwar Europe would then be seen as a plastering over of the fatal cracks in the edifice. Others have held that the sources of weakness really went far deeper, into the character of the French political and social system itself. The Third Republic, a Frenchman once remarked, was a system of government well adapted to "an independent, rich, and happy people" — but not to a nation in crisis. So long as it faced nothing more complex than the theoretical and doctrinal problems of the later nineteenth century, it worked reasonably well. But an essentially negative instrument of government, designed to prevent abuses rather than to get things done, was scarcely adequate for an era of rapid and profound change. The trouble with the Third Republic (according to this line of argument) was that it succeeded in taking root in French affections just at the moment when it was beginning to be outmoded. Frenchmen clung to it after 1900, just as most of them clung to a social structure and a cluster of attitudes that belonged to the nineteenth century. As a result, they entered the new industrial age — an age of mass production and mass rule — both psychologically unprepared and politically unarmed. For such a nation, the cumulative effect of the Great War and the Great Depression was likely to prove overwhelming.

During the first postwar decade, however, these weaknesses could easily be ignored. Frenchmen, like Americans in the same era, were eager to recover what the Americans called "normalcy." Victory seemed to prove that France needed no fundamental change, that it would be enough to repair the damage and resume the upward trends of the pre-1914 years. By the end of the 1920's the devastated regions had been reconstructed, as nearly as possible on the prewar model; rebuilt factories had raised industrial production well above the 1914 level; the manpower gap left by the war had been filled by the immigration of some two million foreign workers.

Politically, too, the republican system survived the war unaltered. A restless parliament promptly shook off Clemenceau's wartime dictatorship and reasserted its prewar ascendancy over the executive. But if the structure of the system emerged intact, within this old framework the postwar era brought both new forces and new men. The most striking change, superficially at least, was an apparent shift in the political center of gravity toward the right. Since the inception of the Third Republic the trend had been almost steadily leftward; power had shifted from the monarchists to the Opportunists to the Radicals, and on the eve of the war it had begun to seem that the Socialists' turn would be next. Suddenly, in the elections of November, 1919, this trend appeared to be reversed: Frenchmen chose their most rightist Chamber since 1871, giving the Moderates and the conservative right more than two-thirds of the seats.

This startling reversal in parliament did not, however, reflect a major shift of opinion among the voters. In 1919 the left-wing parties actually increased their popular vote over the 1914 figure, and during the next two decades the left won every election except that of 1928. The rightist victory just after the war was a kind of fluke, made possible by the new electoral system adopted in that year. It provided for large multimember electoral districts in place of small single-member constituencies; it gave a clear advantage to those parties that could organize electoral coalitions. The various Moderate and conservative groups managed to do so in 1919, under the label Bloc National; the leftist parties fought each other instead. The Socialists by now were in the throes of a bitter internal conflict; one powerful faction was attracted to Moscow and wanted the party to join Lenin's new Third International. Most Radicals were unwilling to link their fate with a party that might be on the verge of embracing Leninism. So it was that the left cancelled itself out, even though the Radicals won as many votes as in 1914, and the Socialists won more.

If the rightist victory had any real significance, it was to show the declining intensity of the religious issue in French politics. For the Moderates to form electoral coalitions with strongly clerical conservatives represented a sharp change since prewar days. Time and the wartime sacred union had done their work; the extreme right had accepted the secular republic, the Moderate right-center was prepared to meet it halfway. The renewed political influence of the Moderates between the wars was traceable in large part to the fading impact of clericalism as a vital issue. To please the new Chamber of 1919 (the first since 1871 to contain a majority of practicing Catholics), the government quietly restored diplomatic relations with the Vatican and exempted Alsace from the separation laws of 1905.[1]

On the whole, however, the right's victory produced no major change in policy or mood. If the Moderates were willing to ally with the conservative right for electoral purposes, many of them preferred to govern in combination with their Radical neighbors just to the left. The old impulse toward *concentration*, toward collaboration of right-center and left-center groups, became stronger than ever before. From 1899 to 1919 the Radicals had usually dominated such coalitions; from 1919 to 1936 it was more often the Moderates. But since the same fluctuating alliance continued to govern the country, the interwar period proved to be a political prolongation of the prewar era. Even when the left-wing parties managed to recover control of the Chamber (as in 1924

---

[1] When Herriot's Radical cabinet tried in 1924 to revive the clerical issue by extending the separation laws to Alsace, the effect was to consolidate the center and right rather than to rally the left around the old anticlerical banner. The hierarchy encouraged the creation of a pressure group called the National Catholic Federation that effectively influenced parliament and the *bien-pensant* public. Since large segments of the left were indifferent, the cabinet soon abandoned its anticlerical program, though pools of hostility toward the church survived. The one remaining issue that threatened to reawaken the old anticlerical spirit was the question of state aid to church schools; Catholics began to advance this idea in the mid-1920's.

and 1932), their failure to cooperate among themselves, combined with the Socialists' steady refusal to enter any cabinet, always led to a restoration of the Radical-Moderate alliance, with the Moderates usually shaping policy and holding the key positions.

Since the fulcrum of politics lay in the shadowy zone where Radicals and Moderates met, the most likely candidate for the premiership would be a man with a foot in both camps — a man better adapted to compromise than to vigorous, forthright action. There could hardly have been a more fitting aspirant than Aristide Briand, who had already headed six cabinets before and during the war, and who broke all records by forming five more during the 1920's. Briand's political background was strangely variegated. As a young man he had flirted with Boulangism and anarcho-syndicalism; then he had joined the Socialist party of Jaurès, only to leave this group in 1906 in order to accept a cabinet post. His first act on becoming a minister, it is said, was to send an aide to the Bibliothèque Nationale to destroy the violent articles he had once written in an anarchist newspaper. Since then he had hovered between or above parties, maintaining his contacts and friends in all camps. France has rarely produced a more flexible politician; indeed, Briand's favorite maxim was "life is made of rubber." His admirers said that, like an insect, he possessed invisible antennae that enabled him to operate by "feel." It is likely that he had no deep convictions, no doctrine, nothing beyond a highly developed politician's instinct. Yet his personal charm, his oratorical skill, and his adaptability made him in many respects the most successful and the most representative French political figure of the era.

Briand's only serious rival for leadership in the postwar decade was the Moderate Raymond Poincaré, who broke precedent by returning to active politics after his presidential term ended in 1920. Both men headed coalition cabinets of much the same kind, yet they could hardly have been more different in temperament. Where Briand was devious and improvising, Poincaré was rigid and intransigent. A wit of the day remarked that "Briand knows nothing and understands everything; Poincaré knows everything and understands nothing." If few of his

fellow politicians liked Poincaré, most of them respected him for a
personal honesty so scrupulous as to be unusual in the world of politics.
As a young minister in prewar days, he had astounded his secretary
by sorting out his personal letters from his official correspondence and
buying his own stamps for the former kind. His reputation as a financial expert and as a dedicated patriot adapted him for leadership at a
time when the two critical issues were the problem of the franc and the
enforcement of Versailles. Poincaré's cabinets, unlike Briand's, were
few but durable; he held the premiership from 1922 to 1924, and
again from 1926 to 1929.

Alongside these older leaders whose political careers had begun
before the turn of the century, a younger generation of politicians was
beginning to emerge into prominence in the 1920's. On the right, the
most notable new figures were André Tardieu and Pierre Laval; on
the left, Edouard Herriot and Léon Blum. All four were to play first-
rank roles during the crisis decade of the 1930's. Tardieu, scion of an
old family of the middle bourgeoisie, was one of the few native
Parisians to rise high in a political world monopolized by provincials.
After a brilliant prewar career as civil servant and journalist, he had
entered the Chamber in 1914 and had risen to prominence as Clemenceau's right-hand man at the peace conference. As arrogant as he was
able, Tardieu's contempt for lesser men and for public opinion hampered his political career and led him eventually to repudiate the
parliamentary system in favor of an authoritarian republic. Laval, son
of a village innkeeper and butcher from the remote hill country of
central France, had a career that resembled that of his idol Briand. A
Socialist of the most rabidly leftist variety before 1914, he left the
party shortly after the war and underwent a gradual and rather obscure
conversion that eventually turned him into a nonparty Moderate. A
shrewd and unscrupulous manipulator of men, Laval took it for granted
that a politician ought to appeal to man's baser motives. In the 1930's
he was to become Briand's successor as the most remarkable political
manipulator in parliament. However, he lacked Briand's oratorical skill
and his sense of timing.

Edouard Herriot emerged in the 1920's as the new spokesman and standard-bearer of the Radical party. Son of a career army officer, brilliant graduate of the École Normale, professor of literature in a Lyon *lycée,* he had been drawn into politics during the Dreyfus Affair and had entered parliament in 1912 as France's youngest senator. Herriot was a talented if rather rhetorical orator, a man who managed to combine the realist's flexibility with the idealist's respect for doctrine. Twice, after the left's electoral victories in 1924 and 1932, he was to serve briefly as premier at the head of a shaky left-wing coalition.

In the Socialist party it was Léon Blum who sought to fill the gap left by the assassination of Jaurès in 1914 and the aging of Guesde (who died in 1922). Blum was another ex-Normalien, the son of Jewish bourgeois parents whose forebears had come to Paris from Alsace. A brilliant student of esthetic tastes and subtle mind, he had become politically conscious during the Dreyfus uproar and had become a dedicated disciple of Jaurès. After the victory of the Dreyfusards he had returned to his original career as journalist, literary man, and high civil servant (in the Conseil d'État); but Jaurès' assassination and the outbreak of war brought him back to an active role in the party. By the end of the war he was leader of the Socialists' center faction, and in 1919 he won election to the Chamber. Like Jaurès, Blum was a humanitarian socialist for whom Marxism was a method of analysis rather than a dogma. Blum neither sprang from the working class nor had any direct acquaintance with it; his intellectual tastes, his somewhat effeminate voice and manner, made him seem the least likely candidate for the leadership of a proletarian party. Still, French socialism had never been led by proletarians, and during the interwar years it was to become more and more a party of white-collar workers, intellectuals, and elements of the lower middle class. If Blum lacked the personal magnetism and the robust earthiness of Jaurès, he won the genuine respect of his party followers as a subtle theoretician and as a remarkable spokesman for humanitarian ideals.

Blum's first task as party leader was to prevent French socialism from slipping into the Moscow orbit. Since 1917 the Bolshevik experi-

ment had exerted a powerful pull, not only on the new unskilled proletariat in war production plants, but also on many old-time Socialists
of the Guesdist wing. This latter group persuaded itself that Lenin's
communism was basically not much different from Western Marxian
movements: "Socialism with Tartar sauce," one of them ironically
called it. But some Guesdists, together with most of the heirs of Jaurès,
were more dubious; men like Blum detected in Leninism something
new and ominous, and they managed to block the pro-Moscow element
for a time. At the party congress of Tours in December, 1920, however,
they were swamped by a three-to-one vote in favor of joining the Third
International. Blum preferred secession to unity on Lenin's terms; he
led the minority group out of the congress hall, leaving almost everything — party machinery, newspaper, membership — in the hands of
the majority that promptly renamed itself the French Communist party.

At the outset the Socialists' prospects seemed gloomy; the very survival of the party, except perhaps as a tiny splinter group, appeared
doubtful. Communist membership in 1921 outnumbered that of the Socialists by 140,000 to 30,000; the Communist organ *L'Humanité* outsold
the new Socialist daily *Populaire* by 200,000 to 5,000. But the next few
years were to justify Blum's determination to go it alone. By 1924
the Socialists' dues-paying membership exceeded that of the Communists; by 1932 Socialist representation in the Chamber outnumbered
that of the Communists by ninety-eight to ten; by 1936 the Socialists
had become France's largest party, and Blum took over the premiership.
This remarkable recovery stemmed in part from Blum's determined
and intelligent leadership. He refused to permit the party to become a
new version of the Radicals, but clung instead to the policy of nonparticipation in bourgeois cabinets and to the doctrine of revolution
rather than gradualist reform. If such a doctrine was unrealistic and
in some ways misleading, it did preserve the Socialist party as a haven
for disillusioned Communists and for proletarian idealists. More of
the credit, however, should probably go to those lesser party officials
and local militants who, at the grass-roots level, worked doggedly at
the task of party reorganization. And perhaps the major credit must

go to the Communists themselves, for their policies contributed heavily to the Socialist revival. French communism's record during the twenties was one of chronic dissension and division. At the outset its members were united by little more than a romantic enthusiasm for the Russian experiment. They had accepted Lenin's twenty-one conditions in order to gain admittance to the Third International, but most of them had not taken very seriously the prospect that Moscow would insist on dictating party policy within France. A kind of resurrected Gallican spirit marked the outlook of the early French Communists; their aim was formal allegiance to Moscow without domination by Moscow.

Through the 1920's a steady stream of telegrams and investigators poured into France from Russia as the Soviet leaders sought to discipline the French party. One faction after another was expelled, or angrily resigned. By 1923 it was estimated that two-thirds of the original members had left the party, and many of these deserters found their way back to the Socialists. But if Moscow's policy was temporarily disastrous, it was potentially effective. By the end of the decade what was left of the French Communist party had been thoroughly Bolshevized. A new generation of younger leaders, tougher and more Leninist in spirit, more truly proletarian in origin, had replaced the older group — men like the miner's son Maurice Thorez, the metallurgy worker Jacques Doriot, the veterans' organizer and ex-pastry cook Jacques Duclos, the onetime naval petty officer André Marty. These men, untouched by French socialism's deep-rooted humanitarian and libertarian heritage, were dedicated to Leninist doctrines of organization and action. From its low point in the mid-twenties the Communist party began to make slow but steady progress at the polls. Most of its strength remained concentrated in the red belt of workers' suburbs surrounding Paris; but the party was already experimenting with new propaganda appeals destined to attract the largest French voting groups — the petty bourgeoisie, the artisans, the poorer peasants, the intellectuals. By the end of the decade the Communists had forged a small but reliable weapon for use in times of stress or crisis.

431

Communism was not the only new force in politics that emerged in the postwar decade. Other movements of the center and right, though smaller, also foreshadowed future trends. One of these was Christian democracy, which burgeoned in the 1920's in a whole series of forms. The prewar Sillon, after its condemnation by the Vatican, had left behind a small nucleus of militants dedicated to the idea of reconciling their faith with the ideals symbolized by the Great Revolution. Many of them had turned to social rather than political activity, and they worked through the lay organization called Catholic Action. After the war they founded a whole series of new specialized branches of Catholic Action aimed at young people: the Young Christian Workers (J.O.C.), the Young Christian Farmers (J.A.C.), and so on. Some of the ex-Sillonistes also helped to organize a new Catholic trade-union movement, the C.F.T.C., in 1919; and in 1924 they re-embarked in politics when they founded the Popular Democratic party. Between the wars Christian democracy remained a minor current; the Popular Democrats managed to elect only about a dozen deputies, mainly in strongly Catholic provinces like Alsace and Brittany. The old religious feud, though no longer so intense, still tainted men's minds and emotions; neither Catholics nor freethinkers quite trusted a party like this one. But the foundations for expansion were being laid by training a new Catholic elite in the youth movements — an elite that in time of crisis would prove its dedication to the republic's ideals.

On the extreme right, too, there were signs of effervescence during the 1920's; several small but noisy movements emerged, some of them traditionalist and authoritarian, others frankly totalitarian or fascist in spirit. In the latter category, Pierre Taittinger's Jeunesses Patriotes was representative; its model was Mussolini's Fascismo. Potentially much more important, however, were those groups that professed purely French and authoritarian doctrines, with only tinges of fascist theory. Notable among them was the Croix de Feu, still a nonpolitical organization of decorated veterans in that era, but one that was marked by an authoritarian temper and by a growing tendency toward political action. Another — the most influential of all during this decade — was

432

the Action Française of Charles Maurras. Its rabid nationalism, its refurbished traditionalism, and its arrogant elitism appealed to young activists in much the same way that Leninism attracted another segment of youth. Several eminent literary figures lent intellectual respectability to the movement; and in addition, it offered a chance for action and excitement through participation in a kind of private army called the Camelots du Roi. In 1919 the Action Française managed to get its spokesman into the Chamber of Deputies: Léon Daudet, son of the distinguished novelist and wielder of the most scurrilous and venomous pen in Parisian journalism.

French monarchism had been almost moribund until Maurras came along to revive it. The king's cause was brought to life again by all this agitation; but the pretender was not at all sure that he wanted such unorthodox and dangerous champions. Many Catholics, too, were disturbed at the violence and the brutal cynicism of the Maurrassian doctrine; some of them suspected (quite properly) that Maurras's aim was not to serve the church but to use it for his own purposes. After many years of hesitation the Vatican concluded that young Catholics were being corrupted by an amoral and dangerous ideology; in 1926 Catholics were instructed to abandon the movement and to give up reading its newspaper. Some years later the royal pretender followed suit and repudiated Maurras. Although many Catholic laymen openly refused to follow the Vatican's directive, the Pope's action proved to be a major blow to the Action Française. The clergy generally submitted; Maurrassism was pruned out of Catholic schools and universities, leaving Catholic youth to be exposed to a different set of intellectual leaders. When the crisis decade of the 1930's arrived, the Action Française found itself quickly outdistanced by newer authoritarian groups. Yet the insidious doctrines of the movement had made their way into the minds of an important minority of the French elite and had softened up that element for fascist or proto-fascist agitators. After 1930 the republic would once again be faced by vigorous and unscrupulous enemies on the far right.

Between the extremes of right and left, the old political groups clung to their prewar habits without much change. The Radicals (still technically named the Radical and Socialist-Radical party) remained a kind of loose confederation of libertarian, petty-bourgeois individualists bound together by little more than tradition and electoral interest; party discipline was weak, party policy more negative than positive. On most important votes in the Chamber, the Radicals divided three ways: yes, no, and abstention. Radicalism had long since shifted from an urban to a small-town and rural base, with its greatest strength in the economically static southwest. Through most of the interwar period the Radicals had the largest single organized group in the Chamber, and they attained an even firmer grip on the Senate, largely because they had gotten control of so many municipal and departmental councils in rural France. The Moderates remained divided into several rather loose party groups, of which the Democratic Alliance and the Republican Federation were the largest and most durable. The line of separation between Moderates and Radicals continued to be obscure; one of the most effective parliamentary groups of this era, the misnamed "Radical Left," profited from this obscurity by frankly straddling the gap and furnishing ministers to all kinds of cabinets. On the whole, the Moderates had outgrown their anticlericalism more rapidly than the Radicals, and they were more inclined to reflect the interests of large-scale business while the Radicals responded to the pressures of small enterprise.

One of the few political novelties of the postwar decade was the emergence of fairly sizable and influential organized interest groups. Only a few such organizations had existed in prewar days — the steelmakers' Comité des Forges, for example, and the coal industry's Comité des Houillères. There had also been such loose groups as the Union of Economic Interests, set up shortly before 1914 to provide an electoral slush fund for center and right-wing politicians, and the so-called Mascuraud Committee, which from the late 1890's had financed the election of Radical candidates, and which drew its funds mainly from small business firms. All of these groups continued to function after the war; the Union of Economic Interests even expanded its activities and allegedly subsidized more than half the successful candidates for the Chamber in the 1920's. What was new in the postwar era was the proliferation of important interest groups representing almost every segment of society and of the economy. Business men established the first national employers' confederation (C.N.P.F.) in 1919. In the same year a much less successful National Agricultural Confederation sought to group the farmers; it was quickly outpaced by a whole series of specialized associations representing the wheatgrowers, the sugar-beet producers, and so on. Labor, which needed its own pressure group more desperately than did any other social stratum, continued to divide its strength. To the old C.G.T., which still tried to turn its back on politics, there were now added the Catholic C.F.T.C. and the Communist C.G.T.U. Probably the most effective interest groups of the period were those representing the war veterans. Here again, however, diversity rather than unity was the rule: the Union Fédérale and the Union Nationale des Combattants, which had almost a million members each, were only the largest of a half-dozen groups. Although they were hampered by division, most of the interest groups quickly learned that the French political system was ideally suited to their needs. The decision-making process was widely diffused through parliament and the bureaucracy; there existed no powerful and stable executive authority to speak for the nation as a whole and to resist demands for special privilege. During these last years of the Third Republic the lobbyist became an increasingly familiar and influential figure in the committee rooms of parliament and in the offices of high civil servants.

In that era of recovered normalcy that extended from 1919 to about 1931, Frenchmen once again could believe — as they had before 1914 — that politics was less a serious matter than a kind of game, passionately interesting, perhaps, but not of vital importance. The journalist Robert de Jouvenel had written of his compatriots in prewar days: "France is a happy land, where the soil is generous, the artisan ingenious, and wealth widely shared. Politics one can take or leave, according to individual taste: it is not the decisive factor in

Frenchmen's lives."[2] The novelist-diplomat Paul Morand was later to add, with a touch of irony, that the practice of politics had been brought to its ultimate refinement by Frenchmen, who had made of it "a pure indigenous art." Such epigrams contained a disturbing germ of truth. Although most Frenchmen refused to recognize the fact, the time was at hand when politics could no longer be viewed as little more than a game, a spectacle, a career. For good or ill, it was rapidly becoming the overwhelming factor that would really shape the condition of men's lives.

[2] R. de Jouvenel, *La république des camarades* (Paris: Grasset, 1914), p. 4.

TWENTY-EIGHT

> France victorious must grow accustomed to being a
> lesser power than France vanquished.
>
> JULES CAMBON *(1918)*

The Era of French Hegemony,
1919–1933

For more than a decade after the victory of 1918 France appeared to be the undisputed mistress of the Continent. With Russia disrupted, Germany reduced and disarmed, and Britain inclined to return to its tradition of island aloofness, it did not seem remotely possible for any nation to challenge the pre-eminence of France. Yet by 1939 the French position had disintegrated completely; France had lost its military superiority, diplomatic predominance, even independence of action. Such a disastrous reversal suggests a failure of effective leadership in France; yet it may also suggest that France's hegemony in the 1920's was more factitious than real, and that outside factors partially beyond French control were more important than internal weakness in destroying the French position.

Throughout the interwar years French foreign policy had a double focus: on relations with Britain and on relations with Germany. The prewar entente with the British barely survived the victory; within a year the relationship had taken on a bittersweet flavor. Late in 1919 Clemenceau, a lifelong exponent of cooperation with Britain, remarked privately: "England is the lost illusion of my life! Not a day passes that I do not receive from one of our agents abroad reports indicating veritably hostile acts. I had hoped that the fraternity of arms . . . would suppress the old traditional prejudices. Not at all. The evil is without remedy."[1] Clemenceau almost certainly exaggerated the case, yet his remarks reflected a revived and widespread Anglophobia in those postwar years, inspired by friction in the Near East and over the German reparations settlement. Across the Channel most Englishmen reciprocated this suspicion and hostility. Their outlook was deeply influenced by John Maynard Keynes's best-selling book *The Economic Consequences of the Peace*, which denounced the Versailles settlement as the product of France's unreasoning thirst for revenge. They were skeptical, too, about the sincerity of French motives in demanding large reparations payments from Germany; the French purpose, many Britishers believed, was not so much to restore war-ravaged France as to keep the Germans permanently on their knees.

In fact, the overriding goal of almost every Frenchman was neither revenge nor hegemony, but simply security; and even with several decades of hindsight, it is still not easy to say how they might best have achieved it after 1919. One possible course, advocated at the time by part of the French left, would have been to commit France's future to the new League of Nations and to such collective security arrangements as might be developed around the League. A second alternative was to construct a new alliance system to replace that of prewar days. The small new states of eastern Europe, however, offered a rather shaky substitute for Russia, the keystone of the old Triple Entente. Even if the French had been able to pour into those states as many francs as they had invested in prewar Russia, they probably could not have created a solid bulwark. In any case, such an effort was well beyond France's postwar capacity. Only the active collaboration of Britain in this alliance system might have made the eastern states strong enough to survive and to serve as a barrier against future aggressors. French

[1] A. François-Poncet, *De Versailles à Potsdam* (Paris: Flammarion, 1948), p. 65.

statesmen tried repeatedly to convince the British of the wisdom of such a commitment. They pleaded for a British promise to guarantee the security of the little east European states; the British consistently refused. Lloyd George told Briand frankly in 1921 that Britain had little interest in eastern Europe: "The British people felt that the populations in that quarter of Europe were unstable and excitable; they might start fighting at any time, and the rights and wrongs of the dispute might be very hard to disentangle."[2]

If the French were not strong enough to construct a solid continental alliance themselves, and if they could not persuade the British to help construct one, there remained very few alternatives indeed. One theoretical possibility might have been to abandon eastern Europe as indefensible against a resurgent Germany or Russia; to leave the Poles and Rumanians and Czechs to their inevitable fate and to fall back on a kind of isolationist "fortress France" policy. Such a plan would have required a bigger and better Maginot Line, extended all the way to the Channel. Or, alternatively, the French might have chosen from the beginning to put all their eggs in the British basket; to abandon the initiative in foreign policy to the British, in return for a binding guarantee of British aid if France were attacked. Such a policy would have involved writing off eastern Europe, scaling down German reparations, and relaxing controls on Germany, as the British wished. Toward the end, in the late 1930's, the French were to arrive at something very much like this position; but its wisdom a decade earlier would have depended on the farsightedness of British foreign-policy makers in that era. Still another possibility might have been an attempt to develop a close Franco-German entente, with a view to channelling the resurgent power of Germany into some sort of western European alliance or federation.

If all of these alternatives were theoretically open to French leaders after 1919, they were not all feasible in practice. Like all policy-makers, those of France were limited by their own prejudices and by those of

[2] Foreign Office (Great Britain), *Papers Respecting Negotiations for an Anglo-French Pact* (Cmd. 2169) (London: H. M. Stationery Office, 1924), pp. 112–13.

the nation they represented, as well as by the mood of the nations with which they had to deal. In the early postwar years an intimate rapprochement with Germany was inconceivable; so was a frank abdication of initiative into the hands of the British, or a wholehearted gamble that the League of Nations would bring a new era. Frenchmen emerged from the war divided over the proper course of foreign policy, and that division was increased by the peace settlement and the events of the early 1920's. It is not surprising that the behavior of French policy-makers during their years of hegemony seems groping and ineffective, or that their policy appears to have been shaped by improvisation more than by farsighted planning.

At the peace conference Clemenceau had abandoned France's demand for control of the Rhine and had gotten, instead, a promise of American and British treaties guaranteeing aid if France should be attacked. When the United States Senate repudiated the American guarantee, the British government withdrew its offer as well. Some French nationalists held that France would now be legally justified in seizing the Rhineland by unilateral action; but even a heavily rightist Chamber was unwilling to take such a risk. The government turned, instead, to constructing a military alliance system that eventually came to include Belgium, Poland, Rumania, Czechoslovakia, and Yugoslavia. The idea of adding a line of fortifications along the Franco-German frontier was still several years in the future; the Maginot Line was not begun until 1929.

Meanwhile the problem of setting a German reparations figure (entrusted by the peace conference to an interallied commission) was creating serious friction between France and Britain. The deadline for a decision was finally met early in 1921, but the figure set was resented by both the British and the Germans as unreasonably high and by the French as unjustly low. The critical problem of transfer from the Germans to the victors was evaded rather than settled; part of the payment was to be in specified raw materials, but large-scale financial transfers would be possible only if the Germans cut their living standards drastically, or if they were encouraged to flood world markets with German exports, or if they could borrow large sums from some broad-minded lender. The French apparently assumed that the Germans, as loser, ought to choose the first alternative; that they should resolutely swallow the bitter medicine of defeat and face several years of marginal existence. French spokesmen pointed out quite logically that for the victors to bear the cost of reconstruction while the vanquished went largely unscathed would be a gross inequity. The gap between logic and equity on the one hand, and the hard realities of national attitudes and international relationships on the other, has rarely been so great. Most Germans, rightly or wrongly, were unwilling to behave as the French thought they should; and the British and Americans were increasingly convinced that the French, not the Germans, ought to retreat. No German was likely to resist the temptation to profit by the disintegration of the victors' coalition.

By the end of 1921 French leadership faced a simple choice: either to agree to a drastic scaling down of reparations, or to go it alone in an effort to call the Germans' bluff. Premier Briand, who had been an advocate of rigorous treatment of the Germans, adapted himself to what seemed to be necessity; in a private session with Lloyd George, he agreed to cut reparations in return for a British guarantee of military aid if France should be attacked. The news leaked out before Briand had time to charm parliament into accepting his policy; his cabinet was overthrown, and Poincaré was restored to power in January, 1922. A tenacious legalist, Poincaré stood on the letter of the agreements in force; he made it plain that if Britian would not cooperate, France would have to act alone. Yet even Poincaré hesitated for a year before taking drastic action; it was only in January, 1923, that he ordered French troops to occupy Germany's Ruhr valley, on the legally valid ground that the Germans had chronically evaded and postponed payments due.

It was a divided France that occupied the Ruhr. Almost the entire

441

left vigorously opposed the action; Marshal Foch himself, when con-
sulted by the cabinet, had advised against it. Poincaré evidently had
serious doubts about the wisdom of acting in defiance of British and
world opinion, and he took the plunge only because neither he nor his
cabinet could face the alternative — a major retreat to suit German
demands. If the purpose of the occupation was to seize reparations in
kind that the Germans had refused to supply, the action failed badly.
France's reparations collections in 1923 were scarcely higher than they
had been in 1922, and the cost of collecting them was higher than the
value of the goods. If the hidden purpose was, as many of Poincaré's
enemies alleged, to seize and keep the Ruhr and Rhineland area by
encouraging the growth of a native separatist movement there, it
failed just as completely. Some Frenchmen did take the opportunity
to encourage separatist activity, but the movement never attained
serious proportions. Only if the purpose was to call the German bluff —
to ensure that the Germans would stop evading and delaying — can it
be argued that the Ruhr occupation succeeded; for by the end of 1923
the new Stresemann cabinet in Berlin abandoned passive resistance and
agreed to resume payments.

The victory, however, was a costly one at best — not only for its
economic and psychological effects on the Germans, but perhaps even
more for its impact on French minds. It marked the end of a really
independent French policy in Europe; never again during the interwar years was a French government willing to act on its own, in defiance,
if necessary, of world opinion. French power remained great enough
to permit such action for another decade at least, and probably as
late as 1936; but the French were henceforth reluctant to move without British support. Such a change of attitude in Paris might have had
merit if this had been an era of wise and constructive British leadership; coordinated Franco-British action of a farsighted character might
have shaped a healthy future for all of Europe. But Paris gained little
by grudgingly abdicating the initiative to a series of British cabinets
that meant well but lacked the qualities of tough-mindedness and foresight.

The apparent success of Poincaré's policy of enforcement did not impress French voters. They were struck much more by the fact that the government had to raise taxes by 20 per cent to cover the costs of the Ruhr expedition. Still, the elections of 1924 probably would have turned Poincaré out in any case, for the left-wing parties had learned from the last elections that dispersing their strength was a costly error. This time the Radicals and Socialists succeeded in forming an electoral alliance under the label *Cartel des gauches;* and even though the Moderates and the conservative right managed to poll 51 per cent of the popular vote, the leftist coalition was swept into control of the Chamber. A Radical cabinet under Herriot took office, with Socialist support but without Socialist ministers; and this new government participated in an international conference that worked out the new Dawes Plan, scaling down German reparations payments. Some months later Briand became minister of foreign affairs, a post that he was to hold almost without interruption from 1925 to 1932. Never since Delcassé had there been such continuity at the foreign office, such an opportunity for a man to put his stamp on the whole course of French foreign policy. The so-called Locarno era of the late twenties may quite properly be called the era of Briand.

Yet to crystallize in words the spirit of that era is not as easy as it might seem. Briand, who knew how to attune himself to changing moods, talked much about disarmament, about his faith in the League of Nations, about his self-chosen role as "the pilgrim of peace"; his record as foreign minister was peppered with pacts and schemes like the Locarno Treaties, the Kellogg-Briand Pact, the projected United States of Europe. He set out frankly to appease Stresemann's Germany; indeed, it was Briand who first used and popularized the word *apaisement.* He brushed aside evidence that the Weimar Republic had been evading the Versailles controls on its rearmament. Briand told Foreign Minister Stresemann that he had received "kilos of documents" proving Germany's illegal armament; "I threw them in a corner, I refused to waste my time with these trifles." Briand failed to move as far or as fast as he had hoped on the path of reconciliation. At a private meeting

443

with Stresemann in 1926, he proposed a sweeping across-the-board settlement of all outstanding Franco-German problems, including an immediate end to the occupation of German soil, the return of the Saar at once, and a lump-sum settlement of reparations. This was too much for either the cabinet or parliament of France to swallow. But Briand did accept Stresemann's Locarno scheme for "freezing" the Franco-German frontier; he abandoned France's right to keep military inspectors in Germany; and he withdrew the last French occupation troops in 1930, five years ahead of schedule.

Perhaps the most surprising aspect of Briand's reconciliation policy was that Poincaré's return to the premiership in 1926–29 did not interrupt it. Both Poincaré and his Moderate successors kept Briand at the foreign office; outwardly, it almost seemed that a kind of bipartisan unity had been achieved on policy toward Germany. Poincaré had not changed his mind, but he had lost some of his faith in a tough independent line, and he knew that the temper of the voters required a continuation of Briandism. Besides, since 1925 Germany had been paying reparations without quibble or delay, thanks to the booming prosperity of the era and to copious American loans.

There was another reason, however, for Poincaré's willingness to keep Briand in office. He was aware that Briandism and Poincarism were not so contrary as they seemed; that the difference between them was one of mood and emphasis, not of goal or of fundamental conviction. Briand's appeasement had its limits. He was determined to maintain the French army as the largest in Europe and to preserve the French alliance system. Indeed, it was Briand rather than Poincaré who negotiated new treaties with the Poles and the Czechs tightening France's obligations to those two partners. Though Briand never precisely defined his aims, he seems to have based his reconciliation policy on two hopeful assumptions: (1) that the new Germany, more democratic and peaceful in spirit than that of 1914, would reconcile itself to a secondary role in Europe if treated with generosity; (2) that the British, even though refusing any formal commitments to France or eastern Europe, would intervene in case of a major crisis to prevent France from being overrun. On the second point, time was eventually to prove him right, even though British aid in 1940 turned out to be inadequate to save France from defeat. On the first point, Briand apparently began to develop some qualms after Stresemann died in 1929, for no one of Stresemann's quality and force appeared in German politics to carry on his work. Perhaps that is why, in 1929–30, Briand began to talk in rather vague terms about a United States of Europe; perhaps his concern was to integrate the resurgent power of Germany with that of the rest of Europe before that power could get out of hand.

The wisdom or unwisdom of the Briand experiment in the late 1920's produced a continuing debate during the years that followed — a debate that in many ways resembles the American controversy over the Yalta Conference after 1945. Hitler's rise to power in 1933 led some French rightists to denounce Briand as the appeaser whose concessions had opened the way to the Nazis. If he had not withdrawn French occupation forces from the Rhineland, ran the argument, they would have been on the spot in the years after 1933 and would have choked off Hitler's preparations for aggression. An American historian has added more recently that Briand, by falling back on the hope of British aid rather than continuing Poincaré's independent policy, made France the prisoner of Britain and took "the first step on the road to Munich."

Briandism is easy to criticize, for it did fail in the end. Yet even in retrospect, it is not easy to suggest a workable alternative for that period, except the old Poincaré policy of independent action in the face of world opinion and even of much French opinion. Even if perpetuated, the Poincaré policy could not have endured much longer simply because France's dominant position in Europe was artificial and temporary and was not based on the solid realities of geopolitics. In truth, France by the late 1920's was caught in an almost insoluble dilemma. Whatever the French might do, their fate depended on the nature of German and British leadership; and they could no longer exert much influence over the selection and decisions of German and British policy-makers, if indeed they had ever been able to do so when French strength was at its peak.

It is barely possible that the French missed one last chance to shape the future and to head off Hitler during the early depression years. The Weimar Republic's leaders were desperate; Chancellor Heinrich Bruening, who took office in 1930, argued that a generous loan from the prosperous French, or a German diplomatic victory like a customs union with Austria, might give him time to ride out the crisis. But France blocked the customs union, and the loan negotiations failed to work out for rather obscure but complex reasons. Bruening came to Paris to ask for help, but he was unwilling to pay for aid by making any commitments. The French, in turn, talked of floating a large French-British-American loan, in return for which they suggested taking a kind of mortgage on the German economy and requiring a firm German commitment to respect the *status quo* in Europe for a decade. Negotiations dragged on sporadically, without result save for the virtual cancellation of German reparations in June, 1932 — too late to save the regime. Briand by this time was old and ill and had lost any real power to shape foreign policy when Pierre Laval took over the premiership in 1931. Whether a full dose of Briandism in the years 1929–32 would have saved the German republic it is impossible to say; yet in retrospect, it would probably have been worth trying as a kind of calculated risk.

⋑◦⋐⋑◦⋐⋑◦⋐

France's policies toward the chain of smaller states extending from the Baltic to the Balkans were dependent on French relationships with Germany, Italy, and the new Soviet regime. Poland, largest of them all in size, population, and standing army, became the anchor of the French alliance system in eastern Europe. French military aid to the Poles helped them to survive their critical war with Russia in 1920–21, when for a time it seemed that Poland might be overrun and turned into a Bolshevik satellite. France also acted as a kind of sponsor to the so-called Little Entente, made up of countries carved out of the old Austro-Hungarian empire and dedicated to averting the return of the Hapsburgs. Some French aid was extended to these states in the form of loans and expert military advice, but the flow remained relatively small. French commercial relationships with eastern Europe were also not very highly developed; only in Yugoslavia was French private capital to be found in sizable amounts, mainly in the copper-mining industry there. French policy-makers made sporadic efforts in the late 1920's and early 1930's to fuse parts of eastern Europe into a tighter bloc; their favorite scheme was a Danubian federation that might be strong enough to serve as a barrier against both a resurgent Germany and an adventurous Italy. But internal divisions in the Danube valley combined with hostile pressures from Rome, Berlin, and London to keep the French plan in the blueprint stage.

Although some Frenchmen were tempted by the idea of restoring the old tie with the Russians or the wartime alliance with the Italians, both projects ran into ideological opposition. Herriot's Radical government did recognize the Soviet Union in 1924, and then sought to negotiate a payments agreement on the tsarist debt to French bond-holders. The attempt broke down even before the return of the Moderates to power; relations thereafter grew steadily worse, as the Soviet government sought to use its Paris embassy for purposes of propaganda and espionage. The Communists' hostile line toward the French Socialists blocked the growth of broad left-wing sympathy for a Franco-Soviet tie.

Franco-Italian friendship cooled during the Paris peace conference of 1919, and it suffered a further setback when Mussolini took power in 1922. Although the extreme right in France welcomed the new Italian regime and campaigned actively for a Latin bloc, the bulk of center and left opinion remained skeptical or hostile. Most of Italy's antifascist émigrés fled to Paris, where they carried on active agitation against Mussolini's regime and provoked repeated diplomatic protests from Rome. Continuing friction over the status of the large Italian minority in Tunisia provided another irritant; the French refused to

447

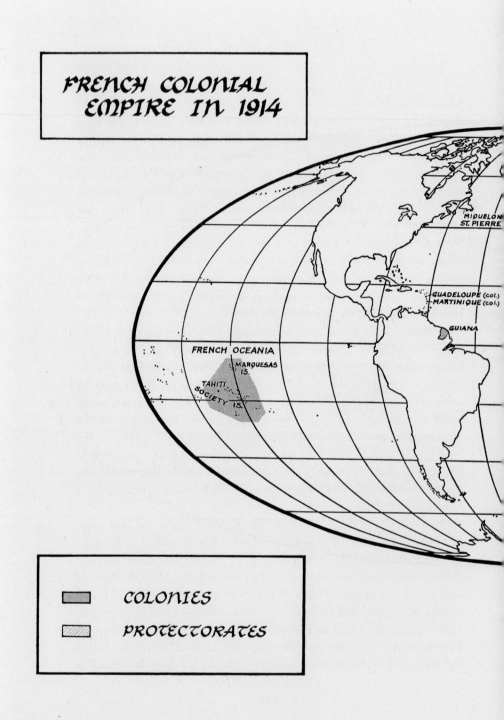

FRENCH COLONIAL
EMPIRE IN 1914

MIQUELON
ST. PIERRE

GUADELOUPE (col.)
MARTINIQUE (col.)

GUIANA

FRENCH OCEANIA

MARQUESAS
IS.

TAHITI
SOCIETY IS.

COLONIES
PROTECTORATES

FRANCE

ROCCO
ALGERIA
TUNIS
ENCH WEST AFRICA
SOMALILAND
FRENCH
EQUATORIAL
AFRICA

CHANDERNAGAR
(col.)
YANAON (col.)   LAOS
(col.)
PONDICHERRY
MAHÉ   KARIKAL
(col.)   (col.)

TONGKING
KWANGCHOWAN
ANNAM
COCHIN
CHINA
CAMBODIA

COMORO IS (col.)
MADAGASCAR
RÉUNION (col.)

NEW
HEBRIDES
(Fr.-
Br.)
NEW
CALEDONIA

grant this minority equal status unless its members would become French citizens. Fascist designs on parts of the French colonial empire and fascist intrigues in the Danube valley added to the suspicion in Paris. Not until the rise of Hitler did the common threat begin to overshadow the differences separating what some Frenchmen liked to call the Latin sisters.

◈◦◌◦◈◦◌◦◈◦◌◦◈

In the realm of overseas empire, French power reached its peak during the years between the wars. To the old colonies absorbed two centuries earlier and the vast areas added in the pre-1914 generation, victory in the Great War brought important new acquisitions: a sizable share of the German empire in Africa and the Turkish empire in the Near East. President Wilson's insistence at Paris forced the French to agree that the new territories would be mandated areas supervised by the League of Nations; but the limitations on French control proved to be slight. France's overseas possessions now totaled four and a half million square miles — twenty times the area of the homeland, with a population almost double that of France. Patriots began to claim proudly that there were now a hundred million Frenchmen under the tricolor.

But if Frenchmen took pride in their imperial strength, most of them still had no real interest in, or understanding of, the empire. With a few exceptions, the colonies were not adapted to large-scale European settlement, even if the French as a people had been inclined to emigrate. The vast stretches of French Equatorial Africa, for example, never attracted more than about five thousand Frenchmen, most of them colonial officials rather than settlers or business men. Only Algeria, and to a lesser extent Tunisia and Morocco, had European minorities of any size. French investment in the empire was not much more extensive than French emigration. Public expenditures on railways, harbors, schools, social services, remained relatively meager after the Great War; private capital preferred other outlets, though some banks and enterprises did invest in mining and large-scale agriculture in Indo-China and Morocco. Most of the old colonies survived like outmoded ghost towns from another era; the vast new ones slumbered on without much change, save for a gradual improvement in public health through the control of endemic and epidemic diseases. These vast underdeveloped areas provided only a meager market for French goods and furnished little except foodstuffs in return. In 1929 only 15 per cent of France's foreign trade was with the empire. A few politicians in the 1920's began to advocate a program of planned economic development (*mise en valeur,* they called it) and contended that private capital could not do the job alone. Some of them even proposed that the colonies be freed from the rather rigid embrace of the French tariff system so that they might buy and sell on the world market. None of these campaigns produced significant results; and the Great Depression was to undermine the slight progress that had been accomplished. As foreign markets for French exports shrivelled up, French business men were jolted into a new awarenes of the value of a closed imperial market. By the mid-1930's almost one-third of France's exports were going to the empire — more than the French could now sell to their three best European customers combined. These figures, however, concealed the fact that the colonial market had simply shrunk less rapidly than the foreign market.

In the broader realms of political and cultural relationships, it scarcely occurred to any Frenchman that paternalistic and bureaucratic rule from Paris might not be the wisest way to run an empire. True, the older policy labelled "assimilation," which aimed to convert the colonized peoples into completely acculturized Frenchmen, was being abandoned in favor of "association," sponsored initially by the French left. But the new doctrine involved no very fundamental change; its goal was to acculturize only a small native elite, which would then share with Frenchmen the task of governing vast populations sunk in primitive barbarism. The idea of a real decentralization of decision-making, a real trend toward autonomy and federalism, was simply outside the mental horizons of French leaders of that era.

For a time after 1918 French politicians seriously discussed extending the military conscription law to the overseas possessions, so as to draw on what they called an "inexhaustible reservoir of men" to supplement France's own dwindling manpower and to shorten the conscription period. About a half-million colonial soldiers (most of them volunteers) had served in France during the Great War; the temptation was great to extend the practice. Even those Frenchmen who favored the idea, however, would not consider racial integration of French and colonial troops or a grant of citizenship to those who served. In the end parliament rejected general conscription, partly on the ground that it would divert native manpower that might be needed for colonial economic development. Some limited conscription did persist, but it varied in different colonies and affected only a few men.

If Frenchmen were guilty of the sins normally associated with colonial rule, their brand of imperialism continued to be more cultural than economic. It was easy to cling to their illusory paternalistic practices so long as the subject peoples remained passive and unorganized; and until the 1930's that was the case almost everywhere. Only in the Near Eastern mandated area of Syria was there an aggressive nationalist movement that threatened French control and that had to be checked by force. In 1925–26 a revolt of the Riff hill tribes under Abd el Krim spilled over from Spanish into French Morocco; but it resembled the American Indian wars rather than a modern nationalist movement. Elsewhere, the premonitory signs of nationalist discontent already detected by men like Lenin remained too feeble to attract the serious notice of politicians in Paris or colonial officials in the field. Tiny nuclei of activists existed in Indo-China and Tunisia and were to grow rapidly in the 1930's; elsewhere, it was easy to believe throughout the interwar years that the native populations had no higher ambition than to remain French subjects.

TWENTY-NINE

In the meantime Penguinia gloried in its wealth. Those who produced the things necessary for life, wanted them; those who did not produce them had more than enough. "But these," as a member of the Institute said, "are necessary economic fatalities."

ANATOLE FRANCE

Economy and Society
in the Postwar Decade, 1919–1931

A wealthy country chronically on the verge of bankruptcy: such is the impression given by France in the interwar years. War and reconstruction had left the state with a heavy burden of public debt, owed both to foreign nations and to its own citizens — a burden that, if assumed without postponement, would have skimmed off much of the nation's wealth and would have imposed a policy of strict austerity on a whole generation. But French leaders of the era, responsive to the pressures of French citizens generally, took the understandable if shortsighted position that if anybody's wealth were to be skimmed off, it should be that of Germany and not of France. No American can properly criticize this French failure to face up to hard and painful facts in the postwar decade, for Americans scarcely did better in that respect. The difference was that France's problem was bigger and more urgent. It needed to be faced without delay, while French wealth and resources were still adequate to meet it without large-scale external aid.

The French failure to take prompt and adequate action was the product of several convergent factors. One of these was lack of experi-

453

ence with a shaky currency and a serious deficit in the public treasury. For decades the franc had been solid as a rock, and the state budget had been steadily balanced despite the failure of French governments to modernize their ramshackle and antiquated tax structure. The "myth of the franc" — the illusion that even major catastrophes like wars, revolutions, and depressions could not shake its value — had a powerful grip on French minds, and it could not be dissipated at once when circumstances changed. A second factor was the persistence of a social structure that made any major change in the tax system politically difficult. In an economy dominated by a few giant firms, a parliament responsive to the voters can get the bulk of its revenue from large enterprise, which controls few votes. In an economy based in considerable part on a huge mass of small private operators, the problem of raising tax levels or redistributing the tax burden becomes much more severe. France's parliament did finally adopt an income-tax law in 1916, but its rates were so low and its loopholes so large that it worked no revolutionary change in public finance. During the interwar years less than a quarter of the government's total tax revenue came from the income tax; the rest was produced by the so-called four old taxes on real property and by various indirect levies such as the business turnover tax adopted in 1920. Still a third factor was the economic illiteracy of most French politicians. Those who were lawyers by profession had been exposed to a highly abstract and outmoded kind of economics in the law schools, while the nonlawyers in parliament had only private business experience and a set of deep-rooted prejudices to guide them. Not one French leader at the end of the Great War was both able and willing to try to educate the electorate in the economic problems that faced the nation. Clemenceau had the courage to do so, but he prided himself on his ignorance of economics. Poincaré probably had the requisite knowledge, but he clung to his legalistic illusion that since "the Boche" ought to pay, he *would* pay. In the early postwar years a curious double-budget device lulled the voters into security; alongside a regular budget that was not merely balanced but showed a surplus, an "extraordinary budget" almost three times as large was devoted to war and reconstruction costs, with no provision for receipts except as the Germans might pay reparations.

So long as the war had lasted, interallied controls kept the franc from depreciating by more than 15 per cent. Within a year after the armistice its value had fallen by more than 50 per cent; and the downward trend continued, more slowly and spasmodically, in subsequent years. A series of reconstruction bond issues were floated and sold to French citizens, in order to finance the rebuilding of the devastated areas without delay. In addition, some of the wartime bonds began to come due, and the government chose to replace them with new issues bearing even higher interest rates. The treasury thus borrowed more from French citizens during the early 1920's than it had borrowed from them during the war itself; and the interest burden piled up in ominous fashion. French suggestions that the United States write off American war loans to France got a cold reception in Washington; eventually, and reluctantly, that burden had to be shouldered, too, though a payments agreement was not worked out until 1926.

It was obvious to everyone — even the politicians — that taxes had to be increased; but until 1923 every proposal to that end was defeated. Most deputies were willing to vote additional taxes; they simply could not agree as to which Frenchmen should pay them. Meanwhile, governments managed to operate by resorting to a disguised form of inflation; the treasury was supplied with steadily larger advances from the Bank of France, which in turn put more currency into circulation. The left wing's victory at the polls in 1924 only made matters worse. The two major parties of the left clashed sharply on financial policy, the Socialists favoring a capital levy and a reduction of the interest rate on government bonds, the Radicals rejecting both ideas as dangerously confiscatory. Many Radical voters possessed a small nest egg of capital, often in the form of a few government bonds. Another factor also operated against the left. The Bank of France, controlled by large private banking interests, began to balk at further advances to the treasury; its directors had little enthusiasm for a government that might be tempted to try a capital levy. A flight of capital set in after 1924, leading to a new and more rapid decline in the franc and a new record for cabinet instability — six cabinet crises in the space of only nine months.

This state of almost permanent crisis, with the franc down to less than one-tenth of its prewar value and threatening to collapse entirely, forced the Radical leadership to make a decisive choice: either to adopt the Socialists' drastic program, or to abdicate power to the Moderates. Most of them preferred the second alternative; Raymond Poincaré was called back to the premiership in 1926, and the Radicals assured him of their support. Poincaré they trusted as scrupulously honest, a dedicated republican, and a lifelong anticlerical. His broadly-based cabinet (which included some Radical representatives) checked the crisis with remarkable ease, and without either foreign borrowing or really fundamental reforms at home. The impact was primarily psychological, through a restoration of confidence that the government would neither "soak the rich" nor let the franc collapse. Taxes were sharply increased (perhaps too sharply, indeed), though without altering the distribution of the tax burden; drastic cuts were made in government expenditures. But what really counted was the return of capital from hiding or from safe havens abroad, to be reinvested at home or to be used to buy government bonds. The franc suddenly rose so rapidly that the government had to step in and check it at about 20 per cent of its prewar value (the equivalent of four cents in place of twenty). The Paris daily *Le Temps* (which reflected the outlook of its industrialist owners) labelled the premier "Poincaré the Well-Beloved" and asserted that "one would have to go back to Saint Louis to find such popular enthusiasm for a sovereign."

Over the next several years the franc seemed to have recovered the stability of prewar days, and the chronic financial problem appeared to be solved at last. True, the franc had not been restored to its full prewar value, in the fashion of the British pound; therefore many Frenchmen (holders of wartime bonds, for example) lost 80 per cent of their original investment. But rather than sulk over this loss, most of these Frenchmen were inclined to congratulate themselves that they had not been wiped out completely, as had many German investors during

the 1923 inflation. The French solution to the war's financial burden
— an inflation that was checked short of disaster — fell midway between that of the Germans and that of the British and was probably
healthier than either. It was, however, a solution that was more
empirical than planned.

France's inflationary experience, nevertheless, had serious long-
range results. For one thing, it left the French with a kind of neurosis
about the franc. After 1926 they suffered from a nagging fear of
another decline and developed a kind of psychological block against
any tampering with the currency. Some years later, when the depression drove nations everywhere to abandon the gold standard and to
devalue their currencies, the French clung to the "Poincaré franc" with
disastrous results. A second serious consequence of the episode was to
consolidate the legend that a greedy band of capitalists had used its
financial power to destroy the left-wing coalition of 1924–26, thus
frustrating the will of the voters. The big bankers, it was alleged, had
erected a *mur d'argent* (barrier of silver) against the left's reform
program by refusing further advances to the treasury from the Bank
of France. The legend contained a little truth; but at least an equal
share of reponsibility for the left's downfall was traceable to the left's
own voters. Thousands of little investors cashed in their government
bonds or withdrew their savings from French banks in order to send it
abroad or buy easily hoarded gold. Rarely had there been a clearer
example of André Siegfried's hackneyed law of politics that even though
Frenchmen's hearts might be on the left, their pocketbooks remained on
the right. The legend of the *mur d'argent* persisted nevertheless; it
contributed to the later rise of the Popular Front (which was bound
together in part by its denunciations of the "two hundred families" that
controlled the Bank of France) and to the eventual nationalization of
the major French banks in 1946.

❧◦❧◦❧◦❧

When one looks behind the problem of public finance to the state
of the French economy as a whole, the impression of crisis and in-

457

stability disappears in favor of a sense of steadily expanding wealth and well-being. By 1929–30 all production and trade figures had reached record levels. Industrial production, which had fallen during the war to 60 (base index 1913 = 100), was up to 140, whereas the British figure still lagged behind the prewar level. Foreign trade had attained 166; even agriculture, the most nearly stagnant sector, was at 110. These gains resulted only in part from the recovery of Alsace with its textile mills, Lorraine with its iron ore and its steel plants, the Saar with its temporary supply of coal. The improvement also derived from the destruction of much outmoded French industry in the north and its replacement by modern factories. There was a general increase in productivity as well, and a slow but steady modernization of a broad sector of French enterprise.

Agriculture lagged behind as the weakest sector of the economy, but this fact reflected a world-wide condition in the 1920's. As a whole, French farming was becoming more efficient; total production increased even though the number of people on the land continued to decline. By 1929 the average yield of wheat per acre, for example, was 30 per cent higher than during the prewar decade. But much of this improvement was concentrated in a limited area in the northeast, the wheat and sugar-beet country, where large-scale mechanized farming was taking over. Most of rural France dragged on with scarcely altered methods and at a marginal standard. Economists calculated that the 35 per cent of Frenchmen who still lived by agriculture were receiving only 18 per cent of the national income. At the time almost no French farmers knew of these statistics, nor were they aware that some of the same sort of disproportion between agriculture and industry existed in every country. But they were beginning to sense acutely that many peasants were worse off than the city population and that the days of farm prosperity during the war were definitely over. The drift to the cities, temporarily checked during the war years, became more rapid than ever before. And the peasants' growing discontent opened a wide gap for the activities of agitators of both left and right, particularly in the 1930's.

458

Although the economy as a whole seemed to be prosperous and expanding in the 1920's, it can be argued that far more might have been done, and that France may have missed a golden opportunity for really fundamental modernization and economic resurgence in that boom era. It is true that French recovery was far more successful than British, but the rate of economic expansion was sharply below the world rate in the postwar decade. Indeed, it had been falling behind the world rate since 1910 at least. One reason was that postwar France failed to invest enough in modernizing its productive plant. This was not because French capital was again flowing abroad; Frenchmen after the war were investing outside France only one-twentieth as much as they had before 1914. Rather, it was because so large a slice of France's national income had to go for paying for the recent war and policing Europe against a new one. Reconstruction, pensions, and the army were absorbing ten per cent of the national income. Another cause of lagging investment was the nervousness of holders of capital and the resulting periodic flight of funds. And more basic still was the survival of so many small plants that failed to make enough profit either to allow self-financed expansion or to attract outside funds. Their existence produced an apparent stability that approached stagnation; their chief economic impact was to keep French price levels inordinately high.

It is true that in some circles during the 1920's France experienced a real drive toward the rationalizing of industry, toward more modern and efficient methods. A current of Saint-Simonianism or Americanism, stronger than at any time since the days of Napoleon III, set in during the boom years after 1925. The most typical representative of this spirit was André Citroën, an automobile manufacturer who had worked for a time in Detroit and who had become inspired by the example of Henry Ford. Citroën was a new industrialist who got his chance during the war years and made the most of it. He adopted production-line methods and large-scale marketing devices aimed at encouraging mass consumption; he even advertised by skywriting and by illuminated signs on the Eiffel Tower. Unlike traditional French enterprisers, his ambition was to undersell competitors and dominate the market rather than to share a limited market through cartel procedures. In politics, the leading exponent of the same renovating spirit was André Tardieu, whose experience as wartime purchasing agent in the United States had convinced him of the virtues of American industrial methods. This new spirit took organized form in 1925 when a group of rightist politicians, industrialists, and bankers of somewhat technocratic outlook formed a pressure group called the Redressement Français (French Resurgence). Its suggestive symbol was a reproduction of the Roman statue "The Dying Gaul"; its program called for a tougher, more vigorous political system (notably a stronger executive) and a new entrepreneurial spirit in the business world (emphasizing a really competitive laissez faire ideal).

This revival of Saint-Simonianism, however, affected only a limited minority in the French business and political worlds. Far larger and more powerful was the older group of industrialists, content with the tradition of limited production, high profit margins, and market-sharing through cartel agreements. Most of France's basic production (e.g., of steel, chemicals, etc.) remained in their hands; the innovators appeared primarily in the conversion or finished-goods industries, where they were seriously hampered by the high cost of their basic materials. Besides, the new entrepreneurs were far more vulnerable to the impact of a major economic crisis. Thus the postwar recovery era merely accentuated the division of the French economy into two increasingly divergent sectors: the dynamic and the static. That division coincided in part — but only in part — with the differentiation between large and small enterprise and between urban and rural areas. Within limits, there was also a gradual tendency toward geographical differentiation — the dynamic enterprises clustering in the northeastern quarter of France, from Paris to the Belgian and German frontiers, the static element holding doggedly to its habits in the central and southern half of the country. Economically and socially, two Frances were emerging within this long-unified nation, the one superimposed on the other as in a double-exposure photograph.

One much debated issue of the postwar decade — an issue with both economic and social implications — was the demographic problem. France emerged from the Great War seriously short of manpower; in the 1920's active campaigns to recruit foreign labor were undertaken by the large steel firms, coal mines, and mechanized farms. Some three million immigrants arrived during that decade from almost every part of Europe; France replaced the United States as the world's melting pot. The newcomers were not, however, easily assimilable. Four-fifths of them were men, unmarried or with families left at home; and French regulations restricted them to the less desirable types of work and to relatively isolated mining towns or large farms. Some of the immigrants also took over abandoned farms in the south, as tenants or crop-sharers.

Many Frenchmen had come to accept immigration as a logical necessity to solve a population problem far older than the war. But the population question promptly got entangled in politics. The trade unions and the left wing generally were skeptical about any planned immigration policy or any scheme to stimulate the birth rate through bonuses to large families; they suspected the capitalists of seeking devices to get cheaper labor or the Catholics of plotting to recover control of France. The unions looked without enthusiasm on experiments with family allowances undertaken in the 1920's by some Catholic employers. Not until after the Second World War did the left become fully aware of the deleterious economic effects of an aging population and of the social justice of some redistribution of income in favor of larger families. After 1945 family allowances were to become the heart of the French social security system, with labor's hearty consent.

If the French working class in the 1920's showed an excessive tendency to be suspicious and resentful toward both employers and politicians, at least it had much justification for such an attitude. Already in the prewar boom era labor had failed to get its full share of the nation's expanding prosperity; in the postwar period of expansion it continued to fall behind. By 1929 the real-wage index had risen only to 109 (1914 = 100), as compared to an industrial production figure of 140. Labor did win one major victory immediately after the war, when Clemenceau in 1919 sought to forestall a major strike wave by legalizing the eight-hour day. That reform, however, had proved to be the end of labor's gains rather than the first step in a whole series of improvements, as the trade unions had hoped. The C.G.T., bolstered by the influx of a million new members during and after the war, embarked on a series of strikes in late 1919 that culminated in May, 1920, in the first French attempt at a general strike. The undertaking had been poorly prepared, and it was met head-on by the right-wing majority in the new Chamber. The collapse of the strike was disastrous to the unions; within a year two-thirds of the C.G.T.'s members had abandoned the organization. Through the rest of the decade, and down till 1936, ninety per cent of French workers remained unorganized And to make matters worse, those who remained union members were divided among three rival organizations — Communist, Catholic, and nonpolitical syndicalist.

This division of the workers and their resistance to organization sterilized the proletariat as a pressure group; it meant that labor could exert little influence on parliament to offset that of big business, small enterprise, or even some farm producers who learned at last during the 1920's that organization pays. Yet even if French labor had been unified and organized, it might have been frustrated in its demands. Parliament, by the nature of the electoral system and the social composition of the electorate, remained dominated by small-town and rural France, and these voters were steadily reluctant to tax themselves to help the urban workers. Furthermore, most French employers showed little sign of social conscience; their central interest in the 1920's seemed to be to secure the repeal of labor's single gain, the eight-hour day, on the ground that it was responsible for the high cost of production in France.

Undoubtedly, labor gained a little from the general growth of production in the postwar decade — though more in increased leisure than in improved living standards. The urban workers also gained, in the short run at least, by the perpetuation of wartime rent controls; in an era of inflation, rents were held at so low a level that they eventually absorbed only 5 to 7 per cent of the worker's budget. In the long run, however, this advantage boomeranged against both workers and lower bourgeoisie. Rents were too low to permit any maintenance by landlords, so vast areas in the cities rapidly deteriorated into noisome slums, sometimes concealed behind façades that remained externally impressive. There was no longer any incentive for low-cost housing construction, which dried up completely except for a few municipally-financed projects. By the end of the interwar period France was facing a critical housing emergency. Rent controls, a sop to the voters by the politicians, ended by breeding a whole series of social problems; and these in turn fed proletarian resentment toward a society that would permit such evils to exist.

If a doctrine or mystique was needed to reinforce these unpleasant facts, it was provided by the Soviet example. "Just as a new generation was beginning to forget the Paris Commune [Val Lorwin tells us], the Russian Revolution added its spell. In no country did this great twentieth century myth make a deeper impression than in skeptical France; among no group a greater impression than on the workers who had never made a successful revolution of their own."[1] The new mystique combined with an old and brooding sense of injustice to prevent a lessening of social tensions even in a time of prosperity. Through the years of normalcy the active minority of French labor remained alienated from the republic, indifferent to its fate and hostile to its leadership. The consequences in an era of depression and crisis were to be disastrous.

---

[1] V. Lorwin, "Labor and Economic Development in France."

THIRTY

A governing class in decline lives by half-measures,
from day to day, always postponing the examination
of vital questions until tomorrow.

IGNAZIO SILONE

Depression Politics,
1931–1936

From 1926 to 1931 France experienced what seems in retrospect to
have been a kind of Indian summer. *La belle époque* had apparently
returned; a stable franc, a booming economy, a brilliant culture, coincided to produce a wave of euphoria and a new sense of confidence.
Paris once more could regard itself as the capital of Europe, or even
of the world. The reconstruction of the war-torn areas was complete;
German reparations payments arrived on schedule; the "Locarno spirit"
seemed to promise a long era of relaxation and harmony in Europe.
Not only was the governmental budget balanced annually, but an
impressive surplus was piling up in the treasury. It was beginning to
attract so many demagogic politicians that in 1929 Premier Tardieu
proposed a great five-year spending program to devote the surplus to
public works and economic expansion.

As the repercussions of the New York stock market crash spread
throughout the world, France seemed more and more like a protected
island in a stormy sea. The boom continued through 1930 and well
into 1931; only after two full years of world crisis did the French

464

dikes begin to break down. But more important than the late arrival of the depression in France was the fact that when it came, it stayed; it developed into the longest and deepest economic crisis France had known for a century. The downswing was not checked until the end of 1935, much later than in other nations; and when recovery did set in, the upswing was slower than in almost any other country.

Until 1931 some Frenchmen reacted to their good fortune with a certain smugness; the advantages of France's economic and social structure, they argued, were being proved over those of societies that claimed to be more dynamic. Much was made of the healthy balance between farm and factory, between large and small enterprise; such an economy was held to be less susceptible to the great economic swings of modern capitalism. Defenders of the French system pointed out that the small producer or trader, the little polycultural farmer, was better able to adapt himself to stringent times than was the big operator with a large overhead and a constant need for a mass market. They pointed, too, to the merits of the cautious and conservative business approach of Frenchmen, whose prudence had protected them against the wild speculative gambling of business men elsewhere. Now Frenchmen could gloat a bit and enjoy the fruits of their virtue.

This case was not entirely invalid. A less dynamic economy is likely to weather a long crisis better than an advanced, highly complex system dependent on a stable world with freely-flowing trade currents. France's archaic small farms served as a kind of cushion to absorb the shock of the crash; the peasants could fall back on even more complete self-sufficiency than usual, and they could feed part of the urban unemployed who returned to the farm to sit out the crisis. The conservatism of French bankers in the 1920's did make the banking structure more solid; hardly any banks failed during the 1930's, and few even needed direct governmental aid.

But if the nature of the French economy and of French business psychology helped to soften the impact of the depression once it arrived, other factors were responsible for postponing that impact. The crisis came late to France because of a series of lucky accidents. For one thing, the franc had been stabilized in 1928 at a relatively low level — probably too low to reflect its real exchange value at the time. France thus became a cheap country for foreign buyers and visitors; a large backlog of orders poured in, carrying French producers along into 1931 without much slackening in production. A second factor was the steady flow of gold back into France, attracted because the franc remained stable and business good. The French gold supply therefore continued to rise after 1929 and gave the illusion of wealth that tended to conceal the crisis for months after the first danger signs began to appear. Still a third factor was a lucky turn in the weather in 1930; a bad harvest postponed until 1931 the problem of agricultural surpluses that had plagued the rest of the world since the crash.

The unfortunate consequence was that French governments did almost nothing until 1932, and not very much more until 1935, to work out a consistent crisis program like those of other nations. What they did do was of a piecemeal, opportunistic nature, fitting into no kind of long-range policy or plan. In part, this immobility derived from the fact that in a divided country, with a weak executive power, agreement on vigorous economic measures of any kind is hard to reach. But it also derived from the conviction of many Frenchmen that there was no French crisis at all; that a healthy France was simply unlucky enough to be caught in a world of sick nations. That doctrine suggested that France needed only to seal itself off from the rest of the world in order to keep out the germs of disease.

The primary aim during the early 1930's, therefore, was to isolate France behind a tariff wall, and behind that wall to prevent any changes in the French economy. Above all, French governments sought to keep the French price level from dropping, even if that might mean a loss of foreign markets and a sharp reduction in the size of the domestic market. When world prices fell so low that foreign farm products began to spill across the high tariff wall, the French added a system of quotas as well. Within this closed area, meanwhile, governments let industry take care of itself through domestic cartel arrangements. Participating producers agreed to cut production, share the shrinking home market, and keep prices at the predepression level. Government and industry cooperated to avert any serious unemployment problem; thousands of foreign workers were sent back to their countries of origin, while many French workers voluntarily returned to their ancestral farms. French unemployment figures even at the worst moment in the depression decade never rose much above a half-million — a total lower by far than that of any other industrial nation. Most small farmers and shopkeepers of the precapitalist type also took care of themselves by the simple process of belt-tightening, aided by only a little governmental action. The government's help was primarily negative and took the form of a kind of legalized tax exemption. Whereas 700,000 farmers had paid an income tax in 1927, the figure dropped to 97,000 in 1935.

For the more dynamic sector in agriculture — the large capitalist farms or the smaller, one-crop producers, dependent on the market — the problem of adjustment to the depression was much more serious. Successive governments had to step in with a system of controls to limit production or to bolster the prices of such items as wheat and wine. Although these schemes often functioned badly and aroused much criticism, they worked their way into the habits of the farm population and became quasi-permanent aspects of French agricultural policy. Since the depression a free market system has never been restored for certain important farm products. One particular group of specialized farmers did take care of itself — too well, indeed, for the welfare of the nation as a whole. The sugar-beet growers, few in number but prosperous and shrewd, managed to organize a kind of producers' cartel that limited acreage effectively. Far more important, however, they learned to operate as a political pressure group. By recruiting the support of the winegrowers, whose voting power was far greater than their own, they persuaded parliament to authorize purchase of all excess sugar-beets and wine at a favorable price. These products were then distilled into alcohol, which the government either stored, sold at a loss, or mixed into the gasoline supply that automobile owners then had to buy at double the regular gasoline price. This arrangement, once adopted, became a kind of inviolable vested interest even after the economic emergency ended. "Alcohol," remarked the French demographer Alfred Sauvy twenty years later, "makes two kinds of lunatics: those who drink it and those who pay for it."

In industry as in agriculture, the dynamic sector was harder hit than the static sector by the depression. One traditional indirect advantage of old-style "panics" had been their function of cutting away economic deadwood; hard times forced many inefficient enterprisers out of business or drove them to modernize and rationalize their methods. That purpose was not served by the French depression of the 1930's. If anything, the effect was just the opposite: it was the least fit that tended to survive. This happened in part because the government took measures to help the weak, and in part because the static industries kept each other afloat through cartel arrangements. Those who went under (and there were some resounding crashes) were often the most vigorous and imaginative entrepreneurs — those in the uncartelized sector of the industrial system. The most notable case was that of André Citroën. His spectacular career had won him the ironic sobriquet "King of Paris," but it had brought him few friends among the traditional industrialists and bankers. When trouble came Citroën proposed to meet it not by retrenching but by capturing the market with a new front-wheel-drive model. As the crisis deepened, he borrowed money to retool his entire plant; but before the conversion process was complete, disaster struck. His creditors closed in and refused his pleas for a ninety-day extension to get his new car on the market. In 1934 his empire crashed into bankruptcy; and shortly afterward Citroën carried his symbolic Americanism to its ultimate conclusion by failing to survive an operation for ulcers.

✥⊃∘⊂✥⊃∘⊂✥⊃∘⊂✥

During the early depression years the political machinery of France remained in the hands of the Moderates. Poincaré's successful stabilization of the franc, and the years of prosperity that followed,

468

had enabled the right-center groups to triumph in the 1928 elections. Again there was no important shift in the popular vote, but a return to the traditional electoral system of small single-member districts benefited the center parties. Illness forced Poincaré to abandon the premiership in 1929, but his prestige enabled his Moderate friends to retain control of the cabinet until the 1932 elections. The key figure of the period was André Tardieu, who headed three cabinets between 1929 and 1932. A brilliant man of somewhat overbearing and cynical temper, Tardieu for years seemed to be on the verge of becoming one of the republic's really first-rank statesmen, yet he never quite lived up to his promise. The economic crisis reinforced his conviction that the French political and economic system must be transformed in the direction of either the British or the American model. Political reform, he believed, was the essential first step toward economic rejuvenation; what France needed was a two-party system with a strong and stable executive.

Tardieu's plan for modernizing the Third Republic was not a new one; it consisted of introducing the Anglo-American electoral system of electing representatives by simple plurality, without a second run-off ballot. Such a plan, he believed, would force all parties to fuse into two major political movements; and he was convinced that the bulk of the Radicals in such case would be driven to join the Moderates, thus ensuring a clear right-center majority. At his urging, the Laval cabinet in 1931 managed to get this electoral reform adopted by the Chamber, but it was rejected in the Radical-dominated Senate. The Radicals much preferred the run-off ballot, which enabled their candidates to ally with either left or right and thus maximize their chances.

Beaten by the politicians, Tardieu sought to sell his program to the country at large. He had no illusions about the wisdom of the man in the street; "public opinion," he remarked privately, "is a harlot that must be driven with a whip." But he had no choice; and so he led the Moderates into the 1932 elections, preaching the virtues and the necessity of reform. In spite of an almost unprecedented slush fund furnished by Tardieu's business friends, the voters failed to respond.

By this time the impact of the depression was being clearly felt, and the parties in power suffered the natural consequences. The Moderate groups were beaten, and Tardieu angrily withdrew from active political life, devoting himself henceforth to an increasingly bitter one-man press crusade against the shortcomings of the invertebrate republic.

The left's electoral victory in 1932 brought the Radicals back into power. They outnumbered the Socialists in the new Chamber, even though for the first time the Socialists emerged as France's largest party as measured by popular votes. The Communists, still isolated by choice and badly split by internal dissension, lost votes for the first time since the party was founded. The Socialists, faithful to the doctrine of Guesde as revised and elaborated by Léon Blum, refused to enter any coalition cabinet which they could not dominate; but as in 1924, they promised to support a radical government without participating in it. Once again Herriot became premier; and once again France entered upon a two-year period of governmental instability that had been equalled only in 1924–26. Six cabinets in twenty months was the dismal record. The source of the trouble was once again the inability of the Radicals and Socialists to agree on an economic program and particularly on that essential question, who should bear the cost of recovery?

This chronic instability, combined with the steadily worsening economic situation and the ominous growth of Nazism across the Rhine, led many Frenchmen and foreigners, too, to conclude that the republic was on the verge of complete disintegration and that some sort of authoritarian regime had become almost inevitable. Whether France really skirted the edges of fascist revolution in those years is a controversial question that has been debated ever since. According to one viewpoint, a carefully-planned fascist coup was barely averted in 1934 and was thwarted thereafter only by the organization of a Popular Front alliance that fused the strength of the entire left. According to a second interpretation, the threat has been much exaggerated; organized fascism in France was relatively small and weak, it made no serious attempt to seize power, and it would probably have failed if it had tried to strike. According to the exponents of this second view, the experience of the 1930's proved that France was virtually immune to fascism, except as it might be imported by a foreign conqueror. The controversy hinges in part on varying definitions of "fascism," and in part on varying views of what really happened in 1934 when the attempted coup d'état allegedly took place.

The depression decade did encourage the growth in France of a whole series of movements or "leagues" that were loosely labelled "fascist" by their enemies. Some of them were frankly modelled on the doctrines and systems of Mussolini and Hitler: Pierre Taittinger's Jeunesses Patriotes, for example, and Marcel Bucard's Francistes, and Major Jean Renaud's Solidarité Française, and the C. S. A. R. (popularly called the Cagoulards or hooded men) of the later 1930's. Although some of these groups were subsidized by wealthy extremists like the perfumer François Coty, they failed to attract mass support. No dependable membership figures exist, but probably none of them enrolled more than fifty thousand real activists, and some had only a few hundred. The one exceptional case was Jacques Doriot's Parti Populaire Français (P.P.F.), which attracted a half-million disciples. Until 1934 Doriot had been one of the top figures in the Communist party and was viewed by many as the potential Stalin of France. Increasingly, however, it became clear that he saw the party as an agency to serve his own ambitions. Like Mussolini before him, he was an opportunist and an activist rather than a fanatic and a doctrinaire; his goal was power rather than utopia. After his expulsion by the Communists in 1934 he tried for a time to compete with them for the labor vote, then followed Il Duce's example by shifting abruptly to the extreme right. It is not surprising that Mussolini secretly subsidized his movement after 1936; what *is* surprising is the fact that so many Frenchmen accepted his frankly totalitarian line. If Doriot had founded the P.P.F. earlier and had been ready to strike in 1934–35 when the republic's defenses were down, it is at least conceivable that he might have been able to seize power.

All of the aforementioned leagues were truly fascist — or, to use a less ambiguous word, totalitarian. They were revolutionary in spirit; they aimed to uproot the old system completely and to overturn all traditional institutions; they proposed to create a new elite and not to restore or confirm the power of the old traditional elites. They were marked by a kind of distorted neoromanticism in their stress on change and on action for action's sake. They truly represented that twentieth-century current called the radical right.

But alongside these totalitarian groups there emerged a number of more ambiguous movements that attracted much wider support, and that belonged more properly in the older French tradition of the authoritarian nationalist right. The largest by far was the Croix de Feu movement of Colonel de la Rocque; the most durable was that hardy perennial the Action Française of Maurras. Such organizations deserved the fascist label only in the loosest sense of the term. Their leaders were not right-wing radicals but conservatives or reactionaries. They yearned not for upheaval and the creation of a new elite, but for order, stability, authority, and a return to the old elites. They favored not the totalitarian ideal that would create a monopoly of power, but a more pluralistic and decentralized system that would respect the nation's deep-rooted institutions. Some men of totalitarian temper were attracted to these groups for a time, but most of them withdrew as soon as they detected the lack of revolutionary spirit there. Many of Doriot's P.P.F. adherents, for example, were dissatisfied deserters from the Croix de Feu, and the Cagoulard faction was composed mainly of impatient ex-members of the Action Française.

The Croix de Feu, founded in 1928 as an organization of decorated veterans, was gradually converted into a political movement after Colonel de la Rocque became its president in 1931. By 1933 it had between forty thousand and sixty thousand members; by 1935 it claimed several hundred thousand. Its appeal depended in part on its amorphous vagueness; any patriot who wanted strong government and disliked communism could feel at home here. It was in a sense (as René Rémond puts it) a political boy-scout movement for adults. Its most massive growth was to come after 1936, when it was suppressed along with the other leagues and re-emerged at once as a regular party — the Parti Social Français or P.S.F. Its claim of three million members in 1938 was certainly exaggerated, but its following just as certainly exceeded that of all the radical-right groups combined.

That most Frenchmen of the right preferred a De la Rocque to a Doriot or a Bucard may not prove that France was immune to fascism; it may prove only that "France found a Mosley, but not a Mussolini." Still, the record does seem to suggest that France was more resistant to the totalitarian germ than were some other nations. It might be argued that a greater degree of political maturity, a longer experience with free government, explains the difference. Or perhaps the essential factor was the lack in France of the essential sociological and psychological base for fascism's success. Totalitarian movements have a special at- traction for *déclassé* groups, for a broken or threatened middle class and a large mass of unemployed workers; and that attraction is rein- forced in a period of social upheaval and national frustration. Although France in the 1930's suffered from growing social stresses, French society on the whole remained stable, and there was no widespread sense of frustrated nationalism to increase the degree of discontent.

There remains a second question of highly controversial nature: Did the republic's enemies (whether totalitarian or merely authoritarian) try to destroy it by violence on February 6, 1934? For French leftists, it has always been an article of faith that a coup was tried and thwarted. A parliamentary investigating committee in 1947 even con- cluded that there could be ". . . no room for doubt. It was not a question of a spontaneous demonstration but of a genuine insurrection, minutely prepared." Yet every rightist involved in the riots of that day has steadily denied that there was a planned coup, even though some of them might normally be expected to boast of a plot to smash the hated republic.

The 1934 riots grew out of a scandal, much like the Panama affair of the 1890's, that reflected on the honesty of a number of politicians and on the purity of French justice. Serge Stavisky, high-level confi- dence man, had a long police record for shady financial schemes, but

473

he had never been brought to trial on any of the charges. Trial dates had been set repeatedly and had been repeatedly postponed through the influence of powerful friends. His last venture was to establish a series of pawn shops conveniently located near gambling casinos and to sell unlimited issues of stock in these enterprises. The ramshackle edifice collapsed late in 1933, and a great outcry went up from the bilked investors. Rumors spread that Stavisky had been abetted and protected by leading Radical politicians, including even a cabinet minister. The outcry grew worse when Stavisky was cornered in an Alpine hideout and committed suicide to avoid capture. It was widely believed that the police had shot him on orders from the besmirched politicians, in order to prevent a damaging confession. Soon afterward, the mutilated corpse of a government attorney connected with the case was found on a railroad track; the story spread that he, too, had been killed because he knew too much. Eventually, as in the Panama case, parliament set up an investigating committee that heard scores of witnesses but reached no convincing conclusions.

The whole affair was minor compared to Panama, or even to a number of other earlier scandals. But it came at just the right moment to crystallize the nation's growing discontent and to furnish good copy for the right-wing press. For several weeks there were small street riots almost every evening, and the politicians' attempts to restore order only made things worse. Late in January Edouard Daladier organized a new and presumably tougher cabinet and dismissed the Paris prefect of police who had allegedly favored the rioters. All of the extremist papers, along with certain veterans' organizations, responded by calling on their followers to gather on the evening of February 6 for a massive demonstration against the corrupt regime. If anyone was really planning an insurrection, the planners were incredibly inept. There was no apparent coordination of the protesting groups; each chose its own route of march and its own destination, and none struck at such obvious targets of a coup as the railway stations and the public utilities.

In the huge Place de la Concorde, just across the river from the Chamber of Deputies, a mob of demonstrators and curious sightseers milled about through the late afternoon, hemmed in by mounted police-men. The Croix de Feu meanwhile approached the Chamber from the rear but was diverted by a police barricade; its columns gradually disintegrated, and many members went home. The Communists, not to be outdone, called out their small veterans' organization to march in the Champs-Élysées. In the Place de la Concorde, meanwhile, tensions were building up to the verge of spontaneous revolution. The crowd, spearheaded by members of the right-wing veterans' organization called the Union Nationale des Combattants, tried several times to break through police cordons on the bridge, only to be beaten back by fire hoses and bullets. By midnight the scene resembled a battlefield; there were fifteen dead and fifteen hundred injured on the two sides. Not since the Commune of 1871 had so much blood been shed in Paris. Soon after midnight, nevertheless, the mob broke up as its members rushed to catch the last subway train home.

If this was really "a genuine insurrection, minutely prepared," it disintegrated with surprising speed. The aim of the demonstrators was almost certainly a more modest one; they sought not to topple the regime but to force out the Radical cabinet in favor of a more rightist combination. This at least they achieved; Daladier's cabinet resigned the next day to make way for a broad "national union" ministry under ex-President Gaston Doumergue, an aged wheelhorse politician resur-rected from rural retirement to save the republic. Although the cabinet included such symbolic figures as Tardieu and Marshal Pétain, it also included some Radicals and a majority of Moderates; it stood for the existing republic rather than for the authoritarian revolution desired by the right. Yet the rioters seemed to be satisfied with this "Dou-mergue experiment"; the disorders of February 6 were not renewed in the days that followed.

The Radicals were not reluctant to abdicate power at such a moment; they preferred to let the Moderates wrestle with the worsening crisis. They had abdicated to Poincaré in the same way in 1926, and Poincaré had succeeded admirably. But Doumergue was no Poincaré. nor was his problem any longer quite so simple. The new premier, "a vain and complacent antique," let his temporary prestige go to his head, and he developed a mild version of a messiah complex. Since he lacked interest in economic problems, he turned his attention to the political problem: how to give France stable government. Perhaps he was influenced by De la Rocque, as the left suspected; more probably he listened to Tardieu, who urged him to bolster the executive power. There was nothing shocking about Doumergue's reform proposals, the core of which was to reinvigorate the premier's authority to dissolve parliament. But the manner in which he tried to achieve reform was unwise. He embarked on a program of direct radio talks to the nation, over the heads of the politicians, and he aroused suspicion among the Radicals by failing to take them into his confidence. A series of resignations shook his ministry in the autumn, and by November the Radicals felt it safe to bring down the government by withdrawing their ministers. Thus the much publicized Doumergue experiment collapsed after only nine months, leaving behind it a record of futility.

If 1934 had been the year of Doumergue, 1935 was that of Pierre Laval. This shrewd parliamentary manipulator, this disciple of Briand who had by now completed his migration from left to right, was the strongest figure in the government throughout the year, though he became premier only in June. After several months of significant activity as foreign minister, Laval turned his attention to the nation's domestic problems. Industrial production had fallen by about a quarter since 1929, foreign trade by half; unemployment, though not high, was still on the rise. Whatever Laval may have lacked in wisdom, he at least showed courage; for the first time a French cabinet made a really coherent and systematic attack on the economic crisis. Laval's program called for severe deflation in an effort to get the French price level down to the world level. The Chamber, impotent to take action itself, empowered him to legislate by decree, and Laval used or abused that power to cut state expenditures drastically. He hoped that this example would have wide repercussions in private enterprise as well.

The effects of the Laval experiment have been disputed ever since. His defenders point out that during the year from June, 1935, to June, 1936 (when the Popular Front took office), the curve of industrial production at last hit bottom and started upward again. They insist that recovery would have continued at an increasing rate if the Popular Front had not scuttled Laval's program. Laval's critics, on the other hand, believe that the industrial upturn of 1935–36 was misleading and inadequate; that by every statistical measurement except that of industrial production, France's economy continued downward or remained stagnant. They argue that far more drastic action would have been needed to make the deflationary plan succeed: a severe wage cut, a devaluation of the currency, and a ruthless clearing away of the barbed-wire entanglement of laws and exemptions protecting the static sector of the economy. Without these measures, they believe, French production costs were doomed to remain high, and French prices well above the world level. Worst of all, say the critics, was the psychological impact of the Laval experiment, for it seemed to require the mass of little Frenchmen to bear the burden of recovery. At any rate, the rising resentment of many voters led the Radicals to withdraw from Laval's cabinet in January, 1936, and to wreck the Laval experiment.

The Radicals' repudiation of Laval was linked with their decision to turn back toward the left and to join the new Popular Front. For the first time since the Dreyfus era the entire left wing consolidated its strength with the declared purpose of defending the republic against its enemies both at home and abroad. The Popular Front was, in a sense, the product of the alleged coup d'état of February 6, 1934, but it was by no means an automatic reflex resulting from that day of bloodshed. Several months went by after the riots before the Socialists and Communists could agree on even an embryonic alliance, and it was not until January, 1936, that Radical adherence made the Popular Front complete. Complex and arduous negotiations were required to reconcile

477

THE LEFT IN 1849

Proportion of vote cast for
"democratic socialist" candidates
to the Legislative Assembly, May 13, 1849

Over 37.5%
22.5 to 37.5%
Below 22.5%

Not within French boundaries in 1849.

0   50   100   150   200
SCALE OF MILES

Based on Georges Dupeux,
Le Front Populaire et les élections de 1936
(Paris: Colin, 1959), p. 169.

THE LEFT IN 1936

Proportion of votes cast for
Popular Front candidates to the
Chamber of Deputies, April 26, 1936

English Channel

BELGIUM

GERMANY

LUXEMBOURG

Pas de Calais

Somme

Seine Inférieure

Aisne

Ardennes

Manche

Calvados

Eure

Oise

Meuse

Moselle

Bas-Rhin

Côtes Du Nord

Orne

Seine et Oise

PARIS

Marne

Meurthe et Moselle

Finistère

Ille et Vilaine

Mayenne

Sarthe

Eure et Loir

Seine et Marne

Aube

Haute Marne

Vosges

Haut Rhin

Morbihan

Loiret

Aube

Loire Inférieure

Maine et Loire

Indre et Loire

Loir et Cher

Cher

Yonne

Côte d'Or

Haute Saône

Doubs

Vendée

Deux Sèvres

Vienne

Indre

Cher

Nièvre

Saône et Loire

Jura

SWITZERLAND

Charente Inférieure

Charente

Haute Vienne

Creuse

Allier

Loire

Ain

Haute Savoie

Bay of Biscay

Gironde

Dordogne

Corrèze

Puy de Dôme

Haute Loire

Ardèche

Drôme

Isère

Savoie

ITALY

Hautes Alpes

Landes

Lot et Garonne

Lot

Cantal

Lozère

Gard

Vaucluse

Basses Alpes

Alpes Maritimes

Gers

Tarn et Garonne

Aveyron

Tarn

Hérault

Bouches du Rhône

Var

Basses Pyrénées

Haute Garonne

Hautes Pyrénées

Ariège

Aude

Pyrénées Orientales

Mediterranean Sea

SPAIN

Bay of Biscay

Rhône

	Over 52.5%
	37.5 to 52.5%
	Below 37.5%

0   50   100   150   200
SCALE OF MILES

Based on Georges Dupeux,
Le Front Populaire et les élections de 1936
(Paris: Colin, 1959), p. 160.

the differences among the leftist groups, and most of those differences were in fact side-stepped rather than resolved. The heart of the problem was the curious role that the Communist party had played since 1920 and the well-founded skepticism of many Socialists and Radicals about the Communists' sincerity in suddenly changing their tactics.

Until the Popular Front era the Communists had clung stubbornly to a policy of isolated political action. Indeed, their most vindictive epithets had been reserved for the leaders of the non-Communist left; as late as December, 1933, Comintern instructions declared that the principal task of Communist parties everywhere must be to disintegrate social democracy by unremitting attacks on its leaders. As for defending the bourgeois republic, Communist spokesmen had always made it plain that they were uninterested in its renovation or its survival; they alleged that it differed from fascist regimes only in form, not in fundamentals. On the day of the 1934 riots Communist demonstrators had echoed many of the slogans of the rightist mob. The French Communists appeared to be patterning their action on that of the German Communists in the last months of Weimar, when Nazis and Communists had collaborated in the great Berlin traffic strike against the regime.

Immediately after the February riots the first faint signs of a reversal appeared. The Socialists and the C.G.T. called for a symbolic general strike on February 12 as a warning to the republic's enemies, and the Communists ordered their followers to participate — perhaps because they felt it dangerous to resist the wave of energy that swept through the working class. But for several months thereafter the party continued its denunciations of Socialist leadership and its efforts to detach the Socialist rank and file. A sudden though slight softening of tone occurred in June, 1934, and opened the way to a cautious "unity of action" pact with the Socialist organization. The real switch came in the spring of 1935, when the Communists began to push hard for "organic unity," or a complete merger with the Socialist party. Still another obstacle was removed in May, when Stalin publicly announced his interest in the strengthening of France's military power; three days later the French Communists leaped aboard the patriotic band wagon. The Communist trade-union movement, the C.G.T.U., was shortly merged with the older and larger C.G.T.

A few Radicals like Edouard Daladier and Pierre Cot were already seeking to pull their party into the common front, and they finally got their way in January, 1936. A vocal minority of Socialists had meanwhile picked up the Communist cry of working-class unity and was campaigning for a complete merger of the two Marxian parties. But the dominant Socialist group around Léon Blum was more cautious; and besides, the problems that emerged in working out a common program for the Popular Front showed that unity was a long way off. The Socialists and the C.G.T. wanted a precise, coherent, and sweeping plan of economic and social renovation; both the Radicals and the Communists preferred ambiguous generalities, with the emphasis on blocking fascism rather than on reforming the republic. The program that emerged in January, 1936, contained no provisions for substituting even partial socialism for capitalism; but it did include a set of demands in the economic and social sphere that added up to a real new deal. It was enough to frighten the orthodox and to send a wave of hope through a working class that had never before been offered so much as a reward for its electoral support.

The electoral campaign of 1936 was dominated by slogans and emotions rather than by rational discussion of party programs. Yet it would be a serious mistake to underestimate the significance of that campaign or the depth of the passions it aroused. Not since the great contest of 1877 between MacMahon and Gambetta had any election been so bitterly fought. The outcome closely resembled that of 1877: again the left won a narrow but clear-cut victory. As usual there was no great shift of voters from right to left; what happened, rather, was a hardening of existing attitudes and a sharp polarization of the vote around extremes of right and left at the expense of all the center groups. Areas that had traditionally voted to the right simply moved farther to the right, while leftist areas moved farther left. The Socialists emerged as not only the nation's largest party but also as the largest group in the Chamber, with 146 seats. The Radicals slipped sharply to second place with 116 seats. But the Communists' gains were the most dramatic: their popular vote doubled, and their parliamentary representation rose from 10 to 72 seats. No other group benefitted so greatly from the coalition tactics imposed by the Popular Front agreements. To Frenchmen of the time, the elections of April-May, 1936, seemed to mark the end of an era and the beginning of a wholly new phase in the Third Republic's history. Hopes and fears coalesced into an impassioned sense of expectancy.

THIRTY-ONE

> When a country hasn't an army that fits its
> policies, it must have policies that fit its army.
>
> RAYMOND RECOULY *(1936)*

Crisis and Collapse,
1936–1940

"At last — the difficulties begin!" So wrote a leading Socialist intellectual in June, 1936, as his party prepared to take power in France for the first time. Only twice in the history of the party had a Socialist participated in a cabinet, and then only in token fashion. Socialists in several other European nations had become full partners in "bourgeois" coalitions between the wars, but the French party had clung doggedly to Blum's doctrine that it must not take office unless it could dominate the coalition.[1] Now at last, as the largest group in parliament and as the axial party in the Popular Front alliance, the Socialists were marked out to form a government. "Go to work!" Blum was urged by

---

[1] A number of prominent Socialists who chafed at the party's refusal to let them enter cabinets broke away in 1933 to form the Neo-Socialist group. These "participationists" were joined by another group of seceders whose motives were quite different. This second group was attracted by certain aspects of fascist doctrine and was ready to substitute authoritarian for democratic methods in order to achieve a planned society. Marcel Déat was its chief doctrinaire, while Pierre Renaudel headed the "participationists." Renaudel's group eventually returned to the Socialist party; Déat and most of his followers ended as dedicated totalitarians.

483

one of his bourgeois friends. "France is ready for you. She awaits you nervously, but her nervousness is that of a young bride."

Yet it took only a year for the Blum cabinet to be overthrown by the Popular Front-dominated Chamber of Deputies, and only two years for the Popular Front itself to disintegrate completely. Few episodes in modern French history have generated such passionate initial enthusiasm or such rapid disillusionment; few have so promptly crystallized into durable and influential myth. There is a good deal of irony in the fact that this abortive experiment left behind it a legend of hope, derived from the deep conviction that the working class had never been so close to victory, and that success had been snatched away by the self-seeking capitalists. For the next generation, nostalgia for the Popular Front was to be almost the only common denominator that seemed capable of binding together rival segments of the French left.

The Blum cabinet proved to be narrower in composition than the Popular Front coalition that produced it. Despite Blum's appeals, the Communists agreed to support the government but not to join it. Thus they succeeded to the role played by the Socialists for a generation, combining the advantages of power with those of irresponsibility. Socialists and Radicals therefore shared most of the key ministerial posts, and the old problem of reconciling their basic differences on social and economic issues promptly reappeared. Perhaps Blum might have been wiser to try a more daring venture in 1936, by forming a homogeneous Socialist cabinet that could have struck out vigorously on a path of consistent reform. Such a government would have been based on only a minority in the Chamber, but the mood of the moment might have forced both Radicals and Communists to support its program. Had they opposed it and brought down the cabinet, at least they would have been forced to assume open responsibility for blocking vigorous reforms. Blum's motives in refusing such a gamble were admirable ones; he was determined to preserve the *élan* of the Popular Front and to give his government the broadest possible democratic base. But in the end his decision blunted his government's action, diffused responsibilities for its failure, and produced general disillusionment. Most of the Popular Front's reforms turned out to be more spectacular than effective, in part because they remained incomplete. Social reforms proved to be easier to accomplish than were the economic measures required to give them a solid foundation.

The new government's social reforms could not have been postponed — both because they were already long overdue, and because any delay might have produced violent insurrection or civil war. A week after the April-May elections a wave of sit-down strikes inundated the country; when the new cabinet took office almost two million workers had seized control of their plants in the Paris region alone, to the fury and despair of owners and managers. France had known no social upheaval of such proportions since 1848. It was a curious aftermath to a left-wing electoral victory, for it seemed more like the kind of action that might have followed a leftist defeat. The workers had never resorted to such methods against previous governments that had been far more indifferent to labor's interests. It was widely alleged at the time that Communist agitators, convinced that the revolutionary moment had arrived, had stirred up the strikes. In fact, the outbreak was almost certainly spontaneous — the product of a cluster of long-standing grievances and of the emotions aroused during the election campaign. In American terms, it was the tearing down of the goal posts after the football victory. The Communists actually tried to restrain the strikers until restraint proved impossible. As for the trade unions, the head of the C.G.T. first heard of the strikes when he was informed of them by telephone.

This effervescence forced the new government into rapid action, more improvised than planned. Blum brought together labor leaders and representative employers and persuaded them to accept a series of agreements that provided for immediate wage increases averaging 12 per cent and the introduction of generalized collective bargaining. During the next two weeks the cabinet rushed through parliament several other notable reforms, including the forty-hour week in industry, paid vacations for workers, and (later) compulsory arbitration of labor disputes. Certain other measures were products of the Popular

Front's mythology about bankers and munitions-makers. The Bank of France, for example, was brought under state control, and some aircraft plants were nationalized. In the political sphere, the antiparliamentary leagues like the Croix de Feu were dissolved — though most of them promptly reappeared as political parties, with new labels. An effort was made to stabilize farm prices by setting up a wheat office.

Some of Blum's ex post facto critics have argued that his fatal mistake was his failure to go far enough on the road to reform in June, 1936. The outcome of the elections and the quasi-revolutionary situation produced by the strikes, they believe, had stunned the business class and had offered Blum an unparalleled chance to carry through a drastic but peaceful social revolution. This thesis is a plausible one, yet it is easier to assert than to prove that the country would have accepted more sweeping reforms at the time. A more valid criticism can be directed at Blum's failure to accompany his initial social reforms with the kind of economic measures needed to support the new social program and to revitalize the economy. The Popular Front's economic doctrines were, on the whole, rather primitive; it operated on the pump-priming theory that if purchasing power could be put into the hands of the masses, prosperity would follow automatically. In the proper circumstances, so simple a device can be effective; but it was not effective in the conditions existing in France in 1936. The contrary, indeed, was true. Industrial production, instead of being stimulated, dropped sharply at first. In October, 1936, it began to pick up slightly, rose to an index figure of 92 early in 1937, then fell again and bumped along between 80 and 90. When the Popular Front finally disintegrated in 1938, production was about where it had been when Blum took office.

Meanwhile the governmental deficit continued to rise; prices jumped rapidly and soon wiped out labor's gains from wage increases; unemployment stubbornly refused to drop. In desperation, the government finally devalued the franc late in 1936, after having proclaimed for months that it would never take such action. A devaluation carried out several years earlier might have stimulated the French economy; but it now came too late to have any significant effect. Economically speaking, as one French expert has brutally put it, "the Blum experiment was a total failure."

Defenders of the Popular Front have always insisted that the experiment of 1936–38 was consciously sabotaged by its enemies on the right. Business men and investors, they have charged, sent their capital to safe havens outside the country, refused productive investment in home enterprise, and cut production by running their plants only forty hours a week — all this with the aim of wrecking the Popular Front. The thesis undoubtedly has some validity. Many French capitalists were frightened by the Popular Front's program and by the electoral oratory of its more demagogic spokesmen — more frightened, indeed, than they were hurt by the Popular Front in action. A serious flight of capital did occur, thanks to the government's reluctance to set up exchange controls until too late to stop the hemorrhage.

Yet not all the responsibility for economic failure can be attributed to the business group. Labor itself contributed to that failure by focussing narrowly on its own interests, without much reference to the question of national interest, and by failing to work toward some kind of joint action by capital and labor to reinvigorate the economy. In too many cases, as one critic ironically put it, the forty-hour week came to mean four hours of work plus thirty-six hours of discussing the rights of labor. Still another share of responsibility for failure must be assessed against the government for its lack of expertise in economics, which produced a series of fundamental mistakes both in the original conception of the Popular Front's program and in the implementing of that program.

In Blum's defense it ought to be added that perhaps no one could have done much better, given the long postponement of many of the problems his government had to tackle, given the deep class antagonisms that had developed in the nation, and given the divisive impact of international tensions on France in those years. Perhaps Blum's social reforms were, as he later claimed, inescapable — the only alternative to civil war. A few of these social gains did prove permanent, and in that sense the Popular Front experience was not a total failure.

Never again was French labor to be so badly off as it was before 1936. Nevertheless, to some of those who had hoped for a new era in 1936, the shortcomings and the prompt disintegration of the Popular Front produced intense disillusionment. Such Frenchmen concluded that no true reform in France could be achieved without a prior revolution to shake up the country's basic structure. The Popular Front's limitations therefore pushed many leftists into the arms of the Communist party. On the other slope of politics, the episode also strengthened extremism at the expense of moderation. The emotions aroused in 1936 made any moderate rightists more receptive to antidemocratic slogans and drove them to support authoritarian or totalitarian movements like those of De la Rocque or Doriot. In a significant sense, therefore, the Popular Front boomeranged against the republic.

In defense of the Popular Front, it should also be pointed out that it made a serious attempt to carry out a wide variety of reforms designed to clean up long-standing abuses. For example, a bill was introduced to create a healthier and purer press by tightening the libel laws and publicizing newspaper ownership. Measures were also projected to liberalize French colonial policy by broadening the rights of the colonized peoples, notably in Algeria and Syria-Lebanon. These proposals, however, bogged down in parliament and were still pending when the Popular Front fell apart. On the other hand, Blum made no attempt to clear away the barbed-wire entanglement of restrictions and privileges that protected the static sector of the economy and that prevented any rapid invigoration and modernization of French enterprise. On the contrary, the Popular Front added even more barbed wire; laws were adopted, for example, to block the expansion of chain stores and *prisunics* (the French equivalent of five-and-ten cent stores). Such measures reflected the fact that the Popular Front rested not only on the votes of factory workers but also on those of many small enterprisers, marginal survivors of a past economic era, typical representatives of "static France."

The Blum cabinet was overthrown by the Radical-dominated Senate in June, 1937, when at last it sought to introduce such real economic restrictions as controls on foreign exchange. Leadership in the Popular Front passed to the Radicals, who were satisfied with a policy of drift rather than action. In 1938, after a second Blum cabinet far more brief and futile than the first, the Popular Front was formally buried. As in 1924 and 1932, a left-wing victory at the polls ended two years later in a return of the center or right-center groups to power. Once again the Radicals executed their standard pirouette from left to right and accepted as their new partners a segment of the Moderate group.

The new prime minister, Edouard Daladier, was a onetime protégé of Edouard Herriot, but he had risen to be Herriot's rival for leadership of the Radical party. A southerner by origin, he had been a *lycée* professor of history before entering parliament in 1919. Daladier had been one of the first Radicals to advocate a Popular Front, but he had quickly lost his enthusiasm for collaboration with the Communists. Somehow he had acquired a rather misleading reputation for vigor and firmness; events were to show that he possessed more intelligence than character. As premier, Daladier was preoccupied mainly with matters of foreign policy and national defense; in domestic affairs, the dominant figure in his cabinet was Paul Reynaud, a Moderate who stood out in French politics as one of the rare exponents of genuine laissez faire. Reynaud shared with the rest of the center and right a dislike for the Popular Front's tendencies toward state intervention in the economy; but in contrast to his political colleagues, he believed also in clearing away the barrier of privileges and exemptions that prevented real competitive enterprise. Reynaud's aim was to reinstill confidence in the business class and to encourage large-scale private investment and expansion. He urged the cabinet to lower taxes on business enterprise, to abandon some of the Popular Front reforms (e.g., limitations on hours and regulations on overtime pay), and to offer business men guarantees against spoliation if they would bring their capital back from abroad. The Radicals balked for a time; they were just as horrified as they had been when the Socialists had talked of a capital levy. At last, however, they reluctantly agreed to try the Reynaud plan.

The announcement late in 1938 of what Reynaud called "the last experiment in liberalism" threatened to produce a social upheaval as serious as that of 1936. The unions, in protest, resorted to their rarely used ultimate weapon — the general strike. Its failure was complete. The cabinet took a tough line, resorting to its special emergency powers to mobilize many of the strikers for continued service on their regular jobs. But more important still was the apathy of the workers, who failed to respond with enthusiasm to the strike call. The euphoria of the Popular Front victory had long since been dissipated. In the springtime mood of 1936, trade-union membership had grown in almost incredible fashion; the C.G.T. had jumped from one to five million members in a few months. By 1938 about half of the new members had already abandoned the C.G.T., and the failure of the general strike produced a further hemorrhage. For example, the building-trades union, which had boasted a membership of six hundred thousand in 1936, had fallen by 1939 to a mere sixty thousand. Cynicism, bitterness, apathy, marked labor's outlook at the end of the decade.

The Reynaud program, though it lacked much concern for social justice, at least had vigor and coherence. The failure of the general strike and the government's repression of the strikers served as psychological stimuli to ensure the program's temporary success. Capital flooded back into France; industrial production, still at 87 late in 1938, rose to 100 in July, 1939, for the first time since the depression struck France. The franc, which had been slipping ever since 1936, tended to stabilize in value, and prices at last levelled off. In the short run, Reynaud's program was clearly an economic if not a social success.

There were still grave weaknesses, however, in the French economy. Figures on production, national income, population level, all indicated that France in 1939 was still about where it had been in 1913; a quarter-century had gone by with no real progress at all. Such figures suggested a condition of pernicious anemia in an era of rapid world economic expansion. Furthermore, the crisis decade of the 1930's had aggravated the disease. The economy became even more rigid and less adaptable; the crisis was prolonged by many of the measures taken to combat it. Economists calculated, furthermore, that between 1929 and

1939 there had been a net disinvestment in France; that the nation's productive plant had not even been kept up to the 1929 level. In the realm of public works and housing, the record was meager; Great Britain, dominated by the Conservatives, built six times as many housing units as France in the 1930's. The Daladier-Reynaud regime took no direct steps to rationalize and modernize the economy, but relied on the prospect that the free winds of competition would accomplish that end over the years. Possibly a decade or two of Reynaudism might have accomplished such a change; but at best it was likely to be a slow process, given the traditional outlook of the French business group and the powerful hold of static France on the political machinery. In any event, the experiment was scarcely begun when it was interrupted by the outbreak of war.

⋖⋗∘⋖⋗∘⋖⋗∘⋖⋗

The Third Republic's record during the crisis decade was even more dismal in foreign than in domestic policy — though perhaps there was more excuse for failure in the international sphere. The disintegration of France's power position in those years was rapid and dramatic. In 1930 France was still the dominant state on the Continent; by 1940 the country's strength and morale were gravely undermined, and any real independence of action had been lost. The nation's alliance system had crumbled; its military establishment was overshadowed by that of Germany; its unity and determination were dubious. Even in retrospect, there is no simple explanation for this disastrous record, though a good many easy answers have been suggested. Leaving aside for the moment the question of personal or party responsibilities, one might single out three approaches to a general explanation. Each one contains at least a little validity, though none offers a really satisfactory answer.

The root of the trouble, according to one thesis, was France's ideological disunity in face of the fascist threat. The right wing, traditionally most intransigent toward Germany and most thoroughly committed to a strong and independent foreign policy, gradually abandoned

491

this position during the 1930's; many rightists sought an accommodation with Hitler's Germany or Mussolini's Italy, or both. Exponents of this thesis point out that certain aspects of fascism appealed even to the nonfascist elements of the French right, which allegedly (though in fact rarely) adopted the battle cry, "Better Hitler than Blum!" The French left, meanwhile, underwent an opposite evolution, from its traditional pacifism to a stance of belligerent hostility toward the Nazis; but that change was offset by the division and doubt produced by the right's new role.

A second thesis centers attention not on French disunity but on the fundamental issue of French morale. Most Frenchmen, it is argued, were permanently scarred by the traumatic experience of the Great War; whatever their ideological preferences, they desperately sought a way to evade a new clash at almost any cost. Wishful thinking encouraged their effort to escape from their commitments to their eastern allies, in order to retire to safe isolation behind the Maginot Line. No great nation, however, could embark on such a policy of weakness without an adequate excuse; and the French allegedly sought that excuse by abandoning the initiative to the British, who they knew would insist on the appeasement of Hitler. If the French repeatedly received unwise counsel from London, asserts the British historian Sir Lewis Namier, they had no real cause to complain; ". . . for they would not have sought British advice, whose character they could gage beforehand . . . , had it not answered their own unavowed inclinations."[2]

Still a third thesis views the French as more to be pitied than censured; it holds that they were the victims of other nations' errors and of almost inexorable circumstances. According to this view, French leaders recognized the Nazi threat more clearly than did those of any other nation, but they were also realistic enough to recognize France's weakness and inability to act alone. Above all, France needed the support of Britain. Throughout the decade, therefore, French govern-

[2] L. B. Namier, *Europe in Decay* (London: Macmillan, 1950), p. 5.

ments constantly sought to alert London to the danger threatening the West, and in failing to do so, they were dragged unwillingly into the futile line of appeasement.

All three of these strands, along with many other lesser ones, were intertwined in the story of French diplomacy during the crisis decade. Perhaps a more stable regime or a more forceful set of leaders might have slowed or prevented the disintegration of France's position. Or perhaps the combination of circumstances in interwar Europe — the psychological aftermath of the Great War, the disruptive impact of the depression, the widespread hold of certain political myths, the generalized tendency to wishful thinking — would have made the task of even the ablest of French statesmen impossible.

During the first three years of the Hitler era (1933–36) there was fairly broad agreement in France on the question of Nazi Germany. Only a few intellectuals were attracted by the dynamism of the new regime across the Rhine; some of them joined Fernand de Brinon's France-Germany Committee to work for collaboration. The appeasers of these early years included a curious mixture of rightists attracted to Hitler's authoritarianism, of neo-Socialists more interested in planning than in democracy, and of leftists attached to the pacifist ideal that no people would be aggressive if treated fairly. No first-rank political figure was involved; the bulk of the right, center, and left-center favored a stiff policy of bolstering France's alliance system and military strength, while most of the Socialists contended that fascist aggressors ought to be stopped by measures of collective security through the League of Nations.

The League, however, was already a feeble reed by 1933. The French foreign office therefore turned back to a frankly avowed policy of independent French action. Worked out by Alexis Léger, the top career official at the Quai d'Orsay from 1933 to 1940, this program proposed to tighten France's alliances with the eastern European states, to bolster the military strength of those allies, to add pacts with the Soviet Union and Italy, and to seek once more a British commitment to an eastern Locarno that would fence in the Nazis on both their frontiers. Léger was a former protégé and collaborator of Briand, but the threat of Hitler converted him from the Briandism of the 1920's to something more like the old Poincarist line. The new policy was further invigorated early in 1934 when Louis Barthou, one of Poincaré's closest political associates, took office as foreign minister. Barthou made a series of visits to France's eastern allies, opened negotiations with Moscow and Rome, and seemed well on the way to encircling Hitler with a ring of steel. Only the Socialists, the Communists, and the few pro-Nazi in France resisted the Barthou policy. But in November, 1934, Barthou was assassinated along with King Alexander of Yugoslavia, who had just arrived on a state visit. Perhaps that was a fatal turning point in French diplomatic history; or perhaps the Barthou experiment rested on a faulty foundation that would have wrecked it eventually. At any rate, his successor as foreign minister, Pierre Laval, approached the problem in a somewhat different spirit.

It is true that outwardly at least, Laval continued the Barthou policy. He visited Rome and came to an understanding with Italy, though possibly at an exorbitant price. He travelled to Moscow to sign the mutual aid pact with the Soviet Union that Barthou and Léger had initiated. But Laval was much more devious than Barthou in carrying out these moves. Reports got out that he had bought Mussolini's support by secretly handing over Ethiopia to the Italians. Proponents of the Soviet pact noted that Laval, after signing it, kept postponing its presentation to the Chamber for ratification. Late in 1935 rumors spread in Paris that Laval was privately undercutting the Barthou policy by seeking some kind of understanding with Hitler. Laval angrily denied this charge; and there is no reason to believe that he was lying. The available evidence does not suggest that Laval at that time was either attracted to Nazism or convinced that France was too weak to resist Hitler. It does suggest that Laval, true to his own character, was more sinuous and opportunistic than Barthou in shaping French foreign policy, more willing to play a complex double game. Such devious behavior doubtless helped to confuse the French public and to undermine the nation's "multipartisan" firmness in the face of the German menace.

Until 1936 pro-Nazi or pro-appeasement sentiment remained rare in France, even on the right. Indeed, during those years the right's record of firmness had been at least as good as that of the left. When Hitler openly announced conscription in 1935, most right-wing Frenchmen denounced him; when French cabinets asked for credits to expand the armed forces, they gave their support. The Socialists, on the other hand, came around slowly and reluctantly to the need for national defense and voted against military credits until 1936. Their pacifist dogmas hampered their adaptation to the age of aggressors, while their Marxist bias distorted their understanding of the true character of twentieth-century fascism, a movement that transcended economic or class interests. As for the Communists, their sudden right-about-face in 1935 to vociferous support of national defense and a democratic crusade against fascism contributed more to confusion and suspicion than to French unity.

The first serious signs of proappeasement sentiment on the right appeared during the winter of 1935–36. Two causative factors were involved: the loss of Italian friendship, as a result of the Ethiopian conflict, and the formation of the Popular Front in France. Together, these two factors raised a new bogey that to many rightists seemed at least as bad as the Hitler threat. Italy's support, as these rightists saw it, was a vital necessity now that France had decided to ally itself with the Soviet Union. Without Italy as a makeweight, they feared that the alliance might be converted from a realistic anti-Hitler bloc into an ideological coalition devoted to furthering the Communist cause. The formation of the Popular Front seemed to intensify this latter danger. Rightists were frightened into believing that France itself might soon be taken over by a left-wing coalition sympathetic to Moscow's interests, and that such a government might let control of the alliance slip out of French into Russian hands. In an important sense, therefore, the formation of the Popular Front weakened France's resistance to fascism more than it strengthened that resistance. While the antifascist forces were broadened by the adherence of the Communists, they were weakened by the tendency of many Frenchmen of the center and right to be driven even farther toward the right and toward appeasement.

The first precise indication of this changing attitude on the right came in February, 1936, when the Soviet mutual aid pact was at last brought up for ratification. A year earlier most of the right had openly supported such a pact. Now, only a few rightists like Paul Reynaud and P.-E. Flandin joined the left in arguing and voting for it. Ratification came by a bare majority; and the military staff conversations needed to implement the pact were repeatedly postponed by succeeding French governments. Even when the Popular Front took office, Soviet requests for such conversations were evaded, mainly because of Radical and Socialist skepticism about Moscow's motives.

It was thus a divided France that faced the challenge of Hitler's first great gamble: his military occupation of the Rhineland in March, 1936. That act violated not only Versailles but also Locarno; Hitler's excuse was that France had just torn up Locarno by ratifying the Soviet pact. A year or two earlier the French might have reacted sharply to such a challenge; now the growing divergence between right and left, combined with the fact that France was on the threshold of an election campaign, made the government hesitate. The cabinet, a weak interim coalition headed by the Radical Sarraut, met at once and called on the general staff for technical advice. Commander-in-Chief Gamelin disclaimed authority to make a policy recommendation, but told the cabinet that only two paths were open: either all-out action involving total mobilization against the Germans, or no action at all. The army had prepared no plans for a limited police operation, and such an operation was impossible to improvise with an army of draftees. Faced by such a choice, only a handful of ministers favored an open challenge to Hitler by France alone.

The cabinet postponed its decision, however, until an effort could be made to get British support. Foreign Minister Flandin was sent to London to argue the case for action. Whether either Flandin or the cabinet really thought that Britain might help is a highly controversial question; it is conceivable that they were only seeking an excuse for their own inaction. At any rate, the British government urged caution and refused any commitment; Flandin's discouraging report on his return to Paris made it certain that the cabinet would accept the accomplished fact. Some Frenchmen believed then, and many more have argued since, that France should have moved unilaterally; they hold that the British would then have given reluctant support and the German bluff would have been called. Yet it is worth stressing that both French and British opinion were strongly opposed to military action in 1936. It would have required a really unified and courageous cabinet to move in the face of the public mood and at a time of serious division in the country. And it is by no means certain that the use of force would have brought quick success.

Nevertheless, the failure to act had grave consequences. It marked the collapse of the Poincaré-Barthou policy of independent French action in 1936. It would have required a really unified and courageous the sterilization of France's alliance system, for the guarantees of French aid to the Czechs and the Poles would become largely meaningless as soon as Hitler could fortify the Rhine. It converted France into a kind of undeclared British satellite, dependent on prior British consent for any important foreign policy action. Italy had already been lost in 1935; the Soviet tie had been rendered almost useless; the British still boggled at any binding commitments to block German aggression.

As the French examined the alternatives that were still theoretically open to them after March, 1936, they could not be very sanguine. Most rightists seized upon the idea that winning back the Italians would solve the problem. Many of them harbored serious illusions about both Italian strength and Italian aims; they convinced themselves that Mussolini would be a dependable ally, and that recovering his help would redress the European balance. Buttressing this idea was the right's growing tendency to find some virtues in Mussolini's brand of facism; to conclude that it had brought order, authority, and social peace, uncorrupted by ambitious designs of European aggression.

A growing minority in France, however, now began to be infected by sheer defeatism. Flandin, after his unsuccessful mission to London, was the clearest example. He had favored action against Hitler in March, 1936; now he saw no hope for France except in renouncing an independent role and abandoning any pretensions to great-power status. He and others like him proposed to make the best possible arrangement with Hitler, on the theory that France could then retire to secure isolation behind the Maginot Line. Still a third alternative was to accept totalitarianism as the wave of the future; to junk the Third Republic and join the Axis. Such was the doctrine preached by Doriot's P.P.F. and by several lesser extremist groups. There remained, finally, one other path: to patch together what remained of the Barthou encircle-ment policy by maintaining France's commitments in eastern Europe, refusing any further retreats before Hitler's menace, and gambling that if aggression did come, both the British and the Russians would be driven by self-interest to aid France before it was too late. Such was the policy preferred by most of the center and left-center politicians and by a few maverick rightists like Reynaud and Georges Mandel. Since clear proof of Hitler's aims was not then available, it is easy to see how risky and almost irresponsible this firm policy seemed to many contemporaries.

It is just as easy to see why French policy from 1936 onward seemed then, and seems in retrospect, so groping, fumbling, and flabby. Every one of the alternatives still open to France was either risky or potentially disastrous. Frenchmen were therefore quite naturally tempted to slip into a mood of wishful thinking; to avoid choosing any one of these evils and to hope that, perhaps, Hitler might be reasonable in spite of all appearances to the contrary. Even the leading figures of the Popular Front were affected by this mood. Although they were loudly and unanimously antifascist, in fact they were divided into two camps: those who held that any concessions would be dangerous, and those who hoped that Hitler might behave if given a little rope.

The central foreign policy problem of the Popular Front era was the Spanish civil war, which broke out just after Blum came to power. It was natural for a Popular Front government in Paris to want to help its sister regime in Madrid. Yet within a few weeks French aid in arms and volunteers was cut off, and Blum reluctantly accepted a policy of nonintervention by the great powers. Blum's defenders have always argued that his hands-off attitude was dictated by the British, and that Blum accepted it because he clearly recognized France's overriding need of British friendship. But more important, probably, were the Popular Front's own internal divisions over the Spanish issue. Many of the Radicals were reluctant to risk active aid, and if Blum had pushed ahead, the coalition probably would have collapsed. For a time, indeed, the Spanish ambassador in Paris pleaded with Blum to cut off aid, arguing that the worst possible disaster for the Spanish republic would be the disintegration of the Popular Front in France. There is some evidence, too, that Blum feared the outbreak of civil war in France if he continued to aid the Spanish republic.[3]

Blum's decision on Spain has often been branded the worst foreign policy error of the Popular Front period. Superficially, the case of the critics is strong; for the Axis powers evaded their nonintervention pledges, while the *élan* of the antifascist forces in France was weakened by what seemed to be a craven attitude. It is too easy to conclude, however, that bold French intervention would have saved the Spanish republic, and that it would have consolidated the European forces committed to stop naked aggression. In fact, what Hitler wanted most in 1936–38 was a dragging, spreading war in Spain that would involve Britain and France against Italy and would thus give him a free hand to strike toward the east.

By the spring of 1938, when the spotlight shifted from Spain to central Europe, the Popular Front had virtually disintegrated, and the making of French policy had passed into new hands. Alexis Léger was still at the foreign office as secretary-general, but diplomatic decisions

---

[3] C. Audry, *Léon Blum: ou la politique du juste* (Paris: Julliard, 1955), p. 126.

were now shaped mainly by Premier Edouard Daladier and Foreign Minister Georges Bonnet. Both men played a highly controversial role during the last two years of peace. Some have seen them as weak men, appeasers by choice and conviction; others reply that they reluctantly succumbed to unrelenting British pressure. In fact, Bonnet seems to have deserved the first description and Daladier the second, though neither was an absolutely clear-cut case. Certainly Daladier was a much less willing appeaser than his British colleague Neville Chamberlain; and the evidence is clear that he was subjected to continuous British pressure all through the period that culminated in the Munich settlement in September, 1938. Bonnet was a much more pliable and vacillating figure. For a time after he took office he seems to have balanced between appeasement and resistance, but he soon came to incline strongly toward the former course. Daladier privately admitted that he had absolutely no confidence in Bonnet, yet felt compelled to put up with him as foreign minister in order to keep the pro-Bonnet faction of the Radical party behind the cabinet. It would be hard to imagine a more unhealthy state of affairs at a time when firmness and unity were essential.

Hitler's first blow in central Europe, the annexation of Austria in March, 1938, had been foreseen and written off in advance by both the French and the British. But the pressure on Czechoslovakia that began at once and increased through the summer months could not be absorbed so nonchalantly. France had binding commitments to the Czechs; and besides, it was clear that once the Czech bastion was destroyed, there would be only a dim chance of checking further Nazi expansion to the east. So long as the French archives are closed, it is impossible to say whether Daladier made a really serious and sustained effort to persuade the British government to support the Czechs. But it is quite clear that the attitude of the Chamberlain government would almost certainly have made such a French effort futile; for Chamberlain was determined to force the Czechs to accept a compromise satisfactory to Hitler. Bonnet bowed to this British pressure early; even Léger accepted the idea of enforcing a Czech retreat on the ground that France could no longer go it alone and must keep Britain friendly at all costs. The Western capitulation at Munich on September 30, 1938, though welcomed by the bulk of French opinion and approved by the French parliament, was the direct product of British rather than French policy; the Daladier government was essentially an accomplice before the fact. Daladier himself had no illusions; he was thunderstruck at the triumphal reception given him by Parisians on his return from Munich, and privately he expressed the conviction that Munich had been a disastrous setback for the West.

During the six months after Munich the idea of winning back Italy from the Axis to the Western camp entered its most active phase, with Chamberlain as its most active proponent. The French right also urged an all-out effort to court Mussolini; and Foreign Minister Bonnet even sent a private emissary to Rome to explore the ground. The scheme had not the least chance of success; Mussolini was privately contemptuous of the soft Western democracies, and remarked to his son-in-law Count Ciano that France was a nation "ruined by alcohol, syphilis, and journalism." Besides, the British and French could not agree on the bait to be used in attracting the Italians; each government wanted the other to foot the bill through colonial concessions. The sole effect of all these initiatives was to deepen the distrust between Paris and London and to divert attention from the desperate need to prepare for war. The French, meanwhile, were seeking a further accommodation with Germany; in December, 1938, Foreign Minister von Ribbentrop came to Paris for conversations with Bonnet, out of which came a Franco-German agreement for mutual consultation, similar to the one signed by Britain and Germany as a by-product of the Munich conference. It was subsequently alleged that Bonnet had privately encouraged Ribbentrop to turn German power eastward; these charges Bonnet vigorously denied.

The false illusions produced by the Munich settlement were given a rude jolt in March, 1939, when Hitler manufactured an excuse to absorb the rest of Czechoslovakia. Frenchmen were less surprised than Britishers by this cynical act, and they could more promptly draw the consequences of the failure of appeasement. The bulk of Frenchmen on both left and right now rallied to a policy of firm resistance and a last-ditch attempt to fence Hitler in by a pact with the Soviet Union. Even the conservative Catholic daily *La Croix* came out for reinforcing the Soviet tie. There were important exceptions, like the outright fascists and the Flandin-type defeatists, joined now by such new converts as Pierre Laval. The phrase of the neo-Socialist Marcel Déat, "Why die for Danzig?" became the keynote of the defeatist campaign.

From March until August, French policy-makers sought to pull the rather reluctant British government in the direction of a tight East-West pact against aggression. French leaders shared British skepticism about the effectiveness of the Soviet army as a fighting force and about the sincerity of the Kremlin. They took the position, nevertheless, that something would be better than nothing to divert part of Germany's striking power to the east; and they believed that the possibility of Russian duplicity had to be accepted as a calculated risk. They urged the British, therefore, to accept Soviet terms no matter how unreasonable they might seem; and they began to exert pressure on their Polish allies to authorize Soviet troops to enter Polish territory in case of war. Disturbing reports reached Paris of *sub rosa* negotiations between the Russians and the Germans, but the French government discounted these as baseless.

The news of Stalin's pact with Hitler in August, 1939, struck Paris with staggering effect. Daladier remarked privately that France's position had been rendered almost hopeless; that if Hitler now attacked Poland, France alone would have to face the combined power of Germans and Russians, for Poland could not resist for more than two months, while Britain would not be armed short of two years. As Hitler had expected, his diplomatic coup stunned Frenchmen, many of whom concluded that it would now be folly to fight for Poland. But contrary to his expectation, Daladier and the resisters managed to keep their grip on the government, against the efforts of the defeatists. Foreign Minister Bonnet sent a personal agent to Rome in an effort to arrange a second Munich, but the cabinet as a whole repudiated the idea. Most responsible Frenchmen, though dubious about the chances of victory, concluded that another Munich would turn France into a German satellite. They preferred to accept the formidable risks of war.

∞•⊂∞•⊂∞•⊂

France's long-standing pact with Poland, as revised in May, 1939, committed the French to furnish active military aid no later than the sixteenth day after an attack on the Poles. No one, however, had foreseen the tempo of the Nazi blitzkrieg. After sixteen days of war Poland had been half overrun and was on the verge of collapse even before the Soviet armies struck from the east on September 17. The French furnished almost no help at all to their Polish allies. A few border raids into the Saar provided no real diversion; and French appeals for British air strikes against the Ruhr were rejected by London. By the end of September all Polish resistance had ceased.

Formally, the *casus foederis* had disappeared; France could no longer fight for Poland when no Poland existed. Many Frenchmen reasoned thus, and Hitler sought to appeal to their prejudices by offering peace on a forgive-and-forget basis. The appeal was strengthened by a widespread and panicky sentiment in Paris that Germany, supported by the Soviet air force, would turn at once on isolated France, and that the British would stand by across the Channel ready to make peace after France had succumbed. Premier Daladier and Secretary-General Léger at the foreign office were subjected to intense pressure from leading politicians to withdraw from the war at once. Both men, despite their gloom about the chances of victory, resisted the pressure and chose to face the risk of an armed showdown with Hitler. Some French critics later denounced their decision as a grave error, inspired by bravado and shortsightedness rather than courage. Such an argument, however, ignores the consequences of an unresisted Nazi conquest of all Europe. It was a kind of minor miracle, nevertheless, that the French government did manage to stick to its guns in October, 1939.

The winter of 1939–40, variously labelled the "phony war" and the *drôle de guerre,* was replete with false alarms of German attacks, with persistent and bitter squabbles between the French and British, and with efforts to expand and reorganize the Western military forces so that they might hold off a German blow. The German threats were real enough, and they failed to materialize as attacks only because weather conditions interfered; but repeated alerts produced some feeling in France that perhaps Hitler was only bluffing, and that he would never really dare to strike. The controversies with London, produced both by clashes of personality and by differing concepts of warfare, interfered with the smooth operation of the alliance. The heart of the difficulty was a hard core of mutual distrust. French political and military leaders became convinced that Britain would refuse to commit more than a token force of men and aircraft to the continental front and would stand silently by while the French carried the brunt of the coming attack. The British, meanwhile, concluded that the French were eager to devise a plan of action in some distant theater of war, as far as possible from French soil and as dependent as possible on British naval and air power for success. Nazi psychological warfare took advantage of these differences to encourage suspicion on both sides of the Channel.

Meanwhile both French and British desperately sought to remedy the long-standing deficiencies in their armed forces. France at least possessed a large and well-trained land army, which was still believed by many to be the world's best in equipment and morale. All through the 1930's French military leaders like Marshals Pétain and Weygand and Commander-in-Chief Gamelin had resisted pressures for fundamental change in the direction of greater mechanization or increased air power. Their fault was not lack of loyalty to the republic, but lack of imagination and foresight; they clung to their memories of the First World War and anticipated another long defensive struggle of the same type. "For an army," remarked one disillusioned Frenchman, "perhaps a victory is harder to overcome than a defeat." A few maverick officers like Colonel Charles de Gaulle, and a few politicians like Paul Reynaud, had been campaigning for years for a new conception of warfare that would convert the French armies from an essentially defensive instrument into a maneuverable weapon for lightning offense or for roving defense. Their doctrine called for the concentration of tanks and armored vehicles in several mechanized divisions supported by tactical aircraft, and for a shift of emphasis away from a mass of conscripted troops toward a smaller long-term professional army. Perhaps their chief error lay in combining these two reforms; for the idea of a small professional army frightened and irritated good republicans and blurred their understanding of the real advantages of mechanization. In consequence, neither reform was adopted, and reformers like De Gaulle were shunted off into obscurity.

Preparedness had suffered further during the 1930's because of the persistent hold of pacifism on both politicians and public. The warmongering armament-maker and the saber-rattling soldier came to be legendary ogres in the folklore of the French left, as they did in most democracies in the same era. This sentiment made it easy for Hitler to seize the initiative in armaments and to gain a lead of two or three years over the Western powers. The Popular Front's accession to office in 1936 introduced a further diversion, for it focussed attention on social reforms and a shorter work week at a moment when an all-out productive effort was vital. Blum showed no more understanding of the need for a new military doctrine than did most other politicians of the decade. However, Vichy's later charge that the Popular Front, either deliberately or through its fumbling incapacity, sabotaged French preparedness and opened the way to defeat was a blatant distortion.

A much more important factor in French unpreparedness was the government's adoption in 1938 of a plan to modernize the air force by converting to new models of aircraft. This essential change came so late that the outbreak of war caught France in the midst of the conversion process. In September, 1939, the French had fewer than 500 first-line planes available, as compared to the Germans' 4000. Great Britain's contribution of 1100 first-line planes fell far short of making up the difference.[4] In a desperate effort to remedy this imbalance, Premier Daladier in November, 1939, made a dramatic and pressing plea to the American government to come to France's aid by building 10,000 planes at once for sale to the French. The cost, he declared, was immaterial; with some hyperbole, he declared his readiness to mortgage France or sell the palace of Versailles if that should be the Americans' price. It was a hopeless appeal; the American government dared not challenge isolationist opinion in such a brusque fashion, and Daladier sank into a kind of moody spirit of defeatism.

Meanwhile the French army was making belated efforts to adapt itself to the kind of warfare inaugurated in the Polish campaign. The army had some 2300 modern tanks along the eastern frontier to match the Germans' 2700, but when the war began they had been parcelled out in small packets to support a large number of infantry divisions.[5] Steps were taken during the winter of 1939–40 to group them into a few highly-mobile armored divisions, but the conversion process was only half complete when the German attack finally came. Six months proved far too short a time to create an effective mobile force. Furthermore, the French high command still clung to its blind confidence in the superiority of French troops and equipment and to its conviction that Hitler's blitz tactics would be too risky to succeed in the West. Half of the French eastern frontier was impregnably protected by the Maginot Line; the other half, from Sedan to the Channel, was only

[4] By May, 1940, French and British production had narrowed the gap somewhat. France now had 1300 first-line planes (of which 300 were based in North Africa); Britain had an estimated 1350; and the Germans had more than 5000, plus 1000 transport planes. (Lt. Col. J. Le Goaster, "L'Action des forces aériennes," *Revue d'histoire de la deuxième guerre mondiale*, III [June, 1953], 137–40.)

[5] Whether the French possessed as many tanks as the Germans in 1940 has been much disputed. According to one careful study, the French armies that were actually engaged in the critical phase of the German attack (May 10 to June 1) had only 1520 tanks as compared to the Germans' 2683 used during that operation. By June 11, however, the French had brought into action a total of 2262 modern and 540 obsolescent tanks. (Major A. Wauquier, in *Revue d'histoire de la deuxième guerre mondiale*, III [June, 1953], 163–64.)

lightly fortified. Proposals during the 1930's to extend the Maginot Line to the sea had bogged down because of the cost, and because French governments hesitated to alienate the Belgians by leaving them outside France's defensive frontier. The Franco-British war plan of 1939 called for a massive swing of Allied troops across the frontier into Belgium, pivoting on the northern end of the Maginot Line. This move was to begin only if and when Belgium and the Netherlands should be invaded by Hitler, and it was predicated on the assumption that the Allied forces would have several days to reach advanced defensive positions along the Meuse River. Both the French high command and the British government opposed this swing into Belgium and would have preferred to await the German onslaught from stronger defensive positions along the Franco-Belgian frontier. But once again political considerations dominated; the French government insisted on immediate action to aid the Low Countries, lest the latter feel themselves abandoned by France. In the event, the decision proved to be disastrous and played directly into Hitler's hands.

An equally serious matter during the phony-war winter was the problem of civilian morale. Some Frenchmen were lulled into security by the repeated postponement of Hitler's attack; others persisted in a quasi-public campaign in favor of a negotiated peace. Dissension was increased by the curious role played by the Communists. From 1935 to 1939 they had spearheaded the antifascist crusade and had denounced the appeasers who had sacrificed Czechoslovakia and were allegedly scheming to sacrifice Poland. The Nazi-Soviet pact in August, 1939, converted them overnight into advocates of neutrality; "brave little Poland" suddenly became "Poland, that monstrous bastard of the Versailles treaty." The Daladier government, naturally but perhaps unwisely, outlawed the party as soon as the war began and interned many of its leaders. Communist agitation against the war nevertheless continued, especially in the trade unions, and contributed to doubt and defeatism. Morale was further injured by the persistent Franco-British squabbles over the conduct of the war and by a resurgence of parliamentary factionalism. Daladier's rivals sought to displace him as premier and also to substitute a more vigorous commander-in-chief for the scholarly but indecisive Gamelin.

These domestic feuds finally produced a cabinet crisis in March, 1939. Daladier was overthrown, in part because he had failed to help Finland resist Soviet attack. Paul Reynaud replaced him as premier, introducing a new mood of energy and optimism in place of Daladier's moody doubts. The balance of political forces, however, forced Reynaud to keep Daladier in the cabinet as war minister; and a kind of political cold war between the two rivals ensued, to the further detriment of effective leadership. This conflict produced a new cabinet collapse on May 9, but before the press could even announce the news, Hitler struck at last into the Low Countries, and the shaky Reynaud government had to be left in office to face the emergency. Winston Churchill's personal representative, General Spears, who arrived in Paris at about this time, was appalled by what he described as "the slimy mess of disastrous incompetence" that passed for leadership in France. His savage comment was manifestly exaggerated and unfair. Yet it is clear that in this new emergency France turned up neither a Clemenceau, nor a Foch, nor a Poincaré. Even if men of this caliber had been available, it was doubtless too late to improvise an effective defense.

Within a week after the attack the French lines had been pierced near Sedan, and an armored German spearhead was swinging to the right toward the Channel, disrupting French communications and dividing the Allied armies into two isolated segments. The French and British had moved up into Belgium on schedule, but faulty intelligence had led them to underestimate the speed with which the German panzer divisions could advance. Gamelin left a weak covering force at the Sedan hinge, on the assumption that this area would be protected by the rugged Ardennes forest region in southern Belgium. Once the initial breakthrough occurred, the result was spreading chaos. Headquarters could no longer communicate with the various command posts; each unit had to fall back on its own initiative. Stunned by the attack and unprepared for improvised action, much of the army disintegrated as a fighting force. Roads choked with thousands of fleeing refugees

508

further disrupted the war zone. In desperation, Reynaud called General Weygand back from Syria to take over direction of the French armies; and he pleaded passionately with the British government to send the bulk of the Royal Air Force from England to join the fight. Both steps were futile. Weygand, almost as soon as he arrived, concluded that the fight was hopeless. He refused to adopt a plan advocated by General de Gaulle that called for a fighting retreat to a redoubt in Brittany and the eventual transfer of both government and armed forces to North Africa. When the second phase of the German offensive got under way after the battle of Dunkirk, France's capacity for armed resistance had virtually disappeared. On June 10 the government left Paris for the south, arriving finally in Bordeaux; the Germans occupied the capital city without a fight. On the sixteenth a majority in the cabinet voted to ask the Germans for armistice terms; Reynaud submitted his resignation at once and recommended that President Lebrun appoint Marshal Pétain as premier. A week later, on June 22, the capitulation was signed in Compiègne Forest, in the same railway car that had sheltered the signers of the 1918 armistice. Never before in modern history had France been so prostrate, so stunned and broken in spirit. Defeat the French had known, in 1814, 1815, 1871. But this was far more than defeat: it was utter humiliation, almost too deep for any Frenchman to comprehend.

THIRTY-TWO

> There are times when one must have the courage
> to bet on two possible winners.
>
> EX-PREMIER CAMILLE CHAUTEMPS

Bifurcated France,
1940–1944

The years from defeat to liberation — described by Alexander Werth as "the strangest and most complicated in the whole history of France" — constitute a curious interlude in the record of the nation. For the second time since 1815 the parliamentary system gave way to an authoritarian regime. But alongside that regime, and challenging its legality, there emerged a rival government-in-exile. On June 18 General Charles de Gaulle, who had fled from Bordeaux to London in a British plane, issued a call for continued resistance and set up a Free French movement that was eventually to attain the status of a *de facto* government. Meanwhile the Third Republic's last regularly appointed cabinet headed by Marshal Pétain was transferring its temporary center of operations to Vichy and was embarking on its own attempt to purge and renovate France.

Parliament, whose sessions had been suspended during the invasion, was convoked at Vichy on July 9–10 to consider Pétain's plans for a new order. Most of the deputies and senators managed to make their way to the meeting in the Grand Casino, though there were two dozen notable absentees who had left Bordeaux for North Africa on June 21 in a vain attempt to set up a government-in-exile there. Among them were such figures as Edouard Daladier, Georges Mandel, and Pierre Mendès-France. Their departure (along with that of President Lebrun) had been approved initially by Pétain, but Pierre Laval and others had persuaded the marshal to abandon the idea. Lebrun remained in France; Mandel and his colleagues, when they sought to land in Casablanca, were arrested by French army authorities acting on orders from Bordeaux, and they were charged with plotting against the security of the state.

Pétain's support among the politicians at Vichy (as among Frenchmen in general in July, 1940) was virtually unanimous. The nation had not yet emerged from the numbing shock of the disaster, which had struck with the startling power of an avalanche. That shock produced an intense desire for vigorous leadership and an equal revulsion against the men and the system that had failed to avert the debacle. Almost every parliamentarian was ready to entrust France to Pétain at least for the immediate future, and many were prepared to see a permanent shift to authoritarian government.

Just what the marshal had in mind for France was not, however, fully clear. The character of his entourage gave a strong hint, but nothing more precise than that. His cabinet contained a curious mélange of politicians, bureaucrats, and army and navy officers. Most of the politicians were rightists who had been appeasers before September, 1939, and defeatists since, though there were one or two notable exceptions. Most of the "technicians" from the civil service and the armed forces were more or less open critics of the parliamentary republic; some had authoritarian, others totalitarian leanings. But the man who was already assuming the dominant role in the cabinet was Vice-Premier Pierre Laval, to whom Pétain entrusted the task of drafting and presenting to parliament a program of reform.

Although most of Laval's adult life had been spent as an astute and successful parliamentary politician, the events of 1940 had destroyed the last remnants of his loyalty to the parliamentary system. Perhaps he was moved by nothing more than sheer opportunism — by an instinctive and catlike reaction that led him always to land on his feet. Much more probably, he was motivated in part by personal resentment against the regime that had shunted him into the background since 1936 and in part by an overhasty conviction that fascism had proved itself the wave of the future. In later retrospect, his protagonists were to argue that he had merely accepted the inescapable fact of defeat and had devoted himself to protecting France against its full consequences. His comments at the time, however, suggested a quite different mood: "Parliamentary democracy has lost the war. It must disappear and give place to a hierarchical authoritarian regime, national and social."[1]

Laval's purpose was to persuade parliament to abdicate its power into the hands of Marshal Pétain, and he proceeded with characteristic shrewdness and skill. In the end, however, he had to accept a degree of compromise. While the parliamentarians were ready for temporary abdication to Pétain, a vocal minority was determined to put the question of a permanent new regime "on ice" for the duration of the war. Laval, by a combination of threats, promises, and concessions, managed to avert this postponement; on July 10 a joint session of parliament approved by a vote of 569 to 80 his revised plan for vesting Pétain with power to draft a new constitution without delay. He agreed, in return, that the new system would be referred to the people by referendum, and he allegedly promised that members of the moribund parliament would meanwhile continue to enjoy their privileges and salaries. Not a single party voted solidly against this grant of virtually unrestricted powers to Pétain. The Socialists furnished the largest single bloc of opposition votes, but even what was left of their solidarity was shattered by the events of 1940.

What followed, however, was not a coherent and sweeping "National Revolution," despite the use of that grandiloquent phrase in all Vichy orations. Although Pétain set up committees to study and draft a con-

[1] R. Aron, *Histoire de Vichy, 1940–1944* (Paris: Fayard, 1954), p. 130.

stitution, the task remained undone when Vichy collapsed four years later. Although certain organs of a corporative nature were established over the next year or so (notably a state-patronized labor movement, a Peasant Corporation, and a series of industrial Organization Committees), no thoroughgoing corporative structure ever emerged. Although Vichy's purpose was allegedly to put an end to the instability, intrigue, and corruption that its leaders attributed to the Third Republic, Vichy promptly developed most of those same weaknesses in aggravated form. Factions and cliques engaged in constant subterranean or open warfare; men and groups followed one another into office and out again with bewildering frequency. Vichy came to resemble (as Alfred Cobban puts it) "a ramshackle copy of an eighteenth century court" over which Pétain presided as a more or less benevolent autocrat, guided apparently by whims more than by principles. What those four years brought was a series of different Vichys, each one giving birth to the next in what might be called a process of parthenogenesis. If the period had any continuity, it was provided by the continuance and the reinforcement of the administrative bureaucracy, which survived the 1940 upheaval almost intact and which steadily tightened its grip on the processes of decision-making. Not only did these men keep their civil service posts, but an increasing number of them moved up into cabinet positions as the years passed.

The original mélange of politicians, idealistic patriots, authoritarians, totalitarians, and sheer opportunists that surrounded Pétain at the outset quickly disintegrated through internal strife. The politicians were the first to go; all of them except Laval were dismissed from the cabinet within three months. The totalitarians of the radical right soon departed also, disillusioned with what they took to be the reactionary traditionalism of the men closest to Pétain. Most of them — Doriot, Déat, Deloncle, and so on — went to German-occupied Paris, whence through press attacks and intrigue they carried on a kind of guerrilla warfare against Vichy. Those who remained around Pétain were mainly authoritarians rather than totalitarians: Charles Maurras and Raoul Alibert of the Action Française, De la Rocque of the P.S.F.,

513

Henri Dorgères of the Peasant Front, Paul Baudouin, white hope of the technocratic elements in industry and the bureaucracy. These men, on the whole, aimed at restoring the old virtues and the old elites. They did not want an all-encompassing state run by a new power elite, but a refurbished old regime: an organic, hierarchical society of somewhat pluralistic character. The Parisian extremists (many of them one-time leftists) were committed to the kind of right-wing radicalism represented by Hitler's and Mussolini's fascism, but they were badly split by personal rivalries. Over the war years the gulf between Vichy and Paris grew steadily wider, though in 1944 the Paris totalitarians at last managed to cross it and to establish a bridgehead of influence within the Vichy government.

Long before that time, however, a whole series of palace revolutions had marked the career of the Vichy regime. The most dramatic of these came in December, 1940, when Vice-Premier Laval was suddenly summoned before Pétain and summarily dismissed from the cabinet. The origins of this overturn remain somewhat controversial. Many of Pétain's close advisers had been intriguing against Laval from the outset, moved by personal dislike, jealousy, and a growing suspicion that Laval was likely to commit France to an open declaration of war against the British. Pétain's own attitude toward Laval seems to have been ambiguous; his behavior toward Laval and his comments about him contained irreconcilable inconsistencies. The most plausible explanation of their relationship is that Laval thought of Pétain as a successor to the presidents of the Third Republic, dignified but powerless, while Pétain thought of Laval as a chief of staff, who ought to be totally dependent on orders from his commander-in-chief. Laval, curiously unaware of (or indifferent to) the palace plots against him, proceeded stubbornly toward his goal of closer rapprochement with the Germans, apparently with a view to softening the rigors of the armistice and ensuring France the role of brilliant second in Hitler's Europe.

Laval thought that he had taken a long step toward that goal when he was granted a personal audience with Hitler at the village of

514

Montoire in October, 1940. That meeting paved the way to a conference between Hitler and Pétain a few days later at the same place, but their conversation failed to produce the kind of Franco-German entente that Laval wanted.[2] Laval was much encouraged nevertheless; he began for the first time to make free use of the word "collaboration." He arranged a meeting with German Foreign Minister von Ribbentrop at which he hoped to get the bulk of the French prisoners of war in Germany released and the German occupation costs reduced by half. It was the prospect of this Laval-Ribbentrop meeting, and the fear of many Vichyites that Laval might offer to join the war against England in order to gain his ends, that seems to have triggered the crisis ending in his dismissal. After a brief period of house arrest he departed for Paris, where from 1940 to 1942 he associated closely with German Ambassador Otto Abetz and with some of the totalitarian critics of Vichy.

Pétain meanwhile turned to another politician of the Third Republic, P.-E. Flandin, as Laval's successor. The Flandin interlude was brief, however; he arrived with the illusion that Vichy was an independent government, and Berlin lost little time in disabusing him of his error. In February, 1941, he was dismissed in favor of Admiral François Darlan, a naval officer with a passion for politics and a talent for intrigue. Darlan, as active head of the government and Pétain's new heir-apparent, lasted for fourteen months. Though shrewd and ruthless, his efforts to turn France into Germany's favorite ally failed to produce results. One German official later remarked that "when we

---

[2] Pétain's admirers later concocted a remarkable myth about the Montoire Conference, comparing it with Verdun in 1916 as the turning point that won the war. According to this legend, Pétain misled Hitler into hoping for a reconciliation with France, and therefore Hitler abandoned his plan to bring Franco's Spain into his alliance system by promising the Spaniards a large part of French North Africa. If Hitler had not been diverted from his Spanish scheme (so runs the thesis), Spain and Germany would have seized North Africa in 1940, would have sealed off the Mediterranean and mounted a southern attack on the Soviet Union via the Caucasus, and would have won the war in Europe. Pétain's own postwar comment about Montoire, when asked in 1947, was simply, *"J'ai été roulé"* ("I was played for a sucker" — i.e., by Hitler).

asked Laval for a chicken, he gave us an egg; when we asked Darlan for an egg, he gave us a chicken." Darlan's policy toward England has been described as one of "all hostility short of war"; he was even willing to commit France to military collaboration in the colonies against British troops, but he failed to secure anything tangible from Berlin in the way of concessions, and his influence gradually deteriorated. During his year in power technocratic elements from industry, banking, and the bureaucracy reached the peak of their influence at Vichy. Pétain himself had little use for such people, but Darlan was willing to work with them to further his collaborationist policy, while the technocrats in turn were willing to harness the French economic machine to Hitler's needs if Hitler would furnish the raw materials and the market.

The entrance of the United States into the war, however, shook the confidence of the technocrats at Vichy; their business acumen made them well aware of the weight that the Americans could throw into the scales. Their retreat toward a policy of *attentisme* (fence-straddling) combined with Darlan's shrinking prestige to bring a new change of leadership in April, 1942. This time it was Laval who returned triumphantly to a post that he was to retain until Vichy collapsed. It was a different Laval, though, from the Laval of 1940. Then he had been convinced of an imminent German victory, and he had sought to win for France a favored place in the New Order. Now the outcome of the struggle was no longer sure, and his altered purpose was, by dissembling and delay, to evade German exactions and to preserve some semblance of French autonomy. As time went by he even developed the idea of bringing about a peaceful transition from Vichy to a restored Third Republic. This new role that he chose in 1942 was played until August, 1944, with considerable skill and cunning, though with steadily decreasing power to shape the course of events.

Laval returned to office just at the moment when German pressures began to intensify sharply. The terrible drain of the war in Russia plus Germany's shortage of manpower brought a demand for the requisitioning of French labor for work in Germany. Laval's efforts at

evasion eventually failed, and he ended by agreeing to conscript workers for the Germans in return for the freeing of some French prisoners
of war. By 1944 seven hundred thousand French workers had been
recruited or impressed into service in Germany. Many potential conscripts preferred, however, to take to the hills in central and southeast
France and to join armed bands of resisters called the *maquis*. The
Germans also stepped up pressure for the arrest of Jews. Again Laval
sought to negotiate and delay, then finally agreed to turn over all
foreign-born Jews in return for a German promise to spare French
Jews.[3] As the anti-German underground in France grew more active,
the Germans declared their intention to seize and execute hostages as a
deterrent to underground sabotage. Again Laval sought to soften the
repression by offering to do the job for the Germans; he set up a
special corps of French police and special courts empowered to arrest
and punish "terrorists." The effect was to free some of Germany's over-
burdened security police and SS agents for service in other parts of
occupied Europe.

That Laval played a double game after 1942, assuring the Germans of his undying allegiance but in fact evading their exactions,
seems undeniable. Whether in the long run the policy was a wise and
justifiable one is much more questionable. Laval believed that in accepting lesser evils he was sparing his countrymen greater ones: that it
was better for the Vichy police to shoot ten resisters than for the
Germans to shoot a hundred hostages. He believed that the Germans'
confidence in him made him the last remaining barrier to the appointment of a gauleiter in France — a Doriot, a Déat, or a Joseph Darnand,
all-out totalitarians dedicated to Hitler's cause. He believed that the
alternative to his tortuous leadership was the "Polonization" of France,

---

[3] After the war, Vichy's Commissioner-General for Jewish Affairs, Xavier Vallat,
asserted that 95 per cent of all French Jews survived the occupation period, whereas
only 5.8 per cent survived in seven other occupied countries. His statistics have
never been verified; and his testimony carefully avoids such embarrassing facts as
the spoliation of French Jews and the role of Vichy police in rounding up and
deporting non-French Jews to concentration camps in eastern Europe.

with mass deportations and the liquidation of anti-Nazis. "If my policy succeeds," he told a friend in 1942, "there won't be enough stones in France to put up statues of me; if it fails, I'll be hanged. But that doesn't bother me — I will have done it for my country." Yet even if "Polonization" was really the alternative to Laval's rule, it might have been no worse for France in the long run; for the limited protection provided by Lavalism was won at the cost of grave division and confusion within the nation. For if Laval successfully misled the Germans, he also misled many of his own countrymen. And whether Laval liked it or not, Vichy France became Germany's most important supplier of both goods and manpower during the war years.

Laval has had his protagonists since 1944; Pétain has had even more defenders, and these have had greater effect on the opinions of postwar Frenchmen. The Pétainists hold that it was the marshal who was the real master of the double game; that he played it from the very outset, and that it was he who saved the nation from "Polonization." Pétain's role is, in fact, not easy to assess. His excessive secretiveness, his talent for dissembling, his contradictions of word and action, are almost impenetrable barriers to understanding. His closest advisers were third-rate figures like his personal physician, Dr. Ménétrel. His own behavior seems to have been more impulsive than carefully calculated; his venerable appearance and charismatic aura seem to have concealed a shallow mind, a kind of peasant cunning, and a deep-seated vanity. There is little evidence that he hoodwinked the Germans, or that he seriously and consistently sought a secret *modus vivendi* with the British, or that he sent Admiral Darlan to North Africa in 1942 with secret instructions to turn the area over to the Allied invaders. Pétain's role had some meaning and even some grandeur until November, 1942; it lost any meaning whatsoever when he remained in office after the Allied landings in North Africa and the resultant occupation of all France by the Germans. At eighty-eight he was doubtless too old to leave for Algeria at that critical moment; but he was tempted for a time to put himself at the head of France's tiny armistice army and to offer token resistance to the Germans as they flooded in to occupy southern as well as northern France. Such an act, however quixotic, would have ended "the Franco-French War," and it might have prepared the way for a broader unity of Frenchmen in the postwar era. Pétain no longer had any real function after November, 1942. His tragedy was not his decision to take power in 1940 but his failure to realize when he and the regime he headed had outlived their usefulness.

❧◦❧ ❧◦❧ ❧◦❧

Alongside Vichy stood a second wartime France — one committed from the outset to what seemed a quixotic determination to continue the war, but one destined to grow in strength until at last its leaders and its ideals would emerge to shape the restored republic. Some kind of government-in-exile was almost certain to emerge from the collapse; but that Charles de Gaulle should lead it was something of an accident (unless one believes, like De Gaulle, in the force of destiny). As the youngest general (aged forty-nine) in the French army, he was outranked by dozens of better-known officers; and he was prepared to follow the orders of any of his superiors if they would carry on the fight. But none spoke out in the moment of crisis, and no well-known political figure managed to escape abroad to serve as rallying point. De Gaulle stepped promptly into the vacuum, and just as promptly he found the task of leadership of the Free French movement much to his liking.

De Gaulle was no ordinary professional officer. His unorthodox views on strategy during the interwar years, when he preached the new doctrine of mechanized warfare, won him some notoriety if not very much support. He was a voracious reader, something of a military philosopher, an author of essays distinguished by an elegant, almost classical style. His views on the nature of leadership, contained in a volume with the unlikely title *The Edge of the Sword* (and dedicated to Marshal Pétain), accurately reflected De Gaulle's own self-image and foreshadowed in almost uncanny fashion his own conduct over the quarter-century that followed. His books betrayed a fervent patriotism,

519

a touch of mysticism, an austere and humorless integrity, a serene conviction of destiny. The personal traits of such a man were sure to shape the character of the movement that he led.

Free France at the outset was an ill-assorted collection of accidental exiles bound together by nothing more than a common response to De Gaulle's rallying cry of June 18. There were few prominent figures among them, and in some cases their loyalty to the republican ideal seemed uncertain. Indeed, De Gaulle's own political views remained unclear for a time; his declarations were fervently patriotic, but what he talked of restoring was France, not the republic. In the end he followed the counsel of his legal adviser, Professor René Cassin, who urged him to take the position that the Third Republic remained France's legal government, and that it had been destroyed by the unconstitutional machinations of the men of Vichy. Over the next two years, however, De Gaulle's contacts with the emergent French underground showed him that the resistance leaders wanted neither the prewar system nor an authoritarian substitute, but rather a new and purified republic. In 1942 De Gaulle responded by issuing a call for the restoration of France's traditional liberties, and thereafter he began to talk openly of a fourth republic. That commitment was necessary if there was to be a merger of Free France in exile with the underground movement at home.

Within De Gaulle's organization there was never perfect harmony. The general had little sympathy for palaver and compromise; meetings of his quasi-cabinet, the French National Committee, resembled briefings by a commander more than discussions of policy. But the fault was not all De Gaulle's; his makeshift organization contained more than the usual quota of prima donnas and mediocrities. Some members resigned and took to denouncing De Gaulle as an incipient dictator surrounded by fascists. Much criticism centered on the man who called himself Colonel Passy, an ex-officer who headed the Free French intelligence service. His enemies accused him of operating a small-scale Gestapo office in London, complete with dungeons for the uncooperative. Eventually De Gaulle was driven to replace Passy with a civilian director, the young anthropologist Jacques Soustelle. There were accusations, too, that De Gaulle aimed to establish a one-party system in postwar France. To offset these fears, Gaullist agents in France were eventually ordered to stimulate the revival of the prewar parties, some of which had disintegrated completely since the collapse. The long-range effect of this decision was to render more likely the restoration of a multiparty parliamentary system after the war, rather than the two-party presidential system favored by many Gaullists. On the other hand, it gave De Gaulle a broader base for his claim to represent all French resisters and enabled him to push aside rival aspirants to leadership.

There was serious friction, too, with the British, almost from the outset. Although Churchill's government supported Free France with loans and grants and furnished office space and broadcasting facilities, De Gaulle quickly concluded that British policy, "malevolent and scheming," was designed to undermine his influence in France and to absorb most of the French empire. A series of clashes brought repeated threats that De Gaulle might move his headquarters to Brazzaville. A disastrous Franco-British sortie against Dakar in September, 1940, added to the mutual resentment. The whole bittersweet relationship inspired one of Churchill's most celebrated witticisms: his remark that the Cross of Lorraine (De Gaulle's symbol) was the heaviest cross he had to bear.

Within France, meanwhile, there was springing up in almost spontaneous fashion a whole series of tiny and uncoordinated underground movements, dedicated to restoring French morale and rebuilding the will to resist the German conqueror. They were usually the work of a single individual or a handful of men; the first of these grouplets appeared within two months after the 1940 collapse. In the unoccupied southern zone the underground was predominantly leftist in composition, for most Frenchmen of right-wing leanings there were committed at first to the Pétain experiment. In the German-occupied north, where Pétain's hold was weaker, the membership was more broadly recruited from right as well as left. In organizational structure, too, south and north differed somewhat. The southern groups were fewer, but larger and better articulated; by 1942 three organizations called Combat, Libération, and Franc-Tireur dominated the resistance movement in the south. The northern groups were smaller, more isolated, more activist. To function under the noses of the Germans required great daring; frequent arrests kept the northern movements small and tough. Of the northern groups, the best known were the Organisation Civile et Militaire or O.C.M. (rightist in tone), Libération-Nord (mainly Socialist), and Défense de la France (composed largely of Parisian students).

Only one movement straddled the two zones from the outset: this was the Front National, founded by Communist activists in 1941. There had been some individual examples of Communist resistance to the Germans before Hitler attacked the Soviet Union in 1941; but the party's official line until then had continued to be one of "revolutionary defeatism." After June, 1941, the party sprang enthusiastically into a type of activity for which no other group in France was so well prepared. Individual Communists joined most of the leading resistance groups, but they held all the key posts in Front National. The party's purpose seems to have been to make Front National the capstone of a united or federated resistance movement that would absorb all other groups and would thus be in a position to shape postwar France.

It was not the Communists, however, who managed to weld the underground into a nation-wide federation. Instead, Gaullist agent smuggled in from London accomplished that difficult task. De Gaulle's hopes for building a new France in the postwar era depended on his ability to fuse and win over the resistance movement. He believed that both British and American intelligence agents were out to forestall him by offering the underground arms and money. As soon as possible, therefore, a Free French representative was parachuted into France with the mission of uniting the underground and committing it to De Gaulle. That representative was Jean Moulin, a young career prefect who had been dismissed by Vichy for his resistance activities.

Moulin's task was not easy. By 1942 there were many personal rivalries to overcome, as well as conflicting conceptions of both organization and aims. Many resistance leaders preferred to remain independent of London; some hoped to set up their own central organization and then to negotiate with De Gaulle as his equal. In the end, however, Moulin got his way — thanks in part to the arms and money he could distribute and in part to the growing prestige of De Gaulle as national symbol. In May, 1943, the underground agreed to the creation of a National Resistance Council under Moulin's presidency, representing not only the major resistance groups but also the principal parties and trade unions. The underground paramilitary forces were also united under a single command and were shortly given the label French Forces of the Interior (F.F.I.).

Moulin's personal triumph was brief. In June, 1943, an informer led the Gestapo to a conclave of resistance leaders near Lyon; Moulin was arrested and so brutally "interrogated" that he died a few days later. The National Resistance Council, instead of waiting for De Gaulle to designate a new president, seized the initiative and promptly chose its own: Georges Bidault, a professor of history and a leading Christian democrat. Sporadic friction between the underground and De Gaulle's headquarters continued during the last year of the German occupation, but it never reached the point of a major clash. Further stresses resulted from the Communists' tendency to play a semi-autonomous role within the federated underground, and from Communist complaints that De Gaulle's agents discriminated against their *maquis* units in parachuting arms.

De Gaulle's headquarters, meanwhile, had been transferred from London to Algiers. The Allied landings in North Africa in November, 1942, had produced several months of severe tension between the Free French and the Anglo-Americans; for De Gaulle had neither been informed in advance about the expedition nor invited to participate in it. The general's sense of grievance was aggravated when the Allied command, finding Admiral Darlan on an unexpected visit to Algiers, made a pragmatic arrangement with him to call off French resistance to the landings. Still more irritating was the fact that the Americans, convinced that De Gaulle's influence in North Africa would be meager, had smuggled a rival general out of France to serve as symbol and leader of the French African war effort: Henri Giraud, a war hero who had dramatically escaped from a German prison.

After some complex negotiations all parties agreed that De Gaulle would go to Algiers to join Giraud as co-president of a new French Committee of National Liberation. Only a few months were needed to prove Giraud's total incompetence as a political leader and his almost complete lack of popular appeal. By the end of 1943 De Gaulle had skillfully elbowed him into the shadows and had firmly established his leadership of the French resistance movement both underground and overseas. The only remaining issue was the question of formal recognition by the great powers, which would enable De Gaulle to assume governmental powers as soon as the Allied armies should land in France. The British were prepared to grant such recognition well in advance of D-Day, but President Roosevelt, still suspicious of De Gaulle's motives and of his popular support, refused even *de facto* recognition until July, 1944, and *de jure* recognition until October.

During the final months at Algiers, De Gaulle and his advisers had worked out the procedure by which liberated France would be governed pending the creation of a new republican framework. The general's own temperament, and the fashion in which he had dominated the government-in-exile, fed the fears of his critics that his real aim was some kind of authoritarian regime. His plan for the postliberation era only partially alleviated these fears. It provided that the French people would determine their future by a free election, but only after the country could be cleared of the Germans, and only after two million French war prisoners and conscripted workers could be brought back from Germany. During the interim months a provisional government headed by De Gaulle would rule with virtually unrestricted authority. The Communists (and many other leftists as well) suspected that De Gaulle would prolong this interim arrangement as much as possible, with a view to getting Frenchmen accustomed to strong-man rule. Their suspicions were to prove unfounded; but on the eve of D-Day, 1944, not even De Gaulle's closest confidants could be sure of his real intentions.

When one considers the wartime stresses and strains between Free French and Anglo-Americans, and between De Gaulle and the underground movement, one has some right to be surprised that the actual process of liberation of French soil went off so smoothly. True, D-Day (June 6, 1944) came near producing an open breach between De Gaulle and Churchill, for the British informed De Gaulle of the invasion only after it had actually begun. De Gaulle's furious reaction so aroused Churchill that the latter allegedly wrote (but did not send) a letter breaking off all personal relations and ordering De Gaulle off British soil. The crisis passed; during the next few weeks Allied forces moved in from the Normandy beaches (and up from the Riviera) in close coordination with the F.F.I. guerrilla forces. Fortunately, Allied headquarters abandoned plans to set up an Anglo-American military government in France, and the liberated areas were promptly turned over to De Gaulle's representatives. In some parts of France, German troop withdrawals left a vacuum that was promptly filled by self-appointed resistance leaders, many of them Communists. De Gaulle moved rapidly to appoint his own regional representatives with orders to take over from these local committees. Some Communists wanted to resist and to strike for power, but they were overruled by the party leaders who permitted the Gaullist agents to take over with no more than a mild protest. Paris itself was liberated on August 25, when De Gaulle made his triumphal entry, marching afoot down the Champs-Élysées, flanked by the members of the National Resistance Council, while Parisians roared their enthusiasm and hunted down the last remaining Vichyite snipers on the rooftops.

Recent French history contains few episodes so dramatic and so heroic as the resistance era. Thousands of Frenchmen, moved by a vague but generous idealism and by a sense of patriotic duty, risked or gave their lives with a courage worthy of the highest cause. There were many late adherents, of course — "resisters of August 32nd," the French called them — and far more who practiced *attentisme* or fence-straddling till the very end. But more than a hundred thousand suffered deportation to concentration camps, from which only forty thousand returned; and the story of the underground is replete with accounts of real heroism.

It has sometimes been suggested, nevertheless, that the whole episode was little more than a futile and quixotic gesture; that the destiny of France would scarcely have been altered if there had been no Free French movement, no active underground at all. Such an assertion is not easy to test. It is true enough that much of the wartime idealism soon curdled; that resistance dreams of a wholly new era, a *république pure et dure,* were quickly shattered; that the Fourth Republic as a political system turned out to be not very much different from the Third. Yet it can be argued that the resistance movement, by pulling together the active elements in the nation and creating at least a temporary consensus in liberated France, did at least ensure a quick and peaceful transition from Vichy to the new republic. It may even be true that the consolidation of a single underground movement "spared France a civil war in the liberation period."[4]

Much more important were the broader or deeper consequences in the postwar era. Any nation's morale can easily disintegrate, its outlook can become badly distorted, if at moments of crisis it fails to discover within itself a civic-minded elite possessed of deep convictions and courageous enough to fight for them. There are powerful arguments for the easier road of *attentisme;* for a national policy of "rolling with the punch" or waiting for outside salvation. Still, a France totally committed to *attentisme* in those critical years might have left a heritage quite different from that derived from the resistance mystique. There is something to be said for the thesis that if France since 1945 has shown some healthy trends and signs of renewal, they are to be traced neither to Vichy nor to the straddlers, but to the men, the action, the ideals of the wartime resistance.

[4] H. Michel, *Histoire de la résistance* (Paris: Presses Univ., 1950), p. 126.

THIRTY-THREE

France is not ungovernable. It can be ruled by
skill and dissimulation.

Attributed to EX-PREMIER EDGAR FAURE

The Life and Death
of the Fourth Republic, 1944–1958

No Frenchman who lived through the liberation era in 1944–45 is
likely to forget the mood of impassioned idealism, confidence, and
hope that suffused the nation in those dramatic months. The disintegration of Vichy seemed to prove the bankruptcy of the republic's
enemies. Many ex-Vichyites who had been active in the prewar antiparliamentary leagues had gradually grown disillusioned with Pétain's
authoritarian system and had become reconciled to a return to free
institutions. The flame of the resistance seemed to have fused together
all patriotic Frenchmen, producing a unity the nation had not known
for a generation. The National Resistance Council's program for the
postwar era, embracing drastic economic and social reforms, had been
accepted by every participating group, even the representatives of the
resuscitated Moderate parties. De Gaulle as provisional president was
acclaimed with such unanimity that there was no need for a plebiscite
to buttress his authority; his was a temporary dictatorship by general
consent. The country's thirst for change was clearly illumined in the
referendum of October, 1945, when more than 96 per cent of the

527

voters rejected a return to the constitution of the Third Republic and called for a brand-new set of political institutions.

Less than fourteen years later the Fourth Republic was to come to an ignominious end when its political leadership abdicated before the threat of civil war. The enthusiasm, confidence, and hope of 1944 had long since evaporated, giving way to a mood of cynical apathy. Politics-as-usual and interest-group rivalries had taken the place of the unselfish crusading temper and the unity of purpose that had seemed to inspire the Fourth Republic's founders. Once again the idealists and the reformers had lost their faith in the existing regime and were prepared to entrust their hopes and illusions to a revolutionary change in system and leadership.

That the Fourth Republic was a disappointing failure seems, on the face of things, to be indisputable. And yet, seen in perspective, the period was one of remarkable achievement. Between 1944 and 1958 France inaugurated one of the world's first experiments in economic planning through democratic processes; France's production records were broken, and the nation enjoyed its most remarkable decade of economic growth since the 1850's; the downward population trend that had seemed to mean stagnation and decadence was dramatically reversed; a long step was taken toward the welfare state ideal by the establishment of an adequate social security system; a possible *coup de Prague* — a crisis opening the way to a Communist seizure of power, Czechoslovak fashion — was headed off; and in foreign and colonial affairs, the nation managed to absorb a whole series of setbacks that might easily have produced a kind of national neurosis. Perhaps less was done than ought to have been done; perhaps the Fourth Republic and its political leadership deserve little of the credit for what was accomplished. Yet the ironic fact remains that few regimes in history have seen so much achieved in so short a time and have gotten so little credit for it.

In a technical sense, the Fourth Republic was not established until October, 1946, when its constitution was finally proclaimed as the law of the land. But the preliminary period of provisional government that lasted from 1944 through 1946 must be seen as an integral part of the Fourth Republic's history, during which the new institutions were shaped and the new political class emerged. Indeed, these provisional years may have been the most important of the whole postwar era. For it was during those years (according to the Fourth Republic's severest critics) that the crucial decisions were made, determining the whole character of France's new regime. "All the cards in the hand of her post liberation destiny," says one such critic, "had been dealt by April 1945; it only remained for time to play them."[1] Such a view, though exaggerated, does contain a modicum of truth.

De Gaulle's dictatorship by consent lasted from the liberation of Paris (August, 1944) until the election of a Constituent Assembly (October, 1945). That Assembly promptly confirmed him in office as a kind of combined president and prime minister, much like Thiers in 1871. But sharp conflict promptly developed over policy issues and over the character of the new constitution; and in January, 1946, De Gaulle startled politicians and public alike by brusquely resigning his office and retiring to obscurity. Through the rest of 1946 a broad left-wing coalition cabinet headed by the Socialist Félix Gouin carried on the provisional government, until the new constitution was ratified and promulgated in October.

Some of De Gaulle's wartime followers had hoped that after the liberation he might found and lead a broad new centrist party, based on the common struggle against the Germans and large enough to furnish a firm governmental majority. They believed that such a movement with De Gaulle as titular head might give France the kind of stable, efficient system that had been lacking before the war. But the general quickly blighted any such hopes; refusing to lend his name or

---

[1] R. Matthews, *The Death of the Fourth Republic* (New York: Praeger, 1954), p. 199.

prestige to any party, he chose a position above the battle and preferred to let political currents swirl and eddy far beneath him. Whether
he missed a chance to build a powerful Gaullist party or coalition just
after the war is, in any case, open to question; for the unity of the
wartime resistance movement was more apparent than real, and fundamental differences of outlook began to emerge almost at once after the
liberation. It would have required a leader with all of De Gaulle's
strength but without his inflexibility to weld these disparate elements
into a single party.

The revival of the prewar parties had begun even before the liberation, and alongside them there promptly appeared several new groups
emerging from the resistance movement. The most vigorous of the
new organizations was the Mouvement Républicain Populaire or M.R.P.,
founded by a group of Christian democrats around Georges Bidault,
president of the National Resistance Council. Its program of social
reform and a directed economy indicated the strongly leftist bent of
its leaders and suggested to some Frenchmen the possibility of an
alliance or fusion with the revived Socialist party of Léon Blum, who
returned in May, 1945, from a German concentration camp. The merger,
however, was never accomplished; the heritage of distrust on the part
of both Catholics and anticlericals was too old and deep. An attempt
by some Socialists (including Blum himself) to give their party a
broader base by freeing it from the remnants of Marxian dogma and
by modelling it after the British Labour party was also blocked by
those doctrinaire party members who clung to the proletarian ideal and
to the traditional cry "no enemies on the left."

Since neither De Gaulle nor the Socialists was willing to try to build
a broad new centrist party, it was once again a fragmented center that
emerged in the Fourth Republic. The opportunities open to extremists of right and left were correspondingly enhanced. On the right, no
group appeared during the early postwar years to take advantage of the
opportunity. Most of the well-known rightists had compromised themselves during the Vichy period and were still working their passage
home. Many of them were still in disgrace and were being tried before

special courts that usually penalized them by loss of civic rights for a fixed period. In any case, the right could scarcely have bucked the strongly leftist current that swept through the country in those post-liberation months. Since Frenchmen of conservative temper had no place else to go, most of them turned to the M.R.P. as the least of evils, thus inflating the size of this new party and giving it an ambiguous character. Several years went by before French rightists recovered their vigor and self-confidence and re-entered politics under their own banner. After 1950 the newly-created Independent Republican and Peasant groups joined forces and built themselves into the strongest single conservative party republican France had ever known.

On the extreme left, the state of affairs was quite different. The Communist party, shaken and divided by its sudden plunge into revolutionary defeatism in 1939–41, had made a dramatic comeback during the resistance years. Whether its members really outdid all other Frenchmen in courage and self-sacrifice may be open to question, but at least the party had managed to create a powerful legend by 1945. No other group had so many martyrs, or declaimed so loudly about them. The new prestige of the Soviet Union also lent glamor to the French Communists, and the general trend of opinion toward the left benefited them as well. De Gaulle helped to remove the stigma of unpatriotic conduct when he gave two Communists posts in his 1944 cabinet and when he permitted Communist leader Maurice Thorez to return from Moscow despite the latter's desertion from the French army in 1939. De Gaulle's visit to Moscow in December, 1944, and his signature of a twenty-year treaty of alliance with the Soviet Union seemed further guarantees that Communists were now to be regarded as good Frenchmen. However, De Gaulle stubbornly resisted Communist pressure for one or more of the key posts in his postliberation cabinet, through which the party hoped to get control of foreign policy, the armed forces, or the police. The party line during these first postliberation years was moderate and ultra-patriotic; only a few extremists pressed for an early attempt to seize power. From their seemingly bottomless treasury, the Communists inundated the country with newspapers and pamphlets and

531

set up front organizations aimed to win support in every sector of the population. A fair number of French idealists (as one British journalist put it) were persuaded to get on the train for 1984 in the conviction that it was bound for 1848. The party's strategy and goal in those years closely paralleled those being used by the Czechoslovakian Communists.

De Gaulle, meanwhile, was governing France without much interference by any faction or governmental organ. He had established a Consultative Assembly, but its membership was not broadly representative and its powers were meager. The task of completing the liberation of French soil continued until the end of 1944, after which French forces shared in the invasion and defeat of Germany. It was this task of liberation and conquest that ranked first on De Gaulle's priority list; for above all, he believed, France's morale, self-confidence, and national greatness had to be reconfirmed. Elections were to be postponed until the return of the prisoners of war, political deportees, and conscripted laborers. Pending that time, the most pressing domestic issues were mainly economic in nature.

It was in this economic sphere that De Gaulle's decisions were least imaginative and enlightened. France emerged from the German occupation a stripped and debilitated country, desperately short of raw materials, consumer goods, and food supplies. Transportation was paralyzed; industrial production had fallen to 40 per cent of the 1938 level; a generalized black market had replaced the usual channels of trade; a disastrously inflated monetary system (the result of the Germans' legalized pillage based on exaggerated occupation costs in the 1940 armistice) threatened to bring the whole economy down into chaos. Some of these problems could not be tackled until final victory over the Axis; others — notably the monetary problem — called for immediate and drastic action. Minister of National Economy Pierre Mendès-France strongly urged such action; he recommended replacement of the inflated currency with new bank notes and the inauguration of a stringent policy of austerity. De Gaulle considered but finally rejected these recommendations, which were regarded as risky by other cabinet members and which would undoubtedly have been intensely unpopular in some circles. The spiralling inflation that followed, the lack of effective controls in a time of severe scarcity, seriously hampered the Fourth Republic during its early years.

By the autumn of 1945 most of the prisoners and deportees had been repatriated, and the initiative could pass on to the voters. The Constituent Assembly elected in October, with French women voting for the first time alongside French men, reflected the powerful leftist surge of the postwar months. Never had a French legislative body been so heavily weighted toward the left: Communists, Socialists, and M.R.P. combined drew almost three-quarters of the nation's ballots. The Communists, with 26.6 per cent of the votes cast, emerged as France's number one party; their strength had doubled since the last elections in 1936, and their support was far more generalized both sociologically and geographically. The surprising new M.R.P. ran second with 25 per cent, and the favored Socialists had to be content with third place (24 per cent).

The results gave added evidence that most Frenchmen were agreed on the need for change. But it soon became clear that they were by no means agreed on the kind of change to be accomplished. In one camp were those who held that the times called for a stronger executive, on the British or even the American model. An opposite camp urged a system of government by assembly: they wanted an all-powerful one-house legislature that would govern France directly through a kind of executive committee and would not be restrained by checks and balances. What made both alternatives unattainable was the fact that the first plan was said to be favored by De Gaulle, the second by the Communists; and both were suspected of having ulterior motives. As the Socialist patriarch Léon Blum put it, the Communists had come to be "a party of foreign nationalists," while De Gaulle "stood for democracy, but did not embody it." Between the two extremes of strong executive and all-powerful legislature, there was virtually no place to go except back to the ground on which the Third Republic had been built—to an essentially negative system of checks and balances. In the end, after several months of haggling, the Assembly wound up with such a compromise. Its constitutional draft was presented to the voters for approval or rejection in May, 1946.

In the eyes of many voters, however, the checks and balances in the new draft were not adequate to guard against the encroachment of a powerful legislature, subject to possible domination by the Communists. Spokesmen for the M.R.P. charged that the Socialists in the Constituent Assembly had been taken in by Communist blandishments; they urged the voters to reject the draft as too risky. They warned also that the constitution did not adequately guarantee property rights or the integrity of the French empire. Their vigorous campaign contributed heavily to the defeat of the draft in the May referendum; and the whole weary process of constitution-making had to begin once more. In the second Constituent Assembly elected in June the M.R.P. replaced the Communists as the largest party, but once again the third-ranking Socialists held the balance of power between them. This time Socialists and M.R.P. worked together to salvage what they could of the first constitutional draft; they sought only to write some safeguards into the system. More effective checks and balances were introduced and the structure of the refurbished French empire (rechristened the French Union) was tightened in order to avert secessionist movements. The changes were slight enough to permit the Communists in the end to vote for it, along with the Socialists and the M.R.P.

This time it was General de Gaulle who suddenly emerged from the political wilderness to denounce the draft as potentially disastrous. For the first time De Gaulle publicly sketched out the main lines of his own constitutional ideas, foreshadowing closely the system that he was to install many years later as the basic law of the Fifth Republic. The second referendum campaign in October, 1946, thus turned into a two-way struggle between the three big leftist parties on the one hand, and De Gaulle and the reawakening right on the other. The outcome was claimed as a victory by everyone: one-third of the voters accepted the constitution, almost as many voted against it, and the rest refused to go to the polls at all. The Fourth Republic had its basic law at last;

but the country's mood had shifted in two short years from passionate idealism to skeptical indifference.

This is not to suggest that nothing constructive had been achieved during those two years. A system of responsible government had been restored, despite the fears of De Gaulle's critics. A rejuvenated French army had participated in the last stage of the war, thus bolstering French pride and ensuring France a share in the occupation of Germany. A purge of Vichyite bureaucrats, business men, publicists, and intellectuals had been carried out in order to make way for a new political and administrative elite born of the resistance.[2] Most Vichy legislation had been repealed, though some of Pétain's lesser reforms were perpetuated by the republic. A spate of new daily newspapers had sprung up out of the resistance movement, seeming to give promise of a purer and more vigorous press. An important segment of the economy — coal, gas, and electricity, the four largest deposit banks, most of the insurance companies — had been nationalized by the coalition government that succeeded De Gaulle in 1946. Labor had been given a broad and coherent system of social security, as well as a voice in plant management through works committees. The first step toward economic planning had been taken by the creation of the so-called Monnet Commission, which brought together representatives of capital and labor as well as technicians to sketch out a four-year plan of investment in key branches of the economy. A new day was heralded for the overseas empire when all the overseas possessions were

[2] Vichy sympathizers have alleged that the liberation era brought the bloodiest purge France had known since Robespierre's Reign of Terror. Some of them contend that as many as 120,000 Frenchmen were executed in 1944-45, mostly by local resistance groups operating without benefit of judicial processes. There was undoubtedly a great deal of vigilante justice dispensed, and some personal scores were settled. But the number of victims almost certainly did not exceed 40,000, and among these were many informers or collaborators who had been flagrantly guilty of atrocities against the resistance groups. French special courts after the liberation sentenced 39,000 persons to prison terms, 40,000 to loss of civic rights, and 2000 to death; but fewer than 800 of the death sentences were carried out.

given representation in the two Constituent Assemblies and were thus allowed to share in drafting plans for the new French Union.

The republic's new institutions went into operation at the end of 1946. Although the constitution contained a number of gadget-type provisions designed to correct the weaknesses of the Third Republic, most of them turned out to be ineffective. Tradition and habit quickly reasserted themselves; after only two or three years the wits were remarking that the Fourth Republic was already dead and had given way to the Third. Cabinets averaged six months in duration, just as they had between the wars; power, instead of being balanced between the executive and legislative branches, was concentrated once more in the lower house of parliament, now renamed the National Assembly. The trend toward fewer and more disciplined parties that had marked the immediate postliberation period gave way to a partial return to the older system of loose and shifting party groups. Governmental reformers who had hoped to revivify local democracy by shifting some power away from Paris to the departments and communes abandoned the task as futile; the centralized tradition was far too powerful to break. Most of the resistance-born newspapers failed or were bought out by powerful economic groups; government efforts to purify the press, to treat it as a quasi-public service rather than a purely commercial enterprise, were quietly abandoned.

Still, this reversion to custom and habit had its limits; the Fourth Republic never became a mere carbon copy of its predecessor. The differences were revealed not so much in the governmental structure as in the substructure of politics: in the party system, in the evolution of social and economic relationships, in the altered psychological outlook of Frenchmen. The trend back toward the loose and amorphous multiparty structure of prewar days was checked halfway — partly because of the Fourth Republic's new electoral system (a modified form of proportional representation) and partly because of the existence

536

of a large and well-disciplined Communist movement. Parties needed to be better articulated now if they were to compete with the Communists; politicians usually needed the support of a party if they were to get themselves elected in the new enlarged electoral districts. There emerged, in consequence, a kind of "hexagonal" party system with six nationally-organized groups: Communist, Socialist, M.R.P., Radical, Independent-Peasant, and some kind of right-wing protest movement (e.g., Gaullist or Poujadist).

A second important contrast between the Fourth Republic and the Third was the striking increase in size and influence of the various interest groups. Behind the parties stood a whole congeries of professional associations representing labor, employers, farmers, small producers and distributors, white-collar elements, veterans, family associations, and other more specialized factions. These groups served as devices for indirect access to power, acting on and through the parties or, even more commonly, on and through the standing committees of parliament and the government bureaucracy. Some students of politics contended that they had become more powerful than the parties themselves, and that a kind of *de facto* corporatism was emerging in France, a more effective corporatism than the artificial variety created by Vichy. In a political system where authority was dispersed rather than concentrated in a powerful executive, the pressures of special interest groups could easily become excessive. The Fourth Republic in this respect differed from the Third in degree rather than in kind; but differences in degree can be significant.

One of the most striking political trends in postwar France was the steady shift of power from left to right, apparently reversing the historic trend in the Third Republic. Just after the liberation the left had attained what seemed to be an unchallengeable monopoly of power; the fulcrum of politics shifted much farther to the left than in the days of the Popular Front or the post-Dreyfus era. Early in 1947 the governing coalition of leftist groups was broken by the ejection of the Communists from the cabinet; the new "Third Force" coalition was made up of Socialists, M.R.P., and Radicals, with the fulcrum still to

537

the left of center. In 1951 the Socialists followed the Communists out of the coalition, leaving power in the hands of the Radicals, the M.R.P., and the Independent-Peasant bloc. In 1956 the Socialists returned to the coalition once more, but as a fourth participant rather than as a substitute for a more rightist group; the fulcrum remained to the right of center until the collapse of the regime in 1958.

A major factor in the left's weakness was, of course, its irreconcilable division between Communists and non-Communists. So long as the Communist party held its grip on a quarter of the electorate and on more than half of the proletariat, there could be neither a solidly left-wing coalition nor leftist domination of a center coalition. Yet unless some government could achieve dramatic economic and social reforms, there was little likelihood that Communist strength could be seriously undermined. A second factor contributing to the weakness of the left was the persistent electoral power of static France — of those precapitalist and early-capitalist elements on the farms, in the towns, even in the cities, that sought survival through political influence. The course of events in France since 1930 — the depression, the Vichy era — had left the static sector more deeply dug in than before, even though no more prosperous or contented. In that segment of society the craze for change and reform that had swept through France during the liberation months had quickly given way to the old defensive, protective mood.

What made the problem of government even more serious was the intermittent appearance of a powerful and aggressive right-wing movement, hostile to the parliamentary system itself. The first such movement was sponsored by De Gaulle, who re-entered politics in 1947 by organizing the Rassemblement du Peuple Français (R.P.F.). The so-called Third Force coalition was the natural reaction of the center groups to this new threat. But the center parties, themselves divided by economic and religious issues, had little room to maneuver between the Communists on the one hand and the Gaullists on the other. Condemned to live together but to avoid actions that might wreck their fragile entente, it is not surprising that *immobilisme* became the order of the day.

Yet even though the Third Force governments of 1947–51 could scarcely act, they defended themselves and the republic with remarkable pertinacity. Twice, in 1947 and again in 1948, the Communists sponsored general strikes that were probably intended to open the way to a seizure of power. Both times the threat was contained through tough measures improvised by Minister of the Interior Jules Moch. At one point Moch was allegedly prepared to abandon the whole country except a few key areas and communications routes to the Communists and to try to hold those areas by armed force; if all else failed, he was ready to call back De Gaulle as savior. Without this determined resistance by the feeble republic, France might have taken the path of Czechoslovakia or might have slipped into full-scale civil war. Against the Gaullists, the Third Force defended itself by more classic methods: namely, by tempting a sizable number of De Gaulle's followers into sharing the pleasures and benefits of power. The R.P.F. won more than a hundred seats in the National Assembly in 1951 (the first general election after it was organized as a party). Within a year a number of R.P.F. deputies accepted ministerial posts; two schisms occurred in the Gaullist parliamentary group, and De Gaulle angrily disowned the whole movement in 1953. A small remnant of the general's followers, led by Jacques Soustelle in the National Assembly and Michel Debré in the upper house of parliament, clung to their identity as a loyal Gaullist group; but the R.P.F. as a movement lost any real importance after 1953.

Meanwhile, the Third Force coalition had been replaced in 1951 by a right-center combination. Not since the period 1919–24 had the right so completely dominated French politics. The Independent-Peasant bloc, heir to the old Moderate tradition with its social and economic conservatism and its rural or small-town bent, shared power with the resuscitated but not rejuvenated Radical party and with the M.R.P., whose leftist character had eroded away in less than a decade. True, M.R.P. doctrine remained Christian democratic, and many of the party

539

leaders continued to be men of social conscience. Besides, the party had long since lost the mass of conservative hitchhikers who had climbed aboard in 1945–47; they had deserted to Gaullism or to the Independent bloc. In some ways the M.R.P. was still the most leftist Christian democratic party in Europe. Yet somehow the M.R.P. had lost much of its original crusading spirit and had become a kind of Catholic equivalent of the Radical party in the Third Republic. Perhaps this was the penalty paid for attaining a share of power too soon and for keeping it too steadily.

The most notable political episodes of the 1950's were the attempt by Pierre Mendès-France to give vigorous direction to the republic and the emergence of a new ultra-rightist protest movement led by Pierre Poujade. For some years Mendès-France had been playing a kind of Cassandra role in parliament, warning the politicians and the nation that a policy of facility, of evasion of difficult issues, of *immobilisme*, would in the end be fatal to the republic. France's resources, he insisted, were not adequate to do everything at once; *"il faut sérier les questions,"* he kept repeating, much as Gambetta had done in an earlier day. By 1954 his constant hammering began to have its effect. France faced the prospect of humiliating disaster in Indo-China, where a revolt that began in 1946 had dragged on and expanded into a full-scale war. The rebel leader, a long-time Communist named Ho Chi-Minh, got enough support from China to besiege the French stronghold of Dien-Bien-Phu and to win a major victory there in 1954. The war-weary French decided to seek an armistice, and Mendès-France became premier with liquidation of the war as his principal task.

Although the Mendès-France cabinet lasted for only seven months, it had a dramatic impact on French political life. The vigor and forthrightness with which he tackled problems shook the apathy of many Frenchmen (especially the younger generation) and seemed to suggest that all France needed was vital leadership. Not only was an Indo-Chinese armistice worked out, but the first steps were taken toward granting both Tunisia and Morocco virtual independence under a face-saving formula, thus averting potential wars for independence in those protectorates. Mendès-France's temporary influence was such that he was able to wrest control of the Radical party machinery from the older leadership, and he undertook a campaign to convert the party into a vigorous, disciplined political movement with a kind of Keynesian program of economic reform hitched to its traditional political liberalism.

The experiment failed, both quickly and completely. Once Mendès-France had extricated France from Indo-China and had announced his intention to turn to economic reform at home, he ran into a blizzard of opposition in parliament. Early in 1955 he was overthrown as premier, and was replaced by another Radical of more cautious and traditional stripe. His efforts to reshape his party led before long to severe internal strife; two discontented Radical factions seceded to form new groups, and eventually Mendès-France was dislodged from the party leadership. A small band of disciples continued to follow his lead, but the prospect of achieving a major change in direction and in the character of the Fourth Republic seemed more hopeless than ever. The failure of the Mendès-France experiment, though perhaps unavoidable, produced a kind of disillusionment among young reformers that helped to open the way three years later to the return of Charles de Gaulle.

The Poujadist episode, equally brief and in its way equally revealing to the student of political and social trends, was in essence an emotional and incoherent protest against the kind of modernizing tendency that Mendès-France represented. Pierre Poujade, a small-town shopkeeper who had fought in De Gaulle's Free French forces during the last years of the war, first won notoriety in 1953 when he rallied a group of merchants in his home town to resist the government's new tax brigades that sought to check the common practice of tax evasion. He promptly organized a regional and then a national Association for the Defense of Shopkeepers and Artisans, whose mushroom growth suggested the depth of the fears and discontent of marginal independents in France. That growth also suggested to Poujade the possibility of moving from tax resistance to active politics.

Shortly before the 1956 parliamentary elections he converted his movement into a party, entered tickets of candidates in almost every district,
and stumped the country with a vague and demagogic appeal to malcontents of every sort.

Poujade's agitation got under way just after the Gaullist R.P.F. had
disintegrated; part of his support came from ex-Gaullists who were
seeking some new organ of protest against the flabby republic. But
Poujadism and Gaullism were fundamentally different in temper and,
for the most part, in membership as well. The R.P.F. had appealed not
only to malcontents and antiparliamentarians, but also to right-wing
and even some left-wing advocates of drastic change: men who wanted
the restoration of France's greatness through reform, modernization,
expansion. Something of the same temper had marked Louis Napoleon's
supporters in the early years of the Second Empire. The Poujadist
appeal was of just the opposite character: it came as a desperate
protest by static France against the threat of change and modernization.
In part this protest had been stimulated by the agitation surrounding
the Mendès-France experiment; in part it reflected a conviction that
the whole trend of the Fourth Republic was against the little independent operator. Poujade argued (with much validity) that tax
evasion and special exemptions were essential to the survival of the
small man, since his margin was so slim; and he appealed unashamedly
to the special interests of static France. His real spiritual ancestor, as one
French political scientist has observed, was that Radical doctrinaire
of the Third Republic, Alain.

The 1956 elections gave the Poujadists a startling success. Almost
three million votes were cast for his obscure candidates; more than
fifty Poujadists won seats in the Assembly. But the disintegration of
Poujadism was to be as rapid as its growth. Poujade himself, though
a talented demagogue, showed not the slightest capacity for leadership;
and his movement contained, as one critic put it, "as much intellectual
content as a scream." Over the next two years more than half of the
Poujadist deputies deserted to other right-wing parties; Poujade himself was disastrously beaten when he ran in a Parisian by-election; the

national organization simply fell apart as its leaders groped blindly for slogans and for allies. Unfortunately, however, the generalized discontent that had produced Poujadism continued to exist and to seek another outlet for its neurotic hatred of the republic.

Meanwhile, the steady rightward trend in the government had been reversed slightly for the first time in a decade. After the 1956 elections the Socialists returned to the governing coalition and even accepted the premiership for a time. Indeed, the cabinet of Socialist Guy Mollet broke the Fourth Republic's endurance record by lasting for sixteen months. But the leftward swing was more apparent than real. The 1956 elections left the Assembly so divided into six roughly equal groups that it was impossible to form any kind of majority cabinet without getting four parties into it. Force of necessity rather than change of direction caused the broadening of the coalition, which from 1956 to 1958 included Socialists, M.R.P., Radicals, and Independent-Peasants. This was a kind of reversion to the Third Force model, but with a much heavier weighting toward the right. The incoherence of this cumbersome arrangement condemned the government to *immobilisme* of the worst sort, for no vigorous action was possible without alienating one component party. Mollet stayed in office merely because there seemed to be no workable alternative and because he suspended any attempt to carry out his own party's program. When at last he sought to introduce some economic measures designed to alleviate labor unrest, he was promptly overthrown, and a new coalition under an obscure Radical politician was painfully patched together.

In quiet times this sort of makeshift government might have carried on indefinitely; for France was prosperous, booming beyond the memory of almost any living Frenchman. Poujadist discontent persisted, but it represented the past, not the future; in the long run Poujadism was doomed by economic expansion and by the steady growth of the population. Chronic inflation persisted, too, and weak governments were unlikely to risk painful correctives; but inflation rarely becomes a serious threat to a regime unless it becomes uncontrollable. The decisive factor in the destruction of the Fourth Republic came from outside France proper; to be precise, from across the Mediterranean, in Algeria. The Fourth Republic was destroyed not by its chronic internal ailments, but by its colonial wars.

Since the end of 1946 French forces had been fighting almost constantly against rebellion in some part of overseas France. The Indo-China uprising had dragged on from 1946 to 1954 and had ended in only partially concealed disaster; revolt in Algeria had broken out late in 1954 and had steadily gained strength in spite of all efforts at repression. What seemed to be the natural solution for Algeria — the same kind of virtual independence that had been granted to Tunisia and Morocco in 1955 — was obstructed by the presence of more than a million European settlers in Algeria, where many of these *colon* families had lived for four generations. When Guy Mollet became premier in 1956 he made an abortive attempt to seek peace by negotiation with the rebels; but the *colons* greeted him with overripe fruit and threats of violence when he visited Algiers, and his conservative cabinet colleagues demanded repressive measures. The bulk of the French army (almost a half-million men) was transferred to Algeria in a futile attempt to corner the small guerrilla army of the rebels. The rebels' decision to resort to terrorism in its more barbarous forms, both in Algeria and in France itself, embittered the contest and produced some counter-atrocities by French troops. By 1958 the drain on French finances, on manpower, and on morale was clearly beginning to portend disaster. A few Frenchmen dared to speak out for a negotiated peace; far more of them admitted privately that the struggle was hopeless, but they feared to say so publicly; the rest (probably a majority) insisted that the fight go on and that Algeria remain French forever.

The key role in the revolution of 1958 was to be played by the French army. This was a fact almost without precedent in modern French history; the army, unlike those in certain other nations, had carefully avoided either direct or indirect intervention in politics and had loyally served each successive regime whether or not it liked that regime. Most members of the officer corps would probably have preferred to go on in that tradition. But years of defeat, of courageous

but futile campaigns, had gradually produced a state of advanced
neurosis. Some of the officers had been fighting almost constantly since
1939 and had known almost nothing but failure. Many of them had
been serving in Africa or in Asia for almost two decades, and had
lost touch with civilian society as with France itself. There was a widespread sentiment among them that the weak and scheming politicians
and the untrustworthy intellectuals of Paris had sacrificed the army by
giving it one hopeless assignment after another and by failing to
furnish the material and moral support needed to do the job. The right
kind of appeal made at the right moment might turn the armed forces
to revolutionary action.

Plots against the regime were already simmering well before 1958.
The schemers (some of them serious men, some of them fanatics and
eccentrics) were for the most part either civilians or ex-soldiers; but a
few officers on active duty had indicated their sympathy. Several different clandestine groups were operating in Paris or Algiers — some of
them overlapping, some of them working at cross purposes, but all of
them dedicated to revolutionary change. Certain groups looked to
De Gaulle as symbol and savior (though De Gaulle, quietly engaged
in writing his memoirs at his country villa, refused them either real or
moral support). Other groups (notably those with a Vichyite heritage)
were bitterly anti-Gaullist and favored an army coup d'état to be
followed by the establishment of some sort of ruling junta.

The opportunity for action came unexpectedly, while the plans of
the revolutionaries were still maturing. A cabinet crisis in April, 1958,
created a kind of vacuum in Paris; negotiations dragged on for a month
before a new coalition (scarcely different from its predecessor) could
be patched together. The designation of the M.R.P. deputy Pierre
Pflimlin as premier offered the activists a chance to strike, since it was
rumored that Pflimlin favored negotiating with the Algerian rebels. A
confusing series of rival plots converged in Algiers on May 13, the day
set for Pflimlin's first appearance before the National Assembly.
Extremist leaders organized a mammoth demonstration outside the
main government building in Algiers; the demonstration turned into a

545

riot, the building was invaded and sacked, and a revolutionary Committee of Public Safety was proclaimed.

Over the next two weeks a complex series of negotiations went on both between Algiers and Paris and in Algiers itself. The anti-Gaullist element wanted a complete break with Paris and a paratroop operation to seize the capital as well as other major French cities. Gaullist agents preferred to use the threat of violence to achieve a bloodless revolution; they hoped that the Fourth Republic's leaders could be persuaded to abdicate power to De Gaulle. The general himself adopted an aloof and ambiguous position; he made it plain that he would refuse to return to power either through a violent coup d'état or through the slow and cumbersome processes of the constitution. His aim, apparently, was to wait until the politicians would voluntarily abdicate to him.

In the end the Gaullist agents proved to be the cleverest maneuverers. Aided by key men in the army high command in Algiers (notably Generals Massu and Salan), they elbowed their way into control of the Algiers Committee of Public Safety, averted a complete breach with Paris, and opened the way for a peaceful transfer of authority. A solution by force was, however, only narrowly averted; at one point, plans were complete and a date was set for a paratroop landing around Paris ("Operation Resurrection") and for a simultaneous advance on Paris by various military units stationed in the provinces. A successful coup by rebel sympathizers in Corsica on May 24 speeded the eventual solution, for Premier Pflimlin was unable to get the insurrection in hand despite his best efforts. President René Coty, working desperately against time in an effort to avert civil war, managed to persuade Pflimlin and his cabinet to resign in favor of De Gaulle, while De Gaulle in turn was persuaded to accept office via the normal route (i.e., designation by the president and approval by the National Assembly). Operation Resurrection, twice postponed at the last minute, was called off for good on May 29; and on June 1 De Gaulle was confirmed as premier by an Assembly vote of 329 to 224.

Technically speaking, De Gaulle took office as the last premier of the Fourth Republic. In reality, that regime went into suspended animation on June 1, when the National Assembly voted the new government full powers for six months. De Gaulle was entrusted with the task of drafting a new constitution for approval by popular referendum; the Assembly adjourned *sine die*, never to reconvene. Only once before, in 1870, had France experienced a completely bloodless revolution. If there is any historical parallel for the events of 1958, however, it would not be that of 1870 but rather of 1940. There was considerable irony in the fact that De Gaulle arrived in power much as Pétain had done — by the abject surrender, the abdication, the suicide of the members of parliament. But the validity of the parallel is limited by the difference in circumstances, and above all by the difference of purpose between the two soldiers who thus assumed power at a moment of crisis. Pétain took office to save the nation by destroying the republic and substituting an authoritarian regime. De Gaulle's aim was to save the nation by bolstering the republic — by giving it the leadership and the firmness to avert either authoritarian substitutes or civil war.

THIRTY-FOUR

> Thus the urgent, the critical dilemma hangs over
> France today: To change and, in changing, die; or
> not to change, and risk a swifter death.
>
> DAVID LANDES

Silent Revolution or Quiet Stagnation?
Social and Economic Trends,
1945–1960

France, long after entering the twentieth century, still seemed to prefer living in the nineteenth. The brief but impressive industrial boom of the decade after 1900 had given way to a generation of stagnation. In 1938 the gross national product was only 6 per cent greater than in 1913. By almost every statistical test, a quarter-century had been devoted to standing still. The Great War had intervened, of course, and was at least partially responsible; it had set back French economic growth by almost a decade. But the war alone was not enough to explain the failure of France to evolve and expand along with other Western industrial nations and to move into the modern age.

France in 1960, whatever its problems and its shortcomings, could no longer be described as a hopelessly stagnant nation. Despite the fact that another great war had intervened, a remarkable era of growth had begun with the Fourth Republic. By most statistical tests, France had been converted into a nation of change, of dynamic progress. Industrial production was almost double that of 1938; farm yields were rising slowly but steadily despite a continuous decline in the number of

Frenchmen on the land; population growth had been continuous since 1946. More important still (though less easily measurable) was the evidence of psychological change — of a new spirit of comprehension of the twentieth-century world and of how an old nation might be adapted to it. All of these convergent factors were beginning to break up the congealed economy and society of the previous generation. In Raymond Aron's phrase, there were clear signs that a silent revolution was taking place in France.

Just when and how this process had begun was not easy to determine. Demographers were inclined to see the new population trend as basic; they argued that a willingness to raise larger families reflected a new sense of confidence in the future and would eventually force Frenchmen to accept an expanding economy and a more open society. The slackening population curve of the century 1846–1946 (during which time the French population had grown by only 15 per cent) was brusquely transformed into a sharply rising curve that boosted the total population from forty to forty-four million in a decade. France's motto, someone remarked, had evidently been modified to read *"liberté, égalité, maternité."* Why Frenchmen should have suddenly altered their deep-rooted habits is not fully clear; but part of the explanation was doubtless economic in nature. One of the last acts of the Third Republic, in 1939, had been the adoption of the so-called family code, generalizing and expanding the family allotment system. Both Vichy and the Fourth Republic preserved and improved this system, thus stimulating a remarkable increase in the birth rate. A more gradual decline in the infant mortality rate (and in the death rate generally) contributed also to population growth. To correct the distortion in France's population pyramid would require a continuation of the new trend over several generations; but a significant start had been made.

Another source of the new spirit, of the urge toward change and growth, may be found in the wartime resistance movement. If few Frenchmen in the underground had any real grasp of the nature of France's postwar problems and needs, at least there was an active elite whose crusading mood was receptive to novelty and progress. The

549

resistance talked much about "structural reforms," about stripping the "economic feudalities" of their overweening and repressive power, of building a new and better society as well as a new governmental system. Too often the difficulties of the task were oversimplified, and it was assumed that political reforms plus the nationalization of monopolies would do the job. Eventually there was to be some disillusionment when such simple remedies proved to be inadequate. Still, the resistance spirit, with its self-reliance and its drive to restore French greatness, forced that elite to delve steadily deeper into the foundations of the country's weakness. If the resistance movement failed to sweep away the old political class and to substitute a brand-new set of politicians, it was more successful in producing a new administrative class — a set of technicians, bureaucrats, and managers in both government and industry whose goal was to adapt France to the modern era.

One of the first and most important products of the new spirit was the creation in 1946 of the Planning Commission, headed for several years by the business man Jean Monnet. This agency, with only a small staff of economists and technicians, drew heavily on the advice of industrial and labor representatives as it shaped its projects. Its first four-year plan for development and modernization was approved by general acclamation, even though the plan involved a long step toward a directed economy. The goal of the planners was to channel investment, both public and private, into certain basic sectors of the economy: such sectors as coal, electricity, steel, and farm machinery. The announced target was an increase in the gross national product of 14 per cent over the 1929 peak figure. A second and then a third plan followed during the 1950's, with investment channelled more broadly into consumer goods, housing, farm production, and overseas development. Although a number of hitches developed during the early stages, and although economists and politicians differed over the degree of success achieved, Frenchmen generally agreed that planning had contributed to economic growth and that it had come to stay.

While public funds played an important role in this developmental process, an increasing share of modernization capital came from private

550

financing. A growing number of French business men shook off their traditional caution and were gradually converted to the gospel of productivity preached by young technicians and by United States missions financed through the Marshall Plan. The example of mushroom growth furnished by German business after 1948 also had its impact on French industrialists. By the end of 1952 (the terminus of the first modernization plan) industrial production exceeded the 1929 all-time maximum by 8 per cent. From 1953 onward, aided by a brief interlude of stable prices unique in the postwar era, French industry entered upon an era of growth unprecedented since the 1850's. Something of the same entrepreneurial spirit that had marked the age of Napoleon III pervaded this new decade; for a time the rate of increase in productivity equalled that of West Germany and outstripped that of any other country in free Europe.

Gains were made in the public as well as the private sector of the economy. For some years after the wave of nationalizations in 1945–46 it had seemed that public ownership might create more problems than it solved. Most of the public enterprises operated for a time at a heavy deficit that had to be covered from the public treasury; politics invaded the boards of directors, and interest groups engaged in successful logrolling tactics at the expense of the taxpayer. But sizable investments and improved managerial techniques eventually gave the public sector a more solid base and quieted the criticism of those who had argued that public and private enterprise could not possibly coexist. Some problems of supervision, of policy formulation, and of labor relations persisted, but the permanence of the mixed economy seemed assured.

The task of renovating an old economy and society was not, however, an easy one. Habit and prejudice, as well as vested interests, were built-in obstacles to change. Many Frenchmen remained persuaded that "balance" and "harmony" were higher virtues than modernization and growth and that a healthy democracy must be based on a bedrock of small independent operators — family farmers, shopkeepers, artisans. The young technicians and modernizers they regarded as

551

"sorcerer's apprentices," thoughtlessly releasing forces of mechanization and monopoly that would soon be uncontrollable. This kind of
social philosophy was deply rooted and widely distributed in France;
its appeal was reflected in the revival of the Radical party and the
reappearance of the traditionalist right wing in politics.

Just as powerful as this genuine doctrinal opposition to basic
change was the more practical force of special interest, derived in the
main from inertia and fear. The slow evolution of France's economy
and society during the Third Republic had left great segments of the
nation almost untouched. The survival of this static sector had been
ensured before 1940 by a governmental policy of protectionism and
subsidy. Static France emerged intact into the postwar era, sheltered
behind a barbed-wire entanglement of special privilege and reinforced
rather than weakened by the effects of the Great Depression and of
Vichy reforms. Planners and reformers can more easily attack vested
interests when those interests are represented by a wealthy minority
than when they are represented by a great mass of little men, by millions of citizens imbued with the democratic ideal and possessed of the
ballot. The restoration of responsible government in 1945 provided
static France with a powerful weapon against change, for a majority
of politicians (especially those of the center and right-wing groups)
could not attain or stay in office without its support.

The more impatient reformers quickly grew disillusioned at these
serious roadblocks in the way of progress, and they wrote despairingly
of the nation's "ideal of painless immobility," of France as a country
"dedicated to the survival of the unfit." Weak governments, they contended, had been content with mere palliatives; the politicians had
appeased their right-wing voters by protecting the static sector and had
placated the left by handing out pensions, bonuses, and wage increases.
They complained that population growth, which began to level off
after 1953, was not great enough to force fundamental change; it would
take 160 years, Alfred Sauvy calculated, for France's population density to reach that of Germany and England. One journalist dramatized
France's dilemma by dividing the country into two contrasting sec-

DYNAMIC vs STATIC FRANCE

Relative standing of French departments
in total per capita production (1948~49)
(Base 100 = average for France as a whole)

GERMANY

BELGIUM

LUXEMBOURG

English Channel

Manche

Pas de Calais

Somme

Seine Inférieure

Aisne

Ardennes

Oise

Calvados

Eure

Seine et Oise

PARIS

Marne

Meuse

Moselle

Meurthe et Moselle

Bas-Rhin

Orne

Eure et Loire

Seine et Marne

Aube

Haute Marne

Vosges

Haut Rhin

Finistère

Côtes Du Nord

Ille et Vilaine

Mayenne

Sarthe

Loiret

Yonne

Côte d'Or

Haute Saône

Morbihan

Loire Inférieure

Maine et Loire

Loir et Cher

Indre et Loire

Cher

Nièvre

Doubs

Jura

SWITZERLAND

Vendée

Deux Sèvres

Vienne

Indre

Cher

Allier

Saône et Loire

Ain

Haute Savoie

Charente-Inférieure

Charente

Haute Vienne

Creuse

Puy de Dôme

Loire

Rhône

Savoie

Isère

ITALY

Bay of Biscay

Corrèze

Cantal

Haute Loire

Ardèche

Drôme

Hautes Alpes

Dordogne

Lot

Lozère

Basses Alpes

Alpes Maritimes

Gironde

Lot et Garonne

Tarn et Garonne

Aveyron

Gard

Vaucluse

Bouches du Rhône

Var

Landes

Gers

Haute Garonne

Tarn

Hérault

Basses Pyrénées

Hautes Pyrénées

Ariège

Aude

SPAIN

Pyrénées Orientales

Mediterranean Sea

Dynamic departments (index 110 or above)
Average departments (index 90 to 110)
Static departments (index 90 or below)

SCALE OF MILES
0   50   100   150   200

Based on a study made by the Institut National
de la Statistique et des Etudes Economiques, L'Espace
économique français (Paris: Presses Univ., 1951).

tions: a small area of nineteen departments in the northeast, from Paris
to the Belgian frontier, and a larger area composed of the remaining
seventy-one departments of center, west, and south. The first section,
he observed, contained less than 20 per cent of the nation's territory
but 38 per cent of its population and almost half of its total productive
capacity. As a separate state, it would compare favorably with any
rival in western Europe; in structure and standards, it would resemble
Denmark or West Germany. But this dynamic area was condemned
to drag behind it the static bulk of France, outmoded and stagnant,
more like Portugal or southern Italy than like an advanced industrial
society.

This schematic division overstated and oversimplified the contrast
between the two Frances, the static and the dynamic. Not all of the
vigorous enterprise was confined to the northeast; stagnancy and
change coexisted almost everywhere. Yet the scheme contained a basic
element of validity; and natural trends during the postwar years made
the contrast more rather than less striking. Capital, manpower, and
enterprise were inclined to flow more readily to the dynamic areas,
which meant that the gap in productivity and living standards grew
greater rather than less. This trend was by no means new; for a
century at least, there had been a steady drain of population and
resources out of the static areas which, by the loss of their most enterprising young people, were rendered steadily more backward. More
than two-thirds of the departments of France in 1960 had a lower
population than in 1880; the decline sometimes exceeded 50 per cent.

The task of the planners and reformers was vastly increased by
this curious heritage from the past and by the dominant political role
played by the static sector. Any attempt to reverse the population flow
and to modernize the more backward areas was bound to be costly and
slow, for it ran counter to natural economic trends; it could be done
only if dynamic France would bear the cost of raising static France
to a higher level and if static France could be persuaded to accept
change. On the other hand, any decision to strip away the barriers of
protection and privilege that sheltered the backward areas and to let

free competitive forces have their way would have been politically suicidal.

It is scarcely surprising, therefore, that the Fourth Republic carried through no revolutionary modification of France's economic and social structure. What is surprising is that so much change did occur during the postwar years, partly through governmental efforts but mainly through the operation of natural forces. Not even the barbed-wire entanglement of tariffs, subsidies, and exemptions sufficed to protect the most marginal forms of enterprise against extinction. From the late 1940's onward there set in a steady decline in the number of small farms, small shops, and small handicraft plants in the country. The flow of population from agriculture into industry and commerce, suspended for a time during the war, resumed once again at about the prewar rate. Government planners meanwhile sought to reinvigorate depressed areas by encouraging the decentralization of industry, by sponsoring regional planning that would take advantage of special resources, and by exerting pressure toward more rational farming and a better distribution of crops.

Evolution rather than revolution has been the keynote of this recent period. If static France has been steadily losing its dominant place, the change has been so gradual that it resembles geological erosion. Until that process of erosion reaches the point where the dynamic element in France comes to dominate the nation's political life and psychological outlook, the static sector must continue to be a source of serious tension and of neurotic fears. Those fears have produced such demagogic movements as that of Poujade, and they have contributed to the strength of extremist groups like the Communist party, which manages simultaneously to preach dynamic change and the protection of the little man against the big monopolist. Those same fears have also buttressed the right-of-center political parties that increasingly dominated the coalition governments of the Fourth Republic in its later years. Decades rather than years may be needed to carry through this gradualist "silent revolution" that erodes away the old structures surviving from nineteenth-century France, and, still more

555

important, that alters the minds of Frenchmen, the outlook and hopes of the nation.

꧁ꋖ꧂ ꧁ꋖ꧂ ꧁ꋖ꧂

If the postwar era brought no revolutionary change in the over-all pattern of French society, it did bring some modifications within that pattern. The most notable of these was the increased rigidity and influence of the professional organizations representing various economic and social strata. In an era of mass democracy, the emergence of such a quasi-corporative structure may be inevitable; individual farmers, workers, business men, sense a need for group effort in a highly organized technological system. Despite the persistent hold of that ferocious individualism whose spirit was so well expressed by Alain, postwar France experienced a clear tendency toward the crystallization of powerful interest groups.

No element in society had resisted organization so long and so effectively as the farmers. Some people have argued that the Vichy regime, which introduced a state-sponsored and virtually compulsory Peasant Corporation, was responsible for the change in the countryside. Well before Vichy, however, there were signs of a new outlook among the peasantry. The unsettling impact of the First World War and of the Great Depression had begun the slow process of converting the farmers from a passive and negative social force into an active and organized body. The first step was usually membership in a local cooperative or mutual-aid group, which involved only a slight commitment to joint action. The second step, already taken by a minority of peasants before 1940, was membership in a regional or national professional organization or in a specialized producers' group like the Winegrowers' Confederation. Some farmers in the 1930's also became active in a small Agrarian party or in other parties with rival reform programs.

The real surge toward organization and unity occurred just after the liberation, when the government sponsored the creation of a new

THE DECHRISTIANIZATION
OF RURAL FRANCE

GERMANY

BELGIUM

LUXEMBOURG

English Channel

Pas de Calais

Somme

Seine Inférieure

Aisne

Ardennes

Oise

Manche

Calvados

Eure

Seine et

PARIS

Marne

Meuse

Moselle

Bas-

Orne

Eure et Loire

Seine et Marne

Aube

Haute Marne

Vosges

Meurthe et Moselle

Rhin

Haut Rhin

Finis-tère

Côtes Du Nord

Ille et Vilaine

Mayenne

Sarthe

Loiret

Yonne

Côte d'Or

Haute Saône

Doubs

Morbihan

Loire Inférieure

Maine et Loire

Indre et Loire

Cher

Nièvre

Cher

Saône et Loire

Jura

SWITZERLAND

Vendée

Deux Sèvres

Vienne

Indre

Allier

Ain

Haute Savoie

Charente Inférieure

Charente

Haute Vienne

Creuse

Puy de Dôme

Loire

Rhône

Savoie

Isère

ITALY

Bay of

Biscay

Gironde

Dordogne

Corrèze

Cantal

Haute Loire

Ardèche

Drôme

Hautes Alpes

Landes

Lot et Garonne

Lot

Aveyron

Lozère

Gard

Vaucluse

Basses Alpes

Alpes Maritimes

Gers

Tarn et Garonne

Tarn

Hérault

Bouches du Rhône

Var

Basses Pyrénées

Haute Garonne

Aude

Hautes Pyrénées

Ariège

Pyrénées Orientales

S P A I N

Mediterranean Sea

"Christian parishes" (majority of adults attend mass and confession).

"Partially-dechristianized areas" (minority of adults attend mass).

"Missionary areas" (few adults attend mass; many children raised outside the church).

SCALE OF MILES
0   50   100   150   200

Based on Abbé F. Boulard, Essor ou déclin du clergé français? (Paris: Cerf, 1950), p. 169. Boulard's survey ignores the urban areas and the Protestant minority.

General Confederation of Agriculture (C.G.A.). For a time the C.G.A. claimed that 80 per cent of all French farmers belonged to its various subsidiary branches. The initial enthusiasm soon withered, however; perhaps as many as half of the members dropped out, and the C.G.A.'s organizers lost their fight to assert centralized control over all farm organizations. By the mid-1950's the subsidiary groups had asserted their autonomy, and the divisions of prewar days had returned. The National Federation of Farmers' Unions (F.N.S.E.A.) emerged as the most influential of the C.G.A.'s branch units; it was dominated by the more prosperous family farmers with right-center political leanings. The more left-of-center farm elements preferred to channel their energies into a revived Federation of Mutual Aid Societies and Cooperatives. Communist efforts to infiltrate the various farm organizations did not get very far, except for a brief period after the liberation. They kept some influence in a Tenants' and Sharecroppers' Union and managed to dominate the largest union of farm laborers. The most effective of all farm interest groups, however, continued to be those of a specialized character, representing the growers of wheat or sugar-beets or wine. Unlike the more general associations, these specialized groups could agree on a simple and precise set of demands and could orchestrate their propaganda activities in press and parliament.

No single farmers' organization was likely to fuse the loyalties of all French peasants, if only because the peasantry continued to be the most variegated (and perhaps the most individualistic) social category in France. No program could possibly appeal to large and small farmers alike, to owners, tenants, and sharecroppers, to modern mechanized operators and primitive marginal peasants, to both single-crop and polycultural enterprisers. Widely varying political and religious traditions in different rural areas added to the almost infinite complexity of the peasant pattern.

But if French agriculture continued to be "a museum with exhibits from every period since the Middle Ages," the postwar year brought convincing evidence of an evolution more rapid than any the French countryside had ever known. The new trend toward organization was only one aspect of a profound psychological conversion that was broadening the outlook of many farmers and that was pulling them — unwillingly, in some cases — into a market economy. Improved channels of communication, travel, and indoctrination were having their effects on the once-isolated village. Changing times were forcing upon them at least a dim understanding of national and international economic relationships and of the farmer's role in the nation. The propagandistic and organizational efforts of the Communists, the Catholics, and the government were producing a new awareness of rural social and economic problems and were stimulating the rise of a young rural elite. If the result of this new awareness was often an aggrieved sense of inferiority and of injustice, at least it was accompanied by a novel determination to modernize the rural sector and to make farm life as attractive as city life. Long-term economic trends reinforced this changed outlook, for the steady disappearance of marginal farms was accompanied by a slow growth in the number of medium-sized farms and in the degree of mechanization. There were signs that the nation's agrarian structure was moving gradually toward that of countries like Denmark. There was some reason to believe that within a generation the typical peasant would no longer be a gnarled old man clinging to his scattered strips of soil outside a decaying, depressing village, but rather a young and enterprising farmer concerned with improved techniques, with marketing problems, and with the state of the profession to which he belonged.

❖❂❖❖❂❖❖❂❖

The industrial labor force, the only segment of French society that outnumbered the French peasantry, experienced less dramatic changes during the postwar era; yet here, too, there were signs of significant evolution. Labor emerged from the Second World War at the peak of its prestige and full of hope for a labor-dominated state. Many workers had played a heroic role in the resistance; the wind was blowing strongly toward social reform; and the business class was chastened by its Vichyite associations. Workingmen flocked into the C.G.T. and, to a lesser extent, into the Catholic C.F.T.C.; the membership figures reached 5,500,000 and 750,000 respectively. Never before, not even during the euphoria of the Popular Front, had so large a proportion of workers been unionized. A series of wage increases and social reforms promulgated in 1944–46 gave labor more security and greater power than it had ever before possessed in France.

Once again, however, labor's hopes of a new era were rapidly dimmed. The cause was, in part, a natural lassitude after the enthusiastic surge of the liberation period. In part it grew out of the reviving strength of the business group and the middle classes, which reasserted their rights against labor's demands. In part it was the product of labor's own division after a brief and atypical period of near-unity. In 1945 the Communists wrested control of the C.G.T. from the older, more moderate syndicalist leadership, and they set out to use the organization for partisan purposes. Cooperation between the C.G.T. and the C.F.T.C. was, in consequence, seriously undermined. In 1948 the anti-Communist element within the C.G.T. seceded to form a rival group called Workers' Force (C.G.T.-F.O.), with syndicalist leanings and unofficial Socialist ties. Interunion squabbles replaced labor unity, and over the years that followed there was a steady drain of membership. Once again, as through most of modern French history, the biggest union came to be "the union of the unorganized."

Labor's interests were further injured by the steady shift of political power toward the right. The Communist party, which kept the support of more than half of the working class throughout the Fourth Republic, was out of the governing coalition after 1947. No other party was primarily a working-class movement with a program devoted to the interests of labor. Cabinets dominated by center and right-of-center groups were naturally inclined to favor the middle classes and the farmers. Labor was, of course, partly responsible for this state of affairs. By voting stubbornly for the Communists, the bulk of the working class isolated itself and sterilized its potential political influence. It refused to believe that support of any non-Communist party would give labor a really effective voice. This alienation of much of the French working class from the state had become so deep-seated as to be almost neurotic; the workers preferred to be "domestic émigrés" rather than to be hoodwinked again (as they saw it) by the bourgeoisie. The origins of this neurosis are easy to find in the modern history of France.

If labor believed, however, that its interests were being cynically ignored and brutally overridden by rival social groups, it was distorting the facts. The welfare-state mystique has had a wide and deep impact in postwar France; in consequence, labor has fared much better than might have been expected in an era of labor weakness. It was a cabinet of the right-center that instituted (in 1952) a reform long sought by labor — a sliding wage scale, linked to the cost-of-living index. It was a Third Force cabinet that restored collective bargaining, suspended since prewar days. The major gains secured by labor in the liberation era were all preserved when political power shifted to the right. Furthermore, the working class shared to a considerable degree in the benefits of the great production boom of the 1950's. Nothing is more difficult to secure than dependable figures on real wages, but the best available statistics suggest that the over-all real wage level of 1938 had been regained by 1951 and had been considerably surpassed by the middle 1950's. Government figures even indicated that at the height of the boom (1953–56), French wage earners were making more rapid gains than workers anywhere else in the world. For the first time opinion polls indicated a widespread belief among French workers that expanding production might be something more than a capitalists' scheme to increase profits — that a growing economy might, in fact, benefit all participating classes. There were signs that some workers were crossing a kind of barrier into a new bourgeois style of life, as they began to buy refrigerators, motor scooters, even automobiles, and on credit at that. Whether this *embourgeoisement*, this rise in material standards and aspirations, represented a gain or a threat to French civilized values remained a matter for debate; but it opened the possibility, at least, of an eventual softening of class conflict, of an eroding of the barrier between proletariat and bourgeoisie.

The prognosis of the late 1950's for French labor could not, however, be unrestrainedly optimistic. The new cycle of inflation that set in after mid-decade — the product, in part, of the Algerian war's drain, but the product also of the boom itself — checked the rise in real wages, for price increases cancelled out any monetary gains. General averages concealed the fact that far too many workers' families were still subsisting on a marginal standard. The contrast between wealth and poverty remained obvious enough to convince suspicious workers that labor was getting only the crumbs of economic growth. The steady deterioration of middle- and lower-class housing in the cities, and the failure of either public authorities or private enterprise to build adequate new low-cost housing, intensified both social problems and class resentment. Infant mortality figures in Paris (1954) continued to show a startling class differential; they ranged from 20.7 per thousand for children of the managerial group to 48.7 per thousand for children of unskilled workers. Meanwhile, trade-union squabbles and Communist efforts to "politicize" the C.G.T. led to growing apathy rather than to an attempt to make the unions democratic and effective. "A true democracy," warned one eminent French economist, "cannot be built so long as the most disfavored citizens put their class status ahead of their membership in the national community."[1] Yet the task of converting the working class from an alienated bloc of domestic émigrés into a healthy and active segment of the French community seemed likely to require a long process of evolution and effort.

❧

The social groups that had put their special stamp on France throughout the modern era were those commonly categorized as "the bourgeoisie." During the Third Republic they had furnished most of

[1] J.-M. Jeanneney, *Forces et faiblesses de l'économie française* (Paris: Colin, 1956), p. 270.

the nation's political class, most of its bureaucratic personnel, almost all of its economic leadership. Frenchmen, despite their deep-rooted theoretical attachment to the egalitarian principle, had become accustomed to living in a fairly rigid society that permitted, but scarcely encouraged, rapid upward mobility. Children of farm or factory families might work their way up the social ladder in two or three generations, but rarely in one. Most of them did not even presume to try.

One aspect of the resistance mystique and of the liberation era was a deepened and intensified egalitarian spirit. Men of every social origin had worked together in the underground: engineers, intellectuals, farmers, workers, learned to judge one another as men rather than as products of a class. Those idealists who were busy planning the new *république pure et dure* were agreed that careers should really be open to talents. There was much talk of creating a thoroughly democratic educational system that would no longer separate the sons of workers from those of the bourgeoisie. One of the early postliberation reforms was the nationalization of the old École Libre des Sciences Politiques, the privately-operated graduate school that had largely monopolized the training of high civil servants and diplomats during the Third Republic. Its successor, the École Nationale d'Administration, was designed to draw its students from every social category; admission was to depend on ability alone, and successful candidates were to be put on the state payroll while being trained.

Political life, too, seemed more easily accessible to all classes at the outset of the Fourth Republic. In the first elected assemblies of the postwar era, factory and office workers and teachers outnumbered the lawyers, notaries, and landowners who had usually dominated the old parliament. In business, the grip of the old bourgeois families was shaken by the nationalization of about one-fifth of France's productive capacity and by the promotion of at least some new men to high managerial posts in state-owned enterprise. Even in private industry, the institution of Works Committees suggested that control would be shared with elected representatives of the labor force.

Here again, as in so many other respects, most of the hopes of the liberation era proved to be illusory. By the end of the Fourth Republic it was clear that no dramatic increase in the degree of social mobility had been achieved. If the various segments of the bourgeoisie no longer controlled all the levers of political and economic power, they had recovered a good share of their prewar influence in both spheres. If the sons of the middle and upper bourgeoisie no longer monopolized the training schools that prepared for entrance into the higher civil service, they far outnumbered the sons of workers there. Indeed, few farm or factory children found their way into any kind of higher education; primary school, with sometimes a year or two of trade school, was all that most of them could expect. In industry and commerce, the number of successful self-made men remained meager.

Yet there were two potentially hopeful signs: one of them psychological, the other structural. The first involved a change in the bourgeois outlook; the second involved the gradual conversion of the French economy from a static, closed system to an indefinitely expanding one.

The structural change, many Frenchmen believed, would in the long run produce a slow revolution in the nature of French society. An economy dedicated to growth and productivity offers steadily expanding opportunities for social mobility; the static ideal of the checkerboard, with a fixed number of squares for a stationary number of players, is forced to give way. Population growth is likely to create additional pressure for a steadily expanding system, with more jobs and fewer restrictions on the chance to rise. The trend may be encouraged by the erosion of France's protective trade barriers and the gradual merger of the French economy with that of western Europe. Skeptics like the demographer Alfred Sauvy continued to warn that the process of change was far too slow to offset the nation's endemic weaknesses. But optimists insisted that no other generation in modern French history had faced the prospect of such extensive alterations in the structure of society and the attitudes of all social groups.

The psychological change within the postwar bourgeoisie had already been foreshadowed during the interwar years by the emergence of a small technocratic element in business and in the civil service and the founding of an organization of progressive factory owners called the Jeunes Patrons. Both groups were inspired by the challenge and the complexities of the modern industrial system; both were impatient to adapt France's economy and society to the new age. Many of the prewar technocrats were more concerned with efficiency than liberty, more interested in ends than in means; and a large number of them were swept into the futile Vichy experiment. Some of them survived and lived down that aberration; they were joined by a new and younger group of economists, managers, and experts who entered business or government just after the liberation and who quietly worked their way up to positions of great influence.

Whether the new generation of technocrats still rated efficiency as a higher good than liberty remained unclear; but the ability and drive of this new administrative and technical elite represented one of the most important new forces of the postwar era. Some French sociologists predict that as the older members of the managerial group retire in favor of new men, this whole segment of society (called in France the industrial and commercial *cadres*) will come to be impregnated with the technocratic outlook. They suggest also that the managerial element is emerging as the most vigorous and articulate group within the bourgeoisie, and that middle-class leadership is in the process of shifting away from the old dominant groups (industrial owners, and members of the liberal professions) to the active and increasingly self-conscious *cadres*.

A less important sign of change within the postwar bourgeoisie (though it received much more publicity) was the persistence and slow growth of the Jeunes Patrons movement. Its membership remained small; its Christian democratic inspiration tended to narrow its influence within the business group and to cut it off from the largely anti-clerical working class. But its lofty ideals, its interest in and concern for both economic advance and social justice, represented at least a nucleus of fundamental change within the industrialist group.

Whether the business group as a whole shared in this process of psychological change was more debatable. There was undoubtedly a revival of the old Saint-Simonian spirit of productivity, partially replacing the traditional Malthusian ideal of limited production for a closed market. It was less clear, however, that a new social outlook or a more genuine civic-mindedness had emerged in industrial circles. Some business men who had visited the United States did show an interest in the new science of labor relations, but skeptical observers doubted that their concern had gone very deep. "Human relations," remarks one such critic, "was one of the mechanical gadgets picked up and brought back with other gadgets in one's luggage."[2]

The reservations of the skeptics received some support from the record of organized business in postwar France. The business men, like every other sector of society, tightened their organizational structure after 1945 and developed remarkable effectiveness as a pressure group. The National Council of French Employers (C.N.P.F.), established in 1946 to replace an indifferently successful prewar predecessor, managed to channel the energies and to serve as the voice of all kinds of industrial and commercial enterprise. Some internal stresses did develop between the C.N.P.F. (dominated by big business) and one of its subsidiary groups, the Confederation of Small and Medium-Sized Enterprises (C.G.P.M.E.), which represented the special interests of the numerous and vocal small-business elements. But collaboration proved to be more profitable than conflict, so the uneasy alliance was never broken. There is not much evidence that the Employers' Council used its influence to encourage vigorous change or progress. Like most interest groups, its energies were devoted to defending the short-run interests of its own members and not the long-run interests of the whole community.

In the lower echelons of the bourgeoisie, evidences of a changed outlook were even more difficult to detect. By the Marxian definition of class, the white-collar workers (*employés*) and the civil servants (*fonctionnaires*) ought properly to belong to the proletariat. But if

[2] V. Lorwin, "Labor and Economic Development in France."

class distinctions are taken to reflect psychological rather than economic factors, if they represent differing sets of mores or ways of life, it is clear that both *employés* and *fonctionnaires* in France have always clung to middle-class status, and they continue to do so in the postwar era. Their influence, channelled through clerical and civil-service unions, has been especially strong in the non-Communist labor organizations, the C.F.T.C. and the C.G.T-F.O.; they have had a powerful voice in the left-center parties, Socialist and M.R.P. Although these elements have been wholeheartedly converted to the welfare-state ideal, their postwar outlook has continued to be defensive and unimaginative; their influence has been exerted against rather than for fundamental change. Perhaps that is why middle-class leadership seems to be shifting to the managerial *cadres*.

⋙◦⋘ ⋙◦⋘ ⋙◦⋘

France in 1960 was a nation at the crossroads of doubt and hope. No one could ignore the persistence of some serious stresses and strains that threatened to rend the social fabric. For a generation the members of every social category had been inclined to consider themselves mistreated in comparison to other groups. Each category had learned to cling stubbornly to those special advantages which, once achieved, quickly came to be regarded as inalienable rights. Only the exceptional citizen could balance national against class interest and could speak out for the greater of the two. Perhaps such balancing of interest among major social groups is an unavoidable aspect of the modern mass age; perhaps, by the operation of J. K. Galbraith's principle of "countervailing forces," an approximate harmony of interests may emerge. But in order to achieve that happy state of relative satisfaction throughout the social structure, some kind of cohesive force is essential. Possibly it was provided in the France of 1960 by the nation's common memory of greatness and suffering, by a stubborn and admirable pride in the fact of being French. Or possibly it was emerging in the form of a common hope for the future: in a broadening and deepening sense that all Frenchmen still possessed a single destiny.

567

THIRTY-FIVE

> We civilizations now know that we are mortal. . . . We
> see that the abyss of history is large enough for every-
> one. We feel that a civilization is as fragile as a life.
>
> PAUL VALÉRY *(1919)*

Trends in French Thought
and Expression, 1919–1960

France in the age of chain wars shared with the rest of the Western world a widely generalized malaise of the mind and spirit. Those who sought descriptive labels for cultural epochs spoke of an age of anxiety or of despair. That France should be affected by such a malaise was hardly surprising, for Frenchmen after 1914 lived con-stantly in or near the edge of crisis. The shattering experience of the Great War left the nation shaken and unsettled even during the post-war decade of quasi-normalcy. There had scarcely been time to settle back into old habits when the Great Depression brought new social and psychological tensions, quickly intensified by the disaster of 1940 and its complex aftermath.

But France's malaise had origins older and deeper than the series of post-1914 crises. Its harbinger had been the new intellectual genera-tion of the 1890's, as it challenged and undermined the dominant mood of the positivist age. By 1914 an avant-garde was in full revolt against the optimistic and confident premises of the Enlightenment in its revised nineteenth-century form. French thinkers and writers after

568

1890 had been among the major contributors to this revolt against rationalism and scientism, though no Frenchman — not even Bergson — could rival the pervasive long-term influence of Sigmund Freud.

The most vociferous crusaders for the new spirit during the interwar years were such fringe groups of artists and poets as the dadaists and the surrealists. Dadaism, though founded in Switzerland and inspired by a Rumanian, had its postwar headquarters in left-bank Paris. Its calculated nonsense was the reflection of a passionate revolt against everything rational and bourgeois; it rejected as false the sensible pretensions of an actually senseless world. Created in the midst of the Great War as an emotional protest against such human folly, dadaism survived only until its novelty wore off. But out of it emerged a far more respresentative and more significant successor, the surrealist movement that managed to "organize the destructive frenzies of Dadaism." According to its French founder, the poet André Breton, "The simplest type of surrealist action consists in going out into the street with a revolver in each hand, and firing as much as possible at random into the crowd." If Breton had his tongue slightly in his cheek, he was at least expressing the surrealists' frankly Freudian impulse to express subconscious drives without permitting the interference of reason to distort their purity. Surrealism, said one of its manifestoes, put its confidence in those forces heretofore restrained by man: ". . . the dream; the subconscious; love, freed from all moral or social fetters; revolutionary fervor; flamboyant atheism. . . ." Although the direct artistic and literary product of surrealism was small, its indirect impact was major. In painting as in poetry, "Surrealism . . . proved to be the great force which, even more than Symbolism in 1890, almost as much as the Romanticism of 1820–1830, launched young creators on their careers."[1]

If surrealism had a powerful liberating effect on French cultural expression, its historical importance lay rather in its noisy advocacy of the new irrationalist mood. But there were others, too, men of major

[1] H. Peyre, "French Poets of Today," *Yale French Studies,* XXI (1958), p. 126.

stature, who both reflected and shaped the new temper. The great names of the 1920's in literature were Marcel Proust and André Gide. Proust's many-volumed masterpiece, *Remembrance of Things Past,* had begun to appear in 1913, but its mood foreshadowed that of the interwar era. "By a neurotic, about neurotics, for neurotic readers," it introduced the stream-of-consciousness technique into modern literature, yet rigorously channelled that stream and retained an over-all architectural structuring that was almost Cartesian in its balanced perfection. Not since Rousseau, at least, had any French literary work revealed such minutely introspective probing into every cranny of an exceptionally complex mind. The beauty of Proust's language, his remarkable evocation of a disintegrating social milieu, his rich and haunting gallery of characters, gave the work much of its distinction; but the trait that made Proust representative of his time was his absorbing interest in the realms of the subconscious and the marginally conscious.

André Gide, who became the literary pope of the interwar period, was a more complex and contradictory figure. A man of bourgeois origin and Calvinist heritage, but tormented by the passionate drives of his own ambiguous nature, he sought throughout his literary career to find an ethic broad enough to reconcile these opposites. "Nostalgic for the previous century's world of secure middle-class values yet forced against his will into opposing those values and declaring new ones,"[2] Gide engaged in a lifetime of introspective wrestling with conscience and instincts that reflected many of the ambiguities of the age in which he wrote. Man, as Gide saw him, was cast into the world without divine guidance or predetermined destiny but with "innumerable possibilities of becoming." In one of his early novels he toyed with the Bergsonian concept of the "gratuitous act" — the action that is performed spontaneously, without forethought or motive. Gide seemed to suggest that only such an unplanned act, lacking in both purpose and calculated result, could be the action of a free man; for

[2] H. S. Hughes, *Consciousness and Society* (New York: Knopf, 1958), p. 360.

all of man's "rational" decisions are forced on him by society or by his previous education and training. Yet Gide was no nihilist; he combined with his revolt against conventional mores and against hypocritical conformism a painful search for a new code that would make even the transgressor a moral, dignified, and responsible man.

It would be surprising indeed if the whole educated elite of any nation, even under the stress of chronic crisis, were to turn to a doctrine of pure irrationalism. It would be especially surprising in the case of France, where the Enlightenment heritage and rationalist tradition are so old and deep. For a century French education had been stressing the Cartesian process of logical deduction as the proper path to knowledge and truth and had placed the highest premium on such virtues as reason, order, and clarity. Some required reading in Pascal may have balanced the Cartesian influence in a few sensitive minds, but Pascal's mystical and irrationalist leanings ("I believe because it is absurd") were usually treated as the regrettable aberrations of a great stylist. The impact of nineteenth-century positivism and scientism had shifted the educational emphasis slightly toward a more empirical and inductive approach; but Cartesian rationalism remained the core of French mental training, just as the literary classics remained the essential fare of the cultivated man.

The French educational system remained highly resistant to reform in the twentieth century, and therefore it acted as a kind of brake on any rapid change of mood. If the new spirit of irrationalism crept into the universities via Bergson and others, it was more than balanced by the survival of a dominant positivistic and rationalistic tradition. Irrationalism's impact in the *lycées* was slight; in the primary schools, almost nonexistent. Durkheimism in the social sciences went almost unchallenged during the interwar period; from its prewar stronghold in higher education, it seeped down even into primary education and reinforced the positivist outlook for another generation. Bergson might be the admired and respected luminary of contemporary French thought, but Descartes was still The Philosopher. Historians remained, by and large, in the scientistic tradition, although tinged by Michelet's passionate romanticism and brought up to date by the leavening influence of synthesizers like Marc Bloch and Lucien Febvre. Literary and artistic criticism, at least in the serious papers, remained essentially traditionalist through most of the interwar era; though new organs like the *Nouvelle Revue Française* (powerfully influenced by Gide) brought increasing prestige to literary experimenters.

Alongside the rebels and the irrationalists, therefore, a major segment of the French literary and artistic world continued to work in a more or less traditional vein and to attract the bulk of the reading public. Probably most Frenchmen of the interwar years regarded as the literary masterpieces and milestones of the era the massive multivolumed novels of Georges Duhamel, Jules Romains, and Roger Martin du Gard — social chronicles, in each case, of the evolving fortunes of a French bourgeois family. Paul Valéry, dean of French poets, managed to combine a powerful symbolist influence with an almost appallingly austere intellectualism. André Maurois and others carried on the skeptical and ironic tradition of Anatole France; the Catholic novelists and poets of the prewar generation had their successors (far more sophisticated and tinged by the tragic mood of their era) in François Mauriac, Paul Claudel, and Georges Bernanos. No essayist of the interwar years was so widely read and discussed as Julien Benda, whose passionate devotion to the rationalist principles of the Enlightenment made him seem a lonely relic of a past age. Benda devoted a lifetime to vindictive denunciations of Bergson and of all philosophers who relied on intuition or dialectics rather than the pure Cartesian method. His *La Trahison des clercs* (1927) was a brilliant but one-sided attack on modern intellectuals for descending into the arena of passion and controversy rather than standing fast on the ramparts of aloof objectivity and pure reason. All of these writers clung, in their separate ways, to a humanistic outlook — to a sympathetic concern for the dignity of man and a sincere attempt to comprehend the human condition.

Yet there were disturbing signs in the 1930's that the ground was slipping away beneath the defenders of the old values and the practitioners of traditional methods in literature or the arts. A new generation of writers, the angry young men of the time, was emerging with an almost vicious onslaught upon both the bourgeois world and its surrealist critics — indeed, upon the humanistic tradition in its every form. The mark of these men was a bitter nihilism, an intellectual anarchism that sought an outlet in violent action or that culminated in utter despair. Pierre Drieu la Rochelle sought to revive as the highest virtues "that divine pair — courage and fear," and he turned to the glorification of physical action: "The sole pleasure given to men on this earth is that passionate vigor that drives a young man to leap on his horse and to send a cry up towards God." To the embittered Louis-Ferdinand Céline, "The sole truth of this life is death," the only moral principle, to save one's own skin. The talented young poet and critic Robert Brasillach returned from a journey through central and eastern Europe entranced with the prospect of "a long, agitated, and sleepless night when every people sings in its own way: Nation, awake!" That such men should be attracted by the activist and nihilistic aspects of fascism is not surprising; their whole coterie plunged after 1940 into impassioned collaboration with Hitler's Germany.

There was, however, another path open to the neoromantic activist who was eager for certainty and a firm principle of action, but who refused to cast off his humanistic heritage. That path led to militant communism or to an impulsive fusion with all those crusaders who would save the world from fascism. The most notable figure to take this path was André Malraux, whose novels were intertwined with his own quixotic exploits in the civil-ideological wars of China and Spain. That Malraux became an active figure in the wartime resistance movement, that he emerged after the war as a leading Gaullist politician and doctrinaire, ought to have surprised no one; temperament once more proved more powerful than ideology.

⮞◦⮜◦⮞◦⮜◦⮞◦⮜

The confusing shocks of the Second World War broke up not only the army and the republic but also the contours of French thought;

and out of the jumbled wreckage new forms and patterns were slow to take shape. But the most striking product of the upheaval was the emergence of existentialism as the dominant force in both thought and literature during the early postwar years. Not since surrealism had any movement had so great an impact; not even surrealism had won such general notoriety.

Existentialism's chief French exponent, the young philosophy teacher and novelist Jean-Paul Sartre, had brought the new doctrine back from Germany in the early 1930's. By a "masterly misinterpretation" of the German philosopher Heidegger, Sartre gave the doctrine an atheistic and humanistic base. His first novel, *Nausée* (1938), portrayed the growing malaise of at least some intellectuals in the interwar period. Its hero, a rootless intellectual alienated to the point of physical repulsion by his senseless, unnecessary existence, drifted aimlessly and almost without conclusion through several hundred pages of futility and frustration. But existentialism's impact was felt in France only after the traumatic experience of the war. Few Frenchmen during and after the occupation ever understood existentialism's highly technical philosophical substructure; what many of them did absorb was the frame of mind, the attitude, the mood that it represented. It was a mood shot through with pessimism, doubt, despair; and yet within it there was contained a kind of stoic response to the challenge of crisis and hopelessness. What man is, whence he comes, whither he may be destined to go — these were things that the existentialists held to be incomprehensible. Man could know only the fact of his existence, of his freedom to make choices, to shape his own life, to "make himself." Freedom to act and choose in a futile, absurd, irrational universe was admittedly a lonely and painful privilege or duty; but Sartre and his disciples nevertheless preached the necessity for *engagement* or commitment — for action rather than escape, for a dedicated literature rather than art for art's sake.

Existentialism has been called "the Counter-Enlightenment come at last to philosophical expression." In a sense, it did contain in capsule form all of the irrationalism, the disillusionment and anxiety and even despair that had been building up in Europe for two generations. French critics promptly found that it had an even older (and truly French) pedigree, reaching all the way back to Pascal. Its generalized appeal, however, was clearly the product of the age of crisis, and it reflected the mood of the age better than any other movement of thought. For a time it took on faddist qualities and was even successfully commercialized by the operators of left-bank tourist traps. Although its great vogue passed within a decade, it was (like surrealism and symbolism) much more than a passing fashion. As an intellectual movement, its long-range effect probably exceeded that of any rival movement in postwar France.

Such rivals did exist, though they were slow to emerge and to crystallize. Even at the height of existentialism's great decade (1945–55), many Frenchmen repudiated it in horror or contempt. One of the largest blocs of resisters were those who preferred an alternative doctrinal system, Marxist materialism, with its code of action and its complete, satisfying set of answers to the problems of man and society. Most Catholics either clung without much reflection to traditionalist values or turned to some form of renovated Catholic thought. Among these newer Catholic currents, the most notable were neo-Thomism, the "personalism" of Emmanuel Mounier (a left-wing maverick Catholic in the Péguy tradition), and the so-called Christian existentialism developed before the war by Gabriel Marcel. A few intellectuals were attracted to the imported system of neopositivism, with its rigorous concentration on science and on mathematical precision. Still others salvaged what they could of the old Enlightenment tradition, as modified by nineteenth-century positivism and by the twentieth century's insights into man's irrational side. There were a few, like Marcel Aymé and Raymond Queneau, who adopted a kind of sardonic nihilism, borrowing the techniques of Kafka to narrate in the most lucid prose the fantastic adventures of ordinary people in an absurd, incongruous, nonlogical world. And as always in times of stress, some chose a kind of epicurean escapism toward the pleasures of the flesh, indifferently turning their backs to a futile and incomprehensible

575

world. "To what do you attach importance?" asks a character in a Françoise Sagan novel. "To nothing," answers the heroine wearily, "I don't think." Perhaps the Sagan mood may properly be labelled "adolescent existentialism"; but it scarcely fits Sartre's own formula that "existentialism is a form of humanism" or his insistence on courageous action in the face of absurdity.

If there were systems of thought, or *Weltanschauungen,* that rivalled existentialism throughout the postwar years, there were still no clearly defined rival schools in literature and the arts. Novelists, poets, painters avoided clear-cut slogans or manifestoes that might indicate developing trends in the current era. Instead of schools of writers or artists, there appeared to be only isolated individuals, each one stressing his own separateness, staking out his own small field of activity. Critics spoke of the intricate and confusing patterns of the period; of the cross-currents that suggested a continuing clash between traditionalism and change; of the "sheer animal vitality of the French literary jungle." If any emergent trend could be detected by 1960, it was an apparent shift toward *dégagement* — a reaction against Sartre's doctrine of commitment to political and social action, a movement toward restoring literature to its own domain, detached from philosophy and politics. Even Sartre himself, after his temporary break with the Communists in 1956, seemed to be moving away from activism. Critics found in his play *Les Séquestrés d'Altona* (1959) a kind of retreat into a modern version of the ivory tower and a mood of disdain toward life and toward his fellow men.

Yet the earnest and courageous search for a new ethic that has deeply marked so much of recent French literature was sure to continue in an anxious age — just as the tragic, the despairing, and the sardonically cynical notes would continue to be sounded by sensitive artists disheartened at the apparent absurdity of their world. It was a French literary man, one who had moved through existentialism to something beyond, who expressed in almost poetic prose the mood of many of his contemporaries:

Whatever we may do, excess will always keep its place in the heart of man, in the place where solitude is found. We all carry within us our places of exile, our crimes and our ravages. But our task is not to unleash them on the world; it is to fight them in ourselves and others. Rebellion, the secular will not to surrender . . . , is still today at the basis of the struggle. Origin of form, source of real life, it keeps us always erect in the savage, formless movement of history. . . . All of us, among the ruins, are preparing a renaissance beyond the limits of nihilism. But few of us know it. . . . [It is for us to choose] the only original rule of life today: to learn to live and to die, and, in order to be a man, to refuse to be a god.[3]

[3] A. Camus, *The Rebel* (New York: Vintage Books, 1956), pp. 301-6.

THIRTY-SIX

> Take the loftiest possible position—it is inevitably
> the least crowded.
>
> CHARLES DE GAULLE

The Fifth Republic,
1958–1960

Changes of regime or leadership, whether violent or bloodless, commonly inspire an extraordinary mixture of hope and illusion. From the accession of Louis XVI in 1774 to the second coming of Charles de Gaulle in 1958, almost every change of leader or of system in France has been accompanied by such a wave of euphoria. It is sobering to recall how rapidly the mood of ebullience has always tended to fade away. Perhaps the strain of living in a state of intense enthusiasm is too great to be endured for very long; perhaps Frenchmen cannot repress their habitual tendency to criticize; or perhaps their new leaders have always turned out to be men with feet of clay. At any rate, the record of two hundred years is likely to leave the student of history a restrained optimist at best.

Parliament's abdication before the threat of civil war left Premier de Gaulle once more a kind of dictator by consent. How he would use his power this time was not at all clear. Some observers, recalling his rigid, self-righteous, and autocratic behavior of 1944–46, looked to the future with foreboding. They feared that years of frustration, marked by bitter outbursts against the Fourth Republic (that "regime of mediocrity and chloroform," that system "floating on the surface of France like scum on the sea"), might have converted him into a ruthless authoritarian dedicated to replacing the parliamentary system with a kind of Bonapartist substitute. But they were quickly reassured: time and experience had apparently mellowed the general somewhat, or had taught him the virtues of at least some flexibility. When an interviewer asked him whether his ideas had changed, he answered: "The only change, you might say, is that I have become more indulgent of others." He did not waste time reminding Frenchmen that he had long since predicted the disintegration of the Fourth Republic. He made no effort to sweep away the personnel of the defunct regime in favor of a completely new elite. Instead, he sought to ensure a smooth transition from one republican system to the next. His interim cabinet of 1958 included not only dedicated Gaullists like Michel Debré, Jacques Soustelle, and André Malraux but also some of the most representative politicians from the old National Assembly, together with a number of nonpolitical "technicians" drawn from the higher civil service.

The task of drafting a new constitution was entrusted, for the first time in French republican history, to an appointed committee of experts rather than to an elected assembly. Its chairman and principal author, Minister of Justice Michel Debré, set out quite frankly to institutionalize the governmental theories of De Gaulle himself. Yet the new system, as it emerged, was much less revolutionary than some Gaullists had hoped or expected it to be. It represented a curious blend of the presidential and the parliamentary regimes, designed to strengthen and stabilize the executive branch without destroying its responsibility to the legislature. The clearest change was a reduction in legislative authority and in the ease with which the Assembly could overthrow cabinets. The most ambiguous change was the altered relationship within the executive branch, between the president on the one hand and the premier on the other. Premier and cabinet were maintained in the role of governing executive; but the president's prestige and right to independent action were markedly increased. The presidential role was tailored to measure for Charles de Gaulle, in what one scholar has called "the first serious attempt to institutionalize a great man."

De Gaulle had promised that the voters would be allowed to ratify the new system by referendum. In September, 1958, they were called to the polls to express approval or disapproval. The response was overwhelming; it far exceeded the expectations of even the most sanguine Gaullist. Almost 80 per cent of those who cast ballots approved the new constitution, despite the vigorous negative campaign conducted by the Communists, a minority wing of the Socialists, and such notable leftist leaders as Pierre Mendès-France. That this was a vote of confidence in De Gaulle's personal leadership rather than in the machinery of the new system was unmistakable.

Fortified by this unprecedented display of near-consensus in a habitually divided nation, De Gaulle could push ahead without delay to erect the institutional framework of the Fifth Republic. During the winter months of 1958–59 a reorganized two-house parliament (National Assembly and Senate) was elected; De Gaulle was named to a seven-year term as president by a broadened electoral college of eighty thousand delegates from local councils; Michel Debré was in turn designated by De Gaulle to be the first premier. The new National Assembly was dominated by a near-majority of dedicated Gaullists, who had hastily organized a new party, the Union for the New Republic (U.N.R.), bound together by its acceptance of De Gaulle's leadership and of the new regime.

The winds of change were felt not only in continental France but in the overseas possessions as well. One of the central purposes of the regime's new leaders was to provide a new, more flexible framework for what had once been called the empire. That framework was written into the 1958 constitution, and the overseas populations were given their chance in the September referendum to accept or reject it. De Gaulle announced during the campaign that any overseas territory except Algeria might choose immediate independence simply by voting down the constitution. A vote to accept the constitution, on the other hand, would open three alternative paths to these territories. They might choose to become integral parts of the French republic itself; or to continue the kind of partially autonomous territorial status granted them piecemeal during the Fourth Republic; or to move forward to full domestic autonomy as self-governing states within the new French Community.

De Gaulle's assurances temporarily checked the surge toward separatism that had been developing in many parts of the old empire; only one overseas territory, French Guinea, chose independence. The others ratified the new constitution by majorities even more overwhelming than that in continental France; and during the subsequent months the twelve largest African territories chose to be advanced to the status of self-governing republics within the Community. The possibility of a contagious spread of the Algerian revolt throughout French Africa was thus averted by De Gaulle's imaginative and generous plan. But in the age of decolonization, no device or policy was likely to do more than delay the overwhelming urge toward full independence. By 1960 the new African republics were already demanding that the French accord them such independence at once. Reluctantly perhaps, but also realistically, De Gaulle and his ministers acceded to this ultimate demand and agreed to amend the new constitution so that independence might be combined with continued membership in the French Community. It remained for the future to determine whether a French commonwealth of sovereign nations would possess the same coherence as the British Commonwealth.

One overseas problem still defied solution. In Algeria the long guerrilla war dragged on, with no apparent prospect of an early settlement. The Algerians, both Moslems and European settlers, voted almost unanimously for the new constitution; but French army supervision of the referendum made many observers doubt the validity of the results. The rebels continued their raids in the hill country and their terrorism in the cities; they ignored an invitation from De Gaulle to negotiate a cease-fire. A few French leftists concluded that De Gaulle, by failing

581

to take dramatic and drastic action immediately after his return to power, had missed the psychological moment for a liquidation of the revolt. They held that his unequalled prestige at that moment might have overawed the army and the *colons* and that he might have been strong enough to grant Algeria a kind of disguised independence. A larger group of critics on the right took a quite opposite view: they began to denounce De Gaulle for his gestures of clemency toward the rebels and for his refusal to adopt the *colons'* slogan of "integration" — i.e., the complete fusion of Algeria with France.

These rightists were even more outraged when De Gaulle, in September, 1959, at last put forth a precise plan for an Algerian settlement. He offered the Algerians, for the first time, full self-determination at the end of four years if they would agree to lay down their arms and permit the peaceful reconstruction and development of the country. A program of extensive and costly economic and social renovation had already been announced; De Gaulle was obviously gambling that its impact might persuade the Algerians to link their destiny with that of France. The principal weakness of this courageous scheme was that it came five years too late. If proposed at the outbreak of the rebellion, it would have been welcomed by virtually every Algerian; by 1959 the rebel leaders had gone almost beyond the point of no return.

While De Gaulle waited fruitlessly for the rebels to accept his terms, the fury of the Algerian *colons* boiled over once more. As in May, 1958, the extremists in Algiers took to the streets in January, 1960, and threw up barricades in an effort to force De Gaulle to accept their program of "integration" and "a French Algeria." The army's sympathies clearly lay on the side of the rioters, and for a time it seemed that the 1958 coup might be repeated. But this time there was a firm hand in Paris; the army, confronted by De Gaulle's angry intransigence, knuckled under, and the rebellion collapsed. De Gaulle promptly transferred most of the top commanders in Algeria to other posts and demanded the resignation of cabinet ministers like Jacques Soustelle who had openly sympathized with the January rioters. The affair left a sediment of intense bitterness in military and right-wing political circles and ended the uneasy collaboration between De Gaulle and the right that had been maintained since May, 1958. Many Frenchmen hoped that the Algerian nationalists, reassured by De Gaulle's forthright action against the *colons*, would now accept his terms and lay down their arms. But subsequent negotiations between the Algerian F.L.N. and the French government ran onto the shoals of mutual suspicion, and both sides returned wearily and bitterly to that ultimate test of righteousness among civilized humans — the battlefield.

Meanwhile, De Gaulle and the Debré cabinet had been wrestling with a second major issue inherited from the Fourth Republic — the financial problem. The inflationary spiral that had set in once again in the later 1950's had been beyond the power of weak coalition cabinets to check; prices mounted steadily, French exports fell sharply behind imports, the stability of the franc was threatened. By 1958 French gold and foreign exchange reserves had dropped to a critically low level, and the treasury deficit was alarming. The Gaullist solution at the end of 1958 was a sharp turn toward deflation and austerity. Taxes were increased, and governmental expenditures were reduced by such heroic measures as suspending veterans' pensions and abolishing the state subsidies that had held down the cost of foodstuffs. The franc was devalued; a tight and fairly effective lid was clamped on prices and wages; import controls were sharply relaxed in an effort to let increased laissez faire reinvigorate the whole economy. Such bold action, challenging a whole series of powerful interest groups, could have been taken only by a strong and self-reliant executive authority.

By the end of 1959 the government was proclaiming the success of its economic experiment. Deflation had brought a brief business slump, but it had soon been checked; prices tended to level off; exports rose so dramatically that they outstripped imports; capital began to flow back into the country; gold and foreign exchange reserves tripled in short order. From the purely economic angle, the policy of deflation and liberalization seemed to be an undeniable success. The psychological effects of the experiment were, however, more mixed. Spokesmen for labor insisted that the plan had been dictated by powerful financial and business interests and that the whole burden of stabilization had been loaded on the working class. Their complaints were not entirely unfounded. The end of subsidies brought a rise in food costs, unemployment rose slightly, and labor protest was stifled by mobilizing workers who threatened to strike. It was easy for labor to believe that a government containing no qualified spokesmen for the workingman was indulging in mere hypocrisy when it talked of temporary sacrifices to attain a more stable prosperity that would benefit all groups. Labor had so long felt itself victimized that it was unlikely to abandon its suspicions at such a moment. The deflationary policy thus represented a rather risky gamble which, given time, might produce remarkable results, but which might meanwhile deepen the existing schisms within the nation.

The revolutionary upheaval of 1958 produced not only a new governmental structure but also an extensive shake-up in the party pattern and in the governing elite — a regular *"Götterdammerung* of ideologies, parties and politicians," as one observer puts it.[1] Three-fourths of the deputies who had served in the previous National Assembly were swept out of office in the 1958 elections (though quite a number made a later comeback by winning seats in the new Senate). The old parties, especially those of the left, suffered a disastrous setback: the Communists fell from 149 to 10 seats, the Socialists from 97 to 44, the Radicals from 57 to 13, the M.R.P. from 75 to 56. Only the heirs of the Moderate tradition, the Independent-Peasant bloc on the right, gained strength and emerged with 118 seats. It was a new party, the Gaullist U.N.R., patched together barely in time for the electoral campaign, that was swept to a victory almost unprecedented in French republican history. Its 212 seats, 188 of which were won in continental France, gave it a near-majority in the Assembly, even though it polled only 26.4 per cent of the popular vote. The Communists and Socialists together still won 34.5 per cent of the popular vote, but these voters

[1] S. Hoffmann, "The French Constitution of 1958," *American Political Science Review*, LIII (June, 1959), 349.

were almost unrepresented in the Assembly and were totally unrepresented in the executive branch. Right-wing dominance at the outset of the Fifth Republic was as great as left-wing dominance at the outset of the Fourth.[2]

This drastic shake-up of men and parties produced an atmosphere of confusion and uncertainty that gave the executive branch even greater freedom to embark on vigorous action. The opposition was too weak to raise an effective voice; the U.N.R. was incapable of taking full advantage of its size because of its own internal dissensions. Its members were bound together by little more than real or professed loyalty to De Gaulle; on specific issues, like the Algerian problem, they differed sharply. Severe tensions developed within the group during 1959, and the Algiers riots of January, 1960, eventually produced an open schism. A small but vocal and well-disciplined group of U.N.R. leaders followed Jacques Soustelle out of the party and raised a standard to which they expected all elements of the embittered right to rally.

As the Fifth Republic approached the end of its second year of existence, its destiny was still clouded by its own ambiguities and by the nation's heritage of division. True, De Gaulle's hold on the public mind was scarcely diminished; the Debré cabinet, though increasingly unpopular, had managed to outlive any ministry of the Fourth Republic; the new constitution was working smoothly, despite the ominous predictions of some observers that there would be serious stresses between president and premier or between cabinet and parliament. Some hopeful Frenchmen could conclude that a workable solution had at last been found for the problem of effective government — that executive paralysis had been cured without resorting to the risky

[2] The turnover in 1958 resulted in part from the adoption of an altered electoral system. Instead of proportional representation, the De Gaulle cabinet chose to resurrect the Third Republic's system of small single-member electoral districts, with a run-off ballot if no candidate polled a majority on the first day of voting. Many Gaullists had long favored a much more revolutionary system of large multi-member districts with election by mere plurality. De Gaulle overruled them, in an attempt to avert a Gaullist sweep that would wipe out the old parties.

remedies of a presidential or an authoritarian system. Most Frenchmen realized, however, that the workability of the system depended to a dangerous degree on the role of one man and that the man in question was probably irreplaceable. Some of them were not sure that even so remarkable a man could cope with the assortment of problems inherited from the past. But the graver question always hovering in the background was whether the Gaullist system could be perpetuated without De Gaulle.

If the Fifth Republic could survive its founder, it seemed almost certainly destined to change in the process of survival and to evolve in one of three possible directions. One path would lead back toward the Third and Fourth republics' tradition of parliamentary dominance, with the executive the creature of the legislative branch. Nostalgia for the old system was already beginning to reappear in the 1959 parliament, and it would inevitably be stronger under an executive more vulnerable than De Gaulle. A second path might lead toward a consolidation of cabinet government, with the prime minister emerging as the real governing executive. France's system would in this case come to resemble those of Scandinavia and the Low Countries, where multiparty structures have been successfully combined with cabinet leadership. A third path would lead in the direction of a frankly presidential system and would somehow institutionalize the role that De Gaulle has been able to play through his unique personal qualities. But alongside these three constitutional possibilities, there remained constantly in the background the shadow of extra-constitutional change as well. If De Gaulle were to disappear, if the Algerian crisis were to remain chronic and apparently insoluble, the prospect of a coup by right-wing extremists and the army would never be absent. That prospect, in turn, would refurbish the myth of the Popular Front and might even raise the spectre of civil war.

"Is the Fifth Republic the last phase of an historical epoch, or rather the first stage in a new era?" The Parisian journalist who raised this question at the end of De Gaulle's first year in power preferred not to offer an answer. But there were others who were less reticent, and who saw no reason to believe that the past had been left behind. "Factionalism," wrote the eminent commentator Raymond Aron, "seems to be endemic in our country. . . . One might almost think that an evil spirit casts a spell on each new French regime and prepares its death on the very day of its birth."

❧◦❦ ❧◦❦ ❧◦❦

A nation's history, if carried to the threshold of the present, cannot properly have a conclusion. Conclusions, like epitaphs, are appropriate only for the dead. France's history over the past two centuries puts one in mind of that medieval masterpiece, the Bayeux tapestry. Both of them offer a closely woven, elaborate pageant of life and action — colorful, dramatic, almost overwhelming in their richness of detail. The tapestry of French history is still in the making; and it may be that the pattern henceforth will be less coherent, the scenes less heroic, the colors more pallid than in the past. Yet if Frenchmen live up to their tradition, the pageant will never lose its passionate interest for humankind.

THIRTY-SEVEN

The Varieties of History,
1919–1960

The writing of contemporary history is a risky enterprise. "Who follows truth too closely at the heels may have his brains kicked out." Most general histories of France — even the recently published ones — taper off after 1919 into thin and sketchy summaries, while most monographs concerning the interwar epoch were written either during that epoch or soon after the 1940 collapse and are marked by the special preoccupations of their time. There are more good studies of the Fourth Republic than of the declining decades of the Third — though, of course, no book on France since the Second World War can yet view the times in perspective.

When and why decay began to rot the foundations of the Third Republic is still a controversial question. David Thomson (*op. cit.*) finds the turning point from stability and success to dissension and decline at about the year 1905, when the old political and ideological issues had been largely settled and when new economic and social problems began to force their way to the forefront. Thomson argues that the republic's negative political system, which mirrored but did not reconcile differences in French society and opinion, was incapable of dealing with these new problems. French historians (e.g., André Siegfried in his *De la troisième à la quatrième république* [Paris: Grasset, 1957]) have been more inclined to see the Great War as the caesura and to regard the period 1919–40 as sharply different in almost every way from *la belle époque* that endured intact until 1914. A few observers have postponed the turning point to 1930 and have treated the 1920's as an appendix to the stable, successful prewar phase of the Third Republic. They point to the painfully close resemblance between the last decade of the Third Republic and the first decade of the Fourth and suggest that the Great Depression inaugurated a long, uninterrupted era of crisis and debility in France.

❧❧❧

The most detailed account of political history between the wars is provided by François Goguel in his *Politique des partis* and his published lectures (see Chapter Twenty-six). A series of contemporary books by Alexander Werth, then Paris correspondent for the *Manchester Guardian,* are of unique value for the 1930's; Werth at the time viewed events from the standpoint of the moderate left. D. W. Brogan has expertly digested these books into a single volume called *The Twilight of France, 1933–1940* (New York: Harper, 1942). The strength, character, and significance of the so-called fascist movements of the 1930's have not been adequately analyzed; but a beginning has been made by René Rémond in his *La Droite en France* (see Chapter Seventeen), by Raoul Girardet ("Notes sur l'esprit d'un fascisme français, 1934–1939," *Revue Française de Science Politique,* V [1955], 529–46), and by Max Beloff (in James Joll [ed.], *The Decline of the Third Republic* [New York: Praeger, 1959]). Eugen Weber's forthcoming study of the Action Française between the wars should throw much new light on the extreme right-wing groups in that period.

On the left, the Communists have found a sympathetic historian in Gérard Walter: *Histoire du parti communiste français* (Paris: Somogy, 1948). A committee of French Communist historians is currently writing an official version of the party's history. Paul Louis's *Histoire du socialisme en France, 1789–1945* (Paris: Rivière, 1949) is sketchy on the interwar period. John T. Marcus's *French Socialism in the Crisis Years, 1933–1936* (New York: Praeger, 1958) examines the

589

party's internal dissension, produced in part by the rise of Hitler and in part by older doctrinal conflicts. There is a concise but rather hostile sketch of Léon Blum's career by Colette Audry: *Léon Blum, ou la politique du juste* (Paris: Julliard, 1955); the slant is that of a left-wing disciple of Jean-Paul Sartre. James Joll's essay on Blum in his *Intellectuals in Politics* (London: Weidenfeld and Nicolson, 1960) is much more sympathetic. The same author, in *The Decline of the Third Republic*, explains how and why the Popular Front was organized and shows that the Communists were its principal advocates. There is a detailed analysis of the Popular Front's origins and of its 1936 electoral victory in Georges Dupeux's *Le Front Populaire et les élections de 1936* (Paris: Colin, 1959). Blum's own reflections on his experience in power, written in prison after 1940, may be found in his *A l'échelle humaine* (Paris: Gallimard, 1945). An American scholar, Joel Colton, is presently preparing a political biography of Blum.

Two of the best books on French labor in recent decades are by Americans: Val Lorwin's *The French Labor Movement* (Cambridge, Mass.: Harvard Univ. Press, 1954) and Henry W. Ehrmann's *French Labor from Popular Front to Liberation* (New York: Oxford Univ. Press, 1947). Michel Collinet's *Essai sur la condition ouvrière (1900–1950)* (Paris: Ed. Ouvrières, 1951; by a strongly anti-Communist leftist) is an interesting attempt to trace changes in class structure, income distribution, and labor conditions generally. On the business group, Henry W. Ehrmann's *Organized Business in France* (Princeton: Princeton Univ. Press, 1957) is a pioneering and penetrating study; it is mainly concerned with the years after the Second World War. On the church and religious issues generally, the best survey is Adrien Dansette's *Destin du catholicisme français, 1926–1956* (Paris: Flammarion, 1957).

On the economic history of the interwar era, the best analyses are those of Charles Bettelheim (*Bilan de l'économie française, 1919–1946* [Paris: Presses Univ., 1947]) and Roger Nathan and Paul Delouvrier (*Politique économique de la France* [Paris: Cours de Droit, 1950]). Bettelheim's approach is that of a non-Communist Marxian; he emphasizes the growing power of monopolies behind a façade of small enterprise and the prevalence of "economic malthusianism" as a kind of quasi-official economic philosophy of the business group. Nathan and Delouvrier's lectures at the Institut des Études Politiques contain a forceful critique of French public policy during the 1930's, stressing the economic failure of the Popular Front.

French foreign policy between the wars must still be examined without benefit of documentary sources, for the French have not chosen to imitate the British in publishing a selection of their diplomatic papers for the period. The best surveys are those of Pierre Renouvin in Volumes VII and VIII of his *Histoire des relations internationales: les crises du XX*ᵉ *siècle* (Paris: Hachette, 1957–58) and J.-B. Duroselle in his *Histoire diplomatique de 1919 à nos jours* (Paris: Dalloz, 1957). There are some enlightening chapters on French diplomacy in Gordon Craig and Felix Gilbert (eds.), *The Diplomats, 1919–1939* (Princeton: Princeton Univ. Press, 1953) and in Arnold Wolfers, *Britain and France Between Two Wars* (New York: Harcourt, 1940). Sir Lewis Namier's essays (e.g., *Europe in Decay* [London: Macmillan, 1950]) are sharply critical of French leadership in the 1930's; Namier accuses the French of wanting appeasement but shifting responsibility for it to the British. Charles A. Micaud's *The French Right and Nazi Germany, 1933–1939* (Durham: Duke Univ. Press, 1943) shows, from press and parliamentary comment, how the right's attitude evolved from firmness to appeasement. French military policy between the wars is critically examined in Richard Challener's *French Theory of the Nation in Arms* (see Chapter Twenty-Six).

There is an extensive and controversial literature on the 1940 collapse, written for the most part by participants in the debacle. Marc Bloch's *L'Étrange défaite* (Paris: A. Michel, 1946, 1957) is still in some ways the most sophisticated brief analysis of responsibilities. Written immediately after the defeat, it demonstrates the glaring inadequacies of France's military leadership, but it also probes deeply into the shortcomings of the nation's social and intellectual elites. Colonel A. Goutard's *The Battle of France, 1940* (London: Muller, 1958) is

591

the work of a dedicated Gaullist who contends that outmoded military conceptions rather than inadequate manpower or equipment were responsible for France's downfall. Jacques Bénoist-Méchin's detailed three-volume study *Soixante jours qui ébranlèrent l'occident* (Paris: Michel, 1955–56) is the work of a prominent ex-Vichyite; it undertakes to rehabilitate the men who chose to suspend the fight in 1940. Pierre Dhers has answered Bénoist-Méchin in his *Regards nouveaux sur les années quarante* (Paris: Flammarion, 1958). General Edward Spears' *Assignment to Catastrophe* (London: Heinemann, 1954), the memoirs of Churchill's personal emissary to France, is an appalling but certainly overdrawn study of disintegration at the top in Paris. John C. Cairns's forthcoming work on the 1940 collapse has been foreshadowed by his brilliant article "Along the Road Back to France, 1940," in the *American Historical Review*, LXIV (1959), 583–603.

⚜⚜⚜

The Vichy episode has produced a veritable flood of self-justifying memoirs by its leaders or adherents. Pétain's admirers have described him as "the crucified savior of France" and have declared that his self-sacrifice after 1940 "will one day count more for his glory than the victory of Verdun." They contend that Pétain, by practicing a double game, protected France against the fate of Poland; some of them even insist that he hoodwinked Hitler into staying out of North Africa and thus made possible the ultimate Western victory in 1945. This latter thesis has been elaborated at length by Louis-Dominique Girard in his *Montoire, Verdun diplomatique* (Paris: Bonne, 1948), while the double-game argument recurs in dozens of books: e.g., Sisley Huddleston's *France: the Tragic Years, 1939–1947* (New York: Devin-Adair, 1955). Laval's defenders have presented his case in more varied fashion. Most commonly he is seen as a martyr who voluntarily chose execration and disgrace in order to protect his countrymen against "Polonization" and who saved hundreds of thousands of Frenchmen from deportation or death. Sometimes he, rather than Pétain, is described as the real master of the double game, or even as the *sub rosa* defender of republican principles at Vichy; his purpose, it is alleged, was to keep the Parisian fascists like Déat and Doriot from taking over as gauleiters. Laval stated his own case in the volume entitled *The Diary of Pierre Laval* (New York: Scribners, 1948); many of his friends have elaborated that case in the collection of documents called *France During the German Occupation* (Stanford: Hoover Institution, 1959). A number of lesser Vichy figures have also found retrospective defenders, but the Paris fascists like Doriot and the dedicated collaborationists like De Brinon still await any concerted attempt at rehabilitation.

Though it is still too early for a dispassionate look at the Vichy experience, a few historians have already made admirable attempts at it. The best of these is Robert Aron's *The Vichy Regime, 1940–1944* (New York: Macmillan, 1958), which confines itself largely to the palace intrigues among the rival factions around Pétain. There is a brief but incisive account by Alfred Cobban in A. and V. Toynbee (eds.), *Survey of International Affairs, 1939–1946: Hitler's Europe* (London: Royal Institute, 1954). Paul Farmer's *Vichy: Political Dilemma* (New York: Columbia Univ. Press, 1955) is readable and balanced; David Thomson's *Two Frenchmen: Laval and De Gaulle* (London: Cresset, 1951) is lucid and provocative, though his partial rehabilitation of Laval stands up better than does his denigration of De Gaulle. Adrienne Hytier's *Two Years of French Foreign Policy: Vichy 1940–1942* (Geneva: Droz, 1958) is an impressively documented study; it concludes that Vichy leaders steadily sought to recover French power and prestige through "profitable collaboration" but were kept at arm's length because most leading Nazis distrusted them. Henri Michel (ed.), *La France sous l'occupation* (Paris: Presses Univ., 1959) is a rejoinder to the Laval documents published by the Hoover Institution (cited above); its thesis is that the existence of Vichy aided the Germans more than it protected the French. A forthcoming study of Vichy by Stanley Hoffmann is foreshadowed by his article "Aspects du régime de Vichy," in the *Revue Française de Science Politique*, VI

593

(1956), 44–69; it is a brilliant analysis of conflicting political and social doctrines at Vichy. Gordon Wright has attempted to reassess Vichy and to compare rival viewpoints about it in "Vichy Revisited," *Virginia Quarterly Review,* XXXIV (1958), 501–14.

Anti-Vichy has drawn far less attention from historians; on the Free French movement and the underground, we are scarcely out of the memoir stage. Henri Michel's brief introductory sketch *Histoire de la résistance* (Paris: Presses Univ., 1950) is the only general account. A French historical commission set up for the purpose has, however, recently begun to produce a series of important monographs. Notable among them are Marie Granet and Henri Michel's *Combat: histoire d'un mouvement de résistance* (Paris: Presses Univ., 1957) and René Hostache's *Le Conseil National de la Résistance* (Paris: Presses Univ., 1958). Robert Aron's *Histoire de la libération de la France* (Paris: Fayard, 1959) is a remarkably thorough and balanced study of an episode still clouded by strong emotions. On the question of summary executions in 1944–45, for example, he corrects both the exaggerated accusations of the ex-Vichyites (that over a hundred thousand were killed) and the excessively modest estimates of the Ministry of Interior (that there were fewer than ten thousand victims). On the Free French movement in London and Algiers, there are memoirs both by long-time Gaullists like Armand Dewavrin and Jacques Soustelle and by embittered ex-Gaullists like Admiral Muselier; but the most remarkable of them all is of course General de Gaulle's own three-volume *Mémoires de guerre* (Paris: Plon, 1954–59). There is an admirable study of De Gaulle's wartime relationships with the British and Americans by Arthur L. Funk: *Charles de Gaulle: the Crucial Years, 1943–1944* (Norman: Oklahoma Univ. Press, 1959). An American scholar, Nicholas Wahl, is preparing an account of the Gaullist movement from its origins to the present.

❧❧❧

France since the Second World War has been prodded, analyzed, and dissected by scholars and journalists of almost every nationality and political predisposition. One of the best volumes on the structure and evolution of political institutions is Philip Williams' *Politics in Post-War France* (London: Longmans, 1954, 1958). Williams believes that France's contemporary problems are traceable to deep-rooted historical and sociological factors rather than to constitutional or institutional flaws; he doubts that any solution can be found except through slow evolutionary processes. A quite contrary view is expressed by Ronald Matthews in his *Death of the Fourth Republic* (London: Eyre and Spottiswoode, 1954); Matthews accuses the immediate postwar leaders of France of fatal errors that doomed the regime. Catherine Gavin's *Liberated France* (London: Cape, 1955) loads most of the blame for the nation's postwar troubles on De Gaulle. Herbert Luethy's *France Against Herself* (New York: Praeger, 1955) is a much more complex, paradoxical, and provocative analysis that stresses the weight of history and of habit under which contemporary France must labor. Alexander Werth's *France, 1940–1955* (New York: Holt, 1956) is well informed and packed with detail, but Werth sees the period through the narrow peephole of the crusading neutralist left. A broader and more balanced view is taken by such authors as André Siegfried (*De la troisième à la quatrième république*), François Goguel (*France Under the Fourth Republic* [Ithaca: Cornell Univ. Press, 1952]), Jacques Fauvet (*Les Forces politiques en France* [Paris: Le Monde, 1951] and *La IVe république* [Paris: Fayard, 1960]), and Donald C. McKay (*The United States and France* [Cambridge, Mass.: Harvard Univ. Press, 1951]).

Monographs and special studies useful for the postwar period include the following: Nathan Leites, *On the Game of Politics in France* (Stanford: Stanford Univ. Press, 1959; a provocative study of political ritualism, too cynical to be entirely fair); Dorothy Pickles, *French Politics: the First Years of the Fourth Republic* (London: R.I.I.A., 1953; solid and thorough); Gordon Wright, *The Reshaping of French Democracy* (New York: Reynal, 1948; on the founding of the Fourth Republic); J.-M. Jeanneney, *Forces et faiblesses de l'économie française* (Paris: Colin, 1956); Warren C. Baum, *The French Economy*

595

and the State (Princeton: Princeton Univ. Press, 1958); Maurice
Duverger (ed.), *Partis politiques et classes sociales* (Paris: Colin,
1955); Laurence Wylie, *Village in the Vaucluse* (Cambridge, Mass.:
Harvard Univ. Press, 1957; a remarkable study of contemporary rural
life based on an American's firsthand observations).

The revolution of 1958 and the Fifth Republic still lie in the
province of the journalist or the political scientist rather than the
historian. To date, the best journalistic account of the 1958 coup is
that of J.-R. Tournoux: *Secrets d'état* (Paris: Plon, 1960). There is a
more dramatic narrative, pro-Gaullist in tone, by Serge and Merry
Bromberger: *Les Treize complots du treize mai* (Paris: Fayard, 1959);
it is based on extensive interviewing of the principal participants. A
Communist version, violently hostile to De Gaulle, may be found in
Maurice Mouillard's *La Mystification* (Paris: Ed. Sociales, 1958). On
the structure and prospects of the Fifth Republic, probably the best
analysis is that of Philip Williams and Martin Harrison: *De Gaulle's
Republic* (London: Longmans, 1960). Other recent works include
Dorothy Pickles' *The Fifth French Republic* (New York: Praeger, 1960);
Roy C. Macridis and Bernard E. Brown's *The De Gaulle Republic* (Home-
wood, Ill.: Dorsey, 1960); Raymond Aron's *France, Steadfast and
Changing* (Cambridge, Mass.: Harvard Univ. Press, 1960); Maurice
Duverger's *La Cinquième république* (Paris: Presses Univ., 1959);
Edgar S. Furniss, Jr.'s *France: Troubled Ally* (New York: Harper,
1960); and Stanley Hoffmann's "The French Constitution of 1958,"
American Political Science Review, LIII (1959), 332–57.

Recent French history, like that of the nineteenth century, is
illumined by certain novels of the period. Some of these works take
social and political problems as their subject matter; others are valuable because they reflect the mood, the intellectual temper, of the era.

No great French literary work came out of the First World War;
but the impact of that traumatic experience on at least some French-

men can be sensed in L.-F. Céline's bitterly cynical *Voyage au bout de la nuit* and in *Le Feu* of Henri Barbusse. Perhaps it is not surprising that Barbusse became a Communist and Céline a fascist; strong protest can carry men to either extreme. Alongside these passionately antiwar novels there was, however, a literature of heroism as well; it was best exemplified in Antoine de Saint-Exupéry's poetic reflections, *Vol de nuit*. No Frenchman of the 1920's produced a paean to war like Ernst Jünger's best-selling *Storm of Steel* in Germany.

The later volumes of Jules Romains's *Hommes de bonne volonté* carry his protagonists through the 1920's; and Georges Duhamel's *Journal de Salavan* also finds its base in the events of that decade. Georges Bernanos' *Journal d'un curé de campagne* provides remarkable insight into some of the tensions of village life; it is the work of a highly unorthodox Catholic. Gabriel Chevallier's *Clochemerle* is a racy and somewhat scabrous satire on village life and politics; Marcel Aymé's *Travelingue* is a more mordant satire on the epoch of the Popular Front. Jean-Paul Sartre's *Nausée* (1938) was the first important existentialist novel, foreshadowing the movement of ideas that had its full impact after the Second World War. The first two volumes of Sartre's later trilogy, *L'Age de raison* and *Le Sursis*, are set in the Munich era. Louis Aragon's *Les Communistes* is a party member's fictionalized account of the "phony war" period.

The occupation years and the resistance movement have inspired a number of topical novels. Albert Camus's *La Peste* is the most notable of these, though it is far more than a parable of France under German occupation. More directly relevant to the French experience of those years are Simone de Beauvoir's *Le Sang des autres*, Jean-Paul Sartre's *La Mort dans l'âme*, Elsa Triolet's *Le Premier accroc coûte deux cents francs*, Jean-Louis Curtis's *Forêts de la nuit*, and Jean Dutourd's satire *Au bon beurre*. Marcel Aymé's *Uranus* is a bitterly satirical portrayal of the months just after the liberation. Roger Peyrefitte's *La Fin des ambassades* is a semifictional, semiautobiographical account of intrigue at Vichy; its author, a professional diplomat, was purged as a Vichyite after the war.

Only a few novels have much direct relevance to political or social issues of the postwar era. Among the exceptions are Simone de Beauvoir's *Les Mandarins* (a thinly-veiled fictional study of leading left-wing intellectuals in Paris); Gilbert Cesbron's *Les Saints vont en enfer* (on the worker-priest movement); and Jean-Louis Curtis's *Les Justes causes* (on the political attitudes of young Parisians in the Fourth Republic).

INDEX

INDEX

A

Abd el Krim, 452

Abetz, Otto, 515

Absolutism: growth of, 9-12

Action Française, 340-41, 375, 415, 433, 472, 513, 589

Acton, Lord, 237

Agrarian party, 556

Agriculture: land ownership before the revolution, 25-26; land redistribution during and after the revolution, 122-23; changes between 1814 and 1870, 221-25; changes between 1870 and 1914, 360-61; changes between 1919 and 1931, 458; the depression, 467-68; postwar organization of farm groups, 556-59; studies of, 417

Aircraft: number possessed by Britain and France at outbreak of World War II, 505-6

Alain, 326-27, 341, 343, 542, 556

Albert (Alexandre Martin), 167, 170

Alexander, king of Yugoslavia, 494

Alexander I, emperor of Russia, 93, 96-97

Algeria: French expedition to, 244-45; French efforts to detach from Ottoman Empire, 247; conquest of, 255-56; colonization of, 256-57; Arab-kingdom plan of Napoleon III, 258; war in, 544-46, 581-83

Alibert, Raoul, 513

Almereyda, 400

Alsace-Lorraine: cession to Prussia, 276; growth of iron and steel industry, 345, 352; French desire to regain, 378-79;

extension of separation laws, 426; French recovery of, 458; studies of, 416

Amiens, Charter of 1906, 365

Amiens, Treaty of, 89

Ampère, André Marie, 240

André, General: reform of the army, 328-29

Anti-Semitism, 319-23

Aquinas, St. Thomas, 376

Aristocracy: position before revolution, 17-19; regains monopoly of high offices, 22; support of Enlightenment, 32-33; created by Napoleon I, 122; restoration to power position after 1814, 211-13; decline in influence, 213, 355

Army: support of Directors, 81-82; role in coup of Louis Napoleon, 181-82; opposition of Waldeck-Rousseau coalition, 328-30; 1917 "mutinies," 398; proposals to mechanize, 504-5; role in revolution of 1958, 544-45; position in Algerian war, 582-83; studies of, 261, 411-12

Aron, Raymond, 549

Artois, Charles Philippe, comte d', 57, 124-25, 133. *See also* Charles X, king of France

Assembly of Notables, 45-46

Assumptionist Fathers, 302-3, 322, 329-30, 341, 397

Auerstaedt, battle of, 92, 96

Aulard, Alphonse, 296

Austerlitz, battle of, 92

Austria: defeat by Napoleon, 94; German annexation of, 500

Aymé, Marcel, 575

B

Babeuf, François Noel, 38, 81
Bainville, Jacques, 3, 6, 8, 378
Balzac, Honoré de, 239
Banking: under Orleanist rule, 203-4; changes under Napoleon III, 206-7, 209
Bank of France, 90, 123, 455, 457, 486
Banque de Paris et des Pays-Bas, 349
Baroche, Jules, 189
Barras, Paul François, vicomte de, 79, 87
Barrès, Maurice, 314, 371-72, 375
Barthou, Louis, 494
Bastiat, Frédéric, 232
Bastille, fall of, 56-57
Baudouin, Paul, 514
Bayle, Pierre, 30
Bazaine, Marshal Achille François, 194, 274
Beauharnais, Eugène de, 96
Becquerel, Henri, 370
Belgium: revolt against Netherlands, 245, 246; alliance with France, 440
Benda, Julien, 572
Bergson, Henri, 371, 372-74, 418, 569, 571, 572
Bergsonism, 372-73, 374
Berlioz, Hector, 229-30
Bernadotte, Marshal Jean Baptiste (Charles XIV of Sweden and Norway), 99
Bernanos, Georges, 572
Bernard, Claude, 240
Berry, Caroline Ferdinande Louise, duchesse de, 149
Berry, Charles Ferdinand, duc de, 132
Berthelot, Marcellin, 240, 366, 370
Bidault, Georges, 523, 530
Bismarck, Prince Otto von, 193, 241, 253-54, 274-76, 381, 384
Blanc, Louis, 167, 169, 171, 173, 175, 187, 236, 246, 288
Blanqui, Auguste, 39, 150, 236, 279
Bloch, Marc, 572
Bloc National, 425
Bloy, Léon, 366
Blum, Léon: view of revolution of 1848, 249; succeeds to leadership of Social-
ist party, 429, 430; struggle with Moscow, 429-30; doctrine of nonparticipation in "bourgeois" cabinets, 470; reluctance to merge with Communists, 481; cabinet policies, 483-89; labor reforms, 485-86; devaluation of franc, 486-87; failure and overthrow, 487-89; policy of nonintervention in Spanish civil war, 499; postwar revival of Socialist party, 530; view of Communist proposals for powerful legislature, 533; studies of, 590
Bonald, Louis Gabriel, vicomte de, 130, 229, 231
Bonaparte, Joseph, 93
Bonaparte, Louis, king of Holland, 96
Bonaparte, Louis Napoleon. See Napoleon III
Bonaparte, Lucien, 85
Bonaparte, Mathilde, 177-78
Bonaparte, Napoleon. See Napoleon I
Bon Marché, 206
Bonnet, Georges, 500-501, 502
Borodino, battle of, 97
Bosnian crisis, 389
Boulanger, General Georges, 311-15, 372, 381, 413
Bourbon-Condé, Prince of, 20
Bourbon restoration, 121-43, 199, 242-43, 263-64
Bourgeoisie: role in prerevolutionary France, 21-23; support of the Enlightenment, 33-34; role in provisional government after 1848, 170-77; categories of, 213-16, 356-59; power of, 1814-1870, 213-16; Third Republic, 355-59; political influence of, 356-59; religious attitudes, 357; role in postwar period, 562-67; studies of, 261-62, 411
Bourget, Paul, 371
Bourmont, Louis August Victor de, Comte de Ghaisne, 139
Brasillach, Robert, 573
Brazza, Savorgnan de, 383
Breton, André, 569
Briand, Aristide, 331, 337, 399, 427-28, 439, 441, 443-46, 494
Briandism, 443-46
Brienne, Archbishop Loménie de, 46
Brinon, Fernand de, 493, 593

Brissot, Jacques Pierre, 67
Brissotins, 64, 67-69
Brogan, D. W., 388
Broglie, Victor François, duc de, 147, 284, 303
Bruening, Heinrich, 446
Bucard, Marcel, 471
Buchez, Philippe, 236, 238
Bugeaud, General, 164
Buonarroti, Filippo, 236
Bureaucracy: growth under Bourbons, 9-12
Burke, Edmund, 28, 73

C

C.F.T.C., 432, 435, 560, 567
C.G.A. (General Confederation of Agriculture), 558
C.G.P.M.E. (Confederation of Small and Medium-Sized Enterprises), 566
C.G.T. (Confédération Générale du Travail): union rivalries, 363; relationship with Socialist party, 365; and doctrine of revolutionary syndicalism, 374; collapse of general strike, 462; 1934 general strike, 480; merger with C.G.T.U., 481; growth and decline in membership, 490; postwar growth, 560; Communist efforts to "politicize," 562
C.G.T.-F.O. (Workers' Force), 560, 567
C.G.T.U., 435. 481
C.N.P.F. (National Council of French Employers), 435, 566
C.S.A.R. (Cagoulards), 471, 472
Cabet, Étienne, 235
Cahiers de doleances, 48, 49-50
Caillaux, Joseph, 337-39, 356, 378, 390-92, 399
Calonne, Charles, 44-45
Cambodia, 254
Cambon, Jules, 437
Camelots du Roi, 433
Camus, Albert, 577
Capet, House of: growth of, 8-11; and the church, 11
Carbonari, 133
Carnot, Sadi, 312

Cartel des gauches, 443
Cassin, Professor René, 520
Catholic Action, 432
Cavaignac, General Louis Eugène, 174-75, 176, 177, 280
Cavour, Conte Camillo Benso, 185
Cayla, Madame du, 133
Céline, Louis-Ferdinand, 573
Celtic revival, 7
Central Powers, 385
Chamberlain, Neville, 500, 501
Chamber of Peers, 125
Chambord, Comte de, 281-82, 285-86, 363
Champollion, Jean François, 240
Charcot, Jean, 370
Charles X, king of France: reign of, 134-43; indemnification of émigrés, 134-35; program of ultra-royalists, 134-39; July Ordinances, 141; exile to England, 142; dissolution of National Guard, 215; coronation of, 230; fall of Algiers, 244; problem of Algeria, 255. See also Artois, Charles Philippe, comte d'
Charter of 1814, 130, 144
Chateaubriand, François René, vicomte de, 29, 130, 136-37, 157, 229, 230, 243-44, 246
Chautemps, Camille, 510
Chauvin, Nicholas, 242
Chevalier, Michel, 189, 208
Chevalier-Cobden Treaty, 208, 252
Chevaliers de la Foi, 99-100, 124
Child labor legislation, 218-19, 362
Christian democracy: emergence of movement, 432
Christian existentialism, 575
Churchill, Winston, 400, 407, 508, 521, 525
Citroën, André, 459-60, 468
Civil Constitution of the Clergy, 60-61
Claudel, Paul, 373, 572
Clemenceau, Georges: and the revolutionary myth, 52-53; opposition to constitution of 1875, 288; and positivism, 300; aid to Boulanger, 312, 313; and policy of ralliement, 317; defeat in 1893, 320; Dreyfus Affair, 322; inventory of church properties, 331; opposition to Jaurès, 334; prewar premier-

ship (1906-9), 337-38; recognition of war to come, 378; relations with Russia and Great Britain, 389, 437-39; wartime leadership, 399-400, 425; peace policy, 405-8; Versailles Treaty, 405-8; postwar economic problems, 454; establishment of eight-hour day, 462; studies of, 414

Cloots, Anacharsis, 64

Clovis, 7

Cobban, Alfred, 19, 66, 513

Cochin, Denys, 396-97

Cochin-China, 254, 257

Code Napoleon, 90

Colbert: effect of mercantilism, 22

Collective bargaining, 485, 561

Colonial expansion: intervention in Mexico, 193, 253, 258; Indo-China, 253, 254, 257, 384, 451, 540, 544; colonial policy, 1814-1870, 254-58; acquisition of Senegal, 254, 257; mercantilism and sugar colonies, 255; conquest of Algeria, 255-56, 258; Ferry's policy, 309-10, 382-84; overseas empire after World War I, 450-52; war in Algeria, 544-46, 581-83; colonial policy of Fifth Republic, 580-81; studies of, 417

Colonial Union, 383

Combat (resistance group), 522

Combes, Émile, 330-33, 335

Comité des Forges, 356, 434

Comité des Houillères, 434

Committee of General Security, 69, 70

Committee of Public Safety (Paris), 69, 70, 71

Committee of Public Safety (Algeria), 546

Committee of Thirty, 48

Committee on French Africa, 383

Commune, 277-81, 318, 412

Communism: emergence of, 429-31

Communist party: birth of, 430; Soviet attempts to discipline, 430-31; reversal of policy under Popular Front, 480-81; push for merger with Socialists, 480; gain in popular votes, 482; refusal to join Blum cabinet, 484; change to policy of support for national defense, 495; outlawed by Daladier, 507; founding of Front National to resist Germans, 522; postwar resurgence, 531-32, 533; as factor in division of the left, 538; general strikes, 539; efforts to infiltrate farm organizations, 558; labor movement support, 560-61; loss of representation under Fifth Republic, 584-85; studies of, 589-90

Comoro Islands: acquisition of, 254

Compagnonnages, 217

Comte, Auguste, 239, 299, 367, 370, 374-75

Concert of Europe, 243

Concordat: of 1516, 11; between Napoleon and Vatican, 89, 102, 330-31

Condorcet, Marquis de, 48

Confédération Générale du Travail (C.-G.T.), 363, 364-65. See also C.G.T.

Confederation of Small and Medium-Sized Enterprises (C.G.P.M.E.), 566

Confederation of the Rhine, 94, 98

Congrégation, 138

Considérant, Victor, 235

Constans, Ernest, 314

Constant, Benjamin, 130, 232

Constitution of 1791, 60

Constitution of 1793, 67

Constitution of 1795, 80-81

Constitution of 1848, 175-76

Constitution of 1875, 287-88

Constitution of 1946, 528-29, 534-35

Constitution of 1958, 579-80

Continental system, 93, 96, 97

Corps Législatif, 188, 190

Cot, Pierre, 481

Coty, François, 471

Coty, René, 546

Courbet, Gustave, 239

Cousin, Victor, 147, 156, 219, 232

Crédit Lyonnais, 206, 417

Crédit Mobilier, 206, 207

Crimean War, 252

Croix de Feu, 432, 472-73, 475, 486

Cubism, 373, 374

Curie, Marie, 370

Curie, Pierre, 370

Cuvier, Baron Georges Leopold, 240

Czechoslovakia: French alliance with,

440, 444; German absorption of, 500, 501

D

Dadaism, 569
Dakar: Franco-British expedition to, 521
Daladier, Edouard: cabinet changes, 474, 475; efforts to pull Radicals into Popular Front, 481; ministry of, 489, 491; prewar foreign policy, 500-501, 502; pressure to withdraw from war, 503; plea for American aid, 506; outlaws Communist party, 507; overthrow, 508, flight to North Africa, 511
Danton, Georges-Jacques, 3-4, 53, 70, 74-75
Darlan, Admiral François, 515-16, 518, 523
Darnand, Joseph, 517
Daudet, Alphonse, 378
Daudet, Léon, 433
Daumier, Honoré, 218
Dawes Plan, 443
Déat, Marcel, 483n, 502, 513, 517
Debré, Michel, 539, 579, 580, 583, 585
Debussy, Claude, 373
Decazes, Élie, 127, 129, 130, 132
Degas, Edgar, 370
De Gaulle. *See* Gaulle, Charles de
Delacroix, Eugène, 229, 239
Delcassé, Théophile, 378, 385-89, 416
Délégation des gauches, 328
Deloncle, Eugène, 513
Democratic Alliance, 340n, 434
Déroulède, Paul, 311, 381
Descartes, René, 571
Desmoulins, Camille, 58
Diderot, Denis, 29
Dien-Bien-Phu, 540
Directory, 71-72, 79-85
Djibouti, 383
Dorgères, Henri, 514
Doriot, Jacques, 413, 431, 471, 498, 517, 593
Doumergue, Gaston, 475-76
Dreyfus, Alfred, 321-24

Dreyfus Affair, 321-24, 328, 329-30, 338, 340n, 388, 414, 429
Drieu la Rochelle, Pierre, 573
Drumont, Edouard, 319-20, 321-22
Duclos, Jacques, 431
Ducos, Pierre Roger, 88
Dufaure, Jules, 291
Duhamel, Georges, 572
Dumouriez, Charles François, 69
Dunkirk, battle of, 509
Durkheim, Émile, 374-75, 418, 571
Duruy, Victor, 190

E

École Libre des Sciences Politiques, 563
École Nationale d'Administration, 563
École Polytechnique, 240
Economic conditions: prerevolutionary cycles of boom and depression, 24-25; industrialization under Napoleon I, 196-97; tariff policy under Bourbon restoration, 197-200; industrial progress under Louis Philippe, 200-205; Second Empire, 205-9; between 1870 and 1914, 344-53; postwar currency problems, 453-57; postwar boom, 457-60; expansion under Fourth Republic, 550-56. *See also* Tariff policy
Eden Treaty, 27, 197
Egypt: Napoleon's expedition to, 87-88; revolt against Ottoman Empire, 247; Franco-British dispute, 381-82; Marchand expedition, 386, 387
Electoral procedure: restriction under Napoleon III, 179, 188; increase in suffrage under Louis Philippe, 214; Third Republic, 290-91; Tardieu proposals for reform, 469; Fourth Republic, 536; Fifth Republic, 580, 585n
"Émigrés's Billion," 134-35
Engels, Friedrich, 239
England. *See* Great Britain
Enlightenment: Freemasonry and diffusion of ideas, 29, 33-34; "alienation of the intellectuals," 29; doctrines of, 29-

31; impact of Rousseau's ideas, 31-32; support by aristocracy, 32-33; support by church and bourgeoisie, 33; criticism of, 34-39, impact on French society and politics, 39; and natural frontiers concept, 304; studies of, 112-13.
Entente Cordiale, 382, 388, 389, 390
Estates-General: convocation of, 46-47; dispute over organization of, 47-49; elections for, 49; grievance petitions, 48, 49-50; meeting of, 54-55
Esterhazy, Major Marie Charles Ferdinand Walsin, 321, 323
Ethiopia, 494
Estournelles de Constant, Baron d', 377
Existentialism, 574-77

F

F.F.I. (French Forces of the Interior), 523, 525
F.L.N., 583
F.N.S.E.A. (National Federation of Farmers' Unions), 558
Faidherbe, General Louis Léon, 257
Falloux Law, 178, 179-81, 301, 304
Fascism: growth of movements, 471-72
Faure, Edgar, 527
Fauvet, Jacques, 423
Fauvism, 373, 374
Favre, Jules, 275, 281
February riots (1934), 473-75
Febvre, Lucien, 572
Federation of Mutual Aid Societies and Cooperatives, 558
Félix Potin, 206
Ferry, Jules: member of Republican Left, 286; Ferry Laws and school reform, 304-6, 311, 362; colonial expansion policy, 309-10, 382-84, 386; supporter of appeasement, 378; downfall, 381
Ferry Laws, 304-6, 311, 362
Fifth Republic: De Gaulle chosen premier, 578-79; constitution of 1958, 579-80; changes in institutional framework, 580; colonial policy, 580-81; war in Algeria, 581-83; deflation policy,

583-84; shake-up in party representation, 584-85; future of, 585-87; studies of, 596
First Estate: under Louis XV, 17, 19-20; election to Estates-General, 49
First International, 220
Flandin, P.-E., 496-97, 498, 515
Flaubert, Gustave, 163, 168, 239, 300, 370-71
Fleury, Cardinal, 12, 13
Foch, General Ferdinand, 396, 400, 405, 442
Foreign investment, 349, 450-51
Fouché, Joseph, 33, 71, 95
Fould, Achille, 189
Fourier, Charles, 233-35
Fourth Republic: achievements of, 528; constitution of 1946, 528-29, 534-35; contrast with Third Republic, 536-37; Indo-China, 540, 544; war in Algeria, 544-46; revolution of 1958, 544-47; De Gaulle named premier, 545, 546-47; Planning Commission, 550; postwar boom, 551; opposition to economic change, 551-56; changes in agriculture, 556-59; growth and division of labor movement, 559-62; social change, 562-67; studies of, 595-96
Franc: collapse in value, 455-56; partial recovery in value, 456-57; devaluation of, 486-87
France: and geographical determinism, 4-5; influence of ethnic factors, 5-8; growth of royal absolutism, 9-12; decline of the monarchy under Louis XV and Louis XVI, 40-46; summoning of Estates-General, 46-50, 54-55; National Assembly, 55-62; constitution of 1791, 60; war with Austria and Prussia, 64-65; rise of the Jacobins, 66-68, 70-72; National Convention, 65, 67-72; death of Louis XVI, 68; fall of the Girondins, 69; rise and fall of Robespierre, 69-71; end of the Terror, 71; the Directory, 71-72, 79-85; constitution of 1795, 80-81; under Napoleon I, 86-106; Bourbon Restoration, 121-43; Hundred Days, 126-27; Second Republic, 167-83; June Days, 160, 174-75, 179, 278,

280-81; constitution of 1848, 175-76; Louis Napoleon's coup d'état, 181-83; Second Empire, 184-95; Franco-Prussian War, 193-95, 273-76, 283; rise of a proletariat, 216-21; foreign policy, 1814-1870, 241-58; entente with Great Britain, 252; intervention in Mexico, 193, 253, 258; penetration in Indo-China, 253, 254, 257, 451; policy toward Prussia, 253-54; colonial policy of Second Empire, 254-58; Paris Commune, 277-81; Opportunist Republic, 296-324; struggle between positivism and the church, 298-304; Ferry Laws and school reform, 304-6; premiership of Gambetta, 306-8; colonial expansion under Ferry, 309-10, 382-84; Boulanger Affair, 311-15; Panama Scandal, 319-21; Dreyfus Affair, 321-24; effect of separation of church and state, 330-33; revival of nationalism, 339, 390-92, 416-17; Méline Tariff, 346-47; question of reconciliation with Germany, 379-80, 385-92; years of isolation, 380-82; Russian pacts of 1891, 1894, and 1899, 384-85; Entente Cordiale, 382, 387, 388, 389, 390; the Great War, 393-400, 401-4;; Versailles Treaty, 404-8; postwar relations with Great Britain, 437-40, 441, 442; German reparations question, 440-41; occupation of the Ruhr, 441-43; conciliatory policy toward Germany, 443-46; Little Entente, 447; relations with Italy, 447-50; expansion of colonial empire, 450-52; fiscal policy, 454-57; the depression, 464-82; growth of fascist groups, 471-72; attempted coup of 1934, 473-75; Popular Front, 483-89; disintegration as a world power, 491-503; indecision, invasion, and defeat, 503-9; pact with Soviet Union, 494, 496: Pétain and Vichy government, 510-19; Free French movement, 519-26; the resistance movement, 521-23, 525-26, 549-50; liberation, 525; Fourth Republic, 527-47; provisional government of De Gaulle, 527-29, 531, 532; postwar alliance with Soviet Union, 531; constitution of 1946,

533-35, 536; postwar purges, 535n; Indo-China, 540, 544; war in Algeria, 544-46, 581-83; revolution of 1958, 544-47; De Gaulle named premier, 545, 546-47, 578-79; Fifth Republic, 578-87; constitution of 1958, 579-80

France, Anatole, 368-69, 370, 371, 374, 453, 572

France-Germany Committee, 493

Francistes, 471

Franco-Prussian War, 193-95, 273-76, 419

Franc-Tireur, 522

Franz Ferdinand, archduke of Austria, 392

Free French movement, 510, 519-25, 594

Freemasonry: and diffusion of Enlightenment ideas, 29, 33-34; and positivism, 300; army espionage system, 329; bourgeois support of, 359

French Committee of National Liberation, 524

French Communist party. See Communist party

French Community, 581

French Congo: cession of section to Germany, 390

French Equatorial Africa, 450

French Forces of the Interior (F.F.I.), 523, 525

French Guinea, 581

French National Committee, 520

French Revolution (1789): effects of, 51-54; Estates-General, 54-55; National Assembly, 55-61; constitution of 1791, 60; war with Austria and Prussia, 64-65; rise of the Jacobins, 66-68, 70-72; National Convention, 65, 67-72; death of Louis XVI, 68; fall of the Girondins, 69; rise and fall of Robespierre, 69-71; end of the Terror, 71-72; conservative view of, 72-74; liberal view of, 74-75; radical view of, 75-76; Marxian view of, 76-79; studies of, 108-10, 110-12, 113-14, 116-17

French Union, 534-36

French Workers' party, 318

Fresnel, Augustin Jean, 240

Freud, Sigmund, 569

Freycinet Plan, 353

Friedland, battle of, 93
Fronde rebellion, 17
Front National, 522
Fustel de Coulanges, N.-D., 374

G

Galbraith, John Kenneth, 567
Gallicanism, 11, 137, 157-58, 332
Gambetta, Léon: role in Franco-Prussian War, 272-75; leader of Radicals, 286; support of constitution of 1875, 288-89; efforts to unify republicans, 290-91, 297; victory of republicans, 293; view of the little man, 298; and positivism, 300; and Catholicism, 303; premiership, 306-8; and petty bourgeoisie, 358; loss of Alsace-Lorraine, 378; diplomatic hopes after 1871, 380-81; British dispute over Egypt, 382
Gamelin, Maurice Gustave, 496, 504, 507
Gaulle, Charles de: conception of presidency, 292; proposals for army mechanization, 504-5; plan for fighting retreat to Brittany, 509; Free French movement, 510, 519-21; friction with the British, 521; growth of the resistance, 521-23; move to Algiers, 523-24; liberation of France, 524; American recognition of, 524; chosen provisional president, 527, 532-33; resignation, 529; alliance with Soviet Union, 531; opposition to draft of 1946 constitution, 534; re-entrance into politics, 538; disowns R.P.F., 539; chosen premier, 545, 546-47, 578-79; constitution of 1958, 579-80; changes in institutional framework, 580, 585n; colonial policy, 580-81; war in Algeria, 581-83; deflation policy, 583-84; shake-up in party representation, 584-85; future of Fifth Republic, 585-87; studies of, 594-96
Gautier, Théophile, 231
Gaxotte, Pierre, 28, 182, 227
Gay-Lussac, Joseph Louis, 219, 240
General Confederation of Agriculture (C.G.A.), 558

Geographical determinism: and shaping of modern France, 4-5
Germain, Henri, 356
Germany: question of reconciliation with France, 379-80, 385-92; Morocco disputes, 388, 390; reparations question, 440-41; French occupation of the Ruhr, 441-43; military occupation of the Rhineland, 496; Soviet nonaggression pact, 502; invasion of Low Countries, 508; fall of France, 509; requisition of French labor, 516-17. See also Prussia
Geyl, Pieter, 86, 100
Gide, André, 373, 570-71
Giraud, General Henri, 524
Girondins, 64, 67-69, 74
Goguel, François, 328
Gouin, Félix, 529
Gramont, Duc de, 193
Great Britain: pressure to evict French ultras from power, 242; opposition to French expedition to Spain, 243; conflict with France over Egypt, 247-48, 381-82, 387; the Pritchard Affair, 248; Spanish marriage question, 248; opposition to construction of Suez Canal, 252n; Entente Cordiale, 382, 388, 389, 390; end of entente with France, 437-38; refusal to bolster alliance of east European states, 438-39; withdrawal of guarantee of aid, 440; German reparations question, 440-41; opposition to military action in 1936, 496-97; Munich, 500-501; prewar Anglo-French disagreements, 504; number of first-line aircraft, 505-6; friction with Free French leaders, 521
Great War, 393-400, 401-4, 415
Grévy, Jules: fear of strong executive, 176, 294; member of Republican Left, 286; successor to MacMahon, 294; opposition to Gambetta, 297, 306; resignation, 312
Guadeloupe, 255
Guérard, Albert, 227
Guesde, Jules: formation of French Workers' party, 318-19; rivalry with Jaurès for Socialist party leadership, 334-35; doctrine of nonparticipation in

"bourgeois" cabinets, 335-36, 470; membership in wartime cabinet, 396; and white-peace advocates, 398

Guizot, François: doctrinaire of moderate royalists, 130, 232, 240; years of leadership, 152-53; educational reform of 1833, 154; court opposition to, 161; fall from power, 164; member of upper bourgeoisie, 214; Spanish marriage question, 248; repression of liberal unrest, 249

H

"H.S.P." (haute société protestante), 357

Hanotaux, Gabriel, 378, 385-86

Hapsburg, House of, 447

Haussmann, Baron Georges Eugène: rebuilding of Paris, 220

Hébert, Jacques René, 70

Hébertists, 76

Heidegger, Martin, 574

Henry, Major, 322, 323

Herriot, Edouard: extension of separation laws to Alsace, 426n; Radical leader, 428, 429; German reparations plan, 443; recognition of Soviet government, 447; second cabinet, 470

Hervé, Gustave, 338-39

Herz, Dr. Cornelius, 320

Hitler, Adolf: early French opposition to, 493, 494, 495; occupation of the Rhineland, 496, 497; French appeasement, 498; civil war in Spain, 499; annexation of Austria, 500; absorption of Czechoslovakia, 501; pact with Russia, 502; invasion of Poland, 503; invasion of the Low Countries, 508; Montoire Conference, 514-15

Ho Chi-Minh, 540

Holbach, Baron d', 30

Holstein, Baron von, 384

Hottinguer (banking firm), 203

Housing conditions: between 1870 and 1914, 344; after the Great War, 463

Howard, Miss, 176

Hugo, Victor, 75, 163, 187, 229, 230, 366, 373

Humanism: and philosophes, 30-31; and teachings of Rousseau, 31-32

Hundred Days, 126-27

Huss, John, 301

I

Immigration: policy to solve labor shortage, 461

Imperialism, 382-84. See also Colonial expansion

Impressionists, 369-70

Income tax: Machault's attempt to levy, 14-15; proposals for, 283; weakness of, 454

Independent-Peasant bloc, 531, 538, 539, 540, 543, 584

Indo-China: French penetration, 253, 254, 257; French acquisition of, 309; nationalist movements, 452; revolt in, 540; armistice, 540, 544

Industrial production: prerevolutionary growth, 24; under Louis Philippe, 200-204; the Second Empire, 205-9; decline by 1914, 350-52; depression slump, 476-77; postwar boom, 550-51; studies of, 262, 267

Inflation, 453-57

Iron and steel industry, 345, 352

Isabella II, queen of Spain, 248

Italy: friction between fascist regime and France, 447-50

J

J.A.C. (Young Christian Farmers), 432

J.O.C. (Young Christian Workers), 432

Jacobin clubs, 66-68, 73, 84

Jacobins, 66-68, 70-72, 77

Jansenism, 153

Jaurès, Jean: view of revolution of 1848, 249; unification of Socialists, 319; view of Dreyfus Affair, 322; leadership

of Socialist party, 333-37; assassination, 429; studies of, 414-15
Jeanneney, J. M., 196
Jena, battle of, 92
Jesuits, 20, 35, 138, 330, 397
Jeunes Patrons, 565
Jeunesses Patriotes, 432, 471
Jews: Vichy policy toward, 517
Joffre, General Joseph Jacques, 395-98
Jouvenel, Robert de, 435
July Monarchy: reign of Louis Philippe, 144-66; conflict between right-center and left-center, 148-49; the Legitimists, 149; republican agitation, 149-50; Guizot ministry, 152-54; religious issues, 155-61; discontent with the regime, 162-63; fall of the monarchy, 163-66. See also Louis Philippe I, king of the French
July Ordinances, 141
June Days, 160, 174-75, 179, 278, 280-81

K

Kafka, Franz, 575
Kellogg-Briand Pact, 443
Keynes, John Maynard, 438

L

Labor movement: Lyons insurrections, 150, 218; rise of proletariat, 216-21; conditions of factory workers, 217-18; child labor legislation, 218-19, 362; temporary reforms of 1848, 219; social reform under Napoleon III, 219, 221; First International, 220; employer welfare schemes, 220-21; between 1870 and 1914, 362-65; C.G.T., 364-65, 374, 462, 480, 481, 490, 560, 562; C.F.T.C., 432, 435, 560, 567; C.G.T.U., 435, 481; divisions of workers after Great War, 462; establishment of eight-hour day, 462; reforms under Blum government, 485-86; responsibility for economic failure of 1936-38, 487; rise and fall in trade-union membership, 490; C.G.A., 558; postwar evolutionary changes, 559-62; C.G.T.-F.O., 560, 567; C.G.P.M.E., 566; studies of, 261, 266-67, 411, 590
Labor shortage: immigration policy to recruit workers, 461
La Bourdonnaye, 139
Labrousse, Ernest, 183
Lacordaire, Jean Baptiste, 159
Lafayette, Marquis de, 32, 48, 49, 130, 142
Laffitte, Jacques, 139, 199
Laissez faire: under Louis XVIII, 197, 199; under Louis Philippe, 200; Second Republic, 204; Second Empire, 206-7
Lamarck, Jean Baptiste, chevalier de, 240
Lamartine, Alphonse de: prediction of 1848 revolution, 162; view of Great Revolution, 163; leader of provisional government, 165, 168, 170; foreign policy, 171-72; public works plans, 173-74, 203; June Days, 174; downfall of, 175, 176, 177; romanticism, 227, 230
Lamennais, Félicité de, 157-58, 173, 238
Landes, David, 203, 548
Land ownership: before the revolution, 25-26
Land redistribution: during and after the revolution, 122-23
Laplace, Pierre Simon, 240
Laval, Pierre: change from Socialist to Moderate party, 428; 1931 premiership, 446; electoral reform, 469; depression policies, 476-77; prewar foreign policy, 494-95; defeatism, 502; early dominance in Vichy government, 511-12; dismissal by Pétain, 514; meeting with Hitler, 514-15; return to power, 516; policy of evasion, 516-18; studies of, 593
Lavisse, Ernest, 374
Law, John, 24
League of Nations, 406, 438, 443, 450, 493
League of Patriots, 381

Lebrun, President Albert, 509, 511
Le Chapelier Law, 216
Leconte de Lisle, Charles, 369
Ledru-Rollin, Alexandre Auguste, 173, 177
Lefebvre, Georges, 28
Left-Center, 286, 287, 288
Léger, Alexis, 493-94, 499, 503
Legion of Honor, 90
Legislative Assembly, 64, 65, 181
Legitimists: attempts to gain power, 149, 177, 355, 363
Lenin, Nicolai, 53, 425, 430, 431, 452
Leo XIII, Pope: policy of *ralliement*, 315, 316-17
Léon, Léonie, 308
Le Play, Frédéric, 238
Lesseps, Ferdinand de, 252n, 319
Lettres de cachet, 50
Libération, 522
Libération-Nord, 522
Libertarianism: Alain, 326-27
Lit de justice, 12
Little Entente, 447
Littré, Émile, 367
Lloyd George, David, 439, 441
Lobbyists, 435
Locarno Treaties, 443
Locke, John, 30
Lorraine: growth of iron and steel industry, 345, 352; French recovery of, 458
Lorwin, Val, 463
Loti, Pierre, 370
Louis XIV, king of France, 12, 13, 14
Louis XV, king of France: reign of, 13-15; attempts at reform, 40-42; studies of, 111
Louis XVI, king of France: restoration of *parlements*, 42, 47; dismissal of Turgot, 43; appointment of Necker, 43-44; Calonne and the Assembly of Notables, 45-46; summoning of Estates-General, 45-46, 54; National Assembly, 55-57; dismissal and recall of Necker, 56, 57; and failure of constitutional monarchy, 63-64; death of, 68
Louis XVIII, king of France: character and motives, 124; and ultra-royalists, 124-25, 127-33; the Charter, 125; Hundred Days, 126-27; second restoration, 127-33; tariff actions, 197
Louis Napoleon Bonaparte. *See* Napoleon III, emperor of the French
Louis Philippe I, king of the French: accession of, 145-46; character and motives, 145-46; attempts to assassinate, 152; Guizot ministry, 152-54; fall of the monarchy, 163-66; economic policies, 200-204; creates peerage, 212-13, 355; increase in suffrage, 214; reconstitution of National Guard, 215-16; conditions of factory workers, 217-18; foreign policy, 245-49; Belgian crisis, 245; Franco-British alignment, 246-48; Egyptian question, 247; Spanish marriage question, 248; colonial acquisitions, 254; occupation of Algeria, 255-56; Thiers's plan for mastering Paris, 280. *See also* July Monarchy
Low Countries: German invasion, 508
Luther, Martin, 301
Luxembourg Commission, 171, 175
Lyons insurrections, 150, 218

M

M.R.P. (Mouvement Républicain Populaire), 530, 531, 534, 537, 539-40, 543, 567, 584
Mably, 30
MacCarthy, Count Robert Joseph, 127n
Machault d'Arnouville, Jean Baptiste, 14-15
MacMahon, Marshal, 194, 284, 285, 289, 291-94
Madagascar, 309, 383
Maginot Line, 440, 492, 506-7
Maistre, Joseph Marie, comte de, 121, 125
Mallarmé, Stéphane, 373
Malraux, André, 573, 579
Malvy, Jean-Louis, 399
Mandel, Georges, 498, 511
Manet, Edouard, 370
Manuel, Jacques, 130
Marat, Jean-Paul, 58

Marcel, Gabriel, 575
Marchand expedition, 386, 387
Marie Antoinette, queen of France: attempts to influence king, 43, 45, 46, 47, 55
Marie Louise, empress of the French, 95, 99
Marin, Louis, 407
Maritain, Jacques, 376
Marne, battle of the, 396
Marshall Plan, 551
Martignac, Vicomte de, 139
Martin du Gard, Roger, 572
Martinique, 255
Marty, André, 431
Marx, Karl: view of revolution of 1848 and Second Republic, 167-70; view of Louis Napoleon, 178-79; model for investigation of society, 211; First International, 220; and Proudhon, 237; and the Commune, 279; antimilitarism and antipatriotism, 338-39
Massu, General Émile, 546
Maupeou, René Nicolas, 41-42
Mauriac, François, 572
Maurois, André, 572
Maurras, Charles: founding of Action Française, 340-41; professed adherence to Comte, 375; continuing influence of Action Française, 433, 472; role in Vichy government, 513; studies of, 415
Mehemet Ali, pasha of Egypt, 247
Méline Tariff, 346-47, 353, 361, 417
Mendès-France, Pierre, 511, 532, 540-41, 580
Ménétrel, Dr., 518
Mercantilism: effect of, 22; and sugar colonies, 255, 256
Metternich, Prince Clemens von, 98, 249
Metz: fall of, 194, 274
Mexico: French intervention in, 193, 253, 258
Meyerbeer, Giacomo, 240
Michelet, Jules, 4, 9, 23, 24, 163, 230, 239, 240, 370, 571-72
Millerand, Alexandre, 325
Millet, François, 222
Mirabeau, Comte de, 49, 53, 62-63
Missions de France, 138

Moch, Jules, 539
Moderates: turn toward the right, 316-18; renewal of leadership, 320; and Dreyfus Affair, 323; collaboration with Radicals, 337; and the little man, 347-48; victory in 1919 election, 425; renewal of political influence, 425-26
Mollet, Guy, 543, 544
Moltke, Count Helmuth von, 274
Monet, Claude, 370
Monnet, Jean, 550
Monnet Commission, 535, 550
Montalembert, Charles, 159-60, 179
Montesquieu, Charles Louis, baron de, 3, 30, 36-37, 60, 113
Montoire Conference, 515n
Morand, Paul, 436
Morazé, Charles, 215
Morelly, 30
Morny, Charles, duc de, 186, 189
Morocco: Franco-German disputes, 388, 390; French investment in, 451; Riff rebellion, 452; move toward granting independence, 540-41
Moulin, Jean, 522-23
Mounier, Emmanuel, 376, 575
Mouvement Républicain Populaire (M.R.P.), 530, 531, 534, 537, 539-40, 543, 567, 584
Mun, Albert, comte de, 317, 363, 396
Munich settlement, 500-501
Murat, Joachim, king of Naples, 98
Mussolini, Benito, 447, 471, 494, 497, 501

N

Namier, Sir Lewis, 492
Napoleon I, emperor of the French: revolutionary changes, 62; and the Paris mob, 72; coup d'état of 1799, 79, 84-85; defeat of Austria, 87; Egypt, 87-88; First Consul, 88-89; Concordat with Vatican, 89; domestic reforms, 89-90, 122-24; colonial plans, 90-91; plans to invade England, 91-92; the Empire, 91, 94-96; defeat of Prussia and Austria, 92; Treaty of Tilsit, 93;

continental system, 93, 97; invasion of Spain, 93-94; abduction of the Pope, 94; invasion of Russia, 96-97; defeat at Leipzig, 98; exile to Elba, 99; history's view of, 100-106; creation of aristocracy, 122; Hundred Days, 126-27; industrial policy, 196-97; labor regulation, 216; studies of, 114-16, 117

Napoleon III, emperor of the French: attempted coups, 151-52; election of, 176-77; character and motives, 177-78; Marxian view of, 177-78; Falloux Law, 179-81; successful coup d'état, 181-83; authoritarian phase of Second Empire, 185, 186-89; liberal phase of Second Empire, 185, 189-92; intervention in Mexico, 193, 253, 258; war with Prussia, 193-95, 273-76; economic growth during Second Empire, 205-9; creation of peerage, 213; social reforms, 219-21; agricultural conditions, 221-25; population changes, 225-26; and doctrine of productivity and welfare, 234; foreign policy, 250-58; entente with Great Britain, 252; European congress system, 252; penetration of Indo-China, 253, 254, 257; policy toward Prussia, 253-54; colonial policy, 257-58; decline and death of, 281, 286-87; middle bourgeoisie, 357; studies of, 265-66

National Agricultural Confederation, 435

National Assembly: establishment of, 54-56; end of feudalism, 58; removal to Paris, 59; and Civil Constitution of the Clergy, 60-61; effect of reforms, 61-62; factions during Third Republic, 286-95. See also Legislative Assembly

National Catholic Federation, 426

National Convention, 65, 67-72

National Council of French Employers (C.N.P.F.), 566

National Defense, Government, 273, 276

National Federation of Farmers' Unions (F.N.S.E.A.), 558

National Guard, 150, 164, 215-16

Nationalism: revival of, 339, 390-92, 416-17

National Resistance Council, 522, 525, 527, 530

National Workshops, 169, 171, 173-74, 257

Nations, battle of the, 98

Natural frontiers concept, 3-4

Navarino, battle of, 244n

Necker, Jacques, 22, 43-44, 48-49, 56, 57

Nelson, Admiral Horatio, 88

Neopositivism, 575

Neo-Socialists, 483n

Neo-Thomism, 375-76, 575

Ney, Marshal, 97

Nivelle, Robert George, 398

Noblesse de robe, 12, 18-19, 49

O

O.C.M. (Organisation Civile et Militaire), 522

Offenbach, Jacques, 240

Ollivier, Émile, 190

Operation Resurrection, 546

Opportunists: split from Republican Union, 288; control of the Third Republic, 296-324; failure to strengthen political system, 296-98; failure to move toward social reform and economic modernization, 296-98; struggle between positivism and the church, 298-304; Ferry Laws and school reform, 304-6; premiership of Gambetta, 306-8; colonial expansion under Ferry, 309-10, 382-84, 386; Boulanger Affair, 311-15; change in attitude and name, 316; *ralliement*, 315, 316, 317; Panama Scandal, 319-21; Dreyfus Affair, 321-24; and the little man, 347-48; lesser bourgeoisie, 359; notions of understanding with Germans, 380-81; studies of, 413. See also Moderates

Organisation Civile et Militaire (O.C.-M.), 522

Orleanist Monarchy, 144-66, 200-205, 264

Orléans, Louis Philippe, duc d', 141-42. See also Louis Philippe I, king of the French

Orléans, Louis Philippe Joseph, duc d' (Philippe Égalité), 48, 148
Ottoman Empire, 427
Ozanam, Frédéric, 157, 160, 179, 238

P

P.P.F. (Parti Populaire Français), 471, 472, 498
P.S.F. (Parti Social Français), 473, 513
Painlevé, Paul, 399
Palmerston, Henry John Temple, viscount, 247, 249
Panama Scandal, 319-21, 358, 385
Papal States: annexation by Napoleon I, 94
Paris: fall of, 275; the Commune, 277-81, 318, 412; change in political sentiment, 315-16; capture by Germans, 509; liberation of, 525
Paris, Comte de, 281
Parlement of Paris: role as power element, 11-12; and Louis XVI, 42, 46-47
Parlements: power of, 11-12; opponents of reform, 14-15; repression by Louis XV, 41; and Louis XVI, 42, 46-47
Parti Populaire Français (P.P.F.), 471
Parti Social Français (P.S.F.), 473
Pascal, Blaise, 376, 571, 575
Passy, Colonel, 520
Pasteur, Louis, 240, 370
Peasant Corporation, 513
Peasant Front, 514
Peasantry: position before 1789, 20-21, 25-26; role in nineteenth-century France, 221-25; numerical decline, 360-62; growth of political awareness, 361-62; impact of Great War, 403-4
Pecqueur, Constantin, 236
Péguy, Charles, 376
Périer, Casimir, 144, 145, 149, 199, 218, 356
Persigny, Jean Gilbert, duc de, 189, 190-91
Pétain, Marshal Henri Philippe: battle of Verdun, 397; succeeds to command of French armies, 398; member of 1934

cabinet, 475; resistance to mechanization efforts, 504; heads Vichy government, 509, 510-14; dismissal of Laval, 514; meeting with Hitler, 515; appointment of Darlan, 515-16; return of Laval, 516-18; evaluation of leadership, 518-19; reforms, 535; studies of, 592, 593
Pflimlin, Pierre, 545-46
Philosophes, 3, 30, 33, 73
Pichegru, General Charles, 81
Picquart, Colonel, 322
Pitt, William, 83, 84
Pius IX, Pope, 179-80, 301
Pius X, Pope, 341
Plan XVII, 395, 396
Planning Commission, 550
Poincaré, Henri, 370
Poincaré, Raymond: chosen president, 339, 390-92; effort to build national strength, 378; differences with Clemenceau, 399, 400, 405; return to politics, 427-28, 444-45, 456; occupation of the Ruhr, 441-43; postwar economic problems, 454; resignation, 469; studies of, 414
Poland: French alliance with, 444, 446; Nazi blitzkrieg, 503
Polignac, Jules de, 139-40, 244
Pompadour, Madame de, 14
Popular Democratic party, 432
Popular Front: rise of, 457; the Laval experiment, 477; Blum cabinet, 483-89; sitdown strikes, 485; labor policies, 485-86; failure of economic program, 486-88; attempts at social reform, 488; growth of appeasement sentiment, 495; Spanish civil war, 499; effect on preparedness efforts, 505; studies of, 590
Population: prerevolutionary growth, 16-17; decline after 1814, 225-26; growth between 1871 and 1914, 344; postwar labor shortage, 461; Fourth Republic, 528; growth since 1946, 549; studies of, 262-63
Positivism, 298-304, 367, 374-75, 571, 575
Poujade, Pierre, 540, 541-42, 555
Poujadism, 542, 543
Press: suppression by Napoleon I, 96;

censorship under Louis XVIII, 133; suppression by Charles X, 135; repression by Napoleon III, 187; freedom restored, 190; growth of resistance newspapers, 535, 536
Pressure groups, 434-35, 460, 537
Prévost-Paradol, Lucien, 232, 241
Proudhon, Pierre-Joseph, 236-37, 279, 364
Proust, Marcel, 372-73, 570
Prussia: defeat by France, 92; defeat of France, 193-95, 273-76. *See also* Germany

Q

Queneau, Raymond, 575
Quesnay, François, 29

R

R.P.F. (Rassemblement du Peuple Français), 538, 539, 542
"Race": as factor in shaping modern France, 5-8
Radicals: party position, 286; support of 1875 constitution, 288; split with Opportunists, 288; collapse of coalition cabinet, 311; and the church, 317-18; change in viewpoint, 318, 326-27; Dreyfus Affair, 323; rise to power, 325-26; withdrawal of Socialist support from coalition, 333, 336; collaboration with Moderates, 337; leadership of Clemenceau, 337-38; fall of Caillaux cabinet, 339; and the little man, 348; control by lesser bourgeoisie, 359; opposition to Russian pact, 385; pressure for white peace, 398; shift in base of support, 434; fiscal policy, 455-56; opposition to Tardieu's plan for electoral reform, 469; return to power, 470; decline in power, 482; studies of, 414
Radical Socialist party, 340n
Railroad construction: public expenditures for, 200, 202-3, 204, 205; social effects of, 224-25; Freycinet Plan, 353
Rassemblement du Peuple Français (R.P.F.), 538, 539, 542
Ralliement, policy of, 315, 316-17
Raspail, François, 177
Rationalism, 229
Reclus, Maurice, 377
Redressement Français (French Resurgence), 460
Reinach, Baron, 320
Rémond, René, 472
Rémusat, Charles de, 232
Renan, Ernest, 5-6, 239, 367-68, 371
Renaud, Major Jean, 471
Renaudel, Pierre, 483n
Renoir, Pierre Auguste, 370
Renouvier, Charles Bernard, 303
Republican Federation, 340n, 434
Republicanism: triumph in 1877, 292-95
Republican Left, 286, 288, 296
Republican Union, 286, 287, 288. *See also* Radicals
Resistance movement, 521-23, 525-26, 549-50, 597-98
Revolution of 1789. *See* French Revolution
Revolution of 1830, 141-43
Revolution of 1848, 163-65, 174-75, 264
Revolution of 1958, 544-47
Reynaud, Paul: economic recovery policy, 489-91; support of mutual aid pact, 496; opposition to appeasement, 498; named premier in 1939, 508, 509
Rhineland: Hitler's military occupation, 496
Ribbentrop, Joachim von, 501, 515
Richelieu, Cardinal, 9
Richelieu, Louis François, duc de (1815), 126, 129
Riff rebellion, 452
Right-Center, 286-87
Right-wing groups: studies of, 260-61, 411
Rimbaud, Arthur, 373
Rivarol, Antoine de, 51
Robespierre, Maximilien, 38, 39, 53, 69-71, 73, 74, 76, 77, 78n
Rocque, Colonel de la, 472, 476, 513

Rohan, Cardinal de, 20
Romains, Jules, 572
Roman Catholic church: concordat of 1516, 11; position of clergy between 1760 and 1789, 19-20; support of Enlightenment, 33; Civil Constitution of the Clergy, 60-61; Concordat between Napoleon and the Vatican, 102; changes under Napoleon, 123-24; revival under Bourbon restoration, 137-38; loss of special privilege, 156; gradual acceptance of revolution, 156-57; Lamennais' attempts to reconcile the church with political liberalism, 157-58; school question, 159-60; Falloux Law, 178, 179-81, 301, 304; and Napoleon III, 185, 187; struggle with positivism, 298-304; Ferry Laws and school reform, 304-6; *ralliement*, 315, 316-17; Assumptionist Fathers, 302-3, 322, 329-30, 341, 397; opposition of Waldeck-Rousseau coalition, 329-30; separation of church and state, 330-33; neo-Thomism, 375-76, 575; studies of, 261, 267-68, 411. *See also* Vatican
Romanticism, 227-31
Roosevelt, Franklin D., 524
Rothschild, House of, 203, 214, 356
Rouher, Eugène, 189
Rousseau, Jean Jacques, 3, 29, 31-32, 34, 36, 38-39, 73, 112-13
Rouvier, Maurice, 356, 378, 389-90
Roux, Jacques, 78n
Royer-Collard, Pierre Paul, 130, 232
Ruhr: French occupation, 441-43
Rumania: alliance, 440
Russia: Treaty of Tilsit, 93; French invasion of, 97; pressure to evict French ultras from power, 242; policy toward Turkey, 247; French investment in, 349, 384, 402

S

S.F.I.O., 336
Sacré Coeur, Church of the, 277, 302
Sadowa, battle of, 253
Sagan, Françoise, 576

Saint-Arnaud, General Jacques, 182
Saint-Just, Antoine Louis, 70, 73, 76
Saint-Simon, Comte de, 233-34
St. Vincent de Paul, Society of, 157
Salan, General, 546
Sand, George, 163, 230, 231
Sangnier, Marc, 341-42
Sansculottes, 77, 215
Sarrail, Albert, 397
Sarraut, Albert Pierre, 496
Sartre, Jean-Paul, 574, 576
Sauvy, Alfred, 468, 552, 564
Say, J.-B., 199, 232
Scheurer-Kestner, Auguste, 322
Schlieffen, General Alfred von, 396
Schneider brothers, 200, 214
Scientism, 368-70, 374-75, 571
Second Empire: historical views of, 184-85; authoritarian phase, 185, 186-89; liberal phase, 185, 189-92; intervention in Mexico, 193, 253, 258; Franco-Prussian War, 193-95, 273-76; economic growth, 205-9; social reforms, 219-21; agricultural conditions, 221-25; population changes, 225-26; foreign policy, 250-58; entente with Great Britain, 252; European congress system, 252; penetration of Indo-China, 253, 254, 257; policy toward Prussia, 253-54; colonial policy, 257-58; studies of, 266
Second Estate, 17-18, 49
Second Republic: Marxian view of, 167-70; June Days, 160, 174-75, 179, 278, 280-81; provisional government, 170-71; National Workshops, 171, 173, 174; Lamartine's foreign policy, 171-72; economic policies, 204-5; agricultural schools, 223; studies of, 264-65
Sedan, battle of, 194
Seignobos, Charles, 6
Seize mai crisis, 292, 294
Senegal, 254, 257
Shopkeepers and Artisans, Association for the Defense of, 541
Siegfried, André, 6, 356, 457
Sieyès, Abbé, 33, 48, 84, 88
Sillon (Furrow), 340-42, 432
Silone, Ignazio, 464
Simon, Jules, 281, 286, 291-92

Small business: decline of, 555

Smith, Adam, 199

Socialism: rise of, 318-19; studies of, 415

Socialist International, 336

Socialist party: withdrawal from Combes coalition, 331, 333, 336; leadership of Jaurès, 333-36; triumph of Guesde, 334-36; policy of nonparticipation in "bourgeois" cabinets, 336-37, 427, 430, 470; relations with labor unions, 365; view of German socialism, 380, 389; opposition to Russian pact, 385; pressure for white peace, 398-99; view of Versailles Treaty, 406; split over question of joining Third International, 425-26; revival under Blum, 430-31; hostility of Communists, 447; fiscal policy, 455; change in Communist policy toward, 480-81; gain in strength, 481; Blum cabinet, 483-89; reluctant support of national defense, 495; opposition to grant of powers to Pétain, 512; postwar attempts to change, 530; membership in Third Force coalition, 537-38; influence of lower bourgeoisie, 566-67; decline in representation under Fifth Republic, 584-85

Socialist Radicals, 318

Social structure: prerevolutionary France, 17-23; changes between 1814 and 1870, 210-26; changes between 1870 and 1914, 354-65; postwar unrest, 461-63; after 1944, 562-67

Social theory: during nineteenth century, 233-38; Saint-Simon, 232-34; Fourier, 234-35; Cabet, 235; Blanc, 235; Pecqueur, 236; Blanqui, 236; Proudhon, 237; Le Play, 238; studies of, 267

Solidarité Française, 471

Sorel, Albert, 4

Sorel, Georges, 364, 373-74, 375, 415, 418

Sorre, Maurice, 325

Soustelle, Jacques, 521, 539, 579, 582, 585

Soviet Union: French recognition of, 447; pact with France, 494, 496; nonaggression pact with Germany, 502; postwar alliance with France, 531. *See also* Russia

Spain: French invasion, 93-94; French expedition of 1823, 133, 243; Spanish

marriage question, 248; civil war, 499

Spears, General Edward, 508

Stalin, Josef, 480, 502

Stavisky, Serge, 473-74

Stendhal, 239

Stresemann, Gustav, 442, 443, 444, 445

Strikes, 218, 219-20, 338, 462, 485

Sue, Eugène, 163, 231

Suez Canal, 252n

Surrealism, 569-70

Symbolism, 373

Syndicalism, 237, 373-74. *See also* C.G.-T.; Labor movement

Syria: French expedition (1860), 253; repression of nationalist movement, 452

T

Tahiti; acquisition of, 254

Taine, Hippolyte, 28, 367, 368, 369, 371

Taittinger, Pierre, 432, 471

Talleyrand, Charles Maurice de, 20, 48, 49, 92, 94, 95, 100, 105, 139, 245

Tanks: number possessed by French in 1940, 506n

Tardieu, André, 428, 460, 464, 469-70, 475-76

Tariff policy: Eden Treaty, 27; under Louis XVIII, 197-98; growth of tariff walls, 198-99; under Louis Philippe, 200; Second Republic, 204; reduction of tariffs under Napoleon III, 207-8, 345; Gambetta, 298; Méline Tariff, 346-47; depression, 466

Taylor, A.J.P., 379

Technocrats, 565

Tenants' and Sharecroppers' Union, 558

Terror, Reign of, 71, 76

Textile industry: modernization of, 200; social reform efforts, 220-21; importance, 352

Thermidor, 71-72, 76, 77, 81

Thiers, Adolphe: press campaign to overthrow Bourbons, 139-40, 141; spokesman for left-center, 145; president of council, 149; plan for mastery of Paris, 164; backer of Louis Napoleon, 176-77; support of Falloux Law,

179; exile, 187; recognition of Prussian threat, 194, 253; intellectual contribution, 232; Egyptian policy, 247; role in consolidating monarchist republic, 272-73; chosen provisional executive, 276-77; Paris Commune, 277-81; leadership of, 282-84; death of, 293; member of upper bourgeoisie, 356; influence of Comte, 367; Bainville's view of, 378; postwar diplomatic hopes, 380

Third Estate: composition of, 20-23; growth of dissatisfaction, 26; demand for unicameral Estates-General, 48, 54-55; representation in Estates-General, 49-50; dismissal of Necker, 56; liberal view of role in revolutionary struggle, 75, 78

Third Force coalition, 537, 538-39, 561

Third International, 425, 430, 431

Third Republic: power of bourgeoisie, 214, 355-59; factions in Assembly, 286-88, 295; constitution of 1875, 287-88; presidency of MacMahon, 289-94; electoral procedure, 290-91; victory of republicanism, 291-95; economic conditions, 1870-1914, 343-53; structure of society, 1870-1914, 354-65; Great War, 393-400; three phases of development, 423; depression, 464-82; Popular Front, 483-89; disintegration as world power, 491-503; indecision, invasion, and defeat, 503-9; Vichy government, 510-19; reasons for decline, 588-89; studies of, 409-18, 591-92; novels of, 418-19

Thorez, Maurice, 39, 431, 531

Tilsit, Treaty of, 93, 96

Tocqueville, Alexis de, 20, 23-24, 40, 145, 161, 227, 232-33

Triple Entente, 389

Tunisia: annexation by France, 309, 382-83; Italian minority question, 447-50; nationalist movement, 452; move toward granting independence, 540-41

Turgot, Anne Robert Jacques, 3, 42-43, 44-45

U

U.N.R. (Union for the New Republic), 580, 584, 585

Ulm, battle of, 92

Ultra-royalists: under Louis XVIII, 124-25, 127-29, 130, 132-33; under Charles X, 134-39, 242

Union Fédérale, 435

Union for the New Republic (U.N.R.), 580, 584, 585

Union Nationale des Combattants, 435, 475

Union of Economic Interests, 434-35

United States: refusal to write off war loans, 455; refusal of French plea for planes, 506

Utopianism, 233-38

V

Vaillant, Edouard, 396

Valéry, Paul, 568, 572

Vallat, Xavier, 517n

Valmy, battle of, 68, 145, 274

Vatican: concordat of 1516, 11; concordat with Napoleon, 89, 102, 330-31; Pope Leo XIII and policy of *ralliement*, 315, 316-17; effect of separation of French church and state, 330-33; view of Sillon, 341-42, 432; restoration of diplomatic relations, 426; condemnation of Action Française, 433. *See also* Roman Catholic church

Vercingetorix, 7

Verdun, battle of, 397

Vergennes, Charles Gravier, comte de: support of American revolution, 44

Verlaine, Paul, 373

Versailles Treaty, 404-8

Veuillot, Louis, 160, 179, 181, 301-2, 341

Vichy government: leadership of Pétain, 510-14, 518-19; early dominance of Laval, 511-12; Laval's dismissal and return to power, 514-18; studies of, 592-94

Vidal de la Blache, Paul, 374
Vigny, Alfred de, 231
Villèle, Jean Baptiste, comte de: leader
of ultras, 130; "émigrés' billion," 134;
financial reforms, 135-36; feud with
Chateaubriand, 136-37, 243-44; fall
from power, 138-39; attitude toward
business, 199; foreign policy, 242-43
Villeneuve-Bargemont, Vicomte, 218
Vingtième (income tax), 14-15
Viollet-le-Duc, Eugène Emmanuel, 229
Voltaire, 20, 29, 30, 35, 113, 330

W

Wagram, battle of, 94
Waldeck-Rousseau, René, 323, 325, 328-
30, 335, 378
Walewski, Comte, 189
Wallon, Henri, 271
Walpole. Robert. 153
Waterloo, battle of, 126, 127
Weimar Republic, 443, 446
Wellington, Arthur Wellesley, duke of,
94, 98, 129

Wendel, 200, 202, 214
Werth, Alexander, 510
Weygand, Maxime, 504, 509
"White Terror," 127
Wilson, Daniel, 312, 313
Wilson, Woodrow, 450
Winegrowers' Confederation, 556
Workers' Force (C.G.T.-F.O.), 560
World War I, 393-400, 401-4
World War II, 508-26

Y

Yalta Conference, 445
Young, Arthur, 55
Young Christian Farmers (J.A.C.), 432
Young Christian Workers (J.O.C.), 432
Yugoslavia: alliance, 440; French invest-
ment in, 447

Z

Zola, Émile, 366, 368-69, 370-71

PRINTED IN U.S.A.